Praise for *The Psychology of Diversity*

Unlike older and traditional texts on prejudice and intergroup relations, *The Psychology of Diversity* offers a sharply different approach—one much better suited to the complexities and subtleties of present-day intergroup phenomena. It is also authoritative as one would expect from a text written by leading social psychological experts in the field.

Thomas F. Pettigrew, University of California, Santa Cruz

This is the most comprehensive survey of diversity since the groundbreaking Jones *Prejudice and Racism* volume, the undisputed bible of the field for decades. *The Psychology of Diversity*, authoritatively written by some of the field's foremost leaders, will rightfully take its place as the go-to resource for students, researchers, and practitioners alike, to meet the challenges of the 21st century.

Professor Susan Fiske, Eugene Higgins Professor, Psychology and Public Affairs, Princeton University

One could not hope for better guides through the maze of social-psychological work on diversity in America. Jones, Dovidio, and Vietze prove to be map-makers of "Lewis and Clark" quality, never losing their way over difficult terrain, and steering the reader through defining research on psychological processes, and an analysis of diversity in terms of culture, power, and institutions.

Miles Hewstone, Professor of Social Psychology, University of Oxford, UK

The successful management of increasingly diverse societies is a major imperative of our times. In their extraordinarily comprehensive volume, *The Psychology of Diversity*, Jones, Dovidio, and Vietze do a masterful job of presenting the latest scientific evidence concerning both the challenges to and opportunities for moving beyond prejudice and racism. This volume is essential reading for anyone interested in social diversity or intergroup relations.

Jim Sidanius, Department of Psychology, Harvard University

The Psychology of Diversity: Beyond Prejudice and Racism is an illuminating book on the psychological processes behind power, bias, and cultural difference, as well as the broad influences and challenges that diversity presents. In this outstanding book, distinguished authors James M. Jones, John F. Dovidio, and Deborah L. Vietze provide us with a historical perspective alongside up-to date information on the psychological principles that influence our diverse society. This book is unique in that it not only addresses the negative consequences of bias and discrimination, but also contributes research-based solutions to these problems by providing techniques to improve intergroup relations. *The Psychology of Diversity* has a wide applicability and utility; I highly recommend this book not only for students, but for professionals and all individuals who care about reducing prejudice and respecting and benefitting from diversity in our society.

Florence L. Denmark, Ph.D., Robert Scott Pace Distinguished Research Professor of Psychology, Former President of the American Psychological Association

About the Authors

James M. Jones is Professor of Psychology and Director of the Center for the Study for Diversity at the University of Delaware. He was Executive Director for Public Interest, and Director of the Minority Fellowship Program at the American Psychological Association. After earning his Ph.D. in psychology at Yale University, he taught at Harvard University, and Howard University. He was awarded the Guggenheim Fellowship in 1973 to study Calypso Humor in Trinidad. His book, *Prejudice and Racism* (1997) is a classic text on this subject. His awards include the Lewin Award from the Society for the Psychological Study of Social Issues, a Lifetime Achievement Award from the Society for the Psychological Study of Ethnic Minority Issues, and the Distinguished Psychologist Award from the Association of Black Psychologists.

John F. Dovidio is Professor of Psychology at Yale University. His publications include *Reducing Intergroup Bias* (with Samuel Gaertner, 2000) and *The Social Psychology of Helping and Altruism* (with David A. Schroeder, Louis A. Penner, and Jane A. Piliavin, 1995). He is co-editor of Blackwell's *On the Nature of Prejudice* (with Laurie A. Rudman and Peter Glick, 2005) and chair of the Society for the Psychological Study of Social Issues' publications committee. Jack is also the editor of the *Journal of Personality and Social Psychology* and has been editor of *Personality and Social Psychology Bulletin*. He is a Fellow of the American Psychological Association and of the Association of Psychological Science. He received SPSSI's Kurt Lewin Award in 2004 for his career contributions to the study of prejudice and discrimination.

Deborah L. Vietze is Professor of Psychology at the City University of New York in the Human Development and Urban Education Ph.D. programs. Her most recent work focuses on cultural influences on social behavior, social and spiritual orientations that predict recycling behavior, and the perception of institutional bias. She was a co-editor of the 2006 *Child Development Special Issue on Culture, Ethnicity and Race*. She is the 1990 recipient of the American Psychological Association's Minority Achievement Award for excellence in integrating research and service for ethnic minority populations and the 1991 C. Everett Koop (former Surgeon General of the U.S.) National Health Award for health-related services research. Deborah has also served as an American Psychological Association representative to the United Nations.

The Psychology of Diversity

Beyond Prejudice and Racism

James M. Jones, John F. Dovidio, and Deborah L. Vietze

WILEY Blackwell

This edition first published 2014
© 2014 Blackwell Publishing Ltd

Blackwell Publishing was acquired by John Wiley & Sons in February 2007. Blackwell's publishing program has been merged with Wiley's global Scientific, Technical, and Medical business to form Wiley-Blackwell.

Registered Office
John Wiley & Sons Ltd, The Atrium, Southern Gate, Chichester, West Sussex, PO19 8SQ, UK

Editorial Offices: 350 Main Street, Malden, MA 02148-5020, USA
9600 Garsington Road, Oxford, OX4 2DQ, UK
The Atrium, Southern Gate, Chichester, West Sussex, PO19 8SQ, UK

For details of our global editorial offices, for customer services, and for information about how to apply for permission to reuse the copyright material in this book please see our website at www.wiley.com/wiley-blackwell.

The right of James M. Jones, John F. Dovidio and Deborah L. Vietze to be identified as the author(s) of this work has been asserted in accordance with the UK Copyright, Designs and Patents Act 1988.

Library of Congress Cataloging-in-Publication Data

Jones, James M.
    The psychology of diversity : beyond prejudice and racism / James M. Jones, John F. Dovidio and Deborah L. Vietze.
        pages cm
    Includes bibliographical references and index.
    ISBN 978-1-4051-6214-2 (pbk. : alk. paper) – ISBN 978-1-4051-6213-5 (hardback : alk. paper)
1. Multiculturalism–Psychological aspects.   2. Prejudices.   3. Stereotypes (Social psychology)
I. Title.
    HM1271.J656 2013
    305.8–dc23

                                2013006406

A catalogue record for this book is available from the British Library.
Cover image: Joy Baer, Dream Tree, fresco. Private Collection / The Bridgeman Art Library.
Cover design by www.cyandesign.co.uk

Set in 10.5 on 12.5 pt Dante by Toppan Best-set Premedia Limited
Printed in Singapore by Ho Printing Singapore Pte Ltd

1   2014

Brief Contents

Contents   vii
Preface   xv
Dedication   xviii
Acknowledgments   xix

Part One   Framing Diversity   **1**
Chapter 1   The Psychology of Diversity: Challenges and Benefits   3
Chapter 2   Central Concepts in the Psychology of Diversity   27
Chapter 3   Historical Perspectives on Diversity in the United States   55

Part Two   Psychological Processes   **87**
Chapter 4   Personality and Individual Differences: How Different
             Types of People Respond to Diversity in Different Ways   89
Chapter 5   Social Cognition and Categorization: Distinguishing
             "Us" from "Them"   117
Chapter 6   Social Identity, Roles, and Relations: Motivational
             Influences in Responses to Diversity   147
Chapter 7   Is Bias in the Brain?   173
Chapter 8   Coping and Adapting to Stigma and Difference   205
Chapter 9   Intergroup Interactions: Pitfalls and Promises   239

Part Three   Culture, Power, and Institutions   **263**
Chapter 10   Cultural Diversity: Preferences, Meaning, and Difference   265
Chapter 11   Social Roles and Power in a Diverse Society   299
Chapter 12   The Challenge of Diversity for Institutions   327
Chapter 13   The Psychology of Diversity: Principles and Prospects   355

Glossary   377
Index   401

Contents

Preface   xv
Dedication   xviii
Acknowledgments   xix

Part One   Framing Diversity   **1**

Chapter 1   The Psychology of Diversity: Challenges and Benefits   **3**

Introduction   4
The Goals of This Book   6
   What is Diversity About?   6
   A Taxonomy of Diversity   9
   When Diversity Does Not Add Up To Equality   10
Perspectives on Diversity   11
   Behavioral Science and Diversity   11
   Diversity within Diversity   13
The Diversity Divide: Benefits versus Challenges   14
   What Are the Benefits of Diversity?   14
   What Are the Challenges of Diversity?   17
Organization of this Book   19
Summary   22

Chapter 2   Central Concepts in the Psychology of Diversity   **27**

Introduction   27
Understanding Diversity   30
   What is the Psychology of Diversity?   30
   What's in a Social Group Label?   33
Social Biases: Stereotypes, Prejudice, and Discrimination   34
   What Are *They* Like? Stereotypes   34
   How Do I Feel About Them? Prejudice   35

How Do I Treat Them? Discrimination and Fairness   37
Biases Below and Above the Surface   40
The Structure of Social Bias   41
Racism: A Case Example of Social Bias   41
The Different Layers of Social Bias   42
Research Methods for the Study of Social Bias   45
The Scientific Enterprise   45
Making Sense of the World Scientifically: Theories and Research Methods   46
Testing Our Ideas: Research Designs   47
Making Meaning from Research: Measures and Analysis of Data   49
Summary   49

Chapter 3   Historical Perspectives on Diversity in the United States   55

Introduction   55
Push–Pull: Dynamics of Diversity   57
Immigration, Importation, and Citizenship   57
U.S. Population Growth is Fueled by Immigration   58
Who Are Citizens of the United States?   59
Immigration and Ethnic Diversity   61
Benevolent Sexism as Legal Argument   62
Cultural Conditioning of American Indians   63
Negative Responses to Diversity   64
Immigration Policy   65
Civil Rights   68
Diversity and Civil Rights   68
Expanding Diversity and Inclusion in U.S. Society Through Civil Rights   72
Affirmative Action as a Diversity Approach   74
A Nation of Minorities   78
Challenges of Diversity   80
Individual Rights, Diversity, and Prejudice Collide   80
Diversity and Difference   81
Majority and Minority   82
Summary   83

Part Two   Psychological Processes   87

Chapter 4   Personality and Individual Differences: How Different Types of People Respond to Diversity in Different Ways   89

Introduction   89
Origins of Prejudice: Allport's Lens Model   90
Personality and Prejudice   92

The Abnormality of Prejudice: The Psychodynamic Model   93
  Psychodynamic Theory and Prejudice   93
  Prejudice against Difference: The Authoritarian Personality   94
  The Legacy of Authoritarianism: Contemporary Measures   96
The Normality of Prejudice   99
  Conformity and Norms   99
  Social Dominance   100
  Authoritarianism and SDO: Sometimes a Lethal Combination   104
  Religion and Prejudice   106
  Politics and Prejudice   107
  Individual Differences in Blatant and Subtle Prejudice   109
Summary   111

Chapter 5   Social Cognition and Categorization: Distinguishing "Us" from "Them"   **117**

Introduction   117
We Are Social Animals   118
How We Think About People: Social Cognition   119
  Acquiring Information: Attributions   120
  Integrating Information: Cognitive Consistency   124
How We Think About Groups: Social Categorization and Group
Membership   128
  Who Is "In" and Who Is "Out"? Social Categorization   129
  Thinking Differently About Us and Them   132
What Can We Do? Reducing Bias and Embracing Diversity   133
  "Me" and "You" Instead of "Us" and "Them": Decategorization   134
  Playing on the Same Team: Recategorization   136
  Implications and Applications of Category-based Models for
    Reducing Bias   138
Summary   141

Chapter 6   Social Identity, Roles, and Relations: Motivational Influences in Responses to Diversity   **147**

Introduction   147
Feeling Good about Us: Social Identity   148
  Who Am I? Personal and Social Identity   149
  Many Me's: Multiple Identities   151
  My Group Is Better Than Yours: Creating Positive Identity   152
Confusing "What Is" with "What Should Be": Social Roles and System
Justification   155
  Blaming the Victim: Attributions to Groups   155
  Judging Who People Are by What Jobs They Do: Social Roles   156
  Maintaining the Status Quo: System Justification   158
Slipping into the Darkness: Groups in Competition   161
  "You Dirty Rattler": Conflict between Groups   162

Threatening What We Have and What We Are: Realistic and
Symbolic Conflict   162
What Can We Do? Changing How Groups Relate   164
Achieving More Together Than Alone: Superordinate Goals   165
Putting the Pieces Together: Jigsaw Classroom   165
You Complete Me (Us): Mutual Intergroup Differentiation   166
Which Approach Is Best?   167
Summary   168

Chapter 7   Is Bias in the Brain?   **173**

Introduction   173
What's Under the Hood? The Organization of the Human Brain   175
How We Know How the Brain Functions   176
Brain Structure and Function   177
Brain Structure, Diversity, and Intergroup Relations   178
Warning! Difference Ahead!   179
Who Are You? Race and Face Perception   183
Brain Function and Intergroup Bias   187
Explicit and Implicit Bias   188
Contemporary Prejudice   192
What Can We Do? Addressing Implicit Bias   195
Acknowledging Implicit Bias   196
Controlling Implicit Bias Through Unconscious Goals   197
Summary   198

Chapter 8   Coping and Adapting to Stigma and Difference   **205**

Introduction   205
Social Stigma and Cultural Difference   207
The Social "Stain" of Stigma   208
How Social and Cultural Difference Divides Us   210
Racial Socialization and Acculturation   211
Preparing Children for a Racialized Society: Racial Socialization   212
Adapting to a Different Culture: Acculturation   212
Stresses Caused by Stigma and Difference   213
Perceiving Discrimination is Bad for Your Health   213
Stereotype Threat Is "in the Air"   214
Coping with Perceived Discrimination   220
How Group Membership Influences the Ways We Cope
with Discrimination   220
The Ways We Cope with Discrimination Individually   223
Collective Identities   224
How We Relate to Our Racial Group: Racial Identity   225
How We Relate to Our Ethnic Group: Ethnic Identity   228
Summary   231

Chapter 9   Intergroup Interactions: Pitfalls and Promises   239

Introduction   239
Psychological Challenges of Intergroup Interaction   241
  Preparing for the "First Date"   241
  Where Do We Go from Here? Experiences in Intergroup Interactions   242
  You (Can) Complete Me   246
  Under the Radar? Implicit Bias and Intergroup Interaction   248
  Some Conclusions About Intergroup Interactions   251
The Promise of Positive Intergroup Interaction   252
  How Does Contact Work?   253
  Friends of My Friends   255
  Just Imagine!   256
Summary   257

Part Three   Culture, Power, and Institutions   263

Chapter 10   Cultural Diversity: Preferences, Meaning, and Difference   265

Introduction   265
What is Culture?   268
  When Do Race Preferences Begin?   270
  Why Do Early Preferences Matter?   271
How Do Cultures Differ?   272
  What We Value   272
  How We See Power   274
  How We Relate to Others: Individualism–Collectivism   276
  How We Perceive "the Other": Enemyship   278
  How We Understand Time: Psychological Time   279
  How We Create Meaning: Religion   280
Cultural Diversity   283
  Now We See It, Now We Don't: Perspectives on Cultural Diversity   285
  Culture Wars Promote Conflict and Contest   287
  Culture Peace Promotes Representation and Belonging   289
  Preventing Bias and Favoritism   291
Summary   293

Chapter 11   Social Roles and Power in a Diverse Society   299

Introduction   299
Power Matters   302
Who's Got the Power? Power Dynamics and Diversity   305
  It's Just Natural: The Power of Social Roles and Social Groups   306
  Who's at the Top and Why? CEOs, Lawyers, and Janitors   307
  Multiple Me: Intersectionality and Power   308
  A Social Hierarchy: What's Diversity Got To Do With It?   310

Psychological Sources of Power   310
  Skin Color, Social Role, and Power   312
  Social Dominance: My Group Versus Your Group   314
  Social Class as a Source of Power   315
Pathways to Fairness: Reducing Bias in Power Dynamics   316
  You Have More Power—What Should I Expect?   317
  Maybe the Status Quo Has Too Much Power   318
  Stereotyping: Can It Help and Not Harm?   319
Summary   320

Chapter 12   The Challenge of Diversity for Institutions   327

Introduction   327
Portraits of Institutional Bias   329
  Texaco: Recognizing Diversity Bias and Doing Something About It   329
  An All-Girls Math Class: Educational Bias on Purpose   330
How Institutional Bias Operates   332
  The Origins of Institutional Bias: A Case Example   333
  Types of Institutional Bias   333
Most Bias is Standard-of-Practice Bias   335
  Can Affirmative Action Address Institutional Bias?   336
  Home Ownership and Mortgage Lending   337
  Race, Ethnicity, Gender, and Age Disparities in Unemployment 339
  The Criminal Justice System and Ethnicity Disparities   340
  Ethnic Disparities in Capital Punishment   341
  Healthcare, Marriage, and Environmental Safety   341
  What Makes Institutional Bias so Challenging?   343
  Effects of Institutional Bias Are Far-reaching   344
  Emotions May Run High   345
  Maybe Poverty Leads to Institutional Bias   347
Preventing Institutional Bias is a Challenge   348
  Valuing Diversity   348
  Diversity Training in Higher Education   349
Summary   350

**Chapter 13   The Psychology of Diversity: Principles and
Prospects   355**

Introduction   356
Diversity Is Diverse   357
Diversity When It Is All Good   359
Diversity Is Normal   361
Doing Diversity Is Hard   362
  Diversity Demands Change   363
  Diversity Sometimes Stands Opposed to Fairness   363
  Bias Has Deep-seated Psychological Roots and Consequences   363
  Diversity Complicates Interpersonal and Intergroup Interactions   364

Principles of Diversity: What Have We Learned in This Book? — 365

Bias Against Diversity Is Not Inevitable — 365

Diversity Presents Opportunities to Learn — 366

Interaction Improves Attitudes Toward Other Groups — 366

Diverse Contexts Promote Flexibility, Adaptability, and Creativity — 366

Personal Motivation Can Limit or Prevent Bias — 367

Belief That Biases Can Be Changed Increases People's Interest in Diversity — 367

People Can Learn To Be Unprejudiced — 367

Approach and Avoidance Motivations Are Keys to Diversity Dynamics — 368

Individual Ideology and Values Determine Diversity Attitudes, Support, and Actions — 368

People Are Resilient in the Face of Discrimination — 368

Respect Promotes Diversity Among Members of Racial and Ethnic Minority Groups — 369

Support for Diversity Is Greatest When it Includes Your Group — 369

Programs to Promote Intergroup Relations Can Succeed — 370

Trust Is Crucial for Dealing with Difference and Change — 370

Organizational Values, Goals, and Practices Determine the Success of Diversity Efforts — 371

Conclusion — 371

Glossary — 377

Index — 401

Preface

The idea for this book began when James Jones was asked about updating his earlier book, *Prejudice and Racism* (Jones, 1997). He was loath to do so because, in his view, *diversity* was the compelling challenge of the twenty-first century. The three of us met at a multicultural conference in New York and talked about what a new book addressing diversity issues would look like and how it could be accomplished. Thus began a collaboration that has produced the current volume.

The very last pages of *Prejudice and Racism* included a major heading, "Diversity is a Strength in the Species and Society." This section argued for both the inevitability of diversity and its fundamental benefits. Subheadings began to explore the idea that diversity exists not only between groups but also within groups. Upon reflection, we realized that prejudice and racism, while continuing to be major deterrents to social justice and a better society, were not sufficient to capture the complexity and challenges of the twenty-first century. The United States and the whole world had changed too much. We began discussing the relationship of diversity to prejudice and racism, and how a textbook could help students and others understand the challenges of diversity and how managing and supporting it across all levels of society would make this a better nation.

"Diversity" is a label that can be applied to any <u>noticeable differences</u> in a context or setting—a forest, a community, the world, the planet. Trying to understand and study diversity in its broadest sense is daunting. When we take too broad an approach, it is difficult to bring clarity to the discussion. When we take too narrow a view, then its meaning and relevance is challenged by all that is excluded from its purview. Finding the proper balance and perspective has been our aim. We know that differences matter and the world has struggled to deal with differences from the beginning of time. We have plunged into an effort to educate readers about the ways in which members of our society have collectively responded to differences among us, and the promise that our differences may combine to create better institutions, societies, and a better world.

What Is This Book About and Who Is It For?

Increasingly, diversity is a fact of life in the United States and globally. *The Psychology of Diversity: Beyond Prejudice and Racism* examines the challenges created by differences among us, and the opportunities these differences offer for creating stronger, more effective institutions and full participation of diverse members of society. This book is about the challenges diversity poses socially and psychologically and how people can choose to address and benefit from those challenges. The book is mainly for students in classes on prejudice, stereotyping, and discrimination; multiculturalism and society; and intergroup relations. It should also appeal to a broad audience of people who are interested in understanding social diversity. The coverage is evidence-based; it is about the facts as we currently know them. These facts tell a story that we attempt to recount, of the past, present, and future of our society and the challenges and opportunities of diversity in everyday life.

What Is the Purpose of this Book?

The purpose of *The Psychology of Diversity* is to help people understand the ways in which differences among people produce a broad array of psychological responses that determine how they are perceived and the effects they have. Diversity is not simply about the experiences of members of selected traditionally disadvantaged groups or about people who bring different values and cultures to new countries when they immigrate. Diversity affects and includes us all. People usually find comfort from being around others similar to themselves, and seek support for their views of the world and their place in it. We document that sharing varied perspectives, talents, and worldviews is beneficial to human interaction and institutional performance. We also demonstrate the resistances that diversity elicits and the benefits that arise when we overcome them. We also focus on approaches that have been shown to produce positive outcomes; that we can learn and benefit from what makes us different from one another. This challenge of diversity is not simply to control or manage it; it is to understand and profit from it. Increasing diversity is inevitable. We use research, case studies, and historical illustration to show that by understanding diversity, we can more constructively navigate our everyday lives and prepare, individually and socially, for a world that is more diverse, more interdependent, and more complex.

What Is Special About this Book?

Many books, including other ones we have written, focus more narrowly on bias and its consequences. This book is subtitled *Beyond Prejudice and Racism*, and also devotes considerable attention to the problems of prejudice and discrimination toward diverse groups. But each chapter also discusses the solutions to these problems; they describe research on techniques for improving intergroup relations in different ways. Moreover, this book goes beyond prejudice and discrimination to emphasize how an understanding of diversity offers unique insights and opportunities to better prepare people for a diverse society.

The story of diversity and its challenges is both broad and complex. This book can't tell it all, so it has particular emphases. The book is primarily social psychological in its orientation, but we consider how historical, political, educational, economic, and societal factors shape the way people think about and respond to diversity. The approach is multilevel, with coverage of the neuroscience of prejudice through the sociology and politics of diversity. Our discussions primarily center on racial and ethnic biases in the United States, partly because most research on these topics is based on people from the United States.

Another reason is because we believe that an understanding of the challenges of diversity should consider the particular historical, political, institutional, societal, and cultural context in which individual-level biases—the emphasis of social psychological approaches—are embedded. To tell that story within a limited number of pages, we have used race and ethnic relations within the United States as a thematic case study. However, we do not limit our discussion to these issues. We examine the implications to a range of other "isms" (e.g., sexism, heterosexism, weightism) regularly through-out the book and discuss diversity and social bias globally. And finally, we have included evidence-based examples that point the way to approaches to differences that have been shown to be effective in bringing people together for mutual benefit.

Dedication

To my students who really want to live fulfilled and meaningful lives in a diverse society and seek guidance in how to do that. We hope this book will help show the way.

J.M.J.

To Rita Kerins (my favorite sister) who spent a career in education learning about the challenges of diversity in everyday life.

J.F.D.

To my husband, daughters, and sons for unwavering support and love during the writing of this book.

D.L.V.

Acknowledgments

We are grateful to the many people and organizations supporting us in writing this book. We deeply appreciate the wisdom, patience, and guidance offered by Elaine Silverstein who helped us craft and organize the content of the book. Deirdre Ilkson at Wiley-Blackwell helped keep us on track with gentle prodding and sensitive guidance all in a soothing British accent. Thanks to Linda Dovidio for supporting our planning and writing with delicious meals and amiable company. Peter Vietze offered helpful editing and Rebecca Vietze provided "in-house" research assistance. We also thank our graduate students who helped with some of the research and provided useful comments on selected sections of chapters: Jordan Leitner at the University of Delaware and Beatriz Coronel at CUNY. Appreciation also goes to several anonymous reviewers who provided valuable insights and suggestions we have taken very seriously and have helped us make this a better book.

James M. Jones acknowledges support from the Department of Psychology, the Office of the Dean of the College of Arts and Sciences, and Morris Library at the University of Delaware for support during the writing of this book. He is especially grateful to Olaive Jones for her patience and expert editorial hand and good judgment about words and ideas.

John F. Dovidio acknowledges the financial support provided by grants from the National Science Foundation (BCS-0613218) and the National Institutes of Health (NIH RO1HL 0856331-0182 and 1R01DA029888-01) during the course of writing this book. He also acknowledges the support provided by Yale University.

Deborah L. Vietze acknowledges the helpful resources provided by the Mina Reese Library at the CUNY Graduate Center. She also appreciates the support of the Psychology Programs at the City University of New York.

Part One

Framing Diversity

Chapter 1

Psychology of Diversity
Challenges and Benefits

Introduction	4
The Goals of this Book	6
Perspectives on Diversity	11
The Diversity Divide: Benefits versus Challenges	14
Organization of this Book	19
Summary	22

We hold these truths to be self-evident, that all men are created equal, that they are endowed by their Creator with certain unalienable Rights, that among these are Life, Liberty and the pursuit of Happiness.

Thomas Jefferson
Declaration of Independence, July 4, 1776

Major American businesses have made clear that the skills needed in today's increasingly global marketplace can only be developed through exposure to widely diverse people, cultures, ideas, and viewpoints. High-ranking retired officers and civilian military leaders assert that a highly qualified, racially diverse officer corps is essential to national security. Moreover, because universities, and in particular, law schools, represent the training ground for a large number of the Nation's leaders, . . . the path to leadership must be visibly open to talented and qualified individuals of every race and ethnicity. Thus, the Law School has a compelling interest in attaining a diverse student body.

Justice Sandra Day O'Connor
Grutter v. Bollinger (2003)

The Psychology of Diversity: Beyond Prejudice and Racism, First Edition. James M. Jones, John F. Dovidio, and Deborah L. Vietze.
© 2014 Blackwell Publishing Ltd. Published 2014 by Blackwell Publishing Ltd.

Introduction

This book is about diversity. **Diversity** refers to those things that make us different from one another. Race, ethnicity, and gender are the most common differences that are mentioned in diversity conversations. But diversity is much more than demographic differences. We are different by virtue of our country of origin, our culture, sexual orientation, age, values, political affiliation, socioeconomic status, and able-bodiedness. Our psychological tendencies, abilities, or preferences also mark diversity.

There are more than 7 billion people on the planet and each person is uniquely different from every other. Diversity is a global reality. Diversity becomes significant in Germany and the Netherlands when increasing numbers of immigrants arrive from Turkey, Africa, and South America. African, West Indian, and South and East Asian immigrants diversify the United Kingdom and Canada. Sub-Saharan Africans immigrate to South Africa and challenge locals for jobs and opportunities. Ethnic differences in the Pacific Islands, Eastern Europe, Canada, and many countries of Africa highlight both differences and similarities. To this we add the pressures created by trying to meld the diverse countries of Europe into a common union, the European Union (EU). Differences in politics, economic policy, cultural traditions, and religious beliefs challenge the fabric of a common identity. All of these diversity trends reflect global dynamics of difference. A recent Google search of the term yielded 229,000,000 hits, evidence of its relevance to our everyday experiences. So how can we possibly address diversity of this magnitude?

Our approach is to narrow it down. Although our goal is to help people understand diversity and people's responses in the broadest global context, much of this book is a case study of diversity issues in the United States. In this book, diversity is examined primarily with respect to racial and ethnic differences, although we also cover differences in gender, religion, ability, and sexual orientation. Diversity, and how people respond to it, depends on the history, economics, and politics of a society and the psychology of its members. For this reason, we focus primarily on diversity in the United States. However, we also refer to diversity in other nations and cultures and how responses to diversity may be similar or different.

As the book's subtitle implies, prejudice and racism play an important role in the context of diversity; they are a challenge to achieving its positive potential effects. One of the challenges of diversity in everyday life is to understand and reduce the biases that hinder the creation of diversity in groups, institutions, organizations, and societies. But equally challenging is to find the proper balance of approaches to diversity that simultaneously strengthen the fabric of our institutions and society and enrich our individual lives, while preserving the cherished values of equality of opportunity and social justice for all.

Diversity is based in difference, but a variety of similarities intersect these differences. Tsui and colleagues, for example, propose that both demographic differences *and* similarities between co-workers and supervisors affect task performance and behavior in organizational settings, but in somewhat different ways (Tsui, Porter, & Egan, 2002). They call this idea **relational demography**. Objective similarities—actual similarity in a given context—are important, but subjective similarities, the extent to which people *perceive* how similar they are to others, and how people weigh them against differences often matter even more. In general, perceiving greater similarity among workers in an organization is related to better performance and commitment to the organization. But perceiving greater similarity does not mean that people do not recognize or respect differences, as well.

What differences and similarities mean in a given relationship will depend on the norms and expectations in that context. A Black and a White female nurse may work together better and show greater support for the organization because of their normative similarities—both are women in a field in which women are the norm—than might a White male and a White female nurse, who are demographically similar by race but normatively dissimilar in the nursing context. In this case, gender similarity is more important than racial similarity. The simple fact of difference then does not create problems. Differences relative to what, when, and where play an important role in determining what the effects are. Diversity offers many ways for us to see similarities with others; it's not just about differences.

The two quotes at the beginning of this chapter, one from the *Declaration of Independence* and the other from Justice O'Connor, illustrate a major challenge we face as a democracy. These statements, made at widely varying times, demonstrate that the United States has a fundamental commitment to equal opportunity and equal rights, and a compelling interest in diversity. As enunciated by Justice O'Connor, **compelling interest** provides the legal basis for determining when and how taking race into account may be used to further diversity objectives in higher education. This commitment to diversity raises three fundamental questions that are the subject of this book: How can we create equality in a society that is so diverse? What are the impediments or barriers to realizing this goal? What are the benefits when we achieve it?

The biggest barriers to equality, given the diversity of our society, have historically been prejudice and racism, because they are premised on the belief that people are *not* equal. Prejudice and racism shape how we think about diversity and difference. When the institutions of society, such as law and education, reinforce these beliefs, the result is a self-perpetuating social hierarchy in which some groups have more, privileges and wealth for example, and other groups have less. One national ideal is to treat everyone equally, and yet everyone is not equal, because we *are* a diverse society. There are real and imagined differences among us. The challenge is to treat people fairly, recognizing that we are not all equally qualified for the same job, and respect the differences among us. Diversity has come to be valued in global and local businesses, in educational institutions, and in the military. Justice O'Connor's statement recognizes this and argues that we have a compelling interest to engage every citizen in the social, educational, and economic institutions that provide direct paths to leadership. Do you agree? America has always been diverse, but over time we have become diverse in different ways. Despite our increasing diversity and the recognition by many that dealing effectively with diversity is essential to our security and economic well-being, engaging diversity remains controversial and raises challenging problems.

Sturm and colleagues refer to successfully achieving diversity in colleges and universities as **full participation**: "an affirmative value focused on creating institutions that enable people, whatever their identity, background, or institutional position, to thrive, realize their capabilities, engage meaningfully in institutional life, and contribute to the flourishing of others" (Sturm, Eatman, Saltmarsh, & Bush, 2011, p. 3). Diversity is not a static, or a fixed number. We think of diversity as a catalyst for full participation in our communities, institutions, society and in our lives.

This book's main purpose is to help readers understand the psychology of diversity by reviewing what we know about human behavior and how it shapes our experiences with diversity in a variety of settings and contexts. This book highlights some psychological reactions to diversity and the emotions, perceptions, and behaviors they activate. It also presents evidence that guides us toward promising pathways for reducing some of the adverse impacts that may accompany increased diversity, as well as demonstrates some of the important benefits that diversity can produce.

The Goals of this Book

We have three main goals for this book. First we want to demonstrate the depth and breadth of diversity in the United States. Our perspective is that diversity has always been a feature of American society (see Chapter 3). This diversity has dramatically increased along race and ethnic dimensions since the 1960s. If the expanding diversity is properly understood and well managed, it will strengthen our security, economic prosperity, and innovation.

A second goal of this book is to describe how diversity is reflected in people, groups, institutions, and cultures, and how and why we react to these forms of diversity in the ways that we do. Prejudice and discrimination result not only from the actions of bigots, but also from the unexamined actions and attitudes of those of us who consider ourselves "unprejudiced." We show that prejudice is "normal" in that it is rooted in basic human cognitive, neurological, and emotional processes. As a consequence, we must overcome powerful and ordinary predispositions in order to reduce prejudices. We present research-based strategies for overcoming some of these prejudices and thus create a more favorable environment for diversity to flourish. In this way, we hope to empower students to actualize their goals regarding equity and democracy.

Third, and finally, our goal is to present some of the problems, challenges, and differing perspectives on diversity, and we provide some historical and cultural perspectives about diversity in the United States. This book may lead you to ask more questions than we have raised here and perhaps it will help you understand and become aware of diversity's challenges. It may also encourage thinking about solutions to some of the challenges we raise. We hope this will help you better live in increasingly diverse settings, institutions, and societies. We want your understanding of diversity to be based on research findings that explain how diversity affects human behavior, and we also want you to appreciate the challenges that these findings present.

What is Diversity About?

Fundamentally, diversity is about differences between and within individuals, institutions, and societies. However, talking about diversity simply as difference is not what we mean in this book; we consider the kinds of social differences that society identifies as important for determining the experiences and futures of individuals and groups. There are many ways in which a person or group is related to diversity. This book will invite you to learn more about what is meant by diversity, our psychological responses to it, what we know about human behavior and diversity, and how it impacts us as people and as a nation. Although diversity often offers opportunities for positive benefits, it is not just any differences that are beneficial. We do not want more felons or bullies among us. But other things equal, we do believe that diversity of perspectives, experiences, talents, and backgrounds can enrich most contexts, institutions, and relationships.

However, as we will show in later chapters, there seems to be a general human tendency to avoid differences or react negatively to them. Moreover, when we focus on differences, we often fail to appreciate the similarities among us. These biases occur at all social levels: (a) individual attitudes and behavior, (b) institutional policies and programs, and (c) cultural beliefs and practices that often lead to biases in relationships and in institutions. Two of the major challenges of diversity in everyday life are to understand and reduce the many biases that hinder the creation and support of effective diversity in groups, institutions, organizations, and societies and then to maximize the benefits of diversity and to minimize the difficulties and adverse effects growing diversity can produce.

This book focuses on the **psychology of diversity**—basic psychological processes that are triggered when we encounter people who are different from us in significant and salient ways, or experience being treated differently by others because of our social status. It further explores the dynamics of mental representation and social interaction across individuals, institutions, and cultures, and how differential bases of power, privilege, and status affect these interactions. Finally, it identifies the effects of diverse contexts on the thoughts, actions, and feelings of people in them.

We begin with four real stories, based on student-to-student interviews done in a course on racism and prejudice, about experiences of prejudice. These stories come from student-led interviews about diversity and help to illustrate what we mean by diversity's challenges at these three levels.

Fahad H. is an exchange student from Pakistan who has lived in the United States for less than a year and is getting his Masters Degree at an ivy-league university. He has strongly defined typical Middle Eastern facial features and a golden hue to his skin. His hair is dark. He also has a slight Pakistani or Indian accent. His western dress, charming manner, excellent spoken and written English, and handsome features also define him. Fahad describes his experiences on his campus and those when not on the campus as being very different:

> When I am not at the university I feel more conscious of my accent. I'm sometimes asked where I am from, but not in a kind or curious way, but with suspicion. I'm watched on the train. I've been stopped by transit cops asking where I am going and where I came from. This has never happened to me in Pakistan, my home. I know people treat me differently because of 9/11.

Fahad has a number of Pakistani friends, some of whom wear traditional dress, are Muslim, or have English-speaking characteristics similar to his, who have had similar experiences. Fahad is aware of the well-documented strong negative bias against

Middle-Eastern and Muslim persons since 2001. Fahad and his friends are experiencing bias at the individual level.

Susanna G. is a college student who has worked for 5 years as an administrative assistant in a graphic design and marketing firm in New York City. She was born in the United States and her parents were born in the Dominican Republic. She came across an article in *The New York Times* about bias against and exclusion of Blacks and other minorities in her industry. Susanna brought the article to a class on racism and prejudice to discuss it with her professor. She stated,

> My firm is an example of exactly what they are describing in this article. There has never been a person of color ever hired in or promoted to a management position in my company. All of the cleaning staff and most of the administrative assistants are Black or Hispanic. All of the supervisors are White. When there are meetings with other firms or when I have to cover a conference, I never see anyone who is not White calling the shots.

She asked, "Is this an example of institutional bias based on race in the workplace?"

Tameeka A. is a senior at a private university where she is a marketing major. She has always worked in fashion sales, and over the summer between her junior and senior year she applied for and was hired as a salesperson for a large national clothing chain that caters to preppy fashion for "all American" young men and women. She arrived on her first day dressed to impress. Her hair was neatly braided cornrows, she wore large gold hoop earrings, and a colorful skirt and blouse with coordinating African print. Tameeka was called into her manager's office and told she could not wear cornrows or large hoop earrings on the sales floor because they did not represent the image the store wanted to promote. She was also told to "tone down her clothing" because ethnic clothing was not allowed on sales personnel. Tameeka was also told that if she didn't want to change her style she would only be able to work in the stockroom. Is it fair to Tameeka that conforming to the company standards prohibits her personal expression in how she dresses? Does the manager not have the right to dictate appropriate dress code for the company? Is Tameeka experiencing a form of cultural bias?

Robert S., when he is asked, describes himself as White. His mother is Italian and his father is Irish, but he says, "I'm White," when asked his racial and ethnic identity. Robert has no ethnicity that he acknowledges day to day—it is only part of his background, called up when asked, but he does not see it as self-defining. When interviewed he cannot describe any ways in which he has experienced individual, institutional, or cultural biases. Robert says in this interview, "I don't see color, we live in a society where everyone has equal rights and a chance to prove himself." Is Robert unbiased? What is his place in the social diversity of America?

These brief descriptions illustrate how people perceive or experience bias on an individual, institutional, and cultural level. They also illustrate that some majority group members may not experience such biases, based on their racial status. But we also go beyond this three-prong framework to propose that not all challenges to diversity are because of biased perceptions, intentions, or beliefs. There are two basic ideas that reflect this viewpoint. First, at times it is not the right and wrong of a situation that we must consider but rather the difference between two positions or among several that may be reasonable, appropriate and worthwhile and therefore difficult to resolve. Second, the more diverse perspectives and points of view there are, the more difficult it is to formulate policies and programs, articulate values, and accept principles that are equitable for all.

A Taxonomy of Diversity

The psychology of diversity considers different meanings and aspects that diversity can assume. Often diversity is used only to refer to ethnic and racial differences and it is also often confused with affirmative action. Scott Page (2007) provides a useful taxonomy for distinguishing among different types of diversity. He proposes four main diversity categories: cognitive, identity, demographic, and preference.

Cognitive diversity reflects differences in patterns of thinking, analysis, perception, and point of view, including:

- Perspectives: ways of representing and understanding the world around us.
- Heuristics: thinking tools or strategies for solving personal problems or achieving desired goals.
- Interpretations: creating categories into which we place and give meaning to things, events, experiences.
- Predictions: inferences we make about what goes with or causes what.

Identity diversity represents differences among people based on sex, gender orientation, religion, race, ethnicity, age, sexual orientation, immigrant status, and so on that are reflected in their affinity for and identification with those social categories.

Demographic diversity occurs when differences among people are based on social categories or social roles without regard to their psychological salience for the person. These differences usually consist of the same categories as identity diversity.

Preference diversity reflects differences in taste and values, including:

- **Fundamental preferences**: the *outcomes* we value or prefer.
- **Instrumental preferences**: the *means* by which we pursue preferred outcomes.

We are used to thinking about identity and demographic diversity. Complications arise when we introduce cognitive or psychological diversity and preferences or values. Even when people agree about valued outcomes like fundamental preferences, they may disagree about the best way to achieve them—instrumental preferences.

Another useful taxonomy is provided by Milem (2003). He proposes three interrelated ways to view diversity: **structural diversity** (numerical and proportional representation), **diversity-related initiatives** (cultural awareness workshops, ethnic studies courses, etc.), and **diversity interactions** (exchanges between and among people who are different). Structural diversity does not guarantee either of the other two forms. And you cannot have the last two if structural diversity does not exist, thus all three are interconnected. Research supports the positive benefits of both diversity initiatives and diverse interactions (Chang, 1999; Gurin, Nagda, & Lopez, 2004).

Diversity is not one thing, it is many things. Its varied nature is one of its challenges; diversity introduces a higher level of complexity to various contexts than does homogeneity. However, the varied nature of diversity is also a principal source of its benefit; from complexity comes better problem solving, greater understanding, and better citizens.

When Diversity Does Not Add Up To Equality

Political and economic power is unevenly distributed in society but social hierarchy is normal (Sidanius & Pratto, 1999). Groups vary in their ability to make decisions that affect the well-being of others. In this case, the group may have considerable influence that can disadvantage less-powerful groups, and advantage their own group. In the United States, men, particularly White men, have historically had greater educational and professional opportunities than have women. On average men get paid more and have more prestigious jobs. Is the reason for this simply because they are better at these jobs? Or is it because they have had more advantages? Or is there something about our cultural values and beliefs that assign greater prestige to things men do? It is hard sometimes to distinguish the influences of privileged opportunity, societal practices and cultural beliefs, and merit-based accomplishment.

We believe in merit, equality of opportunity, and fairness. But accomplishing all of these is challenged by historical patterns of advantage and disadvantage, and by ongoing biases. Many of these biases occur without awareness or intention.

Take a moment and think about the social groups with which you identify and their relative position in the U.S. social hierarchy. Do you belong to or identify with groups that have traditionally been disadvantaged? Groups that have been advantaged? Do you believe that one may be advantaged by virtue of not being disadvantaged? In those instances, disadvantage is hidden. People's understanding of advantage and disadvantage is often limited to what is salient. So calling attention to yourself or your group may be a way to transform disadvantage into advantage.

This book addresses many questions you have probably thought about as you have encountered diversity such as the following.

- When people disagree about the value of increasing diversity, what do they disagree about?
- Does diversity mean the same thing to members of underrepresented groups and majority groups? What are some differences in how it might be understood?
- How can we really be fair to everyone when our society is so diverse?
- Do racism and prejudice remain factors in race relations in the United States? Or, are we now a post-racial society?
- What kinds of diversity strengthen an organization, institution, or society? If so how does it?
- Are there right ways and wrong ways to manage diversity? How do we balance an emphasis on what we have in common with what makes us different?
- Where does individual bias come from? What role does culture play?

- Do some groups have more power than others? Are historical disadvantages or advantages for some groups perpetuated in today's society? If so, does it continue? Can anything be done about this?
- Is it fair to consider race/ethnicity or gender in college admissions? Is it fair not to?
- What role do Whites play in our analysis and understanding of diversity? Is it really true that diversity benefits all? In what ways?

You may have a number of other questions about diversity and more may come to mind as you read this book. Try to remember them—write them down in fact—so that when you finish reading this book, you can determine if your questions have been answered or if you need to look elsewhere for additional resources to answer them.

Perspectives on Diversity

Diversity is a topic of enormous scope and complexity. We cannot cover all of these aspects of diversity in this book. Instead we focus on core psychological processes and institutional practices that inhibit or facilitate effective diversity in schools, organizations, and society at large. Our goal is to present a coherent story about diversity and how people react to it for better or for worse.

Behavioral Science and Diversity

Although we draw on work from a range of disciplines, we approach diversity primarily from the perspective of psychology, hence *The Psychology of Diversity*. We emphasize the central role of *individual* perceptions of, and reactions to, diversity. We consider research from the micro-level of neuroscience, which studies the structure and function of the brain and their relation to behavior, to the macro-levels of social and political psychology, which examine how our identification with various groups influence how we respond to others. The scope of our perspective is broad. We also consider institutional and cultural influences on diversity. Nevertheless, consistent with our psychological perspective, we discuss how historical events, institutions such as the legal system, and culture affect responses to diversity by shaping the way people think, feel, and act.

We illustrate the roles of history and politics largely through examples of events and policies that have shaped U.S. society. As such, the concept of race and issues about race relations occupy central places in this book. Race relations have been the defining form of intergroup relations in the United States politically and socially since the arrival of people from Europe and Africa. Most of the psychological research on intergroup relations has been about race, because of the primacy of Black–White relations during the Civil Rights Movement in the United States and because of our history of enslavement based on skin color. The Black–White divide, known for decades as "the color line," was identified by W. E. B. DuBois (1903) as the problem of the twentieth century. This divide is the primary lens through which we see race.

Race is very real as a practical point of departure for social identity, social classification, and meaning making.

In a discussion about diversity, race can play a central role in highlighting the meaning of diversity, but it is not the only aspect of diversity we consider. We emphasize throughout the book that diversity is, well, diverse; understanding one form of diversity does not automatically mean we understand other forms. Therefore, we consider diversity of many types both internationally as well as nationally. Nevertheless, race in the United States represents a consistent thread across the chapters in this book that allows us to draw on a large body of work to develop a more comprehensive narrative of how history, politics, economics, and human psychology operate, often in concert, to shape diversity and reactions to it.

Returning from time to time to issues of race allows us to illustrate how culture and history influence the ways people think about diversity. It informs us about misconceptions and why they develop. For example, many people still think that race is a biological concept that represents differences among people. But research has clearly shown that a biological basis for race is an inadequate explanation of the wide range of human variation. Asian and European gene variations are very similar to each other, and all the genetic variations found in Asians and Europeans are also found among Africans. The amount of variation found *within* any race group, Asians for example, will be greater than the variation *between* any two groups, Asians and Europeans for example. The human genome is 99.9% the same for all human beings (for more information, see National Institutes of Health Human Genome Project http:// www.genome.gov/). We are, in fact, more biologically alike than we are different.

Even though race means little in a biological sense, in a social sense race matters a lot. As historian Robin Kelley explained in the 2011 PBS documentary, *Race – The Power of Illusion*, race is not about how you look, but "how people assign meaning to how you look" (http://www.pbs.org/race/000_About/002_04-background-02-05. htm). As we saw in our four student profiles, the significance of race lies in its social meaning. Societies construct significance for any concept or thing by imbuing it with beliefs and assumptions and by applying actions and organizational structures to it. Racism is the most pernicious outcome among the beliefs about race. In a racialized society, where life outcomes are determined in part by racial classification, racial inequality is embedded in and a product of social institutions (Jones, 1997; Smedley & Smedley, 2012).

In our discussions of race, we do not imbue the term or the groups Black or White with biological significance (see Helms, Jernigan, & Mascher, 2005). However, we recognize that race groups such as Black, White, Hispanic, Asian, and so forth are socially meaningful when they result in differences in treatment and different social outcomes within a diverse society.

We adopt the general framework of diversity science in our analysis of the psychology of diversity (see Plaut, 2010). According to Plaut, a **diversity science** should (a) avoid employing and perpetuating an abstract conception of race; (b) locate the sources of inequality not only in individual minds but also in the practices, policies, and institutions that they create; (c) unearth cultural ideologies that help perpetuate systems of inequality; (d) interrogate the mask of privilege that Whiteness carries; (e) investigate the perspectives of both minority and majority groups in dynamic interaction; and (f) document the experiences of groups beyond the Black–White binary. In this way, Plaut argues, diversity science will be able to provide descriptions of diversity-related psychological processes.

Diversity within Diversity

All members of diverse groups are not alike, far from it. Diversity is not sufficiently captured by looking at racial, ethnic, or cultural groups as a whole. Not only is there diversity within groups but, at the individual level, a person belongs to multiple diversity groups. Think about yourself. You have a gender, cultural background, sexual orientation, age, way of thinking, and so forth. You belong to multiple groups that, taken together, represent diversity in U.S. society. Of course there are even more groups that you may belong to, such as student, so this concept of diversity gets rather complicated. The fact that each of us belongs to multiple diversity groups complicates any consideration of diversity but must be incorporated into our understanding of it. There is, therefore, diversity "within" and "between" people or groups. We are a diverse society and within the customary demographic markers, there are even more layers of diversity.

Here are some examples. Asians from Korea are different from those from Japan who are different from those from China, and a multitude of diversity exists within each of these Asian groups. South East Asians from India are different from persons from Malaysia, Vietnam, Cambodia, and so on. Whether they are first- or second-generation immigrants to the United States also matters. The so-called "model minority," Asian or Asian American, covers a broad spectrum of socioeconomic statuses, languages, cultures, and immigrant statuses (Sue, Sue, Sue, & Takeuchi, 1995). Hispanics are considered an ethnic group as well as a race category in the U.S. Census, but they may be Black or White or Asian, come from Mexico, Central or Latin America, Spain, Puerto Rico, or Cuba. They may live in the southwest, on the west coast, the east coast or the southeast, each with different challenges and presenting a different cultural context. Like members of all other groups, they vary by sexual orientation.

While we frequently discuss Black–White relations in this book, it is also important to keep in mind the diversity within these groups. Blacks are young and old, rich and poor, immigrant and native born. They may live in Black urban environments or Black suburban enclaves or integrated suburban settings. Robinson (2011) describes this diversity as comprising at least four groups: (a) mainstream, the middle-class majority with a full ownership stake in American society; (b) emergent, persons of mixed-race heritage and communities of recent Black immigrants; (c) transcendent, a small elite group with massive wealth, power and influence; and (d) abandoned, a minority with defeatist dreams and pessimistic hope. According to Robinson, these "four Black Americas are increasingly distinct, separated by demography, geography and psychology . . . leading separate lives" (Robinson, 2011, p. 5). Touré (2011) goes further to describe 40 million ways to be Black based on the uniqueness of each and every Black person.

Whites too are rich and poor, urban and suburban, well educated and not, gay and straight, and members of many different ethnic groups, such as Italian, Polish, or

German. American Indians are from different nations, live in different parts of the United States, and have different traditions and needs. They too vary in socioeconomic status, acculturation, and sexual orientation.

Finally, a large and growing number of people consider themselves to be of mixed race, a group also richly diverse as described for the other groups we mention. By 2050, one in five Americans will describe themselves as multiracial (Lee & Bean, 2012). And we add one further wrinkle: diversity exists not only between and within groups—reflecting ways in which they are different from one another, but also within each individual—reflecting the diversity of experience, identity, and consciousness of each person. So when we talk about diversity, it is not one thing but many. The challenges our society faces in making a harmonious mixture are enormous. This book cannot "solve" these challenging diversity perspectives and issues. We can, however, share psychological research findings that shed light on the challenges and provide some answers to some of our questions about diversity.

But we do not want to leave you with the impression that diversity is only about problems and difficulties. Diversity among us in a variety of settings creates opportunities and better outcomes. So the challenges are not only to lessen the adverse impacts and meet the problems that diversity presents, but to capitalize on the opportunities that multiple perspectives, different experiences and talents, understandings, and even hunches or intuitions can offer.

The Diversity Divide: Benefits versus Challenges

Although we argue that diversity is a reality and an important social value, we also are well aware that everyone does not share the belief that diversity is necessarily good (Crisp & Turner, 2011). The value of diversity is contested in this society; some think it is merely a code for promoting special interests, while others think it is important to promote fairness and level the playing field for different groups. Further, whether you endorse diversity as a valuable goal or oppose it as an infringement of individual rights depends on what it means to you. Some people embrace and promote diversity as valuable and necessary, while others think it is divisive and a threat to core American traditions and values. This makes promoting diversity a challenge. Let's consider some of the reasons that are associated with the benefits viewpoint first.

What Are the Benefits of Diversity?

Among the reasons offered for the value of diversity are that it (a) facilitates adaptability, flexibility, and creativity in thinking and acting; (b) produces better citizenship in a more diverse world; (c) fosters **human capital**, which are the resources that people bring to enterprises, by engaging participation of marginalized groups; and (d) is morally correct and consistent with the core U.S. values of equity and fairness. A brief summary of the reasoning for each of these benefit perspectives follows.

Adaptability, flexibility, and creativity   Flexibility is the trait that allows a person to perceive others in non-stereotypical ways, to view situations in novel ways, and to offer creative solutions to complex problems. This trait, as does adaptability and creativity, often follows exposure to diversity (Page, 2007). For example, in one study racially diverse and non-diverse (all-White) mock juries were exposed to pre-trial questions about racism. The diverse jury exchanged a wider range of information, were more lenient to both Black and White defendants, cited more case facts, made fewer errors of fact, and were more amenable to discussing racism than when they were all-White juries (Sommers, 2006).

Another study examined the effects of both diversity of opinions and racial diversity in small group discussions (Antonio, Chang, Hakuta, Kenny, Levin, & Milem, 2004). Members of groups that included minorities, whether based on race or divergent opinions, saw the minority person as contributing novel ideas to the discussions of a social issue, such as the death penalty or child labor practices in developing countries. Furthermore, diverse groups showed greater integrative complexity as evidenced by more differentiation and integration of multiple perspectives. Even younger children show benefits of diverse perspectives. When taught to classify information along multiple dimensions, 5- to 10-year-old children created counter-stereotypical combinations of social roles. They created combinations such as a female manual worker and a male secretary and were much less likely to make gender-stereotyped judgments and responses (Bigler & Liben, 1992).

Better citizenship   The United States is increasingly diverse, not only in its population but in every aspect of social, organizational, and institutional functioning. Good citizenship in a diverse world requires that one understands and respects differences. Being afraid of differences or seeing them as threatening is counterproductive. Those optimistic about diversity believe that diversity experiences and training prepare a person for living and functioning in a diverse world.

Research supports this claim. Gurin et al. (2004) developed an Intergroup Dialogues Course, designed for first-semester college students from diverse backgrounds to bring diversity and democracy into alignment using a curriculum consisting of readings, lectures, papers, and intergroup dialogues. The **Intergroup Dialogues Course** is based on five principles: (a) presence of diverse others in this course based on pairing people of color and White people; women and men; African Americans and Jews; gay men, lesbians, bisexuals, and heterosexuals; and Whites and Hispanics; (b) discontinuity from pre-college experiences; (c) equality among peers; (d) discussion guided by civil discourse rules; and (e) normalization, and negotiation of conflict.

Students who participated in the Intergroup Dialogues Course, compared with those who did not participate, were more likely to believe that differences are not divisive, that conflict is not necessarily bad, and that learning about other groups is desirable and worthwhile (Gurin et al., 2004). After participating in the Intergroup Dialogues Course, students were more likely to be interested in politics and to participate in campus civic and political activities. They also indicate that they are more likely to be active in the community and to promote racial and ethnic understanding once they graduated.

Full use of human capital   Systematic exclusion of segments of society from its most important institutions, such as education, military service, professions, and so forth, takes a toll on everyone. The Tuskegee Airmen story illustrates this point very well. The Airmen, a special all-Black cadre of fighter pilots, integrated a racially segregated Army Air Corps during World War II (see the Hollywood movie *Red Tails* for a dramatization of their story). At first they were marginalized and limited to simple non-combat and low-risk assignments. Eventually, they were sent out on very dangerous missions, in somewhat faulty planes, to protect White pilots from harm. While doing this they proved that they were excellent and brave pilots. As their feats continued, and with expanding duties and assignments, the Tuskegee Airmen became one of the best squadrons in the Air Corps.

A similar situation occurred when the U.S. military adopted the "Don't ask don't tell" policy toward gay and lesbian service members in the 1980s. This compromise policy allowed gay and lesbian military personnel to serve, as long as they did not live openly as non-heterosexuals. In effect, the policy required members of a minority group to hide a part of their identity. Its repeal made it possible for gay men and lesbians to serve with integrity and human dignity and some were observed to be among the bravest and best. And it was not until 1994 that women were permitted to occupy combat positions, such as serving on warships, in the military.

A society is better and stronger when it promotes and encourages broad participation from all citizens. It costs more to incarcerate a person for a year than to send him or her to college for that same year (Resnick, 2011). In 2011, for example, the cost for a student attending Princeton University in New Jersey was $37,000; the expense associated with a prisoner in a New Jersey state prison was $44,000. Certainly most incarcerated criminals deserve and need to be in prison. However, for many prison inmates, it would have been much better to find opportunities for them early in life to participate as citizens and become engaged in society.

It is morally correct and consistent with the value of equality   Equality of opportunity is a core value of the United States. As we will see in Chapter 3, throughout U.S. history, equality has been a core value but not a reality. A guiding diversity principle is desirable because it sets our sites on equality. According to this view, inequality is not a natural consequence of human variations in abilities, character, and culture. Rather, the characteristics that make a strong person and a strong society are found in all groups. When we narrowly identify the attributes that are considered as criteria for opportunity, the diversity among us is shortchanged. Even if the criterion is relevant and important, such as SAT scores or grades, potential diversity of access and participation is limited.

A current university president who is from a diversity group that is often marginalized, was a poor test-taker, and was denied access to educational opportunities for many years, even though he obviously had the ability to succeed. Diversity as a social goal requires looking for ways to increase participation and outcomes for people and groups who have been excluded or marginalized. We don't know what we may be missing by overlooking these groups. Including diversity as a guiding social principle is morally correct and reflects the highest value for which we stand as a nation.

Institutions of higher learning are increasingly including diversity as an educational and institutional goal. For example, in 2011, the 165-year old City College of New York renewed a long-standing commitment to diversity by establishing a Council on

Inclusion and Excellence. This linked the College's mission of excellence with one of inclusion. The Council's mission includes "[enhancing the College's] ability to fully incorporate the full diversity of backgrounds, traditions and experiences of faculty, staff, and students in realizing the goal of an inclusive community that values excellence in scholarship, creative arts, teaching and learning, and student development." The Council also makes recommendations that promote an understanding of how inclusion and participation of the diverse groups within the College community fosters excellence. It further works to encourage a culturally rich and cohesive environment that nourishes student retention and academic success (*Report of the President's Council on Inclusion and Excellence*, September 2012, City College of New York; http://www.ccny.cuny.edu/inclusion/mission.cfm).

What Are the Challenges of Diversity?

Among the reasons offered that bolster the opinion that diversity is undesirable are that it (a) excludes non-minority groups, typically but not always Whites; (b) defines which differences matter on the basis of convenience or ideology; (c) violates the principle of reward based on merit; and (d) highlights differences, fostering stereotyping and driving people farther apart. A brief summary of the reasoning for each follows.

The practice of diversity can be exclusionary   Is diversity a characteristic of our nation that is both expanding and beneficial, or is it a specification of which groups should be given preferential treatment? People who do not belong to a "diversity group" often feel like diversity is "not about them." If you are White, male, able-bodied, young, heterosexual, and middle class, you are in the default non-diverse group. Diversity then refers to other people and excludes you. From this viewpoint diversity goals are at best irrelevant, or at worst threatening (Norton & Sommers, 2011; Plaut, Garnett, Buffardi, & Sanchez-Burks, 2011).

Diversity goals may seem suspect even to those they seem to benefit, particularly Black persons. When diversity becomes a central goal, the discourse of social justice and civil rights diverges from a focus on race. In the name of diversity, it seems that a focus on specific groups is blurred, so Blacks may feel as threatened as Whites. Thus, one may be suspicious about diversity because of what it excludes—it's not about me, it fails to include me—or how it dilutes historical and ongoing efforts on behalf of certain groups. Diversity then can be both exclusionary because it is too *narrowly* defined or too inclusive because it is too *broadly* defined. Either way, individuals may have good reasons to feel that diversity does not apply to them or their group.

Which differences matter?   People are different from each other in myriad ways. Deciding which differences to privilege is not easy. The question becomes, What kinds of diversity matter? A former nominee of President Richard Nixon to the U.S. Supreme Court, G. Harrold Carswell, was rejected for, among other reasons, being a mediocre jurist. Senator Roman Hruska (R. Nebraska) came to his defense: "Even if he were mediocre, there are a lot of mediocre judges and people and lawyers. They are entitled to a little representation, aren't they, and a little chance?" (*Time Magazine*, 1970).

Obviously, mediocrity is not a diversity value, but what kinds of diversity should be valued? Furthermore, is it necessary to set specific diversity goals? If we don't have specific goals and instead simply say we respect differences and want more of them, when can we say we have reached our goal? Which person best represents diversity: a transgendered individual or a lesbian? Do Asians add to diversity? If so, in what settings? What about older adults or persons with physical or mental challenges? In some cases we may want to recruit more members of certain groups to diversify a setting. In other situations, it may be enough to simply treat all groups respectfully and allow them to be welcomed and successful.

Diversity of perspective or point of view, values, beliefs, and so on can also be aspects of diversity to consider. For example, college campuses are considered to be bastions of liberal thought and politics. Some argue that diversity could or should include more conservative perspectives. The same might be said of conservative institutions of higher learning.

Diversity undermines meritocracy   **Meritocracy** is a core belief about how benefits should be earned and bestowed. In theory, merit is objectively determined on an individual basis. If you work harder, if you are smarter, you should get more or have more. Higher SAT scores combined with a high grade point average should give a person an advantage over a person who does not have these credentials. What does social group or race have to do with it? The answer is, a lot. Context matters.

Many people have argued that modern-day baseball records set during the so-called steroid era should be set aside because these players had an unfair advantage. Others argue that every era was different and aspects of the earlier records can be called into question as well. Racial segregation in baseball meant that some of the best players who were Black could not compete during the time many old-time players, like Babe Ruth, set their records. We cannot really answer the fairness question from this perspective, but it raises an important point: Fairness is not easily calculated and differences among us may contribute to that calculation in a favorable or unfavorable way. The context by which we judge fairness is very important.

Focusing on differences may promote conflict   Does highlighting differences lead to stereotyping and ultimately drive people farther apart? Research has shown, for example, that emphasizing a **multicultural perspective**, in which people focus on others' different racial, ethnic, and cultural heritages, leads people to stereotype others more (Wolsko, Park, Judd, & Wittenbrink, 2000). Conversely, adopting a **colorblind perspective**, in which group differences are ignored, is associated with greater prejudicial behavior. Moreover, the colorblind approach is considered a requirement for achieving true meritocracy.

Although the term is generally applied to race issues, it is a more general ideology that minimizes any group differences in favor of individual assessments. For example, working together in diverse groups for a period of time can reduce the effects of surface-level factors like race, and strengthen deep-level factors like attitudes which can produce more group cohesion (Harrison, Price, Gavin, & Florey, 2002).

Essentially, these divergent beliefs about diversity challenge our ability to allow diversity to flourish. They are flip sides of the same issue, making diversity very complex and not amenable to simple solutions. Those holding beliefs in the colorblind approach may be indifferent or apathetic about diversity initiatives; and in some instances, actively oppose them. Those holding a multicultural perspective usually support initiating of diversity activities, but may fail to see some possible unintended but adverse consequences of them such as those mentioned above.

Organization of this Book

As we have seen, diversity is challenging to understand and analyze. Our approach is based primarily on the research literature in social psychology, which has largely focused on prejudice exhibited by Whites because of the history of racial discrimination in the United States and the general presence of Whites in positions of power and authority. We recognize that members of other groups can also be prejudiced and we believe that a full understanding of the psychology of diversity should examine prejudices of diverse groups, not just Whites. Also studied, but not nearly as much, has been how people respond when they are the targets of prejudice and discrimination. This research increased significantly after 1990 (Swim & Stangor, 1998). However, diversity research really began around the beginning of this century (Plaut, 2010).

Diversity research, from a scientific perspective as discussed in Chapter 2, incorporates research on race and ethnicity but goes beyond it. Plaut (2010) offers a framework for diversity research: It should avoid abstract conceptions of race; locate the sources of inequality not only in persons, but also in the practices and policies of institutions; and unearth cultural ideologies that help perpetuate systems of inequality. With respect to the race and ethnicity diversity, it should examine the mask of privilege that Whiteness carries, and investigate the perspectives of both minority and majority groups in dynamic interaction. It should also document the experiences of groups beyond the much-studied and analyzed Black–White binary.

We know much less about how people experience diversity than we do about the dynamics of prejudice and discrimination. Therefore, although we take a research-based approach, at times we must accept that we do not have the research to support certain ideas, ideals, or practices. At these junctures, we ask you to think for yourself, search for research or perhaps do research, discuss issues, and to come up with your own opinions. We hope you will use these as opportunities to think deeply about the questions, answers, and complexities of the diversity debate.

This book is organized into four parts. Part One provides an orientation and presents the background to diversity and the approach that we take in our analysis and discussion. Parts Two and Three focus on the different ways in which bias can be expressed on an individual, institutional, and cultural level. Part Two emphasizes how individual psychological processes—how we think, feel, fear, need, and desire—shape our responses to difference and diversity. Part Three discusses how organizational, institutional, and cultural forces influence the ways groups are positioned in society and how power determines the degree to which societies and people benefit from diversity. Part Four presents an appraisal of the future of diversity, based on existing literature, and offers some key principles that can guide us into that future. Each chapter concludes with a series of questions that ask readers to reflect upon the implications of the material in the chapter and apply new insights to relevant personal situations, events, and social issues.

Part One, Framing Diversity (Chapters 1–3), consists of three chapters and builds on the ideas we have presented in this introductory chapter. This section provides a context for understanding diversity and describes our approach to discussing challenges to it. Chapter 2, Central Concepts in the Psychology of Diversity, introduces key concepts and terms that recur throughout the book and that are central to our analysis. Chapter 3, Historical Perspectives on Diversity in the United States, focuses on the historical evolution of diversity in the U.S. population. Understanding how we respond to diversity today requires knowing how we got to where we are historically, politically, and socially. We explore themes such as the historical reasons for our diversity and how it has been managed, and how this past history of diversity affects us now.

Part Two, Psychological Processes (Chapters 4–9), consists of five chapters that explain how individual and group processes present challenges to diversity and its benefits. These biases are related to personality, basic psychological processes, and even brain structure and function. We also consider the consequences of individual and group biases for people who are often its targets. These chapters raise and discuss a number of questions. Are there biological and neurological reasons that a person expresses prejudice? Do biological responses explain why some people are racist? How do in-groups and out-groups form? How have they been studied? How do they affect their members and others?

Chapter 4, Personality and Individual Differences, identifies the types of people who actively resist diversity. However, personality is only one of many processes that determine people's reactions to diversity, and the current challenges to diversity go far beyond a limited number of "bad apples" with prejudiced personalities. Chapter 5, Social Cognition and Categorization, reviews how the average person thinks about people and social contexts, this is, social cognition. The mental shortcuts that people use to navigate a complex and diverse world can often lead to bias against people who are unfamiliar to us or different in the way they look, speak, or act. Nevertheless, this chapter also shows that diversity does not have to be divisive. For example, a single personalized interaction with a member of a different group can dramatically change how a person thinks about that group as a whole.

Chapter 6, Social Identity, Roles, and Relations, describes how people, through normal and seemingly rational processes, can devalue members of other groups and resist diversity. For instance, social discrimination in the past can lead to justifications for different treatment of diverse group in the present and future. However, it is possible for people to value, rather than devalue, diversity. When we work cooperatively with others who offer different types of knowledge or perspective, we appreciate the ways that diversity benefits us all. Diversity doesn't have to produce divides; it can be seen as an important social resource, one that should be embraced rather than avoided.

Chapter 7, Is Bias in the Brain?, addresses the question of whether we are biologically programmed to be biased. It discusses how different areas of the brain are activated spontaneously when we encounter a person from a different group and how that can automatically arouse bias. But this chapter also shows that we can short-circuit these biases. Although the structures and activities of the brain are often recruited in our social biases, biology is not destiny. What we choose to think about and experience determines how the brain responds to diversity.

Chapter 8, Coping and Adapting to Stigma and Difference, shifts the focus to how people respond to bias in the short and long term. Perceiving persistent racial discrimination directed at one's group generally has negative psychological consequences. But a substantial body of research shows both the negative effects of perceiving or expecting biased treatment or judgment and ways in which one may counter these negative influences. For example, adopting a strong racial or ethnic identification can protect a person from the adverse effects of perceived discrimination. In general, the negative psychological consequences of belonging to a stigmatized minority group and perceiving that you have been treated unfairly are balanced by psychological adaptations that preserve well-being and self-esteem.

Chapter 9, Intergroup Interaction, shows that diversity is relational; it is about intergroup relations, not just about the separate biases that people hold toward each other or about the ways people cope with being the target of these biases. Intergroup interactions are more fragile than exchanges between members of the same group, and people in intergroup interactions often misunderstand each other despite positive intentions. However, when intergroup contact occurs under appropriately structured circumstances, such as those involving cooperation and the exchange of personal information, it can substantially improve intergroup attitudes and become uniquely rewarding.

Part Three, Culture, Power, and Institutions (Chapters 10–12), extends the analysis of intergroup relations and diversity by asking a number of questions. How do we consider the broader influence of culture and institutions and culture on bias? How do we make judgments of fairness, merit, and deservingness when people are different, and power resides within some groups more than others? Diversity is not just about how a person thinks or feels about another person in a different group, it is also about where groups are situated in society and how institutions reflect this hierarchy.

We address the issue of cultural diversity in Chapter 10. This chapter describes how differences between people pose challenges to ideas about equality, fairness, merit, and value. This chapter focuses on ways in which our differing cultural backgrounds, perspectives, traditions, and predispositions vary as a function of where and how we grew up. Do these differences pose challenges for recognizing diversity? Does it create challenges for fairness? How can we avoid biases against some cultural groups while favoring others? This chapter also summarizes the research that illustrates some obstacles to diversity, and different ways in which we believe it can be successfully achieved.

Chapter 11, Social Roles and Power in a Diverse Society, explores the ways different groups strive to maintain advantage or seek recognition and influence in society. Power and privilege are central characteristics of any social order. The challenge for societies concerned with fairness is to balance the motivations for groups to maintain or enhance their social power while accommodating, indeed welcoming, diversity and the social change and advantages that may accompany it. In this chapter we explore how power is acquired and maintained and its relationship to social roles. The effects of power are pervasive. Therefore, a critical step in addressing bias in power dynamics is developing an awareness of the problem and ways in which diverse groups can negotiate power and privilege in the context of fairness.

Chapter 12, The Challenge of Diversity for Institutions, further examines how biases against diversity can be embedded in the policies that institutions and organization adopt. Institutional bias can be intentional or unintentional, subtle or easy to detect, and it may have negative or positive outcomes. Detecting bias in institutions is a complex task, and it is often difficult to prove. This chapter reviews evidence of adverse outcomes for members of minority groups in the economic system, educational sphere, and justice system and gives a few brief examples from other areas in U.S. society. In the final analysis, addressing institutional biases requires consideration of the broad cultural context in which it occurs.

The final chapter, The Psychology of Diversity: Principles and Prospects, summarizes what we have learned and what it means. It organizes the challenges we face in addressing diversity and points toward promising pathways to surmount obstacles and forge new opportunities. The goal of these analyses is to create a vision of a richly diverse society and a way to secure it that makes the diversity among us a cause of celebration and the achievement of a richer, better society for all.

In summary, in this book, we consider the psychology of diversity as it reflects our past, functions in our current everyday experiences, and forecasts our futures, personally and collectively. We are a nation that values both diversity—this is the "land of opportunity"—and equality; we believe, as Thomas Jefferson said, that all people "are created equal." Yet, we often respond to diversity, politically and individually, with racism and discrimination. Much of the research on diversity has focused on understanding these obstacles, and this book reflects much of that emphasis. However, the psychology of diversity also teaches us how to move beyond prejudice and racism, and achieve the benefits of interactions across the boundaries of diversity, transacting social hierarchies to create greater degrees of fairness and opportunity. This book reflects our belief that fear of difference can be tempered by excitement about new opportunities to learn and experience others. That "tolerance" of diversity can grow into appreciation of diversity, respect for difference, and a willingness to engage others across traditional group-based fault lines. We believe that to the degree we do that, we become more knowledgeable, creative, prosperous, moral, and socially responsible. Diversity is not about "them" or "others" but includes us all.

Summary

Diversity is a global and U.S. reality. There are more than 7 billion people on the planet and each person is uniquely different from every other. Our approach is to narrow it down. Although our goal is to help people understand diversity and people's responses in the broadest global context, much of this book is a case study of diversity issues in the United States.

The psychology of diversity—the basic psychological processes that are triggered when we encounter people who are different from us in significant and salient ways, or experience being treated differently by others because of our social status—is examined primarily with respect to racial and ethnic differences, although we also cover differences in gender, religion, ability, and sexual orientation. Diversity, and how people respond to it, depends on the history, economics, and politics of a society and the psychology of its members. For this reason, we focus primarily on diversity in the United States.

Prejudice and racism play important roles in the context of diversity and are a challenge to achieving its potential positive effects. It is a challenge to find the proper balance of approaches to diversity that simultaneously strengthen the fabric of our institutions and society and enrich our individual lives, while preserving the cherished values of equality of opportunity, individual liberty, and social justice for all. The United States has a fundamental commitment to equal opportunity and equal rights, and a compelling interest in diversity.

This commitment to diversity raises three fundamental questions that are the subject of this book: How can we create equality in a society that is so diverse? What are the impediments or barriers to realizing this goal? What are the benefits when we achieve it?

This book's main purpose is to help readers understand the psychology of diversity by reviewing what we know about human behavior and how it shapes our experiences with diversity in a variety of settings and contexts. This book highlights some psychological reactions to diversity and the emotions, perceptions, and behaviors they activate. It also presents evidence that guides us toward promising pathways for reducing some of the adverse impacts that may accompany increased diversity, as well as demonstrating some of the important benefits that diversity can produce.

Diversity is a topic of enormous scope and complexity. The psychology of diversity approach focuses on core psychological processes and institutional practices that inhibit or facilitate effective diversity in schools, organizations, and society at large. We emphasize the central role of individual perceptions of, and reactions to, diversity. We consider research from the micro-level of neuroscience to the macrolevels of social and political psychology, and institutional and cultural influences on diversity.

This book reflects our belief that fear of difference can be tempered by excitement about new opportunities to learn and experience others. That tolerance of diversity can grow into appreciation of diversity, respect for difference, and a willingness to engage others across traditional group-based fault lines. The psychology of diversity helps identify the means by which these important goals can be reached.

Questions for Thinking and Knowing

1. Draw a diagram, for your own use, that identifies ways in which you belong to diverse social categories. Some sources you might consider include family characteristics; race, ethnicity, and cultural background; and qualities that are unique to you as an individual but which you share with groups with which you identify. What sources of diversity included in your diagram were not included in the chapter? Does this help you define diversity?
2. Why is diversity challenging? How can we define and understand it so that it is less challenging?

3. Make a list of all the ways you can see that diversity is important and valuable today in your community, school, or work setting?
4. Which of the chapters outlined most appeal to you and which do you think will be the most challenging for you to understand? Think about why this might be the case.
5. List the five questions that you most want answered by this book. Save this list and review it at the end of the semester. Write us to let us know how well your initial questions were answered.

Key Terms

Cognitive diversity
Colorblind perspective
Compelling interest
Demographic diversity
Diversity
Diversity interactions
Diversity-related initiatives
Diversity science
Full participation
Fundamental preference

Human capital
Identity diversity
Instrumental preference
Intergroup Dialogues Course
Meritocracy
Multicultural perspective
Preference diversity
Psychology of diversity
Relational demography
Structural diversity

References

Antonio, A. L., Chang, M. J., Hakuta, K., Kenny, D. A., Levin, S., & Milem, J. F. (2004). Effects of racial diversity on complex thinking in college students. *Psychological Science, 15*, 507–510.

Bigler, R. S., & Liben, L. S. (1992). Cognitive mechanism in children's gender stereotyping: Theoretical and educational implications of a cognitive-based intervention. *Child Development, 63*, 1351–1363.

Chang, M. J. (1999). Does diversity matter? The educational impact of a racially diverse undergraduate population. *Journal of College Student Development, 40*, 377–395.

Crisp, R. J., & Turner, R. N. (2011). Cognitive adaptation to the experience of social and cultural diversity. *Psychological Bulletin, 137*, 242–266.

DuBois, W. E. B. (1903). *The souls of Black folk*. New York: Bantam Classic.

Gurin, P., Nagda, B., & Lopez, C. (2004). The benefits of diversity in education for democratic citizenship. *Journal of Social Issues, 60*, 17–34.

Harrison, D. A., Price, K. H., Gavin, J. H., & Florey, A. T. (2002). Time, teams, and task performance: Changing effects of surface- and deep-level diversity on group functioning. *Academy of Management Journal, 45*, 1029–1045.

Helms, J. E., Jernigan, M., & Mascher, J. (2005). The meaning of race in psychology and how to change it: A methodological perspective. *American Psychologist, 60*, 27–36.

Jones, J. M. (1997). *Prejudice and racism* (2nd ed.). New York: McGraw-Hill.

Lee, J., & Bean, F. D. (2012). *The diversity paradox: Immigration and the color line in twenty-first century America*. New York: Russell Sage Foundation.

Milem, J. F. (2003). The educational benefits of diversity: Evidence from multiple sectors. In M. J. Chang, D. Witt, J. Jones, & K. Hakuta (Eds.), *Compelling interest: Examining the evidence on racial dynamics in colleges and universities* (pp. 126–169). Stanford, CA: Stanford University Press.

Norton, M. I., & Sommers, S. R. (2011). Whites see racism as a zero-sum game that they are now losing. *Perspectives on Psychological Science, 6,* 215–218.

Page, S. E. (2007). *The difference: How the power of diversity creates better groups, firms, schools and societies.* Princeton, NJ: Princeton University Press.

Plaut, V. C. (2010). Diversity science: Why and how difference makes a difference. *Psychological Inquiry, 21,* 77–99.

Plaut, V. C., Garnett, F. G., Buffardi, L. E., & Sanchez-Burks, J. (2011). "What about me?" Perceptions of exclusion and Whites' reactions to multiculturalism. *Journal of Personality and Social Psychology, 101,* 337–353.

Resnick, B. (2011, November 1). Chart: One year of prison costs more than one year at Princeton. *The Atlantic.* Retrieved from http://www.theatlantic.com/national/archive/2011/11/chart-one-year-of-prison-costs-more-than-one-year-at-princeton/247629/

Robinson, E. (2011). *Disintegration: The splintering of Black America.* New York: Doubleday.

Sidanius, J., & Pratto, F. (1999). *Social dominance: An intergroup theory of social hierarchy and oppression.* Cambridge: Cambridge University Press.

Smedley, A., & Smedley, B. D. (2012). *Race in North America: Origin and evolution of a worldview* (4th ed.). Boulder, CO: Westview Press.

Sommers, S. R. (2006). On racial diversity and group decision making: Identifying multiple effects of racial composition on jury deliberations. *Journal of Personality and Social Psychology, 90,* 597–612.

Sturm, S., Eatman, T., Saltmarsh, J., & Bush, A. (2011). Full participation: Building the architecture for diversity and public engagement in higher education (White paper). Columbia University Law School: Center for Institutional and Social Change.

Sue, S., Sue, D. W., Sue, L., & Takeuchi, D. T. (1995). Psychopathology among Asian Americans: A model minority? *Cultural Diversity and Mental Health, 1*(1), 39–51.

Swim, J. K., & Stangor, C. (Eds.). (1998). *Prejudice: The target's perspective.* Santa Barbara, CA: Academic Press.

Time Magazine. (1970, March 30). The Supreme Court: A seat for mediocrity? Retrieved on March 16, 2012 from http://www.time.com/time/magazine/article/0,9171,942208,00.html

Touré. (2011). *Who's afraid of post-Blackness? What it means to be Black now.* New York: Free Press.

Tsui, A. S., Porter, L. W., & Egan, T. D. (2002). When both similarities and dissimilarities matter: Extending the concept of relational demography. *Human Relations, 55,* 899–929.

Wolsko, C., Park, B., Judd, C. M., & Wittenbrink, B. (2000). Framing interethnic ideology: Effects of multicultural and color-blind perspectives on judgments of groups and individuals. *Journal of Personality and Social Psychology, 78,* 635–654.

Chapter 2

Central Concepts in the Psychology of Diversity

Introduction   27
Understanding Diversity   30
Social Biases: Stereotypes, Prejudice, and Discrimination   34
The Structure of Social Bias   41
Research Methods for the Study of Social Bias   45
Summary   49

A lot of people in our industry haven't had very diverse experiences. So they don't have enough dots to connect, and they end up with very linear solutions without a broad perspective on the problem. The broader one's understanding of the human experience, the better design we will have.

Steve Jobs

Introduction

This chapter describes key concepts and methods used to study the psychology of diversity. Diversity can mean many things. From early childhood we see others and ourselves as members of social groups often based on skin color, gender, and other easily viewed traits. We note those differences and incorporate them in our everyday perceptions, thoughts and actions. The psychology of diversity examines these responses to human difference—our own and others.

The psychology of diversity examines the basic psychological processes that are triggered when we encounter people who are different from us in significant and

The Psychology of Diversity: Beyond Prejudice and Racism, First Edition. James M. Jones, John F. Dovidio, and Deborah L. Vietze.
© 2014 Blackwell Publishing Ltd. Published 2014 by Blackwell Publishing Ltd.

salient ways, or experience being treated differently by others because of our social status. It further explores the dynamics of mental representation and social interaction across institutions and differential bases of power, privilege, and status. Finally, it identifies the effects of diverse contexts on the thoughts, actions, and feelings of people in them. Victoria Plaut (2010) describes the psychology of diversity as an integral part of **diversity science**, which incorporates the perspectives of many different disciplines. Diversity science examines the ways in which people create, interpret, and maintain group differences and the psychological and societal consequences of these distinctions. Plaut further notes that

> these significant social distinctions . . . are not simply natural, neutral, or abstract. Instead they are created and re-created in the process of everyday social interactions that are grounded in historically derived ideas and beliefs about difference and in a set of practices and institutions that reflect these ideas and beliefs and that therefore shape psychological experience and behavior. (Plaut, 2010, p. 77)

In a complex and dynamic world we can't afford to see everyone as a distinct and unique person. This would sorely tax our cognitive abilities. Seeing people as a member of a group lets us make decisions quickly. It also helps us feel we understand the world. It gives us a sense of order and the feeling we know more about the person because they belong to a group. The flaw here is the focus on group membership, instead of personal qualities, that sacrifices accuracy for ease (Taylor & Fiske, 2007).

Our tendency to see people as group members makes immediately visual cues that are very important in social relations. **Social categorization** occurs when individuals view and arrange themselves and others into social categories based on many different labels such as, most commonly, race, religion, socioeconomic status, political affiliation and attitudes, sexual orientation, gender, and the like. Which of these labels is applied depends on which category is most salient. This helps organize our world.

When these social categories fall along dimensions of numerical representation (majority–minority), power (variation in social hierarchy), normative status (generally accepted or marginal traits or statuses), or nationality (citizen and immigrant status) disparities define important aspects of diversity. We are attuned to shared characteristics distinguishing our group from others (Abrams & Hogg, 2010). After categorizing a person into a group we automatically highlight differences between this person and members of other groups (Tajfel, 1969). Social categorization is a complex process and plays a major role in how we process and understand diversity.

A fundamental challenge of diversity occurs when you rely on social categorization, because this creates in-groups and out-groups. When this happens people tend to view the world in socially biased ways. We see the characteristics of our in-group as better and more socially valued, and as a result our differences from others make us feel better about ourselves (Dovidio & Gaertner, 2010; Tajfel & Turner, 1979). The more readily apparent the characteristics that define a group, the more central their role is in how we perceive and treat others.

Efforts to improve intergroup relations focus on the ways people respond to out-groups. For example, since the 1980s **diversity training**, such as anti-bias education and cultural competence training, has been used in corporate, educational, military, and other settings to help sensitize everyone to the importance of treating persons fairly regardless of their group status, and to supply them with lessons on how this can be done (Stephan & Stephan, 2001). But as we become increasingly diverse across more and more personal traits, social categories, and settings, we need a broader definition of diversity.

While acknowledging the long history of discrimination based on race, ethnicity, and gender in the United States (discussed in Chapter 3), diversity training currently encompasses a wider range of potential biases based on, for example, disability status, sexual orientation, cultural background, religious affiliation, and age (Barak, 2011; Clements & Jones, 2008). A broader definition reflects the fact that the face of the U.S. workforce is rapidly changing and becoming more diverse.

In 1950, 87% of men worked and just 30% of women did. In 2000 the percentage of men working decreased to 73% while that of women working doubled to 60%. The median age in the 1980 labor force was 32 years. It was 41 in 2010 and is projected to be 42 years in 2040 (DiCecio, Engemann, Owyang, & Wheeler, 2008). Increasing numbers of Blacks, Latinos, and Asians are included in an expanding array of jobs, industries, and social roles. And as organizations become more tolerant and sensitive, gay and lesbian workers are more comfortable being public with their sexual orientation and persons with disabilities expect and receive better accommodation and treatment.

These labor force trends reflect our society's increasing diversity and this results in challenges as diverse groups attempt to adjust to and fairly accommodate each other. Increasing diversity initially may make people feel threatened but more contact among diverse groups decreases negative feelings (Putnam, 2007; cf. Pettigrew & Tropp, 2011). The more contact people have with diverse groups, the less threatened they are by those whom they see as different (Pettigrew & Tropp, 2011). With increasing intergroup contact people may begin to see others as less threatening because there is recognition of shared membership in a group encompassing diverse groups (Ukes, Otten, van der Zee, Giebels, & Dovidio, 2012). For example, people from diverse ethnic groups can be loyal to the same home team, value the annual fall festival, and appreciate the many ways in which they share experiences. However, we know that, under some conditions, intergroup contact can further increase hostility and bias, although this occurs less often than positive results (Pettigrew & Tropp, 2011). So it's important to understand how intergroup contact has positive effects. We discuss this more in Chapter 9. When perceptions of diversity lead to conflicts, biased behavior, and unfair outcomes, equality is threatened. This threat is one of the major challenges that makes managing diversity difficult.

The purpose of this book is to review and clarify the ways in which the psychology of diversity affects us in everyday life. We use behavioral research to present these challenges. Much of what we know about this comes from social psychology and research on Blacks and Whites. In this chapter, we introduce the major concepts, terms and methods that scientists use to acquire knowledge for understanding diversity, social bias and fairness.

One goal of research on the psychology of diversity is to explain why people behave as they do when confronted with social groups different from them. This chapter reviews the way in which social scientists do this. Scientists have tackled this problem by addressing the different causes of, and relationships among, human behaviors. Scientists studying human development have proposed that **dynamic systems theory** is useful for explaining the origin of factors affecting human behavior (Thelen & Smith, 2006; van Geert, 2011). This theory states that human behavior is jointly linked to factors occurring within the person (endogenous) and to those occurring in the person's environment (exogenous).

It is difficult to disentangle the independent effects of these mutual influences. Dynamic systems theory proposes that human development, indeed all of human behavior, is a complex interchange between characteristics of the person and the environment. Human behavior is influenced and evolves as a result of these constant dynamic interactions. This epigenetic approach is an extension of the nature–nurture paradigm. **Epigenetic** refers to the concept that genes result in personal traits, and cultural, social, and environmental contexts shape these traits and how we behave (Rutter, 2012; Toyokawa, Uddin, Koenen, & Galea, 2012; Wolf & Linden, 2012). This complex process is discussed throughout this book.

The diversity of physical characteristics that characterize human beings developed millions of years ago. This diversity helped people survive environmental challenges like extreme heat or cold, windy conditions, or lack of sunlight, which is a major source of vitamin D. The genes for these traits were genetically passed on to future generations. The focus of this book, however, is not on what *causes* physical or cultural differences that operate as diversity cues but rather on the ways we *respond* to diversity. Biological and social forces shape both our traits and how we respond. Miller and Kanazawa (2007) asked a number of common questions about diversity and fairness: Why do men earn more money than women and attain higher status? Why are neurosurgeons mostly men and kindergarten teachers mostly women? Why are ethnic and national conflicts so common? Answers to questions like these require understanding of biological and environmental influences. We consider both in discussing diversity and biases like prejudice and racism that can be responses to it. We examine how these influences help us cope with diversity's challenges. Diversity is viewed from a variety of vantage points ranging from the micro-level of neurons to the broader level of neighborhoods, communities, and societies. We believe, as do most scientists, that to understand any complex human behavior we need to consider biological and environmental factors and their interaction.

Understanding Diversity

Diversity is used in some settings to refer to multiculturalism or differences based on culture, language, skin color, income, and gender. But the term is also used to describe differences in the ways that people think and do things. For example, we vary greatly in political ideology and have different ideas about raising children and practicing religion.

What is the Psychology of Diversity?

Human diversity refers to the study of the human species, one of the most widely distributed and varied animal species. Scholars have tried to simplify and organize this variation by grouping humans into categories. In ancient Greece, Aristotle attempted to systematically categorize people by temperaments believed to be related to physical traits. By the early seventeenth century, race was a highly influential form of social categorization. **Race** is a form of social grouping in which observable physical characteristics that distinguish a group of people are linked to a range of other non-visible, but also assumed to be genetically determined, characteristics such as intelligence. **Ethnicity** follows the same principles as race, but the social groupings are based on cultural criteria. The concept of race, and associated beliefs about a hierarchy of races, supported the exploitation of some groups, determined immigration quotas, and justified the subordination of slaves, as discussed in Chapter 3.

Emerging sciences in the eighteenth and nineteenth centuries reinforced the concept of race and a racial hierarchy, with Caucasian or White at the top of this hierarchy. Today, almost no scholars continue to rely on race as a biologically meaningful category (Coon, 1939; Gould, 1981). In the United States around the early 1900s psychologists contributed to the social and intellectual notion that genetic and biological group differences and a "natural" hierarchy of racial and ethnic groups existed. For example, armed with culturally biased IQ test results, psychologists concluded that 87% of Russian, 83% of Jewish, 79% of Hungarian, and 79% of Italian immigrants to the United States were of lower than average intelligence (Goddard, 1913, 1917).

This approach to human diversity was not successful. Using advanced tools in genetics, scientists found that the physical characteristics defining race were not genetically distinguishable in the ways people assumed: "in most cases biological and cultural variation is continuous, natural groupings rarely occur" (Alland, 1971, p. 3; see Koenig, Lee, & Richardson, 2008, for a review). In other words, the concept of separate and unique human races was rejected over 40 years ago because it was not supported by biological evidence and did not explain the continuous nature of human variation. Differences between groups do exist, but they are mainly rooted in social and cultural adaptations to different environments and circumstances.

It is now recognized that the concept of race is a **social construction** by the ways in which it is talked about, portrayed in media, represented in stereotypes, and formulated in laws and reflected in institutional practices and social customs. For example, Black men are stereotyped as violent criminals. In 1988, this stereotype played a large role in the presidential election between George Dukakis, Governor of Massachusetts, and George Herbert Walker Bush, the incumbent president. President Bush's campaign ran an ad that featured Willie Horton, a Black man who had been given a weekend pass from a Massachusetts prison under a program sponsored by Governor Dukakis. While on furlough, Horton kidnapped a couple, stabbed the husband and raped the wife (see the ad at http://www.youtube.com/watch?v=EC9j6Wfdq3o). The ad contrasted Bush who favored the death penalty, with this soft-on-crime policy of Dukakis. While it was meant to gain political leverage in the campaign, it reinforced a negative social meaning of race. Socially constructed categories are often used to justify a social group hierarchy resulting in some groups being treated unfairly.

In Nazi Germany race was socially constructed to distinguish the Aryan Germans (us) from the inferior and dangerous Jews (them). This construction was then implemented in the genocide of Jews that followed. When the U.S. Constitution was drafted African slaves were diminished of two fifths of their humanity by legal, social, economic, and political means. Black meant inferior by all measures of human worth. Chapter 3 traces different waves of U.S. immigrants from China, Ireland, Italy, Eastern Europe, and South and Central America to show how beliefs, media portrayals, and political and criminal action and mob violence defined their ethnic and racial meanings. Their negative treatment was often justified by the meanings they were given.

Understanding research on human diversity requires an appreciation of two important assumptions: (a) there are some genetically based variations that differentiate people and sometimes groups, but there is more similarity and overlap than distinct differences; and (b) biology is not destiny. Biology may facilitate the development of some characteristics and predispose people to behave in certain ways, but environmental forces substantially shape human characteristics and actions.

There is considerable flexibility in how genetics and environment combine to determine human diversity in appearance, traits, and actions. Scholars have proposed that gender role differences—widespread in all human cultures—result from biological differences, such as physical size and reproductive differences. However, women are also ascribed culturally determined social activities like childcare. Although these differences are widespread, they are not universal. For example, women play a primary role in hunting in areas in which game is plentiful close to home (see Wood & Eagly, 2002, for a discussion). So gender is also a social construction. Gender roles are not rigidly prescribed by biology. The complexity of these assumptions about gender and other social roles is reviewed in Chapters 6 and 11.

Human diversity is best understood as adaptations to specific environments. Skin color is an adaptation to climate over generations. Humans migrated from Africa to cold climates where there is less sun exposure. An adaptation to lighter skin, with less melanin, allowed better absorption of ultraviolet rays from the distant sun in these regions to produce essential vitamin D. Our physical traits are natural adaptations so one set of characteristics can't be considered a standard that makes one group better than others. Human diversity results from many adaptations that occur at different times in human history. Different adaptations, such as skin color, stature, amount of body fat, tolerance to cold, resistance to malaria, and the ability to digest milk sugar among others, offer both benefits and challenges.

In an attempt to bring order to a complex world we simplify our perceptions of others by putting them into distinct race, gender, and other groups. As we will see in Chapter 5, this social categorization can create a range of social biases. Social biases often result in social **stereotypes**, "qualities perceived to be associated with particular groups or categories of people" (Schneider, 2004, p. 24). Stereotypes may also result in **prejudice**—negatively biased attitudes toward, and general unfavorable evaluations of, a group that is then ascribed to individual members of the group. Stereotypes and prejudice often lead to preferential treatment for some groups and discrimination against others. Whereas stereotypes are beliefs and prejudice is an attitude, discrimination involves actions. **Discrimination** occurs when individuals are treated differently, and usually more negatively, because of their membership in negatively valued groups. Discrimination may result from the actions of individuals, or the differential application of laws, social policies, or institutional practices. Prejudice leads to discrimination because it is the motivation for creating systems that maintain a social hierarchy that favors some groups over others.

An example of a negative social bias is treating men and women with a same-sex orientation differently, whether by law, social policy, or convention, as they are in many countries. In China a person can be fired from a job for being gay. In the United States, most states do not have laws preventing employment discrimination against gays and lesbians. Personal biases contribute to social discrimination but discrimination can also result from social structures and institutional practices and laws that favor one group or another. Preferential treatment, being hired based on group membership, is more informal but it often systematically favors one group over others. Sometimes the preference reinforces existing hierarchies, and sometimes it attempts to reduce them. This is discussed further in Chapters 11 and 12.

What's in a Social Group Label?

Research on intergroup relations uses labels: Asian, Black, Hispanic White, Latina, African American, Asian Pacific Islander American, minority, and the like. Some labels stem from unscientific race categories. "Minority" is often used to mean a not-White group. Cultural theorists have suggested that these broad social categories tend to gloss over or hide many unique variations and diversity in each category (Fisher & Ragsdale, 2006). The term "minority" may also quickly become a misnomer for "not White" because, as the demographic profile of the United States shifts, so-called "minority" groups are becoming the "majority" of the U.S. population. The U.S. Census Bureau reported that in 2010 there were three states and the District of Columbia that were "majority–minority." Hawaii led the nation with a population that was 75% minority, followed by the District of Columbia with 65%, New Mexico and California with 60%, and Texas with 55%. Minorities currently represent one third of the U.S. population and this is quickly rising, as shown in Chapter 3 (http:// www.census.gov/newsroom/releases/archives/2010_census/cb11-cn125.html).

As authors, we had to make choices about labels and gave serious consideration to using labels that have history and significance for readers of this book. We use the labels for "race," "ethnicity," "nationality," and "culture" as they are used by the researchers or scholars we cite and are categories used by the U.S. Census survey. When reading labels it is important to keep in mind that each labeled group contains significant variability or **diversity within diversity**. Latino/Latina persons differ in (a) heritage (Mexican, Puerto Rican, Cuban, and so forth), (b) generations in the United States, (c) physical appearance, (d) identification with their heritage, and (e) cultural practices—to name a few differences. It is up to each person to decide how they want to name their group when it comes to describing ethnic, national, and cultural backgrounds.

A limited number of terms are used as group labels to simplify our communication. These are sometimes inaccurate descriptions that ignore within-group differences. They may simply rely on skin color, other physical characteristics, or a shared language, all of which can limit our understanding of diversity. For race and ethnicity, we generally use the labels designated by the U.S. Census. Chapter 11 discusses bias in social power dynamics. When this is based on physical appearance we use the term "dark" or "light" skin to refer to ways that bias sometimes operates.

American is often used to mean U.S. citizens. It actually refers to all persons living in North, Central, and South America. In general, we refer to groups in the United States of America as U.S. citizens and try to avoid referring to them generically as Americans. However, at times we find it easier to simply use American when referring to U.S. residents, or research participants. When referring to U.S. groups, or at times Americans, we may be referring to citizens and non-citizens. Readers of this text should feel free to discuss various labels used for a person or group and to share reasons they agree or don't with our choices and those of researchers we cite.

Social Biases: Stereotypes, Prejudice, and Discrimination

Stereotype, prejudice, and discrimination have been fundamental concepts in inter-group relations research. These concepts share some common elements but have distinguishing aspects. In this section we share some details to explain more about how these terms have been used and will be used in this book to discuss the psychology of diversity.

What Are *They* Like? Stereotypes

"Stereotype" is a term first used in describing a mental picture that comes to mind about a social group (Lippmann, 1922). A stereotype is the information we carry about known social roles that a group member usually occupies—leader, officer, cleaner—and traits associated with the group—obsequious, aggressive, or intelligent. Stereotypes distinguish a group from others. They represent social perceptions about consistent qualities presumed to be shared by all members of a group. Early stereotyping research found that it was a faulty thought process. Recent research focuses on how stereotypes simplify a complex environment. Students have to synthesize diverse facts and abstract some basic rule or principle from complex information. Simplifying disparate information in this way is useful. If a heavy desk needs to be moved, you would probably choose a man to do it rather than a woman because of the stereotype: Men are stronger than women. Evaluating each of 100 persons physically capable of this task would be time-consuming and cognitively taxing. Imagine making several such decisions a day without relying on some basic stereotypes. In the example above the stereotype, as some may be, is based on some reality. On average men are stronger than women. In some cases, of course, this is not true.

Stereotyping may be useful but can be a problem if generalizations are negative and harm people. Stereotypes cue us to perceive behaviors or characteristics associated with a group. When a stereotype is activated we judge individual group members in terms of group-based expectations or standards: They're all like that. Stereotypes include emotional reactions like disgust and fear, as well as cognitive representations of a group, for example they are ambitious, aggressive, calculating. Groups do indeed have unique characteristics related to a history and specific intergroup context. The history of slavery and discrimination against Blacks in the United States is an example of how history and context shape stereotypes about a group. Discrimination against

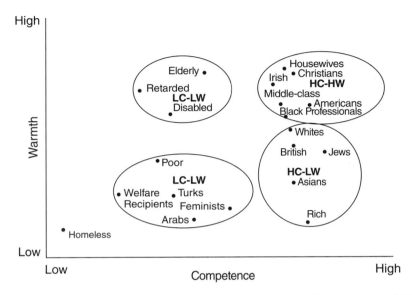

Figure 2.1. The Content of Stereotypes Is Determined by the Perceived Competence and Warmth of the Group. HC, High Competence; HW, High Warmth; LC, Low Competence; LW, Low Warmth. From "The BIAS Map: Behaviors from Intergroup Affect and Stereotypes," by A. J. C. Cuddy, S. T. Fiske, & P. Glick, 2007, *Journal of Personality and Social Psychology, 92,* pp. 631–648.

Jews in Europe left many no choice but to occupy the then disdainful position of moneylender.

According to the **stereotype content model**, a stereotype is a function of how a group is perceived on two dimensions, warmth and competence (Cuddy, Fiske, & Glick, 2007; Fiske, Cuddy, Glick, & Xu, 2002). When focusing on another group we process feelings about it and assumptions about the group's ability to perform some task. Figure 2.1 illustrates that groups high in warmth and high in competence elicit pride and admiration. Groups high in warmth but low in competence, in this case housewives or the elderly, produce pity and sympathy. Those low in warmth but high in competence, illustrated here as Asians or Jews, elicit envy and jealousy. We feel disgust, anger, and resentment for groups low on warmth and competence (welfare recipients and poor people). Stereotypes are beliefs about specific characteristics and attributes of a group thought to be shared by its members. These beliefs elicit people's emotions and conclusions about a group and may influence how members of the groups are treated and how they fare in the social hierarchy.

How Do I Feel About Them? Prejudice

The term "prejudice" is commonly used and has many different meanings in everyday life. A recent Google search identified over 36,000 references to the term. Personal definitions abound because of its widespread use. Some people use the term to

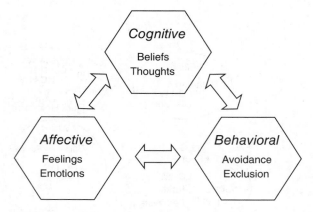

Figure 2.2.   Components of Prejudice: Cognitive, Affective, and Behavioral.

indicate arbitrary and often petty personal dislikes. The iconoclastic journalist H. L. Mencken devoted six volumes to his 1926 book of essays, *Prejudices*. A boss accepts a resignation with prejudice. This means that the person who has resigned will not get a good recommendation. Prejudice usually means something bad happens.

Prejudice has a very specific meaning for social psychologists. The current psychological view of prejudice emphasizes feelings, cognitions, and behavioral predispositions as shown in Figure 2.2. Prejudice, like other attitudes, has three components: (a) a cognitive component—irrationally based beliefs about a target group; (b) an affective (emotional) component—feelings of dislike; and (c) a behavioral disposition—a tendency to avoid or harm the target group. Researchers focus on prejudice as a negative orientation toward others. Allport's (1954) classic definition still stands: "Ethnic prejudice is an antipathy based on a faulty and inflexible generalization. It may be felt or expressed. It may be directed toward a group as a whole, or toward a person because he is a member of that group" (p. 10). According to Allport, prejudice puts a target at an undeserved disadvantage. Prejudice is a negative attitude that is unfair and unjust, and contributes to persistent disadvantage among people and groups.

The sociological view of prejudice focuses on the primacy of groupings that create a social and structural bias: "Race prejudice exists basically in a sense of group position rather than in a set of feelings which members of one racial group have toward members of another racial group" (Blumer, 1958, p. 3). Sociologists focus on how prejudice creates institutional structures to maintain the power of a group at the expense of other groups. We explain this sociological perspective in Chapters 11 and 12. Other definitions of prejudice bridge the individual-level emphasis of psychology and the structural view of sociology by concentrating on the dynamic nature of prejudice. Prejudice is a mechanism maintaining roles and status differences among groups (Eagly & Diekman, 2005).

The stereotype content model applies here. Persons who deviate from their group's traditional role arouse negative reactions. When they behave according to expectations for their group, the status quo is reinforced and they get positive reactions. Prejudice toward women, consistent with this view, has both "hostile" and "benevolent" components (Glick & Fiske, 1996; also Chapter 4). Hostile attitudes may be aroused when women deviate from a traditional subordinate role and benevolent attitudes celebrate women if they are nurturing but still subordinate. In the first instance, this statement might best express the attitude: Most women fail to appreciate fully all that men do for them. A benevolent attitude might be expressed as: Women should be cherished and protected by men. The contemporary perspective on sexism is that current prejudices do not always include a completely negative view about the target group. We discuss this further in Chapters 4 and 9.

When prejudice represents an **individual bias**, members of traditionally disadvantaged groups can develop attitudes that limit their success. It has been shown that African American boys often reject the academic achievement values of the dominant social group because they do not anticipate succeeding due to past prejudice and discrimination against their group (Ogbu, 2004). They most likely reason, "If I am not going to get into college or get a good job because of my skin color, why try to do well at school?" Also, minority-group members often harbor and show overt prejudice toward majority group members. However, much of this prejudice is reactive, reflecting an anticipation of being treated badly (Johnson & Lecci, 2003). So prejudice is an individual-level set of negative evaluations resulting in an attitude that has been generalized to a group and that functions to maintain unequal and sometimes unfair status relations among groups.

How Do I Treat Them? Discrimination and Fairness

As we defined the term earlier, discrimination involves action, specifically the mistreatment of another group. Others offer similar but more elaborated definitions of the term. Allport (1954) described discrimination as denying "a person or groups of people equality of treatment which they may wish" (p. 51). Jones (1972) defined discrimination as "those actions designed to maintain own-group characteristics and favored position at the expense of the comparison group" (p. 4). This definition adds a structural component to the first. Discrimination is thought to be unfair by most people. But fairness is hard to define. Some people think about fairness as equality— all people get the same thing. A focus on equity is another perspective—you get an equitable return on the efforts and resources you invested.

Another view of fairness is through the lens of social justice. Researchers who study social justice distinguish between procedural and distributive justice. **Procedural justice** emphasizes the importance of seeing that decisions about rewards are made fairly whether the outcome is favorable or not. **Distributive justice** concerns whether outcomes in the end are perceived as fair. In general, members of disadvantaged groups tend to judge fairness more in terms of equality of outcomes across social groups. Members of advantaged groups tend to view equity and the process of reward as more important than outcomes.

The relationships among procedural justice, distributive justice, and discrimination get even more complicated when we consider these processes historically. As the next chapter explains in more detail, the harmful effects of our legacy of racial discrimination are undeniable. Here is but one example. Discrimination is most dramatically illustrated in the institution of slavery. During slavery Blacks could be severely punished for simply learning to read and write. Thus, discrimination put these people and their descendants at educational disadvantage not only during the period of slavery but also for many future generations. The immediate outcomes of discrimination were blatantly unfair and the long-term effects could also be viewed as unfair.

The historical and current use of standardized tests for admission to college is another case to consider. The testing industry functions to provide achievement information to colleges so the colleges can make decisions based on test performance about who will likely succeed in college. Test performance in national samples is highly positively correlated with first-semester grades. Often, however, colleges are interested in preparing their graduates for careers and a life of learning and productive contributions to society. The tests are much less associated with those long-range goals.

Originally, these tests were adopted for widespread use by colleges to create a democratic system in which personal academic achievement, rather than a parent's previous attendance or a family's wealth, would primarily determine who was deserving of admission (Lemann, 2000). This seems like a sincere effort to achieve procedural justice, and it worked for a while with some groups. But the tests don't seem to work fairly for everyone. If they do not, then the goal to create democratic access to higher education may not be achieved. The problem is that standardized tests can be culturally biased because they often rely on knowledge or experiences outside the educational system, such as international travel and advanced technology at home. Not all groups wanting to go to college have access to this experience. In addition, from a distributive justice viewpoint, the results of the tests may not create equity in college attendance across social groups. The tests may also work to favor groups with cultural values that stress achievement motivation; Asians have higher test scores than Whites.

Efforts have been made to eliminate cultural bias in tests but scores on standardized tests are substantially predicted by parents' education and income. So if you are economically disadvantaged or have parents who have less education, you may not do as well on the test. This seems to give an unfair advantage to students with more family income and education. Black and Latino students taking the exam have lower scores than do White students. Average family income and education for these groups is substantially lower than it is for White families. So the differences among these groups' test scores may be influenced by family wealth and education and not just academic ability. Therefore, if colleges rely solely on standardized test scores for admission, traditionally disadvantaged groups are less likely to be admitted to college. In this way unfair disparities among groups may continue discrimination. In this book we call this **institutional bias** and explain more about it in Chapter 12.

During the 1960s President Lyndon Johnson explained how he thought the educational disparities began and outlined the challenge of eliminating them with this analogy:

> Imagine a hundred yard dash in which one of two runners has his legs shackled together. He has progressed 10 yards, while the unshackled runner has gone 50 yards. How do they rectify the situation? Do they merely remove the shackles and allow the race to proceed? Then they could say that "equal opportunity" now prevailed. But one of the runners would still be forty yards ahead of the other. Would it not be the better part of

justice to allow the previously shackled runner to make up the forty-yard gap or to start the race all over again? (Franklin & Starr, 1967, p. 226)

Creating and maintaining fairness is complex and involves more than just the absence of current discrimination. We consider the broad and pervasive impact of other types of institutional discrimination, such as employment bias and the disparate impact of various social policies and practices, in Chapter 12. In Chapter 13 we offer some approaches to addressing equity and equality. For many reasons this is a challenge, as Box 2.1 demonstrates.

Box 2.1. *Ricci v. DeStefano*

In the summer of 2009, the Supreme Court decided a case, *Ricci et al. v. DeStefano et al.*, that demonstrates the complexity of legal issues involving diversity. In 2003 the city of New Haven, Connecticut, administered an examination to 118 city firefighters. Results of the exam were to be used for promotion to captain or lieutenant. The test was constructed in a way that was intended to avoid cultural biases. After no self-identified Black candidates scored high enough to qualify for any of the 15 promotions, the city's Civil Service Board decided that the exam was flawed and invalidated the results. The city was concerned about the "adverse impact" of the exam, reflected in racially disproportionate promotions, and felt that it needed to administer a new test to produce more racially equitable results.

Firefighters who were initially led to believe that they had earned promotion through the test learned that they would not be promoted on the basis of the results. Twenty firefighters—19 non-Latino Whites and one White Latino—filed a lawsuit to uphold the results of the test and promotions. Frank Ricci, the lead plaintiff among the firefighters, reported that he had dyslexia, studied up to 13 hours a day for the exam, and paid someone to help him prepare for the exam. He passed. Thus, the outcome in which no Blacks passed the exam did not necessarily mean, from his perspective, that the test was flawed. It could reflect differences in how or how much they prepared for the exam.

The *Ricci v. DeStefano* case involved principles of distributive justice and procedural justice in complex ways. On the one hand, the city of New Haven, with Mayor DeStefano named in the suit, argued that the disproportionate success rate on the test and consequent promotions would be unfair. Distributive justice would be violated. Although they did not conclusively identify the specific cause of the bias, they did note that the substantial weight given to multiple-choice items could put racial minorities at a disadvantage. However, the firefighters who passed the test claimed that the test was originally designed to be culturally unbiased (i.e., procedurally fair) and thus the disproportionate outcome did not necessarily mean that the test was flawed. The New Haven firefighters who passed the test thus claimed that they were wrongfully denied promotions because of *their* race.

This complex case went through many courts and judicial decisions. New Haven's U.S. District Court dismissed the case brought by the firefighters; this decision would permit the city to invalidate the test results. The firefighters filed an appeal, and the U.S. 2nd Circuit Court of Appeals, which included Judge Sonia Sotomayor (who became the first Latina to serve on the U.S. Supreme Court in 2009), upheld the initial decision. Subsequently, the U.S. Supreme Court, in a 5–4 decision, overruled the judgment, supporting the position of the firefighters. New Haven was obligated to consider the test results valid and promote the firefighters who scored the highest to the ranks of captain and lieutenant.

The passions on both side of the argument that this situation and the court's judgments aroused revealed the deep commitment that people have to fairness, albeit defined in different ways. The different judgments by different courts and the narrowest margin in the Supreme Court decision reveals how experienced and well-informed people can reach different conclusions. *Ricci v. DeStefano* illustrates how the dilemmas posed by issues of diversity can challenge people's perceptions of fairness.

1.   How can a seemingly "objective" test be considered discriminatory?
2.   Does fairness require people from different social categories to be treated in an identical way?

Biases Below and Above the Surface

Prejudice and stereotypes exist on an individual level within a person's mind. If we act on them they become apparent to ourselves and to others. **Explicit biases** are preferences for or against a social group that a person is aware of and consciously controls. They can be expressed as an attitude, an evaluation, or a behavior. **Implicit biases** are preferences for or against a social group that a person may be unaware of and thus cannot consciously control. They too may be expressed in one's attitudes, evaluations, or behaviors.

People have difficulty openly expressing some attitudes toward a social group, particularly when the group is an out-group. Stereotypes and prejudice are explicit expressions of bias toward a group. They exist as feelings and thoughts. We control the situations in which they are expressed. However, people are not able to control implicit bias; they may not even be aware of it (Wittenbrink & Schwarz, 2007). Both explicit and implicit biases can result in discrimination toward another group.

Researchers use direct self-report scales to detect explicit biases. To detect implicit bias different methods are used, ones where a response is not under the direct control of a person. These include monitoring brain activity, responses to visual cues, and analyzing linguistic cues. The strategy most widely used to observe implicit biases is a response latency measure called the **Implicit Association Test** (IAT) (Greenwald, McGhee, & Schwartz, 1998). These response-timed tests are based on the assumption that people respond more quickly to a picture, or other stimuli, with information in it that they expect than they do to something with information that is unexpected. For example, a person is likely to respond more quickly to words that are often associated in the mind. These pairs of words, doctor–nurse or table–chair, are expected to be linked so would be responded to more quickly than would word pairs like doctor–chair or nurse–table which are unexpected pairs. Over 100,000 Whites have completed the race IAT on the web (for more details on this test go to https://implicit.harvard.edu/). On average, Whites show a significant implicit bias preference for Whites over Blacks. Implicit biases may affect behavior in ways that can directly contribute to everyday, often unintentional, forms of discrimination. We discuss implicit biases and their implications in detail in Chapter 7 and 9.

Many psychological and social processes influence how people feel, think, and act toward others based on group membership. These come together in complex ways to systematically shape personal and group experience and opportunities. However, societies represent more than the people within them. They are organized, and governed by laws and practices. When these organized rules result in some unfair outcomes or procedures they are social biases. Social biases can be both explicit and implicit.

The Structure of Social Bias

Social biases occur at different levels. They are personal attitudes, laws, institutional policies, and informal practices that perpetuate race, ethnic, and gender biases. They happen without people intentionally driving these processes. In fact, action by a person is required to stop social bias from operating because passivity allows it to shape the lives of groups and their members. In this section we first discuss racism in some detail to show how different levels of social bias can operate in concert to create and perpetuate unfairness. Then, we consider more general principles of social bias and how it operates at the individual, institutional, and cultural level.

Racism: A Case Example of Social Bias

Racism is based on three assumptions: (a) a group's behavioral characteristics are assumed to be biological, and nature created distinct and unbridgeable differences between races; (b) my race is superior to any other; and (c) society creates institutional policies and cultural practices that allow a hierarchical domination of one group based on the first two assumptions. Racism in the United States has a long history of explicit practices and is currently implicitly ingrained in our society. While these statements are true of other countries and cultures, particularly those that enslaved Africans between the sixteenth and eighteenth centuries, racism in the United States has distinctive qualities. Moreover, because racism is a systemic social bias, not simply a personal bias, it has created power differences between Whites and other groups. Institutional and cultural forces have reinforced and perpetuated disparities between groups. We discuss these power differences and institutional and cultural bias in Chapters 11 and 12.

Racism is the coordinated interaction of individual-level biases such as stereotypes, prejudice, and discrimination with societal- and cultural-level biases. This process creates disadvantaged and advantaged groups based on presumably distinct biological traits (Feagin & Vera, 2001). Historically, Black–White intergroup relations have been the defining paradigm for understanding group attitudes and social policy. However, in this book we go beyond the Black–White analysis to recognize that recent events have broadened the issues that relate to fairness in our society. Recent immigrants, the poor, other ethnic groups, women, and sexual minorities reflect our greater diversity. These groups have also experienced social bias. In the interest of providing opportunities and improving outcomes for all, we believe that research on Black–White intergroup relations and social bias can be applied, at least in part, to all social bias experienced by groups. We also recognize that to understand different types of social bias requires consideration of the unique aspects of a group's history and contemporary experiences.

The Different Layers of Social Bias

Social biases have many different layers. In this book social bias and fairness is considered at three different societal levels: (a) individual social dynamics, (b) institutional outcomes, and (c) cultural contexts. These levels of bias are interrelated and illustrated with examples of racism toward Blacks. In principle, however, these represent the different levels by which social bias operate as well.

Individual bias   Bias person to person is the first level of analysis that can be used to understand diversity and bias. It closely aligns with race prejudice and stereotypes against Blacks. The outcome of individual-level bias is expressed as a negative attitude about an entire group, resulting in behavior that directly discriminates against a person belonging to that group. Personal expressions and actions of superiority and/or inferiority often represent centuries-old attitudes that have been perpetuated through parenting practices and both institutional and cultural bias. An example of this explicit individual bias is found in the text of a speech:

> I am not, nor ever have been in favor of bringing about in any way the social and political equality of the white and dark skinned races; I am not, nor ever have been, in favor of making voters or jurors of Negroes, nor qualifying them to hold office . . . [This quotation is attributed to President Abraham Lincoln.] (Hay, 1894, pp. 369–370, 457–458)

A more recent example of individual-level bias is the meltdown of comedian Michael Richards, who played Kramer in the TV series *Seinfeld*. Richards lost his temper during a live-comedy routine in 2006, and screamed at two Black men who had heckled him (profanity and racial slurs deleted):

> Throw his a** out. He's a n*****, he's a n****. Shut up, fifty years ago we would have had you upside down with a fork up your f** a**. (http://www.tmz.com/2006/11/20/kramers-racist-tirade-caught-on-tape/)

This remark refers to lynching and other forms of torture used against Blacks in the United States. Richards use of the word "we" shows that he saw the heckling about

Whites and Blacks as groups and not about him. Richards later apologized for the incident, expressing remorse and stating that he was not a bigot.

Institutional bias   This bias is not always obvious and so tends to be implicit bias. People with individual bias come to accept institutional policies or outcomes that help one group to get ahead as normal. When only one group tends be in control, institutions such as corporations and universities tend to favor their own group, even in the absence of strong negative feelings toward other groups. They support institutional policies that benefit their group, often at the expense of other groups. When institutional bias results in a standard of practice that perpetuates in-group advantage it is more difficult to recognize than individual bias. Chapter 12 focuses on institutional bias in detail.

One main indicator that institutional bias exists is unequal outcomes for different groups over time. Differences that exist in **social indicators** can help reveal the existence of institutional bias. Social indicators are the measures of social outcomes for members of a society such as employment rates and healthcare statistics. A variety of different influences contribute to disparities between groups on social indicator measures. But individual and institutional social bias can play a role.

Institutional bias is the extension of personal biased beliefs that become incorporated into social institutions or practices so that some groups maintain a consistent advantage over others. Institutional bias is a byproduct of institutional practices that restrict the access of some groups' members to social benefits such as education and employment opportunities that should accrue to all equally in an egalitarian society. Public schools illustrate this bias. Because schools are funded by local property taxes, schools that are in poorer neighborhoods are less well funded than those in wealthier ones. The consequence is that less money is available to support the education of poor students and this may contribute to different levels of academic achievement for poor and wealthy students. Institutional biases, whether intentional or not, can create disparities in social outcomes.

An example of institutional bias comes from the advertising industry in New York City. The city's Human Rights Commission reported in 2006 that while 25% of the city's population was Black, only 2% of the city's top advertising executives were. Other disparities were also noted. The number of Black workers had barely improved since a similar survey 40 years ago found the same pattern. Only 2.5% of Black workers made more than $100,000 a year compared with 22% of those who were White. Faced with the findings many agencies set up ways to correct these disparities (Caldwell & Elliott, 2006). These disparities could have occurred as a consequence of explicit beliefs about the superiority of Whites and prejudice against Blacks. But it could also be the result of business practices that promote bias without arousing any personal negative feelings. So, to understand bias it is also important to examine institutional effects on social outcomes.

Cultural bias   **Cultural bias** subsumes elements of individual bias and institutional bias but is more far-reaching. Culture is to humans as water is to aquatic life. We are immersed in it so we are often unaware of its presence or its effects. Bias at this level is often particularly difficult to detect but it can lead to individual and institutional bias and these biases reciprocally lead to further cultural bias. Cultural bias operates when the belief that one's cultural heritage is superior to that of other groups is normalized as part of a society's institutions and practices. In some cultures there is a defined social order that promotes the superiority of one skin color, ethnicity, religion, gender, or sexual orientation over others. Cultural bias shapes the policies and laws that maintain both institutional and individual bias. We discuss culture in Chapter 10, but because it is central to the psychology of diversity, we provide a brief introduction to it next.

Culture shapes social reality by transmitting beliefs, knowledge, and standards between people and over time. Many definitions of culture are based on Kroeber and Kluckhohn's work (1952), which describes culture as a consistent system of values and way of thinking, feeling, and acting that is maintained by symbols, such as writing, and is transmitted through various artifacts and other cultural tools to future generations. The study of culture has expanded to include many diverse perspectives (Baldwin, Faulkner, Hecht, & Lindsley, 2006). The Canadian Commission for UNESCO has promulgated A Working Definition of Culture, which we adopt: "Culture is a dynamic value system of learned elements, with assumptions, conventions, beliefs and rules permitting members of a group to relate to each other and to the world, to communicate and to develop their creative potential" (Rentein, 2004, p. 5).

Cultures differ in the emphasis placed on the function and meaning of behaviors (Matsumoto, 2001; Matsumoto, Yoo, & Fontaine, 2008). For example, one culture might define success as how well you climb a tree or how many children you have. Another might value property and land as success indicators. Social scientists have attempted to categorize cultures along different dimensions. One way on which cultures differ is along the individualistic versus collectivist dimension. Individualistic cultures emphasize each person's unique qualities and independence while collectivist cultures promote the importance of the group and the interdependence of all persons (Markus & Kitayama, 1991; Triandis, 1994). The United States is an individualistic culture while many Asian countries have more collectivist cultural values. In fact, the United States has one of the most individualistic cultures in the world.

Systematic differences between U.S. culture and its embedded Black culture along five dimensions of interpersonal perspective are described by Jones (1997, 2004; see also Chapter 8): (a) sense of time, (b) rhythm, (c) improvisation, (d) oral expression, and (e) spirituality. U.S. culture tends to value a future time orientation, stable and predictable rhythms of activity, planning ahead rather than improvising, written over oral expression, and a belief in personal control instead of an emphasis on spirituality. To the extent the U.S. cultural standards are rewarded and considered normal cultural bias may be operating.

Individual-level bias often stems directly from cultural bias. Anti-gay bias, or homophobia, is an example of individual bias that is rooted in cultural bias. Religious values are cultural values. When a religious value is expressed as strong disapproval of same-sex romantic love in favor only of heterosexism, this leads to individual, institutional, and cultural bias against same-sex oriented persons. Because these biases are so strongly sanctioned and are taught at an early age, they often become an ingrained culture value. This leads to it seeming natural for people to express personal bias and want to create institutional bias (e.g., not allowing marriage or other privileges) so that a cultural bias or even violent behavior toward gay persons is allowed. Herek (1990) describes this complex interplay among the three levels of bias that can operate:

> Cultural heterosexism fosters anti-gay attitudes by providing a ready-made system of values and stereotypical beliefs that justifies such prejudice as "natural." By imbuing homosexuality with a variety of symbolic meanings, cultural heterosexism enables expressions of individual prejudice to serve various psychological functions. Furthermore, by discouraging lesbians and gay men from coming out to others, heterosexism perpetuates itself. (p. 316)

We will explore these topics further in Chapters 10 and 13 as we discuss how personal and collective efforts on the cultural level influence us and can also shape our society to better accommodate its cultural diversity.

As vivid as cultural differences are, researchers have also noted important **cultural universalities**—principles, activities, and other elements that all cultures share. For example, the principle of reciprocity, in which kindness is repaid with kindness and injury produces a desire to harm in return, is common across all cultures. In addition, all cultures wrestle with the dilemma of conservatism versus openness to change and the tension between personal gain and benevolence to others (Schwartz & Sagie, 2000). One question you might ask yourself as you read this text is: Which aspects of diversity and bias are universal and which are unique to U.S. society or my country of origin?

In this chapter we have referred to social and behavioral science research. In this book we use research findings, rather than personal experience, to explain and illustrate our main concepts. We share research findings about feelings, attitudes, intergroup relationships, and social behavior that are related to diversity and social bias. We share anecdotes and case studies to illustrate research findings. It is important for you to have a basic understanding of the social and behavioral science research process as you read this book.

Research Methods for the Study of Social Bias

During the twentieth century, behavioral science researchers, many of whom were social psychologists, developed effective methods for studying feelings, attitudes, and social behavior that helped create a body of evidence about prejudice, racism, intergroup conflict, and intergroup relations. A variety of research methods provide scientific evidence that explains the origin, function, and structure of prejudice and its impact on targets of prejudice and prejudiced persons. These studies help us with understanding psychology of diversity.

The Scientific Enterprise

Behavioral research about intergroup relations and social bias is primarily empirical. It relies on gathering observable evidence according to the **scientific method**, which is a particular problem-solving approach that is common to all sciences. The scientific method follows a particular logic and a series of prescribed stages. The goal of science is a practical one: It is to understand the world. Thus, the scientific method begins and ends in the "real world."

The scientific method begins with a formal or informal observation about specific events or a pattern of outcomes that is sufficiently important. A researcher might notice that when teachers expect children to do well in math they do better than children who are taught by teachers who don't have this positive attitude. At this point the questions that naturally occur are: Can this observation be demonstrated with confidence? Why does this happen?

Good research involves coming up with an explanation about the cause of the observation of interest. These possible explanations can come from many sources including the researcher's ideas, other research, or theories proposed to explain what was observed. A theory is an abstract explanation about a natural social phenomenon. A **theory** must be a coherent and internally consistent; it must also be testable. For instance, one theory may be that hiring managers often treat Latinos/Latinas unfairly. A **hypothesis** is an expectation, or prediction, derived directly from a theory. It is an inference based on a set of earlier observations about what will happen under certain conditions. In this case, a hypothesis might be that employers are more likely to rate resumés of persons with Latina/Latino surnames less favorably than those without such surnames.

The goal of science is to understand the world by collecting observations in a systematic way that tests the hypothesis. When using the scientific method an important step in the process is testing the researcher's hypothesis systematically in the real world or under simulated conditions while controlling other variables not being tested. In our example above, a researcher might construct Latino and White resumés with exactly the same level of qualifications for evaluation by managers with positive, neutral, or negative attitudes toward Whites and Latinos. Resumé ratings of managers with negative attitudes would then be compared with resumé ratings of those with positive or more neutral ratings. If the two groups differ, and this difference is statistically significant, the researcher has some empirical evidence to support the hypothesis. The hypothesis is not proved, but simply supported, because we can't generalize to all managers or all situations. These findings may help to establish that the theory makes sense or does not. After the results are reported new questions are raised and the research cycle continues. The scientific method is typically a cyclical process that leads us successively to a better understanding of the world. These research steps are outlined in Figure 2.3.

Making Sense of the World Scientifically: Theories and Research Methods

Theories about bias in individual and intergroup relations represent abstract ideas about how people behave in the real world. Much of the theory and research in this area focuses on how social circumstances influence a person's behavior. In this book we present theories from a number of different areas of social psychology.

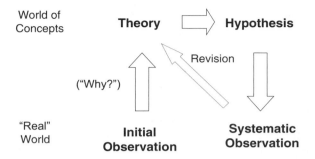

Figure 2.3.   Steps in the Scientific Method: (a) Initial Observation, (b) Theory Development, (c) Derivation of Hypothesis, and (d) Systematic Observation.

- Social cognition and attribution: understanding the social world.
- Self-awareness: identity and understanding.
- Attitudes: how we feel and what we believe.
- Conformity: what influences us to act like others?
- Group processes: the dynamics between people as they interact in groups.
- Social neuroscience: the neurobiological bases of social behavior.

This book also presents scientific research that tests these theories. Researchers who study these topics use a number of research methods and consider a number of ethical challenges before conducting their research. As you read about the research presented, we urge you to consider, with others and your instructor, the methods used to collect the data and the ethical considerations related to the research design and methods used.

Testing Our Ideas: Research Designs

A **research design** is a plan for how data will be collected. Research designs use different standards of control that are somewhat similar to quality control standards for any industry. Some of the studies you will read about use the experimental design, which is a method representing the highest standard of control in research. This design is used because the researcher wants to infer that one factor or variable caused another to change in the direction predicted by the hypothesis. The basic logic of an experimental design is straightforward. It begins with two or more situations that are initially comparable. The members of each group undergo **random assignment** to the groups, so that any observed difference in performance by the groups cannot be explained by any prior differences among people who were in the two groups. The researcher then changes some aspect of the situation that changes the experiences of participants in the two groups. For example, one group of participants is told that they failed a test and another group that they passed it (independent of whether or not they actually failed or passed). This element is called the **independent variable**, because it changes or varies in the way that a researcher has decided to manipulate it. Next, a particular outcome is measured (e.g., prejudice toward another group) to see if it differs between the groups as a consequence of the research manipulation. This outcome is called the **dependent variable** because it is hypothesized that it would change or vary depending on the independent variable that was manipulated.

To illustrate, one study had a Black or a White woman who, as she was leaving a grocery store, drop her bag of groceries in the near vicinity of a White customer (see Crosby, Bromley, & Saxe, 1980). The experimenters were interested in whether or not the White shopper stops to help, and whether this will occur with different frequencies as a function of the race of the woman who dropped the groceries. The race of the shopper who dropped the groceries is the independent variable; whether people help is the dependent variable. The researchers set up this manipulation of the grocery-dropper's race in this condition. They used actors so they could control this variable. Race is not normally manipulated but it is when the researcher sets up a condition in which persons of different races are performing some act to see how others respond. The researcher tested the hypothesis that race of a person needing help is related to whether or not they get help. They found that Black shoppers were helped less often and less quickly than White shoppers when they dropped their bags.

Experiments use strict methods of control so that the causal factor can be isolated from other reasons that could explain the behavior of interest. The experimental method is considered the only one that allows a researcher to accurately infer that one factor or circumstance caused a behavior. You will read in more detail about examples of this type of method in subsequent chapters on social cognition, psychological biases, and intergroup relations.

Some research described in this text uses quasi-experimental or correlational designs. Quasi-experimental research is similar to experimental research, but the researcher has less control over extraneous variables because randomization is not used. For instance, participants vary in how diverse their neighborhoods were as they were growing up. This is not something that can be manipulated by an experimenter. Correlational designs are used to show how a naturally occurring variable is related to another variable that has not been manipulated but simply observed. **Correlations** are a numerical index, ranging from −1.0 to +1.0, showing the strength and the direction of relationship between two variables. They don't provide any evidence about causal relationship between variables. For example, correlational research has looked across different periods of history and shown that as feelings of threat increase, expressions of prejudice and discrimination also increase. Threat and prejudice are correlated. All of these types of research are classified as quantitative methods, because they show how much a factor changes when another factor changes. The changes that occur in experiments and the relationships that are found in correlational studies can be summarized numerically with other statistics, or quantitative methods. In some chapters survey research is reported as proportions or percentages. This information is merely descriptive of trends.

Most research reported in this book uses quantitative methods. However, qualitative research also provides useful information about natural phenomena. Qualitative research stresses the nature of reality from the participants' perspective and is based on a relationship between the participant and the researcher (Denzin & Lincoln, 2005). Case studies and participant observations are examples of qualitative research methods.

Making Meaning from Research: Measures and Analysis of Data

Once a research design is selected a decision must be made about what approach to use to systematically collect data. Possible approaches include direct observation in real-life settings or a laboratory; surveys, attitude scales, and other self-report measures; and searching archival records. Researchers use direct observation in experimental design laboratory studies to study group dynamics and the neurobiological bases of bias behavior. Attitude scales and self-report measures are used to study how targets of prejudice cope, how feelings and beliefs about one's own group compare with those about other groups, and how self-aware participants are about their feelings for example. Percentages or proportions are used to show trends in patterns of employment, mortgages, or arrest rates.

The tables and figures in this book are based on two types of statistics: descriptive and inferential. **Descriptive statistics**, such as the mean and standard deviation, describe the characteristics and general shape of the data the researcher has collected. For example, do the data represent a normal distribution? **Inferential statistics**, such as the t test, χ^2 (chi-square), and F statistics, are used to test the researcher's hypothesis. Percentages show the proportion of a population for a social indicator. In reading descriptions of research it is a good idea to try to understand the researcher's purpose, research questions and, most importantly, the hypothesis on which the research is based. Also, be sure to see if you can determine how the data were collected and how they were analyzed. These two strategies will help you appreciate the empirical nature of the scientific results you read about and the confidence you can have in the reported results and conclusions. To determine some of this information, you may want to read the original article we describe.

Summary

This chapter describes key concepts and methods used to study the psychology of diversity. Diversity can mean many things. Often it refers to skin color, gender, sexual orientation, ableness, or religion that make a person or group different from our group. In a complex and dynamic world we can't afford to see everyone as a distinct and unique person. The psychology of diversity identifies social categorization as a means by which we create in-groups and out-groups. When this happens people tend to view the world in socially biased ways. Diversity is used in some settings to refer to multiculturalism or differences based on culture, language, skin color, income, and gender. But the term is also used to describe differences in the ways that people think and do things. Human diversity is best understood as adaptations to specific environments.

Research on intergroup relations uses labels: Asians, Blacks, Hispanic Whites, Latina, African American, Asian Pacific Islander American, minority. When reading labels it is important to keep in mind that each labeled group contains significant variability or diversity.

Stereotype, prejudice, and discrimination have been fundamental terms in intergroup relations research. These concepts share some common elements but have distinguishing aspects.

Prejudice has a very specific meaning for social psychologists. The current psychological view of prejudice emphasizes feelings, attitudes, and behaviors. Prejudice, like other attitudes, has three components: (a) a cognitive component—irrationally based beliefs about a target group; (b) an affective component—feelings of dislike; and (c) an orienting function—behavior that avoids or harms the target group.

Discrimination is favorable or unfavorable actions directed differentially at others. Often they favor one's in-group at the expense of other groups. Discrimination is thought to be unfair by most people. But fairness is hard to define. We can be aware or unaware of our biases. Both explicit biases that we are aware of, and implicit ones that we are not aware of, can result in discrimination toward another group. Social biases occur at different levels: personal attitudes; laws and institutional policies; and informal or formal cultural practices that perpetuate race, ethnic, and gender biases. They happen without people intentionally driving these processes.

Behavioral research on intergroup relations and social bias is primarily empirical. It relies on gathering observable evidence according to the scientific method, which is a particular problem-solving approach common to all sciences. The scientific method follows a particular logic and a series of prescribed stages. This book presents scientific research that tests these theories and hypotheses that help us understand diversity and its challenges.

Questions for Thinking and Knowing

1. We have suggested that the Black–White situation may be similar to other race/ethnicity/gender/sexual orientation situations. Explain why you agree or disagree.
2. To what extent do you think racial or ethnic groups display the same forms of bias against each other? Why do you think that occurs?
3. Identify any stereotypes with which you are familiar and describe the group to which they have been applied and why you think they originated. What do you think would change such stereotypes, both culturally and in your own mind?
4. Have you ever experienced a situation in which you thought implicit bias was operating? Why do you think this concept might apply?
5. Should we base how we understand the challenges of diversity only on scientific evidence? Why or why not? What other types of evidence should help us decide how to handle diversity's challenges?

Key Terms

American	Descriptive statistics
Correlations	Discrimination
Cultural bias	Distributive justice
Cultural universalities	Diversity science
Culture	Diversity training
Dependent variable	Diversity within diversity

Dynamic systems theory
Epigenetic
Ethnicity
Explicit bias
Human diversity
Hypothesis
Implicit Association Test
Implicit bias
Independent variable
Individual bias
Inferential statistics
Institutional bias
Prejudice

Procedural justice
Race
Racism
Random assignment
Research design
Scientific method
Social bias
Social categorization
Social construction
Social indicators
Stereotype content model
Stereotypes
Theory

References

Abrams, D., & Hogg, M. E. (2010). Social identity and self-categorization. In J. F. Dovidio, M. Hewstone, P. Glick, & V. M. Esses (Eds.), *The SAGE handbook of prejudice, stereotyping, and discrimination* (pp. 179–194). London: Sage.

Alland, A., Jr (1971). *Human diversity*. New York: Columbia University Press.

Allport, G. W. (1954). *The nature of prejudice*. Cambridge, MA: Addison-Wesley.

Baldwin, J. R., Faulkner, S. L., Hecht, M. L., & Lindsley, S. L. (Eds.). (2006). *Redefining culture: Perspectives across the disciplines*. Mahwah, NJ: Erlbaum.

Barak, M. E. M. (2011). *Managing diversity: Toward a globally inclusive workplace* (2nd ed.). Los Angeles, CA: Sage.

Blumer, H. (1958). Race prejudice as a sense of group position. *Pacific Sociological Review, 1,* 3–7.

Caldwell, D., & Elliott, S. (2006, September 8). New York City ad firms agree to hire more Black managers. *New York Times,* p. A1.

Clements, P., & Jones, J. (2008). *The diversity training handbook: A practical guide to understanding and changing attitudes*. London/Philadelphia: Kogan Page.

Coon, C. S. (1939). *Races of Europe*. New York: Macmillan.

Crosby, F., Bromley, S., & Saxe, L. (1980). Recent unobtrusive studies of Black and White discrimination and prejudice: A literature review. *Psychological Bulletin, 87,* 546–563.

Cuddy, A. J. C., Fiske, S. T., & Glick, P. (2007). The BIAS map: Behaviors from intergroup affect and stereotypes. *Journal of Personality and Social Psychology, 92,* 631–648.

Denzin, N. K., & Lincoln, Y. S. (Eds.). (2005). *The SAGE handbook of qualitative research* (3rd ed.). Thousand Oaks, CA: Sage.

DiCecio, R., Engemann, K. M., Owyang, M. T., & Wheeler, C. H. (2008). Changing trends in the labor force: A survey. *Federal Reserve Bank of St. Louis Review, 90,* 47–62.

Dovidio, J. F., & Gaertner, S. L. (2010). Intergroup bias. In S. T. Fiske, D. Gilbert, & G. Lindzey (Eds.), *Handbook of social psychology* (5th ed., pp. 1084–1120). Hoboken, NJ: John Wiley & Sons.

Eagly, A. H., & Diekman, A. B. (2005). What is the problem? Prejudice as an attitude-in-context. In J. F. Dovidio, P. Glick, & L. A. Rudman (Eds.), *On the nature of prejudice: Fifty years after Allport* (pp. 19–35). Malden, MA: Blackwell Publishing Ltd.

Feagin, J. R., & Vera, H. (2001). *White racism: The basics*. New York: Routledge.

Fisher, C. B., & Ragsdale, K. (2006). Goodness-of-fit ethics for multicultural research. In J. E. Trimble & C. B. Fisher (Eds.), *The handbook of ethical research with ethnocultural populations and communities* (pp. 3–26). Thousand Oaks, CA: Sage Publications.

Fiske, S. T., Cuddy, A. J. C., Glick, P., & Xu, J. (2002). A model of (often mixed) stereotype content: Competence and warmth respectively follow from perceived status and competition. *Journal of Personality and Social Psychology, 82,* 878–902.

Franklin, J. H., & Starr, I. (Eds.). (1967). *The Negro in twentieth century America.* New York: Basic Books.

Glick, P., & Fiske, S. T. (1996). The Ambivalent Sexism Inventory: Differentiating hostile and benevolent sexism. *Journal of Personality and Social Psychology, 70,* 491–512.

Goddard, H. H. (1913). The Binet tests in relation to immigration. *Journal of Psycho-Asthenics, 18,* 105–107.

Goddard, H. H. (1917). Mental tests and the immigrant. *Journal of Delinquency, 2,* 243–277.

Gould, S. J. (1981). *The mismeasure of man: New and expanded.* New York: W. W. Norton.

Greenwald, A., McGhee, D., & Schwartz, J. (1998). Measuring individual differences in implicit cognition: The implicit association test. *Journal of Personality and Social Psychology, 74,* 1464–1480.

Hay, J. (1894). Lincoln and the Civil War in the diaries and letters of John Hay. In T. Dennett (Ed.), *John Hay, from poetry to politics* (1933). New York: Dodd, Mead & Company. Retrieved on September 9, 2009 from http://www.questia.com

Herek, G. M. (1990). The context of anti-gay violence: Notes on cultural and psychological heterosexism. *Journal of Interpersonal Violence, 5,* 316–333.

Johnson, J. D., & Lecci, L. (2003). Assessing anti-White attitudes and predicting perceived racism: The Johnson–Lecci scale. *Personality and Social Psychology Bulletin, 29,* 299–312.

Jones, J. M. (1972). *Prejudice and racism.* Reading, MA: Addison-Wesley.

Jones, J. M. (1997). *Prejudice and racism* (2nd ed.). New York: McGraw-Hill.

Jones, J. M. (2004). TRIOS: A model for coping with the universal context of racism. In G. Philogene (Ed.), *Kenneth B. Clark: Essays in honor of a social activist and scholar* (pp. 161–190). Washington, DC: American Psychological Association.

Koenig, B. A., Lee, S. S.-J., & Richardson, S. E. (Eds.). (2008). *Revisiting race in a genomic age.* New Brunswick, NJ: Rutgers University Press.

Kroeber, A. L., & Kluckhohn, C. (1952). *Culture: A critical review of concepts and definitions.* Cambridge, MA: Peabody Museum.

Lemann, N. (2000). *Big test: The secret history of American meritocracy.* New York: Farrar, Straus, and Giroux.

Lippmann, W. (1922). *Public opinion.* New York: Harcourt, Brace.

Markus, H. R., & Kitayama, S. (1991). Culture and the self: Implications for cognition, emotion, and motivation. *Psychological Review, 98,* 224–253.

Matsumoto, D. (2001). Epilogue. In D. Matsumoto (Ed.), *Handbook of culture and psychology* (pp. 447–448). New York: Oxford University Press.

Matsumoto, D., Yoo, S. H., & Fontaine, J. (2008). Mapping expressive differences around the world: The relationship between emotional display rules and individualism versus collectivism. *Journal of Cross-Cultural Psychology, 39,* 55–74.

Mencken, H. L. (1926). *Prejudices.* New York: A. A. Knopf.

Miller, A. S., & Kanazawa, S. (2007). *Why beautiful people have more daughters.* New York: Perigree.

Ogbu, J. (2004). Collective identity and the burden of "acting White" in Black history, community, and education. *The Urban Review, 36,* 1–35.

Pettigrew, T. F., & Tropp, L. R. (2011). *When groups meet: The dynamics of intergroup contact.* New York: Psychology Press.

Plaut, C. C. (2010). Diversity science: Why and how difference makes a difference. *Psychological Inquiry, 21,* 77–99.

Putnam, R. D. (2007). *E pluribus unum*: Diversity in the twenty-first century. The 2006 Johan Skytte Prize Lecture. *Scandinavian Political Studies, 30,* 137–174.

Rentein, A. D. (2004). *The cultural defense.* New York: Oxford University Press.

Rutter, M. (2012). Gene–environment interdependence. *European Journal of Developmental Psychology, 94,* 391–412.

Schneider, D. J. (2004). *The psychology of stereotyping.* New York: Guilford.

Schwartz, S. H., & Sagie, G. (2000). Value consensus and importance: A cross-national study. *Journal of Cross-Cultural Psychology, 31,* 465–497.

Stephan, W. G., & Stephan, C. W. (2001). *Improving intergroup relations.* Thousand Oaks, CA: Sage.

Tajfel, H. (1969). Cognitive aspects of prejudice. *Journal of Social Issues, 25*(4), 79–97.

Tajfel, H., & Turner, J. C. (1979). An integrative theory of intergroup conflict. In W. G. Austin & S. Worchel (Eds.), *The social psychology of intergroup relations* (pp. 33–48). Monterey, CA: Brooks/Cole.

Taylor, S. E., & Fiske, S. T. (2007). *Social cognition: From brains to culture.* New York: McGraw-Hill.

Thelen, E. S., & Smith, L. B. (2006). Dynamic systems theories. In R. M. Lerner & W. Damon (Eds.), *Handbook of child development, Vol. 1. Theoretical models of human development* (6th ed., pp. 258–312). Hoboken, NJ: John Wiley & Sons.

Toyokawa, S., Uddin, M., Koenen, K. C., & Galea, S. (2012). How does the social environment "get into the mind"? Epigenetics at the intersection of social and psychiatric epidemiology. *Social Science and Medicine, 74,* 67–74.

Triandis, H. C. (1994). *Culture and social behavior.* New York: McGraw-Hill.

Trimble, J. E. & Fisher, C. B. (Eds.). (2006). *The handbook of ethical research with ethnocultural populations and communities.* Thousand Oaks, CA: Sage Publications.

Ukes, E. G., Otten, S., van der Zee, K., Giebels, E., & Dovidio, J. F. (2012). Urban district identity as common ingroup identity: The different role of ingroup prototypicality for minority and majority groups. *European Journal of Social Psychology, 42,* 707–716.

van Geert, P. (2011). The contribution of complex dynamic systems theory to development. *Child Development Perspectives, 5,* 273–278.

Wittenbrink, B., & Schwarz, N. (2007). Introduction. In B. Wittenbrink & N. Schwarz (Eds.), *Implicit measures of attitudes* (pp. 1–13). New York: Guilford.

Wolf, C., & Linden, D. E. J. (2012). Biological pathways to adaptability: Interactions between genome, epigenome, nervous system and environment for adaptive behavior. *Genes, Brain and Behavior, 11,* 3–28.

Wood, W., & Eagly, A. H. (2002). A cross-cultural analysis of the behavior of women and men: Implications for the origins of sex differences. *Psychological Bulletin, 128,* 699–727.

Chapter 3

Historical Perspectives on Diversity in the United States

Introduction   55
Push–Pull: Dynamics of Diversity   57
Civil Rights   68
Challenges of Diversity   80
Summary   83

Our patchwork heritage is a strength, not a weakness; and because we have tasted the bitter swill of civil war and segregation, and emerged from that dark chapter stronger and more united, we cannot help but believe that the old hatreds shall someday pass; that the lines of tribe shall soon dissolve; that as the world grows smaller, our common humanity shall reveal itself.

President Barack Hussein Obama
Inaugural Address, January 20, 2009

Introduction

The story of the United States is one of difference and similarity straining against two opposing tendencies, exclusion and inclusion. Culturally, U.S. values proclaim and honor freedom of expression, belief, values, and customs. However, differences between and among people whose cultural expressions diverge from the mainstream have often been denigrated. Our history tells of people striving to be included and to realize the American dream, while they navigate the barriers of exclusion, discrimination, and negative stereotyping.

The Psychology of Diversity: Beyond Prejudice and Racism, First Edition. James M. Jones, John F. Dovidio, and Deborah L. Vietze.
© 2014 Blackwell Publishing Ltd. Published 2014 by Blackwell Publishing Ltd.

The United States is a nation formally founded on a principle of cultural uniformity and uniform rights, privileges, and protections: *E Pluribus Unum*: Out of many, one. John Jay, a Founding Father, stated in a 1787 essay:

> Providence has been pleased to give this one connected country to one united people; a people descended from the same ancestors, speaking the same language, professing the same religion . . . similar in their manner and customs. . . . To all general purposes we have uniformly been one people each individual citizen everywhere enjoying the same national rights, privileges, and protection.

John Jay, writing to persuade the people of New York to support a strong federal government, supported his argument with his observation that New York citizens shared a common origin, language, religion, manners, and customs. To Jay, the United States was defined by the commonalities among its people. President Obama made quite a different claim in his presidential address in 2009 quoted at the beginning of this chapter. We are diverse, not uniform, and the divisions and strife of that diversity shall give way to commonality based on recognizing the humanity we share in spite of, and perhaps even because of, our differences. The tension between wide-ranging differences among us and cultural uniformity is critical to understanding the history of diversity in America.

The experiment in democracy and the "perfect Union" imagined by the Founders consists of justice for all, domestic tranquility, welfare, liberty, and security, all the ideals listed in the preamble to the Constitution. Yet, diversity, by its very nature, presents challenges to securing these liberties and freedoms. Diversity is challenging because it requires more from us to make it work.

W. E. B. DuBois aptly identified the twentieth century's most challenging issue as the *"problem* of the color line" (DuBois, 1903). The defining *challenge* of the twenty-first century, we propose, is the complexity imposed by a rapidly increasing diversity in the U.S. population. The election of Barack Obama as the 44th President of the United States signaled to the world and to ourselves that diversity is at the core of this country. Diversity is a compelling interest, not just a diversion or a source of division.

In Chapter 2, we defined diversity as individual or group differences that exist for any human trait, characteristic, value, or behavior. Americans in the United States are highly diverse, which makes it challenging to determine which characteristics signal, or even if we should define, what it means to be "American." As we noted in Chapter 2, the term encompasses people from North and South America. In the United States, large numbers of immigrants from South and Central American countries also constitute what it means to be "American." The Constitution of the United States (Article 1, Section 2) states that enslaved persons were not citizens, they were not even considered to be fully human; slaves were classified as 40% property and 60% persons for purposes of taxation and representation, respectively (see Hamilton, 1778, for an account of this compromise). Native Americans were considered uncivilized during the nineteenth century and were also not considered to be "American." And immigrants were at best under suspicion of not having what it took to be American well into the twentieth century.

This chapter considers diversity in U.S. history from a variety of perspectives. The responses to diversity have tended to be exclusionary, discriminatory, and problematic. But we also note that inclusion and vigorous anti-bias projects have also been a consistent part of U.S. history. Population diversity in the United States has nevertheless continued to grow and there is much evidence that the United States is better for it. How we respond to diversity as individuals and as a society is a central subject of this book. This chapter provides an overview of the continuing diversification of this society and the responses that have accompanied it.

We first review the dynamic origins and responses to our diverse population. We review the experiences of immigrants and the demographics of diversity over the last 300 years to illustrate how patterns of immigration have changed the U.S. population. We also revisit the familiar ideas of prejudice and racism, sexism and other forms of systematic, deeply ingrained biases against different groups. We next consider ways in which the increasing diversity of the U.S. population challenges our legal, legislative, social, political, economic, and educational systems, and patterns of responses to those challenges. Finally, we conclude that in spite of the resistance to diversity, and because of important doctrines of liberty and ideals of social justice, we have become more diverse, and that diversity has been a strength of this country.

Push–Pull: Dynamics of Diversity

The story of diversity in the United States is a complex example of approach–avoidance motivation. In this section, we provide an overview of the push–pull nature of inclusion and exclusion of various groups in the United States. We focus primarily on legislative and judicial actions taken with respect to immigration and naturalization—criteria for citizenship. **Immigration** is the act of settling in a new country with the desire to remain there permanently. People who enter a country in this manner are called immigrants. We also discuss barriers to participation and individual rights for those who have attained citizenship.

Immigration, Importation, and Citizenship

The origination story of the United States of America and the drama of diversity begin with the settling of Jamestown Plantation in Virginia in 1607 and Plimoth Plantation in Massachusetts in 1620. Differences in the two settlements' environments, their intentions and religious ideas gave rise to different cultural styles and practices, social organizations, and economic institutions. The Southern plantation was a slave-based agrarian economy that produced a Southern aristocracy. The Plimoth Plantation featured enterprising capitalism, and town-centered participatory democracies (Demos, 1970).

These initial differences grew into regional variations that have contributed to a diverse economy, social organization, political attitude, and behavior. We generally think of racial, ethnic, and cultural groups when we discuss diversity. However, social and economic diversity also played a large role in the development of this country.

By 1776, the importation of Africans as slaves and some Europeans as indentured servants had given way to a system of slavery in perpetuity for Africans. In 1787, the idea that slaves were not fully human was incorporated into the U.S. Constitution as the infamous three-fifths compromise between North and South: Northerners wanted Southerners to pay a tax on slaves, and Southerners wanted slaves to count for purposes of political representation. The three-fifths compromise bartered African humanity for economic and political utility. But unease with the idea of slavery led to a plan to end the slave trade. On March 3, 1807, Thomas Jefferson signed a law that forbid importing slaves to the United States effective on January 1, 1808.

Two major events, both in 1793, changed the human landscape in the United States: the first textile factory was built in Rhode Island and Eli Whitney invented the cotton gin. The emerging need for wage labor in the North and the continuing need for slave labor in the South set the two regions on divergent paths. In 1800 about 12% of the U.S. labor force worked for wages. The need for labor to fuel the industrial revolution stimulated dramatic increases in immigration. By 1860, nearly one third of adult White men in the free states were immigrants (Clark, Hewitt, Brown, & Jaffee, 2008).

In the South, the cotton gin fueled the need for more land to grow cotton and created vast markets for the ginned fibers. Indians occupied much of the land and were removed by force to accommodate expanding agrarian economies. Slaves had picked the cotton but with the gin, and the end of slave importation looming, main-taining or acquiring a large pool of "slave labor" was a necessity.

The Naturalization Act of 1790 established the standard for who could become naturalized as a citizen: Caucasians only. However, the dramatic changes that were occurring in the United States by the beginning of the nineteenth century—the removal of Indians from their land, the growth of the slave trade within the United States, and rapidly increasing immigration—raised critical questions about who was or could be a U.S. citizen.

U.S. Population Growth is Fueled by Immigration

From 1820 to 1880, 10.2 million people immigrated to the United States, accounting for 25% of the population growth (Figure 3.1). The need for slaves for the burgeoning plantation economy was accompanied by a need for land occupied by American Indians. On May 28, 1830, President Andrew Jackson signed The Indian Removal Act, which gave the President the power to negotiate removal treaties. Nearly 50,000 Indians were relocated to west of the Mississippi River during Jackson's presidency, freeing up over 25 million acres for predominantly White settlement. The Indian Removal Act forced the relocation of **The Five Civilized Tribes** (Cherokee, Muscogee or Creek, Seminole, Chickasaw, and Choctaw nations) from the southeastern United States to Indian Territory, in what is now eastern Oklahoma. Known as **The Trail of Tears**, the forced march west led to great suffering from exposure, disease and starva-tion, and large-scale deaths en route to their destinations (De Rosier, 1970).

E Pluribus Unum, "Out of many, one," has been represented by the metaphor of a melting pot (Zangwill, 1914). The melting pot refers to the blending of different nationalities, cultures, and races into a new virtuous community, leaving behind their prejudices and cultures, embracing the new land, the new culture, the new way.

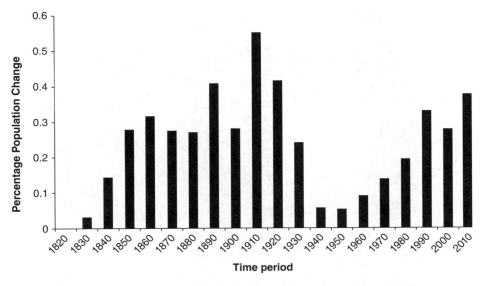

Figure 3.1. Immigrants to the United States as a Percentage of Population Change 1820–2010. From U.S. Census, 2010.

Figure 3.2 shows immigrants to the United States being processed on Ellis Island in New York Harbor, watched over by the Statue of Liberty that beckons: "Give me your tired, your poor, your huddled masses yearning to breathe free . . ."

In the late nineteenth and early twentieth centuries, immigration constituted over 40% of the total population growth of the United States (see Figure 3.1). This period saw the most vigorous immigration in U.S. history. Between 1900 and 1920, immigrants accounted for nearly 50% of the growth in the U.S. population. In 1910, this figure was 55%!

The diverse population in the United States was accomplished by differing means. We know that Africans were brought here not of their own accord. Native Americans were here when British settlers arrived. In 1790, African Americans and American Indians constituted 20% of the U.S. population in the original 13 states (Parrillo, 2006). Over the next century, immigration from various countries in Europe dominated the growing U.S. population.

Who Are Citizens of the United States?

The question of citizenship and rights for Africans remained unsettled until they were crystallized in the Dred Scott decision of 1857. Dred Scott was a slave who had lived in Illinois, a free state, and in Minnesota, part of the free Wisconsin territory. When his master died he sought to buy his freedom but was refused. Scott sued for his freedom but the U.S. Supreme Court rejected his claim, ruling that people of African descent imported into the country and held as slaves or their descendants could never

Figure 3.2.   Immigrants Being Processed at Ellis Island, 1904. Library of Congress: Digital ID (b&w film copy neg.) cph 3a17784, http://hdl.loc.gov/loc.pnp/cph.3a17784. Reproduction Number: LC-USZ62-15539 (b&w film copy neg.). Repository: Library of Congress Prints and Photographs Division Washington, DC 20540, USA. http://www.loc.gov/pictures/item/97501095/resource/

be citizens of the United States. Chief Justice Roger B. Taney put the degraded status of Black people in bold relief when he opined that:

> beings of an inferior order, and altogether unfit to associate with the white race, either in social or political relations, and so far inferior that they had no rights which the white man was bound to respect. (*Dred Scott v. Sandford*, 1857)

Chief Justice Taney argued that granting Dred Scott his freedom would give all black people the freedom to do whatever they wanted, like other U.S. citizens. Justice Taney answered the question "Who is a citizen?" by implying quite emphatically "not Blacks."

On September 22, 1862, President Abraham Lincoln announced the declaration of freedom in the **Emancipation Proclamation**—"all persons held as slaves within any State or designated part of a State . . . shall be then, thenceforward, and forever free." The idea that "stateways" (laws) could change "folkways" (customs and culture) was tested in a series of legislative enactments. Immediately following the Emancipation

Proclamation, the U.S. Congress passed the Civil Rights Act of 1866, which granted citizenship to newly freed slaves. Following in short order, three Amendments to the U.S. Constitution were adopted to secure the rights of citizenship for African Americans and former slaves. The 13th formally ended slavery (1865), the 14th provided due process and equal protection of the laws without regard to race (1868), and the 15th granted voting rights without regard to race or former slave status (1870). Although the right to vote was extended to all races in 1870, it was not until 1920 that the right to vote was extended to women by the 19th Amendment to the Constitution (U.S. Congressional Documents and Debates, 1774–1875).

The **Chinese Exclusion Act,** passed by the Congress in 1882, excluded Chinese laborers from entering the United States. The restriction was limited to 10 years but in 1892, the Geary Act extended and strengthened the Chinese Exclusion Act for another 10 years. Ten years later it was extended indefinitely, but was finally repealed in 1943.

Native Americans were legally excluded in 1884. John Elk, an American Indian, was born on an Indian reservation but moved off the reservation and renounced his tribal affiliation. When he attempted to register to vote, he was denied because Indian tribes were considered "alien nations," and thus Indians could not be U.S. citizens nor exercise the right to vote granted by the 15th Amendment (*Elk v. Wilkins*, 1884). In 1887, however, the U.S. Congress passed the Dawes General Allotment Act, which granted citizenship to Native Americans, but stipulated that they must take up residence separate from any Indian tribe, and adopt the "habits of civilized life" (*United States Statutes at Large* 24:388-91, chapter 119). Finally, the Indian Citizenship Act of 1924 gave full unconditional rights of citizenship to Native Americans.

This is the push–pull pattern of diversity in the United States. Initial responses were to exclude those who were different. Over the centuries, fundamental U.S. principles of liberty, rights, and justice created opportunities and conditions that permitted citizenship to be expanded and more inclusive. However reluctant we may be, and however hard we have tried to circumvent it, the United States has become a more diverse nation.

Immigration and Ethnic Diversity

Immigrants arrived on U.S. shores from different places and for different reasons. Original Irish settlers in the United States were principally Protestants of Scottish background, but by 1820 Irish Catholics began to immigrate in large numbers. Scandinavians immigrated after 1865, driven by religious conflicts, crop failures, and other economic hardships (Parrillo, 2006). Greeks immigrated to the United States in the early twentieth century.

Although Italians were mostly poor farmers from rural areas, they were forced to settle in urban areas because much of the farmland in the Midwest had been claimed by previous waves of immigrants (Germans, Swedes) and veterans of the Civil War. Of necessity they developed urban enclaves, "Little Italies," to cope with the harsh realities of the new world, thus preserving their cultural traditions and affinities, but inhibiting their advancement in society (Petrini, 2001). Similarly, most immigrant Poles were generally poorly educated peasants who established ethnic enclaves, principally in Chicago. They were ghettoized, and their unfamiliarity with the language and customs created significant problems for Polish culture in the New World (Thomas & Znaniecki, 1918). They persevered, however, and their offspring assimilated into and expanded their involvement and success in mainstream culture.

Other Central and Eastern European immigrants (e.g., Hungarians, Russians, Slavs) also tended to be poor and uneducated, and they joined the growing force of wage laborers and felt the ire and wrath of American workers (Parrillo, 2006). Cultural or ethnic immigrant groups that preferred or had the capacity to assimilate into the mainstream of America fared better, both collectively and individually, than those who did not assimilate. By the mid-1960s, however, the melting pot myth was beginning to fade (Glazer & Moynihan, 1963), and by the 1970s embracing one's ethnicity accounted for the growing diversity and cultural difference in the U.S. population (Glazer & Moynihan, 1975).

Religious diversity has also created conflict historically in the United States. From the time of the earliest European settlement, the United States was a majority Protestant nation, and Catholic immigrants were looked upon as outsiders. Some of the most discriminatory treatment of immigrants was meted out against Catholics, particularly if they came from Ireland or Eastern and Central Europe (Higham, 1955; Jenkins, 2003).

Economic differences were sewn into the American fabric from the beginning. Many immigrants were landowners, professionals, or entrepreneurs, but others were laborers, peasants, criminals, or misfits. Some were learned, while others were illiterate. Although most immigrants were, by statute, Whites from Europe, there was substantial diversity among them.

The period 1880–1920 brought a huge influx of immigrants from Southern and Eastern Europe. The proportion of White Protestants in the population dropped significantly, and these new immigrants were perceived as a threat to American values. Psychologist William McDougall (1921) proposed a number of psychological qualities that made for superior cultures, including introversion, strength of will, curiosity, intellectual capacity, self-assertion, and providence, which he assigned to Nordic "races." The opposite qualities—extroversion, sociability, persuadability, being closed to new experiences, low intelligence, low cognitive function, docility, externality, and impulsivity—he assigned to the Mediterranean "races." Detecting mental superiority and inferiority was the work of psychological testing, which he labeled "mental anthropology." For McDougall, deviations from the Nordic norm were signs of deficiency and a reason to restrict immigration by those inferior groups. The 1924 Immigration Act, which we expand on later in this chapter, was one result of this pattern of analysis and thinking.

Benevolent Sexism as Legal Argument

Suspicions about the benefit of diversity extended to women, although the reasoning was somewhat different and cloaked in "faintly favorable" language. Myra Bradwell's husband was a lawyer in Illinois where she worked with him. She read the law and applied to the Illinois state bar for her own license to practice law. In 1869, Bradwell passed the Illinois bar exam with honors. She then applied to the Illinois Supreme

Court for admission to the bar; however, the Court denied her admission, noting, among other things, that the "strife" of the bar would surely destroy her femininity.

Bradwell appealed the decision to the U.S. Supreme Court, arguing that her right to practice law was protected by the privileges and immunities act of the 14th Amendment. In *Bradwell v. State of Illinois* (1872), the Supreme Court disagreed, upholding the decision of the Illinois court. Concurring in the Court's judgment, Justice Bradley claimed that

> The natural and proper timidity and delicacy which belongs to the female sex evidently unfits it for many of the occupations of civil life. . . . The paramount destiny and mission of women are to fulfill the noble and benign offices of wife and mother. This is the law of the Creator and the rules of civil society. (pp. 141–142)

This view reflects contemporary social psychological analyses of **benevolent sexism**: stereotypical attitudes espousing restricted roles for women that are expressed in a subjectively positive feeling tone and accompanied by pro-social (e.g., helping) or intimacy-seeking (e.g., self-disclosure) behaviors (Glick & Fiske, 2001). We also note the applicability of **social role theory** to this non-legal argument: sex-differentiated behavior results from men's and women's adaptations to the division of labor assigned to or expected of each sex (Eagly, 1987). These social roles are accompanied by expectations based on cultural prescriptions that crystallize as gender stereotypes which channel individuals into roles considered to be "suited" for those characteristics and abilities.

Cultural Conditioning of American Indians

During the nativism period, the term "Native American" was reserved by White settlers for Whites only. American Indians, who are now often referred to as Native Americans, were considered savage and uncivilized due in large part to their dramatically different cultural practices and worldview, and equally to their aggressive resistance to the genocidal policies of the U.S. government. This view of Indians as uncivilized savages was advanced in 1881 by Commissioner of Indian Affairs Henry Price and Secretary of the Interior Carl Shurz, who stated: "Savage and civilized life cannot live and prosper on the same ground. One of the two must die. . . . To civilize them, which was only a benevolent fancy, has now become an absolute necessity, if we mean to save them" (Adams, 1988, p. 172).

A group of reformers known as the Friends of the American Indians believed that the only way to solve the so-called Indian problem was to assimilate Native Americans into Euro-American society. This "civilizing" mission was directed at educating young Indian children in boarding schools. The Friends commandeered Army Captain Richard Pratt to head this educational mission. Pratt had been put in charge of 72 Apache prisoners held at Fort Marion near St Augustine, Florida. The prisoners were suspected of having murdered White settlers, a claim never proven. When the Fort Marion prisoners were allowed to return home in 1878, he convinced 22 of them to continue the schooling he had begun at the fort. On November 1, 1878, he opened the Carlisle Indian School at an abandoned military post in Pennsylvania (Prucha,

1984). The Hampton Institute, a school for freed slaves in Virginia, accepted several Apache prisoners as well.

Pratt's educational philosophy was to "kill the Indian, not the man." Indian students at Hampton Institute in 1985 were educated to believe that while all people belong to the human race, the human race could be classified in groups based on their descending order of dominance: Whites, Asians, Blacks, and Reds. Lessons learned are reflected in one answer to a question asking students to say something about White people:

> The Caucasian is away ahead of the other races—he thought that somebody must have made the earth, and if the white people did not find that out, nobody would never know it—it is God who made the world. (Adams, 1988, pp. 175–176)

Negative Responses to Diversity

Prejudice and racism have been a recurring response to diversity. To this we add **nativism**, a feeling that large-scale influx of "foreigners" was a threat to the emerging life and culture of the United States.

During the late nineteenth century, nativists made overt efforts to contain or ghettoize certain immigrants. An initial distrust of "foreigners," based largely on differences in culture and appearance, grew into strong feelings of menace and hatred which often erupted in violence (Higham, 1955). Immigrants from Ireland, Eastern Europe (Slavic peoples and Jews), and Southern Europe (principally Italians) bore the brunt of this burgeoning nativist sentiment. Nativists perceived a threat to the United States in the differences between these new immigrants and those more familiar Western Europeans from Great Britain, Germany, France, and Switzerland. Nativists assumed that the more culturally different immigrants were, the more hostile or alien to the national culture they would be, and the greater the likelihood that they could not be assimilated to the national culture. Nativists feared, demonized, and attacked people from foreign shores (Takaki, 1993). Nativism fostered an exclusionary attitude and corresponding behaviors that curtailed the growth of diversity.

Ethnophaulisms are words that constitute slurs against ethnic groups, and exclusion from U.S. society, for example, "mick" (Irish), "dago" (Italian), "frog" (French), "kike" (Jew), and "asshole bandit" (Greek). Mullen and Rice (2003) looked at ethnophaulisms linked with immigrant groups from 1821 to 1970. They found that the more negative and complex ethnophaulisms associated with an immigrant group, the greater their exclusion as indicated by naturalization rates, immigration quotas, intermarrying, residential segregation, and employment. Other research showed that negative ethnophaulisms were significantly related to suicide rates among immigrant groups (Mullen & Smyth, 2004).

In the 1890s alone, there were six different acts of mob violence directed at Italians. In one incident, New Orleans Police Chief David Hennessey was fatally shot, but before he died he whispered "the dagos did it" (Haas, 1982, p. 53). Many Italians were arrested and held in jail. On March 14, 1891, an angry mob attacked the jail with no resistance, and while the police stood by they shot or clubbed 11 Italian prisoners to death (Haas, 1982).

Terence Powderly was a Grand Master Worker of the Knights of Labor, a labor union organized to protect and extend workers' rights and to reform their social and economic conditions. Powderly waged a campaign against newly arrived immigrants from various Central and Eastern European countries who were hired as strike-breakers. One day in 1890, the striking miners, led by Powderly, attacked the immigrants, killing more than 100 of them in the mining town of Homestead, Pennsylvania (Papp, 1981).

Jews faced hostility, and often had their businesses and homes attacked, particularly in the South, but in the North as well. In a small New Jersey town in 1891, a mill hired 14 Russian Jewish boys and 500 local boys went on a rampage, forcing them to leave the town and their jobs (Higham, 1955).

On May 4, 1886, a rally of laborers in support of an 8-hour work day was held in Haymarket Square in Chicago. Led by anarchists who were mostly German and Eastern European immigrants, a bomb was thrown at the police and a riot ensued. Known as the **Haymarket Affair**, it fueled nativist anti-immigration sentiment, reflected in the virulent voices of editorial writers of the time: "The enemy forces are not American [but] . . . cutthroats of Beelzebub from the Rhine, the Danube, the Vistula and the Elbe. These people are not Americans, but the very scum of Europe" (quoted in Higham, 1955, pp. 54–55).

Stereotypes fed the anti-immigrant frenzy and fueled the violence. Eastern Europeans were considered unruly and uncivilized; Italians were deemed impulsive, violent, and driven by revenge; and Jews were declared charlatans, greedy, and in control of money. Immigrants such as Slavs and Magyars were stereotyped as unruly, uncivilized, and dangerous. These fears and stereotypes arose largely because immigrants competed for wage labor jobs. Often they were willing to accept lower wages and often replaced striking U.S. workers. Undermining the striking workers fanned the flames of animosity and frustration.

Immigrants from Western Europe too were not immune to resistance and violence. Germany had been the source of the most immigrants to the United States since 1820. Yet in 1855 a mob attacked the Germantown section of Louisville, Kentucky, killed 22 people, wounded hundreds more, and burned down several houses.

The Irish immigrants were predominantly Catholic and anti-British, and they came in large numbers during the nineteenth century, raising suspicions and anti-Irish sentiment. Many wished to restrict immigration from Ireland. Hale (1926) reasoned that Whites should not complain about the large numbers of immigrant Irish because

> when they [Irish] come in among us, they come to lift us up. . . . Their inferiority as a race compels them to go to the bottom; and . . . we are, all of us, the higher lifted because they are here. (Hale, 1926, p. 463)

Immigration Policy

Recall that U.S. immigration policy under the Naturalization Act of 1790 restricted naturalization to immigrants of Caucasian heritage. In 1923, Bhagat Singh Thind, an Asian Indian immigrant, sought U.S. citizenship, arguing that scientific evidence showed that Asian Indians were properly classified as Caucasians. The Supreme Court rejected Thind's claim (*United States v. Bhagat Singh Thind*, 1923), arguing that despite the fact that anthropologists had defined the people in India as belonging to the Caucasian race, Thind was not a "White person" as the term was commonly used and understood by the common man.

The nativism of the late nineteenth and early twentieth centuries found voice in the **Immigration Act of 1924**. The Act established a formula for immigration that (a) capped total immigration to the United States at 150,000 per year; (b) assigned quotas to specific nations; (c) restricted immigrant visas from quota nations; (d) made it easier to immigrate from non-quota nations by requiring simple proof of residence in the country of origin for at least 2 years prior to emigration to the United States; and (e) limited immigration from Asiatic nations to professionals, clergy, and students. It dramatically restricted immigration from Southern, Central and Eastern Europe and denied entrance from Japan. Immigration was limited to those who were thought to be able to assimilate into the culture of the United States. Table 3.1 shows the official quotas mandated by the 1924 Immigration Act.

Needless to say, immigration declined during the period 1920–1960 as quotas and World War II restricted entry to the United States (Figure 3.3). But immigration policy expanded in 1943, when the U.S. Congress repealed the Chinese Exclusion Act that had been in force since 1882 (U.S. Department of State; retrieved on November 1, 2009 from http://www.state.gov/r/pa/ho/time/wwii/86552.htm). The legislation also established a quota of 105 Chinese immigrants per year.

In 1952, the Immigration and Nationality Act accorded full citizenship to persons born in the U.S. territories of Guam, Puerto Rico, the Virgin Islands, and the Northern Mariana Islands. In addition, this legislation revised the quota system stipulated in the Immigration Act of 1924 to allow for national quotas at a rate of one sixth of 1% of each nationality's population in the United States in 1920. As a result, 85% of the 154,277 visas available annually were allotted to individuals of Northern and Western European lineage. Immigration policy limited U.S. diversity again by favoring Whites from Europe, but the Act also broadened U.S. diversity by granting citizenship to Central American and Pacific Islanders.

The 1952 Immigration and Nationality Act also repealed the last of the existing measures to exclude Asian immigration by allotting each Asian nation a minimum quota of 100 visas each year. However, the new Asian quotas were based solely on race, instead of nationality. An individual with one or more Asian parent, born anywhere in the world and possessing the citizenship of any nation would be counted under the national quota of the Asian nation of his or her ethnicity. As a result, immigration from Asian countries remained very limited.

Although the Act enhanced diversity in some ways, it continued quotas for non-Western European nations. McCarran, one of the authors of the 1952 Immigration and Nationality Act, supported the origins provision when he declared that

we have in the United States today hard-core, indigestible blocs which have not become integrated into the American way of life, but which, on the contrary are its deadly enemies. Today, as never before, untold millions are storming our gates for admission and those gates are cracking under the strain. (Senator Pat McCarran, Cong. Rec., March 2, 1953, p. 1518)

Table 3.1. Immigration Quota by Country, 1924 Immigration Act

Country	Quota
Northwest Europe and Scandinavia	
Germany	51,227
Great Britain and Northern Ireland	34,007
Irish Free State (Ireland)	28,567
Sweden	9,561
Norway	6,453
France	3,954
Denmark	2,789
Switzerland	2,081
Netherlands	1,648
Austria	785
Belgium	512
Finland	471
Free City of Danzig	228
Iceland	100
Luxembourg	100
Total (number)	142,483
Total (%)	86.5
Eastern and Southern Europe	
Poland	5,982
Italy	3,845
Czechoslovakia	3,073
Russia	2,248
Yugoslavia	671
Romania	603
Portugal	503
Hungary	473
Lithuania	344
Latvia	142
Spain	131
Estonia	124
Albania	100
Bulgaria	100
Greece	100
Total (number)	18,439
Total (%)	11.2
Other countries	
Africa (other than Egypt)	1,100
Armenia	124
Australia	121
Palestine	100
Syria	100
Turkey	100
Egypt	100
New Zealand and Pacific Islands	100
All others	1,900
Total (number)	3,745
Total (%)	2.3
Total annual immigrant quota: 164,667	

Note. From *Statistical Abstract of the United States* (p. 100), 1929, Washington, D.C: Government Printing Office.

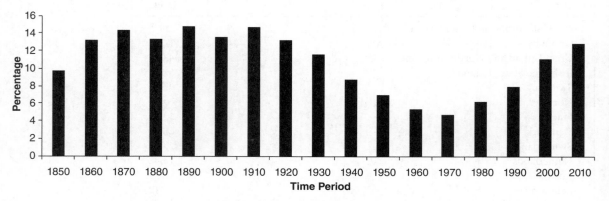

Figure 3.3.   Foreign-born Percentage of the U.S. Population From 1850 to 2010. From U.S. Census, 2010.

President Harry Truman disagreed with this sentiment and vetoed the bill, declaring the national origins quota system and the racially constructed quotas for Asian nations discriminatory. However, the Congress overrode his veto and the law was enacted. Fear and exclusion collided with principles of fairness and inclusion. And the downturn of immigration evident in the first half the twentieth century continued up until 1970 (see Figure 3.3).

Civil Rights

The diversity story is about civil rights as well as immigration. The "isms"—nativism, racism, and sexism—marginalize and restrict participation in our institutions and society by discrimination and exclusion (see Chapter 2 about "isms"). **Racial integration**, the idea that people of all races should comingle across all aspects of society on an equal basis, not only concerns principles of fairness and basic civil and human rights but goes directly to what diversity is about. **Beneficial diversity** requires not only acceptance of differences among people, but a belief that those differences add value to the contexts in which they occur, that organizations, society, and our country are better off when they are diverse. Perhaps it is because we believe in this idea and the underlying principle of fairness, equality and individual rights that we have continued to become a more diverse society even as the "isms" threaten to curtail diversity. Diversity is not just a matter of immigration and opportunities to become citizens of the United States. The full rights of citizenship are at stake when we have a diverse society. Securing those rights of citizenship is a recurring theme of the twentieth century push for civil rights.

Diversity and Civil Rights

On June 7, 1892, Homer Plessy boarded a car of the East Louisiana Railroad that was designated for use by White patrons only. Although Mr Plessy was only one-eighth

Black, under Louisiana state law he was classified as an African American and required to sit in the "colored" car. When he refused, he was arrested and jailed. Plessy argued that his constitutional rights under the 13th and 14th Amendments had been violated. He lost. When Plessy appealed to the Supreme Court (***Plessy v. Ferguson, 1896***), his appeal was rejected with these words:

> We consider the underlying fallacy of the plaintiff's argument [be] that the enforced separation of the two races stamps the colored race with a badge of inferiority. If this be so, it is not by reason of anything found in the act, but solely because the colored race chooses to put that construction upon it.

Thus the "separate but equal" doctrine of racial segregation was made a legal practice in the United States until it was overturned almost 60 years later, by ***Brown v. Board of Education of Topeka* in 1954**.

Anti-Asian sentiment persisted into the twentieth century. In 1907 the United States struck an agreement with Japan, known as the **Gentlemen's Agreement**, promising not to restrict Japanese immigration as long as Japan voluntarily restricted emigration to the United States to upper-middle-class Japanese. This was followed a decade later by the **Immigration Act of 1917**, which restricted immigration from Asia by creating an Asiatic Barred Zone. Added to the 1882 Chinese Exclusion Act, Asians in general were effectively barred from immigration to the United States.

The 1920s had an ominous beginning for both immigration and civil rights. The sentiments of nativism combined with ongoing prejudice and racism made the early 1920s more restrictive and exclusionary than ever. The most restrictive immigration and racial segregation laws since 1790 were passed. Lynchings were widespread. By the end of this period, however, the way was paved for dramatic changes in the 1960s in both immigration policy and civil rights. We review the immigration policy first, then conclude with a discussion of civil rights.

The Civil Rights and Women's Movements of the 1940s, 1950s, and 1960s were founded on the idea that inclusion of racial and ethnic minorities and women as full participants in U.S. society was a natural and necessary condition for meeting U.S. principles of democracy, justice, and liberty. Progress in the area of civil rights was inconsistent, but it included some significant court decisions and presidential and legislative acts that created a foundation for later major societal change.

In 1942, President Franklin Roosevelt issued **Executive Order 9066** which author-ized the forcible relocation and internment of approximately 110,000 Japanese nation-als and Japanese Americans. Of those interned, 62% were U.S. citizens. The exclusionary order was upheld by the U.S. Supreme Court in 1944. But consistent with the push–pull theme of diversity, in 1988, Congress passed and President Ronald Reagan signed legislation which apologized for the internment, stating that government actions were based on "race prejudice, war hysteria, and a failure of political leadership." A total of $1.6 billion in reparations were later disbursed by the U.S. government to surviving internees and their heirs.

Violence against African American veterans of World War II was common. In February 1946, African American World War II veteran Isaac Woodard was attacked and blinded by policemen in Aiken, South Carolina. In July 1946, two African American veterans and their wives were taken from their car near Monroe, Georgia by a White mob and shot to death; they were shot 60 times. In December of that year, President Harry S. Truman appointed a Commission on Civil Rights. The Commission's report, *To Secure These Rights*, issued in 1947, called for an end to all racial discrimination and segregation in the armed forces.

On July 26, 1948, President Truman signed **Executive Order 9981**, which mandated "equality of treatment and opportunity for all persons in the armed services without regard to race, color, religion, or national origin" (Harry S. Truman Library and Museum, http://www.trumanlibrary.org/whistlestop/study_collections/desegregation/large/index.php?action=chronology). In 1953, the army announced that military units were 95% racially integrated (Truman Library, Desegregation of the Armed Forces: Chronology, November 20, 2009).

A pivotal moment in the history of civil rights in the United States occurred in the mid-1950s. Oliver L. Brown was an African American welder and assistant pastor whose daughter Linda, a third grader, was required by law to take a bus to a Black school a mile from her home rather than attend a White school only seven blocks away. Figure 3.4 shows Linda and her older sister walking to school across town on

Figure 3.4. Brown Sisters Walk to School, Topeka, Kansas, 1953. © Carl Iwasaki/Time Life Pictures/Getty Images.

the other side of the tracks. Mr Brown sued the Topeka Board of Education to reverse its policy of racial segregation. On May 17, 1954, the Supreme Court ruled, in *Brown v. Board of Education of Topeka*, that state laws that established separate public schools for Black and White students denied black children equal educational opportunities. The unanimous ruling stated that "separate educational facilities are inherently unequal," thus declaring that *de jure*, or legal, racial segregation violated the 14th Amendment. This ruling overturned the "separate but equal" doctrine, enunciated in the 1896 *Plessy v. Ferguson* decision.

Also decided in 1954 and less well known, but an important expansion of the civil rights for Mexican Americans, was **Hernandez v. Texas (1954)**. This landmark Supreme Court case decided that Mexican Americans, as ethnic minorities, had a right to equal protection under the 14th Amendment. It held that Mexican Americans had been systematically excluded from serving on juries in Texas. There was no legal requirement that a person was entitled to be tried by a jury of peers, only that no racial ethnic or gender groups could be excluded from serving on juries. The Hernandez case granted full rights of citizenship to Mexican Americans.

Citizenship has been a contested condition of diverse groups throughout our history. Racial and nationality groups have been denied or excluded, but have also been reduced to a second-class citizenship status. **Jim Crow Laws** (so called after a Black character in minstrel shows) maintained second-class citizenship for Blacks by imposing legal restrictions on racial interactions. The most common laws forbade intermarriage and ordered business owners and public institutions to keep their Black and White clientele separated. The following are examples of Jim Crow Laws (Randall, 2009).

> It shall be unlawful for any amateur white baseball team to play baseball on any vacant lot or baseball diamond within two blocks of a playground devoted to the Negro race, and it shall be unlawful for any amateur colored baseball team to play baseball in any vacant lot or baseball diamond within two blocks of any playground devoted to the white race (Georgia).

> All railroad companies and corporations, and all persons running or operating cars or coaches by steam on any railroad line or track in the State of Maryland, for the transportation of passengers, are hereby required to provide separate cars or coaches for the travel and transportation of the white and colored passengers (Maryland).

> The marriage of a person of Caucasian blood with a Negro, Mongolian, Malay, or Hindu shall be null and void (Arizona).

But all of this began to change when, on December 1, 1955, an African American woman, Rosa Parks, was arrested for refusing to give up her seat on a Montgomery, Alabama bus in violation of Jim Crow segregation laws.

For Rosa Parks, being asked to give up her seat for a White man was the straw that broke the camel's back. Ms Parks was sitting in the colored section of the bus as required by Jim Crow laws but, as more White riders entered, the bus driver demanded she move back further and give up her seat. She refused to give up her seat and was arrested for violating the Montgomery City code, which required her to give her seat to Whites who were standing. As the officer took her away, she asked him, "Why do you push us around?" Ms Parks recalled his response, "I don't know, but the law's the law, and you're under arrest." She later said

> I only knew that, as I was being arrested, that it was the very last time that I would ever ride in humiliation of this kind in segregation and being arrested for just wanting to go home and wanting to be comfortable and wanting to be treated as any passenger should. (CNN live transcript, aired October 25, 2005, retrieved December 29, 2009)

Plans to boycott the Montgomery bus service were put into operation on December 5 demanding that black riders be treated with courtesy, black drivers be hired, and seating in the middle of the bus be handled on a first-come basis. The **Montgomery bus boycott** expanded to sit-ins, marches, and other forms of passive non-violent resistance. The Civil Rights Movement gained momentum against growing and often violent resistance by Whites.

By the end of the 1950s, the United States was poised to begin the most open and inclusive period in its history. This period was marked by a significant change in U.S. policies toward diversity, not only toward Blacks but also toward other groups. This period was punctuated by the Civil Rights Movement, the Women's Movement, affirmative action, and an inclusionary immigration policy. Diversity of the U.S. population was ready to explode.

Expanding Diversity and Inclusion in U.S. Society Through Civil Rights

The 1960s were generally viewed as a watershed period in American history. No era so dramatically expanded the participation of diverse people in our society. The Civil Rights Movement brought about a fundamental shift in the nation's tolerance for overt legal racial discrimination.

The **Civil Rights Act of 1964** ended legal discrimination on the basis of race, color, gender, religion, and national origin. The **Voting Rights Act of 1965** outlawed literacy tests and provided for the appointment of Federal examiners with the power to register qualified citizens to vote. It also applied a nationwide prohibition of the denial or abridgment of the right to vote because of race or color. The law had an immediate impact. By the end of 1965, a quarter of a million new Black voters had been registered, one third by Federal examiners.

The **Immigration and Nationality Act 1965** (Immigration and Naturalization Service, 1965) abolished the national-origin quotas that had been in place since the 1924 Immigration Act. An annual limitation of 300,000 visas was established for immigrants, including 170,000 from eastern-hemisphere countries, with a limit of 20,000 per country. By equalizing immigration policies, the act resulted in new immigration from non-European nations that changed the ethnic make-up of the United States. Figure 3.5 shows the dramatic change in percentages of immigrants from European and non-European countries during the 1900s. In 2009, 12.5% of the U.S. population was born outside the United States. Of those, 27.7% were born in Asia, 53.1% in Latin America, 3.9% in Africa, 12.7% in Europe, and 2.6% in other regions. Immigration doubled between 1965 and 1970; it doubled again between 1970 and 1990 (Frum, 2000).

During the 1950s and 1960s, increasing numbers of married women entered the labor force, but in 1963 the average working woman earned only 63% of what a man

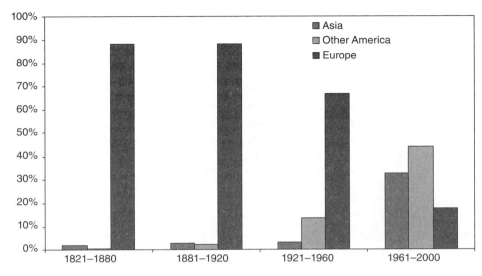

Figure 3.5. Percentage of Total Immigrants to the United States From Europe, Asia, South and Central America, and the Caribbean, 1820–2000. From Bureau of Census, 2010, http://www.census.gov/prod/2010pubs/acsbr09-15.pdf

made. A movement emerged to secure women's rights, inspired in 1963 by Betty Friedan's *The Feminine Mystique*, which urged women to seek out new roles, new possibilities for participating more broadly in U.S. society. Inspired also by the Civil Rights Movement, the Women's Movement pushed for equal rights. This effort culminated in a proposal to amend the U.S. Constitution. The **Equal Rights Amendment (ERA)** to the Constitution declared that "Equality of rights under the law shall not be denied or abridged by the United States or by any State on account of sex." The law was passed by Congress in 1972 and over a roughly 10-year period was ratified by 35 of the necessary 38 states required to become law. Finally in 1982, the effort to obtain ratification from three more states was abandoned.

Title IX of the Education Amendments of 1972 stipulated that no person shall, on the basis of sex, be excluded from participation in, be denied the benefits of, or be subjected to discrimination under any education program or activity receiving Federal financial assistance. Title IX is most notably invoked to support participation of women in athletics. But it also prohibited any educational institution receiving Federal financial assistance from denying admission to any course of study on the ground of blindness or severely impaired vision.

The idea of protecting persons with disabilities from discrimination or more general indifference was formalized in 1990 by the **Americans with Disabilities Act**. The Act provides protections for persons with disabilities in much the same way the 1964 Civil Rights Act did for race, gender, and national origin.

Enacted in 1993, **"Don't ask, don't tell"** (DADT) was the official U.S. policy on gay men and women serving in the military. The policy prohibited military personnel from discriminating against or harassing *closeted* gay or bisexual service members or applicants, but it barred *openly* gay, lesbian, or bisexual persons from military service.

On July 22, 2011, President Barack Obama, Secretary of Defense Leon Panetta, and Chairman of the Joint Chiefs of Staff Admiral Mike Mullen certified that repeal of DADT would not harm military readiness, and on September 20, 2011, the policy officially ended.

Young people and women rebelled against restrictions to their freedom to exercise judgment, and to pursue the life and lifestyles they wanted! The 1960s included broad movements among the younger generation to assert their independence through "counterculture": It was the era of hippies, "flower power," and anti-Vietnam War protests. Thus the movements were not just about promoting the rights of racial, ethnic and other groups, they were also about individual freedom. The removal of racial, ethnic, and national restrictions and quotas in immigration partially answered the age-old question of who is an American. President Lyndon Johnson undertook systematic efforts to end discrimination and social inequality in the name of his Great Society programs. Affirmative action was born and resistance to it began. But the familiar strains of resistance grew as participation in American society widened to be more inclusive, more diverse.

Many people believed that, because the Civil Rights Act of 1964 legally ended racial discrimination or at least provided the enforcement tools to punish people and institutions that continue to discriminate, the problem was solved. However, racial discrimination and other forms of bias continue—by design or default, with or without awareness, in our minds and through our actions, by practice and by belief. Social psychological research over the past 40 years has demonstrated that while overt racial and ethnic prejudice has subsided, subtle expressions of bias persist (Dovidio & Gaertner, 2004; Greenwald, Poehlman, Uhlmann & Banaji, 2009).

The Civil Rights, Voting Rights, Immigration, and Americans with Disabilities Acts, along with the gains forged by the Women's Movement, combined to usher in an unprecedented period of growth in diversity in the history of the United States. Simon Rosenberg, founder of the progressive New Democrat Network (NDN), called the Immigration Act of 1965 "the most important piece of legislation that no one's ever heard of . . . [that] set America on a very different demographic course than the previous 300 years" (quoted in Canellos, 2008). In signing the 1965 Act, President Johnson offered the following judgment:

> This [old] system violates the basic principle of American democracy, the principle that values and rewards each man on the basis of his merit as a man. It has been un-American in the highest sense, because it has been untrue to the faith that brought thousands to these shores even before we were a country. (President Lyndon B. Johnson, October 3, 1965)

Affirmative Action as a Diversity Approach

President Johnson ushered in the age of affirmative action when he signed **Executive Order 11246** on September 24, 1965. The Order required that all federal contractors take affirmative action to ensure that job applicants are judged and employees are treated fairly without regard to their race, color, religion, sex, or national origin. Affirmative action policy established a standard of equal treatment for groups that had been historically disadvantaged and discriminated against, as well as sanctions for violations of non-discrimination practices. Enforcement of the Order was placed with the new Equal Employment Opportunity Commission (EEOC), which was charged with investigating discrimination complaints based on an individual's race, color, national origin, religion, sex (and, more recently, age, disability, and retaliation), and for reporting and/or prosecuting discriminatory practices.

Title VII of the Civil Rights Act of 1964 prohibited employers who did business with the federal government from discriminating on the basis of race, color, religion, sex, or national origin. Title VII has been used to argue so-called **reverse discrimination** cases, which have claimed that Whites are discriminated against by affirmative action policies that give "preferential treatment" to minorities and women in violation of the statute that one may not discriminate on the basis of race, gender, or any specified social demographic category.

Allan Bakke, a White man, applied to the University of California at Davis Medical School in both 1973 and 1974 and was denied admission. In both years, Black and Latino/Latina applicants whose grade-point averages and standardized test scores were lower than Bakke's were admitted under a special admissions program that set aside 16 of the 100 available admissions slots for minority applicants. Bakke filed a racial discrimination lawsuit and it was upheld by the California Supreme Court. The university appealed to the U.S. Supreme Court.

The U.S. Supreme Court ruled 5–4 in favor of both Mr Bakke and the University of California (***Regents of the University of California v. Bakke,*** 1978). Justice Lewis Powell argued against the use of race in admissions if it created a racial quota. Racial quotas discriminated not only against Whites (reverse discrimination) but also against all applicants who were not admitted under the regular admission standards. Justice Powell also argued that universities *could* consider race as long as it did not result in the application of a racial quota. Race could be used in college admissions as one of several factors that influence admissions decisions. Justice Harry Blackmun noted the dilemma that affirmative action placed on society:

> I suspect that it would be impossible to arrange an affirmative-action program in a racially neutral way and have it be successful. . . . In order to get beyond racism, we must first take account of race. There is no other way. And in order to treat some persons equally, we must treat them differently. (p. 69)

The Bakke reasoning was tested in 1996 when the University of Michigan Law School rejected Barbara Grutter, a White Michigan resident. The Center for Individual Rights (http://cir-usa.org/) filed suit on her behalf, alleging that the university had discriminated against her on the basis of race. She said she was rejected because the Law School used race as a factor, and that the university had no compelling interest to justify the consideration of race in the admissions process.

The U.S. Supreme Court decided this case by upholding the reasoning in the Bakke case, that affirmative action programs could use race as a "plus" factor (***Grutter v. Bollinger,*** 2003; http://www.vpcomm.umich.edu/admissions/new/). In her majority opinion, Justice Sandra Day O'Connor wrote that the Constitution does not "prohibit the law school's narrowly tailored use of race in admissions decisions to further a compelling interest in obtaining the educational benefits that flow from a diverse student body." But, the Court ruled, it did on a companion case, *Gratz v. Bollinger* (2003), which found that the affirmative action approach at the undergraduate level was not "narrowly tailored" and struck it down.

The important implication of the Grutter decision is that diversity is a compelling interest in higher education, and that race, among other factors, may be taken into account in admissions decisions. University of Michigan president Mary Sue Coleman hailed the decision as a victory for the value of diversity: "We fought for the very principle that defines our country's greatness. Year after year, our student body proves it and now the court has affirmed it: Our diversity is our strength" (University of Michigan News Service, retrieved from http://umich.edu/news/index.html?Releases/2003/Jun03/supremecourt2).

Can we achieve racial diversity through race neutral means? Is ignoring race or adopting a colorblind approach the best way to insure fairness and equal opportunity? We continue to debate these approaches today as they challenge our ability to achieve the benefits of diversity.

For many years after the *Brown v. Board of Education of Topeka* (1954) ruling, school districts initiated school desegregation plans, often mandated by the courts. Desegregation was an approach that attempted to combat the massive racial segregation in schools caused primarily by racial segregation in residential communities (Massey & Denton, 1993). School jurisdictions initiated affirmative plans to create diversity among their students because they believed they had a compelling interest to do so. Box 3.1 describes one plan, the case of Lynn, Massachusetts.

Box 3.1. The Case of Lynn, Massachusetts

Background

Lynn, Massachusetts is a working-class town of 89,000 people, located about 10 miles northeast of Boston. The median family income is $45,000 compared with $74,463 for the Commonwealth of Massachusetts and $64,000 for the United States. It is a racially and ethnically diverse city, with Whites comprising 65%, Hispanic/Latinos 18%, African Americans 11%, Asian Americans and Pacific Islanders 6.5%, and Native Americans less than 1% of the population. Even though the city was rather diverse, the schools were less so. Beginning in 1988, the Lynn public school system used a voluntary plan to improve racial diversity in its schools and eliminate minority isolation. Under the Lynn Plan, all students had the unconditional right to attend their neighborhood school. However, students could transfer out of their district school and into another if their transfer would have the effect of *decreasing* racial isolation or *increasing* racial balance. Conversely, students could not transfer if doing so would detract from either of these goals. As a result of the plan, the student bodies of Lynn schools had become more racially diverse.

How the Plan Worked

In the 2001/2002 school year, 15,444 students were enrolled in the Lynn public schools: 42% were White and 58% were "minority" (15% African American, 29% Hispanic, and 14% Asian American). In the Lynn Plan, a school is "racially balanced" if the percentage of "minority" students in the school is within ±15% of their overall percentage in the Lynn school system in elementary school. If a school's minority population was above this range, it was racially imbalanced; if it was below this range, it was racially isolated.

A student could transfer to any school if that transfer was considered diversity neutral ("desegregative") and reduced either racial imbalance or racial isolation in either the sending or receiving school. A student was denied a transfer if it was judged "segregative" by increasing either imbalance or isolation.

Opposition to the Plan

Parents whose children were denied transfers on race-conscious grounds challenged the transfer provisions of the Lynn Plan, claiming that those provisions violate rights secured to them under the Equal Protection Clause of the 14th Amendment to the United States Constitution.

Court Rulings

In 2003, the U.S. District Court upheld the School District's transfer plan. However, a three-judge panel of the U.S. Court of Appeals reversed this ruling in 2004. The Lynn School Committee petitioned for a rehearing, and in June 2005 a full panel of judges for the U.S. Court of Appeals upheld the Lynn plan, declaring it to be "narrowly tailored to meet this compelling interest in securing the educational benefits of racial diversity."

The Diversity Challenge

The Lynn Plan was based on the idea that diversity in the schools was a good thing. No one really argued against that idea. What was contested was the means by which it was achieved. So, the challenge did not pit a bad idea (legal racial segregation) against a good idea (racially diverse schooling) as was the case in 1954 in *Brown vs. Board of Education of Topeka*. Rather it pitted diversity of its schools and attendant benefits for social and civic engagement (a good thing) against the ability of students to attend the school of their choice (also a good thing).

1. What rights, if any, were violated here?
2. The pursuit of diversity often comes down to an inherent conflict between two desirable goals. How should these challenges be addressed?
3. What could school districts do differently to achieve their goal of more diverse schools?
4. What could parents and students do to gain more control over their ability to choose schools while not undermining the diversity goals?
5. Is racial/ethnic diversity a goal worth achieving? Why or why not?

A Nation of Minorities

The seemingly inexorable growth of diversity in the U.S. population has gained momentum in the last 30 years so that now we are on the verge of becoming a nation of minorities, defined both by our differences as well as our similarities. Increasingly, difference and diversity describe who we are as a nation.

The rate of immigration has steadily increased, and from 1970 to 2010 immigrants contributed roughly one quarter of the increase in the U.S. population (see Figure 3.1). Today, over 13% of the U.S. population come from other shores (see Figure 3.3). That number more than doubles when we add those citizens born in the United States of parents who were born in other countries. These immigration patterns, combined with divergent birth and death rates, have significantly affected the make-up of the U.S. population.

In 2010, Whites accounted for about 70% of the U.S. population (Figure 3.6), but this percentage continues to decline. In 2012, for the first time live births to racial and ethnic minority mothers exceeded the number born to Whites. The life expectancies for these groups are also extending more rapidly and, as we have seen, immigration continues from Asia, Central, South, and Latin America, and Africa.

By 2042, Whites of European descent will constitute only 46% of U.S. citizens (Figure 3.7). The groups that we refer to as minorities (African and Asian Americans, Native Americans, Alaskan Natives, Native Hawaiians, and Latino/Hispanics) will make up 54%, a majority. Hispanics alone will constitute fully 30% of the population, African Americans 13%, and Asian Americans 8%. American Indians will represent 1% of the population, and 4% will be classified as multiracial (Stein, 2008). Ethnic, racial, and cultural diversity is the prevailing trend in twenty-first century America. How did this happen?

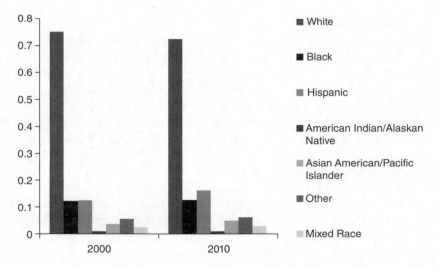

Figure 3.6. Percentage U.S. Population by Race/Ethnicity 2000–2010. From Bureau of Census, 2010.

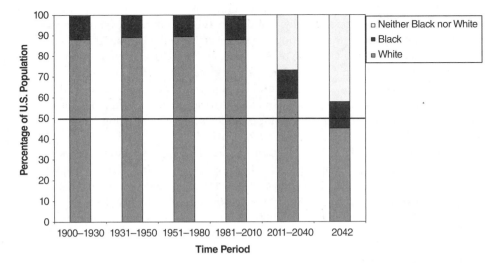

Figure 3.7. The United States Becomes a "Nation of Minorities" 2042. From Bureau of Census, 2010.

The Immigration and Nationality Act of 1965 set immigration policy in the United States on the basis of four general objectives:

1. to facilitate the reunification of families by admitting people who already have a family member living in the United States;
2. to attract workers to fill positions in certain occupations for which there are shortages;
3. to increase diversity by admitting people from countries with historically low rates of immigration to the United States; and
4. to provide a refuge for people who face the risk of racial, religious, or political persecution in their home country.

However, the demand for immigration spots exceeded the supply and a rising tide of illegal immigration, about 60% of which was from Mexico, emerged. In 1996, the U.S. Congress passed an illegal immigration law (**Illegal Immigration Reform and Immigrant Responsibility Act of 1996**) that beefed up border patrols, and enhanced enforcement and penalties, inspection, apprehension, and detention. It further forbid employment and sanctioned U.S. businesses for violations. In spite of the law, however, illegal immigration persisted. In 2010, 11.2 million illegal immigrants were living in the United States. Reforming immigration policy has become a major political, legal, and cultural issue in the twenty-first century debates about diversity.

The State of Arizona tackled this issue head on. The Arizona immigration law SB1070, titled "Support Our Law Enforcement and Safe Neighborhoods Act," was approved on April 19 by the Arizona Legislature and signed on April 23, 2010 by Arizona's Governor Jan Brewer. Arizona faced an increase in illegal immigration from less than 100,000 in 1990 to nearly half a million in 2010. The primary aim was to identify people in the state illegally and deport them. But controversy was created when the law stipulated that the police had the right to determine if a person who was legally detained for a violation of Arizona law was a citizen or a legal immigrant. Opposition was based on concern that authority vested in police officers would contribute to racial profiling. Although the U.S. Supreme Court ruled that in the main the law was unconstitutional, it let stand the provision that allowed police officers to demand proof of citizenship of detainees under suspicion of being illegally in the United States (*Arizona et al. v. United States*, 2012).

Demographic diversity is often accompanied by language diversity (American Psychological Association, Presidential Task Force on Immigration, 2012). For example, between 1979 and 2008, the percentage of children who spoke a second language at home rose from 9% to 21%; 62% of these spoke Spanish, while 15% spoke an Asian or Pacific Island language. Overall, in the United States 26 different languages were spoken by 100,000 or more people (American Psychological Association, Presidential Task Force on Immigration, 2012).

One recurring question that confronts us is, Who is an American? (see Fineman, 2008, for a contemporary discussion of this problem). The answer to this question used to be Whites of Western European lineage. The answer now is anyone from any background who is a citizen of the United States. We have come a long way from John Jay's vision of a unified and homogeneous society. The fact that we are a diverse society challenges us to find ways to accommodate both differences and similarities, to encompass differences in traditionally homogeneous contexts. We conclude this chapter by discussing some of these challenges.

Challenges of Diversity

In this chapter, we have explored several different aspects of diversity: how we achieved the level of diversity that exists in society today, the resistance to diversity, and the legal means used both to suppress and to foster diversity. We have seen that diversity— human variation—has been rejected as well as encouraged at different levels of our government, society, and law. Racial discrimination is undesirable and currently forbidden by law, but remedies are now mainly restricted to race-neutral means. We have to take prejudice and racism into account to reach a balanced and viable understanding of diversity, because they constrain and marginalize broad access to and participation in our society. But we have to go beyond them. The challenge of achieving a diverse society with equal opportunity for all is daunting. In the following sections, we identify three of the continuing themes in this book that reflect central challenges of, and to, diversity: (a) individual rights, diversity, and prejudice; (b) diversity and difference; and (c) majority and minority relations.

Individual Rights, Diversity, and Prejudice Collide

The courts have upheld that individual citizens, not groups, are guaranteed equal protection under the law. Therefore, in the Supreme Court's majority view, remedies to racial segregation cannot be based on race unless they are in response to individual instances of unlawful discrimination, that is, **narrowly tailored** (see RaceBlind.Org for wide-ranging arguments representing this viewpoint). It is more important to our idea of democracy and individual liberty that individual freedoms come first, whether the exercise of such freedoms increases racial segregation or not.

When U.S. courts consider the constitutionality of diversity initiatives, the pivotal arguments hinge on the impact of these policies or programs on individuals. The ruling in *Grutter v. Bollinger* (2003) argued that racial diversity, provided by a "critical mass" of minority students, was a compelling interest on college campuses because it promoted a diversity of viewpoints. The Massachusetts court in **Comfort v. Lynn School Committee (2003)** proposed racial diversity is valuable because it enables students to learn racial tolerance by building cross-racial relationships. Is diversity beneficial because it fosters diverse perspectives or friendships across group boundaries? Or could it provide for both?

Diversity can, under the right conditions, promote tolerance and understanding across groups and lessen interpersonal as well as intergroup biases that undermine equality and opportunity (see Chapter 9). As educational institutions set diversity as a compelling interest, individual applicants will be selected, in part, on the basis of their group membership and how it contributes to a diverse student body. But as we have seen, this selection standard must not conflict with traditional academic selection criteria that people argue must remain the central criterion of individual merit. So, diversity in a variety of settings is good, individual rights are good, but at times achieving one may be at the expense of the other. We confront this challenge throughout this book, for example when we discuss colorblind versus multicultural ideologies (Chapter 10) and institutional forms of bias (Chapter 12).

Diversity and Difference

Diversity is inevitably about difference, but people are different in many ways. Diversity can be based on cultural practices and experiences, individual temperaments, preferences, skills, membership in groups that have been historically discriminated against, conspicuous economic wealth or lack thereof, age or gender, sexual identity, physical capabilities, religion, and so forth. From an institutional or societal viewpoint, which differences do or should matter?

Many people argue that the legacy of the 1960s civil rights era is that color does not and should not matter. That sentiment is often attributed to Martin Luther King, Jr, who, in his famous "I have a dream" speech in 1963 imagined that one day children would be judged by "the content of their character, not the color of their skin." This vision has been interpreted by some who oppose using race as a basis for affirmative action programs specifically, and college admissions generally, to mean that we should be colorblind to race to create an equal and just society. This principle of "colorblindness" has been extended to cover other elements of difference, such as ethnicity, sexual orientation, and religion.

But, is it really possible for one's race or gender or ethnicity to make no difference? Is the election of a Black man as President of the United States the fulfillment of this idea that race makes no difference? Does it signal that we have achieved a colorblind, "post-racial" society? And, can people be truly "blind" to another person's accent, ethnicity, gender, weight, and other signals of diversity?

Research in social psychology demonstrates emphatically that the answer is no to each of these questions. These differences continue to matter, and ignoring them or claiming to do so does not address the challenges of diversity. There is a growing body of research in social psychology that shows a colorblind ideology often leads to more, not less, intergroup bias (Chapter 10). There is an even more compelling body of research that shows convincingly that race matters in our perceptions and actions, often without awareness (Chapters 5 and 7). And we know that sometimes positive or benevolent attitudes toward women actually lead to biased behavior against them (Chapter 4). And what should we think about ignoring race for those persons who are often defined by their race? Can you really tell someone that a central aspect of who they are and have been for all their lives does not matter, makes no difference? Will race become more important to Whites when they become a minority? Does permitting legal discrimination against gay men and lesbians represent the principles of liberty and justice for all?

Majority and Minority

The meanings of "majority" and "minority" are changing. In John Jay's America, "majority" referred to Whites as one people with commonalities that bound them together. However, the new majority is by any measure not one people but a diverse body of people who vary across all the characteristics Justice Jay enumerated. "Minority" has generally referred to racial and ethnic groups (African Americans, Hispanic/ Latinos, Asian Americans, and Native Americans). It has also been applied to other demographic and/or affinity groups such as gender, disability, sexual orientation, cultural background, immigrant status, and age (see Chapter 2). Most generally, though, it is associated with numerical underrepresentation relative to a majority norm based on Whites. In some circumstances, minority is used as a euphemism for "disadvantage." Although immigrants are not formally counted in the "minority" framework, they are crucially connected to the growing diversity that is reflected in the broad meaning of minority.

As we noted earlier, non-Hispanic Whites, now slightly over two thirds of the U.S. population, will represent less than half of the population by 2042. And already in 2012, less than half of all babies born in the United States are White. We have been and will continue to be challenged to remain a united people with a variety of ancestors and languages, multiple religions, and divergent manners and customs. As Justice Blackmun observed, sometimes to treat people equally you have to treat them differently. How can we treat people who are different the same, or people who are the same differently, and produce outcomes that are fair, equal, and just? That is the challenge of diversity in everyday life.

Another challenging issue is the variation among individuals who belong to the same groups—*diversity within diversity*. We tend to see groups as more or less homogeneous, even though we know they are not. When we discuss or take action on diversity issues, we tend to treat groups as single entities. Many of the recent legal decisions that curtailed affirmative action have been based on the idea that lumping people into racial, gender, or even age categories is to stereotype them and not recognize their individuality and uniqueness (*Hopwood v. Texas*, 1996).

Which groups are viewed as a "majority" and which as a "minority" has profound psychological impact. It affects the characteristics that people associate with the way people interact (Chapter 9), how people feel and react to the ways they are treated (Chapter 8), power relations between groups in society (Chapter 11), and the ways people create and enforce policies and laws (Chapter 12). Thus, the rapid demographic shifts experienced not only by the United States but also internationally will exert unprecedented pressure on reactions to, and the experience of, diversity now and into the future. The empirical evidence, largely from psychology, we present in this book not only helps us understand our history but our potential future as a nation.

Summary

As the U.S. population has evolved over time, the meaning of diversity has changed and legislative and judicial barriers to diversity have gradually been removed. Throughout our history, Americans have felt the strain of excluding people who were different from a White mainstream Anglo-Saxon norm or including people of diverse backgrounds and cultures based on core principles of equality, liberty, and the pursuit of happiness. The growing diversity will create a nation of minorities by 2042; no single ethnic or racial group will constitute a majority of the U.S. population.

The problem of the twenty-first century is the challenge of diversity. Two important aspects of diversity are the recurring negative effects of social bias based on race, gender, sexual orientation, and other social demographic categories and the additional challenge posed when two desirable concepts collide. For example, removing race as a barrier to opportunity collides with creating positive opportunities. Multicultural strategies for promoting diversity often conflict with colorblind approaches. Social psychological research and theory provide a way to address these difficult problems.

Questions for Thinking and Knowing

1. Students often feel that people make too big of a deal about diversity. They feel that if we leave students alone, diversity will take care of itself. Do you agree with this sentiment? Given our history with race and ethnicity and other forms of diversity, are you confident that young people will get it right and diversity in the twenty-first century will just happen so that fairness prevails?
2. Does your school have a statement on its diversity mission or goals? Do you find this statement compelling in light of the historical perspectives on diversity presented in this chapter? How would you redefine the mission statement to be more compatible with your perspectives? Think about why diversity would or would not be integral to this new mission.
3. Reflect on any personal history that links your family to the historical trends outlined in the chapter. Have the ways in which your family addressed these challenges been effective and satisfying?

4. Do you think the terms "minority group," "majority group," and "White" will be relevant and accurate to describe our diversity in the future?
5. Identify five facts about our history of diversity that were new to you. Do you feel that you should have had an opportunity to learn about this history before now? In what grade and or setting? From whom?

Key Terms

Americans with Disabilities Act
Beneficial diversity
Benevolent sexism
Brown v. Board of Education of Topeka, 1954
Chinese Exclusion Act
Civil Rights Act of 1964
Comfort v. Lynn School Committee, 2003
Don't ask, don't tell
Emancipation Proclamation
Ethnophaulisms
Executive Order 9066
Executive Order 9981
Executive Order 11246
Gentlemen's Agreement
Grutter v. Bollinger, 2003
Haymarket Affair
Hernandez v. Texas, 1954
Illegal Immigration Reform and Immigrant Responsibility Act of 1996

Immigration
Immigration Act of 1917
Immigration Act of 1924
Immigration and Nationality Act 1965
Jim Crow Laws
Montgomery bus boycott
Narrowly tailored
Nativism
Plessy v. Ferguson, 1896
Racial integration
Regents of the University of California v. Bakke, 1978
Social role theory
The Equal Rights Amendment (ERA)
The Five Civilized Tribes
The Trail of Tears
Title IX of the Education Amendments of 1972
Voting Rights Act of 1965

References

Adams, D. W. (1988). Fundamental considerations: The deep meaning of Native American schooling, 1880–1900. *Harvard Educational Review, 58,* 1–28.

American Psychological Association, Presidential Task Force on Immigration. (2012). *Crossroads: The psychology of immigration in the new century.* Washington, DC: American Psychological Association.

Arizona et al. v. United States, 567 U.S. No. 11–182 (2012).

Bradwell v. State of Illinois, 83 U.S. 130 (1872).

Brown v. Board of Education of Topeka, 347 U.S. 483 (1954).

Canellos, P. S. (2008, November 11). Obama victory took root in Kennedy-inspired Immigration Act. *The Boston Globe.* Retrieved from http://www.boston.com/news/nation/articles/2008/11/11/obama_victory_took_root_in_kennedy_inspired_immigration_act/

Civil Rights Act, 42 U.S.C. 21 § 1981 (1866).

Clark, C., Hewitt, N. A., Brown, J., & Jaffee, D. (2008). *Who built America? Working people and the nation's history, Vol. I to 1877* (3rd ed.). New York: St Martin's.

Comfort v. Lynn School Committee, U.S. Court of Appeals, Appeal No. 03-2415 (2003).

Demos, J. (1970). *A little commonwealth: Family life in Plymouth Colony.* New York: Oxford University Press.

De Rosier, A. H. (1970). *The removal of the Choctaw Indians.* Knoxville, TN: University of Tennessee Press.

Don't ask, don't tell, Pub. L. 103-160 (10 U.S.C. § 654) (1993).

Dovidio, J. F., & Gaertner, S. L. (2004). Aversive racism. In M. P. Zanna (Ed.), *Advances in experimental social psychology* (Vol. 36, pp. 1–51). San Diego, CA: Academic Press.

Dred Scott v. Sandford, 60 U.S. (19 How.) 393 (1857).

DuBois, W. E. B. (1903). *The souls of Black folk.* Chicago: A. C. McClurg and Company.

Eagly, A. H. (1987). *Sex differences in social behavior: A social-role interpretation.* Hillsdale, NJ: Lawrence Erlbaum Associates.

Elk v. Wilkins, 112 U.S. 94 (1884).

Fineman, H. (2008). *The thirteen American arguments: Enduring debates that define and inspire our country.* New York: Random House.

Frum, D. (2000). *How we got here: The '70s.* New York: Basic Books.

Glazer, N., & Moynihan, D. P. (1963). *Beyond the melting pot: The Negroes, Puerto Ricans, Jews, Italians, and Irish of New York City.* Cambridge, MA: MIT Press.

Glazer, N., & Moynihan, D. P. (Eds.). (1975). *Ethnicity: theory and experience.* Cambridge, MA: Harvard University Press.

Glick, P., & Fiske, S. (2001). The Ambivalent Sexism Inventory: Differentiating hostile and benevolent sexism. *Journal of Personality and Social Psychology, 70,* 491–512.

Gratz v. Bollinger, 539 U.S. 244 (2003).

Greenwald, A. G., Poehlman, T. A., Uhlmann, E. L., & Banaji, M. R. (2009). Understanding and using the Implicit Association Test: III. Meta-analysis of predictive validity. *Journal of Personality and Social Psychology, 97,* 17–41.

Grutter v. Bollinger, 539 U.S. 306 (2003).

Haas, E. F. (1982). Guns, goats, and Italians: Tallulah lynching of 1899. *North Louisiana Historical Association, 13*(2&3), 45–58.

Hale, E. E. (1926). A plea for the Irish immigrant. In E. Abbott (Ed.), *Historical aspects of the immigration problem: Selected documents* (pp. 460–465). Chicago: University of Chicago Press.

Hamilton, A. (1788). The Federalist paper #54. Reprinted in M. Beloff (1987) (Ed.), *A. Hamilton, J. Madison and J. Jay, The Federalist or, The new constitution.* New York: Basil Blackwell.

Hernandez v. Texas, 347 U.S. 475 (1954).

Higham, J. (1955). *Strangers in the land.* New Brunswick, NJ: Rutgers University Press.

Hopwood v. Texas, 78 F.3d 932 (5th Cir. 1996).

Illegal Immigration Reform and Immigrant Responsibility Act of 1996, Pub. L. 104-208, 110 Stat. 3009 (1996).

Immigration and Naturalization Service (1965) Immigration and Nationality Act, Pub. L. 89-236, 79 Stat. 911.

Jay, J. (1787). *Federalist paper #2.* New York: J. & A. McLean.

Jenkins, P. (2003). *The new anti-Catholicism: The last acceptable prejudice.* New York: Oxford University Press.

Massey, D. S., & Denton, N. A. (1993). *American apartheid: Segregation and the making of the underclass.* Cambridge, MA: Harvard University Press.

McDougall, W. (1921). *Is America safe for democracy?* New York: Scribner.

Mullen, B., & Rice, D. R. (2003). Ethnophaulisms and exclusion: The behavioral consequences of cognitive representation of ethnic immigrant groups. *Personality and Social Psychology Bulletin, 29,* 1056–1067.

Mullen, B., & Smyth, J. M. (2004). Immigrant suicide rates as a function of ethnophaulisms: Hate speech predicts death. *Psychosomatic Medicine, 66,* 343–348.

Papp, S. M. (1981). *Hungarian Americans and their communities of Cleveland.* Cleveland Ethnic Heritage Studies. Cleveland, OH: Cleveland State University.

Parrillo, V. N. (2006). *Strangers to these shores* (8th ed.). Boston: Pearson Education, Inc.

Petrini, C. M. (2001). *Immigrants in America: the Italian-Americans*. San Diego, CA: Greenhaven Press.

Plessy v. Ferguson, 163 U.S. 537 (1896).

Prucha, F. P. (1984). *The Great Father: The United State Government and the American Indians*. Lincoln: University of Nebraska Press.

Randall, V. R. (Web Ed.). (2009). Examples of Jim Crow Laws. In *Race, Racism and the Law: Speaking Truth to Power!!* Retrieved from http://academic.udayton.edu/race/02rights/jcrow02.htm

Regents of the University of California v. Bakke, 438 U.S. 265 (1978).

Statistical Abstracts of the United States (2009). United States Census Bureau. Available at http://www.census.gov/compendia/statab/2009/2009edition.html

Stein, S. (2008) Census projections: U.S. will be half minority by 2042. Huffington Post.com. Retrieved on October 11, 2010 from http://www.huffingtonpost.com/2008/08/14/census-projections-us-wil_n_118878.html

Takaki, R. T. (1993). *A different mirror: A history of multicultural America*. Boston: Little, Brown & Co.

Thomas, W. I., & Znaniecki, F. (1918). *The Polish peasant in Europe and America*. Chicago: University of Chicago Press.

United States v. Bhagat Singh Thind, 261 U.S. 204 (1923).

U.S. Congressional Documents and Debates (1774–1875). *A Century of Lawmaking for a New Nation: Statutes at Large, 41st Congress, 2nd Session*. Washington, DC: U.S. Library of Congress.

Zangwill, I. (1914) *The melting-pot: Drama in four acts*. New York: Macmillan.

Part Two

Psychological Processes

Chapter 4

Personality and Individual Differences
How Different Types of People Respond to Diversity in Different Ways

Introduction   89
Origins of Prejudice: Allport's Lens Model   90
The Abnormality of Prejudice: The Psychodynamic Model   93
The Normality of Prejudice   99
Summary   111

> *One of the facts of which we are most certain is that people who reject one out-group will tend to reject other out-groups. If a person is anti-Jewish, he is likely to be anti-Catholic, anti-Negro, anti any out-group. . . . Prejudice is basically a trait of personality.*
>
> Gordon Allport
> *The Nature of Prejudice*, pp. 68, 73; italics in the original

Introduction

The violence that has victimized members of diverse groups throughout U.S. history (see Chapter 3) can easily be seen as the outcome of deranged minds. Indeed, such violence continues today. In 2010 alone, the FBI documented 2,600 hate crime offenses directed against Blacks, 922 against Jews, and 1,470 against gay, lesbian, and bisexual individuals (FBI, 2012).

The case of Matthew Shepard provides a vivid example. A little after midnight on October 7, 1998, in Laramie, Wyoming, Matthew Shepard, a 21-year-old college student, met two men at a local bar and accepted a ride in their car. After Matthew

The Psychology of Diversity: Beyond Prejudice and Racism, First Edition. James M. Jones, John F. Dovidio, and Deborah L. Vietze.
© 2014 Blackwell Publishing Ltd. Published 2014 by Blackwell Publishing Ltd.

disclosed that he was gay, the two men robbed, pistol whipped, and tortured him, finally tying him to a fence where they left him to die. Eighteen hours later, Matthew, barely still alive, was discovered by a passer-by who initially mistook him for a scarecrow. Matthew never regained consciousness; he died a few days later. The police arrested the two assailants a short time later. When they went to trial, the defendants pleaded a "gay panic defense," claiming temporary insanity allegedly caused by Matthew's sexual advances. Both assailants were found guilty of murder.

Extreme acts of violence like this led psychologists and other behavioral scientists to theorize that prejudice reflects *abnormal* psychological functioning, a type of **psychopathology**. For many years, prejudice was considered a direct result of abnormalities in personality (such as low self-esteem), in development and socialization (such as harsh parental discipline), and in daily social functioning (for example, the consequence of "mob violence").

From this perspective, prejudice is a kind of "social cancer," an aberrant blight on society. Indeed, the vast majority of Americans today claim that they are not prejudiced. Psychological research thus came to focus on identifying biased individuals who expressed their prejudice. The assumption was that "treating" these supposedly isolated cases would control or even eliminate prejudice as a societal problem (see Dovidio, 2001; Duckitt, 2010). Even today, there is serious discussion about whether to include prejudice as a formal type of psychopathology (Widiger & Mullins-Sweatt, 2009). According to the *Diagnostic and Statistical Manual of Mental Disorders* (DSM), "A mental disorder is defined as a behavioral or psychological syndrome or pattern that occurs in an individual" and is considered a manifestation of a behavioral, psychological, or biological dysfunction in the individual. In fact, it was proposed but ultimately rejected that *racism* be added as a diagnostic category for mental illness (Bell, 2004).

However, research on the prejudiced personality—those who recognize group differences but oppose diversity in its many forms—shifted its emphasis from prejudice as a form of unusual psychopathology to one in which prejudice is viewed as embedded in normal social functioning. From this perspective, most normal people are highly susceptible to being prejudiced and discriminatory toward others who are different from them.

It is easy to see how abnormal people may be prejudiced, but it is hard to imagine that we, ourselves, are biased; yet this is the case more often than we would like to think. In this chapter, we discuss both perspectives and reflect on the kinds of processes that can lead even good and well-meaning people to be biased.

Origins of Prejudice: Allport's Lens Model

Gordon Allport was one of the most prominent psychologists working on the topic of prejudice in the 1950s, and he understood that it originates from many sources and has many causes (Figure 4.1). These causes, which he outlines in his **lens model**, range from very broad and distant to more narrow and immediate. Moving from the broadest to the most specific, the sources of prejudice are categorized as historical, sociocultural, situational, personality based, phenomenological, and based on the qualities of the target of prejudice.

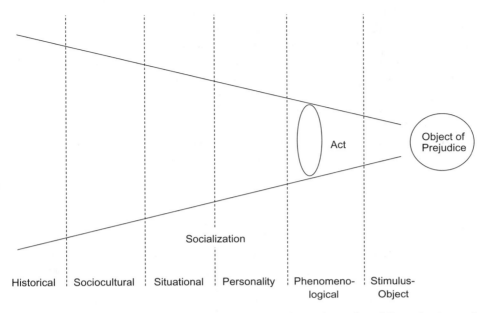

Figure 4.1.   Allport's Lens Model of Prejudice: Sources of Prejudice. Adapted from *The Nature of Prejudice*, by G. W. Allport, 1954, Reading, MA: Addison-Wesley.

The *historical* category suggests that only when the total background of social conflict is appreciated can its current expression be understood. From this perspective, prejudice has been and continues to be promoted to preserve the dominance of the majority group that was established long ago.

The *sociocultural* category suggests that prejudice is the result of ethnocentric preferences for standards of progress and materialism. Beliefs and values associated with upward mobility, economic success, and the material representations of such success define merit and goodness. People who lack these symbols of success are looked down upon. According to this approach, prejudice is directed at those who are situated at the bottom of the sociocultural–socioeconomic ladder. Chapter 3 discussed many of the historical and sociocultural (including economic and political) forces that have shaped prejudice, stereotypes, and discrimination against various groups over time.

Much of the psychological research on prejudice, stereotypes, and discrimination focuses on the remaining steps in Allport's model. The *situational* approach looks at contemporary patterns of social and economic forces as explanations of prejudice. According to this view, prejudice arises from actual or perceived competition and immediate needs for positive feelings about group and personal status.

The *personality dynamics and structure* approach focuses on how and why some individuals become prejudiced but others do not. It emphasizes individual differences in prejudice—how people systematically differ from one another in the ways they are biased toward other groups.

The *phenomenological* approach explains prejudice as arising from immediate experiences in a situation, that is, how the target person is perceived or what expectations are aroused. This view assumes that historical, sociocultural, and character-based factors define and determine the immediate reaction in the situation and provide a causal explanation for the prejudiced person's behavior.

The *stimulus-object* approach, which Allport (1954) identified as the most immediate cause of prejudice, focuses on the target of prejudice. This approach looks for real differences between groups that may provide a basis for intergroup antipathies that could explain negative treatment in a given situation.

In this chapter, we consider the work of psychologists at two key levels in Allport's outline: first, the personality dynamics and structure approach, and then the phenomenological approach.

Personality and Prejudice

Personality refers to the characteristic way that a particular individual interacts with the social and physical world. Personality researchers assume that people differ from one another in systematic ways and that these individual differences influence the way people behave across time and situations. There are many different types of personalities, and some of these types involve unrealistic, distorted, and maladaptive ways of viewing the world. Some people, for example, generally dislike others who are different from themselves and oppose diversity in almost any form. Why do people tend to discriminate not only against one particular group but also against a range of groups? People who are racists, for example, also tend to be sexist, anti-Semitic, homophobic, Islamophobic, anti-immigrant, and biased against homeless people (Zick, Wolf, et al., 2008). This chapter is about those personality types who demonstrate generalized prejudice and resist diversity.

Two of the most influential approaches to individual differences in personality, one based on Freud's psychodynamic theory and the other described as social dominance theory, offer very different perspectives on explaining the origins of prejudice. **Psychodynamic theory** explains prejudice, stereotyping, and discrimination as intra-individual processes, as ways to satisfy individual needs grounded in basic "instincts." In Allport's model, it reflects the personality dynamics and structure level of analysis. The psychodynamic view implies that strong opposition to diversity is a form of abnormal psychological functioning.

Social dominance theory (Sidanius & Pratto, 1999) links prejudice and discrimination to intergroup relations and sees them as an ideology, or worldview, of how groups should relate to one another. In Allport's model, it represents the phenomenological level of analysis. Social dominance theory emphasizes the different ways that people perceive group relations, particularly in terms of zero-sum competition (the view that every gain for your group means a loss for my group). According to social dominance theory, prejudice and opposition to the advances of other groups are normal. Similarly, we discuss how religion and politics shape the ways people see the world, and ultimately how people respond to diverse groups.

In the next section, we discuss psychodynamic theory, which explains how people develop abnormal patterns of thinking, feeling, and behaving. Psychodynamic theory is no longer the preferred explanation in this area, but it left an important legacy. Other scholars, building on Freud's insights, developed scales to measure personality traits that they believed were the underlying reasons why people become prejudiced and oppose diversity.

The Abnormality of Prejudice: The Psychodynamic Model

Sigmund Freud was a psychoanalyst who worked to cure patients with psychological disorders. These disorders were mainly **neuroses**, which are psychological problems that impair a person's activities but do not prevent him or her from functioning in society. Although Freud never considered prejudice or discrimination as neuroses, these biases reflect the type of abnormal behavior he focused on—not full breaks from reality but systematic distortions of the world that have negative social impact.

Psychodynamic Theory and Prejudice

Freud proposed that psychological processes represent flows of psychic energy that are powered by two basic motivations that shape all of human behavior: the life instinct (Eros) and the death instinct (Thanatos). Childhood experiences and conflicts influence how these forces combine to determine an individual's personality and, ultimately, his or her biases toward people who are different, and preferences for people who are similar.

Psychodynamic theory, when applied to explaining prejudice, has three premises. First, it assumes that humans have a disposition to be hostile, particularly in the face of real or perceived danger. Hostility arises from concerns with economic or material advantages (I want the job, but you might get it), fear and defensiveness (your success threatens me), and the need for prideful self-aggrandizement (I am better than you are). Second, the psychodynamic approach to prejudice assumes that, at birth, humans seek comfort, love, and nurturance. But, as they fail to receive these in sufficient degree, they become frustrated, and this frustration activates their latent hostility. And third, this approach assumes that only some people—those whose basic needs are not readily met in other ways—become prejudiced. Prejudice is thus viewed as a kind of abnormality.

While many people outside the field still think about Freudian ideas when the topic of psychology is mentioned, by the 1930s many aspects of psychodynamic theory fell out of favor with experimental psychologists. Freud's ideas did not readily produce specific, testable predictions that would allow the psychodynamic model to be verified or refuted. Still, Freud's ideas were not completely abandoned. One influential group of researchers (John Dollard, Leonard Doob, Robert Sears, and their associates) adapted some of Freud's ideas to develop a new theory of aggression.

Whereas Freud attributed the basis of aggression to an expression of the death instinct, a factor that arises within the individual, Dollard, Doob, Miller, Mowrer, and Sears (1939) proposed that aggression is stimulated by external causes that lead to frustration. According to their **frustration–aggression hypothesis**, frustration causes aggression and all aggression can be traced back to some form of frustration. Borrowing directly from psychodynamic theory, these researchers also recognized that people were often inhibited from expressing aggression. For instance, your boss may complain about your work, frustrating your hopes for a promotion. However, you would not act out against your boss, so wanting to keep your job may cause you to suppress the desire to act out against our boss in frustration. When people are inhibited from expressing their aggression directly, displacement occurs. **Displacement** is the process by which an emotion that is inhibited is redirected. In this case, your anger toward your boss might be displaced to aggressive driving or an argument with your partner (Miller, Pedersen, Earleywine, & Pollock, 2003). It is pretty easy to think of an occasion when we displaced our aggression onto others.

From the frustration–aggression perspective, prejudice often leads to **scapegoating**. Scapegoating occurs when people who are frustrated by one source are unable to retaliate directly (e.g., because the person or source is unavailable or too powerful), so they displace aggression onto a more convenient and socially available person or group. For example, a White person who is frustrated by unemployment and financial insecurity might choose a Black person as the target of aggression. Indeed, from 1882 to 1930, there was a substantial relationship between the economic conditions in 14 Southern states and the incidence of lynchings of Blacks: As economic conditions for White Southerners deteriorated, the number of lynchings of Blacks increased (Hovland & Sears, 1940; cf. Green, Glaser, & Rich, 1998). In other words, the lynchings did not result originally from frustration with or anger toward Blacks as Blacks, but rather from frustration caused by low and unstable cotton prices. The fact that Blacks were not the source of frustration (they were, in fact, much of the labor force supporting the cotton industry) illustrates the seeming "abnormality" of prejudice. This impressive demonstration of how adaptations of Freudian psychoanalytic theory could illuminate the origins of prejudice stimulated a highly productive wave of research that sought to determine who becomes prejudiced and why.

Prejudice against Difference: The Authoritarian Personality

The origins of prejudice against differences are central concerns for the psychology of diversity. The atrocities of the Holocaust and the unwillingness of large numbers of citizens to prevent them are well documented. What kind of person is capable of such extreme prejudice and such malicious actions against others who are different? Theodor Adorno and his colleagues, some of whom had escaped from Nazi Germany, answered that question by drawing on psychodynamic theory in a large and intensively researched book *The Authoritarian Personality* (Adorno, Frenkel-Bruswik, Levinson, & Sanford, 1950). They focused on characteristics that made people susceptible to prejudice.

On the basis of in-depth interviews and empirical tests, Adorno and colleagues identified a particular pattern of family experiences and personality that made people susceptible to extreme prejudice. People described as "high authoritarians" typically had parents who enforced strict discipline, often using harsh punishment. In part the result of this socialization, high authoritarians have an exaggerated respect for those above them but behave aggressively toward and disdain others below them in a social hierarchy. High authoritarians generally submit to authority, adhere to conventional traditions and values, and think in rigid, all-or-nothing ways.

According to research on the **authoritarian personality**, the prejudice of high authoritarians represents a projection of unacceptable impulses (such as anger) onto powerless out-group members (Newman & Caldwell, 2005). For example, after Germany invaded Poland during World War II, a number of Poles collaborated actively with the Germans in the extermination of Jews in Poland. Historian Jan Gross (2001) noted that many of these Poles explained their actions on the basis of their perceptions that Jews had, in the previous years, collaborated with the Soviets to oppress Poles. Gross found that this perception did not reflect actual events; instead the "non-Jewish population projected its own attitude toward Germans in 1941 . . . onto an entrenched narrative about how the Jews allegedly behaved" (Gross, 2001, p. 104).

One of the most significant influences of *The Authoritarian Personality* was that it attempted to identify basic personality differences between prejudiced and less-prejudiced people. Adorno and his associates developed a questionnaire they called the **F-scale**. "F" stood for "susceptibility to Fascist propaganda," a political ideology that emphasized strong leadership and a singular national identity to enhance national prestige and power, and became aligned with Hitler's Nazi Party in World War II. The F-scale measured anti-Semitism and ethnocentrism without mentioning specifically the groups to which antagonisms were expressed. Sample items in the scale included "Obedience and respect for authority are the most important virtues children should learn" and "Every person should have complete faith in some supernatural power whose decisions he obeys without question." The F-scale was considered to be more general and more broadly predictive than other measures of prejudice. People who scored high on the F-scale seemed to be the kind of prejudiced person who responds negatively to differences and feels threatened by diversity.

The study of authoritarianism transformed research and ideas about prejudice for the next two decades. The F-scale was a powerful instrument because those who scored high on it displayed antipathy to a broad range of groups, including Blacks, homosexuals, and elderly people. In addition, evidence supported Adorno and colleagues' hypotheses about the roots of the authoritarian personality in fear and uncertainty.

For example, qualities of authoritarianism, such as power, toughness, and support for traditional values, were reflected more strongly in comic book characters during historical periods in which people felt that their economic well-being and way of life were threatened than during periods of prosperity and social stability (Sales, 1973; see also Doty, Peterson, & Winter, 1991). After the terrorist attacks of 9/11, Americans and Canadians became more suspicious of foreigners, and opposition to immigration, regardless of where immigrants came from, increased dramatically (Esses, Dovidio, & Hodson, 2002). During this period, Americans became more hawkish in their attitudes toward international affairs and more strongly supported restrictions to civil liberties (e.g. the Patriot Act) that made them feel more secure. Moreover, the increased support for these policies associated with the war on terror occurred more strongly for people *low* in authoritarianism (Hetherington & Suhay, 2011); under threat, their attitudes aligned with those of high authoritarians, who already held these positions!

Support for the F-scale as the primary tool to measure prejudice began to wane by the mid-1960s. Alternative scales measuring general dispositions as well as scales developed to capture the essence of different types of prejudice came into vogue. Even more damaging, though, were criticisms about the specific scales used to measure authoritarianism. For instance, people who had a tendency to agree with statements (an acquiescence bias) would score high on these measures of authoritarianism. So it was no longer clear what the authoritarian scales were really assessing. Also, at a broader level, researchers began to question key aspects of the original work on the authoritarian personality. This personality approach tended to slice the world into two types of people: those who were prejudiced and those who were not. Yet there was accumulating evidence that people who scored low in authoritarianism also demonstrated bias against other groups and that those who scored high in authoritarianism, often lower-class and lower-middle-class people with limited education, were not responsible for the widespread discrimination in society. In addition, the F-scale seemed only able to detect people with extremist orientations in a politically conservative (a political orientation to the right) direction; leftist extremists scored low on the F-scale. Thus, a new generations of researchers sought to correct these deficiencies with new measures (e.g., **Dogmatism Scale**; Rokeach, 1956, 1960).

The Legacy of Authoritarianism: Contemporary Measures

Even though the instruments that Adorno et al. (1950) developed to measure authoritarianism were largely abandoned, many of their ideas, with contemporary modifications shaped by new evidence, continued to be influential. Researchers increasingly emphasized the continuous nature of personality dimensions and recognized gradations in prejudice. The idea is that all people are susceptible to being prejudiced to some degree. One of the most influential contemporary approaches, which was stimulated by the work of Adorno and his colleagues, is right-wing authoritarianism.

The right-wing authoritarianism scale   A number of the characteristics originally identified as aspects of the authoritarian personality were highlighted in new instruments designed to measure how people differ in their prejudice. One prominent measure, derived from a critical analysis of the work of Adorno et al. (1950), is the Right-wing Authoritarianism Scale (Altemeyer, 1981, 1996, 1998). Altemeyer found that there were core "attitudinal clusters" that defined **right-wing authoritarianism** (RWA): authoritarian submission (an inclination to submit to those of greater authority or status), authoritarian aggression (general hostility toward deviants and members of other groups), and conventionalism (a strong commitment to the traditional norms and values of one's group). Table 4.1 presents sample items from the RWA Scale that illustrate the basic themes.

RWA differs in two important ways from the original conception of the authoritarian personality. First, RWA is unrelated to the harsh, punitive, parental socialization that Adorno et al. (1950) believed was at the root of the authoritarian personality. Instead, RWA arises when a person is socialized, by whatever means, to see the social world as a dangerous and threatening place. Second, the scale is not designed to assess

Table 4.1.   Sample Items from the Right-wing Authoritarianism Scale

1. The established authorities generally turn out to be right about things, whereas the radicals and the protestors are usually just "loud mouths" showing off their ignorance.
2. Our country desperately needs a mighty leader who will do what has to be done to destroy the radical new ways and sinfulness that are ruining us.
3. Gays and lesbians are just as healthy and moral as anyone else.[a]
4. The only way our country can get through the crisis ahead is to get back our traditional values, put some tough leaders in power, and silence the troublemakers spreading bad ideas.
5. Our country needs free thinkers who will have the courage to defy traditional ways, even if this upsets many people.[a]
6. Our country will be destroyed someday if we do not smash the perversions eating away at our moral fiber and traditional beliefs.
7. The "old-fashioned ways" and "old-fashioned values" still show the best way to live.
8. What our country needs is a strong, determined leader who will crush evil and take us back to our true path.
9. Some of the best people in the country are those who are challenging our government, criticizing religion, and ignoring the "normal way things are supposed to be done."[a]
10. A "woman's place" should be wherever she wants to be. The days when women were submissive to their husbands and social conventions belong strictly in the past.[a]

Note. From "The other 'authoritarian personality.'" by B. Altemeyer, 1998. In M. P. Zanna (Ed.), *Advances in experimental social psychology* (Vol. 30, pp. 47–92). San Diego, CA: Academic Press.
[a]Reverse-scored item.

political attitudes but rather to measure a related set of traits that people on the political left or right might possess. Although people higher in RWA do tend to be politically conservative, the "right-wing" in the measure's name is viewed more as a general personality orientation toward conservatism (see also Jost, Glaser, Kruglanski, & Sulloway, 2003) than as a formal political commitment. Both Democrats and Republicans can score high on RWA. Importantly, the types of orientations represented by RWA are ones that the average person can reasonably hold. Do you know anyone whom you suspect would score high on this scale?

In general, people higher in RWA are both fearful and self-righteous (Altemeyer, 1988). They are thus quick to support aggression toward another country that they see as threatening their country's material status and core values, but only when they see such action as supporting these principles, not when this aggression appears improper or vengeful (Motyl, Hart, & Pyszczynski, 2010).

Also, there is substantial evidence across different cultures (see Chapter 2) that RWA predicts prejudice toward a range of different social groups (Altemeyer, 1996, 1998): ethnic minorities, women, disabled people, deviants, and, in particular, gays and lesbians (Duckitt, 2006).

Need for closure   Adorno and colleagues emphasized that high-authoritarian persons were very rigid in their thinking and had little tolerance for ambiguity. The Need for Closure Scale (Kruglanski, 1990) assesses a related quality that is relatively independent of political attitudes. The **need for cognitive closure** is a characteristic of people who like to adhere to rules that produce clear conclusions and get them there quickly and with certainty. The 42-item scale includes items such as "I think that having clear rules and order at work is essential to success"; "I do not like situations that are uncertain"; and "Even after I've made up my mind about something, I am always eager to consider a different opinion" (Kruglanski, Webster, & Klem, 1993). Because they tend to use cognitive shortcuts and limit the information they collect in order to make decisions quickly, people who score higher on need for cognitive closure rely heavily on stereotypes when thinking about groups, see members of other groups as similar to one another, and apply stereotypes when evaluating members of another group (Roets & Van Hiel, 2011).

Other personality measures   Through the 1990s, researchers identified a number of personality measures that predicted the tendency to be prejudiced and to stereotype others. Although many of these measures are not based on psychoanalytic theory, many bear some resemblance to characters described in *The Authoritarian Personality*. For example, people with great personal need for structure (the extent to which people prefer simple-structured beliefs and activities; Neuberg & Newsom, 1993), preference for consistency (the extent to which people want to see the world as reflecting consistent relations; Cialdini, Trost, & Newsom, 1995), and intolerance of ambiguity (uneasiness with uncertainty; Budner, 1962) demonstrate generally high levels of prejudice and stereotyping.

One critical aspect of the personality approaches is that they demonstrate that people who are prejudiced against one group of people are also prejudiced against other groups. That is, some people are biased generally against difference. These individuals dislike people who are dissimilar to them, who deviate from what they perceive to be a traditional social standard, or who challenge them to question their values or think in new ways. In short, individuals who are uncomfortable with diversity may represent a distinct personality type. In the face of increasing societal diversity, these people may respond in aggressive and violent ways. As Chapter 3 illustrated, the changes that come with diversity threaten some people. The research we have just described suggests that some of us do not like difference of any kind.

Besides helping to identify personality types that are generally prejudiced toward other groups, psychodynamic theory also stimulated insights into the nature and dynamics of prejudicial attitudes. Earlier we mentioned how prejudice, stereotyping, and discrimination are similar to scapegoating. In addition to its extremely violent expressions, scapegoating has more everyday effects. For instance, college students who learn that they did not do well on an intelligence test are more likely to negatively stereotype a person whom they think might be gay, while they do not disparage another student whom they believe is straight (Fein & Spencer, 1997). In other words, disparaging a member of a stigmatized group actually can make people whose self-image is threatened by failure feel better about themselves!

In addition, psychodynamic theory suggested the complexity of attitudes toward members of different groups. Freud proposed that people often do not have simple positive or negative feelings about others. They are frequently *ambivalent*, which means that they have a mixture of positive and negative feelings toward the same person, group, or object. Although Freud was most concerned about ambivalence toward intimate others, such as one's father or mother, the principle has been applied to how a person feels about members of groups that differ from one's own. With increasingly strong norms and laws against discriminating against others based on their race, ethnicity, religion, gender, or sexual orientation, ambivalence has become more common. In addition, Freud talked about how feelings can be unconscious, operating outside people's awareness. Can we be biased and not know it?

We pursue these ideas throughout this book. For example, in Chapter 7, we discuss how people try to balance a positive view of themselves and adherence to prevailing norms of fairness and justice while harboring, often unconsciously, negative feelings about other groups. In Chapter 10, we explain how prejudice has gone beyond its borders to create bias in our social institutions. Thus, although Freud's explanations for the origins of behavior fell out of favor, many of the ideas from psychodynamic theory have informed contemporary researchers about the nature of prejudice and how people systematically differ in prejudice.

The Normality of Prejudice

A recent alternative to the psychodynamic approach comes from a different perspective on how a person views relations between himself or herself and a different group. This approach assumes that prejudice stems from ideas one has about other groups based on one's experiences (phenomenological origins; see Figure 4.1) rather than from intra-psychic conflicts and psychodynamic tensions. In this section, we consider four different perspectives on the ways people think about diverse groups based on (a) conformity, (b) beliefs about how groups should be socially organized (social dominance orientation), (c) religious orientation, and (d) political orientation. We also consider how biases can be expressed in more blatant or subtle ways.

Conformity and Norms

Humans are inherently social beings. We rely on others to help us understand the world (see Chapter 5) and need to coordinate our actions with others (Chapter 6). It is important that we be synchronized with others for groups and societies to function effectively. Thus, group **norms**—informal rules, standards, and expectations within a group—powerfully determine how we interact with others, including members of other groups. When prejudice and discrimination are normative, which was the case for much of U.S. history, people express their biases openly and consistently. But norms also change. The civil rights legislation of the 1960s, which we discussed in Chapter 3, made prejudice non-normative; since then, overt expressions of bias have declined substantially. However, immediate situational norms can play an even larger role. Being with others who exhibit bias and discrimination can lead even good and well-intentioned people to behave in biased ways, both passively, by not intervening to prevent discrimination, and actively, by engaging behaviors that support disparate treatment (Crandall & Stangor, 2005; Killen & Rutland, 2011).

Because the effect of conformity depends upon whether the social context emphasizes norms opposing or supporting prejudice, individual differences in conformity do not relate overall to responses to diversity (Miller, Grover, Bunn, & Solomon, 2011; Sibley & Duckitt, 2008). People who are more conformist are less open to experience and more "tough-minded" about enforcing conventional standards. When the norms favor maintaining the existing social order, more conforming people are more biased against diversity. Conversely, across a range of different countries (including the United States, Sweden, Finland, China, and South Korea), individuals who value uniqueness ("to think up new ideas and be creative; to do things one's own way") more and endorse conformity less are less prejudiced toward immigrants, people of a different race, and different in sexual orientation (Shin, Dovidio, & Napier, 2012).

In addition to how much people value adhering to social norms, the ways people feel about how society should be structured also affects the way they respond to diversity.

Social Dominance

Social dominance theory (Sidanius & Pratto, 1999) proposes that within all societies, groups (typically identified by age, sex, ethnicity, race, and religion) are organized hierarchically. According to this theory, the development of group hierarchies is motivated by basic group-based evolutionary processes, and groups higher in the hierarchy have greater privilege and access to resources. Prejudiced beliefs associated with racism, sexism, and other types of "isms" all result from this principle of social hierarchy. Social hierarchy involves recognizing differences between groups, but because it includes status differences, it does not value differences in a way that promotes cultural diversity. Every group has its separate place in the social hierarchy.

The nature of these hierarchies may vary from culture to culture. In some cultures, they may be based on family clans, whereas in other societies groups may be distinguished by their roles or occupations. In some countries, Christians have higher status than do Muslims; in other countries the opposite is true. However, some status relations, such as men having higher status than women, and older people having more power than younger people, occur in all cultures (Sidanius & Pratto, 1999). These similarities suggest that evolutionary forces play a role in social dominance relations between groups (see Chapter 2).

Social dominance theory thus proposes that group hierarchy is normal and functional: Societies in which groups are hierarchically organized are more stable and efficient than those characterized by group equality. Group-based hierarchies are self-perpetuating. High-status groups develop laws, cultural values, and social norms that reinforce their positions. Negative reactions to members of other groups are byproducts of the operation of social hierarchy.

Social dominance theory reflects three basic principles:

1. Societies are composed of group-based hierarchies, At least one group is domi-
    nant over all others, and that group enjoys a disproportionate share of the positive
    assets (e.g., wealth, prestige, education, health). In such hierarchies, also, at least
    one group is subordinate and experiences a disproportionate share of negative
    consequences (e.g., poor health, poverty, social stigma).
2. Groups compete over scarce material and symbolic resources to enhance their
    own relative positions.
3. In this competitive relationship, groups use ideological strategies, such as those
    that support the national, racial, or ethnic superiority of their group, or political
    ideologies to limit the advancement of other groups perceived to be in
    competition.

Social dominance orientation (SDO) refers to how much a person's view of the social
dominance hierarchy influences his or her behavior or attitudes. In other words, SDO
may be thought of as a measure of how much a person agrees with the tenets of
social dominance theory. SDO reflects the extent to which an individual desires his or
her in-group to dominate out-groups (Sidanius & Pratto, 1999). SDO is a general
orientation toward intergroup relations. It reflects whether one generally prefers such
relations to be hierarchical or equal. Table 4.2 presents selected items from the SDO-6
Scale used to measure social dominance orientation.

People who score higher in SDO tend to see intergroup relations as a zero-sum
game in which if one group wins, the other group automatically loses. Not surprisingly, cross-culturally groups that are in more advantaged social positions (e.g., men
versus women, members of racial/ethnic majority versus minority groups) score
higher in SDO (Lee, Pratto, & Johnson, 2011).

In fact, perceptions of competition and SDO operate in similar ways (Esses,
Dovidio, Jackson, & Armstrong, 2001). To study reactions to another group uncon-
taminated by previous experience with that group, researchers created fictitious ethnic
groups, which participants actually believed to be real. Specifically, in a newspaper
article Canadian participants learned about a new group of people, Sandirians, who

---

Table 4.2.   Sample Items: Social Dominance Orientation

1. Some groups of people are just more worthy than others.
2. We should do what we can to equalize conditions for different groups.[a]
3. If certain groups of people stayed in their place, we would have fewer problems.
4. We would have fewer problems if we treated different groups more equally.[a]
5. To get ahead in life, it is sometimes necessary to step on other groups.
6. Group equality should be our ideal.[a]

Note. From *Social Dominance: An Intergroup Theory of Social Hierarchy and Oppression* by J. Sidanius &
F. Pratto, 1999. New York: Cambridge University Press.
[a]Reverse-scored item.

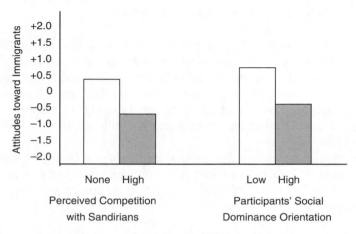

Figure 4.2. Attitudes Toward Immigrants Are Less Favorable When Canadians Perceive They Are in Competition With Them or When Participants Are High in Social Dominance Orientation. Adapted from "The Immigration Dilemma: The Role of Perceived Group Competition, Ethnic Prejudice, and National Identity," by V. M. Esses, J. F. Dovidio, L. M. Jackson, & T. M. Armstrong, 2001, *Journal of Social Issues, 57*, pp. 389–412.

would soon be immigrating in large numbers to Canada because of a natural disaster (a volcanic eruption) in their country. In one case, participants were informed that Sandirians would be competing for jobs; in another case, participants learned that they would fill jobs that were needed because there were not enough Canadians with these skills. A second set of participants, categorized as high or low in SDO, read a non-competitive description of Sandirians.

As illustrated in the left-hand panel of Figure 4.2, participants in the competition condition had a much more negative attitude toward Sandirians, toward immigrants in general, and toward immigration than did those in the non-competition condition. As seen in the right-hand panel of Figure 4.2, high SDO participants had more negative views of Sandirian immigrants than low SDO participants. Moreover, they held these more negative attitudes because they believed, despite the same description of Sandirians, that these immigrants would compete more with Canadians for jobs. Thus, people higher in SDO generally perceive groups as inherently being in greater competition. In this case, the problem is not Sandirians themselves, but rather the frame of mind through which people high in SDO see them.

People who score high in SDO tend to be sexist, racist (toward Blacks, Aboriginals, Indians, Arabs, Asians), and prejudiced toward immigrants, lesbians, gay men, feminists, housewives, and physically disabled people (see Sidanius & Pratto, 1999). Moreover, people who score high on SDO are expected to favor hierarchy-enhancing ideologies and policies that permit groups in power greater authority and control over low-power groups. A good example of a hierarchy-enhancing policy is the recently passed law in Arizona that requires non-citizens to register and carry their documents with them, makes being an undocumented alien a violation of Arizona law, and gives police in Arizona substantial freedom to target individuals suspected of being an undocumented alien. High-SDO individuals are particularly likely to pursue careers as police officers or prosecutors, whereas low-SDO individuals are more prevalent in occupations such as a social worker or public defender. People who score higher in SDO are more likely to pursue college majors that lead to hierarchy-enhancing occupations, such as criminal justice, and their SDO scores increase throughout their course of study in those majors (Sidanius, van Laar, Levin, & Sinclair, 2003). They are also more likely to oppose hierarchy-attenuating policies, such as social welfare and affirmative action.

In addition to being directly related to prejudice, SDO predicts a person's political actions and endorsements of particular social policies. A person scoring high on SDO is likely to oppose immigration, affirmative action, and school desegregation, because each of these would undermine the in-group's hierarchical advantage. Box 4.1 illustrates how personality and social circumstances can align to produce strong and socially consequential expressions of bias.

Box 4.1.   Personality, Social Groups, and the Capacity for Evil

S. Alexander Haslam and Stephen Reicher (2007) conclude that neither personality nor societal influences alone account for extreme actions toward members of other groups. The combination of individual differences and social circumstances is critical. Three key dynamics promote extreme responses to other groups. First, according to Haslam and Reicher, people who support hierarchical relations between groups, such as those high on SDO, are initially drawn to tyrannical groups. Second, people become transformed by their group membership. Once they identify strongly with a group, they see themselves as group members who embody the values, standards, and attitudes that are central to the group. They see these beliefs as normal, and they aspire to live up to and enforce these standards on others. Third, groups become capable of extreme intergroup violence when social conditions enable people who support such actions to assume positions of leadership and influence.

The election of Barack Obama as President of the United States illustrates how rapidly a single event can mobilize extremist groups. The Southern Poverty Law Center estimates that Obama's election stimulated a 25% growth in the number of hate groups and increased the size and activity of existing groups. In 2011, the Southern Poverty Law Center counted 1,018 active hate groups in the United States. These hate groups advocate White supremacy, often overtly support racist positions, and oppose immigration and accommodation for non-Christian groups. A small percentage of hate groups openly encourage violence (Gerstenfeld, Grant, & Chiang, 2003).

People are often drawn to hate groups because they are searching for structure in their lives and in society (Hogg & Blaylock, 2011). Hate groups promote hierarchical relations between groups, with White Christians reigning supreme, but they also enforce a strict hierarchical and authoritarian structure within their group. They demand allegiance and a strong sense of group identity among members.

The internet has played a critical role in the growth of hate groups. It allows individuals with extremist views, who might otherwise recognize their views as improper, immoral, or un-Christian, to create virtual communities in which they feel normal, accepted, and supported. Hate groups recruit and organize their members through these virtual communities. In addition, hate group websites typically contain multimedia materials that exaggerate threats (e.g., the impact of Obama's election) and spread misinformation (e.g., about Obama's citizenship and religion) to stimulate the group members to more extreme positions and activities (Gerstenfeld et al., 2003; Glaser, Dixit, & Green, 2002). Thus, the capacity for prejudice and discrimination in their most extreme expressions reflects more than the influence of a few abnormal but charismatic individuals; it reflects the way in which personality, social conditions, and group processes come together so that people engage knowingly and willfully in violence based on their group membership.

1. What kinds of events or personal experiences that people encounter in life might lead them to be susceptible to appeals from hate groups? What kinds of people may be more likely to succumb to these appeals?
2. How can you determine whether a group is a hate group versus a group that holds particular political values strongly but legitimately?

Authoritarianism and SDO: Sometimes a Lethal Combination

So which is the real source of individual differences in prejudice: authoritarianism or social dominance orientation? Although psychologists started to debate just this point, they soon recognized that both were important, but perhaps for different reasons and in different ways.

Both SDO and RWA are robust predictors of prejudice, and they are correlated with each other (Roccato & Ricolfi, 2005). However, they arise from fundamentally different sources. SDO reflects how people see the legitimacy and desirability of group hierarchy: It is about beliefs in how groups should relate to each other, and what the hierarchy between groups should be. In contrast, RWA primarily represents how people see their relations with other individuals: It involves being submissive to those higher in authority and aggressive toward those lower in status, while enforcing the conventional standards of the group and punishing deviants.

SDO and RWA, in fact, reflect two different worldviews (Duckitt, 2001). People high in SDO see the world as a place where groups must compete directly against other groups to protect their welfare and prosper. Competition is seen as an essential tool for their own survival. People high in RWA, in contrast, see the world as a dangerous place, in which others, for no good reason, are out to get them. They are therefore highly suspicious of others' motives and wary of people who are different from them. Whereas people high in SDO see competition as the rule for the game of life, those high in authoritarianism see the world as "dog eat dog," with conventional authorities having the right to make the rules.

Although both RWA and SDO identify people who resist diversity, they represent quite different qualities. As a consequence, although both scales are effective at predicting prejudice toward a range of groups, including many of the same groups, each has its particular focus. RWA, more than SDO, predicts prejudice toward unconventional groups, groups that are seen to deviate from traditional moral standards (gays and lesbians, people of a different religion). SDO, more than RWA, predicts prejudice toward groups that are likely competitors for resources and social control. Together, SDO and RWA scores are powerful predictors of prejudice.

Understanding how SDO and RWA operate shows that groups composed of persons with both SDO and RWA personality types might be especially capable of causing harm, in the form of discrimination or other forms of immoral actions. The combination of high-SDO leaders and high-RWA followers results in a "lethal union" (Son Hing, Bobocel, Zanna, & McBride, 2007; see Altemeyer, 1998). In an experiment that demonstrated this effect, college students played the role of a CEO confronted with different ethical dilemmas. Participants acting as CEOs made a series of decisions, such as how much the company would "pollute the environment and exploit third world labor to avoid increasing expenditures" or whether to "continue marketing a lucrative but potentially harmful product aimed at elderly customers" (Son Hing et al., 2007, p. 21). Of participants with high SDO scores, 70% chose the unethical alternative in the first scenario, whereas only 28% of participants with low SDO scores chose that option.

Another study further demonstrated that followers with high RWA scores tend to support such an unethical decision. When working with a confederate posing as a leader who decides to pollute the environment and exploit the labor pool in another country, two thirds of followers who were high in RWA acquiesced, whereas only one third of those low in RWA did so.

Taken together, these studies reinforce the idea that people who score high in SDO, who see the world in competitive terms, are generally willing to exploit other groups to benefit their own group, while people who score high in RWA, who support the status structure within their group, will acquiesce. As Adolph Eichmann, a Nazi official, claimed in defense of his role in managing the deportation of Jews to prison camps during the Holocaust, "I was only following orders" (see Cesarani, 2004). Thus, high-SDO leaders coupled with high-RWA followers constitute a truly lethal union in their treatment of members of other groups: One leads with little ethical constraint and the other follows in support of the authority.

Many of the qualities originally associated with authoritarianism that relate to prejudice, such as respect for authority and conventional values and belief in the supernatural, seem to represent qualities that are basic elements of both religious and political thought. Religion and politics often suggest hierarchies of virtue; being "chosen," and wielding power. Can these forces lead to greater bias? Yet diversity of thought with respect to both religious and political orientations is a cherished American value protected in our founding documents. How, then, does diversity in religious and political orientations relate to the ways people view racial and ethnic diversity?

Religion and Prejudice

In the same book in which he described the lens model of prejudice that opened this chapter, Gordon Allport (1954) observed that religion "makes prejudice and it unmakes prejudice" (p. 444). While the intolerance of religious extremists, including Islamic, Jewish, and Christian extremists, capture the headlines, all major religions teach tolerance, fairness, and compassion. In fact, *what* religion a person practices is not strongly predictive of the ways people think of racial and ethnic diversity. However, *how* a person practices that religion does relate strongly to prejudices (Batson & Stocks, 2005).

People may practice their religion for different reasons. For some people, the reasons are intrinsic. **Intrinsic religiosity** represents a deep commitment to the principles of religion for the meaning it provides in one's life. An item reflecting intrinsic religiosity is "My religious beliefs are what really lie behind my approach to life." People higher in intrinsic religiosity, who are more invested in religious values, report lower levels of prejudice toward other groups.

For other people, the reasons for being religious are extrinsic. **Extrinsic religiosity** involves using one's religion to connect to a community, gain social status, or increase personal security. An item measuring extrinsic religiosity is "The church is most important as a place to formulate good social relationships." Perhaps because it reflects a commitment to conventional social standards and commitment to a particular group (Hall, Matz, & Wood, 2010), people higher in extrinsic religiosity tend to express more prejudice toward a range of other groups.

In addition, people often promote their political agenda and aggression toward other groups in the name of religion, in ways that deviate vastly from the basic tenets of the religion. For example, much of the colonization by European countries of Africa and South America was justified as efforts to promote Christianity. More recently, Bill Clinton (August 22, 1998) in a speech to the American people about terrorism observed that

> it is very important that Americans understand that the threat we face is not part of the Islamic faith. Hundreds of millions of Muslims all over the world, including millions right here in the United States, oppose terrorism and deplore the twisting of their religious teachings into justification of inhumane, indeed, ungodly acts. (http://berkleycenter.georgetown.edu/resources/quotes?page=6&topic_id=religion-and-politics-in-us-history)

Indeed, independent of the type and degree of personal religiousness, merely the thought of religious symbols can make college students more biased. Johnson, Rowatt, and LaBouff (2010) presented college students with Christian religious concepts such as faith, church, heaven, and prayer on a computer screen so rapidly that they could not report seeing the words while the words registered unconsciously. Students who were subliminally presented with religious words, compared to those primed with non-religious words, subsequently displayed greater prejudice toward Blacks.

So, the relationship between religiosity and prejudice is not simple. It does not seem to matter what particular religion someone practices. Instead, the relationship between religiosity and prejudice depends on the role that religion plays in individuals' lives. People who practice religion to achieve social stature and to be accepted into a social community often show high levels of prejudice toward other groups. However, people who have a personal commitment to the principles of religion are more open to diversity. In addition, people who have an even more spiritual emphasis, seeing their religion more as a "quest" for addressing complex questions about the meaning of one's existence rather than as an answer to these questions, demonstrate unusually *low* levels of bias toward other groups (Batson & Stocks, 2005). So, Allport's observation over 50 years ago is correct: Religion can make or unmake prejudice.

Politics and Prejudice

Political orientation plays an important role not simply in how people vote in elections but also how people think about diversity. The most basic distinction, which cuts across cultures, is conservatism versus liberalism. Conservatives are motivated to uphold tradition, support systems that protect individual rights, and reward individual achievements. By contrast, liberals are open to change, endorse systems that promote collective welfare, and are optimistic about human nature. In the contemporary United States, the Republican Party is more conservative than the Democratic Party.

Many of the characteristics of political conservatism overlap with traits identified with authoritarianism. This observation has led political scientists, sociologists, and psychologists to explore the relationship between political conservatism and prejudice. Indeed, there is a robust relationship—people who are more conservative appear more prejudiced toward a range of groups and oppose policies promoting diversity. For example, conservatives are more supportive of policies that restrict immigration (Pettigrew, Wagner, & Christ, 2007) and which require immigrants to assimilate socially and linguistically (e.g., opposing bilingual education) than are liberals. In addition, people often draw on principles of conservatism to justify their prejudice and negative treatment of minorities (McConahay, 1986).

However, the consistent relationship between conservatism and prejudice should not lead us to jump to the oversimplified and erroneous conclusion that liberalism is good and conservatism is pathological, or that conservative beliefs are necessarily false, irrational, or unprincipled. The story is much more nuanced. Most human beliefs are subjectively rational. Both conservatives and liberals may be moral but differ in the principles they rely on to make their moral judgments. Graham, Haidt, and Nosek (2009) identified five different "foundations" of morality, representing (a) fairness/reciprocity, (b) harm/care of others, (c) in-group/loyalty, (d) authority/respect, and (e) purity/sanctity. Liberals weigh the principles of fairness and care about harm to others most heavily in how they view right from wrong; conservatives consider in-group loyalty, respect for authority, and purity most heavily in their moral judgments. These are all admirable and important values.

In addition, adherence to these different principles may lead both liberals and conservatives to be prejudiced but toward different groups. Because much of the psychological literature focuses on biases toward particular groups, such as racial or ethnic minorities, the psychological literature typically portrays political conservatives as more prejudiced than political liberals. However, the biases of liberals are more evident when other target groups are considered. Indeed, Chambers, Schlenker, and Collisson (2013) found that more politically conservative people were more biased against Blacks and homosexuals. One of the reasons they were biased against these groups was because they perceive these groups as politically liberal. By contrast, more politically liberal people were biased against business people and Christian fundamentalists, in large part because they viewed these as conservative groups. Thus, both liberals and conservatives were equally biased toward groups perceived to be on the opposite end of the political spectrum.

One of the reasons why so much of the literature is devoted to studying biases toward a certain set of groups is because personality and social psychologists are disproportionately liberal; only 6% describe themselves as conservatives. Moreover, the dynamics of intergroup relations plays out directly within the field. Conservatives in the field fear negative consequences for revealing their political ideology, and indeed there may be good reason: Inbar and Lammers (2012) revealed that more liberal personality and social psychologists admitted that they would tend to discriminate against their more conservative peers in reviewing their papers and making hiring decisions. While only a subset of personality and social psychologists exhibit such biases—most are fair and open to political diversity—these findings reveal that we are not immune to the problems we study. Personality and social psychologists are susceptible to the "normality of prejudice" too.

Understanding that conservatives and liberals rely on different principles in making judgments and have different general worldviews helps us understand the complex motivations behind reactions to diversity. Just because conservatives generally oppose policies such as affirmative action does not necessarily mean they are doing so *because* they do not like minorities. Political conservatives, who focus on individual initiative and merit, are less likely to perceive group-based discrimination and acknowledge the influence of bias in limiting the advancement of racial and ethnic minorities. However, when they recognize that discrimination is operating in ways that violate the principle of individual merit, they are more likely to support corrective policies, including affirmative action (Son Hing, Bobocel, & Zanna, 2002).

Indeed, Shelby Steele, a Black scholar, strongly opposed affirmative action based on the concern, characteristic of conservatism, that the policy did not take individual circumstances sufficiently into consideration and can undermine individual initiative. He wrote:

> In a few short years, when my two children will be applying to college, the affirmative-action policies by which most universities offer black students some form of preferential treatment will present me with a dilemma. I am a middle-class black, a college professor, far from wealthy, but also well removed from the kind of deprivation that would qualify my children for the label "disadvantaged." . . . Still, their society now tells them that if they will only designate themselves as black on their college applications, they will probably do better in the college lottery than if they conceal this fact. I think there is something of a Faustian bargain in this. . . . I believe another liability of affirmative action comes from the fact that it indirectly encourages blacks to exploit their own past victimization. . . . Blacks can have no real power without taking responsibility for their own educational and economic development. Whites can have no racial innocence without earning it by eradicating discrimination and helping the disadvantaged to develop.

Because we ignored the means, the goals have not been reached and the real work remains to be done. (Steele, 1990, *New York Times*, retrieved from http://www.nytimes. com/1990/05/13/magazine/a-negative-vote-on-affirmative-action.html?pagewanted= all&src=pm)

We should also not jump to the conclusion that liberals, despite their general overt support for diversity, are necessarily good and pure in their actions. A number of years ago—in 1973, before there were cellphones—Samuel Gaertner and Leonard Bickman conducted a study in which Black and White individuals made apparently wrong-number phone calls to members of liberal and conservative political parties in New York City (Gaertner & Bickman, 1971). The callers explained that their car had broken down, and that they had no more change to call Ralph's Garage for help. The callers asked the person on the line to make the call for them. Conservatives were indeed less willing to make the call than were liberals. However, liberals were more likely to hang up on a Black caller before the caller even had a chance to request help. Thus, in the end, Black callers received less assistance than did White callers, but conservatives and liberals discriminated in different ways. Conservatives were more direct in their bias. Liberals were more subtle, terminating the conversation before they could be put in a position to help; however, if they got to the point where they heard the request, they helped Black as much as White callers. This set of findings stimulated a line of research on subtle discrimination (Gaertner, 1973). We will return to the work of Gaertner and his colleagues on aversive racism, a form of subtle bias against Blacks, in more depth in Chapter 7. In the next section, we consider extensions of the idea of distinguishing blatant from subtle bias in different domains.

Individual Differences in Blatant and Subtle Prejudice

Drawing on research in North America that emphasized the distinction between blatant and subtle forms of discrimination, Pettigrew and Meertens (1995) developed scales to measure individual differences in **blatant** and **subtle prejudice** using data from a large-scale survey of European respondents. According to Zick, Pettigrew, and Wagner (2008), "blatant prejudice is the more traditional form; close, hot, and direct. By contrast, subtle prejudice is the modern form; distant, cool, and indirect" (p. 240). The Blatant Prejudice Scale reflects feelings of threat (e.g., "West Indians have jobs the British should have") and opposition to intimacy (e.g., the reverse-scored item, "I would not mind if a Turk who had similar economic background as mine joined my close family by marriage"). The Subtle Prejudice Scale focuses less directly on feelings about other groups but instead emphasizes things about their culture and values that are problematic ("Asians living here teach their children values and skills different from those required to be successful in France"). The scale also indicates the degree to which one denies positive emotions, such as sympathy and admiration, rather than expresses negative emotions, such as fear or hatred (which are associated with blatant prejudice). So both blatant and subtle prejudices are biases, but they predict different ways of discriminating. People high on blatant prejudice generally oppose immigration and support policies that will send immigrants back to their countries of origin, but those high on subtle prejudice are more indirect and selective in their exclusion. They favor the exclusion of immigrants when it can be justified on the basis of some other factor, such as a criminal record (Pettigrew & Meertens, 1995) and respond negatively to symbolic issues, such as women wearing the Islamic veil (Saraglou, Lamkaddem, Van Pachterbeke, & Buxant, 2009).

The idea of blatant versus subtle prejudice also applies to attitudes toward women. It expresses itself in different ways, though. Whereas people may be motivated to increase physical distance from members of other racial or ethnic groups, men generally welcome physical proximity with women. Discrimination instead often takes the form of segregation into different social roles and hence access to power, money, and social status (see Chapter 6).

Traditional views of sexism argued that many men disliked certain types of women, particularly feminists, and resisted efforts to achieve gender equality. These attitudes were held much more strongly by more politically conservative men. Peter Glick and Susan Fiske (1996; see also Lee, Fiske, & Glick, 2010) distinguished between blatant and subtle forms of sexism. The blatant form, **hostile sexism**, reflects openly negative attitudes about women. Items representing hostile sexism include "Women are too easily offended" and "Once a man commits, she puts him on a tight leash." The subtle form of sexism, benevolent sexism, is characterized by seemingly positive attitudes toward women that restrict the roles of women through protective paternalism and chivalry by men.

This bias is part of the fabric of our history. Recall the case, described in Chapter 3, of Myra Bradwell who was denied the opportunity to practice law in Illinois. In 1869, the Supreme Court upheld the ruling preventing her from practicing her profession because it challenged prevailing values of femininity proper and threatened the "delicacy" that defined, and constrained, women of that period. Benevolent sexism survives today, with some people endorsing it more than others. Items on the Benevolent Sexism Scale include "Women should be cherished and protected by men" and "Every man ought to have a woman he adores." Hostile and benevolent sexism are the two major components of the Ambivalent Sexism Inventory, which has been tested across 19 cultures.

As you might expect, men higher in hostile sexism typically oppose policies to help women achieve equality in social power and resources in society, as well as discriminate against women in specific situations such as hiring recommendations (Masser & Abrams, 2004). Also, men higher in hostile sexism are more likely to endorse rape myths, such as women inviting sexual advances by men, and reported personally engaging in sexual coercion of women more (Forbes, Adams-Curtis, & White, 2004).

Benevolent sexism undermines the status of women in patronizing ways. It operates as a *system-justifying ideology*—a general belief that the status quo in society is how it should be—that subtly reinforces gender inequality. Women, who generally see society as less fair than men, see it as fair as men do after they are exposed to examples of benevolent sexism (Jost & Kay, 2005), and women who associate romantic partners with chivalrous images (e.g., Prince Charming) have less ambitious career goals, in part because they count on men for support (Rudman & Heppen, 2003). Thus, the form that bias takes can shape intergroup relations and the opportunities that members have in subtle but critical ways.

Summary

Historically, responses to diversity and difference have been blatantly negative and often destructive and abhorrent. Because of the notoriety of these actions, psychologists focused on identifying the types of people who actively resist diversity, typically with the assumption that these people suffered not only from a moral deficit, but also from some form of psychological problem. Guided by Freudian psychodynamic theory, landmark research by Adorno and colleagues identified a relevant personality type, the high authoritarian. High authoritarians are not simply prejudiced against just a particular group; rather, they dislike many groups: They oppose diversity.

Despite its transformative impact on the field, research on the authoritarian personality eventually faced theoretical and methodological challenges. Nevertheless, many of the ideas associated with psychodynamic theory and the authoritarian personality have resonated in the study of prejudice and diversity over the years. Right-wing authoritarianism, which reflects core elements of the original work on the authoritarian personality, is currently one of the most important approaches to the prejudiced personality.

Over time, researchers understood that prejudice is caused not only by the needs, motivations, and conflicts *within* a particular individual but also by perceptions that groups are in competition. Individuals differ in social dominance orientation, or the extent to which they endorse hierarchical relations between groups. People who are high in social dominance orientation tend to see intergroup relations as a zero-sum game; if one group wins, the other group automatically loses. These people are generally biased toward groups other than the dominant social group. They tend to be sexist, racist, and prejudiced toward immigrants, lesbians, gay men, feminists, housewives, and physically disabled people.

The research on the prejudiced personality—those who recognize group differences but oppose diversity in its many forms—shifted its emphasis historically from a focus on prejudice as a form of unusual psychopathology to one in which it is embedded in normal social functioning. In this chapter, we have considered the relationship between religious and political orientations and prejudice. It is not the religion that people belong to that matters, it is *why* they practice that religion. People who practice religion to integrate themselves into a social community tend to be more biased; those whose involvement in religion is to bring meaning to their lives are less prejudiced. Political conservatives tend to be biased toward a range of groups and to policies promoting diversity, but liberals also have their biases. These biases are often expressed subtly rather than blatantly.

This "normality of psychology" perspective dovetails with the approach that much of social psychology has adopted. Social psychological approaches, which consider what most people do most of the time, views prejudice as embedded in processes that help people come to understand their social environment. These social processes are discussed in the next chapter.

Questions for Thinking and Knowing

1. Does SDO seem like a plausible explanation for how some persons view other groups? Identify reasons and examples to support your answer.
2. Would it be useful for you to know, privately, your SDO or RWA orientation? Why or why not?
3. Do you think it is possible to change someone's SDO or RWA orientation? Could this help us with the challenge of diversity? If yes, how? What would be the social and ethical consequences of such assessments?
4. Imagine, or reflect on, a person you know who is extremely prejudiced against a particular group, such as women or gays. Should this person be considered mentally ill? Socially incompetent? Dangerous? Is this extreme prejudice harmful to other people and persons from these groups? Why or why not?
5. Identify some forms of benevolent sexism that you see operating. Are there other forms of benevolent "isms" that you think occur as well? Think of specific examples and examine them using the criteria outlined in the chapter.

Key Terms

Authoritarian personality
Blatant prejudice
Displacement
Dogmatism Scale
Extrinsic religiosity
Frustration–aggression hypothesis
F-scale
Hostile sexism
Intrinsic religiosity
Lens model
Need for closure

Neuroses
Norms
Personality
Psychodynamic theory
Psychopathology
Right-wing authoritarianism
Scapegoating
Social dominance orientation
Social dominance theory
Subtle prejudice

References

Adorno, T. W., Frenkel-Brunswik, E., Levinson, D. J., & Sanford, R. N. (1950). *The authoritarian personality*. Oxford: Harpers.

Allport, G. W. (1954). *The nature of prejudice*. Oxford: Addison-Wesley.

Altemeyer, B. (1981). *Right-wing authoritarianism*. Winnipeg: University of Manitoba Press.

Altemeyer, R. (1988). *Enemies of freedom: Understanding right-wing authoritarianism*. San Francisco, CA: Jossey-Bass.

Altemeyer, B. (1996). *The authoritarian specter*. Cambridge, MA: Harvard University Press.

Altemeyer, B. (1998). The other "authoritarian personality." In M. P. Zanna (Ed.),

Advances in experimental social psychology (Vol. 30, pp. 47–92). San Diego, CA: Academic Press.

Batson, C. D., & Stocks, E. L. (2005). Religion and prejudice. In J. F. Dovidio, P. Glick, & L. Rudman (Eds.), *On the nature of prejudice: Fifty years after Allport* (pp. 413–427). Malden, MA: Blackwell Publishing Ltd.

Bell, C. (2004). Racism: A mental illness? *Psychiatric Services, 55*, 1343.

Budner, S. (1962). Intolerance of ambiguity as a personality variable. *Journal of Personality, 30*, 29–50.

Cesarani, D. (2004). *Eichmann: His life and crimes.* London: Heinemann.

Chambers, J. R., Schlenker, B. R., & Collisson, B. (2013). Ideology and prejudice: The role of value conflicts. *Psychological Science, 24*, 140–149.

Cialdini, R. B., Trost, M. R., & Newsom, J. T. (1995). Preference for consistency: The development of a valid measure and the discovery of surprising behavioral implications. *Journal of Personality and Social Psychology, 69*, 318–328.

Crandall, C. S., & Stangor, C. (2005). Conformity and prejudice. In J. F. Dovidio, P. Glick, & L. A. Rudman (Eds.), *On the nature of prejudice: Fifty years after Allport* (pp. 293–309). Malden, MA: Blackwell Publishing Ltd.

Diagnostic and Statistical Manual of Mental Disorders IV (2000). Washington, DC: American Psychiatric Publishing, Inc.

Dollard, J., Doob, N. E., Miller, D. H., Mowrer, O. H., & Sears, R. R. (1939). *Frustration and aggression.* New Haven, CT: Yale University Press.

Doty, R. M., Peterson, B. E., & Winter D. G. (1991). Threat and authoritarianism in the United States: 1978–1987. *Journal of Personality and Social Psychology, 61*, 629–640.

Dovidio, J. F. (2001). On the nature of contemporary prejudice: The third wave. *Journal of Social Issues, 57*, 829–849.

Duckitt, J. (2001). A dual process cognitive-motivational theory of ideology and prejudice. In M. P. Zanna (Ed.), *Advances in experimental social psychology* (Vol. 33, pp. 41–113). San Diego, CA: Academic Press.

Duckitt, J. (2006). Differential effects of right wing authoritarianism and social dominance orientation on outgroup attitudes and their mediation by threat from and competitiveness to outgroups. *Personality and Social Psychology Bulletin, 32*, 684–696.

Duckitt, J. (2010). Historical overview. In J. F. Dovidio, M. Hewstone, P. Glick, & V. M. Esses (Eds.), *The SAGE handbook of prejudice, stereotyping, and discrimination* (pp. 29–44). Thousand Oaks, CA: Sage.

Esses, V. M., Dovidio, J. F., & Hodson, G. (2002). Public attitudes toward immigration in the United States and Canada in response to the September 11, 2001 "Attack on America." *Analyses of Social Issues and Public Policy, 2*, 69–85.

Esses, V. M., Dovidio, J. F., Jackson, L. M., & Armstrong, T. M. (2001). The immigration dilemma: The role of perceived group competition, ethnic prejudice, and national identity. *Journal of Social Issues, 57*, 389–412.

FBI. (2012). Hate crime statistics 2010. Retrieved on September 6, 2012, from http://www.fbi.gov/about-us/cjis/ucr/hate-crime/2010/tables/table-1-incidents-offenses-victims-and-known-offenders-by-bias-motivation-2010.xls

Fein, S., & Spencer, S. J. (1997). Prejudice as self-image maintenance: Affirming the self through derogating others. *Journal of Personality and Social Psychology, 73*, 31–44.

Forbes, G. B., Adams-Curtis, L. E., & White, K. B. (2004). First- and second-generation measures of sexism, rape myths and related beliefs, and hostility toward women: Their interrelationships and association with college students' experiences with dating aggression and sexual coercion. *Violence Against Women, 10*, 236–261.

Gaertner, S. L. (1973). Helping behavior and racial discrimination among liberals and conservatives. *Journal of Personality and Social Psychology, 25*, 335–341.

Gaertner, S. L., & Bickman, L. (1971). Effects of race on the elicitation of helping behavior: The wrong number technique. *Journal* of Personality and Social Psychology, 20, 218–222.

Gerstenfeld, P. B., Grant, D. R., & Chiang, C.-P. (2003). Hate online: A content analysis of extremist Internet sites. *Analyses of Social Issues and Public Policy, 3,* 29–44.

Glaser, J., Dixit, J., & Green, D. P. (2002). Studying hate crime with the internet: What makes racists advocate for racial violence? *Journal of Social Issues, 58,* 177–193.

Glick, P., & Fiske, S. T. (1996). The Ambivalent Sexism Inventory: Differentiating hostile and benevolent sexism. *Journal of Personality and Social Psychology, 70,* 491–512.

Graham, J., Haidt, J., & Nosek, B. A. (2009). Liberals and conservatives rely on different sets of moral foundations. *Journal of Personality and Social Psychology, 96,* 1029–1046.

Green, D. P., Glaser, J., & Rich, A. (1998). From lynching to gay bashing: The elusive connection between economic conditions and hate crime. *Journal of Personality and Social Psychology, 75,* 82–92.

Gross, J. T. (2001). *Neighbors: The destruction of the Jewish community in Jedwabne, Poland.* New York: Penguin Books.

Hall, D. L., Matz, D. C., & Wood, W. (2010). Why don't we practice what we preach? A meta-analytic review of religious racism. *Personality and Social Psychology Review, 14,* 126–139.

Haslam, S. A., & Reicher, S. (2007). Beyond the banality of evil: Three dynamics of an interactionist social psychology of tyranny. *Personality and Social Psychology Bulletin, 33,* 615–622.

Hetherington, M., & Suhay, E. (2011). Authoritarianism, threat, and Americans' support for the war on terror. *American Journal of Political Science, 55,* 546–560.

Hogg, M. A., & Blaylock, D. L. (Eds.). (2011). *Extremism and the psychology of uncertainty.* Oxford: Wiley-Blackwell.

Hovland, C. I., & Sears, R. R. (1940). Minor studies of aggression: VI. Correlation of lynchings with economic indices. *Journal of Psychology: Interdisciplinary and Applied, 9,* 301–310.

Inbar, Y., & Lammers, J. (2012). Political diversity in social and personality psychology. *Perspectives on Psychological Science, 7,* 496–503.

Johnson, M. K., Rowatt, W. C., & LaBouff, J. (2010). Priming Christian religious concepts increases racial prejudice. *Social Psychological and Personality Science, 1,* 119–126.

Jost, J. T., Glaser, J., Kruglanski, A. W., & Sulloway, F. (2003). Political conservatism as motivated social cognition. *Psychological Bulletin, 129,* 339–375.

Jost, J. T., & Kay, A. C. (2005). Exposure to benevolent sexism and complementary gender stereotypes: Consequences for specific and diffuse forms of system justification. *Journal of Personality and Social Psychology, 88,* 489–509.

Killen, M., & Rutland, A. (2011). *Children and social exclusion: Morality, prejudice, and group identity.* New York: Wiley-Blackwell.

Kruglanski, A. W. (1990). Motivations for judging and knowing: Implications for causal attribution. In E. T. Higgins & R. M. Sorrentino (Eds.), *Handbook of motivation and cognition: Foundations of social behavior* (Vol. 2, pp. 333–368). New York: Guilford.

Kruglanski, A. W., Webster, D. M., & Klem, A. (1993). Motivated resistance and openness to persuasion in the presence or absence of prior information. *Journal of Personality and Social Psychology, 65,* 861–876.

Lee, I.-C., Pratto, F., & Johnson, B. T. (2011). Intergroup consensus/disagreement in support of group-based hierarchy: An examination of socio-structural and psycho-cultural factors. *Psychological Bulletin, 137,* 1029–1064.

Lee, T. L., Fiske, S. T., & Glick, P. (2010). Next Gen Ambivalent Sexism: Converging correlates, causality in context, and converse causality, and Introduction to the Special Issue. *Sex Roles, 62,* 395–404.

Masser, B. M., & Abrams, D. (2004). Reinforcing the glass ceiling: The consequences of hostile sexism for female managerial candidates. *Sex Roles, 9/10,* 609–615.

McConahay, J. B. (1986). Modern racism, ambivalence, and the modern racism scale. In J. F. Dovidio & S. L. Gaertner (Eds.), *Prejudice, discrimination, and racism* (pp. 91–125). Orlando, FL: Academic Press.

Miller, C. T., Grover, K. W., Bunn, J. Y., & Solomon, S. E. (2011). Community norms about suppression of AIDS-related prejudice and perceptions of stigma by people with HIV or AIDS. *Psychological Science, 22,* 579–583.

Miller, N., Pedersen, W. C., Earleywine, M., & Pollock, V. E. (2003). A theoretical model of displaced aggression. *Personality and Social Psychology Review, 7,* 75–97.

Motyl, M., Hart, J., & Pyszczynski, T. (2010). When animals attack: The effects of mortality salience, infrahumanization of violence, and authoritarianism on support for war. *Journal of Experimental Social Psychology, 46,* 200–203.

Neuberg, S. L., & Newsom, J. T. (1993). Personal need for structure: Individual differences in the desire for simpler structure. *Journal of Personality and Social Psychology, 65,* 113–131.

Newman, L. S., & Caldwell, T. L. (2005). Allport's "living inkblots": The role of defensive projection in stereotyping and prejudice. In J. F. Dovidio, P. Glick, & L. A. Rudman (Eds.), *On the nature of prejudice: Fifty years after Allport* (pp. 377–392). Malden, MA: Blackwell Publishing Ltd.

Pettigrew, T. F., & Meertens, R. W. (1995). Subtle and blatant prejudice in western Europe. *European Journal of Social Psychology, 25,* 57–75.

Pettigrew, T. F., Wagner, U., & Christ, O. (2007). Who opposes immigration? Comparing German with North American findings. *DuBois Review, 4,* 19–39.

Roccato, M., & Ricolfi, L. (2005). On the correlation between Right-Wing Authoritarianism and Social Dominance Orientation. *Basic and Applied Social Psychology, 27,* 187–200.

Roets, A., & Van Hiel, A. (2011). Allport's prejudiced personality today: Need for closure as the motivated cognitive basis of prejudice. *Current Directions in Psychological Science, 20,* 349–354.

Rokeach, M. (1956). Political and religious dogmatism: An alternative to the authoritarian personality. *Psychological Monographs, 70(18),* 1–43.

Rokeach, M. (1960). *The open and closed mind.* New York: Basic Books.

Rudman, L. A., & Heppen, J. B. (2003). Implicit romantic fantasies and women's interest in personal power: A glass slipper effect? *Personality and Social Psychology Bulletin, 29,* 1357–1370.

Sales, S. S. (1973). Threat as a factor in authoritarianism: An analysis of archival data. *Journal of Personality and Social Psychology, 28,* 44–57.

Saraglou, V., Lamkaddem, B., Van Pachterbeke, M., & Buxant, C. (2009). Host society's dislike of the Islamic veil: The role of subtle prejudice, values, and religion. *International Journal for Intercultural Relations, 33,* 419–428.

Shin, H., Dovidio, J. F., & Napier, J. L. (2013). Cultural differences in targets of stigmatization between individual- and group-oriented cultures. *Basic and Applied Social Psychology, 35,* 98–108.

Sibley, C. G., & Duckitt, J. (2008). Personality and prejudice: A meta-analysis and theoretical review. *Personality and Social Psychology Review, 12,* 248–279.

Sidanius, J., & Pratto, F. (1999). *Social dominance: An intergroup theory of social hierarchy and oppression.* New York: Cambridge University Press.

Sidanius, J., van Laar, C., Levin, S., & Sinclair, S. (2003). Social hierarchy and assortment into social roles: A social dominance perspective. *Group Processes and Intergroup Relations, 6,* 333–352.

Son Hing, L. S., Bobocel, D. R., & Zanna, M. P. (2002). Meritocracy and opposition to affirmative action: Making concessions in the face of discrimination. *Journal of Personality and Social Psychology, 83,* 493–509.

Son Hing, L. S., Bobocel, D. R., Zanna, M. P., & McBride, M. V. (2007). Authoritarian dynamics and unethical decision making:

High social dominance orientation leaders and high right-wing authoritarianism followers. *Journal of Personality and Social Psychology, 92,* 67–81.

Steele, S. (1990, May 13). A negative vote on affirmative action. *The New York Times.* Retrieved from http://www.nytimes.com/1990/05/13/magazine/a-negative-vote-on-affirmative-action.html?pagewanted=all&src=pm

Widiger, T. A., & Mullins-Sweatt, S. N. (2009). Five-factor model of personality disorder: A proposal for DSM-V. *Annual Review of Clinical Psychology, 5,* 197–220.

Zick, A., Pettigrew, T. F., & Wagner, U. (2008). Ethnic prejudice and discrimination in Europe. *Journal of Social Issues, 64,* 233–251.

Zick, A., Wolf, C., Küpper, B., Davidov, E., Schmidt, P., & Heitmeyer, W. (2008). The syndrome of group-focused enmity: The interrelation of prejudices tested with multiple cross-sectional and panel data. *Journal of Social Issues, 64,* 363–383.

Chapter 5

Social Cognition and Categorization
Distinguishing "Us" from "Them"

Introduction	117
We Are Social Animals	118
How We Think About People: Social Cognition	119
How We Think About Groups: Social Categorization and Group Membership	128
What Can We Do? Reducing Bias and Embracing Diversity	133
Summary	141

I have a dream that my four little children will one day live in a nation where they will not be judged by the color of their skin, but by the content of their character.

Dr Martin Luther King, Jr

Introduction

In the late 1960s, at the time that Dr Martin Luther King was assassinated, Jane Elliot was a third-grade teacher in Riceville, Iowa. Riceville was a small rural community and virtually all White. Jane Elliot wanted to teach her students a lesson about discrimination. In a classic demonstration, captured on film as *The Eye of the Storm*, she divided her class into two groups: those with blue eyes and those with brown eyes. Mrs Elliot told the class that the blue-eyed children were superior, gave them the best seats in the room, and often cited examples of famous people who had blue eyes ("George Washington had blue eyes"). By contrast, she described brown-eyed children as inferior, and when one child with brown eyes forgot his lunch, Mrs Elliott rebuked him and attributed his forgetfulness to his brown-eyed status. Soon the blue-eyed

The Psychology of Diversity: Beyond Prejudice and Racism, First Edition. James M. Jones, John F. Dovidio, and Deborah L. Vietze.
© 2014 Blackwell Publishing Ltd. Published 2014 by Blackwell Publishing Ltd.

children became suspicious of the brown-eyed children. They wanted the cafeteria workers to limit how much food the brown-eyed students could have and asked Jane Elliot to keep a yardstick close by in case the brown-eyed kids "got out of hand." They teased the brown-eyed children until a fight broke out at recess.

The next day, Jane Elliot resumed the exercise but explained that she had made a mistake: It was the brown-eyed children who were superior! The second day was a mirror image of the first, with the brown-eyed children acting superior to the blue-eyed children. On the second day, the brown-eyed children's school performance improved, while the blue-eyed children did worse. Even the meaning of being "blue-eyed" changed in students' minds. At recess, a brown-eyed child taunted another student in the class with the chant, "blue-eyes, blue-eyes"! The blue-eyed child retaliated, admitting to the teacher, "I hit him. I hit him in the gut."

Over the next two decades, Jane Elliot repeated this exercise for a range of audiences. She demonstrated time and time again how easy it is to get people, adults as well as children, to discriminate on the basis of an arbitrary distinction.

What makes us behave this way? Some suggest that it reflects a basic flaw in human nature. In his widely read book *The Lord of the Flies*, William Golding suggests that without the constraints society provides we are destined to spiral toward evil. In this chapter, we evaluate the psychological evidence. We describe fundamental psychological processes that can predispose us to look for differences and to be wary of diversity. We consider basic ways that people think about their world and about their group, and the social consequences of those ways of thinking. Seeing difference, however, does not inevitably lead to bias and discrimination. We conclude the chapter by illustrating how many of the same processes that lead to bias between groups can be harnessed to increase harmony and create positive relations between groups.

We Are Social Animals

Who we are today reflects a long evolutionary process. Whereas other species adapted to their environments by developing great speed or strength; acute senses of sight, smell, and hearing; or capacities for flight or aquatic life, our evolution as *Homo sapiens* was aided by two primary developments. One was the development of intellect, the power of understanding. By understanding our environment, we can predict and ultimately substantially control our fate. The other development was social: By living in groups in which people share responsibilities and coordinate activities, we can accomplish much more collectively than individually. These coordinated interactions, whether for work or for play, are the foundation of culture (Huizinga, 1938).

These are not uniquely human adaptations; they are effective for other animals. For example, whereas a single baboon is easy prey for a lion, three or more baboons working together can ward off the attack of a lion, fostering both their own survival and the survival of their troop. By contrast, isolation puts social animals at risk, particularly against others who work in coordinated ways. A single lioness, separated from her troop, is easy prey for a pack of hyenas. What distinguishes us from other animals, however, is how quickly and how well we developed these capacities. The field of **evolutionary psychology**, which focuses on how evolutionary adaptations can influence current behavior, shows how our past influences our everyday interactions, often in universal ways.

Whereas the previous chapter focused on individual differences in how people think about others, this chapter emphasizes cognitive processes that most people share. Specifically, we consider how two factors that allowed our species to survive, evolve, and prosper—the need to understand and the need to live in groups—can predispose us to be threatened by, to avoid, or to feel hostile toward people who are different. Because difference is the basis of diversity, these natural tendencies are core features of a psychology of diversity!

The next section in this chapter is about social cognition. **Social cognition** is the way we think about others and come to understand our social world. The way I interpret your actions determines how I behave toward you. If I believe that you intentionally jostle me, I push back; if I see it as accidental, I might overlook it or even apologize as if it were my fault: "Sorry!" We pay a lot of attention to others and fit new information about them into our worldviews in systematic ways. Understanding these thought processes can help us become aware of possible sources of prejudice or bias.

Another aspect of our evolutionary legacy is the critical importance of groups, not only materially but psychologically. Diversity usually refers to differences that are group based: gender, age, sexual orientation, race, ethnicity, and so on. And often, belonging to one group means that you feel closer to other group members and distance yourself from members of other groups. These group-based dynamics, if they go unexamined, challenge our ability to diversify places such as neighborhoods, schools, and offices. Our natural psychological tendencies guide us toward the comfort and safety of similarity, and away from the tensions and uncertainty of difference. Thus, after we talk about social cognition generally, we discuss social categorization, which is the way our own and others' group membership influences how we think about people. In the last section in this chapter, we consider the malleability of social cognition and categorization. We will see that difference does not have to translate into discrimination.

How We Think About People: Social Cognition

The need to understand our environment is such a fundamental force that we often take it for granted. Its operation is essentially automatic. When we do not understand something, we immediately become anxious and upset. Walk into an empty room where you expected a class to be, and instantaneously you become confused and disturbed. You are immediately motivated to reduce this unpleasant state, and you react by searching your environment for clues (a note left on the whiteboard) or seeking information from others (calling another student) for an explanation. Once you find a suitable explanation, you feel better; this feeling reinforces the process of understanding.

Because of the importance of connecting to other people, social cognition is critical. You cannot function in your social environments if you don't understand others, recognize their intentions or motives, and don't know how others view and evaluate your own behavior. In an interaction with a person of another race or ethnicity, for example, you may want to show that you are not biased. How do you do that? What do you say or do to communicate your non-biased attitude? The tasks of understanding others and how others understand you are made all the more complicated when the interaction involves someone of a different race, age, or gender. If social cognition is the process by which people come to understand others, then obviously it is a central process in the dynamics of diversity.

Social cognition describes the processes by which people come to understand others. There are two basic activities involved: forming impressions and fitting those impressions into our worldview. Forming impressions involves acquiring information. I look at you and I see a scowl on your face; I conclude that you are a hostile person and avoid you. Once I form an impression, I must integrate this information in a way that is compatible with other things I already know about the world. I see the scowl on your face, but you are my best friend. I change my interpretation. There must be something wrong. You're not hostile, you're upset by something, and I approach you to find out what I can do to help.

Acquiring information is related to **attribution processes**, whereas integrating information relates to **cognitive consistency**. These processes are closely intertwined. How I interpret what you do depends on what I already know about you, and what I think I know about you depends on the attributions I make for your actions. These processes are especially complicated when we do not understand others well because of their differences. The information we acquire may be flawed, colored by suspicion or fear. Cultural biases may exaggerate differences, thus skewing our "social knowledge" even more. Obviously, in a diverse context, all of these dynamics are likely to be operating. So, one could argue that social cognition is key to understanding perceptions and responses to diversity.

Acquiring Information: Attributions

One of the most fundamental elements of the attribution process is that because we do not have the capacity to process *all* the information around us, we tend to use abstract basic principles to explain isolated facts. For example, if you live in the northern hemisphere, you have a general understanding that the climate gets warmer as you travel south. You know that there are exceptions, but you still find the basic idea useful. Indeed, this is a basic process that is reinforced in our education. Because of limited cognitive capacity, we often sacrifice total accuracy for relatively efficient rules for knowing our environment. In this respect, we are **cognitive misers** (Allport, 1954). We have the tendency to use mental shortcuts (e.g., generalizations) that reduce the effort needed to process complex information in an efficient but not necessarily fully accurate way.

We limit the effort we expend while maximizing our understanding of the world. By developing basic principles based on facts we already know, we are better prepared for new situations. We use these principles to sort the often overwhelming details we perceive and abstract meaning from them in novel situations.

In social cognition, the ways that people acquire information about others and create stable ways of organizing this information are crucial. **Attribution theory** explains how we come to understand the causes of people's behavior, others' as well as our own. In general, we attribute behavior either to internal reasons (the person's personality or disposition) or external reasons (some situational influence). Early research on attribution theory demonstrated that the types of attributions people make are greatly influenced by three dimensions: consensus, consistency, and distinctiveness. For instance, when you learn that Mary is laughing at a nightclub comedian and that she (a) is the only one laughing (consensus is low), (b) always laughs at this comedian (consistency is high), and (c) laughs at many other comedians (distinctiveness is low), you are likely to attribute Mary's laughter to a dispositional factor, her sense of humor (McArthur, 1972).

Of particular relevance to the study of prejudice and discrimination, however, is the vast amount of research that shows not only that the attributions that people make are systematic, but also that they are *systematically biased*. These **attribution biases** are so automatic and common that you probably don't recognize how they shape the way you see the world. We explain three basic ways that these biases operate.

The fundamental attribution error   One widespread, virtually universal attributional bias, which psychologists believe is rooted in the motivation to understand the social world, is that we tend to attribute others' behavior to their disposition. To return to the example in the last paragraph, you would be likely to attribute Mary's laughter to her disposition even if you didn't know that she laughs at many other comedians. A dispositional (personality) attribution is more effective than a situational attribution at making you feel that you understand a person's behavior. The bias in overestimating the role of another's stable character as the cause of his or her behavior is so widespread that it is called the **fundamental attribution error** (Ross, Amabile, & Steinmetz, 1977).

Let's consider why this bias is so common. If I see you give money to a homeless person and attribute this to something unique about the situation, such as the way the person approached you, I can only understand your behavior in situations exactly like this one. If, however, I attribute your action to your disposition—if I conclude that you are a generous or compassionate person—I will feel that I can predict your actions in other situations. Feeling that I can predict what you do leads to the feeling that I understand my social world and potentially have more control over it. Young children, in fact, tend to explain anything a person or often even an inanimate object does to a characteristic or intention of the person or object. A child bounces a ball too hard and it hits her in the face; the first thing that comes to mind is "dumb ball!"

Although adults clearly have a more sophisticated and complex view of causal relations, they still fall prey to the fundamental attribution error. Ask a college student why her roommate, friend, or family member did something, and she will say it is because of the person's personality. But ask her why *she* did a comparable behavior, and she will say that something in the situation caused it. Why did your best friend do poorly on the exam? Because he's not real bright. Why did you do poorly? The exam asked trick questions.

Moreover, things that challenge your feelings of control, such as incidents that you see as threatening, lead you to compensate by attributing the threat to another person's particular characteristics (i.e., disposition). If a violent crime is caused by a bad person, that person can be locked up and the threat thereby eliminated; if it is caused by bad luck or poverty or is "just one of those things," then it might happen to you. The dispositional attribution restores your sense of control.

Imagine this scenario. A man drives uphill in a car with a standard shift, parks, and enters his house. While he is inside the house, the car begins to roll down the street, picking up speed as it approaches the intersection at the bottom of the hill. Now suppose one of two different things happens. The first possibility is the car damages a fence (low-harm condition). The second is that the car seriously injures a person (high-harm condition). How negligent do you feel the driver of the car was? Despite the fact that the driver's actions are identical in both conditions, participants in studies consistently make a much stronger attribution of negligence to the driver's personality in the high-harm compared with the low-harm condition (Shaver, 1985). Because the high-harm condition is perceived as threatening, people tend to attribute this negative behavior to another person's disposition.

There is a selectivity to this fundamental attributional bias that is directly relevant to the psychology of diversity. Pettigrew (1979) refers to the **ultimate attribution error** as the tendency to for persons to attribute negative *behaviors* of out-groups to dispositional qualities (bad behavior is because he is a bad person), and positive behaviors to external forces (the teacher felt sorry for him so gave him a good grade). By engaging in strategic attributional biases, a person can maintain the foundations of their prejudices and preserve a world that appears to them to be just.

A just world   Our need to see the world as understandable and predictable is not only important for how we explain particular events but also applies to how we see the world operating more generally. I need to see it as fair. Fairness and justice are the fabric of social life. For example, children learn to take turns. That really big guy at the end of a long line waits his turn and doesn't push me out of his way to get ahead of me. Reciprocity is universal: you help me and I will help you in return; you hurt me, I will hurt you. Reciprocity occurs in all cultures and, as far as we know, throughout history. In the end, we have a fundamental need to see the world as just.

According to the **just-world hypothesis** (Lerner, 1980), people need to see the world as a just place in which we get what we deserve and deserve what we get. Believing that the world is just makes it seem more predictable and controllable. After the death of Bin Laden, President Obama made a proclamation designed to reassure the American people and create a sense of closure and stability: "Justice has been done." Even the illusion of a just world is comforting. People who believe more strongly in a just world and see the world as fairer report being less stressed and being physically, as well as psychologically, healthier (Lucas, Alexander, Firestone, & Lebreton, 2008).

However, the need to believe in a just world has some counterintuitive consequences. Normally when I see someone suffer, I help. But what if I can't help? In a just world, bad things happen to bad people but not good people, right? According to the just-world hypothesis, I need to see the world as just, and therefore when I cannot restore justice by helping I come to see a person who suffers as deserving of his or her fate: We make negative attributions about them. Good people don't suffer without a reason. So we often blame victims, such as victims of sexual assault or robbery, of causing their misfortune as a way to restore our larger belief that the world is indeed just and fair (Van den Bos & Maas, 2009).

Threat and attributions   We often experience unexpected events as anxiety-provoking and threatening. In our evolutionary past, in which we lived in physically challenging and hostile environments, surprises were not usually good things. As a consequence, we still tend to be wary of things that are unusual or unexpected and of people who are different. In addition, some differences are viewed as more important than others. Historically, people tended to see members of other groups, particularly those nearby, as competitors for scarce resources. As a consequence, they attended to physical differences and perceived these not only as characteristics that distinguished the groups but also as indications of the biological inferiority of the other group (Gil-White, 2002). These beliefs justify unequal distribution of resources favoring one's own group and rationalize discrimination against potentially competing, threatening groups.

Some evolutionary psychologists also propose that, like chimpanzees and some other primates, humans cross-culturally display prejudice toward people with physical disabilities. The disability marks someone as different and potentially threatening. What can be threatening about a person with, for example, a visual disability? Evolutionary psychologists suggest that because in the past humans could not identify the causes of contagious diseases, which are typically transmitted by microscopic organisms, we are sensitive to cues of difference. We respond to people with physical disabilities and other groups as if they have a contagious disease: we avoid them and sometimes socially ostracize them (Schaller & Neuberg, 2012; Schaller & Park, 2011). Thus, Huang, Sedlovskaya, Ackerman, and Bargh (2011) found that simply reminding participants that they had been recently vaccinated (against swine flu) reduced their bias against immigrants. We respond to disability, often automatically and certainly not always consciously, as if there is something inherently wrong with the person (a form of dispositional attribution) and that it is catching.

Besides immediate material threats, humans experience more general existential threats—feelings of threat at the thought of our own mortality. Humans are unique in that they not only have the natural and fundamental instinct for self-preservation but also the awareness of the inevitability of their own mortality (Greenberg, Landau, Kosloff, & Solomon, 2009). Simple exposure to a person with a physical disability, for example, activates thoughts of death and arouses fear of one's own death among people without disabilities (Hirschberger, Florian & Mikulincer, 2005).

According to **terror management theory**, anything that makes us aware of our mortality and increases existential threat leads us to reaffirm things we believe in so we can continue to "live on" after our material deaths. After the 9/11 terrorist attacks (Figure 5.1), Americans displayed flags and engaged in other visible forms of solidarity, celebrating American values. However, the flip side of this enhanced commitment to American values is the devaluing of those who are different. After 9/11, U.S. citizens exhibited greater suspicion and dislike of others who seemed different or who questioned these values in any way (Pyszczynski, Solomon, & Greenberg, 2003). Walter Isaacson, who was Chairman and Chief Executive Officer of CNN at the time, commented on the scrutiny that the press received: "There was a patriotic fervor . . . and

Figure 5.1.   The 9/11 Terrorist Attacks on the World Trade Center Has Had a Lasting Psychological Impact on Americans. © Ken Tannenbaum/Shutterstock.com.

if you challenged anything you were made to feel as if there was something wrong with that. And there was almost a patriotism police . . . as if it were disloyal" (retrieved from http://www.pbs.org/moyers/journal/btw/transcript1.html).

These reactions to people generalize to anyone who deviates physically from cultural standards of normality (Martens, Greenberg, Schimmel, & Landau, 2004). People whose skin color or facial features are different or who speak in a way that is difficult to understand may be treated negatively because of systematic biases in how we see and respond to difference. Simply thinking of others as a member of a different race makes us see them as physically different too. People see the same person as darker skinned when they are told that the person has more Black ancestry (e.g., 75% vs. 25% Black ancestry; Sanchez, Good, & Chavez, 2011; see also Ho, Sidanius, Levin, & Banaji, 2011). The effect goes the other way as well: White voters who voted against Barack Obama in the presidential election perceived him as darker skinned than those who voted for him (Caruso, Mead, & Balcetis, 2009).

In this section, we have seen that people often automatically perceive differences as threatening and use these first negative dispositional attributions as a lens for interpreting a person's subsequent actions. Difference is at the heart of diversity. Thus, diversity, if not properly understood, may be seen as a threat rather than as a potential resource.

Integrating Information: Cognitive Consistency

Another facet of people's basic need to understand the world is their fundamental motivation to maintain consistency among their thoughts, interpretations, and actions.

Think for a minute about these statements. Portland, Maine is on the Atlantic Ocean. However, it is located in *western* Maine. Detroit, Michigan is *north* of Windsor, Ontario. How can these be? How does thinking about these examples make you feel? (These *are* true; look at a map.)

When two ideas or views about another person are inconsistent, we experience an aversive psychological state of *cognitive dissonance*. **Cognitive dissonance theory** (Festinger, 1957; Harmon-Jones & Mills, 1999) proposes that holding inconsistent thoughts or beliefs arouses psychological tension and discomfort, which people strive to reduce, often by changing their attitudes to be more consistent with their actions. Feeling tense, anxious, or uncomfortable motivates us to do something to make us feel better. In this case, inconsistency signals that we do not really understand the world, and we immediately become motivated to restore consistency and have the world make sense again.

The need to restore cognitive consistency helps explain why organizations often use strict initiation practices (sometimes hazing) to create loyalty among new members. Suffering for something worthless doesn't make sense, while suffering to attain something valuable does. Thus, if you can induce people to suffer to become members of a group, they will value the group more. In a classic test of cognitive dissonance theory, Elliot Aronson and Judson Mills (1959) invited female students to discuss a sensitive topic, sex, as a step required to join a group. In the "severe initiation" condition, which was designed to be very embarrassing, they had to read lurid sexual passages to a male experimenter. In the "mild initiation" condition, they read everyday words related to sex. In a third condition, the participants were directly admitted to the group. Participants then listened to a boring audio segment of the group discussing "sex behavior in lower animals," after which they indicated how much they liked the group. The women in the severe initiation group reported that they liked the group more than did women in the mild initiation and no-initiation conditions. They distorted their views of the group to make them consistent with the effort they invested to be a member of the group (see also Keating et al., 2005). Apparently, people do not like to think they suffer for no reason. According to cognitive dissonance theory, then, we are not necessarily rational beings; instead we are *rationalizing* beings.

How does such a basic process illuminate the psychology of diversity? We consider four different ways: illusory correlations, confirmatory biases, behavioral consistencies, and self-fulfilling prophecies.

Illusory correlations   Like our attributions, our need for consistency can fuel our biases. We often see relationships that do not exist because it makes the world *seem* consistent. One such phenomenon is the **illusory correlation**, the tendency to associate qualities that we see as rare with groups that are small in number; conversely, we link the qualities we view as common with groups that are large (Hamilton & Gifford, 1976). Unusual things go together, and frequent things go together. The connection between unusual things is particularly strong, because we have little experience to refute or dilute the association. Risen, Gilovich, and Dunning (2007) found that when people read sentences about members of relatively small social groups with some unusual quality (e.g., "Ben, a Jehovah's Witness, owns a pet sloth") they thought harder about the connection than when a common group and behavior were paired (e.g., "Jennifer, who was born in New York, drinks coffee every day"), exerted more effort to interpret the connection, and relied more heavily on the person's group membership (in this case, being a Jehovah's Witness) as an explanation.

This simple consistency bias paves the way for bias. How? Because we tend to see the world as good, with bad people and qualities being rare, we associate the majority group with positive characteristics and the minority groups with negative traits. Thus, when a member of a minority group does something that could be seen as bad, people are quick to associate this negative quality with the group. This automatic tendency not only affects our initial thoughts about the group but also guides our future impressions.

Confirmatory biases   Because people's first impressions, by definition, come first, cognitive dissonance theory suggests that people will adjust their subsequent perceptions, attributions, and beliefs to be consistent with their initial attributions. That is, people have a **confirmatory bias**: We attend to and seek out information that is consistent with what we expect, dismissing information that is inconsistent. Even if you are hesitant to allow initial attributions to color your feelings and beliefs about another person, the expectations derived from these attributions guide how you weigh subsequent information. The results are ultimately the same, however: biased assessments of the other person that confirm the initial impression.

Darley and Gross (1983) tested this process by having college-age subjects evaluate the academic progress of a fourth-grade child, Hannah. Hannah was described as coming from either high or low socioeconomic circumstances. Participants were first asked to evaluate Hannah's ability based on the information about her socioeconomic background. Then they watched a videotape showing Hannah performing several academic tasks and made their judgments.

Darley and Gross (1983) argued that participants would be hesitant to judge (or prejudge) a person on the basis only of her socioeconomic background. And they were right: Participants did not differ in their evaluations between the low and high socioeconomic conditions. For the most part, they expected Hannah to perform at a fourth-grade level regardless of her background. In addition, a substantial number of participants checked off "insufficient information" to make such an appraisal. However, after they watched the videotape of Hannah performing the tasks (which was the same for all participants), they felt that they had a better basis for evaluating her. At this point, those participants who believed that Hannah came from high socioeconomic circumstances perceived her to perform better on the test and evaluated her more favorably than did participants who believed that she came from low socioeconomic circumstances. Specifically, the first group felt that the test was harder and that Hannah got more problems correct, and they reported more of Hannah's positive behaviors when she was presented as someone with high, as opposed to low, socioeconomic status.

Now consider the person who says, "Oh, I don't see color, I just see a person." This person is claiming to be colorblind and implying that his judgments are objective, uninfluenced by a person's race. In the same way, the participants who judged Hannah "proved" they were not biased because of her low socioeconomic background in their initial assessment. But when they observed her behavior, their biases came out; they confirmed the stereotype that perhaps lay hidden from their awareness. They believed they were unbiased, but they behaved in a biased way.

Behavioral consistency and bias   In everyday life, people adjust their behavior, probably often unintentionally, to match their expectations of others. We treat people with physical impairments like helpless children, for example, we may offer assistance that promotes dependency. When asking for directions on a college campus, for instance, confederates using a wheelchair received more concrete, redundant answers than their able-bodied counterparts (Gouvier, Coon, Todd, & Fuller, 1994). Also, college students gave directions that resemble those they would give to a 12-year-old child (e.g., using more words, speaking louder, and in a higher-pitched voice) when under the impression that the recipient was an adult using a wheelchair, even when the adult was clearly identified as a working professional (Liesener & Mills, 1999).

Similarly, people automatically assume that elderly people have major physical limitations: they are thought of as "doddering but dear" (Cuddy, Norton, & Fiske, 2005) and treated as helpless. Younger people often talk to elderly people with "elder-speak," something that resembles baby-talk: simple vocabulary, content, and sentence structure. They speak slower and louder, reflecting their presumption of physical limitations. We often think that such accommodations are comforting, and the elderly deserve to be comforted. Also, native speakers interacting with members of other ethnic or national groups often engage in "foreigner talk": overly simple phrases spoken loudly and with exaggerated intonation (Gallois, Ogay, & Giles, 2005). This, however, is patronizing behavior that is often insulting to others. Although intentions may be good, people from other countries should not be treated as simple-minded or hard of hearing.

Self-fulfilling prophecies   The effects of the need for consistency reach much farther than affecting just our own behavior, however. It also shapes others' reactions, leading them to behave in ways consistent with what we expected in the first place. This process, by which expectations become reality, is called the **self-fulfilling prophecy**.

A number of studies illustrate this effect with people interacting by telephone with others whom they believe to be a very attractive member of the other sex, very unattractive, overweight, or being treated for mental illness. In these studies, participants are given false information about the person with whom they are talking, and the other person on the line is another student who is unaware of the manipulation. Participants initially expect attractive partners to be personable, socially skilled, and warm; they do not have these expectations about unattractive, overweight, or mentally ill people. When researchers coded the conversations that these participants had with their naïve partner, they found that people not only had different expectations of the other person but also behaved in ways consistent with those expectations. Participants were more engaged, interested, and warm in their interaction with a person whom they believed was an attractive member of the other sex, and they were relatively disengaged, disinterested, and cold when they believed that their partner was unattractive, overweight, or mentally ill.

What makes this set of studies particularly interesting is what the researchers found when they coded the way the naïve partners behaved in the interaction. Participants got what they expected. Students with participants who expected their "attractive" partner to be personable and socially skilled and who behaved in a warm and responsive way themselves responded in a positive, personable way. Things went well. By contrast, students with participants who expected their "unattractive," "overweight," or "mentally ill" partner to be socially awkward actually acted in a socially unskilled way in the conversation. These conversations did not go well.

Self-fulfilling prophecies can sometimes have dire consequences. Treating people as helpless makes them helpless. A classic study compared the impact of two different kinds of nursing home care. In one kind, the staff took primary responsibility for caring for elderly residents (scheduling their recreation time, helping them dress, cleaning their rooms). In the second kind of care, the staff encouraged the residents to take personal responsibility and exert personal control over their activities (Langer & Rodin, 1976; Rodin & Langer, 1977). At the end of the 18-month study, nursing home residents who had things done for them had a less positive outlook on life and were more depressed and hopeless than those who were encouraged to take personal responsibility. Even more important, the mortality rate for the dependent group was twice as high (30% vs. 15%). Moreover, people who earlier in life (up to 38 years earlier) thought of elderly people as "helpless" became more susceptible to life-threatening heart attacks and strokes when they became elderly (Levy, Zonderman, Slade, & Ferrucci, 2009). In the long run, people get what they expect.

Throughout this section, we have seen that basic processes in social cognition make us wary of difference. Furthermore, our need to see ourselves in a consistent, integrated way means that information about ourselves that does not fit this view becomes distorted. This need for consistency may further distort our view of others.

Although these processes help us function daily, we tend to interpret the behaviors of others, particularly actions we see as bad, as a function of who they are as people. We then interpret their subsequent behavior in ways consistent with this negative impression. If you do something good, I dismiss it as being manipulative; if you do something bad, I see it as further evidence of your bad character. I treat you poorly, and in turn you treat me poorly. Ah hah! I now have even clearer evidence that you are bad. It is easy to see how this spiral can make us feel threatened by diversity and respond unfairly to others. As we will see in the next section, this process can become even more treacherous when we think of each other in terms of group membership.

How We Think About Groups: Social Categorization and Group Membership

Being human is more than about being smart. How we get along with others is also critical. Today and throughout human history, group living has been essential to our survival. Human activity is rooted in interdependence. Being cooperative gives us substantial survival advantages; we can accomplish more together than alone. However, cooperation requires trust, because we depend upon others cooperating with us in return. Giving a lot more than we get is not usually good for personal survival. In this section, we discuss two important psychological processes crucial to group living: how we spontaneously categorize people into groups (social categorization) with immediate and longer-term consequences, and how we incorporate our group identity as an important element of who we are (social identity).

Who Is "In" and Who Is "Out"? Social Categorization

Social categorization, a fundamental building block of social life, is the process by which we classify people into groups. We engage in social categorization for the same reason that shapes social cognition generally: there is just too much information to process and comprehend at any one time, and we need to simplify the world to understand it. Social categorization also makes us *feel* we understand the world, because once you categorize a person into a group (e.g., Italian, Latino, Red Sox fan), you see that person as similar to other members of the same group whom you know. Moreover, as with the attributional biases we discussed earlier, you see the common qualities of the group as something in the nature of that group, as the "essence" of that group. How many times have you heard people say, "Oh, he did that because that's the way *those people are!*" Seeing a person as a member of a social category allows "top-down" perceptions; you fill in gaps about what you know about that person with information about what people in that group are generally like.

Once we see a person in terms of group membership, we automatically also determine whether that person is a member of our own group or of another group. We view our own group (the in-group) as a community of people who are similar to us, who depend on each other, and who are good and are trustworthy (Brewer & Caporael, 2006). Our group makes us feel like we belong and gives us a sense of security. Have you ever been away at some distant place and unexpectedly bumped into someone from your hometown or school? Whether or not you actually know the person, just seeing her makes you feel good and want to connect with her, a familiar stranger (see Milgram, 1992).

Humans are not the only social animals that make such automatic distinctions between in-group and out-group members. Rhesus macaques behave in the same way (Mahajan et al., 2011). Rhesus macaques not only spontaneously recognize when another monkey belongs to a different social group but are also more wary of monkeys from the out-group. When presented simultaneously with the faces of an in-group and an out-group monkey, they spend more time scrutinizing the out-group faces and become more suspicious of objects associated with the out-group (Figure 5.2).

Macaques appear to use primarily visual cues to decide whether another is a member of the in-group or an out-group. Humans, like macaques, also rely on what people look like to determine their group membership. However, because language is so important to us, we also distinguish whether someone is an in-group or out-group member by the way they speak. Box 5.1 illustrates this point.

Psychologists have found that, for humans, groups do not have to be meaningful for people to begin to think and feel positively about members of their own group and become wary of others. A number of years ago, Henri Tajfel tried to figure out how much these spontaneous feelings of affiliation and liking developed because (a) we have to depend on members of our group, or (b) we feel that we are in

(a)

(b)

Figure 5.2.   The Experimenter Is Testing How Rhesus Macaques Respond to Faces of In-group and Out-group Members (a) and Novel Objects Associated With In-group and Out-group Members (b). From "The Evolution of Intergroup Bias: Perceptions and Attitudes in Rhesus Macaques," by N. Mahajan, M. A. Martinez, N. L. Gutierrez, G. Diesendruck, M. R. Banaji, & L. R. Santos, 2011, *Journal of Personality and Social Psychology, 100,* pp. 387–405.

Box 5.1.   What Did You Say? The Impact of Accents

Immigration is a major social and political issue, not just in the United States but also internationally. The United Nations Department of Economic and Social Affairs (2011) estimates the number of international migrants at about 214 million worldwide. In the United States alone, 43 million people are foreign-born. As we discussed in Chapter 3, immigrants bring valuable diversity to America. They bring new skills, perspectives, and ideas. However, as we have explained in this chapter, despite the fact that the United States is a country composed primarily of immigrants and their descendants, people do not automatically embrace diversity.

One common diversity cue is a non-native (foreign) accent. People typically respond negatively to accents and the people who have them (Gluszek & Dovidio, 2009). This bias occurs in every other country where it has been studied, including the United Kingdom, Australia, Sweden, Germany, the Netherlands, and Israel. People who have non-native accents are viewed as less intelligent, competent, and loyal than are native speakers. The stronger the accent, the more negative the reaction. This bias develops early: children in both the United States and France prefer to be friends with other children who speak with a native accent than with a non-native accent (Kinzler, Dupoux, & Spelke, 2007).

Why would an accent produce such bad reactions? One explanation is that a non-native accent automatically identifies the person as belonging to a different group. People categorize others based on different social cues. We typically group people based on physical characteristics like skin color or, as the example that began this chapter illustrates, eye color. However, hearing an accent can be an even stronger cue.

In a study conducted in Germany (Rakić, Steffens, & Mummendey, 2011), students were asked to remember statements made by a series of individuals. The individuals looked either German (fair skin, light hair) or Italian (darker skin and hair), and spoke either with a German (native) accent or with an Italian (non-native) accent. The outcome of interest was the extent to which participants confused the statement made by different speakers. This is an indirect technique for measuring the social categories participants were using. People tend to confuse statements by others whom they think of as in the same group. For example, when paying attention primarily to others' gender, they frequently confuse the statements of one woman with those of another woman, but they rarely mistakenly attribute a woman's statement to a man.

The researchers found that the participants used both visual cues and accents to socially categorize others, but accents were more important than physical appearance. Participants were much more likely to confuse a speaker's statement with one made by someone else with a similar accent, Italian or German, than with one made by someone else who looked Italian or German. We see similar effects in the United States. In fact, for U.S. children, a non-native accent is a stronger negative cue than race (Kinzler, Shutts, DeJesus, & Spelke, 2009).

1. Why would *your* experience of having difficulty understanding what someone says affect what you think and feel about *them*?
2. Why would accents be a particularly strong basis of bias for young children?
3. Would you think differently about a person with a strong accent if you learned that the person had been in the country only a short time or for a long time? Why?

competition with another group. He kept creating situations stripping them of each of these features. He found that even when he put people into groups that had no previous meaning for them, with other members whom they never met and would never need to depend on, and with no tangible conflict or competition with another group, they still automatically liked others whom they believed were in the same group. These were called **minimal groups**, because they reduced what it means to be in a group as much as possible. In some studies participants were assigned to groups based on their preference for one abstract painting or another (by Klee or Kandinsky); in another experiment they were informed that they tend to overestimate or underestimate the number of dots on a slide, and in other studies they were just told that they were randomly assigned to groups. The results were the same: Just being told that you are in a group with others changes the way you think of people.

Since then, psychologists worldwide have documented what occurs when people think about others in terms of being in-group or out-group members (Dovidio & Gaertner, 2010). People tend to:

- see members of the same group as very similar to each other (**out-group homogeneity**);
- exaggerate differences between in-group and out-group members;
- feel closer to in-group members;
- perceive out-group members as less human;
- value the lives of in-group members more than those of out-group members;
- think more deeply and in a more detailed fashion about in-group members;
- believe that in-group members share their attitudes while out-group members have contrasting attitudes;
- want to approach in-group members but avoid out-group members;
- anticipate out-group members to be biased against them and value in-group members more when they are biased against the out-group;
- be more helpful, cooperative, and generous with in-group members.

In short, I like us, and I tend not to like them. Just using the terms "we" and "us" when you talk with someone makes you both think more positively about each other. We are indeed social animals.

Thinking Differently About Us and Them

Part of the reason why I like "us" so much is because I like me. When you think about yourself in a group, you begin to think about others as part of yourself. Think about a team or a club that you are a member of. Almost invariably, you think about traits, experiences, or activities that you share. You and other group members psychologically overlap. Even the parts of the brain that are usually reserved for thinking about yourself in unique ways become activated when you see other in-group members. Perhaps as a consequence, we extend our attributional biases to how we think about members of our own group and others. Positive behaviors and successful outcomes are more likely to be attributed to internal, stable characteristics of in-group than out-group members, whereas negative outcomes are more likely to be ascribed to the personalities of out-group than in-group members (Hewstone, 1990). Take, for example, a simple negative behavior such as jaywalking. If I see a member of my group crossing the street inappropriately, I am likely to think that the person was in a rush to make an appointment, a situational explanation. If instead I notice that it is a person who is a member of a different group, such as of another race or ethnicity, I would be more likely to attribute the behavior to the person being irresponsible or the type of person who disregards the law—dispositional attributions. These negative dispositional attributions are particularly likely to spread to other members of the out-group because we tend to see out-group members as basically alike. This is a good illustration of the ultimate attribution error discussed earlier in this chapter.

We communicate these biases when we talk to others. When members of my group do something good or members of another group do something bad, I talk about it in abstract ways ("she is good" or "she is bad") that make people think about what happened as something general and normal. By contrast, when someone in my group does something bad or someone in a different group does something good, I describe it as a specific, concrete example ("he did poorly on the math test" rather than "he's stupid," or "she returned the extra change" rather than "she's honest"). Describing the specific event makes it easy to believe that these are rare events. Thus the same cognitive consistency principles that we saw operating earlier lead us to think more highly of in-group members and more poorly of out-group members the more we learn about them.

What Can We Do? Reducing Bias and Embracing Diversity

Thus far, this chapter has discussed a series of findings related to the ways people think in general (social cognition) and how they think about groups (social categorization). The evidence helps us understand why people often, seemingly reflexively, resist diversity and social change. Diversity and change can make us feel uncomfortable: they make the world seem less predictable and controllable and makes our group's position less secure. These processes occur spontaneously, cross-culturally, and toward a range of different groups.

However, the situation is not as bleak as it seems. It seems bad because we are the product of our society, which, as we have seen, limits the way we think of groups. In the United States, race is a historically central social category. Historically, race determined whether a person was free, what kinds of jobs he or she could have, where he or she could sit on a bus, and whom he or she could marry. But it doesn't have to be that way. Many Europeans balk when asked about race and are insulted by that question. In Germany, one is not even allowed to ask a persons' race in a questionnaire— race does not exist! Of course, racism can still exist even if race is not formally acknowledged.

Evolutionary psychologists argue that racial bias is not genetically programmed because humans have traveled very little and slowly across our evolutionary history. We rarely came in contact with other races, so we had no need to develop a particular sensitivity to racial differences. Distinguishing friends from foes and in-group members from out-group members are essential aspects of our history and daily existence, but what defines those groups is a social matter, and thus controllable. Some of the most intense and vicious conflicts we have seen over the past 25 years—the Hutus and Tutsis in Rwanda, Irish Catholics and Protestants in Northern Ireland, and Serbs, Croats, and Bosnians in the former Yugoslavia—involve groups that share similar physical characteristics and history. It is their social differences not their physical differences that make them enemies (see Jones, 1997).

So how do we combat unfair biases based on race, ethnicity, or sexual orientation? One way is to attack these problems at their roots: social categorization. Although thinking about people in terms of their group membership may be our cognitive default, we can think about others in terms of their individual qualities when we are so motivated (Fiske, 1998, 2000). We do this commonly: we know our friends, romantic partners, teammates, roommates, and others whom we want to be close to on an individuated basis. It's a matter of motivation. In addition, we can think of ourselves and others as members of different groups at different times. Depending on what identity is important or salient to me at a particular time determines who is "in" and who is "out." The process of social categorization, although fundamental to human perception, cognition, and social functioning, is fluid. We can't change the basic processes that underlie how we think about people, but we can combat bias by understanding what these processes are and redirecting them.

In the remainder of this chapter, we review two ways to do this: decategorization and recategorization. **Decategorization** is influencing whether people identify themselves primarily as group members or as distinct individuals (Miller, 2002; Wilder, 1986). **Recategorization**, like decategorization, is designed to alter group boundaries but by redefining rather than by eliminating group categorization (Gaertner & Dovidio, 2000, 2009). These approaches help explain how intergroup contact operates psychologically to reduce prejudice (Allport, 1954).

"Me" and "You" Instead of "Us" and "Them": Decategorization

The goal of decategorization strategies for reducing intergroup bias is to get people to stop thinking about others primarily in terms of group boundaries ("we" vs. "they") and instead encourage them to regard one another primarily as distinct individuals ("me" and "you"). For example, learning that members of another group disagree with one another or are dissimilar in other ways makes me see them as unique individuals rather than as a member of the same group. That reduces my bias against them (Wilder, 1986). Another way to weaken group boundaries is to have groups with criss-crossing boundaries. Suppose you are in a group that is discussing bias. The group is composed of four men (two Anglo men and two Latinos) and four women (two Anglo women and two Latinas). As the discussion shifts from ethnic to gender bias and back, the in-groups and out-groups change rapidly. You quickly realize that it is easier and better for the group members to think of each other based on individual qualities than identities that are so fleeting.

One of the problems with decategorization, however, is that categories help us simplify a complicated world. Decategorized impressions cannot be sustained for long. However, they open a door to getting to know someone from a group that you always thought of as being different from you and your group. When you exchange information about each other in a way that conveys your unique personal qualities, called **personalization** (Brewer & Miller, 1984; Miller, 2002), you typically recognize that your stereotypes of the group are incorrect, which undermines your bias against the group as whole. Personalization is one reason why forming a friendship with a member of another group has such a strong effect for reducing bias toward the group (Davies, Tropp, Aron, Pettigrew, & Wright, 2011).

Personalization is most likely to change attitudes toward the group as a whole when the other person who discloses personal information is a typical, rather than atypical, member of a different group. A typical member of a group represents what most people in the group are like. If what you learn about that person contradicts your stereotype of the group, that experience will challenge your biases toward the group as a whole. If that person is an atypical member of the group, there is little reason for your experience with this individual to transfer to the group as a whole, because that person is not like other members of the group.

In one study directly addressing this issue (Ensari & Miller, 2002), secularist college students in Turkey interacted with an Islamic fundamentalist student (actually a research confederate). Secularist college students in Turkey are liberal, believe in a modern lifestyle, and wear European dress. By contrast, Islamic fundamentalists have strong religious beliefs, adopt a conservative and traditional lifestyle, and dress in a religious fashion. Participants were the interviewers, and the confederate was the interviewee. In response to some opening scripted questions by the interviewer, the confederate responded, "I am an Islamic person." This was followed by the manipulation of typicality. In the typical condition, the confederate, who was dressed in traditional attire, expressed the importance of her religious beliefs and her compliance with tradition. In the atypical condition, she wore more European dress and described a more open, liberal, and independent lifestyle. The degree of personalization was varied by the confederate's degree of disclosure in the interview. In the high-disclosure condition, the confederate revealed positive and negative intimate information, such as "The happiest news I had this year was that my father decided to become engaged because after my mother's death he wasn't happy with his life and felt lonely all the time" and "I have made only a few good friends during the past few years and feel lonely most of the time." In the low-disclosure condition, the confederate gave impersonal answers that contained no unique or individuating information. The main outcome of interest was how participants felt about the out-group (Islamic fundamentalists) as a whole after interacting with the confederate.

As expected, participants showed distinctively low levels of bias in the condition in which the confederate disclosed personal and intimate information about herself *and* appeared typical of Islamic fundamentalists (Figure 5.3). This personal disclosure not only brought the confederate closer to the participant but, because the confederate was similar to other Islamic fundamentalists, brought other Islamic fundamentalists closer as well. This did not happen when the confederate was self-disclosing but atypical of Islamic fundamentalists. Even if participants felt close to the confederate, these feelings did not transfer to other Islamic fundamentalists, because she was not like them.

What psychological process is at work when you feel close to a member of another group that you previously did not like? It may arouse cognitive dissonance. Not liking a group and its members is inconsistent with feeling close to a *typical* member of that group. If your view of the group was based on mainly second-hand information, then you will likely change your view to be consistent with your immediate, concrete, and meaningful connection with the out-group member. As we described in Chapter 3, in World War II racism was so strong and accepted in America that the armed forces were racially segregated. Blacks could serve in the military but only in units that were separated by race. Nevertheless, battle conditions often brought Whites and Blacks together side by side, and Whites who fought with Blacks under these conditions became significantly less prejudiced. Once a positive bond is established between members of two different groups, group attitudes change to fall in line. Although we generally try to simplify the way we think about the world—the reason we use social categorization in the first place—we fundamentally want to see the world accurately.

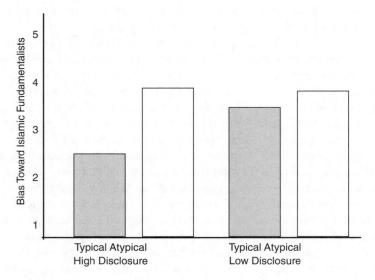

Figure 5.3. Participants Show Particularly Low Levels of Bias Toward Islamic Fundamentalists Whom They See As Typical of the Group who Disclose Personal Information to Them. Adapted from "The Out-group Must Not Be So Bad After All: The Effects of Disclosure, Typicality, and Salience on Intergroup Bias," by N. Ensari, & N. Miller, 2002, *Journal of Personality and Social Psychology*, *83*, pp. 313–329 (Figure 1).

Learning about what another group is like through a close personal relationship overrides what we think about the group generally and abstractly.

In some circumstances, such as intense conflicts or as a result of segregation, we do not have opportunities to engage in these kinds of personalized interactions. In fact, even when we have an opportunity of this type, our group biases and stereotypes may prevent us from disclosing personal information because that could make us feel vulnerable. In these cases, alternative strategies for reducing bias may be useful.

Playing on the Same Team: Recategorization

Whereas decategorization focuses on degrading social categorization, recategorization involves replacing the original categorization of members of different groups with an overriding shared identity. Imagine you are walking down a busy street. As people approach you, you automatically notice their race, and you think about them in terms of their racial group membership. However, as a person from another race approaches you, you notice that he is wearing a sweatshirt from your college. Will you feel differently about him now? According to one theory of recategorization, you will.

The key idea of the **common in-group identity model** (Gaertner & Dovidio, 2000, 2009) is that it is possible to change the ways we think about others by changing the way we think about their group membership. Emphasizing a common group membership can change the way we typically think of others from an "us" versus "them" to a more inclusive, superordinate "we" connection. This approach builds upon the principles of social categorization and social identity theory discussed earlier in this chapter. Once you categorize me as an in-group member (a "we") rather than an out-group member (a "they"), I will benefit from all the pro-in-group biases that make you like me more, discount my flaws, and want to work with me to promote "our" group.

These more positive reactions occur spontaneously and without much thought. Consider a variation of the example that began this section. Suppose you are a White college student walking around the football stadium before a game against a rival team. A White or Black person approaches you and asks for your help by answering a few questions about your food preferences for a survey he or she is doing. Would you help? Would it matter whether the person had on the colors and insignia of your school or the other school? Jason Nier and his colleagues (Nier, Gaertner, Dovidio, Banker, & Ward, 2001) actually conducted this study and found that White participants did not help a White confederate more when he was wearing the home team's signature clothing than when he or she was wearing the other team's insignia; they were already part of the same (racial) in-group. However, when White participants were asked for help by Black confederates, they were almost twice as likely to help (59% vs. 36% of the time) when the confederates wore the same-team (university in-group) insignia than when they wore the rival team's signature clothing. The home-team clothing represented a common in-group identity between White and Black students at the game. But what if the person in need was physically injured and in real trouble? Are you the type of person whose decision about whether to help would be determined by something so superficial as whether he was wearing a soccer shirt of your team or an opposing team? The research shows that, no matter what you think now, the answer is probably "yes" (Levine, Prosser, Evans & Reicher, 2005).

Barack Obama recognized the power of "we" and common identity in his campaign to become the first Black president of the United States. In his speech on the eve of election day (November 4, 2008), Obama stated, "We have never been just a collection of individuals or a collection of red states and blue states, we are and always will be the *United* States of America." In his inaugural address (January 20, 2009), he reinforced this message:

> We are a nation of Christians and Muslims, Jews and Hindus, and nonbelievers. We are shaped by every language and culture, drawn from every end of this Earth. . . . [I]n the face of our common dangers, . . . with eyes fixed on the horizon and God's grace upon us, we carried forth that great gift of freedom and delivered it safely to future generations.

He continued to stress this theme in his acceptance speech of his party's nomination on September 6, 2012. Obama stated that the challenges facing America "will require common effort, shared responsibility" and that the country will have to make "decisions that will have a huge impact on our lives and our children's lives for decades to come." In speeches such as these, Obama's emphasis is on "we," "us," and "our."

There is considerable power in "we." Recategorization in terms of a common in-group identity can promote intergroup forgiveness and trust. For instance, Wohl and Branscombe (2005) showed that increasing the salience of Jewish students' "human identity," in contrast to their "Jewish identity," increased their perceptions of similarity between Jews and Germans, as well as their willingness to forgive Germans for the Holocaust and their willingness to associate with contemporary German students. In addition, first-year college roommates of different racial and ethnic groups who emphasize their college identity—their sameness rather than their differences—are likely to become close friends later in the semester, in fact often closer than roommates of the same race and ethnicity (West, Pearson, Dovidio, Shelton, & Trail, 2009).

Despite the immediate positive impact of creating a sense of common identity between people who formerly thought of themselves as members of different groups, recategorization comes with some limitations. One problem is that it does not eliminate bias; instead, it redirects bias. For example, during the reunification of East and West Germany, East Germans who thought of themselves within the overarching identity of German had less bias toward West Germans. However, those who thought of themselves as Germans became more biased over time toward people from other countries (Kessler & Mummendey, 2001). Kessler and Mummendey noted that "recategorization is a 2-edged process: Although it reduces conflict at the subgroup level, it may initiate conflict at the common in-group level" (p. 1099).

A second problem is getting groups to accept a common identity. Efforts to induce a common identity can be met with resistance that in turn may increase bias between members of the original groups. Social identity theory (Tajfel & Turner, 1979) proposes that people are motivated to maintain the positive distinctiveness of their group relative to other groups. When the integrity of one's group identity is threatened, people are motivated to reestablish positive and distinctive group identities and thereby maintain relatively high levels of intergroup bias or show increased levels of bias (Jetten, Spears, & Postmes, 2004). However, the development of a common in-group identity does not necessarily require each group to forsake its less inclusive group identity. Social identities are complex; every individual belongs to multiple groups simultaneously (Brewer, 2000). It is possible, for example, to see two groups, such as offensive and defensive units on a football team, accountants and marketers in an advertising firm, or Black and Asian Americans, as different subgroups within the same common identity.

Implications and Applications of Category-based Models for Reducing Bias

Although decategorization and recategorization are different ways of reducing bias, they both draw on the fundamental role of social categorization in intergroup bias. Decategorization focuses on eliminating the original we–they distinction, whereas recategorization aims to replace it with a new, superordinate identity. Both strategies reduce intergroup bias, but they do it in different ways. In one direct comparison of these two strategies, Gaertner, Mann, Murrell, and Dovidio (1989) brought two 3-person laboratory groups together to solve a problem. The groups had to decide what items (a gun, newspaper, can of shortening [lard]) were most important for

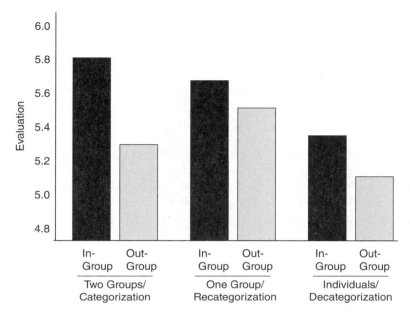

Figure 5.4. Recategorization Reduces Bias by Increasing the Attractiveness of Out-group Members, Whereas Decategorization Reduces Bias by Decreasing the Attractiveness of In-group Members. Adapted from "Reduction of Intergroup Bias: The Benefits of Recategorization," by S. L. Gaertner, J. A. Mann, A. J. Murrell, & J. F. Dovidio, 1989, *Journal of Personality and Social Psychology*, *57*, pp. 239–249.

survival after a crash-landing in the woods of northern Minnesota in mid-January. The experimenters manipulated aspects of the situation to make people feel recategorized as one group (integrated seating, one group name), categorized as two groups (seating on opposite sides of the table, retaining the two previous group names), or decategorized as separate individuals (each person seated at a different table; nicknames for each individual). After the discussion, intergroup bias was measured on the basis of a series or questions about the original in-group and out-group members (How much did you like each participant? How cooperative, honest, and valuable was each person during the interaction?).

In terms of reducing intergroup bias, the one-group and the separate-individuals conditions each had lower levels of bias compared with the two-groups control condition (Figure 5.4). Furthermore, as expected, the recategorized (one-group) condition and the decategorized (separate-individuals) condition reduced bias in different ways. Specifically, in the one-group condition, bias was reduced primarily by *increasing* the attractiveness of former out-group members. In the separate-individuals condition, bias was reduced primarily by *decreasing* the attractiveness of former in-group members. In the decategorized condition, former in-group members no longer benefited from the pro-in-group biases that come with being a "we."

What does this mean in everyday life? Each of these interventions has its own particular challenges. Our basic need to categorize people undermines the ability to sustain decategorized representations over time. In addition, given the traditional and contemporary importance of certain social categories, recategorized as well as decategorized representations may be highly unstable. Also with respect to recategorization, attempts to create new superordinate identities may arouse threats to valued subgroup identities.

Indeed, decategorization and recategorization may be best viewed as complementary strategies that can be applied to different situations and used sequentially at different stages of group relationships. Herbert Kelman (2005, 2010), for example, described the activities and outcomes of a program of workshops designed to improve Palestinian–Israeli relations and to contribute to peace in the Middle East. Because of the intense historical and contemporary conflict between these groups, it was not possible at the beginning for people to ignore group memberships or to trust each other sufficiently to disclose personal information. Thus, as a first step, Kelman focused them on how the fates of the two groups were intertwined and on their common connection and shared identity as workshop participants. Only then, after building this foundation of connection, were Palestinians and Israelis willing and able to develop personal relationships with members of these other groups. Because the workshop participants were national and community leaders, they could rely on these relationships with leaders from the other group to make coordinated efforts toward peace after they returned home. Thus, a strategic application of basic social psychological principles can have significant practical benefits in situations of long-standing intergroup conflict.

Although these processes associated with social cognition and categorization occur spontaneously, who one defines as an in-group or out-group member is primarily socially determined. There is no genetic basis for racism; it is not hard-wired in us. Moreover, we have control over how we choose to perceive others. On a daily basis, we have the motivation and ability to see others as unique individuals. I daily distinguish my best friend from other acquaintances, and I know what is special and unique that makes that person my best friend. Although group boundaries are often an obstacle to getting to know someone personally, they are not complete barriers.

Diversity does not have to divide us. A single, personalized interaction with a member of a different group can undermine stereotypes and dramatically change how I think and feel about the group as a whole, particularly if we see that person as a typical member of their group. We can also take advantage of the fact that we all belong to many groups, and we frequently share membership (students at the same college) with people with whom we differ based, for example, on race, ethnicity, or sexual orientation. Thus, we can change the way we think about these others from different groups to a common group as a function of a situation or our motivation. Once we see someone whom we previously thought of as an out-group member now as an in-group member, we spontaneously think more positively of them. They are now one of "us." However, diversity brings great value and resources to a society, so it is important also to recognize and appreciate qualities that make people and groups different.

Summary

Humans survived, adapted, and prospered throughout our evolutionary history aided by two fundamental qualities: We are intelligent, and we work well in groups. Despite the many benefits of these two characteristics, under some circumstances they divide us unnecessarily and unfairly. Social cognition, which is the way we think about people, is fast and efficient. We use mental shortcuts to understand why people do what they do, and we often gravitate to explanations that make us feel that we can predict and ultimately control our social world. But bias is embedded in these processes. We overestimate the extent that what others do is caused by their personality, and we make stronger attributions to a person's disposition when that person is different in some way or does something we don't like. We need to feel that we understand anything that threatens us, and attributing qualities to someone's personality or disposition allows us to believe that we can predict that person's behavior. To feel that we understand the world, we also need to see the world in consistent ways. Seeing inconsistency disturbs us. This unpleasant state of cognitive dissonance motivates us to distort our views to be consistent and leads us to interpret whatever a person does in a way that is consonant with our initial attributions. Diversity occupies a precarious position in how people think about others.

We rely on members of our group for support and assistance. Relations within a group are highly reciprocal and coordinated, so it is important to distinguish who is in my group (the in-group) and who belongs to a different group (an out-group). We make these social categorization judgments spontaneously, often based on things we see (physical characteristics) and believe (similarity). Once we categorize others as in-group members, we like them more, trust them more, and help them more. We also tend to interpret what they do in ways consistent with our positive connection to them. For out-group members, it's the opposite. It is easy to see how our perceptions of our groups and other groups diverge over time.

Questions for Thinking and Knowing

1. Suppose you meet someone with a lot of tattoos and body piercings. How would each of the following processes affect how you might respond to the person: (a) attributional bias, (b) cognitive dissonance, (c) confirmatory bias, and (d) self-fulfilling prophecy? How likely is it that one or all of them would affect how you respond to the person? How would a person's age, social class, and regional background generally affect how you respond? Where, how, and when did you learn to respond this way?

2. People weigh negative information more heavily than positive information in their daily perceptions, evaluations, and decision-making. Why do you think this is so? How does this affect the way you respond to people of a race, ethnicity, or sexual orientation different from your own?

3. People say "you can't judge a book by its cover." Psychologists, however, say that we often do. Why do you think humans are this way?

4. Think about a recent date or social experience that you had that worked out just as you expected, either good or bad. What kinds of things did you do to create a self-fulfilling prophecy?
5. What are some of the social cognition and social categorization reasons that people are biased against overweight people, gay men or lesbians, and members of a different racial or ethnic group from their own? How are these reasons similar? How are they different?

Key Terms

Attribution bias
Attribution processes
Attribution theory
Cognitive consistency
Cognitive dissonance theory
Cognitive miser
Common in-group identity model
Confirmatory bias
Decategorization
Evolutionary psychology
Fundamental attribution error

Illusory correlation
Just-world hypothesis
Minimal groups
Out-group homogeneity
Personalization
Recategorization
Self-fulfilling prophecy
Social cognition
Terror management theory
Ultimate attribution error

References

Allport, G. W. (1954). *The nature of prejudice.* Oxford: Addison-Wesley.

Aronson, E., & Mills, J. (1959). The effects of severity of initiation on liking for a group. *Journal of Abnormal and Social Psychology, 59,* 177–181.

Brewer, M. B. (2000). Reducing prejudice through cross-categorization: Effects of multiple social identities. In S. Oskamp (Ed.), *Reducing prejudice and discrimination: The Claremont Symposium on Applied Social Psychology* (pp. 165–183). Mahwah, NJ: Erlbaum.

Brewer, M. B., & Caporael, L. R. (2006). An evolutionary perspective on social identity: Revisting groups. In M. Schaller, J. A. Simpson, & D. T. Kenrick (Eds.), *Evolution and social psychology* (pp. 143–161). Madison, CT: Psychosocial Press.

Brewer, M. B., & Miller, N. (1984). Beyond the contact hypothesis: Theoretical perspectives on desegregation. In N. Miller & M. B. Brewer (Eds.), *Groups in contact: The psychology of desegregation* (pp. 281–302). Orlando, FL: Academic Press.

Caruso, E. M., Mead, N. L., & Balcetis, E. (2009). Political partisanship influences perception of biracial candidates' skin tone. *Proceedings of the National Academy of Sciences of the United States of America, 106,* 20168–20173.

Cuddy, A. J. C., Norton, M. I., & Fiske, S. T. (2005). This old stereotype: Pervasiveness and persistence of the elderly stereotype. *Journal of Social Issues, 61,* 267–285.

Darley, J. M., & Gross, P. H. (1983). A hypothesis-conforming bias in labeling effects. *Journal of Personality and Social Psychology, 44,* 20–33.

Davies, K., Tropp, L. R., Aron, A., Pettigrew, T. F., & Wright, S. C. (2011). Cross-group friendships and intergroup attitudes: A meta-analytic review. *Personality and Social Psychology Review, 15,* 332–351.

Dovidio, J. F., & Gaertner, S. L. (2010). Intergroup bias. In S. T. Fiske, D. Gilbert, & G. Lindzey (Eds.), *Handbook of social psychology* (5th ed., Vol. 2, pp. 1084–1121). New York: John Wiley & Sons.

Ensari, N., & Miller, N. (2002). The outgroup must not be so bad after all: The effects of disclosure, typicality, and salience on intergroup bias. *Journal of Personality and Social Psychology, 83,* 313–329.

Festinger, L. (1957). *A theory of cognitive dissonance.* Stanford, CA: Stanford University Press.

Fiske, S. T. (1998). Stereotyping, prejudice, and discrimination. In D. T. Gilbert, S. T. Fiske, & G. Lindzey (Eds.), *The handbook of social psychology* (4th ed., Vol. 2, pp. 357–411). New York: McGraw-Hill.

Fiske, S. T. (2000). Interdependence and the reduction of prejudice. In S. Oskamp (Ed.), *Reducing prejudice and discrimination* (pp. 115–135). Hillsdale, NJ: Erlbaum.

Gaertner, S. L., & Dovidio, J. F. (2000). *Reducing intergroup bias: The Common Ingroup Identity Model.* Philadelphia, PA: Psychology Press.

Gaertner, S. L., & Dovidio, J. F. (2009). A Common Ingroup Identity: A categorization-based approach for reducing intergroup bias. In T. Nelson (Ed.), *Handbook of prejudice* (pp. 489–506). Philadelphia, PA: Taylor & Francis.

Gaertner, S. L., Mann, J. A., Murrell, A. J., & Dovidio, J. F. (1989). Reduction of intergroup bias: The benefits of recategorization. *Journal of Personality and Social Psychology, 57,* 239–249.

Gallois, C., Ogay, T., & Giles, H. (2005). Communication accommodation theory: A look back and a look ahead. In W. B. Gudykunst (Ed.), *Theorizing about intercultural communication* (pp. 121–148). Thousand Oaks, CA: Sage.

Gil-White, F. (2002). The cognition of ethnicity: Native category systems under the field experiment microscope. *Field Methods, 14,* 161–189.

Gluszek, A., & Dovidio, J. F. (2009). The way they speak: A social psychological perspective on the stigma of nonnative accents in communication. *Personality and Social Psychology Review, 14,* 214–237.

Gouvier, W. D., Coon, R. C., Todd, M. E., & Fuller, K. H. (1994). Verbal interaction with individuals presenting with or without physical disability. *Rehabilitation Psychology, 39,* 263–268.

Greenberg, J., Landau, M., Kosloff, S., & Solomon, S. (2009). How our dreams of death transcendence breed prejudice, stereotyping, and conflict: Terror management theory. In T. D. Nelson (Ed.), *Handbook of prejudice, stereotyping, and discrimination* (pp. 309–332). New York: Psychology Press.

Hamilton, D. L., & Gifford, R. K. (1976). Illusory correlation and the maintenance of stereotypic beliefs. *Journal of Personality and Social Psychology, 12,* 392–407.

Harmon-Jones, E., & Mills, J. (Eds.). (1999). *Cognitive dissonance: Progress on a pivotal theory in social psychology.* Washington, DC: American Psychological Association.

Hewstone, M. (1990). The "ultimate attribution error"? A review of the literature on intergroup causal attribution. *European Journal of Social Psychology, 20,* 311–335.

Hirschberger, G., Florian, V., & Mikulincer, M. (2005). Fear and compassion: A Terror Management Analysis of emotional reactions to physical disability. *Rehabilitation Psychology, 50,* 246–257.

Ho, A. K., Sidanius, J., Levin, D. T., & Banaji, M. R. (2011). Evidence for hypodescent and racial hierarchy in the categorization and perception of biracial individuals. *Journal of Personality and Social Psychology, 100,* 492–506.

Huang, J. H., Sedlovskaya, A., Ackerman, J. M., & Bargh, J. A. (2011). Immunizing against prejudice: Effects of disease protection on attitudes toward out-groups. *Psychological Science, 22,* 1550–1556.

Huizinga, J. (1938). *Homo Ludens.* Boston, MA: Beacon Press.

Jetten, J., Spears, R., & Postmes, T. (2004). Intergroup distinctiveness and differentiation: A meta-analytic integration. *Journal of Personality and Social Psychology, 86,* 862–879.

Jones, J. M. (1997). *Prejudice and racism* (2nd ed.). New York: McGraw-Hill.

Keating, C. F., Pomerantz, J., Pommer, S. D., Ritt, S. J. H., Miller, L. M., & McCormick, J. (2005). Going to college and unpacking hazing: A functional approach to decrypting initiation practices among undergraduates. *Group Dynamics: Theory, Research, and Practice, 9,* 104–126.

Kelman, H. C. (2005). Building trust among enemies: The central challenge for international conflict resolution. *International Journal of Intercultural Relations, 29,* 639–650.

Kelman, H. C. (2010). Interactive problem solving: Changing political culture in the pursuit of conflict resolution. *Peace and Conflict: Journal of Peace Psychology, 16,* 389–413.

Kessler, T., & Mummendey, A. (2001). Is there any scapegoat around? Determinants of intergroup conflict at different categorization levels. *Journal of Personality and Social Psychology, 81,* 1090–1102.

Kinzler, K. D., Dupoux, E., & Spelke, E. S. (2007). The native language of social cognition. *Proceedings of the National Academy of Sciences of the United States of America, 104,* 12577–12580.

Kinzler, K. D., Shutts, K., DeJesus, J., & Spelke, E. S. (2009). Accent trumps race in guiding children's social preferences. *Social Cognition, 27,* 623–634.

Langer, E. J., & Rodin, J. (1976). The effects of choice and enhanced personal responsibility for the aged: A field experiment in an institutional setting. *Journal of Personality and Social Psychology, 34,* 191–198.

Lerner, M. J. (1980). *The belief in a just world: A fundamental delusion.* New York: Plenum.

Levine, M., Prosser, A., Evans, D., & Reicher, S. (2005). Identity and emergency intervention: How social group membership and inclusiveness of group boundaries shape helping behavior. *Personality and Social Psychology Bulletin, 31,* 443–453.

Levy, B. R., Zonderman, A. B., Slade, M. D., & Ferrucci, L. (2009). Age stereotypes held earlier in life predict cardiovascular events later in life. *Psychological Science, 20,* 296–298.

Liesener, J. J., & Mills, J. (1999). An experimental study of disability spread: Talking to an adult in a wheelchair like a child. *Journal of Applied Social Psychology, 29,* 2083–2092.

Lucas, T., Alexander, S., Firestone, I., & Lebreton, J. M. (2008). Just-world beliefs, perceived stress, and health behavior: The impact of a procedurally just world. *Psychology and Health, 23,* 849–865.

Mahajan, N., Martinez, M. A., Gutierrez, N. L., Diesendruck, G., Banaji, M. R., & Santos, L. R. (2011). The evolution of intergroup bias: Perceptions and attitudes in rhesus macaques. *Journal of Personality and Social Psychology, 100,* 387–405.

Martens, A., Greenberg, J., Schimmel, J., & Landau, M. J. (2004). Ageism and death: Effects of mortality salience and similarity to elders on distancing from and derogation of elderly people. *Personality and Social Psychology Bulletin, 30,* 1524–1536.

McArthur, L. A. (1972). The how and what of why: Some determinants and consequences of causal attribution. *Journal of Personality and Social Psychology, 22,* 171–193.

Milgram, S. (1992). *The individual in a social world: Essays and experiments* (2nd ed.). New York: McGraw-Hill.

Miller, N. (2002). Personalization and the promise of Contact Theory. *Journal of Social Issues, 58,* 387–410.

Nier, J. A., Gaertner, S. L., Dovidio, J. F., Banker, B. S., & Ward, C. M. (2001). Changing interracial evaluations and behavior: The effects of a common group identity. *Group Processes and Intergroup Relations, 4,* 299–316.

Pettigrew, T. F. (1979). The ultimate attribution error: Extending Allport's cognitive analysis of prejudice. *Personality and Social Psychology Bulletin, 5,* 461–476.

Pyszczynski, T., Solomon, S., & Greenberg, J. (2003). *In the wake of 9/11: The psychology of terror*. Washington, DC: American Psychological Association.

Rakić, T., Steffens, M. C., & Mummendey, A. (2011). Blinded by the accent! The minor role of looks in ethnic categorization. *Journal of Personality and Social Psychology, 100*, 16–29.

Risen, J. L., Gilovich, T., & Dunning, D. (2007). One-shot illusory correlations and stereotype formation. *Personality and Social Psychology Bulletin, 33*, 1492–1502.

Rodin, J., & Langer, E. J. (1977). Long-term effects of a control-relevant intervention with the institutionalized aged. *Journal of Personality and Social Psychology, 35*, 895–902.

Ross, L., Amabile, T. M., & Steinmetz, J. L. (1977). Social roles, social control and biases in social-perception processes. *Journal of Personality and Social Psychology, 35*, 485–494.

Sanchez, D. T., Good, J. J., & Chavez, G. (2011). Blood quantum and perceptions of Black–White biracial targets: The Black ancestry prototype model of affirmative action. *Personality and Social Psychology Bulletin, 37*, 3–14.

Schaller, M., & Neuberg, S. L. (2012). Danger, disease, and the nature of prejudice(s). In J. A. Olson & M. P. Zanna (Eds.), *Advances in experimental social psychology* (Vol. 46, pp. 1–54). New York: Elsevier.

Schaller, M., & Park, J. H. (2011). The behavioral immune system (and why it matters). *Current Directions in Psychological Science, 20*, 99–103.

Shaver, K. G. (1985). *The attribution of blame: Causality, responsibility, and blameworthiness*. New York: Springer-Verlag.

Tajfel, H., & Turner, J. C. (1979). An integrative theory of intergroup conflict. In W. G. Austin & S. Worchel (Eds.), *The social psychology of intergroup relations* (pp. 33–48). Monterey, CA: Brooks/Cole.

United Nations Department of Economic and Social Affairs. (2011). *The age and sex of migrants*. New York: United Nations. Retrieved on September 3, 2012 from http://www.un.org/esa/population/publications/2011Migration_Chart/wallchart_2011.pdf

Van den Bos, K., & Maas, M. (2009). On the psychology of the belief in a just world: Exploring experiential and rationalistic paths to victim blaming. *Personality and Social Psychology Bulletin, 35*, 1567–1578.

West, T. V., Pearson, A. R., Dovidio, J. F., Shelton, J. N., & Trail, T. (2009). Superordinate identity and intergroup roommate friendship development. *Journal of Experimental Social Psychology, 45*, 1266–1272.

Wilder, D. A. (1986). Social categorization: Implications for creation and reduction of intergroup bias. In L. Berkowitz (Ed.), *Advances in experimental social psychology* (Vol. 19, pp. 291–355). Orlando, FL: Academic Press.

Wohl, M. J. A., & Branscombe, N. R. (2005). Forgiveness and collective guilt assignment to historical perpetrator groups depend on level of social category inclusiveness. *Journal of Personality and Social Psychology, 88*, 288–303.

Chapter 6

Social Identity, Roles, and Relations
Motivational Influences in Responses to Diversity

Introduction   147
Feeling Good about Us: Social Identity   148
Confusing "What Is" with "What Should Be": Social Roles and
   System Justification   155
Slipping into the Darkness: Groups in Competition   161
What Can We Do? Changing How Groups Relate   164
Summary   168

We are not fighting for the right to be like you. We respect ourselves too much for that. When we advocate freedom, we mean freedom for us to be black, or brown, and you to be white, and yet live together in a free and equal society. This is the only way that integration can bring dignity for both of us.

John Oliver Killens

Introduction

In a classic children's book, Dr Seuss tells the story of the Sneetches, fictitious yellow creatures with long necks and beaks. Some Sneetches have a green star on their bellies, others do not. The Sneetches notice the difference and, before long, those with the stars hang around together and exclude the Sneetches without the stars. Some Sneetches are "in" while others are "out." But then a character named Sylvester McMonkey McBean offers the Sneetches without stars the opportunity (if they pay)

The Psychology of Diversity: Beyond Prejudice and Racism, First Edition. James M. Jones, John F. Dovidio, and Deborah L. Vietze.
© 2014 Blackwell Publishing Ltd. Published 2014 by Blackwell Publishing Ltd.

to go through his "Star-On" machine. As large numbers of Sneetches take up his offer, the original green-starred Sneetches become alarmed as they lose their ability to distinguish their group from the inferior Sneetches. But Sylvester McMonkey McBean offers them the chance (by paying, of course) to enter his "Star-Off" machine, which removes the star from their bellies and reestablishes their distinctive identity. Of course, then all the Sneetches want their stars off. The Sneetches go back and forth, motivated by the desire to restore or enhance their group's status, paying Sylvester McMonkey McBean to put stars on their bellies, take stars off, and put them on again. McBean rapidly becomes rich.

Of course, Sneetches aren't real. But Dr Seuss did know something about psychology. In this chapter we explore why we, like Sneetches, need to see our group as distinctive and better than other groups. Seeing our own group as somehow superior makes the social world seem just and fair—to us, at least, if not to anyone else. In the first section, we discuss how our feelings of self-worth are closely tied to how we believe our group is valued. In the second section, we review the ways people justify the different social roles and statuses that members of different groups occupy in society. In the third major part of the chapter, we examine how easily groups come to see each other as competitors and the consequences this has on intergroup relations and the way we view diversity. The fourth section identifies ways that people can reduce bias and learn not simply to tolerate but to truly value difference and diversity. As you read on, keep in mind that these basic human tendencies to perceive, value and distinguish their groups, and to respond favorably or unfavorably to differences are basic principles in the psychology of diversity.

Feeling Good about Us: Social Identity

Living in today's world is complicated! We are members of many groups at the same time. Some groups we care about, or identify with, more than others. If I ask you to describe yourself, what groups come to mind first? How much do you care about belonging to them? How has that changed as you have changed, for example from high school to college? Also, being in different situations can make you think differently about your group memberships. You may think of yourself as a student at your school when you are watching your college team play a game, but you think of yourself more as an American during the Olympics. These are questions about *social* identity.

The more strongly you identify with a group, the more strongly you see yourself as a typical member of the group (Hogg, 2010). This usually includes ways of thinking and behaving that are specific to and characteristic of the group. You think like, feel like, and act like members of that group should. You are not simply conforming with people around you; you are actually taking on the character of what you imagine the typical member of the group (the "prototype") is or should be like. **Social identity theory** (Tajfel & Turner, 1979) and **self-categorization theory** (Turner, Hogg, Oakes, Reicher, & Wetherell, 1987) explain when and why individuals identify with and behave as members of specific social groups (see Abrams & Hogg, 2010).

Who Am I? Personal and Social Identity

Social identity theory distinguishes two types of identity that all of us experience. **Personal identity** represents what we believe makes us unique compared with all other people. Your experiences, characteristics, talents, and values are distinctive; there is no one else just like you. By contrast, **social identity** is an identity that you share with others—special others, those in a group that you belong to and care about. These are largely independent ways of thinking. Among Blacks, for example, personal identity and social identity (reference group identity) predict very different things. Personal identity relates to how adventurous a person is and how good a person feels specifically about himself or herself; social identity predicts collectively oriented behaviors, such as activism to benefit one's group (Vandiver, Cross, Worrell, & Fhagen-Smith, 2002). In addition, Blacks with a stronger social identity are buffered psychologically against acts of discrimination against them. They show greater psychological well-being, including lower levels of hopelessness and depression, in the face of discrimination (Branscombe, Schmitt, & Harvey, 1999).

Your motivations and intentions at any point in time are largely determined by whether your feelings of personal or social identity are more strongly activated. When you think in terms of personal identity, your personal motives and goals shape what you feel and do. You get up in the morning and put on clothes that make you feel (and hopefully look) good. However, when you think in terms of your social identity, you act like a representative of the group, often in ways that display your solidarity with the group. If you are a Green Bay Packers fan, on the morning of a big game you wear green and walk around with a cheese hat on your head. It may not make you look good to everyone, but it does to others in your group. Moreover, when your team wins the Super Bowl, you feel a sense of ownership, although you probably contributed little to the effort except eat nachos and chicken wings. College students are almost 50% more likely to wear school identifying clothes and use the word "we" when talking about their college football team after the team wins a game compared to when the team loses or ties a game (Cialdini et al., 1976).

When you think in terms of personal identity, you relate to others on an interpersonal level, evaluating how well their particular opinions and qualities fit with your values. Your personality characteristics (such as authoritarianism; see Chapter 4) guide how you respond to people. However, when you rely on your social identity, which group a person belongs to is what is most important. All you need to know about someone is whether he or she is part of your group. If the person is a member of your group, you tend to like him and want to do things for him. If the person belongs to a different group, you will respond as you think a good member of your group should (Verkuyten & Hagendoorn, 1998). At the next sporting event against an archrival, try this experiment: Wear the colors and insignia's of the other team and see how people treat you.

Because of past experiences or the present circumstances, people differ in their level of identification with a group. Some people identify more strongly than others. In general, people more highly identified with a group work harder for the group, adhere more strongly to group norms and values, and are more affected by the successes or failure of the group. They are also more reluctant to abandon their connection to the

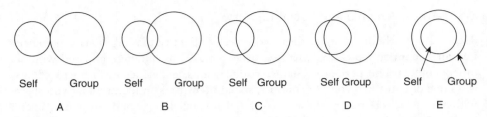

Figure 6.1. A Measure of Identity Fusion: In (E), the Self and the Group Are Completely Fused. Reprinted from Figure 1 of "Identity Fusion and Self-Sacrifice: Arousal as a Catalyst of Pro-Group Fighting, Dying, and Helping Behavior," by W. B. Swann Jr, A. Gómez, C. Huici, J. F. Morales, & J. G. Hixon, November 2010, *Journal of Personality and Social Psychology*, *99*, pp. 824–841, doi: 10.1037/a0020014.

group. The quotation by John Oliver Killens that began this chapter reflects a strong sense of group identity. He wanted the freedom for "us to be black, or brown, and you to be white." The Sneetches, however, had only a weak sense of group identity associated with the stars; they were quick to abandon their starred identity when something better came along.

Strong social identity comes at the expense of personal identity—people "lose" themselves in the group, people can also become "fused" with a group. People with a fused identity retain a sense of personal identity, but the self and the group are indistinguishable; individuals fully incorporate the group's values into their understanding of who they are (Figure 6.1). People who are highly fused with their group, when aroused, will readily take extreme action for their group. For example, highly fused Spaniards are more willing to help other Spaniards, as well as more willing "to fight someone physically threatening another Spaniard" and to potentially sacrifice their lives to save another in-group member but not an out-group member (Swann, Gómez, Huici, Morales, & Hixon, 2010).

Being too identified or fused with a group is not entirely satisfying in the long term, however. People need to distinguish themselves from others to evaluate their unique skills, talents, and achievements, the things that help to define who we are individually. Thus, people often seek a middle point between personal and social selves in order to balance their opposing needs to be different from others and to belong and share a sense of similarity with others. **Optimal distinctiveness theory** (Brewer, 1991) argues that people have simultaneous and competing drives for both distinctiveness and inclusiveness. When inclusiveness exceeds an individual's optimal level—too much "we-ness"—they seek to increase their distinctiveness—more "me-ness." This balancing act implies that when contexts are too homogeneous, too inclusive, diversity should become a more important goal. How do you feel when you think of yourself as a member of your community? As a resident in your state? Thinking of yourself in terms of your community is typically more satisfying because you feel closer to neighbors and others you interact with and share experiences with regularly. But at the same time, you recognize how you are distinctive from others and enjoy your individuality and how you contribute to community life. Achieving this balance between motives enhances one's feelings of connection to the group, reduces feelings of uncertainty, and increases group cohesiveness.

Many Me's: Multiple Identities

Individuals have multiple social identities. You have your high school identity, your college identity, your family identity, and possibly your club or team identity. You might be able to rank these in terms of importance, but the relevance of these different identities changes systematically. The specific social context directly influences which identity is most salient at a given time. According to social identity theory, we can toggle back and forth between these identities in different situations. Social qualities that make you feel distinctive in a particular context (e.g., being a woman in a group of men) or situations that draw attention to a particular group membership (e.g., a women's rights rally) typically make the corresponding identity most important. Activating different identities, in turn, critically determines how you think and behave.

For example, when Asian college students' female identity was made salient, they performed more poorly on a mathematics test (a gender-inconsistent task) than when this identity was not activated. Conversely, when their Asian identity was emphasized, they performed better on the mathematics test than when this group identity was not salient, a result that is consistent with expectations associated with that ethnic identity (Shih, Pittinsky, & Ambady, 1999).

This finding shows that, although we are not always aware of our many different possible social identities, being in specific situations can activate different, alternative identities. Who we are shifts a bit in different circumstances. We not only act but also think and feel differently, depending whether we are at home or at college. For instance, simply asking biracial or multiracial people to think about their father or mother or about different types of food that they like can make them think about themselves as more Black or White or more Asian or American.

This point is particularly important for understanding diversity. People of multiracial backgrounds represent one of the most rapidly growing minority groups in the United States. Because of increasing diversity and greater frequency of intermarriage, by 2050 one in five Americans may be biracial or multiracial (Shih & Sanchez, 2009). Traditionally, people opposed interracial marriage (which has been legal in every state only since 1967) because they claimed that the "racial confusion" of children of these marriages would be distressing and cause them psychological harm. The fact is, however, that multiracial people are as well adjusted psychologically as monoracial people, they do not have lower self-esteem, and are not more depressed or more likely to engage in problem behaviors (Shih & Sanchez, 2005).

Some multiracial people who have difficulty switching their identities across different situations do experience some sense of fragmentation and alienation. They may feel out of place or that they are not quite fitting in. However, multiracial individuals who are able to switch identities easily adapt to new social challenges in creative and effective ways (Shih, Sanchez, & Ho, 2010). They can draw on a wider range of experiences and perspectives, which allows them to adjust better to different situations. An interesting consequence of these shifting identities is that a psychology of diversity can also apply to individuals.

My Group Is Better than Yours: Creating Positive Identity

According to social identity theory, the basic human drive is to feel good about yourself. One way to achieve this is to join groups that are socially valued; another is to increase the perceived worthiness of the social groups to which you already belong. To the extent that people are motivated to regard themselves positively, they are also motivated to differentiate themselves from outsiders; that is, to see as much difference as possible between the groups they belong to and those that they don't (Tajfel & Turner, 1979). Think for a minute about how important it is to you to be a member of your college community. Now think about students at another college. Almost immediately, ideas about how your school is different and better than the other school will pop into your mind! If they don't, or positive features of the other school are more vivid, you may begin considering a transfer, searching for a new and better community. This basic and spontaneous motivation has important consequences for how we treat members of other groups and how we connect to members of our own group.

Feeling superior to other groups   When the integrity of your group identity is threatened, for example, if you learn that an outsider questions the value of your group, you become motivated to reestablish your group's positive and distinctive group identity. One way of doing this is by putting other groups down, either by thinking less positively about them (prejudice) or acting in ways to ensure that they are not as good (discrimination) (Jetten, Spears, & Postmes, 2004). You will find ways to make your group seem distinctive and superior again. Recall the Sneetches at the beginning of this chapter. When the other Sneetches started going through Sylvester McMonkey McBean's "Star-On" machine and it looked like every Sneetch would soon have a star on its belly, the original star-bellied Sneetches paid to go through the "Star-Off" machine to retain their group's distinctiveness.

According to social identity theory, we can use one of three different strategies to enhance our social identity (Jetten, Schmitt, Branscombe, & McKimmie, 2005; Tajfel & Turner, 1979):

- *Social mobility:* You can leave an existing social group and, if possible, join one that is more positively valued. For instance, if you feel that the group you hang around with is not respected by others, you might seek out a new group of friends to be with.
- *Social creativity:* You can seek positive distinctiveness by emphasizing a different basis for social comparison from the one that defines the status relationship, one on which the in-group appears superior (see Mullen, Brown, & Smith, 1992, for a review). For example, people in another group may have more money, but people in your group know how to have more fun.
- *Competition:* Members of your group can feel superior to another group by doing something to assert superiority, such as beating another dormitory in intramural

sports or treating members of the other group poorly—discriminating against them. Thus, the desire to enhance social identity in itself can increase motivations to compete against other groups.

Even learning that a different group beat a rival team makes us feel good. This pleasure that we experience when an out-group suffers, which is actually quite normal (albeit not the most admirable of human traits), is called **schadenfreude** (Smith, Powell, Combs, & Shirtz, 2009). This is why, even when our own team isn't playing, we enjoy rooting against a rival team.

Feeling connected to your group   People can feel better about themselves by feeling closer to members of their group, as well as feeling different from members of other groups. Self-categorization theory, which evolved from social identity theory, goes a bit further by emphasizing how people see themselves relative to other members of their group. Self-categorization theory highlights the role of group prototypes, the standard of what a member of that group should be. According to this theory, categorizing yourself within a group—thinking in terms of your social identity—makes you see yourself as reflecting the group prototype. Because all group members are like that basic standard, you come to feel largely interchangeable with them and believe that all group members think alike, the "right way." People who match the group prototype are more likely to be chosen as leaders, which reinforces what makes the group special and further accentuates why other groups are different and not as good.

This sense of solidarity and like-mindedness makes you feel secure, reducing the uncertainty of dealing with a complex world and with people who are different from you. It meets a basic human need by helping you feel that you understand the world and that you belong with others. Thus, people are particularly likely to seek and develop a strong group identity when they feel uncertain. Uncertainty can involve questions about personal worth, be related to the physical and social changes that occur through adolescence, or relate to social circumstances such as economic concerns.

Becoming an extremist   Although reducing uncertainty by increasing group allegiances is a normal way of coping with anxiety and diminished self-worth, it can have dire consequences. It can attract people to extremist groups. These groups are tightly organized, with clear and rigid rules, homogeneous memberships, a strong sense of mission, and strong and often charismatic leadership, all characteristics that can reduce uncertainty and make people feel secure (Hogg, 2011).

The need to reduce uncertainty promotes ethnocentric motivations, which in turn lead to competitive, discriminatory, and exploitative intergroup relations. Engaging in collective actions of this type not only reduces feelings of uncertainty but also helps to enhance feelings of group superiority, which restores self-esteem and confidence. These collective actions can continue to escalate into extreme violence, particularly when people who already identify strongly with the group encounter additional threat or uncertainty.

Palestinian Muslims and Israeli Jews with strong national and religious identities advocated greater support for violent action when they experienced greater feelings of uncertainty (Adelman, Hogg, & Levin, 2010). As we noted in Chapter 4, Alexander Haslam and Stephen Reicher (2007) have applied these principles to historical atrocities, including analyzing the actions of prominent Nazis during the Holocaust. Haslam and Reicher concluded that it was not blind obedience or extreme conformity that accounted for people's participation in genocide. Instead, it was the sense of identification with a group that had a true hatred for Jews, homosexuals, and gypsies, coupled with a sense of moral superiority that led people to commit atrocities.

Responding to diversity   Social categorization is a natural and necessary process, and feeling part of a group motivates us to think and behave in particular ways. We not only see those in our group as better than members of other groups, we usually like members of our group, and feel more comfortable and secure around them. Thus feeling part of a group makes us feel good about ourselves, like we belong and we work actively to give our group advantages over others. Although there is nothing inherently wrong with this motivation, this goal may be reached at the expense of other groups. We can feel better by thinking and saying bad things about other groups; we can have more resources if we discriminate against and harm other groups. And these measures can become extreme when a group believes that it is morally superior to another group and is justified in harming it.

The motivation to feel good about our group and ourselves often comes at the expense of other groups, both in terms of what we think of them and what we do to them. This is a fundamental diversity challenge. Group identity and affiliation are supposed to make people feel "welcome," but it often devolves into group animus or, at best, indifference. David Brooks (2003) wrote an article in *The Atlantic Monthly* entitled "People like us: We all pay lip service to the melting pot, but we really prefer the congealing pot." In this article, Brooks observes,

> Many of us live in absurdly unlikely groupings, because we have organized our lives that way. It's striking that the institutions that talk the most about diversity often practice it the least. For example, no group of people sings the diversity anthem more frequently and fervently than administrators at just such elite universities. But elite universities are amazingly undiverse in their values, politics, and mores. Professors in particular are drawn from a rather narrow segment of the population. If faculties reflected the general population, 32 percent of professors would be registered Democrats and 31 percent would be registered Republicans. Forty percent would be evangelical Christians. But a recent study of several universities by the conservative Center for the Study of Popular Culture and the American Enterprise Institute found that roughly 90 percent of those professors in the arts and sciences who had registered with a political party had registered Democratic. (Brooks, 2003)

Brooks concludes his essay with this point: "Look around at your daily life. Are you really in touch with the broad diversity of American life? Do you care?" (p. 32).

Psychology helps explain why people who should care often do not. In the next section, we further explore the powerful role of justification in how we see and treat different groups.

Confusing "What Is" with "What Should Be": Social Roles and System Justification

One of the most important developments in human history was the transition from hunting and gathering to agriculture. Agriculture prompted the development of large complex societies. These societies consisted of people in many different roles and many different groups that had to work together (Diamond, 1997). When people began to live in agricultural communities, for the first time they had to value the entire society rather than considering only their own personal welfare and the welfare of the group.

In complex societies, different people perform different roles: farmer, artisan, healer, or ruler. Inevitably, these roles, and the different groups that occupy them, are valued differently from one society to another. The United States tends to view itself as a classless society, yet whether or not it is as openly acknowledged, all societies are hierarchically organized, with different groups having different statuses and opportunities (Sidanius & Pratto, 1999). Power and privilege, which we discuss in detail in Chapter 10, determine intergroup relations in all societies. In the United States, the most blatant example of hierarchy was slavery, but hierarchy continues to determine intergroup relations today in less obvious ways.

Blaming the Victim: Attributions to Groups

The size and complexity of societies has broad implications for how we see diversity. Systematic social stratification of racial and ethnic groups means that members of some groups have more resources than others. In the United States, Whites have more wealth, better education, and better health than do Blacks or Latinos. In Chapter 5, we talked about the fundamental attribution error and the tendency for people to attribute a person's outcomes, particularly negative outcomes, to his or her personality. Imagine that you arrive from Mars and tour the United States. You see that Blacks and Latinos are more likely to live in poverty, be in jail, and have lower-paying jobs than Whites and Asians. If you have the same attributional biases as humans, what would you think? You would most likely think that it must be something about *them*. They must not be as smart or hardworking as Whites and Asians. The fundamental attribution error and its offspring, the ultimate attribution error (see Chapter 5), thus have critical implications for intergroup attitudes and relations.

Living in large societies makes us particularly susceptible to blaming the victim. People can empathize and take the perspective of another individual, but it is harder to empathize with a group of people, a faceless group. A series of studies demonstrated the robustness of this effect (Small, Loewenstein, & Slovic, 2007). The researchers presented participants with either factual information about widespread starvation of African children or a picture of a single little African girl with information about her need for food. Later, participants had the opportunity to donate money to help starving children in Africa. Participants gave over twice as much money, $2.83 versus $1.17, when they had been thinking about one child starving than about thousands of children starving. The researchers concluded that thinking about large groups of people suffering is overwhelming and produces "psychic numbing." Indeed, in this study participants actually felt worse about the situation when they thought about a single child starving than when they learned how widespread the problem was.

Judging Who People Are by What Jobs They Do: Social Roles

Besides the general tendency to blame groups for their disadvantaged status, people also form specific stereotypes of groups based on the social role they tend to occupy. Social role theory (Eagly & Wood, 2011) proposes that people infer the qualities of groups based on the different roles that members of a group occupy. This process seems like a logical inference. For example, in the United States, 96% of secretaries, 82% of elementary- and middle-school teachers, and 71% of waitstaff are women; 97% of construction workers, 96% of firefighters, and 93% of mechanical engineers are men (U.S. Bureau of Labor Statistics, 2010). It is not a coincidence that gender stereotypes portray women as nurturing, helpful, warm, and supportive and men as adventurous, brave, logical, and competent.

Social role theory proposes that it is not these different characteristics of women and men that lead to this pattern of occupational segregation, but rather it is the segregation by role that creates the stereotypes. As illustrated in Figure 6.2, biological, social, economic, and political factors produce systematic divisions of labor and the development of different social roles. Again, reflecting on human history, men's particular physical advantages in body size and strength gave them the edge over women in activities such as hunting, herding, and warfare. Women's responsibilities for child-rearing limited their ability to travel long distances, which these activities often require. By contrast, women assumed the duties needed for storing resources, raising children, and engaging in activities that supported social coordination. Thus, men and women developed not only different but complementary skills and behaviors necessary for the efficient functioning of society. These traditional skills and activities then gave rise to cultural stereotypes. Thus, when people think about the stereotypes of women as warm, they also automatically think of the complementary stereotype of men as competent (Jost & Kay, 2005).

Biology is not the only thing that creates different social roles. Economic and political forces also determine the roles of different groups. Slavery existed for economic reasons: It was the most inexpensive way to obtain the labor needed for the large agricultural expanses of the American South at the time (see Chapter 3). The institution of slavery, in turn, shaped the stereotypes of Blacks in ways that continue to have a profound social legacy. During the period of slavery, Blacks were portrayed as physically strong but intellectually childlike. The belief was that they needed to be controlled and taken care of for their own good. They were good for some jobs, but not for others.

Social role theory has three basic implications:

1. Because different roles give people more or less access to valued resources, roles become hierarchically organized. Because of their role in obtaining resources of

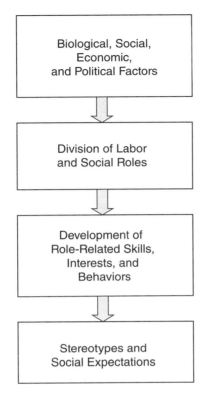

Figure 6.2. Eagly and Wood's Social Role Theory. Adapted from "Social Role Theory," by A. H. Eagly & W. Wood, 2011. In A. W. Kruglanski, E. T. Higgins, & P. A. M. Van Lange (Eds.), *Handbook of Theories in Social Psychology* (Vol. 2, pp. 458–476). Thousand Oaks, CA: Sage.

immediate need (food) and of warding off immediate threats (predators), men gained a traditional hierarchical advantage over women (Wood & Eagly, 2002).

2. Once established, stereotypes are proscriptive: They describe not only what groups of people *are* like but also what they *should* be like. The complementary stereotypes of men and women thus contributed to the stability of society. As a consequence, women who stayed in their traditional social "space" were upheld as social models, whereas those who aspired to positions of power faced resistance, prejudice, and discrimination. An assertive man is admired; an assertive woman, traditionally, has been shunned. Even when women do succeed in achieving social status, it comes at a social cost. They experience **backlash**: If they show that they are competent, then they are seen as less warm (Rudman & Glick, 2001).

3. Biology is not destiny: social roles vary as a function of environment, time, and technology. In environments where food and game were plentiful and people did not have to travel long distances to obtain them, women played a prominent role as hunters (Wood & Eagly, 2002). In our society, day care allows women flexibility

to pursue a range of occupational opportunities. In the United States today, the majority of people in the workforce are women, and the occupational status of women, although still lagging significantly behind that of men, is steadily increasing. As people see men and women in a variety of roles, gender stereotypes will weaken.

Because differentiated roles are essential for all social activities, even in very small groups, the roles people occupy determine what people expect of them and how they are treated. These social forces have very basic effects—biological (e.g., influencing level of testosterone, a hormone related to dominance) and psychological (e.g., shaping aspiration and motivation)—that guide what people feel, do, and even imagine. But, it is not only the case that roles shape people; people can also shape roles. The political movement for women's rights expanded opportunities for women, and the increase in women occupying positions of leadership in industry, government, and the military has fundamentally changed the way gender is perceived. Women are more interested in jobs offering more power and leadership opportunities, and people perceive women and men as increasingly similar in personality attributes (e.g., adventurous), cognitive abilities (e.g., reasoning and problem-solving), and physical qualities (e.g., strong) that were previously associated primarily with men (Diekman & Eagly, 2000; Eagly & Wood, 2011).

Gradual changes in group-based roles are not the only way to change social stereotypes. A single dramatic example can change the way we think of groups. The nomination and election of Barack Obama is a clear example. Obama changed the way Whites spontaneously thought of Blacks: he immediately came to mind as a positive example, which undermined traditional racial stereotypes and reduced prejudicial thoughts (Plant et al., 2009). Moreover, Obama's election provides an important role model for Black children. Black middle-school students who were asked to think about Obama's election demonstrated stronger beliefs in their own ability to succeed academically and were less adversely affected by the knowledge that others stereotype Blacks as academically inferior (Purdie-Vaughns, Summer, & Cohen, 2011). Thus, changing how we see members of different groups fit into the fabric of society substantially changes how we think and feel about these groups.

Traditional social roles and values, however, permeate the way people think about themselves and react to different situations. Women's traditional roles not only involve their positions at work but also how society sees them as sexual "objects." The role of women as sexual objects has profound impact on how they are treated and how they feel and act (see Box 6.1).

Maintaining the Status Quo: System Justification

Although it is possible to change the way we think about different groups in society, psychological forces push to maintain the structure of society as it is. According to system justification theory (Jost & Hunyady, 2002), people not only want to hold favorable attitudes about themselves and their own groups, but they also want to hold favorable attitudes about the overarching social order (system justification). System justification relates to the processes that people engage in to maintain and

Box 6.1. Feeling Like a Body: Objectification

Social expectations of women, based on their social roles, often produce sexual objectification. Sexual **objectification** occurs when a person is treated as a mere body that exists for the sexual use and pleasure of others. In popular magazines, for example, photographs of women are more likely to frame their entire body, while pictures of men are more likely to frame only their faces (Archer, Iritani, Kimes, & Barrios, 1983). Moreover, in contemporary culture, women are regularly treated as sex objects and are routinely portrayed in sexually objectifying ways in the media (Jackman, 1994; Figure 6.3).

Self-objectification influences college women in important ways. It affects how they perform academically and socially. In one study, for example, college women and men were recruited for research supposedly about consumer behavior (Fredrickson, Roberts, Noll, Quinn, & Twenge, 1998). They were asked to try on and rate different garments. Participants were told, "Clothing and style of dress can often have an impact on people's views of themselves. Please take a moment to think about how wearing this particular item of clothing makes you feel about yourself."

Figure 6.3. Advertisers Frequently Objectify Women to Market Even Products That Have Little Directly to do With Sex. Magazine Advertisement for Kahlua. Image Courtesy of The Advertising Archives.

Some participants tried on a sweater and others tried on a swimsuit in front of a full-length mirror. Women in the swimsuit condition felt a particularly high level of body shame, much higher than those in the sweater condition. Men displayed a low level of body shame regardless of whether they wore a swimsuit or a sweater. In addition, after getting dressed in their regular clothes and taking a supposedly unrelated math test, women showed residual effects of self-objectification. What men previously wore had no effect whatsoever on how well they did on the math test. In contrast, women who tried on the swimsuit performed substantially worse on the math test than did women who tried on the sweater. In addition to performing poorly on tests of academic achievement, women who feel objectified also are less socially assertive and more submissive in their interactions, particularly with men (Saguy, Quinn, Dovidio, & Pratto, 2010).

Although the effects of objectification on women are now well documented, information about how women of different ages, races, and ethnicities might differ in their experiences and responses is much rarer. For instance, contemporary standards of attractiveness are especially relevant to young women, and young women place more importance on their physical attractiveness and appearance than do older women (Tiggemann & Lynch, 2001). Thus, younger women likely experience more objectification than older women. With respect to race and ethnicity, Black, Asian, Latino, and White college women generally felt more objectified when they wore a swimsuit than a sweater, but Black and Asian women reported greater objectification than White women, while Latinas felt somewhat less (Hebl, King, & Lin, 2004).

Understanding the experiences of members of different groups thus requires a recognition of **intersectionality**, how different combinations of (for example) race, ethnicity, gender, and age affect not only how people are perceived but also how they experience and respond to different situations. There is important diversity within diversity.

1. What psychological or social factors would lead women to engage in self-objectification?
2. Would feeling objectified have different consequences for women of different races and ethnicities, and, if so, what different effects might feeling objectified have on Black, White, Latina, and Asian women, as well as women from other groups?

reinforce the current social structure. Like social dominance theory, which we introduced in Chapter 4, system justification theory emphasizes how society shapes what we think is right and how society should be: These are called **system-justifying ideologies** because they rationalize, and thus reinforce and perpetuate, the hierarchical structure and corresponding disparities in society as they currently are.

System justification has obvious advantages for members of high status or dominant groups, but **system justification theory** makes the counterintuitive prediction that members of disadvantaged groups will also support the current social system.

For example, southern Italians, who have been traditionally poorer and viewed less favorably than northern Italians, endorse negative stereotypes of their group, particularly those who were more traditional and politically conservative (Jost, Burgess, & Mosso, 2001). Complex societies are essential to our everyday lives, and thus people are motivated to see the different roles of groups within them as legitimate and just.

If, as system justification theory suggests, people try to see the social system as fair and just, then they should see the way society *is* as the way it *should be*. This effect should be particularly strong for people who feel dependent on the current system.

In a study by Kay et al. (2009), for instance, experimenters tried to increase female Canadian students' feelings of dependency by having them read a newspaper article, supposedly from the *Toronto Star*, indicating that the government's actions and the quality of services it provides has a profound influence on Canadian citizens' lives. Students in a low-dependency condition read a similar article, but it emphasized that the policies of the government had negligible effects on what people do on a daily basis. Participants next read a brief description of the responsibilities of Canadian members of Parliament, accompanied by a graph showing that currently only 20% of the members of Parliament were women. Consistent with system justification theory, women who were led to believe that they were highly dependent on the government were more likely to defend the status quo. These women were less likely than those who believed that they were low in dependency to endorse statements that there should be more women in politics and in Parliament. From their perspective, having only 20% female members of Parliament was just fine. System justification theory thus accounts for the fact that low-status group members often support the status quo, often at a cost to themselves and fellow group members (see Jost, Banaji, & Nosek, 2004).

In Chapter 5 we discussed how seeing somebody as a member of your own group rather than as a member of a different group automatically transforms how you think about the person. You tend to like, trust, and care about members of your group. In this chapter, we further show that people are motivated to see their group as better than others, and they will treat members of other groups in ways that promote their group's advantage. Simply thinking about how your group is better than others or taking pleasure at another group's misfortune makes you feel better about your group and consequently about yourself. But what happens when groups actually come in contact? As we will see in the next section, when groups come together, conflict may ensue.

Slipping into the Darkness: Groups in Competition

A brief ride on the subway brings me into contact with people from many different races and ethnic heritages, people who appear rich and those who appear poor, and people of all ages, sizes, and shapes. Contact between groups is inevitable. In Chapter 9, we will focus on how interactions between members of different groups shape the nature of intergroup relations. In this section, we consider what happens when groups encounter each other.

"You Dirty Rattler": Conflict between Groups

How a group responds to others depends most basically on whether the members see the actions of the other group as beneficial or harmful. According to **realistic group conflict theory** (Campbell, 1965; Sherif, 1966), seeing other groups as competitors arouses bias, leads people to discriminate, and often produces open conflict. It doesn't take much to create conflict. As we saw in the section on social identity theory, simply coming in contact with another group can motivate us to see our group as better than the other group. As a result, we will think and behave in ways that give our group an advantage. This process was illustrated in the classic Robbers Cave experiment (Sherif, Harvey, White, Hood, & Sherif, 1961).

In 1954, Sherif and his colleagues conducted a field study on intergroup conflict in an area adjacent to Robbers Cave State Park in Oklahoma. In this study, twenty-two 12-year-old boys attending summer camp were randomly assigned to two groups. The groups were kept apart, and the members of each group were unaware of the other group's existence. During this week, the boys not only got to know one another but also developed their own sense of group identity. One group named itself the Eagles, and the other group called itself the Rattlers.

During the second week the investigators brought the two groups together. The boys were not only surprised to see the other group but also suspicious and concerned. Rumors developed. One of the Rattlers heard voices on a nearby trail, and the next morning he told the others that "those guys were at our [baseball] diamond." Another Rattler responded, "They better not be in our swimming hole!" By the end of the second week, each group insisted that it wanted to challenge the other group in competitive games.

The experimenters satisfied their wish. They had the groups compete against each other in athletic activities such as tug-of-war, baseball, and touch football, with the winning group receiving prizes. The groups quickly developed stereotypes and engaged in prejudiced behavior. Group members regularly exchanged verbal insults ("ladies first") and name calling ("sissies," "stinkers," "pigs," "bums," "cheaters," and "communists"). These exchanges soon escalated into physical conflict. There was genuine hostility between these groups. Each group conducted raids on the other's cabins that resulted in the destruction and theft of property. The boys carried sticks, baseball bats, and socks filled with rocks as weapons. Intergroup conflict began to spiral. Even when they were not in direct competition, the boys showed animosity toward each other. In the dining hall, some of the Eagles protested that they did not want to eat in the same place as Rattlers. Fistfights broke out, and food and garbage fights erupted in the dining hall. Conflict became more and more intense.

Threatening What We Have and What We Are: Realistic and Symbolic Conflict

The Robbers Cave study showed how easy it is to arouse threat between groups through competition. Competition fuels much of the racial and ethnic bias we see in society today (Norton & Sommers, 2011). Like the boys in the Robbers Cave study showed, feelings of threat generally lead to bias and stereotyping between groups, which can escalate to physical conflict (Riek, Mania, & Gaertner, 2006). Threat comes in at least two different forms, though: realistic threat and symbolic threat. **Realistic threat** is the concern that another group will harm our health, take our group's resources (e.g., jobs) or territory (in Robbers Cave, the baseball diamond). After the terrorist attack on the United States in 2001, Americans, who felt severely threatened, showed an unprecedented spike in anti-immigration sentiment. Even today, when the intensity of threat has subsided, other forms of realistic threat can create opposition to immigration. Groups against immigration often argue that immigrants expose us to new and dangerous forms of disease.

This is a relatively common way of mobilizing people to fear immigrants and immigration. Such insinuations about immigrants, even when not based in fact, have a lasting effect. People may wonder about the truth of the statement, but would they want to risk their children's health?

The other kind of threat is symbolic threat. **Symbolic threat** involves perceptions that another group challenges our core values and way of life. For example, have you ever heard statements like these? "They have different family values." "They have a different conception of what American culture should be." These statements indicate symbolic threat to values people cherish (Stephan, Renfro, Esses, Stephan, & Martin, 2005).

Although you might think that physical threats would produce greater bias and ignite conflict more readily than symbolic threat, each type of threat contributes to bias and both predict bias to about the same degree (Riek et al., 2006). In fact, in his well-known book, *The Clash of Civilizations and the Remaking of World Order*, Samuel P. Huntington (1996) argued that the main source of conflict in the future would be about symbolic issues—cultural and religious differences. In an article that summarized his thesis, Huntington (1993) wrote:

> The great divisions among humankind and the dominating source of conflict will be cultural. Nation states will remain the most powerful actors in world affairs, but the principal conflicts of global politics will occur between nations and groups of different civilizations. The clash of civilizations will dominate global politics. The fault lines between civilizations will be the battle lines of the future. (p. 22)

Conflict over symbolic issues may be more likely to escalate and more difficult to resolve than conflict over material possessions. It might be possible, for example, to reach a political compromise between Israeli Jews and Palestinians over statehood and physical boundaries. However, there is no compromise when the discussions about territories involve "holy lands." In the United States, we saw heated debate about building a mosque near "ground zero," the site of the World Trade Center. President Obama identified why the debate was so intense (http://www.nytimes.com/2010/08/14/us/politics/14obama.html): The issues were highly symbolic. President Obama acknowledged on the one hand, "I understand the emotions that this issue engenders. Ground zero is, indeed, hallowed ground." On the other hand, he cited basic principles that symbolize America:

This is America, and our commitment to religious freedom must be unshakable. The principle that people of all faiths are welcome in this country, and will not be treated differently by their government, is essential to who we are.

When two opposing principles are involved, people typically stand on one side or the other; there is little compromise in principles. Where do you stand on this issue?

There's an important issue for the psychology of diversity here as well. Two valid and engrained principles may conflict. With prejudice and racism, issues of biased behavior helped draw lines between right and wrong, good and bad. But here, the conflict is between good and good. Either/or approaches are inadequate to resolve it, and a both/and resolution may be better but is hard to achieve. A role for a psychology of diversity is how we may move toward a both/and approach to issues created by expanding diversity in our institutions and society.

So far in this chapter, we have seen that people not only initially see differences between groups to which they belong (in-groups) and groups to which they don't belong (out-groups), but are also motivated to see their own groups as better. And they work hard to give their group advantages and support and to justify a system that benefits their group, even if it is unfair. In addition, people are easily threatened by other groups, and these feelings of threat to our material possessions or values arouse intergroup bias and conflict. What can be done to reverse this downward spiral in intergroup relations, reduce intergroup conflict, and improve intergroup attitudes?

What Can We Do? Changing How Groups Relate

In the previous chapter on social cognition and social categorization, we noted that these processes reflected fundamental principles of human behavior that were difficult, if not impossible, to change. One solution was, basically, "If you can't beat them, join them": the recategorization strategy was designed to get people who typically thought of others in terms of being members of different groups (Blacks and Whites) to think of themselves as members of a common group (students at the same university). Recategorization does not really eliminate in-group favoritism; instead, it harnesses and redirects it. Once I see you as a member of my group, I begin to show you all sorts of favoritism. However, "we" may still not like other groups very much. The approaches we can use based on principles covered in this chapter involve interventions that build upon the idea that competition increases intergroup conflict while cooperation improves intergroup relations.

The basic idea is that we dislike groups that we see as competitors, because they threaten us; we like groups that we see as cooperating with us, because they help us. How can this idea be applied to the conflict between Eagles and Rattlers in the Robber's Cave study? Recall that the two groups of boys intensely disliked one another, frequently coming to blows. The experimenters tried bringing them together under neutral, non-competitive conditions (to eat, to watch a movie). However, that did not calm the ferocity of the exchanges. It only made matters worse. However, this is not how Sherif and his colleagues wanted or intended to leave things.

Achieving More Together Than Alone: Superordinate Goals

The investigators reasoned that if competition increases bias, then maybe cooperation would reduce it. Still, the challenge was to find a way to get Eagles and Rattlers to cooperate. The solution was to create **superordinate goals**, outcomes that are mutually desired by different groups that can accomplished only if the groups work together. To achieve the goals, the two groups *had* to cooperate.

As one example of a superordinate goal, Sherif and his colleagues arranged for Rattlers and Eagles to depart in separate trucks for an overnight camping trip. Shortly after the boys arrived at the campsite, the driver of one of the trucks said that he would drive down the road to get food. As planned, though, the truck would not start. The boys became hungrier and hungrier. The boys tried, but neither group could move the truck to get food.

Then one of the boys had an idea. He yelled, "Let's get our tug-of-war rope and have a tug-of-war against the truck." Someone else shouted, "Twenty of us can pull it for sure" (Sherif et al., 1961, p. 171). And sure enough, it worked. "We won the tug-of-war against the truck!" said one of the Eagles. Sherif et al. reported, "This cry was echoed with satisfaction by others from both groups. Immediately following this success, there was much intermingling of groups, friendly talk, and backslapping" (Sherif et al., 1961, p. 171). One superordinate goal was not enough to eliminate bias and conflict, but after a few more such activities the boys were all friends again. Whereas competition breeds enemies, cooperation around superordinate goals makes friends. Since then, psychologists have fashioned a number of different interventions (e.g., cooperative learning exercises; Slavin & Cooper, 1999) based on the idea that putting members of different groups together in situations where they have to cooperate to succeed will improve intergroup relations.

Putting the Pieces Together: Jigsaw Classroom

The **jigsaw classroom** is one particularly effective strategy that has been used in schools (Aronson, 2004). The jigsaw classroom gets its name from a jigsaw puzzle, a puzzle for which all of the pieces are needed to complete a picture. The strategy is to replace competition in classrooms with cooperation. Instead of students separating themselves from others to work independently or seeking to distinguish themselves from others with superior performance, the jigsaw classroom mandates interdependence and cooperation. Students are placed into learning groups, with each person having responsibility for a proportion of the information needed to complete a task. Each student thus has a unique and valuable piece of the information that, like a jigsaw piece, is needed to obtain the total correct solution. Children learn that the old competitive ways will not work and they must now listen to others, ask appropriate questions, and regard each other as mutually valuable resources for the learning enterprise.

In an example of this exercise, students are put into a five-person jigsaw group. The group is diverse with respect to gender, race, ethnicity, and other qualities. The students are presented with a complex problem. For instance, the task may be to understand what caused World War II. Each student has a different piece of the puzzle, which can include Hitler's rise to power, Japan's entry into the war, Britain's role, the Soviet Union's stand against the Nazis, and the United States' efforts in the war. Each child then becomes the group expert on a piece of the puzzle. They put the experts' pieces together, asking questions and cooperating, to get the full picture of World War II.

Besides the obvious educational benefits of jigsaw classroom exercises, they have a significant impact on intergroup attitudes. In a classic experiment, researchers introduced the intervention to 10 fifth-grade classes in seven different schools in the then recently desegregated public schools of Austin, Texas (Blaney, Stephan, Rosenfield, Aronson, & Sikes, 1977). The experimental classrooms were conducted three days a week for 6 weeks. At the end, children in jigsaw classroom, compared with students from other classrooms in the same schools, liked others more, both within and outside their own ethnic or racial group (Anglos, Blacks, Latinos), and liked school more.

Another study (Lucker, Rosenfield, Sikes, & Aronson, 1976) showed that the jigsaw classroom also improved the academic performance of Black and Latino students. Therefore, putting students into an interdependent, cooperative relationship and acknowledging the value of each student's different contribution improved their level of liking, degree of friendship, self-esteem, and academic performance, a win–win situation for all students. The jigsaw classroom remains a popular and effective intervention today (Aronson, 2004).

Creating a sense of cooperative interdependence between individuals or groups can create a sense of common in-group identity, something we talked about in the previous chapter. In the Robbers Cave study, after the tug-of-war with the truck described above, the Rattlers and Eagles more frequently used the word "we" to refer to all boys at the camp. On the way home on the bus, they sang together (about Oklahoma, where all the children were from) and no longer talked of themselves as members of different groups.

When people have highly valued social identities, such as racial or ethnic identities, the thought of becoming "one" in a way that makes them abandon their distinctive group identities may be threatening. The next strategy for improving intergroup relations, **mutual intergroup differentiation**, involves maintaining distinct group identities, which limits threats to valued social identity, but within the context of cooperative interdependence between groups (Brown & Hewstone, 2005).

You Complete Me (Us): Mutual Intergroup Differentiation

Because people often feel threatened when pressured to abandon a valued social identity, a way to reduce bias is to allow groups to maintain distinctive identities but to forge a cooperative connection between them. Diversity in the context of cooperation is a good thing. Members of different groups can bring different ways of thinking, experiences, and skills to the same problem, and members of both groups can benefit from the differences that exist between the groups. Instead of being afraid of difference, diversity becomes a strength.

In Chapter 5, we described an experiment in which two groups talked about ranking different objects in terms of their survival value after a crash-landing in northern Minnesota in the winter (Gaertner, Mann, Murrell, & Dovidio, 1989). Normally, when members of two groups come together in this situation, they compete to show which group has the best answer, and their bias increases over time. What if the groups perform slightly different tasks? One group ranks the best items for survival if the survivors decided to wait by the plane to be rescued, while the other group ranks the items that would be best if they tried to hike to safety. There would be less direct competition, but the basic differences between the groups still produce bias. But what if the task involves getting the best answer (which will earn a prize) for survival regardless of whether the survivors stay with the plane or hike to safety. The difference between the groups is now an asset, and when they cooperate to come up with the best answer, intergroup bias disappears (Dovidio, Gaertner, & Validzic, 1998). The meaning of diversity, whether it is seen as bad or good and whether it divides us or brings us together, depends on how the problem and challenges are framed.

Besides not threatening meaningful group identities, another advantage of the mutual intergroup differentiation approach is that it makes it more likely that my positive experience and sense of connection with members of another group will generalize in good ways to my feelings about other members of the group (see our discussion of personalization in Chapter 5). If you think of me as a unique individual or have a close personal connection to me, even though you do not like Muslims as a whole, you may resolve your dissonance by seeing me as an exception. Thus you can like me but still think that other Muslims hate America. If you think of me only in terms of me as a student at your university, you will like me, but maybe not Muslims who are not at the same school. However, if we have a good relationship while you continue to recognize and respect that I am different from you, your good feelings about me will likely generalize to other Muslims. Of course, people do not fully erase our group memberships from their minds when we interact in personalized ways or with a common in-group identity, so some positive generalization occurs in both cases. Nevertheless, this kind of generalization, which is even stronger when you see me as a typical Muslim, is a particular strength of mutual intergroup differentiation—recognizing differences between groups but appreciating their value in our cooperative pursuit of the same goal (Hewstone, Hassebrauck, Wirth, & Waenke, 2000).

Which Approach Is Best?

In this section, we have discussed three ways to reduce bias and conflict between groups: superordinate goals, jigsaw classroom, and mutual intergroup differentiation. In the previous chapter, we considered two other approaches: decategorization and recategorization. So which one is best? Each has its strengths and limitations. In addition, as we mentioned in the previous chapter, rather than viewing different techniques as competing approaches, we see them as complementary tools that we can use to combat prejudice, stereotyping, and discrimination. Sometimes one tool may be more appropriate than the others in a given situation. White, Black, Asian, and Latino college students may all share a university identity. Appealing to common identity is therefore quite easy. Israelis and Palestinians typically see much less in common. Acknowledging difference while encouraging cooperation on a specific task would likely be more effective in that case.

These tools can also be used sequentially. When groups are in heated conflict, members may be less threatened by first getting to know each other on a personal basis, then recognizing common goals, and then securing the relationship through the acceptance of common identity. The bottom line, though, is that just because we see others as different does not mean that those differences have to divide us. Diversity can be a strength because, although we may be different on some dimensions, we may be fundamentally similar on others. Psychology can show us how to bridge difference and use diversity for the benefit of all.

Summary

Our need to simplify our social world and make it more understandable by categorizing people into in-groups and out-groups has profound implications. According to social identity theory, because we derive our sense of self-worth from our social identity, we are motivated to make our group better than others. Discrimination against others who are different ensures the advantage of our group. When we think of ourselves as group members rather than in terms of individual personal identity, self-categorization theory says that we think, feel, and behave the way we believe a good group member should. We feel deeply connected to members of our group in a broad, depersonalized way, and we see ourselves as fundamentally different from people in different groups.

Because of the way we all cognitively and socially differentiate others, groups occupy different roles in society. Social forces segregate different groups into different roles (women and men; immigrants; Blacks, Latinos, Whites, and Asians). When we see members of different groups in these different social roles, we assume that these groups have these different qualities: Women are warm and nurturing, while men are intelligent but cold. These roles and beliefs then become the standards for what we believe *should* be. Our need to see the world as consistent and fair often leads members of disadvantaged groups, as well as advantaged groups, to justify the current social structure and work to perpetuate it, even if it is unfair.

However, diversity brings great value and resources to a society, so it is important to recognize and appreciate qualities that make groups different. This recognition of difference is not threatening when we feel our groups are cooperating to achieve a mutually desired goal. Thus, although we are keenly attuned to seeing similarity and difference, the meaning and consequences of diversity depend on how we choose to frame it as individuals and as a society.

Questions for Thinking and Knowing

1. How do your stereotypes of groups reflect the kinds of jobs or activities that you see them occupy? What might account for the current social roles of these stereotyped groups?

2. Think of groups of students that you know who hang around together. What do you see them doing to increase their feelings of "positive distinctiveness" and enhance their collective self-esteem?

3. We usually think of diversity in terms of race/ethnicity, gender, and, to some extent, religion. However, the article by David Brooks cited in this chapter talks about another dimension of diversity: political affiliation. Brooks reported that university professors are overwhelmingly Democrats. If this is correct, are students being deprived of this form of diversity in college and graduate school?

4. How does objectification of women affect them across the lifespan? How might experiences with objectification at a young age affect a woman as she gets older? Do men ever experience objectification and does it affect them differently or in the same was as it does women? Why would objectification be different for members of different race and ethnic groups?

5. System justification theory suggests that societies develop ideologies and cultural beliefs that help maintain the status quo. Is the American belief that "anyone who works hard enough can succeed" a system-justifying belief?

Key Terms

Backlash
Intersectionality
Jigsaw classroom
Mutual intergroup differentiation
Objectification
Optimal distinctiveness theory
Personal identity
Realistic group conflict theory
Realistic threat

Schadenfreude
Self-categorization theory
Social identity
Social identity theory
Superordinate goals
Symbolic threat
System justification theory
System-justifying ideologies

References

Abrams, D., & Hogg, M. E. (2010). Social identity and self-categorization. In J. F. Dovidio, M. Hewston, P. Glick, & V. M. Esses (Eds.), *The SAGE handbook of prejudice, stereotyping, and discrimination* (pp. 179–194). London: Sage.

Adelman, J. R., Hogg, M. A., & Levin, S. (2010). *Support for political action as a function of religiousness and nationalism under uncertainty: A study of Muslims, Jews, Palestinians and Israelis in Israel.* Unpublished manuscript, Department of Psychology, Claremont Graduate University, Claremont, CA.

Archer, D., Iritani, B., Kimes, D. D., & Barrios, M. (1983). Face-ism: Five studies of sex differences in facial prominence. *Journal of Personality and Social Psychology, 45,* 725–735.

Aronson, E. (2004). Reducing hostility and building compassion: Lessons from the jigsaw classroom. In A. G. Miller (Ed.), *The social psychology of good and evil.* New York: Guilford Press.

Blaney, N., Stephan, C., Rosenfield, D., Aronson, E., & Sikes, J. (1977). Interdependence in the classroom: A field study. *Journal of Educational Psychology, 69,* 139–146.

Branscombe, N. R., Schmitt, M. T., & Harvey, R. D. (1999). Perceiving pervasive discrimination among African Americans: Implications for group identification and well-being. *Journal of Personality and Social Psychology, 77,* 135–149.

Brewer, M. B. (1991). On the social self: On being the same and different at the same time. *Personality and Social Psychology Bulletin, 17,* 475–482.

Brooks, D. (2003). People like us: We all pay lip service to the melting pot, but we really prefer the congealing pot. *The Atlantic Monthly, 292*(2), 29–32.

Brown, R., & Hewstone, M. (2005). An integrative theory of intergroup contact. In M. P. Zanna (Ed.), *Advances in experimental social psychology* (Vol. 37, pp. 255–343). San Diego, CA: Academic Press.

Campbell, D. T. (1965). Ethnocentric and other altruistic motives. In D. Levine (Ed.), *Nebraska symposium on motivation* (Vol. 13, pp. 283–311). Lincoln, NE: University of Nebraska Press.

Cialdini, R. B., Borden, R. J., Thorne, A., Walker, M. R., Freeman, S., & Sloan, L. R. (1976). Basking in reflected glory: Three (football) field studies. *Journal of Personality and Social Psychology, 34,* 366–375.

Diamond, J. (1997). *Guns, germs, and steel: The fates of human societies.* New York: Norton.

Diekman, A. B., & Eagly, A. H. (2000). Stereotypes as dynamic constructs: Women and men of the past, present, and future. *Personality and Social Psychology Bulletin, 26,* 1171–1188.

Dovidio, J. F., Gaertner, S. L., & Validzic, A. (1998). Intergroup bias: Status, differentiation, and a common in-group identity. *Journal of Personality and Social Psychology, 75,* 109–120.

Eagly, A. H., & Wood, W. (2011). Social role theory. In A. W. Kruglanski, E. T. Higgins, & P. A. M. Van Lange (Eds.), *Handbook of theories in social psychology* (Vol. 2, pp. 458–476). Thousand Oaks, CA: Sage.

Fredrickson, B. L., Roberts, T. A., Noll, S. M., Quinn, D. M., & Twenge, J. M. (1998). That swimsuit becomes you: Sex differences in self-objectification, restrained eating, and math performance. *Journal of Personality and Social Psychology, 75,* 269–284.

Gaertner, S. L., Mann, J. A., Murrell, A. J., & Dovidio, J. F. (1989). Reduction of intergroup bias: the benefits of recategorization. *Journal of Personality and Social Psychology, 57,* 239–249.

Haslam, S. A., & Reicher, S. (2007). Beyond the banality of evil: Three dynamics of an interactionist social psychology of tyranny. *Personality and Social Psychology Bulletin, 33,* 615–622.

Hebl, M. R., King, E. B., & Lin, J. (2004). The swimsuit becomes us all: Gender, ethnicity, and self-objectification. *Personality and Social Psychology Bulletin, 30,* 1322–1331.

Hewstone, M., Hassebrauck, M., Wirth, A., & Waenke, M. (2000). Pattern of disconfirming information and processing instructions as determinants of stereotype change. *British Journal of Social Psychology, 39,* 399–411.

Hogg, M. A. (2010). Human groups, social categories, and collective self: Social identity and the management of self-uncertainty. In R. Arkin, K. C. Oleson, & P. J. Carroll (Eds.), *Handbook of the uncertain self* (pp. 401–420). New York: Psychology Press.

Hogg, M. A. (2011). Self-uncertainty, social identity, and the solace of extremism. In M. A. Hogg & D. Blaylock (Eds.), *Extremism and the psychology of uncertainty.* Oxford: Wiley-Blackwell. doi: 10.1002/9781444344073.ch2

Huntington, S. P. (1993). The clash of civilizations? *Foreign Affairs, 72,* 22–49.

Huntington, S. P. (1996). *The clash of civilizations and the remaking of world order.* New York: Simon & Schuster.

Jackman, M. R. (1994). *The velvet glove.* Berkeley, CA: University of California Press.

Jetten, J., Schmitt, M. T., Branscombe, N. R., & McKimmie, B. M. (2005). Suppressing the negative effect of devaluation on group identification: The role of intergroup differentiation and intragroup respect. *Journal of Experimental Social Psychology, 41,* 208–215.

Jetten, J., Spears, R., & Postmes, T. (2004). Intergroup distinctiveness and differentiation: A meta-analytic integration. *Journal of Personality and Social Psychology, 86,* 862–879.

Jost, J. T., Banaji, M., & Nosek, B. A. (2004). A decade of System Justification Theory: Accumulated evidence of conscious and unconscious bolstering of the status quo. *Political Psychology, 25,* 881–919.

Jost, J. T., Burgess, D., & Mosso, C. O. (2001). Conflicts of legitimation among the self, group, and system: The integrative potential of system justification theory. In J. T. Jost & B. Major (Eds.), *The psychology of legitimacy: Emerging perspectives on ideology, justice, and intergroup relations* (pp. 3–32). Cambridge: Cambridge University Press.

Jost, J. T., & Hunyady, O. (2002). The psychology of system justification and the palliative function of ideology. In W. Stroebe & M. Hewstone (Eds.), *European review of social psychology* (Vol. 13, pp. 111–153). Hove, UK: Psychology Press/Taylor & Francis.

Jost, J. T., & Kay, A. C. (2005). Exposure to benevolent sexism and complementary gender stereotypes: Consequences for specific and diffuse forms of system justification. *Journal of Personality and Social Psychology, 88,* 498–509.

Kay, A. C., Gaucher, D., Peach, J. M., Laurin, K., Friesen, J., Zanna, M. P., & Spencer, S. J. (2009). Inequality, discrimination, and the power of the status quo: Direct evidence for a motivation to see the way things are as the way they should be. *Journal of Personality and Social Psychology, 97,* 421–434.

Lucker, G. W., Rosenfield, D., Sikes, J., & Aronson, E. (1976). Performance in the interdependent classroom. *American Education Research Journal, 13,* 115–123.

Mullen, B., Brown, R. J., & Smith, C. (1992). In-group bias as a function of salience, relevance, and status: An integration. *European Journal of Social Psychology, 22,* 103–122.

Norton, M. I., & Sommers, S. R. (2011). Whites see racism as a zero-sum game that they are now losing. *Perspectives on Psychological Science, 6,* 215–218.

Plant, E. A., Devine, P. G., Cox, W. T., Columb, C., Miller, S. L., Goplen, J., & Peruche, B. M. (2009). The Obama effect: Decreasing implicit prejudice and stereotyping. *Journal of Experimental Social Psychology, 45,* 961–964.

Purdie-Vaughns, V., Summer, R., & Cohen, G. L. (2011). Sash and Malia: Re-envisioning African-American youth. In G. S. Parks & M. W. Hughy (Eds.), *The Obamas and a (post) racial America?* (pp. 166–190). New York: Oxford University Press.

Riek, B. M., Mania, E. W., & Gaertner, S. L. (2006). Intergroup threat and out-group attitudes: A meta-analytic review. *Personality and Social Psychology Review, 10,* 336–353.

Rudman, L. A., & Glick, P. (2001). Prescriptive gender stereotypes and backlash toward agentic women. *Journal of Social Issues, 57,* 743–762.

Saguy, T., Quinn, D. M., Dovidio, J. F., & Pratto, F. (2010). Interacting like a body: Objectification can lead women to narrow their presence in social interactions. *Psychological Science, 21,* 178–182.

Sherif, M. (1966). *Group conflict and cooperation: Their social psychology.* London: Routledge and Kegan Paul.

Sherif, M., Harvey, O. J., White, B. J., Hood, W. R., & Sherif, C. W. (1961). *Intergroup conflict and cooperation: The Robbers Cave experiment.* Norman, OK: University of Oklahoma Book Exchange.

Shih, M., Pittinsky, T. L., & Ambady, N. (1999). Stereotype susceptibility: Identity salience and shifts in quantitative performance. *Psychological Science, 10,* 80–83.

Shih, M., & Sanchez, D. T. (2005). Perspectives and research on the positive and negative implications of having multiple racial identities. *Psychological Bulletin, 131,* 569–591.

Shih, M., & Sanchez, D. T. (2009). When race becomes even more complex: Toward understanding the landscape of multiracial identity and experiences. *Journal of Social Issues, 65,* 1–11.

Shih, M., Sanchez, D. T., & Ho, G. C. (2010). Costs and benefits of switching among multiple social identities. In R. J. Crisp (Ed.), *The psychology of social and cultural diversity* (pp. 62–83). Malden, MA: Wiley-Blackwell.

Sidanius, J., & Pratto, F. (1999). *Social dominance: An intergroup theory of social hierarchy and oppression.* New York: Cambridge University Press.

Slavin, R., & Cooper, R. (1999). Improving intergroup relations: Lessons learned from cooperative learning programs. *Journal of Social Issues, 55,* 647–663.

Small, D. A., Loewenstein, G., & Slovic, P. (2007). Sympathy and callousness: The impact of deliberative thought on donations to identifiable and statistical donations. *Organizational Behavior and Human Decision Processes, 102,* 143–153.

Smith, R. H., Powell, C. A. J., Combs, D. J. Y., & Shirtz, D. R. (2009). Exploring the when and why of schadenfreude. *Social and Personality Compass, 3,* 530–546.

Stephan, W. G., Renfro, C. L., Esses, V. M., Stephan, C. W., & Martin, T. (2005). The effects of feeling threatened on attitudes toward immigrants. *International Journal of Intercultural Relations, 29,* 1–19.

Swann, W. B., Jr, Gómez, A., Huici, C., Morales, J. F., & Hixon, J. G. (2010). Identity fusion and self-sacrifice: Arousal as a catalyst of pro-group fighting, dying, and helping behavior. *Journal of Personality and Social Psychology, 99,* 824–841.

Tajfel, H., & Turner, J. C. (1979). An integrative theory of intergroup conflict. In W. G. Austin & S. Worchel (Eds.), *The social psychology of intergroup relations* (pp. 33–48). Monterey, CA: Brooks/Cole.

Tiggemann, M., & Lynch, J. E. (2001). Body image across the life span in adult women: The role of self-objectification. *Developmental Psychology, 37,* 243–253.

Turner, J. C., Hogg, M. A., Oakes, P. J., Reicher, S. D., & Wetherell, M. S. (1987). *Rediscovering the social group: A self-categorization theory.* Oxford: Basil Blackwell.

U.S. Bureau of Labor Statistics. (2010). Employed persons by detailed occupation, sex, race, and Hispanic or Latino ethnicity. Retrieved on July 19, 2011, from http://www.bls.gov/cps/cpsaat11.pdf

Vandiver, B. J., Cross, W. E., Jr, Worrell, F. C., & Fhagen-Smith, P. E. (2002). Validating the Cross Racial Identity Scale. *Journal of Counseling Psychology, 49,* 71–85.

Verkuyten, M., & Hagendoorn, L. (1998). Prejudice and self-categorization: The variable role of authoritarianism and in-group stereotypes. *Personality and Social Psychology Bulletin, 24,* 99–110.

Wood, W., & Eagly, A. H. (2002). A cross-cultural analysis of the behavior of women and men: Implications for the origins of sex differences. *Psychological Bulletin, 128,* 699–727.

Chapter 7

Is Bias in the Brain?

Introduction	173
What's Under the Hood? The Organization of the Human Brain	175
Brain Structure, Diversity, and Intergroup Relations	178
Brain Function and Intergroup Bias	187
What Can We Do? Addressing Implicit Bias	195
Summary	198

Men believe themselves to be free, simply because they are conscious of their actions, and unconscious of the causes whereby those actions are determined.

Baruch Spinoza

Introduction

Incognito: The Secret Lives of the Brain, a book by David Eagleman (2011), describes how the brain guides our behavior in ways well outside our awareness and frequently beyond our control. Eagleman compares the brain to a car engine. You turn the key and feel like you are in full control. However, as you drive down the road, under the hood the engine is making thousands of decisions every second that ultimately determine how fast you will go and where you will go—in fact, *if* you will go. As the Spinoza quote suggests, you feel in total control, unaware of all that lies under your "hood" that actually powers your thoughts, feelings, and actions. Most of the time, the engine works well; your drive is smooth. Sometimes there are problems. Consider these three examples.

The Psychology of Diversity: Beyond Prejudice and Racism, First Edition. James M. Jones, John F. Dovidio, and Deborah L. Vietze.
© 2014 Blackwell Publishing Ltd. Published 2014 by Blackwell Publishing Ltd.

First, the chilling case of Charles Whitman. Late one evening, after visiting a psychiatrist earlier in the day about periodic, uncontrollable, violent impulses, Charles Whitman wrote,

> I don't really understand myself these days. I am supposed to be an average, reasonable and intelligent young man. However, lately (I can't recall when it started) I have been a victim of many unusual and irrational thoughts. These thoughts constantly recur. . . . It was after much thought that I decided to kill my wife, Kathy, tonight after I pick her up from work . . . I love her dearly . . . I cannot rationally pinpoint any specific reason for doing this . . . I truly do not consider this world worth living in, and am prepared to die, and I do not want . . . her to suffer alone in it. I intend to kill her as painlessly as possible. (Whitman letter; 31-07-66, Whitman, C.; retrieved on March 9, 2013 from http://www.answers.com/topic/charles-whitman-suicide-notes)

Later that night, after he killed both his wife and his mother, Whitman continued his note: "I imagine it appears that I brutally killed both of my loved ones. I was only trying to do a good thorough job."

The next morning, Charles Whitman barricaded himself at the top of the University of Texas observation tower. He had a high-powered rifle equipped with a telescopic sight. For 90 minutes, he shot at anything that moved—students, shadows, even an airplane. By the time he was gunned down, he had shot 38 people; 14 of them died.

In the note that Whitman wrote the night before, he stated

> After my death I wish that an autopsy would be performed on me to see if there is any visible physical disorder. I have had some tremendous headaches in the past and have consumed two large bottles of Excedrin in the past three months.

The autopsy revealed a tumor the size of a walnut in the area of the brain called the amygdala.

Second, the infamous case of Amadou Diallo. It was early morning in New York City when four plain-clothed police officers approached Amadou Diallo, a 23-year-old immigrant from Guinea, at the entrance to his apartment building. The officers thought that Diallo matched the description of a serial rapist in the area. News accounts reported that the officers identified themselves as police but that Diallo, apparently confused and frightened, ran up the steps toward the doorway, ignoring the officers' orders to stop and show his hands. It was dark; the porch lightbulb was out, and the officers could only see Diallo's silhouette, backlit by a light inside. At the top of the steps by the doorway, Diallo stopped. He turned and reached into his jacket. As he pulled an object from inside his jacket, one of the officers yelled, "Gun!" Almost immediately, and seemingly instinctively, the four police officers started shooting. One of the officers tripped and fell backwards. The other officers, thinking he was shot, intensified their firing.

In all, the police officers fired 41 shots. Nineteen hit their mark, and Amadou Diallo died at the scene. He was unarmed. The object he took out of his jacket was his wallet, probably to show the officers his identification. An internal investigation by the New York Police Department ruled that the officers had acted reasonably under the circumstances. Later, a grand jury indicted the officers for second-degree murder and reckless endangerment, but they were ultimately acquitted. Many in the community in which Diallo lived were outraged and saddened by this tragedy.

And third, on February 26, 2012 in Sanford, Florida, George Zimmerman, a 28-year-old multiracial Latino American, was patrolling on neighborhood watch when he saw Trayvon Martin, a 17-year-old African American. Zimmerman claimed that Martin was behaving suspiciously, cutting in-between houses and walking very "leisurely" for the rainy weather. Even though a police dispatcher told him not to, Zimmerman followed Martin. What actually transpired next is unclear. Zimmerman claimed that Martin attacked him. Martin's side of the story could not be told; Zimmerman shot him in the chest at close range, and he died. Trayvon Martin was unarmed, and the police report stated that there was no evidence that he was involved in any criminal activity at the time of the encounter.

These examples illustrate the fatal consequences that can occur when activity in the brain is not under our control. Could perceptions of race and ethnicity trigger automatic responses in the brain? To most people, the Diallo case appeared to have something to do with skin color. There was also considerable public outrage and debate about the role of race in the Trayvon Martin case. But what does this have to do with the brain? These unfortunate events led to many research studies on when and how the brain automatically responds with certain biases. In this chapter, we weave these examples together to address the fundamental questions, "Do we have biases in our brains?"

What's Under the Hood? The Organization of the Human Brain

In the previous two chapters (Chapters 5 and 6), we discussed the ways *Homo sapiens* developed intellectually and socially to survive, adapt, and prosper. Our brains evolved in ways that enabled us to make these adaptations, not only to challenging physical environments but also to the complexities of social living (Dunbar & Schultz, 2007). Other animals are also social, but our survival depended on managing a larger and more complicated set of social relationships. Chimpanzees live in groups of about 50, but human social networks include about 150 people. Managing these connections with others requires knowing what we need, what others want, and coordinating our actions for mutual benefit. To accomplish this, we need to develop a theory of mind, which is the ability to understand the thoughts and feelings of others. Infants display evidence of basic elements of this capacity as early as 6 months old. They will need these skills even more in the future. Social networking media are rapidly expanding the size of our social networks and the number of friends that people have, reaching across different geographical locations and cultures instantaneously. The word "friend," as in I will "friend" you, has become a verb, underscoring how human social networks are changing because of advances in communication technology. These advances and cultural changes make the world smaller and our social networks larger and more demanding.

It is easy to take for granted the brain's uniqueness and complexity. Your brain allows you to reach beyond yourself and understand and interact with others. It allows you to comprehend and learn from the past and anticipate the future. Your imagination is almost limitless. Although computers can do many tasks much faster and better than humans, they come nowhere close to the range of things that the human brain handles even in the most mundane daily activity.

This section briefly reviews how we came to be what we are—the evolution of the human brain. This review is a highly selective and simplified review of brain anatomy and function to give you an appreciation of how important the brain is for understanding, how you respond to others, and the ways you experience diversity.

How We Know How the Brain Functions

Much of what we know about how the human brain functions comes from recently developed techniques. One of the most important is **functional magnetic resonance imaging (fMRI)**. An fMRI scanner measures blood flow within the brain to indicate brain activity. Researchers use fMRI to learn what areas of the brain are active when people are exposed to different stimuli, such as a photograph of a person with light or dark skin, or when they engage in certain activities like thinking about social activities or sex, or when they are touched. Researchers can map areas of the brain that are primarily involved in our thoughts and reactions. Figure 7.1 represents the result of an fMRI scan. Areas that change in activity when people perform specific tasks appear in different colors on the brain image (red for increases in activity, and blue for decreases).

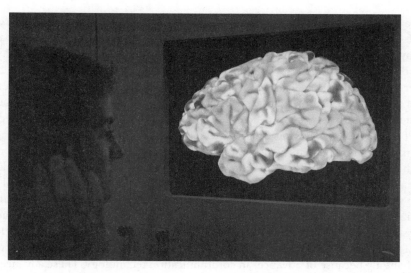

Figure 7.1.   In fMRI Images, Different Colors Show Increases or Decreases in Activity in Areas of the Brain When People Are Exposed to People of Different Groups or Perform Different Tasks. © Miguel Medina/AFP/Getty Images.

A second influential technique is **electroencephalography** (**EEG**). This involves assessing electrical activity in the brain using electrodes pasted temporarily onto the head. Because typically many electrodes are needed, participants often wear special caps with electrodes built in. When neurons in the brain are active, they emit small electrical impulses (measuring only microvolts) that EEG detects and analyzes. Whereas fMRI is particularly good at identifying locations in the brain that are active in response to a particular stimulus, EEG is especially good at detecting rapid changes in brain activity. Together, along with other techniques, fMRI and EEG have transformed how researchers study the brain and opened new doors to understanding what is going on under the hood.

Brain Structure and Function

The human brain evolved in different stages, with different structures and new layers emerging as humans adapted to new challenges. These structures developed from the back and lower part of the brain forward. Let's start with the most basic functions. At the top of the spinal cord just inside the skull, actually a continuation of the spinal cord, is the hindbrain (Figure 7.2). Some parts of the hindbrain control basic life processes such as breathing, blood pressure, and heart rate. Other areas control your ability to move your eyes to track targets. Still other parts help you move different parts of your body. Just above the hindbrain is the midbrain, a relatively small area that controls vital functions. For instance, it helps you move in a coordinated manner, to respond quickly to things like loud noises, and to initiate voluntary actions that involve a number of different movements and actions at the same time, like getting out of a chair.

Being able to move smoothly and purposefully is a prerequisite to social life, but it is the forebrain that adds more dimensions to that life. The social life of the brain begins to really take hold in the forebrain. Many of our basic drives, such as

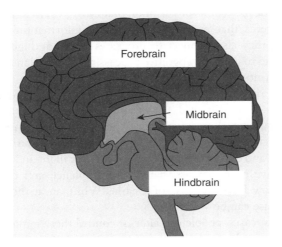

Figure 7.2.   Three Basic Areas of the Human Brain Are the Hindbrain, Midbrain, and Forebrain.

motivations to drink and eat, are located here. So is our sex drive. Other parts of the forebrain provide the capacity for us to develop memories.

One structure within the forebrain, the **amygdala**, is particularly important to how we react to others. The amygdala is sensitive to novel people and objects, and it acts rapidly to signal a threat. When a threat occurs, the amygdala initiates a series of processes that prepare a person for "fight or flight." Recall the case of Charles Whitman at the beginning of this chapter; the tumor in the vicinity of his amygdala likely led to his uncontrollable aggressive thoughts and ultimately his violent actions. The amygdala is part of the limbic system, which plays a key role in regulating emotion and memory.

But in complex societies, we don't just react. We need to think in deliberate ways, to make plans, in order to understand and function in our physical and social environment. The cerebral cortex allows us to do this. The **cerebral cortex** is the outermost layer of the brain, made up of two similar looking halves, called hemispheres. The cerebral cortex is associated with three major functions: (a) analyzing and integrating information from various senses; (b) higher-order thinking and abstract problem solving; and (c) performing voluntary actions. When you look at a brain, you mainly see the cerebral cortex because it covers the forebrain, midbrain, and hindbrain. The size of our cerebral cortex distinguishes the human brain from those of other animals. Our cerebral cortex is much larger than that of other animals, relative to our size. This large cortex plays a critical role in regulating social behaviors, in how we come to understand our world by observing and learning from others (Preston et al., 2007), and in how we think about ourselves in relation to others (Heatherton, Macrae, & Kelley, 2004).

Brain Structure, Diversity, and Intergroup Relations

First, there are very basic systems of the brain that are sensitive to racial or ethnic cues, such as the amygdala and structures related to processing human faces. These systems mostly reside in sections of the brain that evolved early, and they have a direct connection to systems that provide basic sensory information such as sight and hearing. However, they also connect to processes involving higher-order language-related functions and to complex cognitive processing that is related to social behavior like stereotyping (Amodio & Lieberman, 2009).

Moreover, these different systems typically operate jointly to determine our ultimate responses to our social world. For instance, a person from a different racial or ethnic group, because of their novelty or a perceived threat, might automatically trigger amygdala activation. The amygdala then sets in motion basic physiological processes that alert and energize the person for fight or flight and initiates a range of higher-level cognitive processes associated with vigilance and other threat-related responses. As we saw from the case of Charles Whitman at the beginning of this chapter, that response can be violent.

However, in most cases, people can alter or control these initial impulses through cognitive control exerted by the cerebral cortex. Indeed, the cerebral cortex, specifically the prefrontal cortex, evolved to such a degree in humans because it was important to master and regulate these violent impulses so that coordinated social life could develop. This is where a large portion of judgments and decision-making occurs. How people understand difference, whether it represents a novel opportunity for learning or a threat, is often determined by activity in the prefrontal cortex that resolves ambiguity and by specific structures within the prefrontal cortex (such as the anterior cingulate cortex) that detect conflicting information or action tendencies. These modern parts of our brains carry out the kinds of complicated reactions we have when we encounter diversity.

A second fundamental implication of brain structure and function is that memory, our main reservoir of knowledge that guides our behavior, occurs at several different locations in the brain. Some memory and knowledge are stored in basic structures in older parts of the brain. The hippocampus, for example, is involved in short-term memory. But other structures in other areas of the brain are involved in more complex processing and longer-term memory storage. We have survived by our wits, and we have an insatiable hunger for knowledge, which has to be stored efficiently and made readily accessible as we encounter new situations and challenges. Thus there are different memory systems in the brain, and which ones are activated in a given situation determine how we react to other people and other groups. In the remainder of this chapter we consider how the structure and function of what is under our hood, the brain, relates to diversity and intergroup relations.

Warning! Difference Ahead!

As we discussed in Chapter 5, humans evolved with a particular sensitivity to novelty and threat. In a hostile environment that contained many creatures that were much stronger and faster than we are, inattentiveness to potential threats could have mortal consequences. Therefore, the amygdala continuously scans information from our senses for signs of potential threat and things that are out of the ordinary. Although there are pathways between the amygdala and the cortex, activation of the amygdala does not require deep or complex thought. From an evolutionary perspective, reacting immediately to threat is much more important than thinking about the precise nature and meaning of it.

A person who is different from us may represent one such cue that can trigger amygdala activation. In fact, when researchers began to study bias in the brain, the amygdala was one of the first places they looked. Indeed, when White participants were put in an fMRI scanner and exposed to pictures of Blacks and Whites, they spontaneously exhibited differences in amygdala activation (Phelps et al., 2000). The mere exposure to photographs of Blacks to White participants in the safe environment of the laboratory produced a threat response in the older part of the brain. What would cause this reaction? Part of it is explained by novelty. When people are exposed to White and Black faces that are familiar to them, the effect is much weaker. Part of the reaction, however, reflects what the culture has taught the person about Blacks. As this quote from Jesses Jackson reminds us, cultural stereotypes associate Blacks with violence and criminality: "There is nothing more painful to me at this stage in my life than to walk down the street and hear footsteps and start thinking about robbery—then look around and see somebody white and feel relieved." Jesse

Jackson is not alone in this immediate, but unfortunate, reaction. Black adults and youth can also show greater amygdala activation when viewing Black faces than when viewing White faces—they are not immune to cultural influences (Lieberman, Hariri, Jarcho, Eisenberger, & Bookheimer, 2005).

One of the challenges for a diverse society is that what starts in the brain doesn't necessarily stay in the brain. A reaction that was necessary for survival early in human history may not be necessary today. The signals from the amygdala automatically activate a cascading sequence of events, such as increases in levels of epinephrine and other hormones that prepare people for action. This energizing response can come in two forms. Sometimes we mobilize our energy and become more involved or immersed in a task, which is a form of positive engagement. We try to rise to the occasion. This is called a **challenge response**. Other times we seek to escape a situation or to protect ourselves against harm. This is a **threat response**. Challenge and threat responses are distinguished from one another using heart responses and hormone levels (Blascovich & Mendes, 2010).

Our social diversity represents unique opportunities for us to learn and can stimulate new ways of thinking and solving problems. When confronted with diversity, we may automatically experience either a challenge or threat response. Do Whites typically respond to Blacks with challenge or threat response? The automatically activated threat response is the dominant reaction. This happens in the part of the brain that activates our basic survival tools, the amygdala, and translates into a range of physiological responses preparatory for action. This does not have to be the way people respond to diversity—we can think of diversity as a challenge or an opportunity—but Whites typically react to Blacks and members of other racial and ethnic minorities with threat.

Let's return to the case of Amadou Diallo, the unarmed, dark-skinned, 23-year-old immigrant from Guinea who was shot 19 times by four police officers. The shooting began when Diallo reached into his pocket and pulled out a wallet, but one of the police officers thought he saw a gun and yelled "Gun!" to warn his fellow officers. Was it his eyes, or his brain, playing tricks on him? If so, can understanding how the brain functions explain what happened?

One of the functions of a threat response in the brain is to make us vigilant for cues of danger. Sometimes we are overvigilant, seeing things that are not there, because of the mortal costs of missing something that can harm us. In 2011, campus police intervening in a college protest against Wall Street suddenly felt that they were surrounded by students and trapped. They felt threatened and perhaps overreacted by spraying students in the face with pepper-spray. This act seemed unjustified and horrendous to the public who saw students lined up passively in a row on their television screens. The campus police in that situation felt and saw something different. Why? Box 7.1 provides some possible explanations.

Just because neural and physiological mechanisms are involved, it doesn't mean that such responses are beyond our control. Fortunately, our brain evolved in ways that ensures that. In Chapter 6 we explained that although it is easiest for people to think of others in terms of group membership, particularly in terms of a person's in-groups and out-groups, we can focus on the unique characteristics of others as

Box 7.1.   Shooter Bias

Figure 7.3.   White Participants Are Quicker to Recognize Crime-related Objects After Seeing a Black Than a White Face. Reprinted from "Seeing Black: Race, Crime, and Visual Processing," by J. L. Eberhardt, P. A. Goff, V. J. Purdie, & P. G. Davies, 2004, *Journal of Personality and Social Psychology*, 87, pp. 876–893.

Blacks are threatening to Whites, not only because they are simply different but also because negative cultural stereotypes characterize Blacks as criminal and violent. Therefore, people are likely to believe they see things like guns or knives in their hand when the things are actually wallets and combs (Payne, 2001). After seeing a Black face, rather than a White face, quickly on a computer screen, White participants are faster at detecting crime-related objects, like a gun, emerge from an array of dots (Figure 7.3; Eberhardt, Goff, Purdie, & Davies, 2004).

In the context of policing, the consequences can be tragic. The Amadou Diallo case is not an isolated one. Using a number of different simulations, numerous studies in psychology have presented Black and White college students and police officers with situations in which they have to make a split-second decision about whether to simulate shooting a man who may or may not have a weapon in his hand. Both Black and White people are more likely to mistakenly shoot an unarmed Black man than an unarmed White man, and they do so faster. They are also less likely to shoot an armed White man than an armed Black man. This effect, which is called the **shooter bias**, is less strong for trained police officers than for college students, and college students become more accurate in their decisions with practice. However, even after practice the shooter bias persists to some extent (Payne, 2006).

The increased tendency to shoot an unarmed Black over a White man seems like a case of blatantly racist behavior. However, this occurs not simply because the person is Black but because society tells us that Blacks are threatening. You see a dark-skinned person; the amygdala detects threat and prepares you for defensive action. We see things that may not be there and respond because survival may be at stake. Thus the issue is not as simple as seeing Black or White—our reactions hinge on the ways we categorize people and on prevalent cultural messages.

For example, when people are instructed to think about others in terms of age categories rather than racial categories, the shooter bias against Blacks is eliminated (Jones & Fazio, 2010). Also, putting a White man in a threatening background (with dilapidated buildings, dumpsters, and graffiti) increases the likelihood, compared to when there is a neutral background, that he will be mistakenly shot while unarmed (Correll, Wittenbrink, Park, Judd, & Goyle, 2011). However, race still matters. Unarmed Black men with a neutral background are just as likely to be erroneously shot as White men in the threatening situation, and unarmed Black men with the threatening background are still even more likely to be mistakenly shot in these simulations.

Gender also matters. Our culture generally depicts women as less aggressive than men. As a consequence, people in "shooter bias" simulations erroneously shoot an unarmed White woman less often than an unarmed White man, and they are less likely to shoot an armed woman than an armed man. In fact, the shooter racial bias observed in previous research mainly applies to Black men, not Black women (Plant, Goplen, & Kunstman, 2011). Thus, society tells us what is threatening, typically Black men; the amygdala detects that threat and immediately sets in motion defensive thoughts, perceptions, and actions.

1. At the beginning of the chapter, we described how police officers mistakenly shot and killed Amadou Diallo. Based on research on the shooter bias, was race the deciding factor in that incident? Why or why not?
2. What kind of interventions might be designed to help law enforcement officers be more accurate in perceiving and responding to men and women of different races whom they suspect to be armed and dangerous?

separate individuals, and this reduces intergroup bias. But how deep does this effect go? Can it go into the brain and counteract the automatic response?

The answer is yes. Wheeler and Fiske (2005) showed how. Undergraduate students in an fMRI scanner viewed photographs of Black and White faces and were given one of three different processing goals to perform. One goal generally reinforced categorical thinking but did not directly focus on skin color; some students were instructed to indicate whether the person was older (over 21) or younger. Another goal emphasized thinking about the people in an individuated way; these students were instructed to decide whether the person would like a particular vegetable say a carrot. In the third condition, the students had to make a non-social decision by indicating whether a dot appeared on a face that was projected on a computer screen.

The neural responses for each of these conditions were fundamentally different from one another. College students in the categorization condition (asked to classify a face by age) displayed greater activation of the amygdala when responding to Black faces than they did when responding to White faces, consistent with previous research. However, when students were asked to make an individuated decision (Would this person like a carrot?), they showed *less* activation of the amygdala for Black than for

White faces. There were no differences in amygdala reactivity to the faces for students who made the non-social dot-on-the-face judgments. Therefore it seems that how people choose to think about others may direct the brain to function in different ways.

At the most basic neural and physiological levels, our goals, motivation, cultural learning, and experience with diversity matter. As Chapter 3 discussed, Black–White relations has a unique place in the development and history of the United States. Cultural stereotypes today characterize Blacks as aggressive, violent, and angry. Thus it is likely that most Whites perceive Blacks, more than members of other groups, as threatening. In fact, exposure to Asian faces for Whites does not produce evidence of threat responses in the brain (He, Johnson, Dovidio, & McCarthy, 2009) or increase heart rate and hormonal changes associated with fight or flight responses in the way that exposure to Black faces does (Mendes, Blascovich, Hunter, Lickel, & Jost, 2007). However, although cultural exposure matters, so does personal experience. As noted, one of the first studies showing amygdala activation by Whites in response to Black faces found this effect only for *unfamiliar* Black and White faces (Phelps et al., 2000). There was no difference in amygdala response between viewing *familiar* Black and White faces. Difference and diversity are not always associated with threat. In fact, if intergroup contact is fostered under the proper conditions (see Pettigrew & Tropp, 2006), the amygdala can be put down for a nap in diversity settings. The critical factor is how our history, culture, and experience orient us to diversity. We illustrate this principle in the next section on face perception.

Who Are You? Race and Face Perception

It is critical for us to be able to distinguish one person from another. An infant needs to recognize mom and to distinguish those who are familiar from those who are strangers. Face perception plays a special role in this process. Infants are able to categorize faces of different skin color groups (distinguish faces of different races) as early as 3 months old (Kelly et al., 2005). Throughout life people are better able to distinguish and remember faces of people from their own race than from other races, a phenomenon called the **own-race bias** (Young, Hugenberg, Bernstein, & Sacco, 2012). Although this effect occurs more strongly in the United States for Whites, it also occurs consistently for Blacks and Asians (see Chapter 10 for further dicussion).

Not surprisingly, given its central importance to social life, there is an area in the brain that is largely responsible for face processing. The **fusiform face area (FFA)** is a distinct brain area located not too far from the amygdala. Whereas the amygdala is part of the brain's general early-warning system, the FFA is specialized to process information about others' faces. Activation of the FFA is associated with rapidly distinguishing faces from objects, such as houses, and from other body parts, such as arms. The detection of race in this process can occur quite quickly. Differential reactions in the brain based on race appear within about one fifth of a second (He et al., 2009), a speed that is probably necessary for making important split-second decisions about a face—whether it is familiar or not as well as whether it belongs to a trustworthy person.

The FFA is central to explaining the own-race bias effect, that is, superior recognition of faces of people from your own race. Golby, Gabrieli, Chiao, and Eberhardt

(2001) presented Black and White adults with photographs of Black and White faces in an fMRI scanner and measured activation of the FFA and then assessed how well these adults could subsequently recall the specific faces they saw. They found the basic own-race face effect for recognition of the faces: Whites were better at identifying faces of Whites; Blacks were better at identifying faces of Blacks. Also, participants displayed greater activation in the FFA for faces of their own race than for faces of the other race.

Moreover, greater activation of the FFA predicted better memory for faces. Thus, people seem to respond to out-group members more spontaneously with threat (associated with greater amygdala activation) but to devote fewer cognitive resources (reflected in less FFA activation) to distinguishing one out-group member from another. These effects are particularly strong when people think of others primarily in terms of their group membership (e.g., Black or Latino), but both accuracy in recognition and basic differences in brain activation that underlie these differences can be reduced when people focus on individual distinguishing qualities (e.g., between Bob and Joe; Tanaka & Pierce, 2009).

These findings demonstrate that basic processes for face perception in the brain play a critical role in better recall for individuals of their own race than of other races among both Whites and Blacks. But does this mean that there is racism inherent in the way we view others? Not necessarily. Cultural circumstances and forces, however, can produce racist outcomes. The work on own-race bias has direct applications for eyewitness testimony and identification of possible perpetrators. Eyewitness testimony is generally unreliable, but it is particularly so with respect to identifying potential criminals of another race in line-ups. In a line-up of Blacks, Whites frequently misidentify the person who committed the crime. In fact, the Innocence Project, which was founded at the Benjamin N. Cardoza Law School at Yeshiva University to assist prisoners who were wrongfully convicted to prove their innocence through DNA testing, concludes, "Eyewitness misidentification is the single greatest cause of wrongful convictions nationwide, playing a role in more than 75 percent [out of 280 cases since 1992] of convictions overturned through DNA testing" (retrieved on March 9, 2013 from http://www.innocenceproject.org/understand/Eyewitness-Misidentification.php).

Misidentification does not occur randomly, however. The way we think about groups shapes how we see and respond to faces. What do Americans think when they see a woman wearing a headscarf or a man wearing a sheik's headwear? Racial categorization, so important to America historically (see Chapter 3), affects the meaning people attach to faces (Pauker & Ambady, 2009). Imagine yourself looking at the racially ambiguous person. How would you determine if the person was Black or White? And, what effect might this determination have on the ways you think and feel about the person?

Eberhardt, Dasgupta, and Banaszynski (2003) investigated these questions. Simply attaching the racial category label of Black or White to the face changed how people processed and recalled the person. Moreover, for people who believed that race was an essential, fixed category of human difference—we call these persons **entity theorists**—racial category labels dramatically changed how they saw the person. In the Eberhardt et al. (2003) study, college students saw a picture of the racially ambigu-

Ambiguous Target Face

"Black" drawing

"White" drawing

Figure 7.4. People Draw Radically Different Pictures of a Racially Ambiguous Person (top image) After They Label the Person as Black or White (bottom pictures). Reprinted from "Believing is Seeing: The Effects of Racial Labels and Implicit Beliefs on Face Perception," by J. L. Eberhardt, N. Dasgupta, & T. I. Banaszynski, 2003, *Personality and Social Psychology Bulletin, 29,* pp. 360–370.

ous person shown in Figure 7.4 on a computer screen and labeled with the racial category Black in one condition or White in another. While the picture remained on the screen they attempted to draw the face "well enough so that people in the future could successfully match their drawing to the correct target" face shown (p. 365). As illustrated in Figure 7.4, students' drawings of the person in the photograph differed radically depending on the racial label that they were given and theory of human difference they held. Given these distortions, it is not surprising that Whites' identification of Blacks in line-ups is so unreliable.

This inaccuracy is further compounded by the stereotypes associated with different groups. To the extent that cultural stereotypes portray Black men as violent, criminal, and impulsive, as discussed in Chapter 5, a person labeled Black is typically perceived to be criminal, dangerous, and incorrigible. Does this make a difference for Black men? Yes, the difference between life and death. A recent study examined 44 court cases from Philadelphia, Pennsylvania that involved the potential death-sentencing of Black defendants convicted of killing a White victim (Eberhardt, Davies, Purdie-Vaughns, & Johnson, 2006). Pictures of the defendants were rated based on how many phenotypically Black facial characteristics they had. **Phenotypicality** refers to features of the face that are perceived to be most typical for a member of that racial or ethnic group. The face ratings were correlated with juries' decisions about whether or not the defendant would be sentenced to death, over and above other factors such as aggravating or mitigating circumstances, the defendant's socioeconomic status and attractiveness, and the brutality of the murder. Defendants who were high in stereotypical Black appearance were over twice as likely (57.5% vs. 24.4%) to be sentenced to death for killing a White victim.

These biases, like the threat response to Blacks discussed in the previous section, are not inevitable. Although perceptions of racial categories tend to be automatically activated, we can see people in other ways. According to the Common Ingroup Identity Model (Gaertner & Dovidio, 2000, 2009), we can recategorize groups normally seen as different (e.g., Blacks and Whites) within a common superordinate identity if we focus on features we have in common; for example, students from the same university. When we do this, bias in evaluating people based on their racial group memberships is largely eliminated (Hehman, Mania, & Gaertner, 2010).

What happens in the brain in cases like this? Van Bavel, Packer, and Cunningham (2008; see also Van Bavel & Cunningham, 2010) asked and answered this question. They arbitrarily assigned students to one of two groups, Leopards and Tigers, for the duration of the experiment. Once students were assigned to groups, they had 3 min to memorize the group membership of 24 faces presented simultaneously: 12 members of the Leopard group and 12 members of the Tiger group. Within the Leopard and Tiger groups were equivalent numbers of phenotypically Black and White faces. Later, in a neuroimaging phase of the study, participants categorized 24 faces based on team membership (Tiger or Leopard) or skin color (Black or White). The researchers reasoned that this social context, Tigers versus Leopards, was the relevant group membership and that skin color was irrelevant.

Indeed, activation of the FFA occurred only when people were classifying others based on their team membership; under these conditions, there was no difference in activation based on skin color. This research seems to show that the brain responds to socially important categories, and in this case being a Tiger or Leopard was what was more socially relevant than skin color. Although in our daily life race is often a very important and salient social category, it doesn't have to be the dominant one if we recognize commonalities that go beyond race.

There is thus no doubt that the basic structures that emerged relatively early in the evolution of the human brain are sensitive to social novelty, threat, and group membership. Evolutionary psychologists argue, however, that while the brain prepares us to process information about and respond to in-group and out-group members differentially, these structures did not evolve to distinguish between people of different races or ethnicities (Cosmides, Tooby, & Kurzban, 2003). As first discussed in Chapter 5, throughout most of our evolutionary history, humans did not travel very far. Migration was slow and unsystematic. Therefore, people rarely came into contact with others who looked dramatically different from them or were dramatically different by custom. Indeed, the concept of race is actually relatively recent (see Chapter 2). Therefore, although contemporary society tells us that race and ethnicity are important social categories to guide our thinking, our brain is open to other categories. If we choose to think about others in different ways, our brains respond accordingly.

While we are able to exert considerable control over our most basic reactions to diversity, the brain, in the service of efficiency, often functions in ways that don't require or involve our conscious control. In the next section, we return to the quote by Spinoza with which we opened this chapter: although we typically feel in control of our thoughts and feelings, we are typically unaware of the unconscious forces that shape and power them.

Brain Function and Intergroup Bias

The mental processes that result from the brain's evolution allow us to benefit from accumulated knowledge and experience, to maintain a steady and consistent path that provides continuity in our lives. But these same mental processes also allow us to benefit immediately from new circumstances and opportunities and to change course quickly and strategically. We manage a wonderful balancing act between what has worked in the past and what is needed to meet present challenges.

How does the brain accomplish this? There is general agreement among scientists that we developed two different cognitive systems to maintain the appropriate balance (Smith & DeCoster, 2000). One system, the **slow-learning system**, records information slowly and is sensitive to repeated patterns, events, and activities. It produces long-term, stable knowledge that we can access automatically and unconsciously through sensory cues. For instance, suppose you return to a place where you haven't been for some time, like the neighborhood where you grew up. Suddenly you smell a rosebush or hear a gate creaking. Images, feelings, and memories of events come flooding back to you, things you thought you had forgotten. These memories were locked in the long-term memory system, but you didn't have the key to open it. The aroma or the unique sound was that key. These memories are stored in the more basic brain structures of the slow-learning system.

The other memory system is a **fast-learning system**. It is more conscious, effortful, and intentional. This is the system you use when you encounter new challenges that you want to master. This system allows you to learn quickly from limited exposure, drawing from a range of cognitive resources. You use it when you are faced with a new math problem, when you try to navigate your way around a new city, or when you try to speak another language. In contrast to the way those childhood memories automatically popped into your mind with the right cue, the fast-learning system takes effort. This system requires activation of several areas within the cerebral cortex.

In general, the slow-learning and fast-learning systems of the brain operate independently. The slow-learning system guides you through the day without demanding much conscious thought. Think about your journey to school or work each day. Did you ever have the experience of recognizing that you had gotten there without being conscious of the steps you took? Your slow-learning system got you there without a lot of conscious thought. At the same time, your slow-learning system freed your mind to think about the class you are heading toward, paper you are writing, or the party you are planning for Saturday night. The slow-learning system freed up cognitive resources so that you could use the fast-learning system to rehearse the activities for the day and plan future events.

The brain is an amazingly complex organ and a powerful engine for running our social life, as we saw at the beginning of the chapter in the analogy of the car. Billions of brain cells enable us to take in information (to see, hear, and smell), to interpret and remember this information, and to react to it, sometimes reflexively, allowing us to respond in a sophisticated, nuanced, and thoughtful way. These activities go on in parallel, much of the time without our awareness. What is under the hood that provides the power and capacity to accomplish this? Our conscious experience captures only a small proportion of what is going on. In fact, Eagleman's comparison of the brain to the engine of a car doesn't give the brain enough credit. Your brain not only enables you to do what you want to do, but also helps guide your thoughts, feelings, and actions in ways outside your awareness and sometimes beyond your control.

Back in the seventeenth century, Spinoza realized that people are generally unconscious of the real causes of their actions. Modern psychology and neuroscience confirm his view. Much of our experience and behavior is determined by unconscious processes. As we have seen, we process faces spontaneously, without conscious control, but in systematically different ways depending on how familiar they are. In this section, we elaborate on the role of the unconscious and explore how unconscious memories and thoughts shape our actions toward others. We also consider how we accommodate these forces with our conscious thoughts and control our responses to members of other groups.

Explicit and Implicit Bias

In an influential article, Patricia Devine (1989) noted that much of the research on prejudice, discrimination, and responses to diversity focused only on people's conscious attitudes—what they told us they were feeling. These are explicit biases: positions that people consciously endorse and express. Devine argued that explicit bias is not the whole story. In contrast, implicit attitudes and stereotypes are unconscious thoughts, feelings, and beliefs that are automatically activated when we are exposed to a member of a social group unlike ours and for which we have developed a bias. Implicit attitudes and stereotypes represent well-learned and habitual cultural associations that people are not aware of (Karpinski & Hilton, 2001).

Many psychologists consider implicit and explicit attitudes to reflect different components of a system of dual attitudes; this is similar to the distinction between slow-learning and fast-learning systems in the brain. Implicit responses represent older attitudes and stereotypes that may be overwritten by newer, explicit attitudes, either completely or in part. For example, a person who is striving to be more egalitarian in her beliefs might consciously substitute positive for negative thoughts when she interacts with members of a particular group (Wilson, Lindsey, & Schooler, 2000). Whereas implicit attitudes have a strong emotional component, cognition and deliberative thought play a strong role in explicit attitudes (Rudman, 2004).

But how do you measure attitudes and stereotypes that are implicit and often unconscious? You can't directly ask people about attitudes and stereotypes they don't know they possess or can't express. Researchers who study these attitudes have devised a number of different ways to measure implicit biases. Most of these approaches use cognitive techniques but some are physiological. The basic principle behind these techniques is that a person will respond more quickly to ideas or concepts that are associated in the mind than to those that are not. For example, is each of the following strings of letters made up of two words: table–chair, doctor–nurse, chair–nurse? The answer is yes in all three cases, but it takes people a split-second longer to say yes to chair–nurse because those two words are not as strongly associated in your mind as doctor–nurse or table–chair. How about Blacks–good, Blacks–bad, Whites–good, Whites–bad? Notice that you are not asked directly about whether you believe that there is an association between the pairs of words.

The most commonly used method of this type is the **Implicit Association Test (IAT)** (Greenwald, Poehlman, Uhlmann, & Banaji, 2009). In the IAT, people have to make decisions about different groups (such as Anglos and Latinos or Whites and Blacks) in conjunction with positive and negative words (https://implicit.harvard.edu/). For some IATs the ethnic categories are represented by names, such as Jorge and Manuel for Latinos and Adam and Chip for Anglos (Aberson, Shoemaker, & Tomolillo, 2004); for other IATs photographs of group members, such as of Blacks and Whites, are used. If people have an automatically activated bias favoring Anglos over Latinos, they will be quicker in responding when Anglo names rather than Latino names are paired with positive words and Latino names rather than Anglo names are paired with negative words. Because these responses occur in a split-second, they are very difficult to control.

Hundreds of thousands of people have taken the IAT, and a large body of research demonstrates systematic biases against Latinos, Blacks (mainly by non-Blacks), gay, lesbian, bisexual, and transgender (GLBT) persons, overweight people, women, and people with disabilities. These biases in U.S. culture are similar across levels of socio-economic status, educational achievement, and region of the country. However, the IAT is not without controversy (Tetlock & Mitchell, 2008). Some people have questioned whether the IAT reflects mainly the general cultural associations rather than personally-held attitudes (Karpinski & Hilton, 2001). Either way, these automatically activated associations translate cultural biases into individual-level thoughts and action. According to Mahzarin Banaji, one of the creators of the IAT, "The Implicit Association Test measures the thumbprint of the culture on our minds" (Vedantam, 2005).

One of the provocative implications of the distinction between implicit and explicit attitudes is that we live in a society that strongly endorses the principle of equality but at the same time has racist, sexist, and ethnically discriminatory traditions and well-established racial and ethnic divides in wealth, health, and residence (see Chapters 3, 11, and 12). However, it is not acceptable to be prejudiced or act in a biased way toward most social groups. Table 7.1 lists what college students see as the acceptability of prejudice toward 105 different groups (Crandall, Eshleman, & O'Brien, 2002). While it is acceptable to be biased against rapists, child molesters, and wife beaters, it is not acceptable to be biased against Hispanics, Native Americans, and Blacks. Thus, for many groups, such as Blacks and Latinos, people have strong implicit biases but appear largely non-prejudiced in their conscious, explicit attitudes. However, for other groups, such as drug users, who are seen as voluntarily behaving in bad ways, implicit and explicit attitudes converge, and it is OK to express prejudice. Indeed, overall,

Table 7.1. Average Acceptability of Prejudice Toward 105 Target Groups

1.967 Rapists	0.927 Tele-evangelists	0.228 Fat people
1.967 Child abusers	0.900 Guests on Ricki Lake	0.227 People with AIDS
1.933 Child molesters	0.887 Iraqi soldiers	0.227 High school cheerleaders
1.932 Wife beaters	0.824 Politicians	0.220 Cat owners
1.907 Terrorists	0.764 People who smell bad	0.215 Interracial couples
1.840 Racists	0.733 Gamblers	0.207 Auto mechanics
1.827 Members of the Ku Klux Klan	0.733 Feminists	0.196 People who put their kids in daycare
1.820 Drunk drivers	0.725 Rednecks	0.193 Ugly people
1.793 Members of the American Nazi Party	0.653 People who go to Kansas State University	0.167 People on Medicare
1.780 Pregnant women who drink alcohol	0.620 Welfare recipients	0.167 Accountants
1.779 Men who refuse to pay child support	0.607 Homosexuals who raise children	0.148 Canadians
1.713 Negligent parents	0.600 People who smoke	0.147 Trash collectors
1.644 People who cheat on their spouses	0.573 Members of National Rifle Association	0.147 Local residents of Lawrence, KS (non-college)
1.540 Kids who steal other kids' lunch money	0.560 People who got a job due to Affirmative Action	0.147 Asian Americans
1.533 Men who leave their families	0.560 People who call the Psychic Hotline	0.141 Hispanics
1.513 Gang members	0.553 Police officers	0.140 Whites
1.487 Liars	0.547 IRS agents	0.140 Students who attend community college
1.336 Male prostitutes	0.541 British punks	0.133 Doctors
1.307 Men who go to prostitutes	0.520 Gay soldiers	0.128 Catholics
1.253 People who cheat on exams	0.510 People with open sores	0.127 Spelling bee champions
1.235 Female prostitutes	0.460 Lawyers	0.120 Manual laborers
1.227 Careless drivers	0.453 Students who rarely study	0.120 Jews
1.213 Drug users	0.430 Country music fans	0.120 Business women
1.188 People who litter	0.427 Waif fashion models	0.120 Black Americans
1.141 People who cut in line	0.407 Mentally unstable people	0.114 Native Americans
1.134 Members of religious cults	0.407 Hare Krishnas	0.114 Elderly people
1.133 Illegal immigrants	0.367 Jehovah's Witnesses	0.114 Dog owners
1.127 Juvenile delinquents	0.356 FBI agents	0.113 Members of a bowling league
1.080 People who sell marijuana	0.347 Homeless people	0.107 Librarians
0.993 Lazy people	0.329 People who are illiterate	0.100 Male nurses
0.980 Ex-convicts	0.313 Traveling salesmen	0.093 Farmers
0.980 Alcoholics	0.313 Environmentalists	0.081 Family men
0.967 Porn stars	0.275 Rap music fans	0.053 Mentally retarded people
0.947 College teachers with poor English skills	0.247 Beauty contestants	0.053 Deaf people
	0.235 White Southerners	0.047 Women who stay home to raise kids
		0.047 Blind people

Note. The mean ratings reported above are based on the following scale: 2, OK to feel negatively toward these people; 1, maybe OK to feel negatively toward these people; 0, not OK to feel negatively toward these people.

From Table 1 of "Social Norms and the Expression and Suppression of Prejudice: The Struggle for Internalization," by C. S. Crandall, A. Eshleman, & L. O'Brien, 2002, *Journal of Personality and Social Psychology, 82*, pp. 359–378, doi: 10.1037/0022-3514.82.3.359.

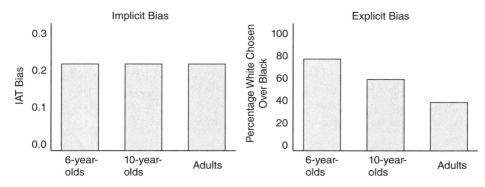

Figure 7.5. White 6-Year-Olds, 10-Year-Olds, and Adults Show Implicit Biases Against Blacks to the Same Degree, But Explicit Bias Decreases for Older Age Groups. Adapted from "The Development of Implicit Attitudes: Evidence of Race Evaluations from Ages 6, 10, and Adulthood," by A. S. Baron, & M. R. Banaji, 2006, *Psychological Science, 17*, pp. 53–58.

implicit and explicit attitudes are only weakly related, but there is greater correspondence for groups against which it is still socially appropriate to express bias.

The idea that implicit attitudes are initially established through socialization is reinforced by developmental trends in implicit and explicit prejudice. Baron and Banaji (2006) tested White 6-year-olds, 10-year-olds, and adults on the racial preference for Whites over Blacks. Significant preference for Whites over Blacks was established by age 6, and the level of implicit prejudice was similar for 10-year-olds and adults (see left-hand panel of Figure 7.5). However, when they looked at explicit attitudes—participants' self-reported preference for Whites over Blacks—older groups expressed less explicit bias (see right-hand panel of Figure 7.5). Presumably, they learned through socialization processes as they grew older that racial bias is not socially appropriate. In general, Black children aged 7–11 do not show the significant pro-White bias that White students of the same age show. On average, they do not show a significant preference for one group over the other. However, the more Black children state an explicit preference for wealth and social status, the more they show an implicit preference for Whites (Newheiser & Olson, 2012).

The distinction between implicit and explicit attitudes, which are related to the slow-learning and fast-learning systems in the brain, is a key one for understanding how people think about and respond to diversity today. The United States was founded on the proposition that "all men are created equal" but, as we discussed in Chapter 3, it has racist traditions and has opposed diversity in its many different forms throughout its history. On the one hand, we are taught that we should not be prejudiced; at a conscious level we know that good people should not be racially or ethnically prejudiced, and we want to be good people. These conscious intentions reflect the fast-learning system in the brain. They change with socialization. Thus, we hold conscious egalitarian views. On the other hand, we are exposed early on to cultural messages that tell us that racial and ethnic minority groups should not be valued as highly as Whites. These messages are absorbed through the brain's slow-learning system as implicit biases.

The idea that Americans view intergroup relations one way at an explicit level but harbor bias that is implicit and often unconscious is currently at the heart of much intergroup bias. In the middle of the twentieth century, people began to recognize that prejudice was evil. Thus, while old-fashioned blatant prejudice has declined over time, modern subtle types of bias largely influence intergroup relations and responses to diversity today. In the next section, we review two forms of contemporary bias, symbolic racism and aversive racism. and consider the role that implicit bias plays today in intergroup relations and responses to diversity.

Contemporary Prejudice

The different types of racism identified in contemporary U.S. society seem tied to different realms of behavior. For example, **symbolic racism**, which refers to the expression of prejudice in the form of opposition to policies that support minority groups, is closely tied to political behavior (e.g., opposition to bilingual education). **Aversive racism**, which considers how people resolve conflicting non-prejudiced explicit attitudes and implicit prejudice, applies to everyday forms of discrimination cross-culturally (at least in Canada, the UK, and the Netherlands, as well as in the United States). One common theme that these approaches share is that racism persists despite significant decreases in overt expressions of bias over time.

Symbolic racism   Symbolic racism theory (Sears & Henry, 2005) developed in response to a practical problem: the failure of traditional measures of "old-fashioned" racism to predict people's actual positions regarding racially targeted policies and Black political candidates. Sears, Henry, and Kosterman (2000) observed, "Few Whites now support the core notions of old-fashioned racism. Our own view is that the acceptance of formal equality is genuine but that racial animus has not gone away; it has just changed its principal manifestations" (p. 77).

Symbolic racism is the combination of politically conservative, individualistic values and negative feelings toward Blacks, Latinos, or other group acquired developmentally. People who are high on symbolic racism are not directly derogatory about other groups, but they express negative feelings indirectly, blaming them on some quality of the group, for example "If Blacks would only try harder, they could be as well off as Whites."

Symbolic racism predicts people's political attitudes and behavior better than do measures of old-fashioned racism, realistic threats, and perceived intergroup competition; non-racial attitudes and values (e.g., individualism, egalitarianism); or political party affiliation and political ideology (see Sears & Henry, 2005). Specifically, symbolic racism uniquely predicts White Americans' attitudes toward a range of racially relevant policies, including busing for school integration and affirmative action, as well as less explicitly race-targeted policies that disproportionately affect Blacks, such as policies relating to crime and welfare. Symbolic racism also predicts opposition to Black candidates, such as Jesse Jackson or Barack Obama, as well as support for ethnocentric White candidates, such as former Ku Klux Klan leader David Duke.

Aversive racism   Aversive racism is sometimes called the prejudice of the well intentioned. Aversive racists support principles of racial equality and genuinely believe that they are non-prejudiced. But at the same time they possess conflicting, often unconscious, negative feelings and beliefs about Blacks that are rooted in basic psychological processes, such as social categorization (see Chapter 5), that promote racial bias (Gaertner & Dovidio, 1986). Whereas symbolic racism characterizes the attitudes of political conservatives, aversive racism reflects the biases of those who are politically liberal (see Dovidio & Gaertner, 2004; Pearson, Dovidio, & Gaertner, 2009).

How do people who are aversive racists resolve the conflict between their conscious non-prejudiced beliefs and their unconscious biases? Because aversive racists are well intentioned and truly want to do the right thing, they behave in an unbiased way when it is clear what the right thing to do is. For example, if I am an aversive racist and see someone from another group trip and fall in front of me, and nobody else is around, will I help? Of course! This person needs help, and I am the only one in position to do it. Only a bad or biased person would not, and I am a good and unbiased person.

However, as an aversive racist, I also have implicit, unconscious biases. These get expressed in more subtle and indirect ways, such as when I can justify my actions based on some factor other than the person's group membership. This time, you turn a corner and you see a person sitting on the ground holding his ankle? Did he fall? Is he hurt? Maybe he is just massaging his ankle because he is tired from walking? Would I be less likely to even ask if he is OK or needs help if he is of a different race or ethnicity than me? The answer from research is yes. Even difference in terms of whether he is wearing a shirt or a cap indicating that he supports a rival sports team or is a student from a different school matters in this case (Dovidio & Gaertner, 2004). I am much less likely to help an out-group member than an in-group member under these conditions. Moreover, because I can justify my behavior on the basis of something other than the person's group membership, such as by convincing myself the person was just taking a rest, I can continue to believe that I am a good and non-prejudiced person. I didn't do anything wrong; I would have helped if he really needed assistance. Thus, aversive racists may engage in behaviors that ultimately harm Blacks but in ways that allow them to maintain their self-image as non-prejudiced and that insulate them from recognizing that their behavior is not egalitarian.

Illustrating how aversive racism operates, Dovidio and Gaertner (2000) presented White college students with information about a candidate applying for a prestigious campus job, Resident Advisor. The candidate's credentials were either impeccable (the person was clearly qualified for the job) or mixed (the person was arguably qualified but perhaps not). A photograph of the applicant, who was either Black or White, was attached to the file. Participants then indicated how strongly they recommended the candidate for the position. They did not discriminate on the basis of race when the candidate had obviously outstanding qualifications; in fact, they recommended the Black applicant slightly more strongly than the White applicant. However, when the case was not clear, they gave the White candidate the benefit of the doubt, recommending him more frequently than the Black candidate. In situations such as these, participants emphasized the strongest qualities of the White applicant and the weakest aspects of the Black applicant as being most relevant to success in the

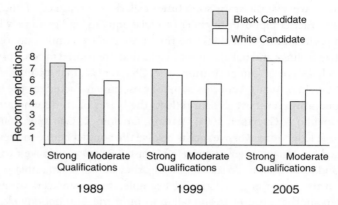

Figure 7.6.   Across Three Different Time Periods (1989, 1999, and 2005) White Participants Do Not Discriminate Against Black Job Applicants Relative to White Job Applicants When the Person Candidate Is Strongly Qualified for the Position. However, They Do Discriminate, and to the Same Degree Across 16 years, When the Candidate Has Only Moderate Credentials and the Decision is More Complicated. Adapted from "New Directions in Aversive Racism Research: Persistence and Pervasiveness," by J. F. Dovidio & S. L. Gaertner, 2007. In C. W. Esqueda (Ed.), *Nebraska Symposium on Motivation: Motivational Aspects of Prejudice and Racism* (pp. 43–67). New York: Springer.

position. They discriminated against the Black applicant who had the same qualifications (Figure 7.6), but they justified it on the basis of some factor other than race (e.g., the Black candidate's lack of experience).

This study was replicated 10 years later with a new group of White college students. Although on explicit self-report measures prejudice appeared to decline since 1989, in 1999 the same pattern of subtle discrimination was obtained (center panel of Figure 7.6). If discrimination goes unrecognized, it will not be corrected. Moreover, the same basic pattern was obtained in 2005 with human resource professionals in Puerto Rico as participants (Dovidio & Gaertner, 2007; right-hand panel of Figure 7.6).

Contemporary racism and implicit attitudes   So what does this have to do with the brain? Recall that implicit attitudes reside in the automatically activated cognitive system. Normally, people make decisions consciously and deliberatively, and they can override implicit biases. However, when a decision is not clear, our gut feelings—things we can't verbalize or may not be fully aware of—tend to guide our behavior. These intuitions often reflect our implicit attitudes. Son Hing, Chung-Yan, Hamilton, and Zanna (2008) basically replicated the findings of Dovidio and Gaertner (2000), but with Asians in Canada as the target group. Asian applicants were recommended as strongly as White applicants when they both had outstanding qualifications. When the applicants had more modest credentials, the White applicant was preferred to the Asian applicant. What these researchers further found, though, is that implicit bias toward Asians (measured with the IAT) strongly predicted bias against Asians when the decision was difficult, but not when it was obvious.

In general, because our brains provide us with two different memory systems, our behavior is jointly determined by both our explicit and implicit attitudes. For instance, a summary of 122 research reports showed that, even though they were only weakly related to each other, explicit and implicit attitudes both significantly predicted a person's behavior (Greenwald et al., 2009). However, which is the better predictor seems to depend on the situation. When issues are socially sensitive, such as those involving race or ethnic relations, implicit attitudes are better predictors than explicit attitudes. In other words, people say the right thing (explicit attitudes), but their negative implicit attitudes often nudge them to behave in less correct ways.

One way to think of the relationship between implicit and explicit attitudes is that implicit attitudes, which are automatically activated, determine the direction and often the first step we take spontaneously; explicit attitudes often put the brakes on and correct our behavior to match our conscious ideals. If a response has to be made quickly, if it is not clear what we should do consciously, or if our cognitive resources have been depleted, implicit attitudes play a larger role in guiding our behavior. Not surprisingly then, implicit attitudes are much more highly related to the early-warning activation of basic brain structures like the amygdala than are explicit attitudes (Phelps et al., 2000), and stimulating the brain to interfere with its associative functioning particularly inhibits implicit bias (Gallate, Wong, Ellwood, Chi, & Snyder, 2011). In addition, when people are in the shooter task (see Box 7.1) and have to make split-second decisions about whether to shoot or be shot, implicit prejudice, but not explicit, predicts the likelihood that people will erroneously shoot an unarmed Black man (Payne, 2006). Implicit biases can have important social consequences.

In summary, in this section we examined how the brain functions in terms of two cognitive systems. One is fast-learning, conscious, and effortful. The other learns slowly by association, but it is stable and becomes activated automatically without intention or effort. These different systems may form the basis for two different types of intergroup attitudes: (a) explicit, conscious attitudes; and (b) implicit, automatically activated attitudes, which may be unconscious. Explicit attitudes are assessed with traditional self-report measures, whereas implicit attitudes are measured with new response–time techniques like the IAT. Contemporary prejudices, such as symbolic and aversive racism, reflect forms of positive explicit attitudes coupled with negative implicit biases. Although the expression of these biases may be more subtle than those of old-fashioned racism, the consequences are as pernicious.

What Can We Do? Addressing Implicit Bias

Just because thoughts, feelings, and behaviors can be automatically activated does not mean they have to determine our behavior or cannot be changed. Earlier in this chapter we discussed ways of preventing these attitudes and stereotypes from being activated by thinking of others in individuated ways rather than as members of another group (Wheeler & Fiske, 2005) or in terms of common group membership rather than as members of separate groups (Van Bavel & Cunningham, 2009; Van Bavel, Packer, & Cunningham, 2008). This kind of reframing or recategorization can prevent activation of the amygdala in response to a person of another race or ethnicity. It can also promote more differentiated face processing in the FFA of an out-group member in the same way it occurs for in-group members. In this section we consider two additional techniques, aimed particularly at addressing implicit bias: (a) acknowledging and addressing implicit bias, and (b) controlling implicit bias through unconscious goals.

Acknowledging Implicit Bias

One of the main problems with contemporary forms of prejudice, particularly aversive racism, is that we are typically motivated to see ourselves as unbiased and therefore we have well-practiced mechanisms for denying or explaining away discrimination. One mechanism that aversive racists frequently use in intergroup interactions is **suppression**, which is directed at one's inner thoughts and which involves conscious attempts to inhibit the activation of negative attitudes, feelings, or beliefs when we sense that we are beginning to experience them.

By itself, suppression is not an effective strategy for eliminating biases. The reason is simple: conscious control requires effort, whereas implicit prejudice and stereotypes are automatic and effortless. Over time our efforts to suppress implicit biases take their toll and deplete our cognitive resources. We run out of cognitive energy. Trawalter and Richeson (2006), for instance, had White students enter an interracial interaction in one of three conditions: (a) they were instructed to avoid being prejudiced (prevention focus); (b) were instructed to try to have a positive interaction (promotion focus); or (c) were given no instructions (control condition). At the end of the interaction, participants performed a simple decision-making task (called a Stroop task). Longer times to make these simple decisions indicate that people are less able to think effectively because they have previously spent their cognitive resources. As the researchers predicted, students in the prevention-focus condition and the control condition (in which participants normally try to suppress negative thoughts in interracial interactions) were much more cognitively depleted than those in the promotion-focus condition. Worrying about difficulties you might have interacting with someone who is different takes a toll. Looking forward to and expecting positive experiences in these interactions can be good for our mental health!

One particular problem with suppression is that when people deplete their cognitive resources, as in the prevention-focus and control conditions, they become unable to control the activation of negative implicit stereotypes and prejudice. Without the ability to control them, implicit biases are activated more strongly than usual—a rebound effect—and they dominate our thoughts in these interactions.

Suppression has another negative, counterintuitive consequence. When people feel like they are behaving in a non-biased way because they believe they have successfully suppressed their negative attitudes, they may be more likely to discriminate in subtle or subsequent ways. For instance, men who are more confident that they are treating women objectively are more likely to discriminate against equally qualified female candidates for a stereotypically male job (chief of police) by inflating criteria that favor male over female candidates (Uhlmann & Cohen, 2005).

Ironically, the act of affirming a non-prejudiced self-image can further increase the likelihood that even seemingly non-prejudiced individuals will discriminate. When given the opportunity to disagree with a prejudicial statement, and therefore affirm a non-prejudiced self-image, individuals were *more* likely to discriminate against women or a racial minority group when making a subsequent hiring decision (Monin & Miller, 2001). The opportunity to reinforce one's egalitarian image, even privately, gave participants a **moral license** to act in a discriminatory manner (see also Effron & Monin, 2010). Moral licensing frees us from controlling our biases because we have engaged in a prior activity that convinces us that we are not prejudiced and thus no longer have to work at being unbiased.

Although attempting to suppress bias can have short-term negative consequences, such as getting us to think about our stereotypes even more (i.e., stereotype rebound), there may be some longer-term benefits of acknowledging that we might be biased. If we deny that we are biased, we will never work hard to be unbiased. However, we need to be motivated to want to change, and, like we need to do to acquire any new skill—from learning math to shooting foul shots in basketball—we need to practice. The good news is that aversive racists, who really want to be non-prejudiced, already have the motivation. So what can we do to help them change to be truly non-prejudiced, even unconsciously?

We need to begin this process by having them discover that they might be unintentionally biased. A number of years ago, Rokeach (1973) developed a value confrontation procedure that helped people recognize contradictions between the core value of equality and their unfair thoughts, feelings, and actions toward other groups. Making people aware of these contradictions increased their motivation to behave in a more egalitarian way and reduced their biases up to a year later. These principles continue to operate today. When people who score low on prejudice acknowledge discrepancies between their behavior toward minorities (what they *would* do) and their personal standards (what they *should* do), they feel guilt and compunction (Monteith, Arthur, & Flynn, 2010). Guilt and compunction are unpleasant psychological states that motivate people to respond without prejudice in the future. With practice, these individuals learn to reduce prejudicial responses and respond in ways that are consistent with their non-prejudiced personal standards. Practiced over time, this process of self-regulation can produce sustained changes in even automatic negative responses.

There is also some evidence of how this may operate in the brain. Cunningham, Raye, and Johnson (2004) found that when Whites were presented with Black faces using exposure times that limited their ability to control their responses (30 ms), they displayed significant amygdala activation, which was correlated with their IAT implicit racial bias. However, when the exposure times were long enough to permit the subjects to control their reactions, they did not show this amygdala activation. Apparently the extra time allowed the subjects to control and correct their responses. When given this time, they showed activation in the frontal cortex (which is related to higher-order executive function) that seemed to inhibit amygdala activation. Thus, there may be some hardwiring in the brain that allows us to make automatic activation less automatic through conscious cognitive control.

Controlling Implicit Bias Through Unconscious Goals

Whereas suppression aims directly at inhibiting or managing implicit bias, using unconscious goals is more indirect. It emphasizes promotion of positive thoughts rather than the prevention of negative thoughts. Its goal is to establish new "habits of mind"—unconscious goals—that are at least as strong as implicit biases and are incompatible with implicit biases. In other words, since implicit attitudes and stereotypes are to a great extent learned through socialization, they can be inhibited by well-learned countervailing influences.

For example, some people have been socialized to hold **chronic egalitarian goals**, habitual ways of thinking that, when activated, inhibit even implicit biases that are normally automatically activated. For these people, seeing a Black person more strongly activates egalitarian thoughts than bias. They are faster to respond to egalitarian-relevant words (e.g., "equality") when primed with Black compared to White faces (Moskowitz, Salomon, & Taylor, 2000). Interventions that arouse these motivations (such as being around others who are blatantly prejudiced) or enhance them (such as having participants describe a personal incident in which they failed to be egalitarian toward Blacks) increase the strength of spontaneous egalitarian thoughts, thereby inhibiting activation of incompatible implicit bias (see Moskowitz & Ignarri, 2009 for a review).

How does one acquire chronic egalitarian goals? The answer is simple to state but difficult to accomplish: practice, practice, practice. For example, either extended efforts to internalize motivations to not be prejudiced (Gonsalkorale, Sherman, Allen, Klauer, & Amodio, 2011) or in associating counter-stereotypic characteristics with racial and ethnic minority groups can inhibit the automatic activation of cultural stereotypes. For example, one successful method is to "say no to stereotyping," being quick to affirm culturally non-stereotypic positive qualities (e.g., intelligent) for minorities, while being fast to reject negative stereotypic qualities (e.g., criminal). However, these efforts have to be made repeatedly and consistently. Too little practice or even an occasional endorsement of cultural stereotypes can undermine the process. In addition, pulling a lever toward you (an approach behavior) rather than pushing it away (avoidance) over and over again (480 times in a single session) reduced implicit racial bias in the IAT and produced more spontaneously open and warm behaviors in an actual intergroup interaction. These implicit motivations to be egalitarian can inhibit the activation of spontaneous racial biases (Kawakami, Phills, Steele, & Dovidio, 2007), even when cognitive resources are depleted (Park, Glaser, & Knowles, 2008). Practice makes perfect.

Summary

Brain structures such as the amygdala and the FFA play key roles in our reactions to diversity. As we explained in Chapter 5, the need to distinguish members of our own group from members of other groups is central to human survival. We need to know, almost instantly, who is friend and who is foe. The amygdala is sensitive to novelty and threat. When it is activated, it initiates a number of physiological responses that prepare us for fight or flight. Similarly, within the in-group, for which we depend upon others in different social roles (Chapter 6), it is critical that we are able to distinguish one individual from another. We don't care as much about differences between members of an out-group; in fact, it is easier to think of them as all basically the same (out-group homogeneity; see Chapter 5). The FFA helps us process faces so we can distinguish one person from another. It is more highly activated when we encounter an in-group member—a person of the same race or ethnicity—than an out-group member.

The brain is functionally organized into two different memory systems, a slow-learning and a fast-learning system. These two memory systems form the foundation for the distinction between explicit attitudes—attitudes that are openly expressed, conscious, and change with socialization and circumstance—and implicit attitudes—attitudes that are automatically activated, often unconscious, and resistant to change. Because the prevailing norms in society are egalitarian and prejudice against most groups is condemned, most people express positive intergroup attitudes and explicitly and consciously embrace principles of equality and fairness. However, because of racist traditions and exposure to pervasive cultural bias, many White Americans harbor negative implicit biases toward other groups. Implicit biases are more directly associated with brain activation related to threat and exert a strong influence on decisions and behaviors that have to be spontaneously enacted.

What distinguishes the human brain from the brains of other animals, however, is the relative size of our cerebral cortex, the part of the brain where higher-order thinking takes place. Higher-order thinking allows us to detect conflicting impulses and to control our reactions. We can think of diversity in many different ways and understand that difference does not always mean threat. Instead we can see diversity as a resource to help us solve new problems in creative ways. Although racial and ethnic categories are automatically activated because of cultural forces, we can choose to see members of different groups as members of our own team, with a common in-group identity. When we do, the amygdala is not activated by racial difference, and we recognize the faces of members of racial and ethnic group members as well as we recognize the faces of members of our own racial or ethnic group. Biology is not destiny.

Just as we learn to become prejudiced, we can learn to be non-prejudiced. But it is not easy. Suppressing our biases takes cognitive effort. When we tire and deplete our cognitive resources, our implicit biases may be activated more strongly, a rebound effect. Nevertheless, if we acknowledge our implicit biases and at the first sign of them practice replacing them with egalitarian thoughts and motivations, we can ultimately inhibit these unwanted thoughts. Repetition and practice in egalitarian non-prejudiced goals make them our automatically activated thoughts. It is difficult to develop egalitarian unconscious goals in a culture in which bias is embedded in so many messages we receive, but it is possible with an awareness of the nature of these biases, the motivation to be better than we are, and extensive practice in thinking and doing the right thing.

Questions for Thinking and Knowing

1. Will the brain adapt to growing diversity and be less likely to show a threat response to difference in the future? What can be done today to make a challenge response more likely than a threat response to diversity?

2.   How do you know whether you are experiencing threat or challenge when you encounter a person of another race or ethnicity? What do these feel like? What are the cues you use to distinguish them? How do you cope with threat, and how does it affect the way you interact with the other person?

3.   Newheiser and Olson (2012) found that when Black children state an explicit preference for wealth and social status the more they showed an implicit bias associating positive words with being White. Can you explain this bias in terms of cultural exposure of Black children?

4.   What social, structural, or psychological forces contribute to the development of implicit biases? How do these forces operate to affect the attitudes of majority- and minority-group members? What kinds of program or policies would you recommend that would prevent children from developing implicit biases against members of other racial or ethnic groups?

5.   Contemporary prejudice is more subtle and less conscious and intentional than old-fashioned racism. How should interventions to combat its negative impact on members of minority groups differ from those used to address old-fashioned racism?

6.   What can *you* do to think and behave in ways to benefit more from diversity in your personal life? What steps can you take? What issues or barriers do you have to overcome? What can you do personally to develop implicit egalitarian goals?

Key Terms

Amygdala
Aversive racism
Cerebral cortex
Challenge response
Chronic egalitarian goals
Electroencephalography (EEG)
Entity theorists
Fast-learning system
Functional magnetic resonance
    imaging (fMRI)

Fusiform face area (FFA)
Implicit Association Test (IAT)
Moral license
Own-race bias
Phenotypicality
Shooter bias
Slow-learning system
Suppression
Symbolic racism
Threat response

References

Aberson, C. L., Shoemaker, C., & Tomolillo, C. (2004). Implicit bias and contact: The role of interethnic friendships. *Journal of Social Psychology, 144*, 335–347.

Amodio, D. M., & Lieberman, M. D. (2009). Pictures in our heads: Contributions of fMRI to the study of prejudice and stereotyping. In T. D. Nelson (Ed.), *Handbook of prejudice, stereotyping, and discrimination* (pp. 347–366). New York: Psychology Press.

Baron, A. S., & Banaji, M. R. (2006). The development of implicit attitudes: Evidence of race evaluations from ages 6, 10, and adulthood. *Psychological Science, 17,* 53–58.

Blascovich, J., & Mendes, W. B. (2010). Social psychophysiology and embodiment. In S. T. Fiske, D. T. Gilbert, & G. Lindzey (Eds.), *Handbook of social psychology* (5th ed., Vol. 1, pp. 194–227). Hoboken, NJ: John Wiley & Sons.

Correll, J., Wittenbrink, B., Park, B., Judd, C. M., & Goyle, A. (2011). Dangerous enough; Moderating racial bias with contextual threat cues. *Journal of Experimental Social Psychology, 47*, 184–189.

Cosmides, L., Tooby, J., & Kurzban, R. (2003). Perceptions of race. *Trends in Cognitive Science, 7*, 173–179.

Crandall, C. S., Eshleman, A., & O'Brien, L. (2002). Sopcial norms and the expression and suppression of prejudice: The struggle for internalization. *Journal of Personality and Social Psychology, 82*, 359–378.

Cunningham, W. A., Raye, C. L., & Johnson, M. K. (2004). Implicit and explicit evaluation: fMRI correlates of valence, emotional intensity, and control in the processing of attitudes. *Journal of Cognitive Neuroscience, 16*, 1717–1729.

Devine, P. G. (1989). Stereotypes and prejudice: Their automatic and controlled components. *Journal of Personality and Social Psychology, 56*, 5–18.

Dovidio, J. F., & Gaertner, S. L. (2000). Aversive racism and selection decisions: 1989 and 1999. *Psychological Science, 11*, 319–323.

Dovidio, J. F., & Gaertner, S. L. (2004). Aversive racism. In M. P. Zanna (Ed.), *Advances in experimental social psychology* (Vol. 36, pp. 1–51). San Diego, CA: Academic Press.

Dovidio, J. F., & Gaertner, S. L. (2007). New directions in aversive racism research: Persistence and pervasiveness. In C. W. Esqueda (Ed.), *Nebraska Symposium on Motivation: Motivational aspects of prejudice and racism* (pp. 43–67). New York: Springer.

Dunbar, R. I. M., & Schultz, S. (2007). Evolution in the social brain. *Science, 317*, 1344–1347.

Eagleman, S. (2011). *Incognito: The secret lives of the brain*. New York: Random House.

Eberhardt, J. L., Dasgupta, N., & Banaszynski, T. I. (2003). Believing is seeing: The effects of racial labels and implicit beliefs on face perception. *Personality and Social Psychology Bulletin, 29*, 360–370.

Eberhardt, J. L., Davies, P. G., Purdie-Vaughns, V. J., & Johnson, S. L. (2006). Looking deathworthy: Perceived stereotypicality of Black defendants predicts capital-sentencing outcomes. *Psychological Science, 17*, 383–386.

Eberhardt, J. L., Goff, P. A., Purdie, V. J., & Davies, P. G. (2004). Seeing Black: Race, crime, and visual processing. *Journal of Personality and Social Psychology, 87*, 876–893.

Effron, D. A., & Monin, B. (2010). Letting people off the hook: When do good deeds excuse transgressions. *Personality and Social Psychology Bulletin, 36*, 1618–1634.

Gaertner, S. L., & Dovidio, J. F. (1986). The aversive form of racism. In J. F. Dovidio & S. L. Gaertner (Eds.), *Prejudice, discrimination, and racism* (pp. 61–89). Orlando, FL: Academic Press.

Gaertner, S. L., & Dovidio, J. F. (2000). *Reducing intergroup bias: The Common Ingroup Identity Model*. Philadelphia, PA: Psychology Press.

Gaertner, S. L., & Dovidio, J. F. (2009). A Common Ingroup Identity: A categorization-based approach for reducing intergroup bias. In T. Nelson (Ed.), *Handbook of prejudice* (pp. 489–506). Philadelphia, PA: Taylor & Francis.

Gallate, J., Wong, C., Ellwood, S., Chi, R., & Snyder, A. (2011). Noninvasive brain stimulation reduces prejudice score on an implicit association test. *Neuropsychology, 25*, 185–192.

Golby, A. J., Gabrieli, J. D. E., Chiao, J. Y., & Eberhardt, J. L. (2001). Differential responses in the fusiform region to same-race and other-race faces. *Nature Neuroscience, 4*, 845–850.

Gonsalkorale, K., Sherman, J. W., Allen, T. J., Klauer, K. C., & Amodio, D. M. (2011). Accounting for successful control of implicit racial bias: The roles of association activation, response monitoring, and overcoming bias. *Personality and Social Psychology Bulletin, 37*, 1534–1545.

Greenwald, A. G., Poehlman, T. A., Uhlmann, E. L., & Banaji, M. R. (2009). Understanding and using the Implicit Association Test: III. Meta-analysis of predictive validity. *Journal of Personality and Social Psychology, 97*, 17–41.

He, Y., Johnson, M. K., Dovidio, J. F., & McCarthy, G. (2009). The relation between race-related implicit associations and scalp-recorded neural activity evoked by faces from different races. *Social Neuroscience, 4*, 426–442.

Heatherton, T. F., Macrae, C. N., & Kelley, W. M. (2004). What the social brain sciences can tell us about the self. *Current Directions in Psychological Science, 13*, 190–193.

Hehman, E., Mania, E. W., & Gaertner, S. L. (2010). Where the division lies: Common ingroup identity moderates the cross-race facial recognition effect. *Journal of Experimental Social Psychology, 46*, 445–448.

Jones, C. R., & Fazio, R. H. (2010). Person categorization and automatic racial stereotyping effects on weapon identification. *Personality and Social Psychology Bulletin, 36*, 1073–1085.

Karpinski, A., & Hilton, J. L. (2001). Attitudes and the Implicit Association Test. *Journal of Personality and Social Psychology, 81*, 774–788.

Kawakami, K., Phills, C. E., Steele, J. R., & Dovidio, J. F. (2007). (Close) Distance makes the heart grow fonder: Improving implicit racial attitudes and interracial interactions through approach behaviors. *Journal of Personality and Social Psychology, 92*, 957–971.

Kelly, D., Quinn, P., Slater, A., Lee, K., Gibson, A., Smith, M., . . . Pascalis, O. (2005). Three-month-olds, but not newborns, prefer own-race faces. *Developmental Science, 8*, F31–F36.

Lieberman, M. D., Hariri, A., Jarcho, J. M., Eisenberger, N. I., & Bookheimer, S. Y. (2005). An fMRI investigation of race-related amygdala activity in African-American and Caucasian-American individuals. *Nature Neuroscience, 8*, 720–722.

Mendes, W. B., Blascovich, J., Hunter, S. B., Lickel, B., & Jost, J. T. (2007). Threatened by the unexpected: Physiological responses during social interactions with expectancy-violating partners. *Journal of Personality and Social Psychology, 92*, 698–716.

Monin, B., & Miller, D. T. (2001). Moral credentials and the expression of prejudice. *Journal of Personality and Social Psychology, 81*, 33–43.

Monteith, M. J., Arthur, S. A., & Flynn, S. M. (2010). Self-regulation and bias. In J. F. Dovidio, M. Hewstone, P. Glick, & V. M. Esses (Eds.), *The SAGE handbook of prejudice, stereotyping, and discrimination* (pp. 493–507). London: Sage.

Moskowitz, G. B., & Ignarri, C. (2009). Implicit volition and stereotype control. *European Review of Social Psychology, 20*, 97–145.

Moskowitz, G. B., Salomon, A. R., & Taylor, C. M. (2000). Preconsciously controlling stereotyping: Implicitly activated egalitarian goals prevent the activation of stereotypes. *Social Cognition, 18*, 151–177.

Newheiser, A.-K., & Olson, K. R. (2012). White and Black American children's implicit intergroup bias. *Journal of Experimental Social Psychology, 48*, 264–270.

Park, S. H., Glaser, J., & Knowles, E. D. (2008). Implicit motivation to control prejudice moderates the effect of cognitive depletion on unintended discrimination. *Social Cognition, 26*, 401–419.

Pauker, K., & Ambady, N. (2009). Multiracial faces: How categorization affects memory at the boundaries of race. *Journal of Social Issues, 65*, 69–86.

Payne, B. K. (2001). Prejudice and perception: The role of automatic and controlled processes in misperceiving a weapon. *Journal of Personality and Social Psychology, 81*, 181–192.

Payne, B. K. (2006). Weapon bias: Split-second decisions and unintended stereotyping. *Current Directions in Psychological Science, 15*, 287–291.

Pearson, A. R., Dovidio, J. F., & Gaertner, S. L. (2009). The nature of contemporary prejudice: Insights from aversive racism. *Social and Personality Psychology Compass, 3,* 314–338.

Pettigrew, T. F., & Tropp, L. R. (2006). A meta-analytic test of intergroup contact theory. *Journal of Personality and Social Psychology, 90,* 751–783.

Phelps, E. A., O'Connor, K. J., Cunningham, W. A., Funayama, E. S., Gatenby, J. C., Gore, J. C., & Banaji, M. R. (2000). Performance on indirect measures of race evaluation predicts amygdala activation. *Journal of Cognitive Neuroscience, 12,* 729–738.

Plant, E. A., Goplen, J., & Kunstman, J. (2011). Selective responses to threat: The roles of race and gender in decisions to shoot. *Personality and Social Psychology Bulletin, 37,* 1274–1281.

Preston, S. D., Bechara, A., Damasio, H., Grabowski, T. J., Stansfield, R. B., Mehta, S., & Damasio, A. R. (2007). The neural substrates of cognitive empathy. *Social Neuroscience, 2,* 254–275.

Rokeach, M. (1973). *The nature of human values.* New York: Free Press.

Rudman, L. A. (2004). Sources of implicit attitudes. *Current Directions in Psychological Science, 13,* 79–82.

Sears, D. O., & Henry, P. J. (2005). Over thirty years later: A contemporary look at symbolic racism. In M. P. Zanna (Ed.), *Advances in experimental social psychology* (Vol. 37, pp. 95–150). San Diego, CA: Academic Press.

Sears, D. O., Henry, P. J., & Kosterman, R. (2000). Egalitarian values and the origins of contemporary American racism. In D. O. Sears, J. Sidanius, & L. Bobo (Eds.), *Racialized politics: The debate about racism in America* (pp. 75–117). Chicago: University of Chicago Press.

Smith, E. R., & DeCoster, J. (2000). Dual-process models and cognitive psychology: Conceptual integration and links to underlying memory systems. *Personality and Social Psychology Review, 4,* 108–131.

Son Hing, L. S., Chung-Yan, G., Hamilton, L., & Zanna, M. (2008). A two-dimensional model that employs explicit and implicit attitudes to characterize prejudice. *Journal of Personality and Social Psychology, 94,* 971–987.

Tanaka, J. W., & Pierce, L. J. (2009). The neural plasticity of other-race face recognition. *Cognitive, Affective, and Behavioral Neuroscience, 9,* 122–131.

Tetlock, P. E., & Mitchell, G. (2008). Calibrating prejudice in milliseconds. *Social Psychology Quarterly, 71,* 12–16.

Trawalter, S., & Richeson, J. A. (2006). Regulatory focus and executive function after interracial interactions. *Journal of Experimental Social Psychology, 42,* 406–412.

Uhlmann, E. L., & Cohen, G. L. (2005). Constructed criteria: Redefining merit to justify discrimination. *Psychological Science, 16,* 474–480.

Van Bavel, J. J., & Cunnigham, W. A. (2009). Self-categorization with a novel mixed-race group moderates automatic social and racial biases. *Personality and Social Psychology Bulletin, 35,* 321–335.

Van Bavel, J. J., & Cunningham, W. A. (2010). A social neuroscience approach to self and social categorization: A new look at an old issue. *European Review of Social Psychology, 21,* 237–284.

Van Bavel, J. J., Packer, D. J., & Cunningham, W. A. (2008). The neural substrates of ingroup bias: A functional magnetic resonance imaging investigation. *Psychological Science, 19,* 1131–1139.

Vedantam, S. (2005, January 23). Many Americans believe they are not prejudiced. Now a new test provides powerful evidence that a majority of us really are. *Washington Post,* p. W12.

Wheeler, M. E., & Fiske, S. T. (2005). Controlling racial prejudice. *Psychological Science, 16,* 56–62.

Wilson, T. D., Lindsey, S., & Schooler, T. (2000). A model of dual attitudes. *Psychological Review, 107,* 101–126.

Young, S. G., Hugenberg, K., Bernstein, M. J., & Sacco, D. F. (2012). Perception and motivation in face recognition: A critical review of the cross-race effect. *Personality and Social Psychology Review, 16,* 116–142.

Chapter 8

Coping and Adapting to Stigma and Difference

Introduction   205
Social Stigma and Cultural Difference   207
Racial Socialization and Acculturation   211
Stresses Caused by Stigma and Difference   213
Coping with Perceived Discrimination   220
Collective Identities   224
Summary   231

"Wow, you really don't look Japanese at all. You look White." He smiled. . . . He was telling me that I looked White, and he meant it as a compliment.

Kohei Ishihara, college student

Introduction

James Garcia and Evaristo Vazquez were fortunate enough to be able to take a week's vacation in Jamaica. Both were born in Pennsylvania, and neither had ever left the United States before. Although they had a dream of a time in sunny Jamaica, they had a nightmare on reentry. When they arrived at Newark Airport, they were surrounded by customs agents, put into separate rooms, and strip-searched. These searches revealed nothing illegal, and neither did a search of their luggage. Nevertheless, James and Evaristo were whisked away in handcuffs to St Francis Hospital to be X-rayed. Again, nothing illegal was found. Without apology, they were taken back to the airport and released. James Garcia asked the U.S. agents why they had been

The Psychology of Diversity: Beyond Prejudice and Racism, First Edition. James M. Jones, John F. Dovidio, and Deborah L. Vietze.

singled out. He was asked, in return, his nationality and age. He replied, "Hispanic and I'm 24." The agent replied, knowingly, "Well, there you go" (as reported by Nat Hentoff, 1994).

Is being Latino, male, and in your early twenties a federal crime? Of course it isn't. Were James and Evaristo victims of stereotyping? Of course they were. Stereotyping, prejudice, and intergroup bias are not just topics that social psychologists study in the laboratory. They are facts of life that affect people every day. This chapter is concerned with how people affected by negative stereotypes adapt and cope psychologically, behaviorally, and emotionally. In the United States, members of ethnic minority groups, gays and lesbians, elderly, women, Muslims, and immigrants often experience bias in many forms. For example, people often suspect Latinos of being illegal immigrants, of being unable to speak or understand English, of harboring criminal intentions, of being unintelligent, of being likely to behave violently, of being unable to lead or to make tough decisions, and of being slow-witted.

As we have repeated throughout this book, diversity concerns differences. Here we examine two kinds of differences. One type involves differences that are stigmatized—differences based on some distinguishing characteristic that devalues the person or group who possesses it (Dovidio, Gaertner, Niemann, & Snider, 2001). The other involves differences that, while based on some distinguishing characteristic, may not be stigmatized, even though they set a person or group apart from others in a given context. Examples include a 60-something person working in a high-tech start-up company among co-workers in their twenties, or a White student in a classroom of predominantly Black students, or some White Southerners growing up in all-Black areas teaching in predominantly White colleges. These differences are not related to inherent devaluation, but, particularly if these are novel experiences, they can still make a person uncomfortable and lead to stress.

Cross-cutting these two kinds of difference is *visibility*—whether the basis for difference or stigma is readily apparent (race, gender, and age versus learning disability, sexual orientation, and mental illness)—and *narrative*—whether a well-known cultural story is associated with the difference (a narrative of inferiority, oppression, and rejection, or of superiority, virtue, and accomplishment). For example, a White man may carry the invisible stigma of dyslexia while at the same time carry the positive narrative of accomplishment. For example, White men (e.g., Tom Cruise, Steve Jobs, Walt Disney, Thomas Edison, John Lennon, and Jay Leno), White women (Cher, Keira Knightly), Black men (Magic Johnson), and Black women (Whoopi Goldberg) may be conspicuously successful, but all have nevertheless been diagnosed as dyslexic.

How people adjust to being stigmatized depends upon how, and how well, they cope with others' bias against them. **Coping** refers to a person's conscious and intentional efforts to regulate behavior (emotion, thought, physiology) or the environment in response to stressful events or circumstances (Compas, Connor-Smith, Saltzman, Thomsen, & Wadsworth, 2001). When the resources needed to manage a particular situation are perceived to be more than you possess, you experience the situation as **stress**. Coping responses are then activated to alleviate the stress. This can happen in one of two ways: (a) you can deal directly with the stress-causing problem (problem-focused coping), or (b) you can regulate your emotions to lessen the distress (emotion-focused coping).

The psychology of diversity examines the basic psychological processes that are triggered when we experience being treated differently by others because of our social status (see Chapter 2). This chapter looks at the reactions and coping processes of individuals who are targets of prejudice, stereotyping, and discrimination. How do they adjust, cope, and keep their psychological well-being intact? Even if one has not been interned in a concentration camp, what effect does knowledge of the internment of one's ancestors have on self-esteem, self-image, and future expectations? What does James and Evaristo's humiliating experience do to their psyches and to the psyches of their Latino friends who hear about it? What are the psychological effects of being an Arab American since the September 11, 2001 terrorist attacks, or of being a gay man or lesbian in the military under the "Don't ask, don't tell" policy? What are the psychological consequences for Black men, who are often under suspicion of violence, criminality, and general wrongdoing? How do these stigmas affect how you are, what you feel, what you think or what you do?

First, we will consider the psychological predicaments caused by prejudice. For example, knowing that you may face prejudice because you are different based on your age, race, ethnicity, gender, or sexual orientation means that you cannot take for granted responses and outcomes that others may consider routine. Simply knowing of negative prejudices against your group can undermine psychological well-being (Link & Phelan, 2001).

We next look into the question of how parents and others socialize young people to live in a society where stigma and features of their difference may affect how they are treated. Most of this work falls under the heading of racial socialization, but we will also consider acculturation and other evidence of cross-generational preparation for adult life. For example, newly arrived immigrants experience the stress of fitting in and learning new cultural ways. What are the costs of acculturating to new ways and shedding old ones? Is this choice an inevitable one or is it possible to have it both ways?

The third section takes a stress-and-coping approach to stigma and difference. Two questions emerge: what factors influence the degree to which stigmatizing or prejudiced contexts are perceived or experienced as stressful, and what strategies do people use to cope with these situations? We will examine specific mechanisms employed by members of various groups to demonstrate when they are able to maintain psychological health and well-being in the face of stigma and unequal status, and when their general well-being and success may be undermined.

The final section focuses on specific aspects of collective identities as broad-based means of combating stigma and difference. We explore a variety of identities including racial, ethnic, gender, immigrant, and their intersections.

Social Stigma and Cultural Difference

Two sources of stress and strain that make diversity challenging are stigma and social/cultural difference. A stigma is a mark that distinguishes a person or group and sets it apart physically, socially, or psychologically. As we saw in Chapter 3, at different times in our history nationality and race were bases for exclusion from the United

States, or segregation from Whites, or internment, or containment on a reservation. A stigma reflects severe social disapproval of personal or group characteristics or beliefs.

Social or cultural difference may challenge diversity even if the basis of difference is not based in stigma. If there is a normative status quo, then people who do not fit that norm are characterized by their difference from it. When people are different, there is often an assumption that they are different in many ways beyond the obvious attribute: that they think differently and have different values and goals. The more deep-seated their principal difference is thought to be, the greater the divide in understanding and the more intractable differences become (Prentice & Miller, 2006). Let's look in turn at stigma and cultural difference.

The Social "Stain" of Stigma

Stigma is a pervasive and powerful phenomenon linked to the value associated with social identities (Dovidio et al., 2001) A social identity is stigmatized if others perceive it as a *stain* (Goffman, 1963). Thus, stigma always refers to how others perceive you or your group. You may be quite aware of this "mark" without adopting it as a part of who you are. Alternatively, you may be aware of it and take active measures to counteract its negative influence, or simply attempt to conceal it. The 2003 movie *The Human Stain* portrays a Black man (Anthony Hopkins) who because he does not appear to be Black, passes for White for 50 years. The "stain" is revealed eventually and his life falls apart. However one chooses to deal with it, being stigmatized challenges your psychological well-being. This chapter is concerned with how those who are the targets of stigma perceive and react to it.

A stigmatized social status is signaled by four conditions: (a) individuals are differentiated and labeled, (b) cultural beliefs attach negative attributes to people who are labeled as different, (c) labeled individuals are placed in groups that are separated between "us" and "them," and (d) labeled individuals experience loss of status and are discriminated against, leading to social inequality (Link & Phelan, 2001). In this model, stigma includes labeling (social categorization; see Chapter 5), stereotyping, disconnection, status loss, and discrimination.

A stigmatized person possesses an attribute that conveys a devalued social identity *within a given context* (Crocker, Major, & Steele, 1998). However, for some stigmatized groups, such as African Americans, the social contexts are pervasive. Prejudice is commonly defined as treating individuals differently on the basis of beliefs about the groups to which they belong or are assigned. Prejudice and stigma challenge efforts to create beneficially diverse settings. And, from our perspective, the challenge is both for those stigmatized and those who hold normative status.

Being stigmatized creates predicaments for people. A **predicament** is an unpleasant, troublesome, or trying situation from which it is difficult to extricate oneself. Prejudice or its potential is a threat a person must pay attention to and often requires corrective or evasive action. Our concern here is with those situations that cause predicaments and those corrective and evasive actions one takes to fix them. Four conditions pose predicaments for people at risk of being targets of prejudice (Crocker et al., 1998):

1. *Awareness of the devalued quality of one's social identity.* You are aware that your group is viewed negatively by others, particularly those who hold positions of authority or who control valued and needed resources.

2. *Stereotype threat.* You are aware of negative stereotypes of your group and the possibility that you may validate that stereotype by your behavior.

3. *Experience with prejudice and discrimination.* You have experienced bias or witnessed public examples of bias against others in your group. This raises an ever-present specter of prejudice that may threaten your self-worth or, worse, lead to real negative outcomes.

4. *Attributional ambiguity.* You feel uncertainty when a member of an out-group behaves negatively toward you or a member in your group. Is that negative behavior because of something about me (possibly valid) or the other person (possibly invalid)?

Let's look briefly at some of these threatening predicaments.

When I (James Jones) go to an outdoor ATM machine at night, and a woman (particularly a White woman) is making a transaction, I wonder if she is anxious from fear that I, a Black male, may harm her in some way. I have no such intention, but how do I put her at ease? Maybe I can't put her at ease, or maybe she has no such expectation. But the thought goes through my mind. Stereotypes affect not only their holder but also their target.

Each person is unique, one of over 7 billion people. Each person's experiences, beliefs, abilities, goals, and social relations are shared by no other person on the planet. But each of us also belongs to many groups whose members share common experiences. Some of these group memberships are chosen (professor), some are inherited (male), and some are socially defined (African American). What distinguishes many of us, though, is that the groups we belong to play an important role in determining our experiences.

If you are Latino or Latina, for example, you may run the risk of being mistaken for an illegal immigrant, especially if you have an accent. You may also face the stigma of being different and wish you could lose the accouterments of culture. A friend once confided that she hated it when her mother made her tortilla-and-bean sandwiches in elementary school. She loved them but knew that they would link her to her Chicana roots. In those days (*c.* 1975), there was constant ambivalence about the melting pot as a cauldron of homogenization and assimilation. Losing one's culture, or at least evidence of it, appeared to be a prerequisite for success or, in some cases, even for opportunity.

For gay men and lesbians, the closet was where one's sexual orientation was housed. Bringing one's sexual orientation out into the open was an invitation to bigotry and prejudice. But with the emergence of trends toward self-definition and legal and judicial acknowledgment of gay rights, there is a more general willingness to declare one's group affiliation publicly and to do so with pride and honor.

So as an individual, one must often decide whether to express one's personal character or to suppress it in the service of reaching desired goals or fitting in. Whether you view this choice as a predicament or as a challenge, it is not simple, and its consequences are often negative or unpredictable. Nevertheless, *not choosing* is often not a psychological option. Race, ethnicity, gender, or sexual orientation is a part of your identity and can be a basis for others' reactions to you or how you think about yourself. We will review some of the ways in which people cope with these predicaments in the next section. Now we turn to the topic of social and cultural differences between groups.

How Social and Cultural Difference Divides Us

Noted American writer F. Scott Fitzgerald is reported to have said to his equally noted writer friend Ernest Hemingway, "The rich are different from us." To which Hemingway is reported to have replied, "Yes, they have more money." Fitzgerald was about to propose some *essence* that distinguished rich people from others. However, Hemingway rejected this approach favoring a simple and objective distinction.

The more we emphasize the essential differences among us, the more divisive differences can become. When differences between two people from different groups are believed to reflect essential differences, these differences are exaggerated and common understanding is undermined; this idea is the **category divide hypothesis** (Prentice & Miller, 2006). Most of us have a tendency to essentialize groups, like Fitzgerald did. We put people in social categories based on surface characteristics like skin color, hair, eye structure, but we often believe that traits (hard working, intelligent, lazy, gregarious, moral, and so on) and characteristic behaviors differentiate members of one group from members of another.

Differences need not always be visible, associated with stigma, or based on traits. Have you ever been in a situation when you felt different from most of the people around you? Just knowing that you are different from others can produce uncertainty, even anxiety, about how to behave, what to say. These feelings of uncertainty often make it much easier to stay within a comfort zone of familiarity and predictability. We associate with those who are like us (see Tatum, 2004).

However, differences are often stigmatized, associated with negative judgments. People may, by virtue of their physical appearance, behavior, or life circumstance, possess attributes that are both statistically unusual and centrally defining (an essential basis for classifying the group; Frable, 1993). Many stigmas, however, are not visible. These stigmas include sexual orientation, mental illness, a criminal conviction, previous drug use, and a medical condition. People with stigmas that are not visible (sometimes called concealable stigmas) also feel vulnerable, particularly when they feel that they cannot control who knows about their stigma and their stigma is more culturally devalued (Quinn & Chaudoir, 2009). However, because it is more difficult to identify other people with the same stigma, people with concealable stigmas frequently experience heightened feelings of uniqueness and isolation. When you have visible features that signal difference, emphasizing similarity to others is a likely coping strategy.

Being a gay man or lesbian is one potentially invisible status. Being gay can present challenges that are stressful (Herek & Garnets, 2007). These challenges include recognizing one's sexual orientation, developing an identity based on it, and disclosing one's sexual orientation to others. Recognizing one's homosexuality often leads initially to negative feelings about oneself. This negative feeling about one's sexual orientation is labeled **internalized homophobia**. Internalized homophobia is associated with less self-disclosure to heterosexual friends and acquaintances, less feeling of connection to the gay and lesbian community, and more depressive symptoms and demoralization. Men higher in internalized homophobia have lower self-esteem (Herek & Garnets, 2007).

However, psychological distress can be alleviated with social support and effective regulation of emotional responses (Hatzenbuehler, Nolen-Hoeksema, & Dovidio, 2009). For lesbian, gay, and bisexual (LGB) participants, stigma-related stress was associated with greater psychological distress, more social isolation, and a tendency to ruminate more on the stigma stress. On days when stigma-related stress occurred, LGB participants felt even more isolated, while African Americans reported greater social support on those days. These findings illustrate differences in availability and utilization of coping responses to stigma-related stress. However, the more one ruminates about stressful events, the more one experiences psychological distress, regardless of social identity. How people cope with stigma is something they learn quite early.

Racial Socialization and Acculturation

Socialization is what parents do with their children to prepare them to function effectively as adults in our society. Socializing children is not only done by parents but also by other family members (e.g., grandparents, uncles/aunts and older siblings) as well as by other adults (e.g., coaches, teachers, religious leaders) and often peers as well. As the saying goes, "It takes a village to raise a child." If you are a parent and belong to a stigmatized group, or if you are entering a new culture, how do you socialize your children for adult status? How do you prepare them for the stigma they may face, as well as the opportunities they should take advantage of? Which behaviors do you reward and which do you punish? What values do you instill and what expectations do you set? Or indeed, why *should* you approach raising a child differently because they do not fit the cultural norm?

Acculturation is similar to socialization but focuses on acquiring knowledge and accepting a different culture. Parents may want their children to function effectively in their own culture (**enculturation**) but also want to teach or expose them to a new culture to prepare them for functioning in a different cultural context. This dual purpose may lead to tension, known as **acculturative stress**. Is it necessary to choose between cultures?

In this section, we will look first at racial socialization to see how parents of different racial groups (mostly Black) frame the socialization task, and what the consequences are for a variety of academic, psychological, and behavioral outcomes. Next we consider acculturation processes and explore how parents instill either their culture of origin or a new one and what processes lead to cultural fluency. The general question is: Do racial socialization and acculturation practices help children become successful academically and healthy psychologically?

Preparing Children for a Racialized Society: Racial Socialization

Racial socialization refers to verbal and behavioral practices of families that inform a child about how race affects personal and group identity, intergroup and interpersonal relations, and position in the social hierarchy (Caughy, Nettles, O'Campo, & Lohrfink, 2006). Racial socialization can be *proactive*, emphasizing pride, knowledge of your culture, and acceptance of who you are; or *protective*, emphasizing discrimination and stigma individuals may face because of their race.

Proactive socialization has positive effects on children's well-being. For example, proactive socialization has been shown to be positively associated with self-esteem (Constantine & Blackmon, 2002), internal attribution for success (Miller, 2001), better cognitive performance, and fewer behavioral problems (Caughy, O'Campo, Randolph, & Nickerson, 2002), stronger reasons for living (Forbes, 2004), and greater prosocial behavior (Stevenson, 1997). Proactive socialization is also negatively associated with psychological distress (Bynum, Burton, & Best, 2007), suicidality, lethargy and low self-esteem (Davis & Stevenson, 2006), and internal attribution for failure (Miller, 2001). Furthermore, proactive, but not protective, messages tend to shield adolescent self-esteem from the adverse effects of racial discrimination (Harris-Britt, Valrie, Kurtz-Costes, & Rowley, 2007; Neblett et al., 2008). In fact, the degree to which experiencing racism increases or decreases a person's regard for being Black is fully determined by their level of proactive racial socialization (Stevenson & Arrington, 2009).

Families and parents matter! How they socialize their children to enter a world in which they may be stigmatized or be different from others in some visible way have consequences for their children's well-being. A child's skills, attitudes, self-confidence, and coping strategies are importantly influenced early on. And the capacity of African American children to cope with real or perceived discrimination is influenced by how they are socialized.

Adapting to a Different Culture: Acculturation

Acculturation is the way in which the culture of a group or individual is modified as a result of contact with a different culture. Entering a new culture often produces opposing desires: to retain one's cultural identity and to seek interethnic contact. Research has attempted to discover how acculturation is successfully accomplished.

One study explored the degree to which different acculturation profiles (Table 8.1) were related to successful adaptation to a new culture (Berry, Phinney, Sam, & Vedder, 2006). An international sample of 276 immigrant youth aged 13–18 from thirteen

Table 8.1.   Profiles of Acculturation Orientations

		Involvement in mainstream culture	
		High	*Low*
Maintain cultural heritage	High	Integration	Separation/Ethnic
	Low	Assimilation/National	Marginalization/Diffuse

different countries were studied. Acculturation was conceived as the degree to which they desired to maintain their heritage culture and identity ("maintenance") and the degree to which they sought involvement with the larger society ("involvement"). Four acculturation profiles emerged: *integration* (high maintenance and involvement), *ethnic* (sense of belonging, positive feelings about being a group member), *national* (a strong orientation toward the new society), and *diffuse* (lack of commitment, direction, or purpose; socially isolated).

Youth with an integration profile were the most satisfied with their lives, had high self-esteem, and showed little evidence of negative psychological states like depression or anxiety. Those with a diffuse profile had the worst adaptation. Those with an ethnic or national profile fell in between. Berry et al. (2006) conclude that immigrant youth should be encouraged to retain a sense of their own heritage cultural identity while establishing close ties with the larger national society. But this may be easier said than done.

Stresses Caused by Stigma and Difference

This section explores a variety of ways in which people cope with stigma. We will look specifically at situations that consistently lead to perceptions of stress and some of the coping consequences they produce. We will focus on how people react when they perceive or anticipate discrimination and discuss several psychological variables associated with different ways of coping.

Perceiving Discrimination Is Bad for Your Health

As we saw in Chapter 2, discrimination involves the systematic mistreatment of a group in a society by law, social policy, or social practice. But **perceived discrimination** involves a person's perception that he or she has been unfairly treated in a given situation. When people perceive they have been discriminated against, whether based on their race/ethnicity (Pascoe & Smart-Richman, 2009) or lower socioeconomic status (Fuller-Rowell, Evans, & Ong, 2012), their physical and psychological health may suffer. Women who perceived that they were targets of sexism experienced physiological stress (in the form of elevated cortisol levels), which interferes with effective problem solving and, longer term, can lead to depression (Townsend, Major, Gangi, & Mendes, 2011).

Perceiving discrimination also affects the way we behave and the choices we make on a daily basis, often with long-term detrimental consequences. Research shows that among Blacks, perceived discrimination decreases self-control, lowering the tendency to perform healthy behaviors and increasing the likelihood of engaging in unhealthy and risky behaviors (Gibbons, Etcheverry, Stock, Gerrard, & Weng, 2010; Gibbons, Roberts, Gerrard, Li, & Beach, 2012). In addition, it adversely affects aspirations and long-term achievements. Controlling for socioeconomic status and other relevant factors, the amount of time Black children perceived discrimination against them prior to and during the time they were fifth-graders decreased the likelihood that they would attend college 7 years later, based in part on their lower aspirations

(O'Hara, Gibbons, Weng, Gerrard, & Simons, 2012). Perceiving discrimination is bad for you. However, if you are actually being discriminated against, and you fail to perceive it, that may be bad for you too.

Stereotype Threat Is "in the Air"

Awareness of cultural stigmatization of your group, even when you do not personally internalize these negative attitudes or directly experience discrimination, can still be stressful and debilitating. The theory of **stereotype threat**, which proposes that situations containing cues making a negative stereotype about your social group salient and awareness of the possibility that your performance will confirm it, creates anxiety and undermines your performance (Steele, 2010). Stereotype threat theory proposes that two responses to the threat are most common: disruptive apprehension and protective disidentification.

The first consequence of stereotype threat is **disruptive apprehension**, the anxiety that accompanies the awareness that you are in a stereotype threating situation. To demonstrate disruptive apprehension Steele and Aronson (1995) had White and Black participants perform a test comprising the most difficult items from the Graduate Record Exam (GRE). The test was introduced in one of three ways. Participants were told that (a) this test is "a genuine test of your verbal abilities and limitations" (*diagnostic*); or (b) you should try hard "even though we're not going to evaluate your ability" (*non-diagnostic*); or (c) you should "please take this challenge seriously even though we will not be evaluating your ability" (*challenge condition*). Only when the test was diagnostic of their abilities was stereotype threat activated, and only then did performance suffer. When stereotype threat was not activated, Blacks and Whites performed equally on the tests. What is going on here? What causes this performance deficit in the stereotype threat condition?

One possibility, supported by a second study, is that stereotype threat activated thoughts of the stereotype, which in turn elicited self-doubt and led to active attempts to avoid the stereotype. A second study showed that when one is experiencing the disruptive apprehension associated with stereotype threat, they are more likely to complete the fragment – – C E with RACE than FACE, and – – – ERIOR with INFERIOR than SUPERIOR. Other studies showed that dissociating oneself from stereotypical activities (rap music, basketball) was another way one could avoid the apprehensions of stereotype threat (Steele & Aronson, 1995).

This research established a paradigm for studying the effects of stigma on a range of behaviors for a number of stigmatized groups. It is one of the most generative frameworks in the field. Research on stereotype threat has not only considered the consequences on problem solving and academic performance for Blacks (Carr & Steele, 2009) but has also been applied to understand academic achievement of Latinos, math performance in women, memory failures for the elderly, eating for overweight people, and athletic performance for Whites (see Inzlicht & Schmader, 2012). Most recently, researchers have further attempted to explain just what goes on during stereotype threat.

The effects of stereotype threat are complex and run deep. Stereotype threat increases feelings of stress, which distracts people from thinking clearly. People spend more time monitoring their environment for other threats while simultaneously devoting their energy to suppressing negative thoughts and feelings, reducing their capacity to perform the assigned task at hand (Schmader, Johns, & Forbes, 2008).

These effects are directly observable in studies of brain imaging (fMRI, which we discussed in Chapter 7). Women who experienced stereotype threat on a math task when they were reminded about the stereotype that women are not good in math showed lower activity in the parts of the brain largely responsible for mathematical calculations and increased activity in areas related to emotional and social concerns (Krendl, Richeson, Kelley, & Heatherton, 2008). As a consequence, women who experienced stereotype threat performed worse on the math test. These efforts to understand and cope with threat deplete resources that could be devoted not only to the primary task but also to resources needed for other activities requiring self-control. For instance, women under stereotype threat for a math test show a "stereotype threat spillover" effect: They not only perform worse on the math test, but they also show less ability to regulate and control their behavior in other ways, such as subsequently showing more aggressive behavior and eating more unhealthy foods (Inzlicht & Kang, 2010).

Another way to protect positive feelings of worth and esteem and buffer the effect of stereotype threat is to engage in **protective disidentification**, in which you define or redefine the self-concept so that performance outcomes are not a basis of self-evaluation or personal identity. If you disidentify with a performance domain, then the threat of confirming a negative stereotype has little personal relevance. Osborne (1995) tested this idea in a large sample of nearly 25,000 students from over 1,000 schools in the United States. For eighth graders, the correlation between academic performance and self-esteem fell in a narrow range between 0.20 (Black boys) and 0.27 (White girls). As shown in Figure 8.1, in the tenth grade the correlations remained roughly the same for Whites (boys and girls), but had fallen slightly for Black girls (from 0.26 to 0.20) and precipitously for Black boys (from 0.21 to 0.075).

If self-esteem exerts an important influence on adolescent behavior, severing the connection between self-esteem and grade point average (GPA) removes an important motivation for academic performance. Indeed, it is primarily members of a stigmatized group who are strongly identified with the domain (e.g., academic achievement) who experience stereotype threat. However, the self-esteem protection strategy of disidentification may have side effects such as diminishing interest, motivation, and, ultimately, achievement. How one copes with stigma can have important consequences for one's academic performance and, over time, for opportunities in life.

Stereotype threat research has expanded the original ideas in a number of different ways. For instance, researchers have considered when stereotype threat is more or less likely to occur. Just because it is possible that a stereotype will be applied does not mean that it will be. It would be inefficient to activate the apprehension associated with stereotype threat every time there was a possibility of a threat. It would be more efficient to calculate the probability a stereotype will be applied, then activate the apprehension responses only if it exceeds some high level. Wout, Shih, Jackson, and Sellers (2009) tested this idea by having Black college students complete an online test of analytical ability that was evaluated by a White or Black evaluator. Performance

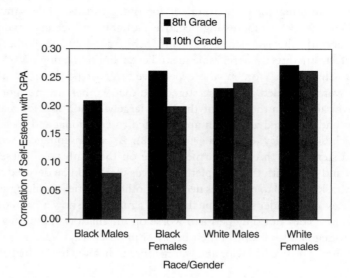

Figure 8.1.   Correlation Between Self-esteem and GPA for Black and White Eighth and Tenth Grade Boys and Girls: Evidence of Disidentification. From "Academics, Self-esteem, and Race: A Look at the Underlying Assumptions of the Disidentification Hypothesis," by J. W. Osborne, 1995, *Personality and Social Psychology Bulletin, 21,* pp. 449–455.

declined with a White evaluator (higher probability of stereotyped evaluation) but not with a Black evaluator (lower probability of stereotype evaluation).

The ideas behind stereotype threat have also been extended to explain the finding that among West Indian immigrants, the longer they have been in the United States, the poorer their psychological well-being. Educational and occupational data show that first-generation West Indian immigrants outperform not only second-generation immigrants but also comparison groups of African Americans.

First-generation West Indian immigrants have less experience with negative stereotypes of Blacks, a stronger ethnic identification as West Indians, and less experience with racial discrimination than their second-generation counterparts (Deaux et al., 2007). Each of these factors could protect them from the adverse effects of stereotype threat. Deaux et al. (2007) tested this idea in a stereotype threat study using the procedures reported by Steele and Aronson (1995) and including first- and second-generation West Indian students. The results, shown in Figure 8.2, confirmed the predicted interaction between generation and stereotype threat condition: First- and second-generation West Indian students performed equally in control conditions, but first-generation students performed significantly better than second-generation students under stereotype threat. However, neither knowledge of negative stereotypes nor strength of ethnic identification played a significant role in these effects. So this generational phenomenon is still in search of an explanation.

It is also possible that being stereotyped is not always bad. What is the effect of positive stereotypes? What about majority group members or members of groups

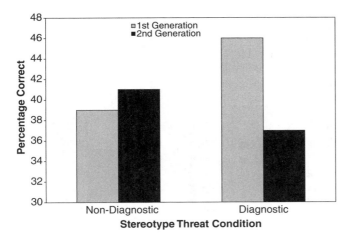

Figure 8.2.   Generational Differences in Stereotype Threat among West Indian Immigrants. From "Becoming American: Stereotype Threat Effects in Afro-Caribbean Immigrant Groups," by K. Deaux, N. Bikmen, A. Gilkes, A. Ventuneac, Y. Joseph, Y. A. Payne, & C. M. Steele, 2007, *Social Psychology Quarterly, 70*, pp. 384–404 (Figure 1 as published).

stereotyped positively on an ability? Does stereotype threat boost performance for people who enjoy a positive association with the domain? Recent research says yes.

Armenta (2010) argues that when one's group is made salient, performance shifts in the direction of the stereotype, either positively or negatively. When the stereotype is negative, performance gets worse and the effect is labeled stereotype threat. But when the stereotype is positive, performance gets better and is labeled **stereotype boost**.

To assess the stereotype boost idea, Armenta (2010) gave a computer-administered math test that activated the positive or negative stereotype to Asian American (positive stereotype) and Latino (negative stereotype) college students. Participants also completed a measure of their ethnic identity. For participants with high ethnic identity, linking a diagnostic math test to ethnic differences led to improved performance for Asian American students, but poorer performance for Latino students (Figure 8.3). Similar results have been found for women (Schmader, 2002), for athletic ability based on IQ (boost for Whites; Stone, Lynch, Sjomeling & Darley, 1999) and for natural athletic ability (boost for Blacks; Stone et al., 1999). Similarly, for Asian women taking a math test, making gender salient reduces performance, but making Asian American identity salient boosts performance (Shih, Pittinsky, & Ambady, 1999).

Whereas stereotype threat focuses on how members of stigmatized groups feel and perform, the stress that people experience in intergroup interaction can contribute to miscommunication across group lines. As Box 8.1 reveals, the stresses that both minority- and majority-group members experience affect the quality of intergroup communication.

But what if you are, in fact, discriminated against, or if you have friends who are, or you read about people who belong to your group who are? How do you avoid these

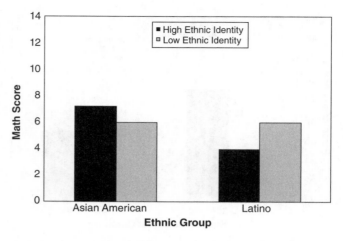

Figure 8.3.   Stereotype Boost for Asian and Stereotype Threat for Latino Students on Math Performance. Adapted from "Stereotype Boost and Stereotype Threat Effects: The Moderating Role of Ethnic Identification," by B. E. Armenta, 2010, *Cultural Diversity and Ethnic Minority Psychology, 16,* pp. 94–98 (Figure 1 as published).

Box 8.1.   Communicating Across the Racial Divide

Research on cross-racial communication identifies three ways that stress influences the quality of intergroup communication: (a) attributional ambiguity, (b) racial paralysis, and (c) pluralistic ignorance.

Attributional ambiguity involves the ways people interpret the statements and behaviors of others when their intentions aren't entirely obvious. It has a strong effect on the responses of members of minority groups. This was demonstrated by Crocker, Voelkl, Testa, and Major (1991), who arranged for Black and White participants to receive negative evaluative information from a student evaluator who was behind a one-way mirror with the blinds open (making the participant visible) or closed (so participants could not be seen). For White students, self-esteem dipped with negative feedback whether the blinds were open or closed. But for Black students, self-esteem dipped only when the blinds were closed and the evaluator could not see them. When Black participants believed that the evaluator knew their race (i.e., the blinds were open), they could attribute their evaluations to the evaluator's prejudice and discount the negative judgment.

Attributional ambiguity creates a predicament, however. While discounting negative evaluations may protect self-esteem, positive evaluations may be discounted also. A person might attribute them to attempts to be "politically correct" and not to personal merit. Thus, Blacks may not be responsive to feedback from Whites, either negative or positive, because they doubt its validity.

The stress that Whites experience also interferes with intergroup communication. Consider a situation in which a White person gets on a bus and there are only two seats available: one next to a White person and the other next to a Black person. Which seat does he take? If he takes the seat by the White person, he might reason that "they will attribute my choice to negative feelings about Blacks and conclude I am a racist!" If he chooses the seat next to a Black person, he might reason, "they may think I am just trying to hide my true racist feelings!" So what does he do? Research by Norton, Mason, Vandello, Biga, and Dyer (2012) suggests that he is paralyzed by these two options, so, unable to choose, he elects to stand!

In an attempt to replicate this bus scenario, White participants were asked to judge how likely two people were to be valedictorians of the class or to commit a crime. When both of the people were White, the subjects made their choice easily (65%). But when one was Black and one was White, racial paralysis set in and they were willing to choose only 15% of the time. Norton and colleagues termed this type of indecision and behavioral "freezing" **racial paralysis** among Whites.

Some stress-related processes affect both Blacks and Whites, jointly contributing to misunderstandings. Consider this college dining hall scenario (Shelton & Richeson, 2005): You enter the dining hall for dinner. You are alone because your close friends are in a review session. As you look around the dining hall for a place to sit, you notice several White (or Black) students who live near you sitting together.

How interested would you be in sitting with these students? How interested do you think these students would be in sitting with you? How likely is it that you would invite yourself over to sit with this group? How likely is it that someone from the group would invite you over to sit with them? College students were asked these questions. The results showed that whether you were Black or White, you thought that students of the other race were less likely to want to sit with you than you were to sit with them. Further, regardless of race, you were less likely to approach them because of fear they would reject you, and you thought they were less likely to invite you to join them because they lacked interest in doing so.

The reciprocal misunderstanding of the intentions and desires of others is called **pluralistic ignorance** (see also Chapter 9). Pluralistic ignorance is exacerbated when two people come from different socially defined groups. The space between people who are different increases because of pluralistic ignorance. So while diversity may increase pluralistic ignorance, underlying the concept is a foundation of mutuality. A challenge of diversity is to overcome pluralistic ignorance, a benefit of diversity is learning about the commonalities that bring people and groups closer together.

1. What other possible explanations are there for the kinds of scenarios described other than pluralistic ignorance?
2. Do you believe that simply telling someone that others feel the same way they do about interacting is a good way to improve intergroup relations? Why or why not?

perceptions and their negative effects? When you belong to an identifiable stigmatized group with an historical narrative or legacy of discrimination, coping becomes a survival mechanism. Following are a few examples of personality characteristics or other variables that influence the impact of perceiving discrimination.

Coping with Perceived Discrimination

People cope with stigma and discrimination in a number of different ways. In this section, we discuss two of them: (a) responses in anticipation of discrimination, and (b) individual assessments and adjustments. As we will see, some responses make things better, others make them seem better in the short run but worse in the long run, and still others exacerbate the problems.

How Group Membership Influences the Ways We Cope with Discrimination

"Once burned, twice shy" the saying goes. If you have experienced status-based discrimination, or thought you have, you might become more vigilant to cues that it is happening again. Further, if you belong to a social group with an historical narrative of being targets of discrimination, you may become more vigilant as well. The following sections discuss three different approaches to the anticipation, expectation, and sensitivity to racial discrimination: racial identification, rejection sensitivity to race, and the universal context of racism.

Rejection identification   The rejection-identification hypothesis argues that consistently attributing discrimination to widespread and recurring prejudice against your group leads to feeling rejected and undermines psychological well-being. But attributing discrimination to prejudice also tends to strengthen identification with your group, which in turn enhances psychological well-being. So if one attributes discrimination to persistent racial prejudice, you may feel bad, but if you also strengthen your identification with your group, you may feel better (Branscombe, Schmitt & Harvey, 1999).

African American college students answered a series of questions about the extent to which they attributed negative treatment to racial prejudice, and their personal experience with racial discrimination (e.g., I feel like I am personally a victim of society because of my race). The researchers also measured their hostility toward Whites, their in-group identification with African Americans, and their personal and collective self-esteem (Branscombe et al., 1999). Results showed that the more they reported experiencing discrimination, and the more they made attributions to racial prejudice, the lower their personal and collective well-being. However, the more strongly they identified with African Americans, the higher their personal and collective well-being.

While perceptions of discrimination not only affect health directly but also produce riskier and unhealthy behavior (e.g., greater substance abuse), strong group identification can buffer these adverse effects. For example, Blacks who think more about experiencing discrimination are more likely to drink alcohol excessively or use illegal drugs. However, this tendency occurs primarily among Blacks low in group identification and not among those high in racial identification (Stock, Gibbons, Walsh, & Gerrard, 2011). In discussions of diversity, people often worry that by emphasizing group differences we run the risk of driving groups further apart. But from the perspective of a person who belongs to a stigmatized group, these results argue that emphasizing differences and strengthening affinity group membership can bolster one's psychological well-being.

Rejection sensitivity to race   Consider the following situation: Imagine you're driving down the street, and there is a police barricade just ahead. The police officers are randomly pulling people over to check drivers licenses and registrations.

How concerned or anxious would you be that the police would be suspicious of you because of your race? **Rejection sensitivity** to race (RS-race) refers to the extent to which a person is anxious about and has high expectations of being rejected, is likely to perceive rejection in ambiguous behaviors of others, and undergoes heightened physiological arousal to threatened rejection because of one's race (Mendoza-Denton, Downey, Purdie, Davis, & Pietrzak, 2002).

A person's degree of RS-race is assessed by the Rejection Sensitivity Questionnaire (RSQ). The RSQ presents 12 scenarios, like the police barricade example, and respondents rate how concerned they would be that their race would determine a negative outcome, and how likely they thought a negative outcome would happen.

What is the consequence of having a high RS-race score? African American first-year college students who were higher in RS-race reported more negative racial experiences and had higher feelings of alienation and lower well-being. Moreover, over a 21-day period, the sense of belonging to the university and positive relations with dorm mates *improved* for low RS-race scorers but *worsened* for those who scored high. RS-race also affected academic performance. At the beginning of the first semester, the average GPA of all students hovered around 2.92. However, five semesters later, the GPA of low RS-race students had increased slightly to nearly 3.0, while the GPA of high RS-race students had fallen to less than 2.8 (Mendoza-Denton et al., 2002).

Other research shows that RS-race can interact with ethnic identity. Ethnic identity was positively related to intentions to stay in school as well as to increases in GPA, but only if RS-race was low (Mendoza-Denton, Pietrzak, & Downey, 2008). Ethnic identification can promote academic success when students have reason to expect that they will not be rejected because of their background and racial identity. These findings "underscore the importance of promoting achievement and institutional affiliation not by discouraging ethnic identification but rather by changing the institutional environment and climate to ensure all students have reason to feel welcome within the institution" (Mendoza-Denton et al., 2008, p. 349).

The universal context of racism   Another approach to sensitivity to race-based discrimination is the **universal context of racism (UCR)** (Jones, 2003). This approach proposes that racism is a chronically accessible explanation for negative outcomes and motivates targets to be vigilant and wary. Belonging to a group that is socially salient and historically stigmatized renders the possibility of race-based bias highly accessible. The accessibility of race bias has the potential to influence interpretations of an individual's experiences and expectations, the goals they set, and the likelihood they attain them. Although every negative experience is not attributed to racism, it is often a plausible explanation when race cues are present whether applied to one's self or to others in one's racial group.

The UCR activates two motivations: one is oriented to detecting, avoiding, and coping with racism (*self-protective*). Self-protection motives may enhance the likelihood of perceiving discrimination, lead one to avoid situations in which the threat may be likely, or internalize the threat as rejection. The second motivation is oriented toward claiming, expressing, and enhancing one's self-worth and humanity (*self-enhancing*). Self-enhancing motives may lead to favorable comparisons with others (Kwan, John, Kenny, Bond, & Robins, 2004), focusing on one's positive qualities (Taylor, Lerner, Sherman, Sage, & McDowell, 2003), or strengthening one's connections with one's group or culture (Branscombe et al., 1999). Self-enhancement is generally associated with positive mental and physical health and longevity.

The UCR Scale consists of eight items that assess the degree to which race or racism is chronically accessible and is used to explain negative outcomes and to motivate vigilant, wary behavior. Four sample items are:

- because of discrimination against my race, I carefully monitor how others treat me;
- I think about my race every day;
- I am suspicious of the motives of people of other races;
- I have often been treated unfairly because of my race.

A sample of 469 African American college students at historically Black colleges and universities and predominantly White institutions completed the UCR Scale, measures of psychological well-being (anxiety, depression, and self-esteem) and reported on the frequency of race-based hassles during the past year. Higher UCR scores were related to higher levels of depression and anxiety, lower self-esteem, and reports of more frequent instances of race-based hassles in the last year (Jones, Campbell, & Sellers, 2012).

Being aware of racism does not automatically lead to poorer psychological outcomes. Formulating a personal identity and approach to race-based situations can provide a buffering effect. For example, **TRIOS** (acronym for Time, Rhythm, Improvisation, Orality, and Spirituality) theory represents cultural capital that Africans brought with them to the New World (Jones, 2003). TRIOS is associated with characteristics that are useful for coping and adapting to threatening and uncertain contexts. TRIOS characteristics include flexible and creative responses to unexpected threats and challenges, using verbal and non-verbal communication to share information and knowledge, establishing group boundaries and creating group cohesion, adopting ways to be in synch with situations and contexts one is in, acute focus on the demands and opportunities of the immediate context, and drawing upon a spiritual belief in a power beyond oneself to make sense of one's predicament and alternative positive possibilities.

Whereas the UCR scores were associated with negative psychological outcomes, TRIOS scores were associated with lower anxiety and depression, higher self-esteem, and unrelated to reports of racial hassles (Jones et al., 2012).

The Ways We Cope with Discrimination Individually

People are resilient and creative in the ways they accomplish this. One way is to limit vulnerabilities to being stigmatized. A second way is to try to reframe potentially biased behavior toward you in ways that protect your feelings of self-worth. And, a third way is to adopt worldviews that disarm feelings of being stigmatized (see Major & Townsend, 2010, for a review). We illustrate each of these strategies.

Psychological disengagement   One common way of coping with stigma is to simply disengage from any feedback in which stigma is likely to be activated (Forbes, Schmader, & Allen, 2008). Psychological disengagement can take two forms: *discounting*, when you assume that a negative judgment or outcome is biased and not to be taken seriously; and *devaluing*, when you reject the ability of negative outcomes in threatening domains to affect your self-worth.

Forbes et al. (2008) tested these ideas in a study of brain activity under stereotype threat conditions. While brain activity (EEG; see Chapter 7) was recorded, participants completed a series of tests that were described either as predictive of intelligence (stereotype threat) or simply as a pattern recognition task (control).

Analysis of the brain activity showed that when performance was framed in terms of intelligence, the more one valued academics the more they were motivated to monitor performance and guard against errors, and reacted more quickly when they made errors and overall made fewer errors. These findings suggest that stigmatized minorities who value academics respond to stereotype threatening cues by becoming vigilant for performance-relevant stimuli and more efficient in responding to them.

Attributional ambiguity and explaining outcomes   If you belong to a stigmatized group, you might perceive more discrimination and suffer lowered self-esteem. Although there is strong theoretical support for this assumption, there is scant empirical evidence (Crocker & Major, 1989). For example, Blacks have relatively *higher* self-esteem than Whites, and the gap has been growing since 1960 (Twenge & Crocker, 2002). Latinos, by contrast, have slightly but significantly lower self-esteem than Whites. Similarly, women do not show lower self-esteem than men do, nor are people who are physically unattractive, facially disfigured, learning disabled, gay or lesbian, or juvenile delinquents lower in esteem than conventionally mainstream groups. Why?

When a stigmatized person receives negative evaluative feedback, is insulted, or is treated badly, the implication for self-worth may be ambiguous. **Attributional ambiguity** offers an explanation for what can happen in such instances (see Box 8.1). If you accept that the judgment is objective and accurate, then you might conclude that you performed poorly and deserved the negative judgment or treatment. If you choose to think that the person was biased, you may discount the judgment, thus rendering it invalid and blunting its negative impact on your self-worth (Crocker & Major, 1989).

This self-protective function may be most successful when negative outcomes can be easily traced to the evaluator's bias. When there is real ambiguity about the evaluator's motives or character, the threat or predicament may be greater. The irony here is that, as we make progress in racial, ethnic, and gender relations, the overt expression of bias may lessen, but ambiguity about motivation and intention correspondingly increases. As a result, the self-protective processes of attributional ambiguity may serve to maintain high levels of vigilance and perceptual acuity for subtle discriminatory acts. That is, as has been said often in the Black community, "I would rather know that someone is a bigot, than have to decipher it from subtle racist behavior." Research shows that Blacks prefer to interact with a White person known to be racially biased than one who ostensibly is not (Shelton, Richeson, Salvatore, & Trawalter, 2005). Maintaining a high level of mistrust can maintain one's awareness of the potential for flawed judgments and hence maintain the self-protective properties of attributional ambiguity (Terrell & Terrell, 1984).

Worldview verification   People who belong to stigmatized social groups may hold different beliefs about the degree to which their chances in society are based on merit (Major, Kaiser, O'Brien, & McCoy, 2007). Perceiving discrimination directed against their in-group (or self) threatens the worldview of those who believe that hard work and talent will lead to success (meritocracy beliefs). But for those who do not believe in a meritocratic society, discrimination experiences confirm their worldview. When a person's worldview is threatened, self-esteem is decreased. Conversely, when a person's worldview is confirmed, it buffers or bolsters their self-esteem.

Major et al. (2007) tested this idea in a sample of Latino college students. After indicating their belief in a meritocratic ideology, their self-esteem and the degree to which they perceived their ethnic group was discriminated against were assessed. For those Latinos who endorsed a meritocratic worldview, the more they believed that Latinos were discriminated against, the lower their self-esteem. However, for those Latinos who rejected the merit ideology, the more they believed that Latinos were discriminated against, the higher their self-esteem. The authors reported similar worldview ideology effects for women.

This finding raises the troubling specter that believing in the American Dream when you belong to a stigmatized group can erode the self-confidence and esteem that is needed to realize the Dream. Rejecting the basic premise of the American Dream may, ironically, be the best way to achieve it!

One consistent theme in this book is that we are social animals with strong affinities to others whom we see as members of our group. Thus, we do not always have to cope individually with being stigmatized. Stigma also shapes our collective identities, not only in ways specifically relevant to a particular incident but also more generally.

Collective Identities

A **collective identity** acknowledges that you belong to a socially defined group and that being a member of that group is important to how you define, describe, and feel about yourself (Ashmore, Deaux, & McLaughlin-Volpe, 2004; Tajfel & Turner, 1986). You may draw positive feelings if a group you belong to is highly valued (your team won the NCAA basketball tournament, your sorority is the most popular on campus, and your group is noted for its expertise in math). Conversely, you may belong to a socially defined group that is associated with stigma or negative stereotypes (Blacks, disabled, gay). How does your group's standing in society affect your willingness to identify with it and to make it an important part of who you are? We will explore how these issues affect people who belong to marginalized groups in the following section.

How We Relate to Our Racial Group: Racial Identity

Racial identity is the degree to which a person identifies with, values, and represents his or her racial group in his or her personal view of self. If your racial group is stigmatized or associated with negative stereotypes, it may be more difficult to draw positive self-esteem and feelings of worth. If it is regarded positively it provides an important avenue to positive self-esteem (Tajfel & Turner, 1986). This section discusses several different ideas about the challenges and opportunities that result from identifying with one's racial or ethnic group.

Black identity   Embracing a collective **Black identity** is challenging. W.E.B. DuBois (1903) spelled out this challenge in his concept of "double-consciousness":

> a peculiar sensation this double-consciousness, this sense of always looking at one's self through the eyes of others. . . . One ever feels his two-ness, —an American, A Negro; two warring ideals in one dark body, whose dogged strength alone keeps it from being torn asunder. (pp. 214–215)

The challenge of diversity goes to the core of collective identity. By what means do Black people, or members of any marginalized group, maintain an integrated and positive sense of who they are, both individually and collectively, in the face of fragmenting and conflicting collective identity pressures. The two most prominent theories of Black racial identity are the multidimensional model of racial identity (Sellers, Smith, Shelton, Rowley, & Chavous, 1998) and the Nigresence theory of racial identity (Cross, 1991).

Being Black in America is complicated. Recall that the rejection-identification model proposes that perceiving racial discrimination makes you feel bad, but leads you to identify more with others in your group. The more you identify with others in your group, the better off you are.

The **Multidimensional Model Of Racial Identity (MMRI)** acknowledges that most people have a hierarchy of social identities, only one of which concerns race (Sellers et al., 1998). The higher racial identity is in your collective identity hierarchy, the more central it is ("centrality"). How central it is depends, in part, on how salient it is in a given context ("salience"). The regard you have for your group is reflected by how positive or negative you feel about your group (private regard), or how positively or negatively you think others feel about your group (public regard). Finally, racial identity includes ideological beliefs, opinions, and attitudes about how they and other members of their race should act. Four ideologies are proposed:

1. *Nationalist*: emphasizes Black uniqueness and the importance of sustaining and supporting the group, for example, "It is important for Black people to surround their children with Black art, music, and literature."

2. *Oppressed minority*: highlights that Blacks have much in common with other nega-
    tively stereotyped minority groups, for example, "Blacks should learn about the
    oppression of other minority groups."
3. *Assimilationist*: involves beliefs that Blacks are like all other Americans and should
    integrate into the mainstream, for example, "A sign of progress is that Blacks are
    in the mainstream of America more than ever before."
4. *Humanist*: associated with beliefs that all people share a common humanity
    regardless of their race, gender, ethnicity, country of origin, or sexual orientation,
    for example, "People regardless of their race have strengths and weaknesses."

The **Multidimensional Inventory of Black Identity** (**MIBI**) was developed to
assess these dimensions of Black identity (Sellers, Rowley, Chavous, Shelton, & Smith,
1997). In general, psychological distress was lower for students when race was more
central to their identity (Sellers, Caldwell, Schmeelk-Cone, & Zimmerman, 2003),
but reports of racial discrimination were more likely for those with a nationalist
ideology (Sellers & Shelton, 2003). Conversely, the more humanist their ideology and
the more favorably they believed others perceived their racial group, the less likely
they were to report experiences with racial discrimination in the previous year (Sellers
& Shelton, 2003). However, the more negative one thought others viewed their
group, the more they reported experiences of racial discrimination (Seaton, Yip, &
Sellers, 2009).

The concept of Nigrescence is central to the **Cross Racial Identity Scale** (**CRIS**), a
scale that measures the structure and development of racial identity in African Americans. **Nigrescence** is the process of becoming Black (Cross, 1991). Nigrescence evolves
from an encounter in which a deracialized identity becomes racialized through some
sort of negative encounter based on one's race. The deracialized identity is shaken
up, challenged, and gives way to a racialized identity—the old identity is demolished
and a new frame of reference is adopted. According to the theory, the new identity is
unequivocally pro-Black and correspondingly anti-White. One becomes immersed in
Blackness as never before. But, over time, one finds this immersion too intense, too
limiting. A need for balance in one's life causes one to emerge from this singular Black
intensity and internalize a new, mature racial identity that can defend and protect a
person from racist insults; provide a sense of belonging to one's racial group; and
afford a foundation for transactions with people, cultures, and situations beyond the
world of Blackness.

The overall structure and specific attitudes are assessed by the CRIS (Vandiver,
Cross, Worrell, & Fhagen-Smith, 2002). The themes are:

1. *Pre-encounter*: I am not so much a member of a racial group as I am an American
    (assimilation); Blacks place more emphasis on having a good time than on hard
    work (miseducation); and, privately, I sometimes have negative feelings about
    being Black (self-hatred).
2. *Immersion–emersion*: I have a strong feeling of hatred and disdain for all White
    people (anti-White sentiment).
3. *Internalization*: I see and think about things from an Afrocentric perspective
    (Afrocentricity); and, as a multiculturalist, I am connected to many groups, such

as Hispanics, Asian Americans, Whites, Jews, gay men, and lesbians (multicultur-alist inclusive).

Each of these racial attitude themes is characterized by identity-specific attitudes that are related to both oneself (personal identity) and one's Black reference group (reference group orientation). According to Nigresence theory, personal identity and reference group orientation can be separated, and only personal identity has direct bearing on psychological well-being. Consistent with this thesis, only self-hatred was linked directly to lowered self-esteem (Vandiver et al., 2002). In other research, it has been found that a deracialized identity was positively related to academic achieve-ment, but also to poorer psychological well-being and weakened in-group ties (Arroyo & Zigler, 1995).

Racial identity and collective threat　A further complication comes when we consider not only our own behavior in relation to our collective identity (e.g., stereotype threat), but the behavior and experiences of other members of our group. When a member of your group behaves in a way that confirms a negative stereotype, how do you feel and what do you do?

Cohen and Garcia (2005) asked and answered this question. White, Black, and Latino high-school students indicated how much they worry that people will draw conclusions about their racial group from the behavior of others of their race (collec-tive threat) or from their own behavior (stereotype threat), or whether others will draw conclusions about them from behavior of others in their racial group (threat of being stereotyped). For Black and Latino students, the biggest threats were for people drawing conclusions about their group from their own and other group members' behavior. Concern that others in your group will confirm negative expectations about your group will motivate you to try harder and dispel those negative stereotypes about your racial group.

They also found that having a strong racial identity could modify negative stereo-type threat effects by engaging in social **identity affirmation**—embracing group stereotypes and seeking out evaluative diagnostic tasks (Cohen & Garcia, 2005, Study 1). These findings provide evidence that a strong racial identification can sustain positive psychological well-being and guide affirmative and effective social behavior.

White identity　When asked "Who am I," White students are less likely to mention their race than are members of other racial groups. What is **White identity**? What does it mean to be White? Grossman and Charmaraman (2009) asked that question of White ninth- to twelfth-grade adolescents from three New England schools: White majority students, White minority in a majority Latino school, or a White minority in a multicultural school. Students identified their race/ethnicity and indicated how important it was to them.

White students in majority schools tended not to claim a racial identity, reporting instead that they had an American identity or that their race/ethnic identity was unexamined. Almost no students in the Latino or multicultural schools did this. The students at Latino schools were more likely to accept diversity (17%) than those at either multicultural or majority schools (3% at each).

When Whites are in a majority context, they are less likely to examine their racial identity, more likely to accept White privilege, and more likely to adopt an American identity. When they are in diverse contexts, Whites are more likely to accept diversity as a valid and relevant concept and less likely to ignore their own racial identity. So, when we discuss diversity, we must understand that it matters to everyone, those in the majority group as well as those in minority groups.

Another approach to White identity borrows from the centrality concept of Sellers et al. (1997). White identity centrality is an automatic association between the concepts *White* and *self* (Knowles & Peng, 2005). The authors used the IAT (see Chapter 7) to establish the degree of association between White and self, and found that White identity centrality is stronger when Whites have more exposure to members of other racial or ethnic groups. The greater White identity centrality, the more time they spent scrutinizing racially ambiguous faces and the less likely they were to accept them as White.

And here we find another diversity challenge. When Whites are exposed to more diverse contexts, they are more likely to formulate race as central to their identity. But, when they do, they are more likely to exclude racial and ethnic others from their in-group. The contexts that foster diversity may also psychologically increase exclusion.

Hartmann, Gerteis, and Croll (2009) conducted a study of racial identity in a national representative sample of 2,081 Whites, Blacks, and Latinos. After identifying their race, respondents were asked how important it was. Racial identity was very important to Blacks and Latinos (72%) but not so much to Whites (37%). The authors analyzed other responses and conclude that White identity can be characterized by invisibility of White identity, the acceptance of White privilege, and belief in a color-blind ideology. However, this is a pattern found only for those who adopt "categorical Whiteness" (only 15% of the sample) by subscribing to each of these tenets of White identity.

How We Relate to Our Ethnic Group: Ethnic Identity

Conceptually, race and ethnicity can be distinguished since race has a biological association as well as a socially constructed meaning. Ethnicity reflects the cultural aspects of language, social patterns, and practices. However, ethnicity and race have a great deal in common and psychologists often use the two terms in combination: "race/ethnicity." **Ethnic identity** refers to the ideas people have of themselves as members of an ethnic group.

Multigroup Ethnic Identity Measure   The most widely used measure of generalized ethnic identity is the **Multigroup Ethnic Identity Measure (MEIM)** (Phinney, 1992). The Phinney approach uses identity development theory (Marcia, 2007) to propose that exploration of identity issues and commitment to relevant identity domains constitute ethnic identity. As illustrated in Table 8.2, the MEIM-R (see Phinney & Ong, 2007) determines the ethnic labels with which individuals identify and the degree to which they have explored and are committed to their ethnic identity. The ethnic iden-

Table 8.2. The Multigroup Ethnic Identity Measure

Exploration
- I have spent time trying to find out more about my ethnic group, such as its history, traditions, and customs
- I have often done things that will help me understand my ethnic background better
- I have often talked to other people in order to learn more about my ethnic group

Commitment
- I have a strong sense of belonging to my own ethnic group
- I understand pretty well what my ethnic group membership means to me
- I feel a strong attachment toward my ethnic group

Note. Adapted from "The Multigroup Ethnic Identity Measure: A New Scale for Use With Diverse Groups," by J. S. Phinney, 1992, *Journal of Adolescent Research*, 7, pp. 156–176.

tity score is used as a measure of ethnic identity exploration, ethnic identity commitment, or overall ethnic identity.

Research has shown that ethnic identity scores do not differ between Asian, Black, Hispanic, and mixed-ethnic group high-school and college students, but are higher for each group than they are for Whites. No differences have been found between high-school and college samples or, for the most part, between male and female samples. For high-school but not college students, higher ethnic identity scores were associated with higher GPAs.

A sample of Mexican and African American students completed the MEIM and analysis revealed three identities: *ethnic* (more ethnic than American), *bicultural* (both American and ethnic), and *ethnocentric* (ethnic and separated from mainstream U.S. society and culture) (Phinney, DuPont, Espinosa, Revill, & Sanders, 1994). The majority of African Americans (54%) considered themselves bicultural, whereas the majority of Mexican Americans (63%) considered themselves ethnic. A bicultural orientation was associated with more positive American identity scores for both Mexican and African Americans. A positive self-concept was most highly associated with an ethnocentric orientation for African Americans and with more favorable attitudes toward other groups for both African and Mexican Americans.

Positive in-group affiliations and preferences (ethnocentrism) are associated with distancing oneself from U.S. society and from Whites. For example, Masuoka (2006) found that perceived discrimination strengthened pan-ethnic identity among national samples of Asian Americans and Latinos. Operario and Fiske (2001) demonstrated that high ethnically identified Asian and Latino youth reported more personal experiences with ethnic discrimination than did those less ethnically identified. However, Lee, Noh, Yoo, and Doh (2007) found that among a sample of Koreans living in China, perceived discrimination was negatively related to ethnic identity.

An ethnic identity is a good thing to have! A large body of research supports this conclusion. For example, ethnic identity has been linked positively to self-esteem and negatively to depression (Roberts, Phinney, Masse, Chen, & Roberts, 1999), to higher GPAs (Smith, Levine, Smith, Dumas & Prinz, 2009), and to greater understanding of intergroup relations (Phinney, Jacoby, & Silva, 2007). Also, ethnic identity has been found to diminish the effects of low socioeconomic status on academic achievement (Ong, Phinney, & Dennis, 2006).

Multiracial identity   World-class golfer Tiger Woods declared himself to be a CABLI-NASIAN (Caucasian, Black, Indian, and Asian), thus proclaiming his multiracial identity. In 1970, there were 500,000 multiracial children in the United States. In 2000, there were 6.8 million, an increase of 1,260%. Many of us have multiracial backgrounds but the historical practice has been to claim one race and stick with it. The so-called **"one drop" rule** meant that a person with any African blood was socially identified as Black (see Chapter 3). Perhaps as a result of the immigration explosion and the desire to claim one's heritage in full measure, as well as greater openness to intimate unions across racial and ethnic lines, "multiracial" is now a recognized identity classification.

But, is being publicly and personally defined as multiracial a coherent classification? Is there an "essential" property of having multiple racial influences or is it simply the combination of individual racial elements. Is it a protective factor like racial or ethnic identity, is it no factor, or does it cause confusion and uncertainty? There is a growing body of theory and research directed at these questions.

Multiracial identity theory has undergone evolution much like racial identity. Like the DuBois double consciousness idea, when caught between two or more cultures, one faces double rejection from the majority culture as well as the minority culture (see Root, 1996). The net consequence of this marginal status was thought to produce psychological deficit, related to stigma, rejection, and identity confusion.

Suppose your father was born to a Japanese mother and a Black father. Or that your mother was born to a Mexican American mother and a White father. What is your racial identity? Consider these four options: (a) you could identify with one of your racial heritages (I am Asian American); (b) you could claim all of them together (I am multiracial); (c) you could enumerate each of them (I am Black, White, Asian American, and Latino—the Tiger Woods option); or (d) you could reject all group labels and proclaim your individual identity (I am a human being).

These four options suggest great latitude of choice. Is that a good thing or is it only confusing? The 2010 Census included multiple racial and ethnic categories, and respondents indicated multiracial status by checking multiple boxes. This decision perpetuates either the choice or the confusion, depending on how you look at it. Over 9 million respondents to the 2010 U.S. Census classified themselves as multiracial (an increase of 33% since 2000).

Shih and Sanchez (2005) analyzed the results of 28 published articles that assessed psychological correlates of **multiracial identity**. They found that psychological adjustment was a complicated result of several factors including racial identity, depression, problem behaviors, school performance, peer relationships, and self-esteem. Some multiracial persons felt rejected because of their racial classifications, but others felt that their multiracial heritage provided them with a wider base of support from multiple racial/cultural communities. More detrimental effects were found in studies that used clinical populations; those using non-clinical samples more frequently reported positive outcomes such as greater happiness and higher self-esteem.

Our understanding of multicultural racial identity is not as advanced as what we know about Black racial identity, but what we know suggests a similar pattern. We begin with some level of stress associated with rejection, stigmatization, and psychological distress related to our racial/cultural identity. Individuals often take a new look at their racialized status and see strengths and resilience that make them feel good about themselves. A balanced integrated view results from the convergence of several developmental, regulatory, and maturation processes. Identity integration represents the successful culmination of racial identity processes whether we consider racial, ethnic, cultural, gender, sexual, or multicultural identities.

Summary

Social or cultural difference may challenge diversity because differences are often a source of stigma, a "stain," a symbol indicating that a person is worthy of rejection or special treatment. People often feel positive about their groups, even if they are stigmatized, but it takes effort, and psychological resilience to do so.

Being different can sometimes cause stress even if the basis of difference is not a stigma. If there is a normative status quo, then people who do not fit that norm are characterized by their difference from it. When people are different, there is often an assumption that they are different in many ways beyond the obvious attribute: that they think differently, have different values and goals. The more deep-seated their principal difference is thought to be (the more "essential" to defining who they are), the greater the divide in understanding and the more intractable differences become. A diversity challenge is finding ways to break down these assumptions of essential differences as a means of encouraging more communication and understanding across groups.

How a given person handles racial or cultural status will depend on how she or he was socialized. Black parents and significant adults train Black children to be prepared for possible biased treatment as well as to feel pride in who they are. Providing positive messages yields positive psychological benefits, while preparing children for biased treatment can sometimes have less beneficial results.

Acculturation presents a set of stressful challenges, including how best to manage the socialization requirements of one's original culture as well as the culture one may be attempting to enter. Successful acculturation depends on both the attitudes and beliefs of the immigrant group as well as those of the host culture.

Perceiving persistent racial discrimination directed at one's group generally leads to adverse psychological effects. But a substantial body of literature shows both the negative effects of perceiving or expecting biased treatment or judgment and ways in which one may counter these negative influences. Several models suggest that adopting a strong racial or ethnic identification can protect a person from the adverse effects of perceived discrimination.

Black identity is associated with changes in how one views oneself, with the goal of acquiring a balanced perspective on positive feelings about being Black, recognizing the potential bias directed against you because you are Black, employing those positive feelings about yourself and your group, and developing effective ways to cope with negative treatment are all demonstrated in a large body of social psychological research. Similar positive effects are associated with ethnic identity. Multicultural identity follows the same general logic as Black identity, but the research is far less conclusive. In all cases, the negative psychological consequences of belonging to a stigmatized minority group and perceiving that your group and perhaps even you have been treated unfairly are balanced by psychological resiliencies that preserve well-being and self-esteem.

Questions for Thinking and Knowing

1. If perceiving discrimination is so consistently associated with negative feelings about yourself, why couldn't a person simply change his or her view? Would that change the overall adverse effects of ambiguous bias?
2. Whites see themselves differently when they are in the minority compared to when they are in the majority. As our society become more diverse, can we expect that Whites will be more aware of their own racial status and the privilege that it confers? Do you expect that changing White attitudes about racial identity is an important way to produce more racial intergroup harmony?
3. DuBois's double-consciousness theory is often used as the starting point for analysis of psychological effects of duality and marginalization. Is the application of this theory appropriate for all groups, or do we need different theories for different groups? What are the pros and cons of each perspective and what evidence would you cite to support your point of view?
4. To what extent does it matter if being different is based on visible or invisible stigma, or simply being different from the norm in a given setting or situation? Think of a time when you felt you were conspicuously or inconspicuously different from others. How did you feel? What did you do to try to make yourself feel more comfortable?
5. Write down your full name. Now finish this sentence with as many features, characteristics or identities as you need to convey who you are to another person. "[name] is . . ." What does this tell you about who you are and what is important to that sense of self?

Key Terms

Acculturation

Acculturative stress

Attributional ambiguity

Black identity

Category divide hypothesis

Collective identity

Coping

Cross Racial Identity Scale (CRIS)

Disruptive apprehension

Enculturation

Ethnic identity

Identity affirmation

Internalized homophobia

Multidimensional Inventory of Black Identity (MIBI)

Multidimensional Model Of Racial Identity (MMRI)

Multigroup Ethnic Identity Measure (MEIM)

Multiracial identity

Nigresence
One drop rule
Perceived discrimination
Pluralistic ignorance
Predicament
Protective disidentification
Racial identity
Racial paralysis
Racial socialization

Rejection sensitivity
Socialization
Stereotype boost
Stereotype threat
Stigma
Stress
TRIOS
Universal context of racism (UCR)
White identity

References

Armenta, B. E. (2010). Stereotype boost and stereotype threat effects: The moderating role of ethnic identification. *Cultural Diversity and Ethnic Minority Psychology, 16,* 94–98.

Arroyo, C. G., & Zigler, E. (1995). Racial identity, academic achievement, and the psychological well-being of economically disadvantaged adolescents. *Journal of Personality and Social Psychology, 69,* 903–914.

Ashmore, R. D., Deaux, K., & McLaughlin-Volpe, T. (2004). An organizing framework for collective identity: Articulation and significance of multidimensionality. *Psychological Bulletin, 130,* 80–114.

Berry, J. W., Phinney, J. S., Sam, D. L., & Vedder, P. (2006). Immigrant youth: Acculturation, identity, and adaptation. *Applied Psychology: An International Review, 55,* 303–332.

Branscombe, N. R., Schmitt, M. T., & Harvey, R. D. (1999). Perceiving pervasive discrimination among African Americans: Implications for group identification and well-being. *Journal of Personality and Social Psychology, 77,* 135–149.

Bynum, M. S., Burton, E. T., & Best, C. (2007). Racism experiences and psychological functioning in African American college freshmen: Is racial socialization a buffer? *Cultural Diversity and Ethnic Minority Psychology, 13,* 64–71.

Carr, P. B., & Steele, C. M. (2009). Stereotype threat and inflexible perseverance in problem solving. *Journal of Experimental Social Psychology, 45,* 853–859.

Caughy, M. O., Nettles, S. M., O'Campo, P. J., & Lohrfink, K. F. (2006). Neighborhood matters: Racial socialization of African American children. *Child Development, 77,* 1220–1236.

Caughy, M. O., O'Campo, P. J., Randolph, S. M., & Nickerson, K. J. (2002). The influence of racial socialization practices on the cognitive and behavioral competence of African American preschoolers. *Child Development, 73,* 1611–1625.

Cohen, G. L., & Garcia, J. (2005). "I Am Us": Negative stereotypes as collective threats. *Journal of Personality and Social Psychology, 89,* 566–582.

Compas, B. E., Connor-Smith, J. K., Saltzman, H., Thomsen, A. H., & Wadsworth, M. E. (2001). Coping with stress during childhood and adolescence: Problems, progress, and potential in theory and research. *Psychological Bulletin, 127,* 87–127.

Constantine, M. G., & Blackmon, S. M. (2002). Black adolescents' racial socialization experiences: Their relations to home, school, and peer self-esteem. *Journal of Black Studies, 32,* 322–335.

Crocker, J., & Major, B. (1989). Social stigma and self-esteem: The self-protective properties of stigma. *Psychological Review, 96,* 608–630.

Crocker, J., Major, B., & Steele, C. M. (1998). Social stigma. In D. T. Gilbert, S. T. Fiske & G. Lindzey (Eds.), *The handbook of social psychology* (4th ed., Vols. 1 and 2, pp. 504–553). New York: McGraw-Hill.

Crocker, J., Voelkl, K., Testa, M., & Major, B. (1991). Social stigma: The affective consequences of attributional ambiguity. *Journal of Personality and Social Psychology, 60,* 218–228.

Cross, W. E., Jr (1991). *Shades of Black: Diversity in African-American identity.* Philadelphia, PA: Temple University Press.

Davis, G. Y., & Stevenson, H. C. (2006). Racial socialization experiences and symptoms of depression among Black youth. *Journal of Child and Family Studies, 15,* 303–317.

Deaux, K., Bikmen, N., Gilkes, A., Ventuneac, A., Joseph, Y., Payne, Y. A., & Steele, C. M. (2007). Becoming American: Stereotype threat effects in Afro-Caribbean immigrant groups. *Social Psychology Quarterly, 70,* 384–404.

Dovidio, J. F., Gaertner, S. G., Niemann, Y. F., & Snider, K. (2001). Racial, ethnic, and cultural differences in responding to distinctiveness and discrimination on campus: Stigma and common group identity. *Journal of Social Issues, 57,* 167–188.

DuBois, W. E. B. (1903). *The souls of Black folk.* Chicago: A. C. McClurg & Company.

Forbes, C. A. C. (2004). Suicidal behavior in African-American adolescents: Racial socialization as a protective factor. *Dissertation Abstracts International: Section B: The Sciences and Engineering, 64(11-B),* 5781.

Forbes, C. E., Schmader, T., & Allen, J. J. B. (2008). The role of devaluing and discounting in performance monitoring: A neurophysiological study of minorities under threat. *Social Cognitive and Affective Neuroscience, 3,* 253–261.

Frable, D. E. S. (1993). Dimensions of marginality: Distinctions among those who are different. *Personality and Social Psychology Bulletin, 19,* 370–380.

Fuller-Rowell, T. E., Evans, G. W., & Ong, A. D. (2012). Poverty and health: The mediating role of perceived discrimination. *Psychological Science, 23,* 734–739.

Gibbons, F. X., Etcheverry, P. E., Stock, M. L., Gerrard, M., & Weng, C.-Y. (2010). Exploring the link between racial discrimination and substance use: What mediates? What buffers? *Journal of Personality and Social Psychology, 99,* 785–801.

Gibbons, F. X., Roberts, M. E., Gerrard, M., Li, Z., & Beach, S. R. (2012). The impact of stress on the life history strategies of African American adolescents: Cognitions, genetic moderation, and the role of discrimination. *Developmental Psychology, 48,* 722–739.

Goffman, E. (1963). *Stigma: Notes on the management of spoiled identity.* Englewood Cliffs, NJ: Prentice-Hall.

Grossman, J. M., & Charmaraman, L. (2009). Race, context, and privilege: White adolescents' explanations of racial-ethnic centrality. *Journal of Youth and Adolescence, 38,* 139–152.

Harris-Britt, A., Valrie, C. R., Kurtz-Costes, B., & Rowley, S. J. (2007). Perceived racial discrimination and self-esteem in African American youth: Racial socialization as a protective factor. *Journal of Research on Adolescence, 17,* 669–682.

Hartmann, D., Gerteis, J., & Croll, P. R. (2009). An empirical assessment of whiteness theory: Hidden from how many? *Social Problems, 56,* 403–424.

Hatzenbuehler, M. L., Nolen-Hoeksema, S., & Dovidio, J. D. (2009). How does stigma "get under the skin"? The mediating role of emotion regulation. *Psychological Science, 20,* 1282–1289.

Hentoff, N. (1994, December 17). This shouldn't be happening in America. *The Washington Post,* p. A27.

Herek, G. M., & Garnets, L. D. (2007). Sexual orientation and mental health. *Annual Review of Clinical Psychology, 3,* 353–375.

Inzlicht, M., & Kang, S. K. (2010). Stereotype threat spillover: How coping with threats to social identity affects aggression, eating, decision making, and attention. *Journal of Personality and Social Psychology, 99,* 467–481.

Inzlicht, M., & Schmader, T. (Eds.). (2012). *Stereotype threat: Theory, process, and application.* New York: Oxford University Press.

Jones, J. M. (2003). TRIOS: A psychological theory of African legacy in American culture. *Journal of Social Issues, 59,* 217–241.

Jones, J. M., Campbell, S. D., & Sellers, R. M. (2012). *Psychological consequences of sensitivity to racism and a culture-based coping strategy: The implications of the universality of racism and the TRIOS worldview.* Unpublished manuscript, University of Delaware.

Knowles, E. D., & Peng, K. (2005). White selves: Conceptualizing and measuring a dominant group identity. *Journal of Personality and Social Psychology, 89,* 223–241.

Krendl, A. C., Richeson, J. A., Kelley, W. M., & Heatherton, T. F. (2008). The negative consequences of threat: A functional magnetic resonance imaging investigation of the neural mechanisms underlying women's underperformance in math. *Psychological Science, 19,* 168–175.

Kwan, V. S. Y., John, O. P., Kenny, D. A., Bond, M. H., & Robins, R. W. (2004). Reconceptualizing individual differences in self-enhancement bias: An interpersonal approach. *Psychological Review, 111,* 94–110.

Lee, R. M., Noh, C., Yoo, H. C., & Doh, H. (2007). The psychology of diaspora experiences: Intergroup contact, perceived discrimination, and the ethnic identity of Koreans in China. *Cultural Diversity and Ethnic Minority Psychology, 13,* 115–124.

Link, B. G., & Phelan, J. C. (2001). Conceptualizing stigma. *Annual Review of Sociology, 27,* 363–385.

Major, B., Kaiser, C. R., O'Brien, L. T., & McCoy, S. K. (2007). Perceived discrimination as worldview threat or worldview confirmation: Implications for self-esteem. *Journal of Personality and Social Psychology, 92,* 1068–1086.

Major, B., & Townsend, S. M. (2010). Psychological implications of attitudes and beliefs about status inequality. In B. Major & S. Townsend (Eds.), *The psychology of attitudes and attitude change* (pp. 249–262). New York: Psychology Press.

Marcia, J. E. (2007). Theory and measure: The identity status interview. In M. Watzlawik & A. Born (Eds.), *Capturing identity:* *Quantitative and qualitative methods* (pp. 1–14). Lanham, MD: University Press of America.

Masuoka, N. (2006). Together they become one: Examining the predictors of panethnic group consciousness among Asian Americans and Latinos. *Social Science Quarterly, 87,* 993–1011.

Mendoza-Denton, R., Downey, G., Purdie, V. J., Davis, A., & Pietrzak, J. (2002). Sensitivity to status-based rejection: Implications for African American students' college experience. *Journal of Personality and Social Psychology, 83,* 896–918.

Mendoza-Denton, R., Pietrzak, J., & Downey, G. (2008). Distinguishing institutional identification from academic goal pursuit: Interactive effects of ethnic identification and race-based rejection sensitivity. *Journal of Personality and Social Psychology, 95,* 338–351.

Miller, J. L. (2001). Understanding achievement attribution and achievement motivation among African-American youth: Racism, racial socialization, and spirituality. *Dissertation Abstracts International: Section B: The Sciences and Engineering, 61(8-A),* 3053.

Neblett, E. W., Jr, White, R. L., Ford, K. R., Philip, C. L., Nguyên, H. X., & Sellers, R. M. (2008). Patterns of racial socialization and psychological adjustment: Can parental communications about race reduce the impact of racial discrimination? *Journal of Research on Adolescence, 18,* 477–515.

Norton, M. I., Mason, M. F., Vandello, J. A., Biga, A., & Dyer, R. (2012). An fMRI investigation of racial paralysis. *Social Cognitive and Affective Neuroscience.* doi: 10.1093/scan/nss010.

O'Hara, R. E., Gibbons, F. X., Weng, C.-Y., Gerrard, M., & Simons, R. L. (2012). Perceived racial discrimination as a barrier to college attendance for African Americans: Mediation by academic orientation and expectations. *Personality and Social Psychology Bulletin, 38,* 77–89.

Ong, A. D., Phinney, J. S., & Dennis, J. (2006). Competence under challenge: Exploring the protective influence of parental support and ethnic identity in Latino college students. *Journal of Adolescence, 29,* 961–979.

Operario, D., & Fiske, S. T. (2001). Ethnic identity moderates perceptions of prejudice: Judgments of personal versus group discrimination and subtle versus blatant bias. *Personality and Social Psychology Bulletin, 27,* 550–561.

Osborne, J. W. (1995). Academics, self-esteem, and race: A look at the underlying assumptions of the disidentification hypothesis. *Personality and Social Psychology Bulletin, 21,* 449–455.

Pascoe, E. A., & Smart-Richman, L. (2009). Perceived discrimination and health: A meta-analytic review. *Psychological Bulletin, 135,* 531–554.

Phinney, J. S. (1992). The multigroup ethnic identity measure: A new scale for use with diverse groups. *Journal of Adolescent Research, 7,* 156–176.

Phinney, J. S., DuPont, S., Espinosa, C., Revill, J., & Sanders, K. (1994). Ethnic identity and American identification among ethnic minority youths. In J. S. Phinney, S. DuPont, C. Espinosa, J. Revill, & K. Sanders (Eds.), *Journeys into cross-cultural psychology* (pp. 167–183). Lisse, Netherlands: Swets & Zeitlinger Publishers.

Phinney, J. S., Jacoby, B., & Silva, C. (2007). Positive intergroup attitudes: The role of ethnic identity. *International Journal of Behavioral Development, 31,* 478–490.

Phinney, J. S., & Ong, A. D. (2007). Conceptualization and measurement of ethnic identity: Current status and future directions. *Journal of Counseling Psychology, 54,* 271–281.

Prentice, D. A., & Miller, D. T. (2006). Essentializing differences between women and men. *Psychological Science, 17,* 129–135.

Quinn, D. M., & Chaudoir, S. R. (2009). Living with a concealable stigmatized identity: The impact of anticipated stigma, centrality, salience, and cultural stigma on psychological distress and health. *Journal of Personality and Social Psychology, 97,* 634–651.

Roberts, R. E., Phinney, J. S., Masse, L. C., Chen, Y. R., & Roberts, C. R. (1999). The structure of ethnic identity of young adolescents from diverse ethnocultural groups. *Journal of Early Adolescence, 19,* 301–322.

Root, M. P. P. (1996). *The multiracial experience: Racial borders as the new frontier.* Thousand Oaks, CA: Sage Publications.

Schmader, T. (2002). Gender identification moderates stereotype threat effects on women's math performance. *Journal of Experimental Social Psychology, 38,* 194–201.

Schmader, T., Johns, M., & Forbes, C. (2008). An integrated process model of stereotype threat effects on performance. *Psychological Review, 115,* 336–356.

Seaton, E. K., Yip, T., & Sellers, R. M. (2009). A longitudinal examination of racial identity and racial discrimination among African American adolescents. *Child Development, 80,* 406–417.

Sellers, R. M., Caldwell, C. H., Schmeelk-Cone, K. H., & Zimmerman, M. A. (2003). Racial identity, racial discrimination, perceived stress, and psychological distress among African American young adults. *Journal of Health and Social Behavior, 43,* 302–317.

Sellers, R. M., Rowley, S. A., Chavous, T. M., Shelton, J. N., & Smith, M. A. (1997). Multidimensional Inventory of Black Identity: A preliminary investigation of reliability and construct validity. *Journal of Personality and Social Psychology, 73,* 805–815.

Sellers, R. M., & Shelton, J. N. (2003). The role of racial identity in perceived racial discrimination. *Journal of Personality and Social Psychology, 84,* 1079–1092.

Sellers, R. M., Smith, M. A., Shelton, J. N., Rowley, S. A., & Chavous, T. M. (1998). Multidimensional model of racial identity: A reconceptualization of African American racial identity. *Personality and Social Psychology Review, 2,* 18–39.

Shelton, J. N., & Richeson, J. A. (2005). Intergroup contact and pluralistic ignorance. *Journal of Personality and Social Psychology, 88,* 91–107.

Shelton, J. N., Richeson, J. A., Salvatore, J., & Trawalter, S. (2005). Ironic effects of racial bias during interracial interactions. *Psychological Science, 16*, 397–402.

Shih, M., Pittinsky, T. L., & Ambady, N. (1999). Stereotype susceptibility: Identity salience and shifts in quantitative performance. *Psychological Science, 10*, 80–83.

Shih, M., & Sanchez, D. T. (2005). Perspectives and research on the positive and negative implications of having multiple racial identities. *Psychological Bulletin, 131*, 569–591.

Smith, C. O., Levine, D. W., Smith, E. P., Dumas, J., & Prinz, R. J. (2009). A developmental perspective of the relationship of racial–ethnic identity to self-construct, achievement, and behavior in African American children. *Cultural Diversity and Ethnic Minority Psychology, 15*, 145–157.

Steele, C. M. (2010). *Whistling Vivaldi: And other clues to how stereotypes affect us.* New York: Norton.

Steele, C. M., & Aronson, J. (1995). Stereotype threat and the intellectual test performance of African Americans. *Journal of Personality and Social Psychology, 69*, 797–811.

Stevenson, H. C. (1997). Managing anger: Protective, proactive, or adaptive racial socialization identity profiles and African-American manhood development. *Journal of Prevention and Intervention in the Community, 16*, 35–61.

Stevenson, H. C., & Arrington, E. G. (2009). Racial/ethnic socialization mediates perceived racism and the racial identity of African American adolescents. *Cultural Diversity and Ethnic Minority Psychology, 15*, 125–136.

Stock, M. L., Gibbons, F. X., Walsh, L. A., & Gerrard, M. (2011). Racial identification, racial discrimination, and substance use vulnerability among African American young adults. *Personality and Social Psychology Bulletin, 37*, 1349–1361.

Stone, J., Lynch, C. I., Sjomeling, M., & Darley, J. M. (1999). Stereotype threat effects on Black and White athletic performance. *Journal of Personality and Social Psychology, 77*, 1213–1227.

Tajfel, H., & Turner, J. C. (1986). The social identity theory of intergroup behavior. In S. Worchel & W. G. Austin (Eds.), *Psychology of intergroup relations* (pp. 7–24). Chicago: Nelson-Hall.

Tatum, B. D. (2004). *Why are all the Black kids sitting together in the cafeteria?* New York: Basic Books.

Taylor, S. E., Lerner, J. S., Sherman, D. K., Sage, R. M., & McDowell, N. K. (2003). Are self-enhancing cognitions associated with healthy or unhealthy biological profiles? *Journal of Personality and Social Psychology, 85*, 605–615.

Terrell, F., & Terrell, S. (1984). Race of counselor, client sex, cultural mistrust level, and premature termination from counseling among Black clients. *Journal of Counseling Psychology, 31*, 371–375.

Townsend, S. S., Major, B., Gangi, C. E., & Mendes, W. B. (2011). From "in the air" to "under the skin": Cortisol responses to social identity threat. *Personality and Social Psychology Bulletin, 37*, 151–164.

Twenge, J. M., & Crocker, J. (2002). Race and self-esteem: Meta-analyses comparing Whites, Blacks, Hispanics, Asians, and American Indians and comment on Gray-Little and Hafdahl (2000). *Psychological Bulletin, 128*, 371–408.

Vandiver, B. J., Cross, W. E., Jr, Worrell, F. C., & Fhagen-Smith, P. E. (2002). Validating the cross racial identity scale. *Journal of Counseling Psychology, 49*, 71–85.

Wout, D. A., Shih, M. J., Jackson, J. S., & Sellers, R. M. (2009). Targets as perceivers: How people determine when they will be negatively stereotyped. *Journal of Personality and Social Psychology, 96*, 349–362.

Chapter 9

Intergroup Interactions
Pitfalls and Promises

Introduction   239
Psychological Challenges of Intergroup Interaction   241
The Promise of Positive Intergroup Interaction   252
Summary   257

We cannot live only for ourselves. A thousand fibers connect us with our fellow-men; and along those fibers, as sympathetic threads, our actions run as causes, and come back to us as effects.

Herman Melville
U.S. novelist and poet (1819–1891)

Introduction

Beginning with the *Plessy v. Ferguson* Supreme Court decision in 1896, the guiding legal policy for interaction between Whites and Blacks in the United States was "separate but equal." Then, in 1954, the historic Supreme Court case *Brown v. Board of Education of Topeka* declared that separate public schools for Black and White students were "inherently unequal" because they unfairly denied Black children appropriate educational opportunities. Thus, the **desegregation** of schools—requiring them to represent appropriate racial and ethnic diversity—became a national priority. Soon after this, sweeping legal changes helped combat the barriers to employment, housing, and other social institutions created by discrimination.

Even though desegregating schools and guaranteeing equal opportunity were truly landmark events in U.S. politics and history, these attempts to eliminate discrimination

The Psychology of Diversity: Beyond Prejudice and Racism, First Edition. James M. Jones, John F. Dovidio, and Deborah L. Vietze.
© 2014 Blackwell Publishing Ltd. Published 2014 by Blackwell Publishing Ltd.

did not mean that the United States formally *valued* diversity. It was not until 50 years after *Brown v. Board of Education of Topeka* that the Supreme Court directly affirmed the importance of diversity. The case was *Grutter v. Bollinger*, one of the University of Michigan affirmative action cases, in 2003. This decision was not simply about protecting the right of minorities for equal opportunity but it also emphasized the importance of experiences with diversity for members of majority groups and for society as a whole because, according to Justice Sandra Day O'Connor, there are "benefits that flow from a diverse student body."

This phrase changes everything. It shifts attention from eliminating segregation to promoting integration. It transforms diversity from something to be tolerated to something to be embraced. This new psychology of diversity was based more on a promotion than prevention motivation (Shah, Brazy, & Higgins, 2004). This positive attitude toward diversity is the focus of this chapter: we review the findings from studies of interethnic and interracial interactions and highlight the value of productive intergroup interaction and exchange for addressing the challenge of diversity. Without harmonious intergroup interactions, few benefits will flow from diversity. When are these interactions negative and threatening? When are they positive? These are the basic questions we consider.

Intergroup interactions are more complicated than encounters between people of the same race or ethnicity. People from different groups often see the world differently, often in contradictory ways. In fact, members of groups in conflict typically view the same incident in fundamentally different, often self-serving ways. In 2000, a series of suicide bombings and shootings by Palestinians killed 39 Israelis. In response, the Israeli military invaded several Palestinian towns; 67 Palestinians died. Only 18% of Israeli Jews characterized the Israeli actions as a form of terrorism, whereas 95% described the Palestinian actions as terrorism; by contrast, 92% of Palestinians saw the Israeli military action as terrorism, but only 13% interpreted the Palestinian violence as terrorism (Shamir & Shikaki, 2002).

Even when groups are not in overt conflict, such as in relations between advantaged and disadvantaged groups within the same society, members of different groups often have divergent perspectives on their relationship. In the United States, for example, nearly three fourths of Blacks but only one third of Whites reported in a national survey that racial discrimination was a major factor accounting for disparities between the groups in income and education levels (USA Today/Gallup, 2008). Whereas a vast majority of Whites (71%) report that they are satisfied with the way Blacks are treated in society, a nearly equivalent proportion of Blacks (68%) report that they are dissatisfied with the way Blacks are treated (Gallup Minority Rights and Relations Survey, 2007). In addition, most White Americans focus on how far the situation of Blacks has come since the days of blatant (and legal) discrimination to the present; they thus think mainly in terms of racial progress. By contrast, Blacks emphasize how far society has to go to achieve true racial equality; they are primarily conscious of continued racial barriers (Eibach & Ehrlinger, 2006). Thus, Whites and Blacks have mirror-image views of equality in the United States.

People not only adopt the different perspectives of their group, they are also often unaware of how members of other groups see the world differently. Thus, there are unique challenges in intergroup interactions. Divergent intergroup perspectives and consequent intergroup misunderstandings contribute directly to intergroup competition and mistrust, from which a single incident can ignite into intergroup conflict. Alternatively, intergroup interactions offer distinctive opportunities to learn more about the world generally and group relations specifically. Encounters with members of other groups can be particularly valuable, personally, and socially. In this chapter, we first discuss the challenges of intergroup interaction, and then we consider the positive potential of these interactions. Much of the research on this topic has featured interactions between Blacks and Whites in the United States, and this chapter reflects that focus. Nevertheless, as our previous examples suggest, we also consider other forms of intergroup relations both inside and outside the United States.

Psychological Challenges of Intergroup Interaction

Understanding others, both members of in-groups and members of out-groups, is a difficult but necessary element of human existence. The psychology of diversity provides a well-developed framework for analyzing and understanding human interaction across individual and group differences. As we explained in Chapter 5, categorizing others as members of one's own group (the in-group) or as members of another group (an out-group) profoundly determines what we expect from them and how we interpret their behaviors. When you interact with other members of your own group, it is easy to feel that it is just about the two of you. But, when you interact with members of another group, these **interpersonal interactions become intergroup encounters**. Whether or not you are aware of it, you are seen to some degree as a representative of your social groups.

As we saw in Chapters 5 and 6, thinking about others or ourselves in terms of group membership activates biases. These biases can influence every stage of the interaction and, as the quote from Herman Melville that began this chapter reminds us, they can ultimately create cascading effects for us and for our groups. In this section, we apply the concepts of social categorization, social identity, and implicit biases (described in earlier chapters) to show how, without ill-intention, intergroup interactions can go awry.

Preparing for the "First Date"

We are inherently social animals; thus social interactions are critically important to us. Merely anticipating an interaction creates a flood of new feelings and thoughts— think of the intense feelings you experience as you get ready for a first date: you feel a flurry of anticipation as you prepare for this important social interaction, which may be positive or negative but which is certainly intense. Similarly, we typically experience intergroup encounters as important social interactions. The psychology of diversity tells us that our reactions differ in fundamental ways in our encounters with in-group compared to out-group members. We expect members of our group to share our attitudes and opinions and be trustworthy; we anticipate members of other groups to hold different views and be untrustworthy and competitive (Foddy, Platow, & Yamagishi, 2009; Judd, Park, Yzerbyt, Gordijn, & Muller, 2005). We start our interactions with out-group members on different footing than those with in-group members. This can be a problem. Think back to how you felt before a recent first date. Were you positive and excited or were you having second thoughts and regretting the arrangement? Very often we get what we expect—our expectations become our reality (see research on the self-fulfilling prophecy in Chapter 5).

What we think as we anticipate encounters is important, but what we believe others think of us is also critical. **Meta-perceptions** are your beliefs about what other people think about you. Many people enter intergroup interactions guardedly, thinking, "He or she may not like me." Negative meta-perceptions of this type commonly occur not only for Black–White relations in the United States but also between White and Aboriginal Canadians, and between Spaniards and immigrants (Frey & Tropp, 2006). They are a common intergroup phenomenon.

Negative meta-perceptions often motivate us to avoid intergroup interaction altogether. These negative expectations make us feel highly anxious simply thinking about impending intergroup interactions (Plant, Butz, & Tartakovsky, 2008). Avoidance is often the easiest way to relieve this anxiety. In addition, we tend to rationalize our avoidance by blaming the other group. White and Black students, for example, say they are really interested in opportunities for interracial interaction, but they also explain that they don't make overtures to members of the other group because they anticipate and fear rejection (Shelton & Richeson, 2005). This is a form of pluralistic ignorance, a phenomenon that occurs when people misinterpret each other's beliefs and actions in ways that prevent them from acting positively together.

Avoiding intergroup interactions, whether because of negative meta-perceptions or pluralistic ignorance, can of course be a major impediment to improving relations. Avoidance limits our opportunities to correct our misperceptions of members of other groups and to understand more accurately how members of other groups view us. Have you ever thought that someone was stuck up and aloof until you got to know her and learned that she was just shy? Avoidance is a personal form of segregation that creates and perpetuates unfair judgments of others. Unfortunately, though, choosing to have an interaction may not be enough to correct these misconceptions. The forces that lead us to avoid intergroup encounters often carry over to affect what we see, believe, and feel in these interactions.

Where Do We Go From Here? Experiences in Intergroup Interactions

When you enter into an intergroup exchange, either by choice or necessity, you literally adopt a different posture than when you interact with a member of your own group. We communicate our attitudes toward others through our **non-verbal behavior**, namely through our physical actions other than what we say. In intergroup exchanges, people position themselves further away from each other, close their arms, maintain less eye contact, and have shorter glances, blink faster, and fidget more. These are signs of tension and anxiety, which often escalate in these interactions (Stephan & Stephan, 2000).

Intergroup anxiety is discomfort associated with anticipating or actually interacting with a member of another group. Majority-group members feel anxious in part because of their unfamiliarity with the situation: The social and occupational segregation that characterizes most societies limits majority-group members' experiences with members of other groups. Members of majority groups also become anxious because they are concerned that they may behave in a way that will lead others to believe that they are biased (Richeson & Shelton, 2010).

By contrast, much of the anxiety that members of traditionally disadvantaged groups feel is related to their vigilance for detecting bias (Vorauer, 2006). Fear of being discriminated against is a central element of Blacks' attitudes toward Whites (Johnson & Lecci, 2003). Thus, no actual conflict has to occur between the two people engaged in an intergroup interaction for them to feel anxious and insecure. Because of the previous history of intergroup relations, both majority- and minority-group members tend to feel vulnerable and defensive. Intergroup interactions often begin a bit off balance.

Interactions with members of your own group are not always easy, but they are relatively straightforward exchanges. By contrast, even casual interactions between individuals of different genders, ethnicities, races, or sexual orientations can feel like a stand-off chess game. Imagine you are a majority-group member in such an interaction. These thoughts may occur to you: "Am I saying the right things? Am I bending over backwards to be *too* nice? Should I mention the recent tragic incident involving his group on campus? I wonder if he likes me?" If you were the minority-group member, you might be thinking: "I wonder what she thinks of my group? Is she prejudiced? Does she have any friends like me? Is she being nice to me because she means it or because she just wants to appear to like a person like me?" Intergroup, and particularly interracial, interactions are often hard work (see Chapter 7), particularly when people concentrate on their group differences and social relations (Babbit & Sommers, 2011). As we saw in Chapter 7, because they consume so many cognitive resources, both Whites and Blacks have more difficulty thinking, such as solving mathematical tasks or even making simple decisions about the color of words (a Stroop task), after interracial interactions than after social encounters with members of their own group (Richeson & Shelton, 2010; Trawalter, Richeson, & Shelton, 2009).

In intergroup interactions, negative group-based expectations often get in the way of mutually satisfying and successful interactions. People typically engage in confirmatory bias (see Chapter 5); they are especially attuned to things that seem to confirm their expectations. For instance, Whites are quicker to perceive hostility in the face of a Black person than a White person, and they are more likely to misperceive neutral facial expressions in Blacks than in Whites as conveying anger (Hugenberg & Bodenhausen, 2004). Also, Blacks who believe that their White interaction partner is racially prejudiced perceive the person as behaving more negatively and are less satisfied with the interaction, even when their beliefs about the White person's attitudes are wrong (Richeson & Shelton, 2010).

The behaviors that a person exhibits when anxious, such as trying to increase physical and psychological distance, failing to maintain eye contact, and using a closed posture, are also signs of dislike. When you interact with in-group members, you expect things to go well. When they look away and cross their arms, you know they are uneasy, but you also assume that they are thinking hard and trying to work things out. When people from another group for whom your expectations are less positive show these same behaviors, you are less sure exactly what these actions mean. You know they are anxious, and you assume that they are anxious because they dislike you. This effect occurs for both Whites and Blacks (Dovidio, West, Pearson, Gaertner, & Kawakami, 2007).

Because of the different ways we interpret another person's anxiety, even minor disruptions can have very different consequences in intergroup compared with same-group interactions. Imagine you are Skyping with a friend of yours. There is a slight delay in the person's responses. No big deal. You assume it is caused by a satellite relay. But what if you are interacting with a person of another ethnicity or race? Is it the satellite, or is the person being unresponsive to you? When people interact with a person of a different ethnic or racial group, these slight delays make them very anxious and disrupt the flow of communication. Moreover, the mutual anxiety that is experienced in these intergroup encounters readily leads to mutual dislike, even without real negative intention or direct evidence of bias (Pearson et al., 2008). Thus, minor disruptions in intergroup and intercultural communication can quickly become "big deals" in intergroup interaction.

These processes, which have been studied primarily in initial interactions between strangers, have persistent effects even as people get to know one another better. As we know from countless anecdotal accounts and personal experience, relations between new college roommates are not always easy. At the very beginning, relations are good. Nevertheless, even when roommates share the same race or ethnicity, on average relations worsen over time. But what about when roommates are from different cultural groups? In general, cross-race relationships deteriorate faster than do same-race roommate relationships. Shook and Fazio (2008a) found that students who were randomly assigned roommates from a different race were twice as likely as same-race pairs to separate after one academic year. Specifically, 15% of interracial roommate pairs dissolved by the end of the academic year, whereas only 8% of the White roommate pairs and 6% of Black roommate pairs dissolved in the same period. One of the problems is that for roommates from different racial or ethnic groups, there is a "contagion" of anxiety. One roommate's anxiety produces increased anxiety in the other roommate. Perceptions of the other roommate's anxiety, which signals rejection in intergroup interactions, in turn produces less desire to live together as roommates in the future. This escalation does not occur for same-race roommates (West, Shelton, & Trail, 2009).

Although both majority- and minority-group members are vulnerable to many of the same processes that contribute to divergent perspectives, there may be distinctive influences as well. People who feel that their group is the target of prejudice are sensitive to cues of discrimination. With respect to minority–majority relations in the United States, minorities' daily encounters with potential discrimination may lead them to interpretations that confirm that prejudice exists and to label ambiguous behaviors as discriminatory (Operario & Fiske, 2001; see also Sue, 2010).

Salvatore and Shelton (2007), for instance, showed White and Black participants the results of a fictitious hiring decision in which a highly qualified applicant was passed over for an applicant who had mediocre credentials. The interviewer who made the hiring decision was of the same race (White or Black) as the mediocre candidate who was hired; the highly qualified applicant was of the other race (Black or White).

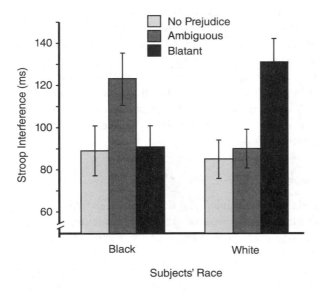

Figure 9.1. Blacks Are Most Cognitively Depleted After Exposure to Ambiguous Bias; Whites Are Most Depleted After Exposure to Blatant Bias. Reprinted from "Cognitive Costs to Exposure to Racial Prejudice," by J. Salvatore, & J. N. Shelton, 2007, *Psychological Science, 18*, pp. 810–815.

In a Blatant Prejudice condition, participants saw the interviewer's notes, which stated that the highly qualified Black applicant had belonged to "too many minority organizations" or the White applicant was "a typical White prep-school kid." In an Ambiguous Prejudice condition, the interviewer made no reference to race. Some participants were also exposed to a No-Prejudice control condition.

To assess how hard participants thought about the case, the researchers assessed participants' performance on a cognitive task. As we saw in Chapter 7, poorer performance on a cognitive task indicates distraction—in this case, the distraction was that the participants thought harder, depleting more of their cognitive resources. As illustrated in Figure 9.1, White participants seemed to be sensitive only to blatant prejudice; they displayed evidence of cognitive depletion only in the Blatant Prejudice condition. Black participants, in contrast, concentrated most in the Ambiguous Prejudice condition. In fact, because it was so obvious (and consistent with their expectations of bias), they did not show more depletion of their cognitive resources in the Blatant Prejudice condition than they did in the No-Prejudice control condition. In other words, this experiment suggests that Blacks are more attuned to detecting prejudice in ambiguous situations than are Whites.

As a result of these tendencies, minority-group members may be better than majority-group members at detecting evidence of prejudice and discrimination. Overall, Blacks show greater accuracy in the detection of bias than do Whites. For instance, Blacks are better able to detect the level of racial bias of White individuals after observing their non-verbal behavior for 20 seconds than are Whites (Richeson & Shelton, 2005).

The differential attunement to cues of bias in intergroup interactions reflects the divergent impressions that Whites and Blacks have about bias in the United States. Whites appear not to recognize intergroup bias, whereas Blacks report that its influence is pervasive. These divergent views produce different expectations and interpretations in intergroup interaction, often leading to confusion, miscommunication, and anxiety. In intergroup interactions, though, one person's uneasiness becomes another person's dislike, and divergent perspectives develop. Over time, mutual uneasiness interferes with the ability of members of different groups to develop positive relations on an interpersonal level.

You (Can) Complete Me

People differ greatly in their individual needs, preferences, and values, but one thing we have in common is that we all need social interaction. In fact, some researchers view human interactions largely in terms of the exchange of resources, such as love and status, that we personally desire.

But we also have group-based needs, needs that become important to us when our social identities are activated. Although scholars differ in what they call these basic group-based needs, there is general agreement that there are two clusters. According to the **needs-based model of reconciliation** (Shnabel, Nadler, Ullrich, Dovidio, & Carmi, 2009), for example, the two fundamental needs are for *acceptance* and *empowerment*. The needs-based model started with the study of interpersonal transgressions and the needs of perpetrators and victims in interpersonal relationships (Shnabel & Nadler, 2008). Think of a time when your partner in a relationship did something that hurt you. What did you want more from that person: affirmation that you were a good person, or an indication that you were truly valued and deserving of dignity and greater status as a human being? For most people, the answer is value and status. Now think back to when you harmed someone you cared about. What did you want from them, affirmation that you had power over them or their acceptance of you as a good person? For most people, the answer is acceptance. Since then, this reasoning has been extended to the psychology of perpetrator and victimized groups in the Middle East and to advantaged versus disadvantaged groups more generally. Members of minority groups feel like victims who have lost status and control. They therefore seek reaffirmation of their power and competence. Members of advantaged groups, when they feel that the moral legitimacy of their status and privilege is questioned, seek acceptance and social approval from members of disadvantaged groups (Shnabel et al., 2009).

Researchers studying race in the United States have drawn parallel conclusions (Bergsieker, Shelton, & Richeson, 2010). In intergroup encounters, Blacks and Latinos are motivated to be respected and consequently make particular efforts to manage the impressions of Whites so that they are seen as competent. Whites, in contrast, are motivated to be liked, and in these interactions go out of their way to be ingratiating.

How does this play out? Bergsieker et al. (2010) videotaped Blacks and Whites in cross-race and same-race interactions and had raters code the videos for self-promoting

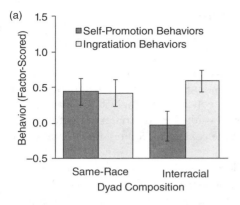

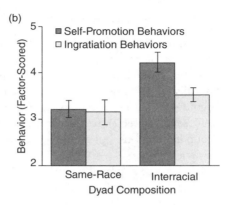

Figure 9.2. Whites Show More Ingratiation Behaviors Than Self-presentational Behaviors in Interracial Interactions, Whereas Blacks Show More Self-presentational Behaviors Than Ingratiation Behaviors. From "To Be Liked Versus Respected: Divergent Goals in Interracial Interaction," by H. B. Bergsieker, J. N. Shelton, & J. A. Richeson, 2010, *Journal of Personality and Social Psychology, 99,* pp. 248–264.

behaviors, which are attempts to convey an image of power, and ingratiating behaviors, which are attempts to get another person to like you. Examples of self-promoting behaviors are describing specific accomplishments, achievements, and talents, as well as showing confidence non-verbally (e.g., upright posture, eye contact). Examples of ingratiating behaviors are attempts at humor, drawing attention to similarities or common acquaintances, and nodding and smiling in response to what the other person says. As illustrated in Figure 9.2, in interracial interactions, Blacks show a high rate of self-promoting behavior (but not ingratiating behavior). Whites in interracial interactions, compared to same-race encounters, display more ingratiating behavior and less self-promoting behavior.

So majority- and minority-group members have divergent goals in their intergroup encounters. However, people don't understand that the other person has different needs. What's my best guess about what another person wants or needs, particularly if I don't know the person well? I am likely to project my own needs onto that person: I assume that he or she wants the same things I want. In fact, Whites, particularly when they feel uncomfortable in interracial interactions, exaggerate friendly gestures such as smiling and laughing (Mendes & Koslov, 2012)—affiliative gestures that would meet their own need to be liked in these interactions. These efforts often backfire, because I am satisfying my own need but not those of my partner. In fact, when Blacks encounter Whites who appear too positive or friendly, they often see this as an indication of prejudice (Crocker, Voelkl, Testa, & Major, 1991). However, when people do respond in ways that satisfy what the other group is looking for—respect and empowerment for minority groups, acceptance and being liked for majority groups—intergroup interactions are more positive and intergroup attitudes generally become more positive (Shnabel et al., 2009).

Under the Radar? Implicit Bias and Intergroup Interaction

In Chapter 7, we discussed the distinction between explicit biases, biases that people are aware of and whose expression they can control, and implicit biases, biases that are activated automatically and sometimes operate unconsciously. Researchers typically assess explicit bias with self-reports and measure implicit biases using cognitive-association, response-latency measures such as the Implicit Association Test (IAT; see Chapter 7). Implicit biases have been studied in the context of actual intergroup interactions, but almost exclusively in the context of Whites' biases in encounters with Blacks.

Implicit racial prejudice can play a critical role in shaping intergroup interactions through interpretations and expressions of non-verbal behaviors (Greenwald, Poehlman, Uhlmann, & Banaji, 2009; cf. Blanton et al., 2009). Earlier, we noted that Whites are generally quicker to perceive hostility in the faces of Blacks than of Whites. But does this effect last? In one study, White participants saw a brief movie clip of an animated face (Figure 9.3) morph a facial expression from unambiguously hostile (on the left) to unambiguously happy (on the right), with ambiguous expressions in between (Hugenberg & Bodenhausen, 2003). Participants indicated when they no longer saw hostility on the face. In general, participants said that the hostility lasted longer on the faces of Black than White characters, and this occurred more strongly for more implicitly prejudiced Whites.

With respect to our own actions, non-verbal behaviors are very difficult to monitor and control. We engage in them spontaneously and rarely reflect on what we are doing. We are poor at consciously controlling our non-verbal behaviors. Instead,

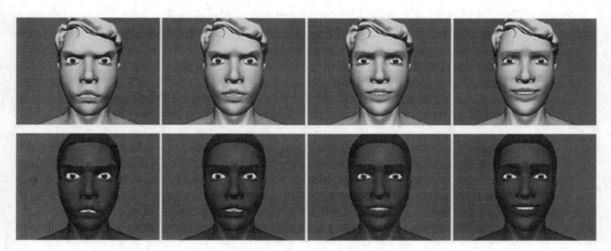

Figure 9.3. Whites Higher in Implicit Prejudice See Hostility (Depicted by Images on the Left) Longer on the Faces of Blacks than of Whites. Reprinted from "Facing Prejudice: Implicit Prejudice and the Perception of Facial Threat," by K. Hugenberg, & G. V. Bodenhausen, 2003, *Psychological Science, 14,* pp. 640–643.

implicit, and often unconscious, attitudes play a large role in non-verbal displays. For Whites, implicit prejudice is a better predictor of non-verbal behavior in interracial interactions than is explicit prejudice. More implicitly prejudiced Whites blink more when interacting with Blacks than with Whites (reflecting anxiety), and they look less at them, have more speech hesitations and errors, and generally appear less friendly non-verbally (see, for example, McConnell & Leibold, 2001).

As we discussed in Chapter 7, many Whites in the United States are characterized by *aversive racism* (Dovidio & Gaertner, 2004). They consciously endorse egalitarian values and appear low in explicit prejudice, but they are significantly biased in implicit measures like the IAT. Thus, in interracial interactions, Whites often show a mismatch between more controllable behaviors, such as the verbal content of what they say, and more spontaneous non-verbal behaviors and expressions. This mismatch contributes to misunderstanding and mistrust in interracial interactions.

This effect is illustrated in a study in which the researchers (Dovidio, Kawakami, & Gaertner, 2002) first assessed the explicit and implicit racial attitudes of White participants. These participants then engaged in an interracial interaction and a same-race interaction. Whites' explicit racial attitudes primarily predicted bias in their more conscious and controllable interpersonal behavior (verbal friendliness) during their interactions with Black and White partners. Whites who reported that they were more prejudiced behaved in a less verbally friendly way toward a Black relative to a White partner. However, it was Whites' implicit racial attitudes (assessed with a response-latency procedure), not their self-reported prejudice, that predicted bias in non-verbal behaviors, which they were less capable of controlling or monitoring.

In addition, the mismatch between Whites' verbal and non-verbal behaviors produced different perceptions of the interaction for them and their Black partners. Whites keyed in on the things they were most conscious of: their generally non-prejudiced explicit attitudes, reinforced by the positive nature of *what* they said. They believed that they acted in a warm and friendly manner. In contrast, when asked their impressions of how friendly the White person's behavior was toward them, Black partners focused more on *how* Whites communicated—their non-verbal behavior. Because these behaviors tended to be negative, reflecting anxiety and avoidance (as we discussed earlier), Blacks typically perceived that their White partners were less friendly than Whites thought they were. As a consequence, Blacks were less satisfied with the interaction than were Whites. Moreover, the Black and White participants were unaware that the other person viewed the experience differently than they did. Thus, these interracial interactions produced divergent perspectives and fundamental misunderstandings. This is another form of pluralistic ignorance in intergroup encounters. Even within the same interaction, Whites and Blacks experience different "realities."

Much of the psychological research on interracial interactions has examined social encounters between previously unacquainted college students. These interactions can lead to lasting intergroup impressions and misinterpretations, but what personal impact does this have? Do similar processes operate in consequential intergroup interactions involving specific tasks and goals outside the laboratory, in the "real world"? Box 9.1 answers that question with a resounding yes.

Box 9.1.   Health Disparities and Implicit Bias in Healthcare

In the United States, Blacks, Latinos, and American Indians have more health problems than do Whites. These differences are referred to as **health disparities**. Racial and ethnic minority-group members typically suffer much higher mortality rates than majority-group members for similar conditions in the US and across 125 other countries (see Penner, Albrecht, Orom, Coleman, & Underwood, 2010). For example, in the US the rate of stomach cancer among Latinos compared to Whites is 63% higher for men and 150% higher for women (National Center for Health Statistics, 2011; Smedley, Stith, & Nelson, 2003). Moreover, the gap in mortality rates for Blacks relative to Whites in several areas (heart disease, female breast cancer, and diabetes) has significantly widened in recent years.

Differences in socioeconomic status, insurance coverage, and access to healthcare contribute to health disparities, but bias among healthcare providers also exerts a significant influence beyond these elements. Indeed, like the average person, doctors display substantially more racial bias on an implicit measure, the IAT, than on an explicit, self-report measure. In fact, doctors score about the same on both measures as the average person (Moskowitz, Stone, & Childs, 2012; Sabin, Nosek, Greenwald, & Rivara, 2009; Sabin, Rivara, & Greenwald, 2008).

So, what does this mean for healthcare? As we have discussed in the context of social intergroup interactions, these biases may "leak out" non-verbally and undermine minority patients' trust in the doctor, which can adversely affect the effectiveness of treatment. When a White physician is higher in implicit racial bias, Black patients feel less respected, like their physician less, and have less confidence in the physician (Cooper et al., 2012). Also consistent with the social effects of implicit bias, doctors higher in implicit prejudice also appear less warm and friendly to Black patients. Explicit prejudice has a much weaker effect: Doctors who are more explicitly prejudiced admit that they are less apt to involve a Black patient directly in their medical decision-making process, but it is still the implicit bias that drives their non-verbal behavior (Penner, Dovidio, et al., 2010).

The research on aversive racism discussed in Chapter 7 and earlier in this chapter further suggests that receiving mixed messages (positive verbal-negative non-verbal) from aversive racists can be particularly detrimental to doctor-patient relations. Penner, Dovidio, and colleagues (2010) measured doctors' explicit and implicit attitudes and then, after the doctors saw Black patients in an inner-city clinic, questioned patients about how satisfied they were with the visit. Patient satisfaction is an important predictor of how well patients adhere to the doctor's instructions and how willing they are to schedule visits for follow-up care. Black patients were less satisfied with a high-prejudiced doctor (high explicit-high implicit prejudice) than with a low-prejudiced doctor (low explicit-low implicit prejudice). This makes sense. But what about doctors who fit the profile of an aversive racist: low explicit-high implicit prejudice? Patients were *least* satisfied with their visits with these doctors—even less satisfied than with consistently high-prejudiced doctors!

The finding that a doctor's implicit prejudice undermines minority patient trust and satisfaction—particularly among doctors who say that they are not prejudiced—helps to explain a range of racial and ethnic disparities that characterize doctor–patient interactions (see Penner, Albrecht, et al., 2010).

1. An additional research finding is that Black patients tend to show less trust in their physician immediately after their visit with the doctor than before. Why would this be so?
2. How can patients from racial and ethnic minority groups behave in medical encounters to build on the conscious egalitarian values of people in the medical community to receive higher quality medical care?

Some Conclusions About Intergroup Interactions

This section paints a rather bleak and frustrating picture of intergroup interactions. Even when people's conscious intentions are positive, intergroup interactions are undermined by cultural mistrust, miscommunication, and misunderstanding. Additionally, interactions between people of different races or ethnicity require much more effort than interactions between members of the same race/ethnic group. Differences between groups are accompanied by suspicion, as people expect and watch for signs of rejection. Hindering intergroup interactions are negative illusions along with the often unrecognized and unacknowledged influence of implicit biases.

And what we expect is what we see: we misinterpret cues of anxiety as indications of dislike. Interpersonal interactions between members of different groups occur across a "category divide" (Miller & Prentice, 1999). As a consequence, when members of different groups disagree in intergroup interactions, they see the situation as being less open to a solution than one involving within-group interactions. Even when intergroup interactions appear to be going smoothly and members of different groups appear to see each other at a closer interpersonal level, a slight disagreement automatically activates stereotypes and reestablishes the interaction as an intergroup exchange (Kunda, Davies, Adams, & Spencer, 2002). This misunderstanding can be quite costly because once people label the disagreement as reflecting group differences, they believe it is especially difficult to resolve (Miller & Prentice, 1999).

Nevertheless, intergroup interactions don't have to turn out this way. While diversity and difference can cause misunderstandings in intergroup interactions, these molehills do not have to become mountains. In addition, despite their challenges, interactions with members of other groups can have unique benefits, the benefits "that flow from diversity." If we are open to it, we can learn more from others who are different from us than from those who are the same. In the next section, we see how intergroup interactions can become more harmonious.

The Promise of Positive Intergroup Interaction

Intergroup interaction has enormous potential for reducing prejudice, improving intergroup relations, and realizing the benefits of diversity. However, as we have seen from our review of intergroup interactions, simply bringing members of different groups together is not enough. Psychologists, sociologists, and political scientists noticed this beginning in the 1930s. However, they also recognized that intergroup contact, for example between Blacks and Whites in coalmines in West Virginia and in combat situations in World War II, changed people's attitudes positively and profoundly. Why does this happen?

Gordon Allport (1954) integrated many of the ideas and existing evidence on intergroup interaction to formulate his highly influential **contact hypothesis** and presented this in his classic book *The Nature of Prejudice*. The contact hypothesis specified four conditions that were necessary for intergroup interaction to reduce bias:

- equal status within the contact situation;
- intergroup cooperation;
- shared goals;
- support of authorities, laws, or customs.

Since then, two additional key conditions have been added (see Pettigrew, 1998):

- exchange of information that allows us to make a personal connection during these interactions;
- having at least one friend who is a member of the other group.

Developing a friendship is particularly important to improving intergroup interaction because it encompasses many of the other elements in the contact hypotheses. For example, we typically see friends as equals, we share personal information with them, cooperate with them, and we share common goals with them. Having friends from another group can play an important role in reducing long-term conflicts (Paolini, Hewstone, Cairns, & Voci, 2004).

The contact hypothesis has given us many theoretical and practical ideas to pursue to better understand intergroup interaction. It has stimulated generations of studies. More important, it has been shown to work! Pettigrew and Tropp (2006, 2008, 2011) summarized the results of 515 studies involving more than 250,000 participants from 38 nations around the globe. Overall, intergroup contact, particularly contact that more closely matched the conditions specified by Allport, produced lower levels of prejudice. When the conditions were not met, such as in some of the ways early school desegregation plans were implemented, prejudice was not reduced and intergroup conflict sometimes ensued (Schofield & Eurich-Fulcer, 2001). In addition, contact is less effective for improving the attitudes of minority-group members than of majority-group members (Tropp & Pettigrew, 2005). However, adding interventions in the classroom, such as the jigsaw classroom and cooperative learning, has significant beneficial effects for both groups (see Chapter 6).

The positive impact of intergroup contact occurs not only for different racial and ethnic groups but also for groups such as homosexuals and people with mental illness. In addition, contact that happens over the internet also works (Tynes, Giang, & Thompson, 2008). The quantity of contact matters, but the quality of the contact (whether it is positive or negative) matters even more. In addition, the positive effects of intergroup contact are highly generalizable. People not only like the out-group members with whom they interact more but they also develop more positive attitudes toward other members of the group whom they have not yet met and to the out-group as a whole. In addition, there are impressive **secondary transfer effects**, which involve the generalization of the benefits of contact to other types of out-groups (Pettigrew & Tropp, 2011). The positive feelings generated by contact with members of one out-group extend to other out-groups that are seen as similar, even though members of these groups were not involved in the intergroup encounter. There is so much evidence in support of it, the contact hypothesis now is called *contact theory*.

How Does Contact Work?

How does contact improve intergroup attitudes? There are two possible routes. One is cognitive and the other is emotional. We are both thinking and feeling beings. People commonly believe that prejudice comes from ignorance of the other group. So, one way contact might work is by expanding our knowledge about what people in another group are like. This is reasonable, and intergroup contact does increase knowledge, but increasing knowledge by itself doesn't play that much of a role in reducing prejudice (Pettigrew & Tropp, 2008).

The cognitive route: greater knowledge Although general knowledge has little impact, particular types of knowledge do matter. When we encounter someone from another group who does not conform to our stereotypic preconceptions, it makes us question whether our views about the group are correct. We learn a lot from what others tell us about what members of another group are like, but a single personal experience of **stereotype disconfirmation** can override second-hand information. Of course, as we noted in Chapter 5, humans strive for cognitive consistency, and so we will tend to dismiss this person as an exception, different from other members of that group. Think back to a time when you met and got to know a person who was from a group that you didn't like much, such as a particular fraternity or sorority. What did you think? For most of us, the tendency is to say, "I like Mary; she's not like the rest of *them*." We retain our negative view of the group by seeing this person as an exception. This is why positive intergroup contact is more effective when the other person is seen as typical of the group (Brown & Hewstone, 2005). We may be a bit more suspicious and guarded when we interact with a typical out-group member, but if we do connect to that person, then we automatically connect better to other members of that group.

The emotional route: reduced anxiety Intergroup contact reduces prejudice also, and in fact more so, through emotional routes. Because successful intergroup interaction dispels our fears of rejection and reduces our uncertainty about others, it reduces our intergroup anxiety (Tausch & Hewstone, 2010). As we saw earlier in this chapter, anxiety leads us to avoid or be suspicious in intergroup interactions, and we often interpret signs of anxiety as cues of dislike. Thus, relieving intergroup anxiety opens us up to overtures from the other person and to see the other group in more realistic and less threatening ways. When we feel more secure with members of another group, we are more open to positive interactions with them.

In addition to reducing negative emotions, intergroup contact allows us to make more positive, human connections with others. Having the opportunity to develop a relationship with a single member of another group allows us to empathize with that person. **Empathy** involves understanding the perspective of the other person so that we respond emotionally to their situation. A recent television show filmed how people responded to various types of discrimination against Blacks, Latinos, and gay men. Some of the bias was subtle, such as White salespeople following a Black woman through a store to make sure she didn't steal anything. Some incidents were blatant— White youths beating up a Latino. Whites who witnessed the event actually occur got upset initially, but the feeling did not last. They typically walked away without doing anything. Most of those who did stop reported that they did so because they knew a person from the victim's group, they understood how the victim felt, and therefore they cared enough to do something. They felt empathy for the victim, which motivated them to help.

When people feel empathy, particularly involving feelings of compassion and concern, they respond more favorably and helpfully not only toward that one person but also to their group as a whole. These acts of compassion and caring extend to other socially devalued groups like people with AIDS, homeless people, and even murderers (Batson et al., 1997). Intergroup contact allows us to make fundamental human connections with others, and this shared humanity leads us to treat each other better.

Recall our earlier description of the challenges that roommates from different races or ethnicities face. They also have a lot to offer each other if they are open to it. And what they can learn can be especially satisfying and can strengthen intergroup relations over time. Think of the excitement you experience when you connect with someone from another group or culture; it opens your mind to understand and value diversity. So if instead of the cultural mistrust and tension that colors our intergroup interactions we start off with a positive frame of mind, such as believing that our differences contribute to our common good (a common in-group identity; see Chapter 5), the possibility of developing close intergroup relations increases.

As we discussed earlier, roommate relations generally tend to get worse over the course of students' first semester in college. When roommates from different racial and ethnic groups (Whites, Blacks, Latinos, and Asians) see themselves primarily in terms of their racial or ethnic differences, things go downhill even faster. However, the results are strikingly different for roommates from different groups who focus on what members of different racial or ethnic groups have in common: These relationships stay positive and close, and often create stronger friendships than those between same-race roommates at the same point in the semester (West, Pearson, Dovidio, Shelton, & Trail, 2009). In addition, positive roommate relations between members of different racial or ethnic groups create more favorable attitudes toward the roommate's group, reducing even implicit prejudice (Shook & Fazio, 2008b) and creating more openness to diversity throughout students' college careers (Van Laar, Levin, Sinclair, & Sidanius, 2005).

Research carried on for over 60 years has shown that intergroup contact is the most effective and robust recipe for improving intergroup relations. This work has guided legal interventions such as school, residential, and employment integration laws and policies. Nevertheless, it has some limitations. One limitation is that the original version of the hypothesis stated that personal, first-hand contact is required. This implies that we can only improve intergroup relations one or two people at a time. However, some of the most exciting new extensions of contact theory involve indirect forms of contact. **Indirect contact** involves learning about others' intergroup contact, observing others engaging in intergroup interaction, or imagining oneself interacting with a member of another group.

Friends of My Friends

The **extended contact hypothesis** presents the idea that an in-group member's mere knowledge of a close positive relationship with a person in an out-group can reduce intergroup bias (Wright, Aron, McLaughlin-Volpe, & Ropp, 1997; see also Dovidio, Eller, & Hewstone, 2011). In other words, White students who know another White person who has a Black, Asian, or Latino friend has more positive attitudes toward that racial or ethnic group than do Whites who do not know such a person. If you are a friend of my friend, I not only like you, I like the entire racial or ethnic group you are in more. Racial and ethnic minority-group members show the same effects in their attitudes toward Whites.

These were only correlational data, however, not direct evidence that learning that other in-group members have friends in the out-group causes more positive intergroup attitudes. To address the issues of causality, Wright et al. (1997) first created two laboratory groups, the blue group and the green group, with six or seven team members each. To produce intergroup rivalry and prejudice, the groups competed against each other on problem-solving tasks (e.g., designing a safe-sex media campaign) and physical tasks (e.g., while blindfolded untangling a rope that tied members of their group together). The members of the different groups did not like each other much by the end of these rounds of competition.

But then one member of each group was pulled out to participate in a friendship-building exercise, in which they gradually disclosed more personal and intimate information to each other. These two participants then explained to the other participants how they had become friends with each other. Although the other green- and blue-team members had no other exposure to each other and the study required further competition, in virtually every session and on every measure of intergroup attitudes, participants became more favorable in their attitudes after learning about the single case of intergroup friendship. This one piece of information caused a significant improvement in participants' attitudes toward the other group. Since this seminal finding, dozens of studies have found that extended contact of this type improves intergroup attitudes, above and beyond the effects of direct personal contact (see Turner, Hewstone, Voci, Paolini, & Christ, 2008 for a review).

In Chapter 5 we discussed the importance of social learning—learning from observing what others do—in how we gain knowledge of our social world. Mass media (television, radio, and the internet) are also primary sources of information that shape our impressions and feelings about other social groups. Learning about intergroup friendships from the media can reduce prejudice. For example, 5- to 10-year-old children who read stories featuring friendships between non-disabled and disabled children displayed more positive attitudes toward and greater interest in playing with children with disabilities (Cameron & Rutland, 2006).

Even in intense intergroup conflicts, the media can play a critical role in peace-building. In Rwanda, approximately 800,000 people were murdered (mainly Tutsis by Hutus) in 100 days in 1994. Since then, relations between Hutus and Tutsis have, understandably, been tense, fueled by deep-seated animosity. There have been a number of attempts to rebuild the society and promote reconciliation. One initiative involved creating a radio soap opera featuring positive contact and friendships between Hutus and Tutsis. Not surprisingly, exposure to this radio show did not immediately improve intergroup attitudes in the aftermath of such brutality. However, it did alter how both Hutus and Tutsis believe they *should* interact and work together in the future (Paluck, 2009). It helped shape the norms for intergroup relations in Rwanda and laid a solid foundation for future reconciliation. Indeed, changing perceptions of intergroup norms may be a more efficient way to promote positive relations between groups than targeting attitudes that are deeply embedded in personal experiences and long-term socialization.

Just Imagine!

One of the most wonderful and important aspects of the evolution of the human brain is our remarkable capacity to think imaginatively. The visual and performing arts as well as literature and poetry attest to how far people will go and how much they will spend for works of the imagination. Thus, we may not have to personally experience positive intergroup contact (direct contact) or know of an actual in-group member who has an out-group friend (extended contact) to develop more favorable intergroup attitudes. We might be able to imagine it. **Imagined contact** is the "mental simulation of a social interaction with a member or members of an out-group category" (Crisp & Turner, 2009, p. 234). For instance, in a study of imagined contact with the elderly, college students were instructed, "We would like you to take a minute to imagine yourself meeting an elderly stranger for the first time. Imagine their appearance, the conversation . . . and what you learn" (Turner, Crisp, & Lambert, 2007, p. 430). Participants in the control condition imagined an outdoor scene instead. After imagining such intergroup contact, people had more positive impressions of the out-group as a whole, held more favorable attitudes, and were more willing to have future contact with them. This method has been applied to ethnic groups, national groups, and gay men as well as the elderly (see also Husnu & Crisp, 2010; Stathi & Crisp, 2008).

Your imagination can take you places you may hesitate to go in reality, because of uncertainty or fear of rejection. Like direct contact, imagined contact reduces anxiety, increases confidence in our ability to have productive exchanges, and leads us to recognize positive non-stereotypic characteristics of members of the other group. Imagination is a powerful tool that, if managed properly, can improve intergroup relations. We often imagine the worst, but we can also imagine the best and reap the benefits of diversity.

Summary

Intergroup biases play out in a variety of ways in social interactions. We expect interactions with people from other groups to be more difficult than encounters with members of our own racial, ethnic, or national group, and we are more cautious and guarded in these personal exchanges. As intergroup interactions progress, we tend to interpret the behaviors of others, such as their facial expressions, in ways that confirm our suspicions of the other group. As a consequence, intergroup interactions typically follow a different trajectory than intragroup interactions. Our systematic misinterpretations of each other's behavior in intergroup interactions have long-term consequences, interfering with the ability to develop intergroup friendships, producing divergent perspectives on the source of the problem, and ultimately reinforcing cultural intergroup biases.

The disintegration of relations between members of different groups is far from inevitable, however. Despite the many pitfalls of intergroup interaction, appropriately structured intergroup contact is a powerful force for improving intergroup attitudes. According to contact theory, cooperative interaction with common goals, equal status participation, and exchange of personalized information is most effective for improving intergroup relations. Having even a single friend who is an out-group member can change our attitudes toward the group to be significantly more positive. These experiences reduce our anxiety, increase our empathy, and allow us to recognize errors in our stereotypic expectations with members of the other group.

Even contact that we are not directly involved in can transform our intergroup attitudes. Research on extended contact, in which we learn that another in-group member has an out-group friend, improves our attitudes toward the outgroup. Observing an in-group and out-group member interact positively makes us feel more confident that we, too, can interact with members of the other group and increases our willingness to do so. Contact does not have to be real for it to have beneficial effects: Imagining an interaction with a member of another group that goes well increases our willingness to seek further intergroup contact and, by itself, makes our attitudes toward the other group more favorable.

In conclusion, intergroup interactions are unusually challenging cognitively, emotionally, and socially. Individuals from different groups approach these interactions with anxiety and trepidation, and they have different needs and goals, of which their partner is typically unaware. In addition, people from different groups are attuned to different cues, which may be emitted by their partner unconsciously and unintentionally, in ways that produce divergent perceptions, create confusion and mistrust, and reinforce negative expectations. Nevertheless, by understanding the processes that lead to divergent intergroup perspectives, we can introduce structural and psychological interventions that can capitalize on the positive motivations that people often have in intergroup interaction. The result can be mutual understanding, common goals, and coordinated efforts to improve intergroup relations for enduring peace and the benefit of both groups. The psychology of diversity effectively identifies the pitfalls and roadblocks that thwart effective intergroup interactions. But it also identifies ways we can reverse or eliminate these undesirable effects.

Questions for Thinking and Knowing

1. Many years of research have shown that intergroup contact is very effective in reducing racism and other forms of intergroup bias. How can this research finding be applied to reduce intergroup bias and potential conflict?
2. This chapter presents and elaborates on a quote from Justice Sandra Day O'Connor: there are "benefits that flow from a diverse student body." What arguments for or against the ones presented in this chapter do you think are valid and why?
3. Identify and describe the in-groups and out-groups to which you belong and within which you are active. How do these groups interact? Do they frequently have contact? What would make the interactions among these groups better?
4. Review your answer to the previous question and reflect on what types of biases are operating to maintain the status quo among these in-groups and out-groups.
5. What are some common rationalizations used to avoid interaction with other groups?

Key Terms

Contact hypothesis (theory)
Desegregation
Empathy
Extended contact hypothesis
Health disparities
Imagined contact
Indirect contact
Intergroup anxiety

Intergroup (versus interpersonal)
   interaction
Meta-perceptions
Needs-based model of reconciliation
Non-verbal behavior
Secondary transfer effects
Stereotype disconfirmation

References

Allport, G. W. (1954). *The nature of prejudice*. Cambridge, MA: Addison-Wesley.

Babbit, L. G., & Sommers, S. R. (2011). Framing matters: Contextual influences on interracial interaction outcomes. *Personality and Social Psychology Bulletin, 37*, 1233–1244.

Batson, C. D., Polycarpou, M. P., Harmon-Jones, E., Imhoff, H. J., Mitchener, E. C., Bednar, L. L., . . . Highberger, L. (1997). Empathy and attitudes: Can feeling for a member of a stigmatized group improve feelings toward the group? *Journal of Personality and Social Psychology, 72*, 105–118.

Bergsieker, H. B., Shelton, J. N., & Richeson, J. A. (2010). To be liked versus respected: Divergent goals in interracial interaction. *Journal of Personality and Social Psychology, 99*, 248–264.

Blanton, H., Jaccard, J., Klick, J., Mellers, B., Mitchell, G., & Tetlock, P. E. (2009). Strong claims and weak evidence: Reassessing the predictive validity of the IAT. *Journal of Applied Psychology, 94*, 567–582.

Brown, R., & Hewstone, M. (2005). An integrative theory of intergroup contact. In M. P. Zanna (Ed.), *Advances in experimental social psychology* (Vol. 37, pp. 255–343). San Diego, CA: Academic Press.

Cameron, L., & Rutland, A. (2006). Extended contact through story reading in school: Reducing children's prejudice towards the disabled. *Journal of Social Issues, 62*, 469–488.

Cooper, L. A., Roter, D. L., Carson, K. A., Beach, M. C., Sabin, J. A., Greenwald, A. G., & Inui, T. S. (2012). The associations of clinicians' implicit attitudes about race with medical visit communication and patient ratings of interpersonal care. *American Journal of Public Health, 102*, 979–987.

Crisp, R. J., & Turner, R. N. (2009). Can imagined interactions produce positive perceptions? *American Psychologist, 64*, 231–240.

Crocker, J., Voelkl, K., Testa, M., & Major, B. (1991). Social stigma: The affective consequences of attributional ambiguity. *Journal of Personality and Social Psychology, 60*, 218–228.

Dovidio, J. F., Eller, A., & Hewstone, M. (2011). Improving intergroup relations through direct, extended, and other forms of indirect contact. *Group Processes and Intergroup Relations, 13*, 147–160.

Dovidio, J. F., & Gaertner, S. L. (2004). Aversive racism. In M. P. Zanna (Ed.), *Advances in experimental social psychology* (Vol. 36, pp. 1–51). San Diego, CA: Academic Press.

Dovidio, J. F., Kawakami, K., & Gaertner, S. L. (2002). Implicit and explicit prejudice and interracial interaction. *Journal of Personality and Social Psychology, 82,* 62–68.

Dovidio, J. F., West, T. V., Pearson, A. R., Gaertner, S. L., & Kawakami, K. (2007, October). *Racial prejudice and interracial interaction*. Paper presented at the annual meeting of the Society for Experimental Social Psychology, Chicago, IL.

Eibach, R. P., & Ehrlinger, J. (2006). "Keep your eyes on the prize": Reference points and racial differences in assessing progress toward equality. *Personality and Social Psychology Bulletin, 32*, 66–77.

Foddy, M., Platow, M. J., & Yamagishi, H. (2009). Group-based trust in strangers: The role of stereotypes and expectations. *Psychological Science, 20*, 419–422.

Frey, F. E., & Tropp, L. R. (2006). Being seen as individuals versus group members: Extending research on metaperceptions to intergroup contexts. *Personality and Social Psychology Review, 10*, 265–280.

Gallup Minority Rights and Relations Survey (2007, June 4–24). A downturn in black perceptions of racial harmony. Retrieved August 30, 2008, from http://www.gallup.com/poll/28072/Downturn-Black-Perceptions-Racial-Harmony.aspx

Greenwald, A. G., Poehlman, T. A., Uhlmann, E. L., & Banaji, M. R. (2009). Understanding and using the Implicit Association Test: III. Meta-analysis of predictive validity. *Journal of Personality and Social Psychology, 97*, 17–41.

Hugenberg, K., & Bodenhausen, G. V. (2003). Facing prejudice: Implicit prejudice and the perception of facial threat. *Psychological Science, 14*, 640–643.

Hugenberg, K., & Bodenhausen, G. V. (2004). Ambiguity in social categorization: The role of prejudice and facial affect in race categorization. *Psychological Science, 15*, 342–345.

Husnu, S., & Crisp, R. J. (2010). Imagined intergroup contact: A new technique for encouraging greater inter-ethnic contact in Cyprus. *Peace and Conflict: Journal of Peace Psychology, 16*, 97–108.

Johnson, J. D., & Lecci, L. (2003). Assessing anti-White attitudes and predicting perceived racism: The Johnson–Lecci Scale. *Personality and Social Psychology Bulletin, 29,* 299–312.

Judd, C. M., Park, B., Yzerbyt, V., Gordijn, E. H., & Muller, D. (2005). Attributions of intergroup bias and outgroup homogeneity to ingroup and outgroup others. *European Journal of Social Psychology, 35,* 677–704.

Kunda, Z., Davies, P. G., Adams, B. D., & Spencer, S. J. (2002). The dynamic time course of stereotype activation: Activation, dissipation, and resurrection. *Journal of Personality and Social Psychology, 83,* 283–299.

McConnell, A. R., & Leibold, J. M. (2001). Relations among the Implicit Association Test, discriminatory behavior, and explicit measures of racial attitudes. *Journal of Experimental Social Psychology, 37,* 435–442.

Mendes, W. B., & Koslov, K. (2012). Brittle smiles: Positive biases toward stigmatized and outgroup targets. *Journal of Experimental Psychology: General* (online first publication, August 13, 2012). doi: 10.1037/a0029663.

Miller, D. T., & Prentice, D. A. (1999). Some consequences of a belief in group essence: The category divide hypothesis. In D. A. Prentice & D. T. Miller (Eds.), *Cultural divides: Understanding and overcoming group conflict* (pp. 213–238). New York: Russell Sage Foundation.

Moskowitz, G. B., Stone, J., & Childs, A. (2012). Implicit stereotyping and medical decisions: Unconscious stereotype activation in practitioners' thoughts about African Americans. *American Journal of Public Health, 102,* 996–1001.

National Center for Health Statistics. (2011). *Healthy People 2010.* Hyattsville, MD: U.S. Government Printing Office.

Operario, D., & Fiske, S. T. (2001). Ethnic identity moderates perceptions of prejudice: Judgments of personal versus group discrimination and subtle versus blatant bias. *Personality and Social Psychology Bulletin, 27,* 550–561.

Paluck, E. L. (2009). Reducing intergroup prejudice and conflict using the media: A field experiment in Rwanda. *Journal of Personality and Social Psychology, 96,* 574–587.

Paolini, S., Hewstone, M., Cairns, E., & Voci, A. (2004). Effects of direct and indirect cross-group friendships on judgments of Catholics and Protestants in Northern Ireland: The mediating role of an anxiety-reduction mechanism. *Personality and Social Psychology Bulletin, 30,* 770–786.

Pearson, A. R., West, T. V., Dovidio, J. F., Powers, S. R., Buck, R., & Henning, R. (2008). The fragility of intergroup relations. *Psychological Science, 19,* 1272–1279.

Penner, L. A., Albrecht, T. L., Orom, H., Coleman, D. K., & Underwood, W. (2010). Health and heath care disparities. In J. F. Dovidio, M. Hewstone, P. Glick, & V. M. Esses (Eds.), *The SAGE handbook of prejudice, stereotyping and discrimination* (pp. 472–489). Thousand Oaks, CA: Sage.

Penner, L. A., Dovidio, J. F., West, T. V., Gaertner, S. L., Albrecht, T. L., Dailey, R. K., & Markova, T. (2010). Aversive racism and medical interactions with Black patients: A field study. *Journal of Experimental Social Psychology, 46,* 436–440.

Pettigrew, T. F. (1998). Intergroup Contact Theory. *Annual Review of Psychology, 49,* 65–85.

Pettigrew, T. F., & Tropp, L. R. (2006). A meta-analytic test of intergroup contact theory. *Journal of Personality and Social Psychology, 90,* 751–783.

Pettigrew, T. F., & Tropp, L. R. (2008). How does contact reduce prejudice? A meta-analytic test of three mediators. *European Journal of Social Psychology, 38,* 922–934.

Pettigrew, T. F., & Tropp, L. R. (2011). *When groups meet: The dynamics of intergroup contact.* New York: Psychology Press.

Plant, E. A., Butz, D. A., & Tartakovsky, M. (2008). Interethnic interactions: Expectancies, emotions, and behavioral intentions. *Group Processes and Intergroup Relations, 11,* 555–574.

Richeson, J. A., & Shelton, J. N. (2005). Thin slices of racial bias. *Journal of Nonverbal Behavior, 29*, 75–86.

Richeson, J. A., & Shelton, J. N. (2010). Prejudice in intergroup dyadic interactions. In J. F. Dovidio, M. Hewstone, P. Glick, & V. M. Esses (Eds.), *The SAGE handbook of prejudice, stereotyping, and discrimination* (pp. 276–293). Thousand Oaks, CA: Sage.

Sabin, J. A., Nosek, B. A., Greenwald, A. G., & Rivara, F. P. (2009). Physicians' implicit and explicit attitudes about race by MD race, ethnicity, and gender. *Journal of Health Care for the Poor and Underserved, 20*, 896–913.

Sabin, J. A., Rivara, F. P., & Greenwald, A. G. (2008). Physician implicit attitudes and stereotypes about race and quality of medical care. *Medical Care, 46*, 678–685.

Salvatore, J., & Shelton, J. N. (2007). Cognitive costs to exposure to racial prejudice. *Psychological Science, 18*, 810–815.

Schofield, J. T., & Eurich-Fulcer, R. (2004). When and how school desegregation improves relations. In M. B. Brewer & M. Hewstone (Eds.), *Applied social psychology* (pp. 186–205). Malden, MA: Blackwell Publishing.

Shah, J. Y., Brazy, P. C., & Higgins, E. T. (2004). Promoting us or preventing them: Regulatory focus and manifestations of intergroup bias. *Personality and Social Psychology Bulletin, 30*, 433–446.

Shamir, J., & Shikaki, K. (2002). Self-serving perceptions of terrorism among Israelis and Palestinians. *Political Psychology, 23*, 537–557.

Shelton, J. N., & Richeson, J. A. (2005). Intergroup contact and pluralistic ignorance. *Journal of Personality and Social Psychology, 88*, 91–107.

Shnabel, N., & Nadler, A. (2008). A Needs-Based Model of Reconciliation: Satisfying the differential emotional needs of victim and perpetrator as a key to promoting reconciliation. *Journal of Personality and Social Psychology, 94*, 116–132.

Shnabel, N., Nadler, A., Ullrich, J., Dovidio, J. F., & Carmi, D. (2009). Promoting reconciliation through the satisfaction of the emotional needs of victimized and perpetrating group members: The Needs-Based Model of Reconciliation. *Personality and Social Psychology Bulletin, 35*, 1021–1030.

Shook, N. J., & Fazio, R. H. (2008a). Roommate relationships: A comparison of interracial and same-race living arrangements. *Group Processes and Intergroup Relations, 11*, 425–437.

Shook, N. J., & Fazio, R. H. (2008b). Interracial roommate relationships. *Psychological Science, 19*, 717–723.

Smedley, B. D., Stith, A. Y., & Nelson, A. R. (Eds.). (2003). *Unequal treatment: Confronting racial and ethnic disparities in health care.* Washington, DC: National Academies Press.

Stathi, S., & Crisp, R. J. (2008). Imagining intergroup contact promotes projection to outgroups. *Journal of Experimental Social Psychology, 44*, 943–947.

Stephan, W. G., & Stephan, C. W. (2000). An integrated threat theory of prejudice. In S. Oskamp (Ed.), *Reducing prejudice and discrimination* (pp. 23–46). Hillsdale, NJ: Erlbaum.

Sue, D. W. (2010). *Microaggressions in everyday life: Race, gender, and sexual orientation.* Hoboken, NJ: John Wiley & Sons.

Tausch, N., & Hewstone, M. (2010). Intergroup contact. In J. F. Dovidio, M. Hewstone, P. Glick, & V. M. Esses (Eds.), *The SAGE handbook of prejudice, stereotyping, and discrimination* (pp. 544–560). Thousand Oaks, CA: Sage.

Trawalter, S., Richeson, J. A., & Shelton, J. N. (2009). Predicting behavior during interracial interactions: A stress and coping approach. *Personality and Social Psychology Review, 13*, 243–268. doi: 10.1177/1088868309345850.

Tropp, L. R., & Pettigrew, T. F. (2005). Relationship between intergroup contact and prejudice among minority and majority status groups. *Psychological Science, 16*, 951–957.

Turner, R. N., Crisp, R. J., & Lambert, E. (2007). Imagining intergroup contact can improve intergroup attitudes. *Group Processes and Intergroup Relations, 10,* 427–441.

Turner, R. N., Hewstone, M., Voci, A., Paolini, S., & Christ, O. (2008). Reducing prejudice via direct and extended cross-group friendship. In W. Stroebe & M. Hewstone (Eds.), *European review of social psychology* (Vol. 18, pp. 212–255). Hove, UK: Psychology Press.

Tynes, B. M., Giang, M. T., & Thompson, G. N. (2008). Ethnic identity, intergroup contact, and outgroup orientation among diverse groups of adolescents on the internet. *CyberPsychology & Behavior, 11,* 459–465.

USA Today/Gallup. (2008, June 5–July 6). Majority of Americans say racism against blacks widespread. Retrieved August 30, 2008, from http://www.gallup.com/poll/109258/Majority-Americans-Say-Racism-Against-Blacks-Widespread.aspx

Van Laar, C., Levin, S., Sinclair, S., & Sidanius, J. (2005). The effect of university roommate contact on ethnic attitudes and behavior. *Journal of Experimental Social Psychology, 41,* 329–345.

Vorauer, J. D. (2006). An information search model of evaluative concerns in intergroup interaction. *Psychological Review, 113,* 862–886.

West, T. V., Pearson, A. R., Dovidio, J. F., Shelton, J. N., & Trail, T. (2009). Superordinate identity and intergroup roommate friendship development. *Journal of Experimental Social Psychology, 45,* 1266–1272.

West, T. V., Shelton, J. N., & Trail, T. E. (2009). Relational anxiety in interracial interactions. *Psychological Science, 20,* 289–292.

Wright, S. C., Aron, A., McLaughlin-Volpe, T., & Ropp, S. A. (1997). The extended contact effect: Knowledge of cross-group friendships and prejudice. *Journal of Personality and Social Psychology, 73,* 73–90.

Part Three

Culture, Power, and Institutions

Chapter 10

Cultural Diversity
Preferences, Meaning, and Difference

Introduction	265
What Is Culture?	268
How Do Cultures Differ?	272
Cultural Diversity	283
Summary	293

[A] globally diverse workforce is a vital, competitive asset, providing a wide array of perspectives, ideas, talents, experiences and skills . . . diversity is and must be recognized as a bottom line force.

Committee on Economic Development

I would hope that a wise Latina woman with the richness of her experiences would more often than not reach a better conclusion than a white male who hasn't lived that life.

Sonia Sotomayor
Associate Justice, United States Supreme Court

Introduction

People are different, and those differences challenge ideas about equality, fairness, merit, and value. Malcolm Gladwell asks: "Why is the fact that each of us comes from a culture with its own distinctive mix of strengths and weaknesses, tendencies and predispositions, so difficult to acknowledge?" (Gladwell, 2008). Good question.

The Psychology of Diversity: Beyond Prejudice and Racism, First Edition. James M. Jones,
John F. Dovidio, and Deborah L. Vietze.
© 2014 Blackwell Publishing Ltd. Published 2014 by Blackwell Publishing Ltd.

As we noted in Chapter 2, the psychology of diversity is based on perceptions of and responses to human differences. There are myriad ways in which we differ, one person from another, one group from another and one culture from another. This chapter focuses on cultural differences: ways in which our backgrounds, perspectives, traditions, predispositions, vary as a function of where and how we grew up, how we behave, what we value and prefer, what we perceive and believe. For the purposes of this chapter, **cultural diversity** refers to contexts in which people from different cultural backgrounds interact with each other. In these contexts, cultural differences between and among people are reflected in the structure of influence and authority, goals and objectives, needs and desires, opportunities and outcomes.

Noticing differences is normal. How a person responds to differences is variable. *Being* different from others and *perceiving* others as different from you are associated with different responses to diversity. These variable relationships among being different and perceiving and responding to differences are the primary focus of the psychology of diversity.

Diversity is significant at multiple societal levels: individuals react to differences including their own as well as others; institutions formulate policies and programs based in part on the diversity of people in them; and society formulates laws, policies, and legal mandates that encourage or inhibit diversity in the United States.

Following are three examples that highlight aspects and implications of the psychology of diversity. They illustrate the anxieties engendered by being different, personal and institutional resistance to diversity, and ways in which culture can influence behavior.

A Latina co-worker recounted growing up in Colorado in the 1980s. One of her most vivid and painful recollections was how embarrassed she felt during her elementary school years when she brought tortilla and bean sandwiches to school, while other children munched on their white bread PB&J or ham and cheese sandwiches. This may seem trivial today, but her anguish over being different illustrates the powerful forces diversity dynamics activate.

Differences sometimes generate anxiety about being excluded or treated badly. Other times, though, differences can produce strong and violent hostility, or subtle forms of bias. Among the many anti-Black acts of violence in the 1950s were the murder and mutilation of 14-year-old Emmitt Till in Mississippi, the bombing of the home of Martin Luther King, and the admission and then suspension of Autherine Lucy, a Black student admitted to the all-white University of Alabama.

The *Brown v. Board of Education of Topeka* Supreme Court decision of 1954 declared racial segregation in public schools illegal. The response to this decree was strong and violent resistance. Bullet holes in the main administration building at the University of Mississippi still symbolize resistance to racial desegregation. In 1957, Arkansas Governor Orville Faubus defied a federal court order to integrate public schools by calling up the National Guard to prevent nine Black students from entering Little Rock High School. President Eisenhower called up the 101st Airborne Division of the U.S. Army to escort those children to school. Figure 10.1 shows 15-year-old Elizabeth Eckford braving the fierce animosity and hatred directed at her for wanting to attend the public high school.

Figure 10.1.   Elizabeth Eckford Withstands Taunts and Insults to Attend a White-only Central High School in Little Rock, Arkansas, September 4, 1957. © Bettmann/CORBIS.

Sometimes cultural variables influence social behavior in ways that affect task performance. On August 5, 1997, Korean Airlines flight 801 crashed into Nimitz Hill on Guam, killing 228 of the 254 people on board. According to the story told by Malcolm Gladwell in his bestselling book *Outliers* (2008), the plane was in good working order, the pilot was experienced, and he had flown into the Guam airport many times. What went wrong?

The weather was horrible and the pilot had to land the plane using a VOR procedure. VOR (VHF Omnidirectional Range navigation system) sends signals from a beacon that allows pilots to calculate altitude as they approach the airport. Using this system in severe weather requires tremendous coordination among all pilots in the cockpit (captain, first officer, and flight engineer). This coordination was absent in that fatal cockpit. Why? The following account describes how culture contributed to the disastrous cockpit dynamics.

The first officer makes a suggestion in the form of a statement: "Captain, the weather radar has helped us a lot." The pilot replies, "Yes it has," failing to get the meaning (we'd better use radar because we can't see anything). The first officer cannot see the runway even though the VOR signal tells them that the plane is 500 feet off the ground. He advises making a missed approach (elevating and flying around for another attempt). He reports with more distress that the runway is still not in sight. The plane crashes less than a second later.

If the first officer or flight engineer had communicated to the captain more directly, more specifically, and more urgently, the pilot might have taken evasive action in time to avoid the crash. Power distance (Hofstede, 2001), the degree to which members of a culture respect or accept a hierarchy of authority and power, may have undermined communication in the cockpit (see Chapter 11 for further discussion of power distance). In high power-distance cultures, people in power command the respect and unquestioned subordination of those with less power. Because he accepted the obligations of a power-distance relationship, the first officer could not adequately convey the danger the plane faced. In this instance, cultural characteristics cost hundreds of lives.

As a result of this tragedy, Korean Airlines vigorously addressed the issue of power distance among pilots. Specifically, pilots were provided an alternative identity that, in the context of the cockpit, allowed them to function outside their cultural legacy. They were required to speak English in the cockpit and were formally freed from the deference that a power-distance hierarchy imposed. Today it is one of the safest airlines in the world.

A challenge posed by diversity is to find commonalities among people with different cultural perspectives, expectations, and traditions. Acknowledging differences is a start, and valuing diversity is important, but neither alone is sufficient to produce an effectively diverse institution or society. Learning about, understanding, and managing differences is the real challenge.

The first section of this chapter defines culture and explores why it is important to understand its role in the psychology of diversity. In the next section, we explore how cultures differ. The recurring theme is that the numerous cultural differences among us make managing the resulting diversity a great challenge in our interpersonal, intergroup, institutional, and societal worlds. Finally, we turn to the enormous problem of defining cultural diversity within a given context, and explore how various approaches offer the best chances to achieve a fair, equitable, and just society. Finally, we summarize some of the challenges and opportunities presented by the expansion of cultural diversity in our society and suggest some constructive responses that make cultural diversity an asset and compelling interest in the United States.

What Is Culture?

Culture is the medium we live in. It includes the form and content of communication, the values we espouse, the beliefs we hold, the rituals we practice, the symbols we honor, and the language we speak and how we speak it. Culture is the avenue through which we grow and learn. It is a primary influence on how we think, what we value, what we feel, and how we behave. Culture is a set of tools, real and symbolic, that allows us to share rituals, practices, and customs. This is true whether you conform to prevailing cultural mores, ignore them, or rebel against them.

Hofstede (1980) proposes that culture represents how the human mind is programmed to distinguish the members of different human groups and their collectively held values. Culture emphasizes the collective—the relatedness of people within a culture, and the means by which they come to share basic human psychological attributes, tendencies, and values.

It is also very important to know that culture is subjective (Triandis, Vassiliou, & Nassiakou, 1968). **Subjective culture** refers to the influence of cultural standards and practices on what is considered right and wrong, good and bad, acceptable and unacceptable; and which human categories are important, how they are perceived and valued, and the course of interactions within culturally diverse contexts. For example, Triandis et al. (1968) found that Greeks view competition as a life and death proposition when it involves those who are different (out-groups) but with family and friends (in-groups) competition is a sign of loyalty and love. Greeks value intimacy and positive affect more than Americans and this shows in the fact that they see more intimacy in a variety of behaviors than Americans do including complaining, competing, arguing, working for, thanking, and so forth. The *meaning* of behaviors is not the same across cultural groups.

Cultural diversity can lead to miscommunication and conflict when people from different cultures interact. And because many of these boundaries are subjective (matters of taste, preference, habit, and experience), it is challenging to consider this source of diversity in institutional settings. The psychology of diversity probes the bases of intercultural communication and interaction, and ways in which cultural differences create barriers to as well as opportunities for better relationships and outcomes.

Culture also teaches us early on about what group distinctions matter in society and how different social groups are valued. A child can learn to regard some groups as inferior or superior without formal learning. Culture also influences how people respond to discrimination. For instance, Black women are more likely to directly confront someone who directs a racist comment toward them than are Asian women. Asian women, by contrast, do not say anything directly but after being insulted they withhold rewards from the other person to the same degree that Black women do (Lee, Soto, Swim, & Bernstein, 2012).

The meaning of symbols depends upon cultural perspectives. The case of American Indian team mascots is a good example. Are these mascots symbols of strength and bravery, or are they demeaning to Native Americans? Jack Kent Cooke, the late former owner of the Washington Redskins football team, responded to the controversy about Indian mascots by claiming that to him, the Indian is a symbol of courage and bravery, what he wanted his football team to represent. In a poll of 768 self-identified American Indians conducted by the Annenberg Public Policy Center (2004), 91% said they were not offended by the Redskin's team mascot. However, in a 1981 poll of readers of the magazine *Indian Country Today*, 81% of respondents felt American Indian mascots and names were offensive to Indian people (cited in Fryberg & Watts, 2010, p. 472). What are we to make of this?

It depends on the cultural context. Fryberg and colleagues (Fryberg, Markus, Oyserman, & Stone, 2008; Fryberg & Watts, 2010) primed American Indian and White high-school students with either an image of Chief Wahoo (mascot of the Cleveland Indians Major League baseball team), a picture of Pocahontas for a Disney movie, or a list of negative stereotypes about Indians, or nothing at all (control). They then assessed respondents' self-esteem and feelings of community worth (Figure 10.2).

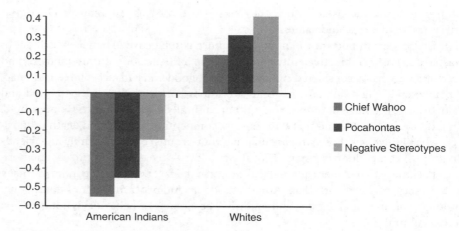

Figure 10.2.   Changes in Self-esteem Among American Indian High-School Students When Exposed to Indian Mascots, Cartoons, and Negative Stereotypes. From "Of Warrior Chiefs and Indian Princesses: The Psychological Consequences of American Indian Mascots," by S. A. Fryberg, H. R. Markus, D. Oyserman, & J. M. Stone, 2008, *Basic and Applied Social Psychology, 30,* pp. 208–218 (adapted from Figure 1).

Indian students who viewed the Indian portrayals had lower self-esteem, relative to those who did not, whereas self-esteem of White students who saw the Indian portrayals where higher than the control condition. The results suggest that the meaning and consequences of symbols depends on the cultural context. What the Indian symbols meant for Jack Kent Cooke may not be what they meant for Indian people.

Culture is also the social reality that you learn from the moment you are born: Culture determined whether your mother swaddled you, breastfed you, and picked you up when you cried. The process of learning one's own culture, called **cultural transmission** or **enculturation**, involves acquiring the knowledge, skills, attitudes, and values that enable a person to become a functioning member of a society. A human baby is capable of learning any cultural formulation in the world.

People learn their culture through interaction with it (secondary learning), as well as from explicit teaching, socialization, and formal learning. You learned the culture into which you were born from significant people in your environment and through general socialization processes. Through their associations individuals learn about social hierarchy, the differences among people, and what they mean. Through formal as well as secondary learning, children acquire knowledge of social structures and normative relationships and expectations.

When Do Race Preferences Begin?

An important aspect of culture is your family. As early as 3 months of age, babies prefer looking at faces that are the same race as they are (Kelly et al., 2005). These researchers showed White infants a series of photographs of male and female adult faces from White, African, Middle Eastern, and Asian racial backgrounds (Figure 10.3).

Figure 10.3. Experimental Sample of a Male White, Middle Eastern, African, and Asian face. From "Three-month-olds, But Not Newborns, Prefer Own-race Faces," by D. J. Kelly, P. C. Quinn, A. M. Slater, K. Lee, A. Gibson, M. Smith, L. Ge, & O. Pascalis, 2005, *Developmental Science, 8,* pp. 31–36 (Figure 1).

Using a specialized camera, the researchers recorded the infants' eye fixations (or time spent looking at the faces). Newborns showed no visual preference for the White faces, but the 3-month-old babies looked significantly longer at the White faces (59%) than at faces of other races (41%), while showing no preference when the two faces were both White.

Similar results were found in a follow-up study conducted with 3-, 6-, and 9-month-old Asian infants, who preferred Asian faces over White, Middle Eastern, and African faces (Kelly et al., 2009). This tendency to spend less time looking at faces from other races may be an early manifestation of the own-race bias (introduced in Chapter 7), which refers to the inability to differentiate faces of individuals from other races as well as you do those of your own race. But this effect was more pronounced at 9 months than at 6 months and was not found at all at 3 months.

Why Do Early Preferences Matter?

What might these early differential preference and recognition abilities mean? The **perceptual narrowing** hypothesis (Kelly et al., 2009) suggests that human perceptual systems are shaped by experience to be optimally sensitive to stimuli most commonly encountered in their cultural environment. The more experience an infant has with same-race persons, the more likely he or she is to pay attention to these persons. And this tendency grows stronger with age.

The tendency to ignore the race of adult faces ends by age 3 months! Thus, the belief that we should and can ignore race is based on an inaccurate idea about how human perception and cognition work. As early as a few months after birth, we see the beginnings of what may eventually become in-group favoritism. Research with college students corroborates these findings.

How does race matter in children's lives? A study of peer relations among 240 elementary school White and Black boys and girls in grades 1–3 and 5–6 investigated whether children befriend or avoid classmates based on race (Aboud, Mendelson, & Purdy, 2003). In general, cross-race friendships declined with grade level. In-group preferences were setting in. Moreover, among fifth-graders, cross-race friendships were much more fragile (more likely to end) than same-race friendships. Although cross-race friendships did not differ from same-race friendships in such things as loyalty and emotional security, they were lower in intimacy. Children with more positive racial attitudes had more cross-race companions and more positive perceptions of their friends. Children with more negative racial attitudes were strongly inclined to exclude their other-race classmates as friends.

As we saw in Chapter 5, the human tendency to categorize is very strong, and this tendency almost always distances people from those who are different, and draws them closer to those who are similar. In-group favoritism, more than out-group rejection, may well be the biggest challenge to achieving functional diversity in a variety of contexts. Expanding the comfort zone beyond same-race companions and friends (or other similarities such as culture, ethnicity, religion, nationality) is an important challenge and the obstacles begin at 3 months of age.

How Do Cultures Differ?

In this section we selectively explore some of these ways in which cultures are similar and different, and the implications of these differences for the psychology of diversity.

What We Value

All cultures have core **values**—desirable trans-situational goals, varying in importance—that serve as guiding principles in people's lives (Schwartz & Sagie, 2000, p. 467). There are certain values that are found in different configurations in all cultures. Schwartz (1992; see also Schwartz & Sagie, 2000) found 10 universal value types across a wide array of cultural groups (Table 10.1).

While these values are found across cultures throughout the world, cultures vary in how central individual values are in their society. Moreover, at times cultural values sometimes clash. Power values (status and dominance) may clash with benevolence values (care for the welfare of others). Universalism values (tolerance and welfare for all people) may clash with values of tradition (commitment to and acceptance of customs and ideas traditional to the culture). These cultural differences in values may occur within a single culture. Thus cultural diversity is challenged by the possibility that different cultural groups may embrace different and at times conflicting values.

The fact that values clash is not surprising. But consider what happens when people from different cultures, with different and conflicting values, interact. Most values are not inherently good or bad, merely different. But when one group is motivated by a value that conflicts with another group's values, it takes effort and consideration to work things out. And if one group has more power, resources, and control, that group's values will dominate.

Table 10.1.	Ten Values Expressed Across Cultures	
Type	*Definition*	*Value*
Self-direction	Independent thought and action (choosing, creating, exploring)	Creativity, freedom, independent, curious, choosing own goals
Stimulation	Excitement, novelty, and challenge in life	Daring, a varied life, an exciting life
Hedonism	Pleasure and sensuous gratification for oneself	Pleasure, enjoying life
Achievement	Personal success through demonstrating competence according to social standards	Successful, capable, ambitious, influential
Power	Social status and prestige, control or dominance over people and resources	Social power, authority, wealth
Security	Safety, harmony, and stability of society, relationships, and self	Family security, national security, social order, clean, reciprocation of favors
Conformity	Restraint of actions, inclinations, and impulses likely to upset others and violate social expectations or norms	Self-discipline, obedient, politeness, honoring parents and elders
Tradition	Respect, commitment, and acceptance of the customs and ideas that traditional culture or religion provide	Accepting one's portion in life, humility, devotion, respect for tradition, moderation
Benevolence	Preservation and enhancement of the welfare of people with whom one is in frequent personal contact	Helpfulness, honesty, forgiveness, loyal, responsibility
Universalism	Understanding, appreciation, tolerance, and protection for the welfare of all people and for nature	Broadmindedness, wisdom, social justice, equality, a world at peace, a world of beauty, unity with nature, protecting the environment

Note. Adapted from "Value Consensus and Importance: A Cross-national Study," by S. H. Schwartz & G. Sagie, 2000, *Journal of Cross-Cultural Psychology, 31*, pp. 465–497 (Table 1).

Cultural difference can also operate subtly to shape different outcomes for members of different groups. American universities are often competitive places that stress individual achievement and competition. However, those are not everyone's values. In fact, first-generation college students whose parents did not attend college and who have working-class backgrounds generally value interdependence more than individual achievement. This mismatch of values creates a disadvantage for first-generation college students. Stephens, Fryberg, Markus, and Johnson (2012) found that first-generation college students underperform academically in these environments. Moreover, first-generation college students with a greater mismatch between their personal values of interdependence and their university's emphasis on independence had lower grade point averages (GPAs). However, they are not academically inferior. When they receive messages that their university values interdependence more than independence, first-generation college students perform as well as, and even a bit better than, students whose parents attended college.

Cultural differences in what values are most important are intimately linked to psychological differences. As a result, cultural diversity is associated with psychological diversity. Interaction between two people from different cultural groups can be quite challenging when their cultural differences are also interwoven with divergent psychological tendencies. We cannot cover all the ways that cultures differ, but we discuss several that relate to diversity. In the following sections we discuss psychological differences related to power distance, psychological time, individualism and collectivism, enemyship, and religion.

How We See Power

Let's return to the Korean pilot example presented at the beginning of this chapter. Power distance was implicated in the failure of communication that might have avoided the disastrous plane crash. **Power distance** reflects the relative degree of power between a dominant and subordinate person in a social system (an office, a classroom, a sports team, an airplane cockpit). A boss and an employee are not equals—the boss naturally has more power. The cultural expression of power distance reflects the accepted degree of hierarchical separation between people and roles, as well as the permeability of the boundaries within the hierarchy. In low power-distance relationships, the power of interacting parties is relatively equal. When power distance is high, the power differences are quite large. The first officer was subordinate to the captain, and because he accepted the captain's superior authority without question, he used extremely subtle ways to tell the captain he was wrong. His communication was so subtle that it failed, and disaster ensued.

Power distance is typically measured from the subordinate's point of view, the first officer in our example (Hofstede, 2001). A higher **power distance index** (**PDI**) is indicated by the degree to which a subordinate (a) is afraid to disagree with a superior, (b) perceives that the superior makes decisions in an autocratic or paternalistic way, and (c) prefers that the superior makes decisions in an authoritative or paternalistic way. Hofstede found that PDI scores were lower for people with more education and higher occupational stature (managers, professionals compared with unskilled, clerical, skilled workers), and higher for people from developing countries (South and Central America, Arab countries, West Africa).

Power differentials between people in strategic situations can have disastrous results. Bringing people together in diverse settings without addressing their perceptions and preferences for power relationships can undermine the goals of individuals and organizations. A given PDI may become a normative value in a culture or organizational setting. The more a person or culture accepts a large degree of power distance, the less concerned they are with equality and fairness across status lines. Conversely, the less power distance a person or culture prefers, the more they demand fairness, justice, and a role in decision-making. Much of the research on power distance addresses these concerns.

Procedural justice   Decision-making procedures are considered just when people believe they are fair and tend to accept their consequences whether the outcome is favorable or not. Lee, Pillutla, and Law (2000) studied a sample of 625 Chinese-speaking employees of a university in Hong Kong. The relationship between procedural justice and trust in the supervisor, the organization, and the perceived fairness of the decisions were both greater for employees with low power-distance orientations.

Voice in decision-making   Giving people a **voice** in decision-making allows them the opportunity to participate in and have influence on decisions that affect them. Further, voice enhances their perceptions that the resulting decisions are fair as well as their satisfaction with their job and the organization. For example, research has shown that in low power-distance cultures (the United States and Germany), having less voice in decision-making results in lower commitment to the organization (Brockner et al., 2001). However, in high power-distance cultures (People's Republic of China, Mexico, and Hong Kong) the absence of voice in decision-making has little impact on people's commitment to the organization.

Closeness   One might expect that workers with high power-distance orientations would feel more distant from their supervisors. While this seems reasonable, Spencer-Oatey (1997) found it was not always the case. She had British and Chinese tutors and postgraduate students complete a questionnaire that probed their conceptions of degrees of power differential and social distance/closeness in this role relationship. Although the Chinese respondents had higher PDI scores, they judged the relationship to be closer than did British respondents.

Interethnic relations   Bochner and Hesketh (1994) had 263 workers employed in a large Australian bank complete a questionnaire measuring superior–subordinate relationships, decision-making styles, work ethic, task orientation, psychological contract, and individual versus group achievement. Employees from high-PDI countries were more cautious about disagreeing with their superiors. They were also more careful about how they expressed themselves when telling either a subordinate or a superior from a different ethnic background about a problem at work.

Power distance is both a cultural variable—cultures vary widely in PDI—and an individual difference variable—people within cultures vary in PDI. Thus as diversity increases in a given setting, constructs like power distance affect the dynamics of the setting at all levels, from leadership, to the effects of giving voice to decision-making, feeling close to one's superiors, and even willingness to share basic information with a person from another cultural group.

How We Relate to Others: Individualism–Collectivism

Another important cultural difference is individualism and **collectivism** (Hofstede, 2001). The United States is a land of pioneers, men and women who left their homelands to seek opportunities in the new world. That spirit of adventure and self-improvement was labeled **rugged individualism**. It is associated with the **Protestant work ethic** that values hard work as the basis of individual accomplishment.

Individualists focus on individual rights more than their duties to others, seek personal autonomy and self-fulfillment, and make accomplishment a central basis for their personal identity (Hofstede, 1980). Collectivists focus more on mutual obligations and expectations between themselves and groups to which they belong and tend to subordinate their interests to those of the group (see Oyserman, Coon, & Kemmelmeier, 2002). Table 10.2 classifies countries by degree of individualistic versus collectivistic orientations.

West European cultures tend to be individual-oriented, while East Asian cultures are relatively more group-oriented (see Brewer & Chen, 2007). These psychological orientations lead to differences in perceptions of one's self and of one's group members. For example, Japanese people are less likely to praise themselves for accomplishments (self-enhancement) but more likely to criticize themselves for poor performance or behavior (self-criticism) (Kitayama, Markus, Matsumoto & Norasak-

Table 10.2.   Individualistic and Collectivist Cultures

Individualist		*Collectivist*
←		→
United States	Argentina	East Africa
Australia	Japan	Portugal
United Kingdom	Iran	Yugoslavia
Canada	Jamaica	Malaysia
Netherlands	Arab region	Hong Kong
New Zealand	Brazil	Chile
Italy	Turkey	West Africa
Belgium	Uruguay	Singapore
Denmark	Greece	Thailand
France	Philippines	El Salvador
Sweden	Mexico	Taiwan
Ireland		South Korea
Norway		Peru
Switzerland		Costa Rica
Germany		Indonesia
South Africa		Pakistan
Finland		Colombia
Austria		Venezuela
Israel		Panama
Spain		Ecuador
India		Guatemala

kunkit, 1997). For North Americans it is reversed; more self-enhancement and less self-criticism.

It is important to note that these cultural differences are not an imperative for behavior. Takata (2003) found that Japanese tend to be self-critical in a competition-free situation and affective bonds with others were strong (**uchi**). But Japanese display self-enhancement as much as North Americans in competitive situations, particularly when affective bonds with others are weak (**soto**). The tendency to bestow honor and public recognition to individual accomplishments may lead to anxiety and some embarrassment for persons with a self-criticism orientation to their relationships with others.

Because the two cultural orientations have different key values and different views of the self and in-groups, individual- and group-oriented societies may have different routes to prejudice. Competition and meritocracy beliefs, which are associated with individualistic societies, are well-established predictors of prejudice (see Dovidio, Hewstone, Glick, & Esses, 2010). Competition often leads to fear that another person's or another group's gain will result in a loss of resources for one's self or for one's group. Meritocracy is based on the belief that people earn their social status based on their individual talents and efforts.

Recent research tested some of these assumptions and findings by comparing prejudice in an individual-oriented culture (the United States) and a group-oriented culture (South Korea) (Shin, Dovidio, & Napier, 2013). Respondents from 100 different countries completed the World Values Survey (http://www.worldvaluessurvey.org), in which they rated the extent to which nine different groups would be undesirable as neighbors. The researchers were able to reduce the nine groups to two clusters: social deviants (drug addicts, heavy drinkers, criminal record, and emotionally unstable), and permanent out-groups (immigrants/foreign workers, Muslims, people of a different race, people with AIDS, and homosexuals). White Americans rated social deviants more negatively, while South Koreans rated permanent out-groups more negatively.

How does culture matter here? First, South Koreans were more likely to emphasize group-oriented dispositions, characterized by beliefs that one's family's well-being is a direct indicator of one's own well-being—going along with your group is important even if you would rather not. Emphasizing group-oriented dispositions was also associated with beliefs in **biological hierarchy**: Biologically defined groups were judged to be superior (men) or inferior (Blacks) and their social status was believed to be genetically determined (superiority and inferiority begins at birth). By contrast, White American participants were more likely to emphasize individual achievements. This emphasis is associated with belief in social hierarchy: Inferiority or superiority is based on individual achievements, such as being poor or having only one parent (inferiority), or graduating from top schools or earning a high income (superiority).

If you come from a culture with an interdependent self-construal, you are likely to hold group-oriented dispositions, to believe in a biological basis of social inequality, and, ultimately, to hold attitudes toward people and groups based on their physical and cultural differences. If you come from a culture with an independent self-construal, you are likely to focus on individual achievement, to attribute social inequality to social conditions, and to judge people based on those social conditions.

What this tells us is that concepts like competition, meritocracy, inequality, even achievement, are loaded with cultural meaning. What you prefer, expect, or value in another person or group depends, in part, on your cultural orientation. And note that believing in, expecting, and valuing diversity is itself a cultural condition.

Prejudice, in general, restricts and constrains diversity. If you hold a prejudice against a group, you tend to exclude members of that group from your activities. Whether you do so because of group-oriented dispositions or a reliance on individual achievement, prejudices still result, and prejudices create and reinforce status hierarchies. Does an emphasis on diversity dissolve status hierarchies, as many might argue? These data suggest that they may not. This is another critical issue that the psychology of diversity should examine.

How We Perceive "the Other": Enemyship

A person's **worldview** is his or her concept of what the world is like. Is the world good or evil? Is there a god? Is family the most important aspect of society? Worldview guides your perception, evaluation, and the interpretation of the world around you. Different cultures have different worldviews, and different worldviews lead to different social judgments and different conceptions of reality.

In his primer *The Prince* on how to be a dominant, powerful, and unchallenged leader of an Italian nation-state, Niccolò Machiavelli advised his ruler to hold his friends close because he could trust them to look out for his interests. But, he advised, he should also keep a careful eye on his enemies so he could protect himself against their malevolent intentions. In contemporary times, this advice was offered by Michael Corleone in *The Godfather Part II*, "Keep your friends close and your enemies closer!" But does the average citizen really have "enemies"? Isn't that just political talk? Gangsta talk? Well, like so many other ideas we have discussed, having enemies, or believing you have enemies, is a function of culture, subjective culture.

Adams (2005) studied differences between the United States and West Africa in the concept of **enemyship**—"a personal relationship of hatred and malice in which one person desires another person's downfall or attempts to sabotage another person's progress" (p. 948). People's ideas about whether one may, does, or even should have enemies varies between the United States and the West African country of Ghana.

In Ghana enemies are not only believed to exist to a greater extent than in the United States, they are an important, and perhaps necessary, part of one's social world. To explore this idea, Adams asked research participants in the two countries several questions such as: Are there people who hate you personally and wish for your downfall or sabotage your progress? How would you respond if you knew someone was an enemy? How would you evaluate two hypothetical people: one who claimed he had no enemies and another who was certain he was the target of malice and sabotage from his enemies?

Ghanaians were nearly twice as likely as U.S. participants to say that they had enemies (48% vs. 26%), and almost three times as likely to say they were a target of enemies (71% vs. 26%). Furthermore, Ghanaian participants regarded the hypothetical person with no enemies as naïve and disparaged him. U.S. participants viewed the hypothetical person who claimed to have many enemies suspiciously and negatively. Furthermore, if a Ghanaian found he had enemies, he would either avoid them or seek protection from them. U.S. participants would more likely confront them or ignore them.

Black Americans are far more likely than White Americans to endorse theories about conspiracies by the U.S. government against Blacks (Crocker, Luhtanen, Broadnax, & Blaine, 1999). Further, conspiracy beliefs are positively associated with the racial self-esteem of Black students but negatively associated for White students. These effects were mediated primarily by the degree to which one blamed the systems of society for inequality and negative outcomes. Negative expectations of the motives of others are more likely for those whose worldview embraces the possibility that they are targets of enemies (see also the construct of the universal context of racism discussed in Chapter 8).

This research shows that culture can strongly influence psychological reality and behavioral responses to it. What is normal in your culture dictates how you view your social world and how you behave in that world. Cultural beliefs, which organize your everyday world, matter. Denying the validity of others' beliefs and insisting on one's own view of everyday existence as normative, natural, and correct is a major source of cultural miscommunication and conflict.

How We Understand Time: Psychological Time

There is an expression in Trinidad that "anytime is Trinidad time" (Jones & Brown, 2005). In Trinidad, time is an attitude about life. Time holds personal and cultural meaning but has no inherent value—a person cannot save time, invest time, or even waste time. This approach has been called a **tempoagnostic** view of time.

Conversely, in many cultures, time is money—it has an inherent value. McGrath (1988) coined the term **temponomic** to describe this view. In the temponomic view, time is an unseen arbiter of values, accomplishments, order, and sometimes character. Time directly affects behavior—efficiency, punctuality, discipline, productivity, and achievement are often measured against a template of time.

In the tempoagnostic view of time, a person's behavior is mostly determined by social relationships, personal intentions, preferences, and motives. Behavior is not contoured to the dictates of time, and time is not a way to measure progress and accomplishment. Rather, time is a silent bystander that observes, follows, and bends to the whim of the person's desires.

The anthropologist E. T. Hall (1983) referred to the connection people have with time as the *dance of life*. This dance intimately connects feelings, emotions, actions, and verbal and non-verbal displays. For Hall, time is at the center of culture: "Because time is a core system of all cultures, and because culture plays such a prominent role in the understanding of time as a cultural system, it is virtually impossible to separate time from culture" (p. 4). He illustrates this cultural aspect of time with the concepts of **monochronic time (M-time)** and **polychronic time (P-time)**. M-time is characterized by doing one thing at a time in a sequential pattern—following schedules, completing one task before starting another, persisting in goal-directed activities, and disregarding distractions. M-time is arbitrary, imposed, and learned through socialization. P-time is characterized by doing many things at once, casual disregard for punctuality and focus on social transactions and affective states. P-time is social and thus is based on "transactions." Hall argues that M-time and P-time are not mutually exclusive and that they often interact. M-time is business time, work time, official; P-time is often playtime, dream time, or social time. We work (M-time) and we play (P-time), and people and cultures have a capacity to do both.

The construct of **Confucian dynamism**, or orientation toward the present or future, is based on an analysis of traditional Asian values across 22 cultures (Chinese Culture Connection, 1987). Cultures that score high in Confucian dynamism value persistence, hierarchical ordering of relationships, thrift, and sense of shame. These cultures have a future orientation that corresponds with M-time. Countries that score low value personal steadiness and stability, protecting one's face, respect for tradition, and reciprocity with others. These cultures have a present or P-time orientation.

Cultures also differ in how they perceive time, and evaluate people who deviate from their concept of how time should be judged. Levine, West, and Reis (1980) showed that Brazilians were less punctual than Americans, and that this could be because of their less accurate perception of time. Not surprisingly, although Brazilians were more often late for appointments and social gatherings, they were more flexible in their definitions of "early" and "late," and expressed less regret over being late than did Americans. Americans had more negative overall impressions of a person who was frequently late and rated punctuality as a more important trait in a businessperson and friend than did Brazilians.

Cultural differences can have significant effects on interaction and on judgments people make of one another. A P-time person in an M-time setting may be seen as unmotivated, irresponsible, and maybe even unintelligent. An M-time person in a P-time setting may be seen as uptight, rigid, and lacking spontaneity. These cultural tendencies become interpersonal judgments with both positive and negative consequences.

How We Create Meaning: Religion

Religion is the human attempt to explain the mystery of existence and guide one's behavior. Every culture has organizing principles for confronting the ultimate forces of creation and being. These principles are value-laden; all religious systems favor some basic values over others. For example, some religions emphasize beliefs, while others emphasize actions. At times we do not make a distinction between **relative values**—those that are right for me—and **absolute values**—those that are right for everyone. Religions often make value judgments, and as a result people use religion to make blanket judgments: homosexuality is wrong, Africans deserve to be slaves, Jews are a threat to Christianity, Catholics are not trustworthy because of their loyalty to Rome, and Muslims are capable of worldwide terrorism. These statements are all based in part on religious beliefs, and they give rise to intergroup and intercultural conflict. Religion is often a foundation of both cultural differences and cultural conflict, as has been demonstrated so powerfully in Northern Ireland, Bosnia, the Middle East, and in the United States (see Box 10.1).

Divergent cultural realities are a major source of cultural diversity (see Chapter 8). It is a significant challenge to understand the cultural reality of people with whom

Box 10.1.   Being Muslim in America

Since the terrorist attack of September 11, 2001, animosity toward and stereotyping of American Muslims has been widespread. Whereas overt sentiment about prejudice toward racial minorities like African Americans and Latinos has waned and is generally opposed, prejudice toward Muslim Americans, regardless of their true religious, national, or personal qualities, is often considered acceptable.

Discrimination in the Workplace
Muslim workers are filing complaints of employment discrimination in record numbers (Greenhouse, 2010). In 2009, Muslim workers filed 803 claims of workplace discrimination, up 20% from 2008 and 60% from 2005.

Diversity Challenges to Individual and Collective Rights
Imane Boudlal was 26, a Morocco-born U.S. citizen. When she wore a headscarf to work at the Storytellers Cafe in observance of the religious celebration of Ramadan, her supervisors told her to remove it, work where customers couldn't see her, or go home. She was later offered an alternative non-religious Disney-supplied headscarf but wasn't given a date for completion of the garment and was told she couldn't wear her own hijab in the interim.

In a prepared statement, Disney spokesperson Suzi Brown said the company "values diversity and has a long-standing policy against discrimination of any kind," and that Disney has been "working directly" with Boudlal, who has been employed at the resort for more than 2 years. "Typically, somebody in an on-stage position like hers wouldn't wear something like that, that's not part of the costume," Ms Brown said. "We were trying to accommodate her with a backstage position that would allow her to work. We gave her a couple of different options and she chose not to take those."

Boudlal isn't the first employee to run afoul of the "Disney Look," a legendarily strict dress code that dates back to Disneyland's inception in 1955. According to David Koenig, founder of mouseplanet.com and author of four books on Disneyland, another Muslim woman filed suit against Disney World in 2004 for not being allowed to wear the hijab at work; the case was settled a year later for undisclosed terms. Describing the Disney culture, Koenig noted that "Walt [Disney] wanted people to be as friendly, clean-cut and all-American as possible, and you couldn't stand out in any way. . . . In the early days, there were few if any minorities . . . it was a Barbie and Ken mold" (quoted in Bly, 2010).

Figure 10.4 shows Ms Boudlal in her hijab. The alternative dress was deemed unacceptable to Ms Boudlal, which she felt denied her a proper expression of her religious beliefs.

A Middle-eastern American: A Troubling Duality
Porochista Khakpour was born in Iran, raised in Los Angeles, and became a U.S. citizen in November 2001, shortly after the bombings in New York.

Figure 10.4.   Imane Boudlal Speaks During a News Conference at the ACLU With Her Lawyer Mark Rosenbaum, Chief Counsel ACLU in Los Angeles on Monday, August 13, 2012. Boudlal, a Former Disneyland Employee Who Says She Was forbidden to Wear a Muslim Head Scarf at Work Plans to Sue the Walt Disney Company for Discrimination. © AP Photo/Nick Ut.

Ms Khakpour recalls singing the national anthem in a federal courtroom in Brooklyn, and feeling a sense of optimism about the future, and the thrill of introducing the hyphen that in her words "would from now on gracefully declare and demarcate my two worlds: Middle-Eastern American" (Khakpour, 2010).

Ms Khakpour is not Muslim, not religious really. She was elated by the successful presidential run of Barack Hussein Obama whose middle name matched that of many of her cousins, but daunted by the growing anti-Muslim sentiment she found around her. She reported mixed feelings brought on by women in full burqa, at times feeling discomfort at the cultural kinship. But that passed into protective rage when she saw teenagers laughing and pointing at these Muslim women. She criticized Muslims but also defended and protected them fiercely. Her dual identity left her feeling indignant, marginalized, and exhausted. And finally this duality, represented by the hyphen, became for Ms Khakpour "a dagger that coarsely divides [what] had once, not too long ago, been a symbol of the most hallowed bond."

1.   Should Disney have the right to dictate employees' appearances? Should Ms Boudlal have the right to celebrate Ramadan in a manner appropriate to her culture and religion? What if an actress wanted to wear a hijab while playing Margaret Thatcher? Wouldn't the authenticity of the onstage character be compromised? How do you think this sort of conflict should best be resolved?
2.   Do you think the double-consciousness described by DuBois (1903) applies to all diversity groups who are not considered mainstream? What are the positive and negative aspects of a double-consciousness?

you interact or for whom you set policies and practices when they are different from you. In culturally diverse contexts, cultural reality and its influences on individual beliefs, perceptions, and behavior are significant and constant challenges.

The history of the United States is different from the history of Japan, China, Russia, or Ghana. Our unique history and our traditions help define the cultural continuity that flows from the past to the present. No one alive today was alive in 1776, yet we embrace the American Revolution as if we staged it. It belongs to us, we own it. History, passed down over generations, is an organic and intimate aspect of the culture we all share. That we have different histories as a result of our racialized and gender-based experiences contributes to the conflict we face in resolving the problems of racism, ethnocentrism, and sexism today.

Histories diverge by race and gender, as well as by place of origin. Immigrants from Russia or China or the Caribbean are different from those from Africa or Cambodia or India. Simply emphasizing our similarities or oneness as citizens of one nation does not recognize this divergent pattern of experience, meaning, culture, and personality. It is to this diversity that we turn in the next section.

Cultural Diversity

There are 7,263,411,177 people in the world and counting (you can count along at http://www.ibiblio.org/lunarbin/worldpop). In the 20 years or so since many of you were born, the world population increased by nearly 2 billion people, or 33%.

The U.S. population is also growing rapidly, from 254.9 milllion in 1992 to 314.7 million in 2012 (23% increase). With increased population comes increased human diversity. Table 10.3 shows dramatic increases in racial and ethnic diversity since 2000.

Table 10.3. United States Population by Race/Ethnicity, Sex, and Age, 2010

	Population	*Percent change from 2000*
Total population	308,745,538	9.7%
White	231,040,398	6.5%
Hispanic/Latino	50,477,594	43.0%
Black/African American	42,020,743	15.4%
Asian American/Pacific Island	17,320,856	45.6%
American Indian/Alaskan Native	5,220,579	26.7%
Sex		
Male	151,781,326	9.9%
Female	156,964,212	9.5%
Age		
Under 18	74,181,467	2.6%
18–44	112,806,642	0.6%
45–64	81,489,445	31.5%
Over 65	40,267,984	15.1%

Note. Hispanic/Latino numbers can be distributed across the race categories. Source U.S. Census, 2010. Retrieved from http://www.census.gov/prod/cen2010/briefs/c2010br-02.pdf

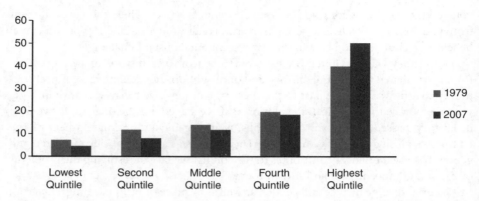

Figure 10.5.   Percent Total U.S. Worker Income Earned by Lowest to Highest Income Groups, 1979–2007. Source: Congressional Budget Office (2011). Retrieved from http://www.cbo.gov/sites/default/files/cbofiles/attachments/10-25-HouseholdIncome.pdf

Table 10.4.   Change in Household Wealth by Socioeconomic Status, 1962 to 2009

	Income status			
Year	Top 1%	Top 20%	Middle 20%	Lowest 20%
1962	$6,000,000	$800,000	$52,000	($7,000)
2009	$14,000,000	$1,700,000	$65,000	($27,000)
Change	133.3%	112.5%	25.0%	−285.7%

Note. Source Congressional Budget Office (2011).

Latinos and Asian Americans have increased by 43% and 46% respectively over the first decade of the twenty-first century, while Whites have increased by only 6.5%. Black gains have been modest at 15.4%, but combined ethnic/racial groups are on pace to become, collectively, a majority of the U.S. population by 2042. Diversity in age, income, and wealth also characterize the U.S. population. In 1979, U.S. workers whose income was in the bottom 20% earned 7.5% of all U.S. income, while those in the top 20% earned 42%, an income gap of 34.5%. In 2007, the gap had grown to 48% (Congressional Budget Office, 2011; see Figure 10.5) Refining it further, growth in income among the top 1% of household incomes was 58%, while among all others it was 6.4% (Congressional Budget Office, 2011). Disparities in wealth have increased even more dramatically in the last several years. Household wealth increased by 133% from 1962 to 2009 among the 1% highest income households. The corresponding change for the lowest 20% of income households was a 285% *decrease* (Table 10.4).

However different their circumstances, all people want to have positive, successful experiences and achieve personal goals. If people have different goals, or divergent perceptions of success, and these differences are importantly influenced by their cultural background, how can these divergences be accommodated in a given context or environment?

In the United States, race, ethnicity, gender, and immigrant status have been the principal social categories contributing to diversity dynamics. More recently, sexual orientation, age, and physical disability status have entered the diversity discourse. Add geographical region, socioeconomic status, and religion and the complexity of diversity grows. How can a person or institution possibly adopt an approach to so much diversity that attempts to treat persons from different backgrounds the same? It is not possible nor, we would argue, is it desirable. People are truly different in ways that matter. We next turn to the perspectives on diversity that influence the way people, institutional leaders, judges, and policy-makers think and act.

Now We See It, Now We Don't: Perspectives on Cultural Diversity

People take different perspectives on the value of diversity, the best way to achieve it, and the benefits to different groups. Three perspectives are **colorblind** (group differences should be ignored and people should be treated as individuals); **multicultural** (preserving different cultures or cultural identities within an organization or society is desirable); and **identity safety** (systematically identify the identity contingencies that undermine well-being and actively alter their adverse effects). Each of these approaches to diversity has strengths and weaknesses. We will discuss each in turn.

Colorblind   Arguments for a colorblind approach to race is often traced to Martin Luther King's "I have a dream" speech in 1963. On that hot August day, Dr King intoned

> I have a dream that my four little children will one day live in a nation where they will not be judged by the color of their skin but by the content of their character. (http:// www.americanrhetoric.com/speeches/mlkihaveadream.htm)

Former Secretary of Education William Bennett picked up on Dr King's dream when he framed the colorblind view of race in a 1985 speech in Atlanta, Georgia, on Martin Luther King's birthday:

> People of good will disagree about the means [but] I don't think anybody disagrees about the ends . . . I think the best way to achieve the ends of a colorblind society is to proceed as if it were a colorblind society . . . *I think the best way to treat people is as if their race did not make any difference.* (Sawyer, 1986, p. A6, emphasis added)

Is viewing the world from a colorblind set of eyes really the best way to achieve a colorblind society? Is a colorblind society really what we want to achieve?

A colorblind perspective proposes that although people do vary in skin color, it is irrelevant and should not be a basis for making important decisions such as hiring for a job or admitting to a school. We should note that a colorblind philosophy is not limited to race, but applies to the use of any group characteristic in decision-making. A large amount of social psychological research suggests we do not, and for the most part cannot, ignore race (see Chapter 5 for accounts of research that supports this idea). We have seen that race is often an implicit, automatic basis of judgment and evaluation. Legal and legislative approaches to diversity based on race seek to mini-mize if not make illegal its application to decisions about access and opportunity. It is challenging to produce fair and equitable laws about race, in the context of subtle biases that perceiving race can produce.

Research shows that a colorblind perspective often leads to more prejudice (boo) but less stereotyping (yea) (Wolsko, Park, & Judd, 2006). But in high conflict situations, it may lessen out-group bias (yea again) (Apfelbaum, Norton, & Sommers, 2012; Correll, Park, & Smith, 2008). Believing that we can and do ignore race in human judgments does not necessarily produce a fairer, more equitable society, but it may promote more tolerance in certain situations.

Multicultural   Multicultural approaches explicitly emphasize and acknowledge the existence and importance of culture differences. A multicultural perspective reflects the belief that preserving different cultures or cultural identities within institutions and societies is desirable and beneficial. Group differences exist and should be acknowl-edged and appreciated. Nathan Glazer (1997) offers one interpretation of what mul-ticulturalism means:

> [Multiculturalism is] . . . a new image of a better America, without prejudice and dis-crimination, in which no cultural theme linked to any racial or ethnic group has priority, and in which American culture is seen as the product of a complex intermingling of themes from every minority ethnic and racial group. (p. 11)

A multicultural approach makes diversity a core value and explicitly advocates for inclusive and welcoming strategies for bringing diverse people together. However, some fear that the emphasis on group distinctiveness will balkanize settings and undermine mutual communication and cooperation and ultimately friendship and unity. Research shows that a multicultural perspective leads to less prejudice and more positive intergroup attitudes (yea), but more stereotyping (boo) (Richeson & Nussbaum, 2004; Wolsko, Park, Judd, & Wittenbrink, 2000).

Other research shows that multicultural experiences have a variety of positive effects such as reduction in support of stereotypes, symbolic racism, and making discriminatory hiring decisions (Tadmor, Hong, Chao, Wiruchnipawan, & Wang, 2012). These positive consequences of multicultural experience result from reducing the **need for cognitive closure** (**NFCC**)—a strong preference and need for having firm answers to questions and understanding of situations compared with confusion and uncertainty. Multicultural experiences are often associated with discrepancy between expectations and actualities in social interactions. With repeated multicultural experi-ences, understanding one's social world is constantly challenged by these discrepancies and simple closure is not possible. As a result, individuals may adjust their need for closure downward in order for their social world to make more sense to them. This positive effect of multicultural experience has been shown for White Americans and native Israelis, when they report multicultural experiences with African Americans, Ethiopians, gays or lesbians, and native Israelis.

Multicultural orientations are based on the ideology that one should not only value but respect differences. This requires a *learning orientation*, making an effort to get to know, understand, and appreciate those who are different. An ironic consequence of this approach is that when there is conflict and relationships are threatening, a multicultural perspective may increases the hostility of responses compared with either a colorblind or an anti-racist approach (Vorauer & Sasaki, 2011).

Believing that we can and should pay attention to and value group differences may produce more civility, but again may not necessarily produce a fairer, more equitable society, or in some instances more positive interpersonal relationships.

Identity safety   It is an unpleasant feeling when you discover that negative contingencies are associated with your identity (Purdie-Vaughns & Walton, 2010). Who I am influences the consequences of what I do. Stereotype threat, which we discussed in Chapter 8, results from a negative identity contingency. Identity safety consists of (a) identifying features of a given environment that give rise to negative identity contingencies; and (b) securing a feeling of social belonging in settings where negative identity contingencies exist.

One negative identity contingency, according to Purdie-Vaughns and Walton (2010), is a colorblind philosophy about workplace polices. Another is the actual representation of diversity in an organization. Purdie-Vaughns, Steele, Davies, Ditlmann, and Crosby (2008) created authentic-looking corporate brochures that were distributed at a corporate booth at a job fair. The brochures pictured either a diverse workforce or a mostly White one and either a colorblind corporate philosophy or one that espoused the value of diversity. When brochures depicted a low minority representation and a colorblind diversity philosophy (a negative identity contingency), African American professionals were unmotivated to work for the company and reported little institutional trust.

Research also shows that women experience negative identity contingencies when representation is low, and when communication emphasizes competition more than relationships. Gay men feel vulnerable when organizations require social intimacy in and out of work (Mock, Sedlovskaya, & Purdie-Vaughns, 2011).

The three approaches to diversity reviewed above each comes with its own benefits and drawbacks. Colorblind approaches reduce stereotyping tendencies, appreciate individuality, but tend to discriminate against people because of their group membership. Multicultural approaches tend to diminish prejudices, but often increase stereotyping. Further, they may increase the likelihood of hostile responses in conflict situations. Identity safety approaches do not have an inherent advantage or disadvantage, but rather point to some conditions that can lead to favorable outcomes when eliminated (negative identity contingencies) or promoted (heightened sense of belonging).

Culture Wars Promote Conflict and Contest

A **culture war** is a clash between two competing ideas about what is moral, right, and good for a society. The idea that America was engaged in a culture war was proposed by Patrick Buchanan, a candidate for the Republican nomination for President of the United States in 1992, in his speech to the Republican National Convention that year:

> My friends, this election is about . . . who we are . . . what we believe . . . [and] what we stand for as Americans. There is a religious war going on in our country for the soul of America. It is a cultural war . . . [we fight] . . . against the amoral idea that gay and lesbian couples should have the same standing in law as married men and women . . . right-to-life, and for voluntary prayer in the public schools, and against putting American women in combat. . . . And as they [18th Cavalry who restored order after the LA riots in 1992] took back the streets of LA, block by block, so we must take back our cities, and take back our culture, and take back our country. (Buchanan, 2004)

Who owns America? *We the People* of the United States, begins our Constitution. WE are the people of the United States, not THEM, not US. We is a fundamentally inclusive idea. How does diversity among us further our we-ness? The psychology of diversity addresses this issue in a variety of ways in this book. Forming a more perfect union was our Founders' goal. That union is different now than then, and diversity is a fundamental fact. Successfully meeting the challenges of diversity is at the heart of achieving that more perfect union.

Is America post-racial? For many, the election of President Barack Obama in 2008 signaled the transition to a **post-racial** era in America, where race was no longer a barrier to progress, opportunity or accomplishment. Race no longer mattered and racism was a thing of the past. However, since the implementation of affirmative action in the 1960s, "reverse discrimination" has been charged by critics of programs and policies designed to diversify U.S. institutions and society. In this so-called post-racial society, racism still exists, but for increasing numbers of people it is no longer anti-Black but anti-White. Recent research illuminates this perspective.

Norton and Sommers (2011) analyzed survey responses from 417 middle-aged Black and White adults, matched on gender, age, and education level. Respondents rated the degree of racism directed at Blacks starting in the 1950s and proceeding through the 2000s. They then rated the degree of racism directed at Whites during this same period. Figure 10.6 shows that in the 1950s, both Blacks and Whites rated anti-Black bias very high and anti-White bias very low, a realistic assessment. Ratings of anti-Black bias steadily declined over the 50-year period for both Blacks and Whites, a sign of progress. Black ratings of anti-White bias remained low and largely unchanged during the period. However, White ratings of anti-White bias showed a sharp upturn in the 1970s and by the mid-1990s, Whites perceived racism against Whites as greater than racism against Blacks. These data suggest that the election of Barack Obama did not usher in a post-racial society, but perhaps actually deepened the racial divide.

But of course it is never that simple. Recent research also suggests that Obama's election may be responsible for more favorable implicit racial attitudes among Whites (Plant et al., 2009). Plant and colleagues found dramatically decreased levels of implicit anti-Black prejudice and stereotyping following President Obama's election. Two effects explained this reduced racial bias: first, when Whites thought of a Black person, they now thought of positive exemplars (like the President) and less of negative exemplars (criminals); second, when Blacks were made salient, more positive individual qualities such as those associated with Obama as a political figure came to mind. The more each of these happened, the lower the anti-Black prejudice.

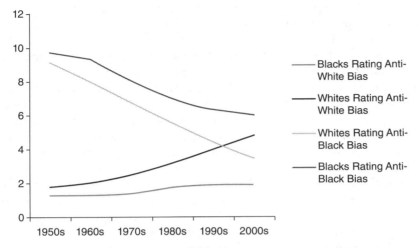

Figure 10.6.   White and Black Perceptions of Bias against Whites and Blacks (10, very much; 1, not at all). From "Whites See Racism as a Zero-sum game That They Are Now Losing," by M. I. Norton & S. R. Sommers, 2011, *Perspectives on Psychological Science, 6*, pp. 215–218 (Figure 1).

Cultures wars are based on differences among us, and a desire to make one group's characteristics dominant as a basis for policies, laws, programs, merit, and opportunity. A colorblind approach to fairness argues that cultural differences should have no bearing on decisions about individuals. But as we have shown in this chapter, cultural differences are intertwined with many differences that define what merit, fairness, values, and respect are. In the multicultural debate, people and groups are often arrayed on different sides of the culture war. Finding a middle ground is a major challenge for achieving the positive possibilities of increasing diversity.

Culture Peace Promotes Representation and Belonging

Ironically, it was the late Rodney King, whose beating by the LAPD (watch it at http://www.youtube.com/watch?v=SW1ZDIXiuS4&feature=related) triggered the Los Angeles riots in 1992, who uttered the peace proposal, "Can't we all get along?" Every group wants to be involved, respected, treated fairly, and receive their fair share. The downside of diversity is typically identified by the way it can distance people from each other by focusing more on differences than on commonalities. Another objection is that diversity is perceived by Whites as a code for concern for others, not them.

In an interesting article titled "What about me?" Whites were found to associate multiculturalism with exclusion, have difficulty pairing multiculturalism with the self, and feel excluded in institutional diversity (Plaut, Garnett, Buffardi, & Sanchez-Burks, 2011). However, when multiculturalism was defined to include Whites or European Americans, support and connection to the self was stronger, and support for diversity programs increased. The researchers conclude that "interest in diversity, or in supporting diversity efforts, does not rely simply on one's membership in a 'minority' or

'White' group but rather may rise and fall with the incorporation of multiculturalism in the self-concept" (Plaut et al., 2011, p. 346).

Recall that Whites have an automatic association of White with American (Devos & Banaji, 2005). Whites also associated Blacks more than Asians with the concept of American. This study also showed that even when you categorized White and Black as athletes representing the United States in the Olympics, White students still had a stronger implicit association of White than Black athletes with American. This study did not assess the associations of race/ethnicity with American for other racial or ethnic groups. If a similar study were conducted with Black, Asian, Hispanic, and Native American participants, what would you expect the results to look like?

All groups can find ways in which they feel included or excluded. For Justice Sandra Day O'Connor, diversity is a compelling interest because it benefits everyone. "Compelling interest" is the basis for legal support of race-based diversity programs. When diversity programs and policies are conceived in "either-or, zero-sum" terms, war may be inevitable. The diversity logic is better conceived of as a "both-and" approach. The goal is to make broad-based diversity a compelling interest for everyone.

Diversity benefits all   It has also been shown that differences between people, in terms of both race and opinions, stimulate perception of novelty and force greater **integrative complexity**, the degree of integration and differentiation of multiple perspectives and dimensions in a person's thinking pattern. Antonio et al. (2004) had White college students discuss their opinions on different issues in three-person groups. The groups were joined by a collaborator of the experimenter who was either Black or White, and expressed an opinion that was the same or different from the other group members. Results showed that following these interactions, essays written by these students showed greater integrative complexity when their groups included either a racial or an opinion minority. Integrative complexity was also greater for those White students who reported having more racially diverse friends and classmates.

Social belonging enhances achievement   Exclusion is painful. And social pain is very much like physical pain, not only psychologically but also in how our brains react to it (Eisenberger, 2012). In academic and professional settings, members of socially stigmatized groups are more uncertain of the quality of their social bonds and thus more sensitive to issues of social belonging. Walton and Cohen (2011) conducted a brief intervention designed to disconnect feelings of uncertainty about belonging from racial group status. African and European American freshmen students were provided survey information from upperclassmen that recalled how they had worried about whether they belonged in college during the difficult first year but grew confident in their belonging with time. This sentiment was widespread regardless of racial or ethnic background. For instance, one senior noted,

> Freshman year even though I met large numbers of people, I didn't have a small group of close friends . . . I was pretty homesick, and I had to remind myself that making close friends takes time. Since then . . . I have met people some of whom are now just as close as my friends in high school were. (p. 1448)

Students were then asked to write their own essays describing how their experiences matched those of the upperclassmen. These essays would be shown to future first-year students to ease their transition to college.

GPAs of African Americans in the intervention group increased from freshman to senior year, while the GPAs of controls did not change. For Whites, GPAs also increased but equally in the intervention and control groups. And 3 years later, African Americans in the intervention group, compared with the control group, reported greater belonging, fewer negative stereotypes, less self-doubt, better general health, fewer doctor's visits, and overall more subjective happiness.

Preventing Bias and Favoritism

Categorizing others into groups, and favoring those in one's own group is quite a natural human tendency (see Chapter 5). We saw earlier in this chapter how preferring others like you develops within the first year of life. Moreover, our brains are wired to make it easier for us to recognize and respond to faces that we see most frequently (e.g., the fusiform face area; see Chapter 7). Perceptual narrowing exaggerates these in-group tendencies as we get older (Kelly et al., 2009).

When participation and interaction occurs across traditional group boundaries, basic psychological processes can affect barriers to smooth communications. But it is also quite possible for out-groups and in-groups to merge, and characteristics of difference that keep us apart subside as newly created or perceived similarities that bring us together become more salient. Some examples of how this is accomplished follow.

Circles of inclusion for children   An elementary school program in northern Delaware called Green Circle was built on the idea that helping children bring people from different groups into their own circle of caring and sharing fosters appreciation of their common humanity as well as respect for their differences. In a series of sessions over 4 weeks, researchers developed a group-enhanced intervention based on the common in-group identity model (see Chapter 5; Houlette et al., 2004). Activities designed to widen their circles of inclusion to include people different from themselves (on race, sex, or body type) were presented to 830 ethnically diverse first- and second-grade children in the Green Circle program. Some children participated in the regular Green Circle program, others received the group-enhanced version of Green Circle, and a control group did not participate in Green Circle.

Children in the regular and enhanced Green Circle programs significantly increased their choice of playmates that were less similar to themselves (in terms of race and sex). Children who did not participate in Green Circle tended to prefer playmates that were similar to them. Focusing on differences and making those differences a part of one's group can effectively produce harmony in diversity.

What parents can do   What happens if parents do not actively seek to broaden these perceptual narrowing tendencies in children? In-group bias increases among both White and Black children whose parents avoid discussing cultural and skin color differences with them (Katz, 2003). As an antidote to perceptual narrowing and to broaden children's views of race and culture, Vietze and Hildebrandt (2009) propose a multicultural conscious parenting strategy. The key components of this strategy are as follows:

1. Parents should examine their own narrowing tendencies, biases, and prejudices and see how they may be communicating them to their children.
2. Parents model multicultural friendships and create a home environment that broadens their children's experiences and perspectives.

Sue (2010) suggests that parents can greatly diminish some of the natural tendencies of children to become fearful about differences and adopt negative judgments about others. He suggests that consistent, honest, and frank communication with children about race, disability, sexual orientation, or social class can be a great help. He further proposes that parents should understand and confront their own prejudices, and model tolerance and acceptance of diversity in their own lives by exposing their children to diverse friends, neighbors, and other acquaintances and actively created situations of diversity. Parents should be comfortable interacting with members of different groups and talking on topics of difference, prejudice, and stereotyping.

You don't have to be prejudiced!   Carr, Dweck, and Pauker (2012) showed that majority-group members' beliefs about prejudice can create "prejudiced" behaviors above and beyond prejudice measured either explicitly or implicitly. Individuals who believed prejudice was relatively fixed (you either were or you weren't) rather than malleable (behaviors are affected by a variety of things and could change) were less interested in interracial interactions, activities relating to race or diversity, or activities to reduce their prejudice. They were also more uncomfortable in interracial interactions. In an experimental study, students who were taught a more malleable belief became more interested in interracial interactions. Students taught a fixed belief were more anxious and unfriendly in an interaction with a Black compared to a White person. An individuals's beliefs about prejudice can affect their behavior, and if they adopt a malleable idea about it, they become more open to experiencing the possibilities of interactions with different other people (see also Neel & Shapiro, 2012).

Breaking the prejudice habit   Implicit prejudices can be thought of as overlearned habits that build up through socialization experiences (Devine, Forscher, Austin, & Cox, 2012). One strategy for reducing prejudice is to treat it like a bad habit! To do this requires learning about the situations that activate prejudices and learning how to replace these often unconscious biases with responses that reflect one's goal not to be prejudiced (see also Chapter 7). Of course, this model presupposes one has that intention. Devine et al. (2012) conducted a habit-breaking intervention aimed to educate participants about implicit bias, and train them to apply bias reduction techniques to break the prejudice habit.

Non-Black college students completed an initial race IAT and a measure of explicit racial bias. They were randomly assigned to an intervention or control group. Those in the intervention group received feedback on their degree of racial bias, saw a video about the prevalence of implicit bias in society, and were trained in five bias-reducing techniques:

- **Stereotype replacement**: replacing stereotypical responses with non-stereotypical responses.
- **Counter-stereotypic imaging**: imagining in detail counter-stereotypic other people.
- **Individuation**: obtaining specific information about group members to prevent drawing stereotypic inferences about them.
- **Perspective taking**: adopting the perspective of a person who is a member of a stereotyped group.
- **Increasing opportunities for contact**: seeking opportunities to encounter and engage in positive interactions with counter-stereotypic group members.

Participants came back at 4 and 8 weeks and were contacted again 2 years later. The results showed that the intervention group was more aware and concerned about their own prejudice behavior, and were more motivated to recognize and change it. They also scored lower, relative to the control group, on implicit prejudice at 4 weeks, 8 weeks and even 2 years later. The prejudice habit was significantly reduced by this brief experimental intervention.

Summary

People are different, and those differences challenge ideas about equality, fairness, merit, and value. This chapter has focused on cultural differences, ways in which our backgrounds, perspectives, traditions, and predispositions vary as a function of where and how we grew up. Noticing differences is normal. How a person responds to differences is variable. These variable relationships among being different and perceiving and responding to differences are the primary focus of the psychology of diversity.

A challenge of diversity is to find commonalities among people with different cultural perspectives, expectations, and traditions. Acknowledging differences is a start, and valuing diversity is important, but neither alone is sufficient to produce an effectively diverse institution or society. Learning about, understanding, and managing differences is the real challenge.

Culture represents socially transmitted ways of thinking, feeling, and reacting. Culture is subjective so differences are not simply observable—they are also often hidden and implicit. Cultural diversity reflects differences among people in their values, ideas about time, individual accomplishments and obligations to others, the acceptability of social hierarchies, the presence of enemies, and the influence of religion in everyday life.

Cultural diversity consists of many different aspects, including diversity in cognitive processes, social identity, demographic differences, and preferences in both goals and means of reaching them. Three main beliefs about cultural diversity are colorblind (race or other social characteristics should be irrelevant), multicultural (importance of maintaining group-based identities and valuing them), and identity safety (identifying sources of negative stigmas and removing them). There are benefits and drawbacks to each approach.

Conflict over culture is reflected by the "culture wars," and reducing those conflicts represented by "culture peace." Conflict arises over which groups face unfair bias, and which cultural values should be promoted by society. Evidence for ameliorating these conflicts is shown by studies that demonstrate diversity is beneficial to everyone—when people feel like they belong in a setting they do better.

Evidence for ways to prevent or reduce bias is shown by the following interventions: inclusion training in children, multicultural parenting, malleable beliefs about prejudice can reduce prejudice behaviors, and habitual implicit biases can be reduced through habit-breaking training.

Questions for Thinking and Knowing

1. U.S. culture consists of many subcultures. How would you describe your cultural background? What cultural practices are common to you now? What do you anticipate will be your future cultural perspectives? Do you see similarities with any other cultural groups with which you are familiar?

2. It is often argued that emphasizing diversity exaggerates differences among us and diverts attention from our similarities. Can you think of situations you have been in where attention to and respect for differences helped you become aware of similarities?

3. Three approaches to achieving a fair society discussed in this chapter are the colorblind, multicultural, and identity safety approaches. What are the positives and negatives of each? Which approach do you favor and why?

4. Feeling like we belong to a group or setting has been shown to have very positive effects. How does culture influence the likelihood of feeling like you belong, either positively or negatively?

5. Consider the 10 universal values described in Table 10.1. Which ones do you endorse? Which ones do you think most people in your social class endorse? Which ones do you think are most endorsed in this country? What happens when people hold different universal values?

Key Terms

Absolute values
Biological hierarchy
Collectivism
Colorblind
Confucian dynamism
Counter-stereotypic imaging
Cultural diversity
Cultural transmission (enculturation)
Culture war

Enemyship
Identity safety
Increasing opportunities for contact
Individualism
Individuation
Integrative complexity
Monochronic time (M-time)
Multicultural
Need for cognitive closure (NFCC)

Perceptual narrowing

Perspective taking

Polychronic time (P-time)

Post-racial

Power distance

Power distance index (PDI)

Protestant work ethic

Relative values

Rugged individualism

Soto

Stereotype replacement

Subjective culture

Tempoagnostic

Temponomic

Uchi

Values

Voice

Worldview

References

Aboud, F. E., Mendelson, M. J., & Purdy, K. T. (2003). Cross-race peer relations and friendship quality. *International Journal of Behavioral Development, 27,* 165–173.

Adams, G. (2005). The cultural grounding of personal relationship: Enemyship in North American and West African worlds. *Journal of Personality and Social Psychology, 88,* 948–968.

Annenberg Public Policy Center. (2004). Most Indians say name of Washington "Redskins" is acceptable while 9 percent call it offensive. Press release September 24. Retrieved from http://www.annenberg publicpolicycenter.org/Downloads/ Political_Communication/naes004_03_ redskins_09-24_pr.pdf on May 25, 2012.

Antonio, A. L., Chang, M. J., Hakuta, K., Kenny, D. A., Levin, S., & Milem, J. F. (2004). Effects of racial diversity on complex thinking in college students *Psychological Science, 15,* 507–510.

Apfelbaum, E. P., Norton, M. I., & Sommers, S. R. (2012). Racial color blindness: Emergence, practice, and implication. *Current Directions in Psychological Science, 21,* 205–209.

Bly, L. (2010) Muslim employee sues Disney for right to wear headscarf. *USA TODAY.* Retrieved on October 30, 2012 from http://travel.usatoday.com/destinations/ dispatches/post/2010/08/muslim-woman- disneyland-hotel-hijab/108827/1

Bochner, S., & Hesketh, B. (1994). Power distance, individualism/collectivism, and job-related attitudes in a culturally diverse work group. *Journal of Cross-Cultural Psychology, 25,* 233–257.

Brewer, M. B., & Chen, Y.-R. (2007). Where (who) are collectives in collectivism? Toward conceptual clarification of individualism and collectivism. *Psychological Review, 114,* 133–151.

Brockner, J., Ackerman, G., Greenberg, J., Gelfand, M. J., Francesco, A. M., Chen, Z. X., . . . Shapiro, D. (2001). Culture and procedural justice: The influence of power distance on reactions to voice. *Journal of Experimental Social Psychology, 37,* 300–315.

Buchanan, P. (2004, March 8). The aggressors in the culture wars. Retrieved on June 16, 2010 from http://www. theamericancause.org

Carr, P. B., Dweck, C. S., & Pauker, K. (2012). "Prejudiced" behavior without prejudice? Beliefs about the malleability of prejudice affect interracial interactions. *Journal of Personality and Social Psychology, 103,* 452–471.

Chinese Culture Connection. (1987). Chinese values and the search for culture-free dimensions of culture. *Journal of Cross-Cultural Psychology, 18,* 143–164.

Congressional Budget Office. (2011). *Trends in the distribution of household income between 1979 and 2007.* Retrieved on October 30, 2012 from http://www.cbo.gov/sites/ default/files/cbofiles/attachments/10-25- HouseholdIncome.pdf

Correll, J., Park, B., & Smith, J. A. (2008). Colorblind and multicultural prejudice reduction strategies in high-conflict situations. *Group Processes and Intergroup Relations, 11,* 471–491.

Crocker, J., Luhtanen, R., Broadnax, S., & Blaine, B. E. (1999). Belief in U.S. government conspiracies against Blacks among Black and White college students: Powerlessness or system blame? *Personality and Social Psychology Bulletin, 25,* 941–953.

Devine, P. G., Forscher, P. S., Austin, A. J., & Cox, W. T. L. (2012). Long-term reduction in implicit racial prejudice: A prejudice habit-breaking intervention. *Journal of Experimental Social Psychology, 48,* 1267–1278.

Devos, T., & Banaji, M. R. (2005). American = White? *Journal of Personality and Social Psychology, 88,* 447–466.

Dovidio, J. F., Hewstone, M., Glick, P., & Esses, V. M. (2010). Prejudice, stereotyping, and discrimination: Theoretical and empirical overview. In J. F. Dovidio, M. Hewstone, P. Glick, & V. M. Esses (Eds.), *The SAGE handbook of prejudice, stereotyping, and discrimination* (pp. 3–28). Thousand Oaks, CA: Sage.

DuBois, W. E. B. (1903). *The souls of Black folk.* Chicago: A. C. McClurg & Company.

Eisenberger, N. I. (2012). Broken hearts and broken bones: A neural perspective on the similarities between social and physical pain. *Current Directions in Psychological Science, 21,* 42–47.

Fryberg, S. A., Markus, H. R., Oyserman, D., & Stone, J. M. (2008). Of warrior chiefs and Indian princesses: The psychological consequences of American Indian mascots. *Basic and Applied Social Psychology, 30,* 208–218.

Fryberg, S. A., & Watts, A. (2010). We're honoring you dude: Myths, mascots, and American Indians. In H. R. Markus & P. M. L. Moya (Eds.), *Doing race: 21 Essays for the 21st century* (pp. 458–480). New York: W. W. Norton.

Gladwell, M. (2008). *Outliers: The story of success.* Boston: Little Brown.

Glazer, N. (1997). *We are all multiculturalists now.* Cambridge, MA: Harvard University Press.

Greenhouse, S. (2010, September 23). Muslims report rising discrimination at work. *The New York Times,* p. A25.

Hall, E. T. (1983). *The dance of life: The other dimension of time.* Garden City, NY: Anchor Press/Doubleday.

Hofstede, G. H. (1980). *Culture's consequences, international differences in work-related values.* Beverly Hills, CA: Sage Publications.

Hofstede, G. H. (2001) *Culture's consequences: Comparing values, behaviors, institutions and organizations across nations* (2nd ed.). Thousand Oaks, CA: Sage Publications.

Houlette, M. A., Gaertner, S. L., Johnson, K. M., Banker, B. S., Riek, B. M., & Dovidio, J. F. (2004). Developing a more inclusive social identity: An elementary school intervention. *Journal of Social Issues, 60,* 35–55.

Jones, J. M., & Brown, W. T. (2005). Any time is Trinidad time: Cultural variations in the value and function of time. In A. Strathman & J. Joireman (Eds.), *Understanding behavior in the context of time* (pp. 305–323). Hillsdale, NJ: Lawrence Erlbaum Publishers.

Katz, P. A. (2003). Racist or tolerant multiculturalists? How do they begin? *American Psychologist, 58,* 897–909.

Kelly, D. J., Liu, S., Lee, K., Quinn, P. C., Pascalis, O., Slater, A. M., & Ge, L. (2009). Development of the other-race effect during infancy: Evidence toward universality? *Journal of Experimental Child Psychology, 104,* 105–114.

Kelly, D. J., Quinn, P. C., Slater, A. M., Lee, K., Gibson, A., Smith, M., . . . Pascalis, O. (2005). Three-month-olds, but not newborns, prefer own-race faces. *Developmental Science, 8,* 31–36.

Khakpour, P. (2010, September 11). My nine years as a Middle-Eastern American. *The New York Times,* p. A23.

Kitayama, S., Markus, H. R., Matsumoto, H., & Norasakkunkit, V. (1997). Individual and collective processes in the construction of the self: Self-enhancement in the United States and self-criticism in Japan. *Journal of Personality and Social Psychology, 72,* 1245–1267.

Lee, C., Pillutla, M., & Law, K. S. (2000). Power-distance, gender, and organizational justice. *Journal of Management, 26,* 685–704.

Lee, E. A., Soto, J. A., Swim, J., & Bernstein, M. J. (2012). Bitter reproach or sweet revenge: Cultural differences in response to racism. *Personality and Social Psychology Bulletin, 38,* 920–932.

Levine, R. V., West, L. J., & Reis, H. T. (1980). Perceptions of time and punctuality in the United States and Brazil. *Journal of Personality and Social Psychology, 38,* 541–550.

McGrath, J. E. (Ed.). (1988). *The social psychology of time.* Newbury Park, CA: Sage.

Mock, S. E., Sedlovskaya, A., & Purdie-Vaughns, V. (2011). Gay and bisexual men's disclosure of sexual orientation in the workplace: Associations with retirement planning. *Journal of Applied Gerontology, 30,* 123–132.

Neel, R., & Shapiro, J. R. (2012). Is racial bias malleable? Whites' lay theories of racial bias predict divergent strategies for interracial interaction. *Journal of Personality and Social Psychology, 103,* 101–120.

Norton, M. I., & Sommers, S. R. (2011). Whites see racism as a zero-sum game that they are now losing. *Perspectives on Psychological Science, 6,* 215–218.

Oyserman, D., Coon, H. M., & Kemmelmeier, M. (2002). Rethinking individualism and collectivism: Evaluation of theoretical assumptions and meta-analyses. *Psychological Bulletin, 128,* 3–72.

Plant, E. A., Devine, P. G., Cox, W. T., Columb, C., Miller, S. L., Goplen, J., & Peruche, B. M. (2009). The Obama effect: Decreasing implicit prejudice and stereotyping. *Journal of Experimental Social Psychology, 45,* 961–964.

Plaut, V. C., Garnett, F. G., Buffardi, L. E., & Sanchez-Burks, J. (2011). "What about me?" Perceptions of exclusion and Whites' reactions to multiculturalism. *Journal of Personality and Social Psychology, 101,* 337–353.

Purdie-Vaughns, V., Steele, C. M., Davies, P. G., Ditlmann, R., & Crosby, J. R. (2008). Social identity contingencies: How diversity cues signal threat or safety for African Americans in mainstream institutions. *Journal of Personality and Social Psychology, 94,* 615–630.

Purdie-Vaughns, V., & Walton, G. M. (2010) Is multiculturalism bad for African Americans? Redefining inclusion through the lens of identity-safety. In L. R. Tropp & R. K. Mallett (Eds.), *Moving beyond prejudice reduction: Pathways to positive intergroup relations* (pp. 159–178). Washington, DC: American Psychological Association.

Richeson, J. A., & Nussbaum, R. J. (2004). The impact of multiculturalism versus color-blindness on racial bias. *Journal of Experimental Social Psychology, 40,* 417–423.

Sawyer, K. (1986, January 15). King scholars steal Bennett's lines. *Washington Post,* p. A8.

Schwartz, S. H. (1992). Universals in the content and structure of values: Theoretical advances and empirical tests in 20 countries. In M. P. Zanna (Ed.), *Advances in experimental social psychology* (Vol. 25, pp. 1–65). San Diego, CA: Academic Press.

Schwartz, S. H., & Sagie, G. (2000). Value consensus and importance: A cross-national study. *Journal of Cross-Cultural Psychology, 31,* 465–497.

Shin, H., Dovidio, J. F., & Napier, J. L. (2013). Cultural differences in targets of stigmatization between individual- and group-oriented cultures. *Basic and Applied Psychology, 35,* 98–108.

Spencer-Oatey, H. (1997). Unequal relationships in high and low power distance societies: A comparative study of tutor–student role relations in Britain and China. *Journal of Cross-Cultural Psychology, 28,* 284–302.

Stephens, N. M., Fryberg, S. A., Marcus, H. R., & Johnson, C. S. (2012). Unseen disadvantage: How American universities' focus on independence undermines the academic performance of first-generation college students. *Journal of Personality and Social Psychology, 102,* 1178–1197.

Sue, D. W. (2010). *Microaggressions in everyday life: Race, gender and sexual orientation.* Hoboken, NJ: John Wiley & Sons.

Tadmor, C. T. Hong, Y., Chao, M. M., Wiruchnipawan, F., & Wang, W. (2012). Multicultural experiences reduce intergroup bias through epistemic unfreezing. *Journal of Personality and Social Psychology, 103,* 750–772.

Takata, T. (2003). Self-enhancement and self-criticism in Japanese culture. An experimental analysis. *Journal of Cross-Cultural Psychology, 34,* 542–551.

Triandis, H. C., Vassiliou, V., & Nassiakou, M. (1968). Three cross-cultural studies of subjective culture. *Journal of Personality and Social Psychology, 8(4, Part 2),* 1–42.

Vietze, D. L., & Hildebrandt, E. J. (2009). Multiculturally conscious parenting: Promoting peace and teaching tolerance to young children. *Encounter, 22,* 33–37.

Vorauer, J. D., & Sasaki, S. J. (2011). In the worst rather than the best of times: Effects of salient intergroup ideology in threatening intergroup interactions. *Journal of Personality and Social Psychology, 101,* 307–320.

Walton, G. M., & Cohen, G. L. (2011). A brief social-belonging intervention improves academic and health outcomes of minority students. *Science, 331,* 1447–1451.

Wolsko, C., Park, B., & Judd, C. M. (2006). Considering the Tower of Babel: Correlates of assimilation and multiculturalism among ethnic minority and majority groups in the United States. *Social Justice Research, 19,* 277–306.

Wolsko, C., Park, B., Judd, C. M., & Wittenbrink, B. (2000). Framing interethnic ideology: Effects of multicultural and color-blind perspectives on judgments of groups and individuals. *Journal of Personality and Social Psychology, 78,* 635–654.

Chapter 11

Social Roles and Power in a Diverse Society

Introduction   299
Power Matters   302
Who's Got the Power? Power Dynamics and Diversity   305
Psychological Sources of Power   310
Pathways to Fairness: Reducing Bias in Power Dynamics   316
Summary   320

The relations and practices of power that influence our lives are often invisible to us. If we do not proactively look at how relations of power operate to create advantages for some and deny these advantages to others, it hinders our work. . . . Without examining the operations of privilege, we are unable to see the circumstances that create constraints on other people's lives. We are unable to appreciate their daily efforts to work and live in the context of these constraints, or to resist them.

Salome Raheim

Introduction

The study of power requires examining inequality. Sociologists and psychologists have documented inequalities among diversity groups in income, college admissions, high-school completion, employment rates and patterns, health outcomes, and health services. On average, these inequalities favor White males (Fiske, 1993). This chapter reviews how power is related to diversity and to distributive justice, a concept we introduced in Chapter 2. The chapter will also provide additional perspectives on the

The Psychology of Diversity: Beyond Prejudice and Racism, First Edition. James M. Jones,
John F. Dovidio, and Deborah L. Vietze.
© 2014 Blackwell Publishing Ltd. Published 2014 by Blackwell Publishing Ltd.

concepts of social dominance, conflict between social groups, social role identity theory, and system justification, concepts, introduced in Chapter 6, that are closely related to the social power of groups. In this chapter, we also explore how power is acquired and maintained and how it is related to social roles. Previous chapters focus on power relations between individuals and among groups. This chapter examines how societal and power dynamics are related.

Power and privilege represent complex social processes made all the more complicated in diversity contexts. **Power dynamics** is a term we use to represent how power is acquired and maintained and the complex relationships among diversity status, power, and **privilege**. As you read this chapter and discuss it, remember to keep in mind that the situations and data we describe cannot be applied to all persons and situations. Statistical averages are just that, a composite picture of a group. It is impossible to make predictions based on these averages as to how each person will behave, react, or be positioned in society. Our purpose is to present you with some perspectives to help you think critically about power and diversity so you have greater awareness of how they intersect and challenge our sense of fairness.

Social power is the ability to control assets and the access that others have to those assets (Houser & Ham, 2004). Social power often leads to *social privilege*: access to resources, opportunities, and possibilities that are not easily available to others (McIntosh, 2009; Ramos, 2010; Wise, 2005). Peggy McIntosh refers to this as the "invisible, weightless knapsack of assets—unearned assets of which one is usually oblivious" (Anderson & Middleton, 2011, p. 1). If power is concentrated in only one or two groups or where two diversity groups intersect, such as White and male, to the disadvantage of others, questions of fairness arise. Many challenges to diversity arise when one group has more social power than others.

Natasha Scott's mom is Asian, her father Black. On college applications she had to decide whether to check the "Black" or "Asian" box, or both. Natasha stated in a *New York Times* article, "I just realized that my race is something I have to think about. It pains me to say this, but putting down Black might help my admissions chances and putting down Asian might hurt it" (Saulny & Steinburg, 2011). How mixed-race students determine which ethnicity group will improve their chances for admission to college is an interesting problem. It arises because diversity has a complicated relationship to the social power of groups (Sandel, 2011). Having to choose between the two boxes, "Asian" and "Black," forced Natasha to think about her race and to wonder which box gives her a better chance to get into college. In situations like this, where there is no interpersonal contact, the social power of your group may matter. This is because the opportunity to be admitted to college is not equally distributed among ethnic groups. Asians are often well represented among college students. Asians, on average, score well on admission tests, have high grade-point averages, and many have economic advantages. Because of the social categorization processes and ethnic stereotypes, discussed in Chapters 2 and 6, Asians may be viewed more favorably by admissions teams. Blacks, especially Black men, are underrepresented among admissions and college degree groups. On average they have less economic advantage and do less well on admissions tests. Because of this disparity, some colleges may seek to correct the disparity by giving some preference to Blacks over Asians. If this is the case, Natasha might benefit from checking the "Black" box. In checking "Asian" she may be placed in a larger pool of very competitive students and thus perhaps lessen her chances of admission to a college. Alternatively if she checks "Asian," chances are she is viewed more favorably and is seen as more academically prepared.

Checking the "Black" box might help Natasha if Blacks are underrepresented and if the institution values increasing this type of diversity. Checking "Asian" might hurt her if Asians are overrepresented or do not fall into a protected class. What if Natasha had a White father and a Black mother and applied to a school where most students identified as White? What if she applied to a historically Black college? Are her chances better if she checks the box for the group with the most power, or if she checks the box for the underrepresented and thus less-powerful group? Natasha's dilemma illustrates one of the complex issues related to power and diversity. These complexities challenge our sense of fairness. Natasha's dilemma also shows how diversity intersects with the social power of groups and complicates our ability to be fair. The link between diversity and power can also result in institutional bias, which is discussed in Chapter 12. When institutional bias is widespread or becomes obvious, then questions of fairness may arouse emotions and social tensions among groups.

Fairness is a complex moral concept related to equity that emerges early in human development. The ability to be fair means that a person detects inequalities that may not be justified. This ability is very subjective and varies with cultural context and situations. Equity is possible when situations are fair. **Equity** refers to whether groups are treated in a way that does not impose economic, social, or other barriers that would prevent them reaching their full potential. Equity does not mean all persons will be treated equally but that they will be treated fairly. Not all people conform to the social norm for seeing whether equity exists in situations. We don't all see fairness in the same way in every situation (Miles, Hatfield, & Huseman, 1989). If a child who just received a cookie witnesses another child receiving three cookies, she is likely to see this as unfair, all other things being equal. She will wonder why does someone else get more? What did that child do that I did not do to earn more cookies? Many, but not all, adults react to privileges like college admissions, employment, and good housing the way children react to cookies. When we do think about fairness, it's usually in a personal way: Why didn't I get more? Why was I singled out for punishment? The feelings one might have in this example have been referred to as **relative deprivation**, which has a long history in sociology (Schaefer, 2008). Relative deprivation is the feeling you might have if you think you have been denied a benefit to which you should be entitled. When we compare our situation or circumstances to someone else's and feel deprived of fair treatment, the opinion that this is unfair usually occurs. There is research on "me-first" bias and perceptions of fairness. Researchers conducted a series of five studies using Harvard Introduction to Psychology students to explore how perceptions of fairness were related to considering other people's perspectives (Epley, Caruso, & Bazerman, 2006). These researchers hypothesized that as consideration of others' perspectives increased, judgments about what others were entitled to gain—perceptions of fairness—would increase. They set up situations where students participated in simulated discussions about how much of a scarce resource their group was entitled to harvest. They found that discussing other groups' perspectives did reduce "me-focused" assessments of fairness. The students who discussed what other groups would think is fair felt it was better for them to use a smaller amount of the scarce resources than the students who did not consider others' assessments.

We rarely think about whether systematic bias disadvantages members of a group who constantly receive fewer privileges than members of other groups. Persons in power are especially prone to not considering other viewpoints. In fact members of dominant groups work to impose their will on members of subordinated groups (Fiske, 1993; Sidanius & Pratto, 1999).

It is exceedingly difficult to understand this if you are privileged rather than oppressed. Power can operate fairly but often does not. If we observe that power leads to privileges that appear to be unearned, we tend to see this as unfair. Power often leads to privilege, but privileges granted do not always result in power. Well-qualified poor or non-legacy students, whose families cannot pay for their tuition, may be admitted to a prestigious college because of a policy to increase diversity. These students are being given the privilege of special consideration and the privilege of admission (Soares, 2007). They will also be given the privilege of financial aid so that they can attend. In this situation, it might also seem that economically disadvantaged White students should be treated the same as disadvantaged Black and Hispanic students. However, they may not be because of their perceived social power as Whites in U.S. society. However, the privileges given to well-prepared non-wealthy students does not bestow the same power as well-qualified students who come from wealthy families or those who are legacy students. Legacy and wealthy students may enter college with what some would view as unearned privileges when compared with students who do not fit this profile. Not all the wealthy or legacy students are "top-notch" scholars so a preference system is operating for them too; it is not based on ethnicity but on social status. Privileges, even if unearned or unrecognized, can place the wealthy or legacy student in a more powerful position than others. When placed in this situation some of these students cannot compete and suffer for it.

Power Matters

Today sitting in a skybox (Figure 11.1) at a sports event is a privilege of the powerful. The powerful don't sit in the "cheap seats." Sandel (2011) termed this the *skyboxifica-tion* of America. He claims that we used to sit together at games, the boss sitting next to the mail clerk; the office secretary next to the chairman of the board. The powerful, however, have always been segregated from the less powerful. The more powerful sit in an air-conditioned skybox or 10 rows above the 50-yard line, nowhere near crowds of the less powerful, from whom they are separated by glass and air conditioning or whom they look down on from the "nose-bleed" section.

In many venues, the affluent and powerful retreat into privilege, away from public schools and from other public institutions into more privileged settings. Rich and poor don't mix. This situation is very similar to racial segregation—this is a form of economic apartheid. The 99% movement, begun in a park near Wall Street, recognized and broadcast this point: the 1% of powerful and privileged persons is very different from the rest of us. The perceived unfairness of massive economic disparities has

Figure 11.1. Skyboxes Denote Special Privilege and Are Often Inaccessible to Persons With Disabilities. © Adam Haylock/iStockPhoto.

caught the public's eye, as noted by protests on Wall Street, across the United States, and around the world. The perception of conflicts between the rich and the poor were documented in a 2012 survey by the Pew Research Center which showed that perceptions of conflict between the rich and the poor had risen by 19 percentage points since 2009 (Morin, 2012). The Center surveyed 2,048 adults and reported that two thirds of this group said that there are "very strong" or "strong" conflicts between the rich and the poor.

The economic downturn hit this country hard in 2004, and has continued into 2013. Everyone saw their overall financial health erode regardless of race. However, the erosion was less for Whites (a loss of 16% of their net worth) than for Blacks who lost 53% and Hispanics who lost 66% of their net worth between 2005 and 2009 (Kochhar, Fry, & Taylor 2011). This race gap in net worth is equaled by the growing disparities in income among the highest and lowest groups. As shown in Chapter 10, between 1979 and 2007, the income of the top 1% earning group increased 275%, while the income of the lowest earning group increased a mere 20%, and the middle income group increased about 40% (see Figure 10.5). In 2010 the Census Bureau reported the gap had further increased. The median net incomes for Whites, Asians, Hispanics, and Blacks were $111,000, $70,000, $8,000, and $5,000, respectively. Economic well-being is an avenue to power and control. Disparities based on race/ethnicity, as well as social class, are well established historically and have continued to widen.

Privilege has many faces. Anderson and Middleton (2011) offer first-hand narratives of how privilege is experienced by those who have it and those who do not. Their stories talk about how it feels to have both privileged and non-privileged status. One story tells about a young White woman who grew up poor and struggles with being thought to be privileged because of skin color but feeling oppressed because of her class status. If you are heterosexual you belong to the majority. Your sexual orientation is not the butt of jokes; something you have to be conscious of to avoid bad experiences. You have less privilege to feel comfortable expressing your identity. This is a form of oppression that can have extremely negative consequences. Matthew Shepard (his story is presented at the beginning of Chapter 4) paid the ultimate price for not being in a privileged heterosexual social group because two homophobic men took his life. Arguments about the naturalness of heterosexual marriage exclude others from this privilege (Cole, Avery, Dodson, & Goodman, 2012). The able-bodied enjoy all sorts of privileges. Infrastructure is built for this group. People with disabilities have to "fit in" and often can't enjoy the same privileges as the able-bodied. While we have tried to mitigate this oppression to some degree with the Americans with Disabilities Act and other legislation, there are still places in our society where people with physical disabilities cannot go. Imagine being in a wheelchair and trying to get to the top row of a stadium where you can afford seats.

Box 11.1 presents one woman's gradual awareness of power and privileges she had that others did not have.

Box 11.1.   Becoming Aware of Power and Privilege

Stories are a good way to better understand power dynamics. Personal stories clarify how bias works and what is equitable in some cases. Stories capture nuances of situations and emotional responses. They let us see others' point of view more clearly. Sharon Anderson and Valerie Middleton present stories of privilege and bias in their book *Explorations in Diversity: Examining Privilege and Oppression in a Multicultural Society*. The first part of the book presents stories of White privilege. There are also stories of able-bodied privilege, heterosexual privilege, male privilege, and age-privilege (described as ageism). Many other stories are included, some from a global perspective, others about how we may reduce bias by becoming allies. The story that begins this book is entitled "An Awakening to Privilege, Oppression, and Discrimination: Sharon's Story." This story is compelling so we share a bit of it here.

Sharon was born into a family she describes as "White European descent and middle-class income" (p. 5). She grew up in a White community, went to an all-White school, attended a White church, and all of her family members were White. As she describes it, in her childhood she never heard her parents disparage other ethnic groups but neither did she hear anything about discrimination or privilege. Sharon was taught that hard work leads one to success regardless of color, ethnicity, gender, or culture. Her situation in early adulthood and college was very similar to her childhood upbringing. For this reason Sharon concluded, much later in life, that she was never made aware of her White privilege in her early years.

Sharon begins her story by sharing an experience an African American friend told her in her early years. Her friend explained that she had been waiting to order food at a fast food restaurant when a White man walked up behind her. She told

Sharon that the cashier looked past her, and took the man's order, as if she was invisible. The friend felt that this had happened because she is Black. Sharon told her friend that perhaps the cashier was confused and thought she was still deciding what to order.

Much later in her life Sharon thought about her friend's experience. She decided that perhaps her reasoning about the incident may have been due to her limited experience with diversity. Her thinking changed after she had more contact with groups different from her own. After completing a Masters degree, Sharon began working for programs that served youth from ethnic and cultural groups different from her own. She continued this work for many years, having authentic and long-lasting contact with people very unlike her. Gradually she began to realize that she had been very isolated from the realities of people's lives that did not have white skin. She had never thought about the obstacles and difficulties they experienced. Her worldview, that all it took was hard work to get ahead, was challenged. She realized that having white skin, speaking Standard English with no accent, and supporting Christian beliefs, had given her advantages that she did not earn through hard work. She also began to realize that she had wanted the students of color to fit into her program, for them to be more like Whites. She did not see the reality of the students' experiences. Sharon gradually experienced "An awakening to privilege, oppression and discrimination" (p. 5).

1. What other privileges do you think Sharon may have enjoyed that were not earned through hard work?
2. Do you have a story to tell about privilege or oppression? If so, find someone you trust with whom to share it. Listen to that person's story as well.

Who's Got the Power? Power Dynamics and Diversity

Power dynamics refers to differences in power across social groups representing our diversity. These dynamics potentially affect a person's life prospects. Understanding power dynamics is important in appreciating the relationship between diversity and fairness. Does the distribution of power differ among the diverse groups in our society? One challenge for diversity is determining if power differences—those that are a legacy of the past as well as those that seem "natural"—challenge our beliefs about fairness. A person with power often controls resources, such as wealth, job promotions, and college admissions, that can open or close opportunities for others (Golden, 2007; Stevens, 2009). Likewise, a person with power has decision-making power over others. For example, a supervisor in a company determines whether you get hired or promoted, whether you get prestigious assignments that may lead to raises and promotions, even when you can take your vacation. If you hold and exercise power over others you decide social policy, such as whether to segregate or integrate schools or to sell homes only to members of particular groups. Power differences among social groups are responsible for complex effects resulting in who lives where and who goes to what school, among others (Guinote & Vescio, 2010). Research using survey and interview methods has found that middle-class and wealthy people tend to emotionally and cognitively distance themselves from the poor and as such care little for how social policy decisions affect them (Lott, 2002). The power dynamics of diversity raises this question: Who has power and what does this have to do with our diversity? The more control a person or group has over their life outcomes and those of others, the more power that person or group has. The opposite is also true: the less control you have, the less power. If power dynamics are such that your diversity status is highly correlated with the degree of power you have, fairness enters the picture. Using the social groups of race, ethnicity, and gender, we next explore some of the demographics of power and their implications for fairness.

It's Just Natural: The Power of Social Roles and Social Groups

A social role reflects one's position in society, as discussed in Chapters 5 and 6. White, heterosexual, able men have historically acquired more power more often than other demographic groups for many historical reasons, as described in Chapter 3. Here's an example: Blacks have tried to buy several major sports teams but only two have succeeded in becoming majority owners compared to hundreds of White owners of franchises in the United States and Canada. Social roles that correspond to diversity group membership have created a social hierarchy where Blacks, Hispanics, women, gays and lesbians, and some other social groups have less power and social status and are afforded less privilege. Less power means you are probably less well employed, wealthy, or college educated. You are less privileged. White women have, on average, had more power and privileges than Black women. White women have group social power because they are White but less power because they are women. White men with power usually belong to several privileged demographic groups—White, male, able-bodied, and heterosexual—whereas a Black woman represents at least two disadvantaged groups—Black and women. This has been referred to as "double jeopardy," suggesting that if you belong to two less privileged groups the effects are additive or interact to create risk for success (Sidanius & Veniegas, 2000).

Social roles predict a person's expected actions and behaviors. We expect parents will be more knowledgeable, nurturing, and empathic toward children than adults who are not parents. Workers are more subservient than bosses. With each social role, you adapt your behavior to fit the expectations you and others have of that role (McLeod, 2008). The power of a social group is acquired, expressed, and maintained by the proportion of high-status social roles occupied by members of that group. These power differences constantly affect the interactions among social groups and between and among people. An example from research on intimate couples illustrates this. Christensen and Heavy (1990) studied the power dynamics of couples when one partner wants a change to avoid the other partner's unpleasant behavior. The researchers theorized that the person who demands change is in a low-power position relative to the other person. If the person with power withdraws from the exchange, so the situation can't change, the power differential remains the same and change is not possible (Eldridge, Sevier, Jones, Atkins, & Christensen, 2007). These power dynamics played out in numerous civil rights movements in the United States and around the world. When those in power do not want change, they withdraw until the less power-ful group creates a situation where change is inevitable because of possible negative consequences for those in power. Diversity power dynamics represent the complex interplay between access to power and diversity status. If you are wealthy, you control your life outcomes and those of others. Your assets and resources allow you to have many privileges. Wealth is associated with power because it often correlates with a social position that has status and decision-making authority: the CEO of a company, a university president, or the owner of a sports team. Wealth allows you to be in control, to be "first in line," to have your opinion and views count.

If you also belong to one of our diversity social groups with more power, your power as a person in some situations may be increased. For example, a person who is wealthy, White, and a man may exert greater power in a business transaction because of his position in the social hierarchy and the role expectations allowed for his diversity group than will a wealthy Hispanic woman. In a different setting, a His-panic woman may have greater authority in her role, and thus more power. Supreme Court Justice Sonia Sotomayor has much more power, based on her role, than does a White man studying law. The relationship between diversity status and power is not perfect. If you occupy a role with power, you have the power of that role no matter what your diversity status may be. The problem is that there are fewer Hispanic women than White men occupying positions of power. This means that some groups have more social group power than others. **Social group power** is the degree of power that is acquired, expressed, and maintained by a group based on the proportion of high-status social roles occupied by members of that group. Groups with a high pro-portion of persons with high-status roles have more social group power. These power differences constantly affect the interactions among social groups and between and among people. For example, the broad social group Hispanic therefore has less social group power than the White social group. As this changes we begin to meet the chal-lenges of diversity (see Chapter 13).

Who's at the Top and Why? CEOs, Lawyers, and Janitors

We expect that persons who occupy a social role will act in a certain way. A **social role** is like an actor's role in a play: it represents a set of expectations for how a person will behave and interact with others. A social role also conveys access to social status, **social dominance**, and to privilege. Social roles are organized into **social role hier-archies**. A social hierarchy is a stratification system reflecting the status and privileges given to persons who occupy particular social roles in a society. These hierarchies order the privileges and status a person receives based on the actual or perceived contributions made to the well-being of society or according to the status given to particular social roles.

Some social roles have more power and prestige than others. Sociologists consider **social status** to be the prestige associated with your position in society. It is a combi-nation of education, job status, and income, in that order. So, if you have a high prestige social role you have certain privileges that are associated with your status. It is fairly easy for a person to identify the powerful social roles in society. These are often associated with occupations. Lawyer and CEO are social roles giving you more

Table 11.1.	Occupations and Wage Estimates for Employment in the United States
Occupation	*Mean annual salary ($)*
CEOs	173,350
Lawyers	129,440
Teachers	38,940
Maintenance/repair	36,630
All occupations	44,410

Note. Source: National Bureau of Labor Statistics (2010).

status and power than a maintenance worker, for example. Table 11.1 shows that the average CEO earns over 4.4 times as much as the average teacher and 4.7 times as much as the average maintenance worker (National Bureau of Labor Statistics, 2011).

We expect lawyers and CEOs to earn more than maintenance workers, because their work requires training and experience. In a diverse society, we are challenged to determine whether it is more likely than not that persons of one diversity group, to the exclusion of others, occupy some status positions. Are CEOs more likely to be White men while maintenance workers are more likely to be Hispanic and female or Black and male? We will review some data to answer these questions in Chapter 12. Is it fair that social roles and occupations are unequally distributed in relationship to a society's diversity? Does this affect personal and societal well-being? If most CEOs are White men, what does this say about the distribution of education and opportunity in society? In other words, do all diversity groups have equal access to the opportunity to obtain high-paying work? Social hierarchies are necessary for a society to function (Kerbo, 2007; Magee & Galinsky, 2008; Parsons, 1939). Not all social hierarchies are bad. The problem is that these structures should operate fairly. We need them but we need them to operate equitably.

Multiple Me: Intersectionality and Power

Each of us has multiple identities: student, sibling, friend, and factory worker, for example. These identities shift depending on situation, according to social identity theory (see Chapter 6). Our self-concept is greatly determined by the social group with which we identify. Each person belongs to more than one of many diverse social groups, such as gender, ethnicity, cultural group, social class, age, and sexual orientation, which represent our diversity. The social groups to which you belong, for example young, female, middle income, gay, Asian American, make up the totality of your social identity. This requires you to see yourself as a collective of social groups representing differing types of expectations and different amounts of social power (Hammack, 2008; Wiley, Philogene, & Revenson, 2011). For example, you understand that, at the same time, you are a man, heterosexual, high-income, White, Irish American, and middle-aged. The power status of these social groups may determine with which group you most strongly identify. In this case probably being a man and White

Table 11.2. Implications of Three Questions on Multiple Group Identity for Each Stage of the Research Process

Research stage	Who is included in this category?	What role does inequality play?	Where are the similarities?
Generation of hypothesis	Is attuned to diversity within social categories	Studies reviewed focus on social and historical contexts of inequality	May be exploratory rather than testing to find differences
Sampling	Focuses on neglected groups	Category membership marks groups with unequal access to power and resources	Includes diverse groups connected by a common relationship to social and institutional power
Collecting data	Measures are developed from the perspectives of the group being studied	If comparative, differences that are described are based on structural inequality rather than primarily on individual-level effort	Views social categories in terms of individual and institutional practices rather than primarily as characteristics of people
Analysis	Attends to diversity within a group and may be conducted separately for each group studied	If comparative, differences are included in the context of structural inequality rather than just focused on individual differences	Interest is not limited to the differences among groups
Interpreting data	No group's findings are offered as representing a universal or normative portrait of human experience	Differences are interpreted as relevant to a group's position in the social structure	Sensitivity to nuanced variations that exist across groups are a focus even when some similarities are identified

Note. Adapted from "Intersectionality and Research in Psychology," by E. R. Cole, 2009, *American Psychologist, 64*, pp. 170–180, doi: 10.1037/a0014564.

are most important because these groups command more social power. **Intersectionality** is the term social scientists use to describe the way these different social groups come together in us to form our identity.

Cole (2009) offers three questions and a research model that are useful for understanding the influence of intersectionality on identity. The top row of Table 11.2 lists Cole's three questions and the column to the far left lists suggestions for how they should be approached in a research paradigm to better understand intersectionality. At each stage of the research process, from generating hypotheses to interpreting results, Cole offers suggestions for how to consider the interplay between inequality and social group membership in research on social groups.

Cole emphasizes the changes in thinking that need to take place if we are to understand social categorization's implications for fairness in a diverse society. You could also use the questions in the table to think about the social groups that you view as relevant to your social identity. For example, Cole's first question implies that we should look for explanations about how those who are classified in different social groups actually differ from one another. Our tendency is to view a group as a monolithic whole. The second question suggests that it is important to factor in the social inequalities in power and privilege across social groups when considering variation across groups. The third question reminds us that there are often more similarities across our groups of diversity than there are differences. These perspectives may be useful for correcting our imperfect and sometimes misguided perceptions of groups that we perceive to be different.

A Social Hierarchy: What's Diversity Got To Do With It?

Social roles are arranged in a hierarchical structure. Suppose you belong to, and identify with, several of the diversity groups in which you fit. One of these social groups may have more power, prestige, or privileges than another social group, all of which apply to one person. For example, a Black woman who has a same-sex sexual orientation belongs to three diversity groups that have traditionally held less power, prestige, and access to privileges. A woman who is White and heterosexual belongs to only one that is relatively disadvantaged.

Gender, social role, and power   Gender is a diversity group with two traditional dimensions, male and female. In early childhood, boys and girls develop a gender identity and learn that men and women's social roles differ and are hierarchically structured (Eagly, 1987; Eckes & Trautner, 2000). These roles put women at a distinct power disadvantage (Eagly, 1987). Research in the 1970s showed that children as young as 3 years of age were able to point out socially relevant gender distinctions and, more recently, gender inconsistencies (Kuhn, Nash, & Brucken, 1978; Riley, 2011). In our culture, children have traditionally come to understand that men play football, fight wars, and fix computers while women cook, clean, and take care of babies. This has changed somewhat in the last 20 years as more women occupy high-status positions in professions like medicine, the military, and the law. For example, some children grow up and never see a male doctor, as many pediatricians are women. Despite these changes, children still learn that men play a more dominant or powerful role in society than do women (Eagly, Wood, & Diekman, 2000; Eckes & Trautner, 2000).

This dominance is reflected in how women are compensated for their work. In 2010, women working full-time and year-round had a median annual income of $36,931 compared with men's median income of $47,715 (U.S. Census Bureau, 2011). Women earned 77% of what men earned. Is this fair? Men with children get a 2% salary advantage when compared with their fellow workers who do not have children, while for women just the opposite is true: Women with children earn less than women without children. Chapter 12 discusses how this status and income gap may lead to institutional bias based on gender.

Psychological Sources of Power

A leader is a person who manages others. Leaders typically use three types of power to exercise control: (a) legitimate authority that comes from the leader's position;

(b) coercive power, based on threats or actual punishment; and (c) reward power, which is the positive opposite of coercive power (Houser & Ham, 2004). These sources of power are based on the **theory of social influence** (French & Raven, 1959), which identifies these three sources of power above but also includes referent and expert influence. **Expert influence** is based on the subordinates' beliefs that the supervisor has some know-how and understanding that is not yet available to them and thus allows the influence of the supervisor to prevail. **Referent influence** is based on the subordinate's interest in identifying with the supervisor. The subordinate's admiration of the supervisor and desire to be like the supervisor give the supervisor influence.

Power can be legitimate or not. Parents occupy positions of power over children through the legitimacy of the parent role. For a similar reason, teachers have positions of power over students and judges and police have legal power over other citizens. There are also sources of power that may be viewed as unfair or illegitimate. Power maintained through coercion, fear, or intimidation is illegitimate. Dictators use threats, punishment, or promise of rewards to gain and maintain power.

In early spring 2011, citizens in several Arab nations rose up against years of illegitimate and coercive power of dictators, held by use of torture, imprisonment, and murder. The uprisings, known as the **Arab Spring**, shifted the illegitimate power of autocratic dictators to the legitimate power of the people (Bynen, Moore, Salloukh, & Zah, 2013; Ehteshami & Wright, 2007; Khalidi, 2011). Figure 11.2 shows protestors engaged in this emotionally uplifting exercise in power.

Stahelski and colleagues studied how supervisors used social power in employment settings (Stahelski, Frost, & Patch, 1989). They asked 127 supervisors, from three different work environments, to describe the **social influence** they used based on French and Raven's (1959) theory of social influence (Raven, 2008). In general social influence is a concept that assumes persons are influenced by the behavior of others. In the Stahelski study the researchers reported that supervisors with the most subordinates

Figure 11.2. Lack of Economic and Social Power Can Lead to Political Protest as Disenfranchised People Seek Political Power. Egyptian Women Gather in Cairo's Tahrir Square, the Epicenter of the Popular Revolt That Drove Veteran Strongman Hosni Mubarak From Power on February 12, 2011. © Mohammed Abed/AFP/Getty Images.

tended to increase their use of coercive power. The social group membership of the supervisor and the subordinate, and the position of the group to which each belong in the social hierarchy, strongly influenced the degree to which an employee shared power with a supervisor. For example, a woman supervised by a man may feel that he is entitled to more power than a woman supervisor would be.

In some men, feeling powerful has been shown to have an automatic connection to sexual aggression and harassment (Bargh, Raymond, Pryor, & Strack, 1995). These researchers found that men who were exposed to a condition that made them feel powerful rated a woman confederate as more attractive than did men who were not primed to feel powerful (Bargh et al., 1995). You might infer from these results that for some men, having power presents challenges for them and for women they may supervise if it triggers responses that may be automatic or unconscious. This study suggests that men may need to become more conscious of the influence that having power has on their responses to women so as to not perpetuate the status of women reduced to appearances and not competence. Understanding power dynamics and their relationship to diverse social groups may help us better understand challenges to fairness in a society.

Skin Color, Social Role, and Power

Skin color or skin tone is a characteristic that distinguishes people between and within social groups. In some situations, having white or lighter skin means that you are likely to be in an advantageous or powerful position—given a privilege you have not earned, just because your skin-color group is more powerful (McIntosh, 2009; Wise, 2008). For example, White adults, compared with Black and Hispanic adults, find it easier to rent an apartment and obtain a mortgage. Evidence for this is based on federal Department of Housing and Urban Development (HUD) field studies (Department of Housing and Urban Development, 2005). In these audit studies, people from different ethnic groups are sent to rent an apartment or obtain a mortgage from the same realtors or lenders. HUD then compares the information or treatment each receives to determine whether discrimination took place. White applicants tend to receive more information, more time, and more favorable rent or mortgage rates. In 2005, the HUD study reported:

> While generally down since 1989, housing discrimination still exists at unacceptable levels. The greatest share of discrimination for Hispanic and African American home seekers can still be attributed to being told units are unavailable when they are available to non-Hispanic whites and being shown and told about less units than a comparable non-minority. Although discrimination is down on most measures for African American and Hispanic homebuyers, there are worrisome upward trends of discrimination in the areas of geographic steering for African Americans and, relative to non-Hispanic whites, the amount of help agents provide to Hispanics with obtaining financing. On the rental side, Hispanics are more likely in 2000 than in 1989 to be quoted a higher rent than their white counterpart for the same unit. (p. 102)

These results could be more about race and ethnicity than simple skin tone. But other studies have shown that lighter-skin women from the same race/ethnic group have social advantages over women with darker skin in other ways. Hunter (2002) used two national databases to examine the effect of skin-color stratification on life outcomes. Her analysis was based on the premise that skin color hierarchies of beauty, established by Europeans during colonial and slavery periods, persist today and create a social role position of power and advantage for lighter-skinned women. Her analysis found that within both African American and Mexican American ethnic groups, women with lighter skin had higher educational attainment. Lighter skin also directly predicted earnings for African American women and indirectly predicted earnings for Mexican American women. When skin color is one basis of power, some people may acquire power not only through hard work but also because they belong to the lighter skin group, the one with greater advantage in the social hierarchy.

Although there is a great deal of evidence that some groups experience social role power based on skin color, it is difficult for people, especially members of the socially dominant group, to accept how this applies to them. This phenomenon has been described as **white-skin privilege** (McIntosh, 2009; Wise, 2005, 2008). People who enjoy white-skin privilege don't have to think about being discriminated against in everyday life.

McIntosh's list of white-skin privileges includes: (a) knowing that when culture or civilization is referred to it's usually about your heritage; (b) being able to be around people that look like you whenever you choose; (c) being pretty sure that if you ask to speak to the person in charge that person will look like you; and (d) if your day is going badly, being sure it is not because of a situation with racial overtones. While there is little empirical research on measuring white-skin privilege and its effects on social interactions, the concept has been useful for opening up dialogues about fairness and diversity. White students' levels of awareness of white-skin privilege range from none to limited. None of the students interviewed in a qualitative study of white-skin privilege were willing to engage in further understanding and acceptance of it or to be involved in proactively dismantling the privilege in the interest of fairness to others (Ancis & Szymanski, 2001).

Privilege that comes from belonging to a powerful social group is often invisible to those that have it (Kimmel, 2011; Wise, 2009). White-skin privilege is to some like water is to fish—you just don't notice it because it seems natural to you. If you have special privileges that you have had for a lifetime, this is the natural order of things for you. Skin color is not the only diversity characteristic that can denote privilege. Although historically White men have been the most privileged group, more recently privilege extends to gender, sexuality, and religious choice or values.

When we talk about privilege feelings of alienation often arise. It's like talking about racism. No one wants to be thought of as racist and it's difficult to admit being privileged because it implies that someone else is not. In a society that values equality we don't like to focus much on who's at the top and who is at the bottom. In this chapter we bring into focus the relationship between diversity and privilege. Unawareness of this relationship may interfere with our ability to manage diversity. Good intergroup relationships between diversity groups are much more likely to occur when diversity status is not closely correlated with membership in a privileged or more powerful group.

Social Dominance: My Group Versus Your Group

Social dominance theory suggests that a group's status in the social hierarchy is determined by the group's access to power (see Chapter 4). There is abundant evidence that social dominance is a characteristic of both human and animal groups (Guinote & Vescio, 2010; Henry & Pratto, 2010; Houser & Ham, 2004; Pratto, Sidanius, Stallworth, & Malle, 1994; Sidanius & Pratto, 1999).

Three hierarchical social structures characterize social dominance in societies around the world now and over many millennia (Sidanius & Pratto, 1999):

- Age: elders and adults have more power than younger persons.
- Gender: men have more social and political power than women.
- Arbitrary organizing system: bases of hierarchy vary from one society to another, but typically are based on race, ethnicity, religion, and **socioeconomic status (SES)**.

Arbitrary organizing systems determine which group characteristics should form the basis of power, status and control. For example, in the United States over the last 400 years White people have been dominant over members of other groups. In Inuit society, an indigenous group in northwest Canada, elders and healers hold the most highly regarded social positions. These systems are fixed and don't change much over time. Groups with higher social status have more wealth and more resources and opportunities to control events for themselves and for others.

The social dominance hierarchy of social roles is well known among members of a society. For example, you don't have a problem determining who earns a higher income: a tenured high-ranking Black male university professor or an entry-level White female secretary. You can also easily determine which person has more prestige and privilege, thus demonstrating the social dominance of the group to which each belongs. Professors belong to the higher status group and the secretary belongs to the lower status group. However, one's social role and social group membership are usually intertwined. Sometimes the social role dominates (professor trumps secretary in earning and status); sometimes the social group dominates (male professor trumps female professor in earning power and status). We are all familiar with the social dominance hierarchy. Our expectations about the power relationships among social roles in the hierarchy of age and gender are well understood, and for the most part most dominance hierarchies that exist in our culture are familiar to us as well.

Social dominance orientation (SDO), or a person's tendency to enhance or weaken the social hierarchy, plays an important part in social dominance theory. People who believe in social hierarchy are the ones who carry it out, hold it as a value, and judge others from that perspective. Their behavior reflects this point of view so they enhance hierarchy (HE) or attenuate it (HA) as a function of their SDO. So a real problem of power is that people who control it are often higher in SDO (HEs). Research has shown, for example, that police officers were more HE and public defenders more HA; Whites were more HE and Blacks and Hispanics more HA (Sidanius, Liu, Shaw, & Pratto, 1994).

Research has shown that even among preschoolers, gender role expectations about social dominance play a role in determining who is liked. Sebanc and colleagues studied dominance, acceptance, and assertive social skills in 100 preschoolers (Sebanc, Pierce, Cheatham, & Gunnar, 2009). They wanted to find out if these characteristics differed for boys and girls, and how these characteristics were related. Same-gender pairs were videotaped interacting in a competitive movie-viewer task. A child's dominance rank was based on the amount of time he or she spent looking into the movie viewer. A child was considered highly dominant if he or she used the movie viewer more than the other children. Using a method that allowed the children to show who was more liked, they found that both gender and dominance rank determined who was liked. Boys who were high in dominance and girls who were low in dominance were most liked.

This research shows that people have different expectations and preferences about power based on gender. Social role expectations largely determine power and how others interact with us. Social roles also allow us to identify with larger social groups made up of persons who occupy the same or similar social roles. Social identity attaches meaning to membership in social groups and occupying social roles (Hammack, 2008; Stets & Burke, 2000; Tajfel, 1979). If you are a schoolteacher, you have more power in most situations than your students, because of the authority of your teacher role. However, the power you actually have may also be influenced by your diversity status. Social hierarchies exist in most institutions and they affect the status of members of social groups in them.

Social Class as a Source of Power

Social class is a complex characteristic comprising two features: (a) material resources or assets and (b) social status in the social hierarchy. Social status is how a person is perceived compared to the social prestige and resources of others (Hodge, Siegel, & Rossi, 1964; Hodge & Treiman, 1968; Jackman & Jackman, 1983; Kraus, Piff, & Keltner 2009; Warner, Meeker, & Eels, 1949). Social class may be measured both objectively and subjectively (Kraus et al., 2009). A person's financial resources, access to educational opportunities, and participation in social institutions represent an objective measure of SES (as described by Oakes & Rossi, 2003). However, objective measures of social class seem outdated to some researchers. Instead, they measure **subjective SES** with an instrument developed by a consortium of researchers that asks participants to mark an "X" on a 10-rung ladder, where each rung represents a position of social prestige, relative to other persons in society (Goodman et al., 2001). Subjective SES refers to the perception that a person has of their position on the social ladder or hierarchy rather than the actual status held based on occupation and financial resources. Both the objective and subjective characteristics of social class provide a snapshot of the power each person thinks he or she exercises in our social hierarchy.

Kraus et al. (2009) studied the relationship between social class and a person's sense of control and how he or she explained success. A national sample of college students who were subjectively lower class reported a lower sense of personal control and tended to explain events—wealth, social outcomes, emotions—as being caused by external forces. In contrast, students with subjectively higher social class felt that they exercised more personal control over life events. In addition, subjective SES was a better predictor of social explanations, feeling in control, than was **objective SES**. One interpretation of these results is that SES is influential in determining whether people *feel* powerful.

The social hierarchy of objective SES was presented in Table 11.1. Research by the Pew Hispanic Center (2012) provides information on the distribution of various occupations by race classifications used in the U.S. Census. Data provided by the Pew Center on its website show the over- or under-representation, relative to their percentage of the population, of Whites, Blacks, Hispanics, and Asians in selected occupations. The data are for U.S. citizens over 16 who worked in the last 5 years. Whites are overrepresented in management and business, Asians in science and engineering, Hispanics in building and grounds and cleaning services, and Blacks in healthcare support. Diverse social groups occupy different strata in the world of work, strata that are associated with more or less status and power. As a result, diversity issues are intimately linked to inequality. Distributive justice, you will recall, is related to the lack of inequality in the delivery of goods in a society. These patterns of stratification associated with status, earnings, and power continue to challenge the idea that the United States distributes justice evenly.

Pathways to Fairness: Reducing Bias in Power Dynamics

Our purpose in this chapter is to bring awareness to the operation of power dynamics in institutions and society. We are still becoming aware of how diversity affects power dynamics. For example, it is not always obvious that a moderate level of organizational diversity does not prevent bias in power dynamics. An organization can be diverse in its workforce, but not diverse in access to power. An example of this was uncovered when one of the authors helped design an analysis to determine if White men controlled most of the decision-making in an academic department that appeared to be fairly diverse. The department had an equal proportion of male and female faculty members; 27% of the staff was African American, 12% Latino, and 10% of Asian descent. On close examination, using criteria other than demographic diversity, it was found that all decision-making in the department, and thus all power, resided among a small group of older White male faculty members. Department chairs determined the teaching schedules of other faculty members and decided whether and which privileges and opportunities faculty members received. In the last 25 years, only White males had been department chairs. During that time, only one woman had been promoted to the rank of professor while at least eight men had been promoted to this rank. Female faculty members were part-time adjuncts or teaching assistants, while most male faculty members were full-time. Faculty search committees largely comprised White men; women search committee members were largely untenured and thus less influential in decision-making. White men were more likely to have release time from teaching and other perks than were women and minority faculty members, which gave them more free time to work on activities that led to promotion, such as research.

This is an interesting case study but not enough information is provided here to draw conclusions about the department's promotion and hiring process. Some additional information is needed to make a convincing case for bias in this situation: What is the length of service of men versus women? How many tenure-track faculty have been added in that time? What was the racial/gender composition of those hires? How many of those were women? How many females/minorities were eligible for promotion to full professor? Can you think of any other critical questions necessary for evaluating this case? Awareness of the possibility of bias in power dynamics stimulates examination and self-study.

Disparities in decision-making and status show how power can be unequally distributed, even when a situation seems diversity-rich. When organizations interested in increasing diversity examine the interaction between diversity and power dynamics, they are more likely to successfully achieve both diversity and fairness.

You Have More Power—What Should I Expect?

An interesting series of studies showed that people with less power, compared to those with more power, had a more negative reaction to a situation where a person with power expressed a negative attitude toward them (Barreto, Ellemers, & Fiske, 2010). These researchers created conditions where people felt that someone else had power over them and compared this with situations where everyone felt a sense of equal power. In one study these researchers asked adults to imagine they had just been hired and were then introduced to a fictitious supervisor, "Peter van Dijk," who was described as a "direct supervisor who will evaluate you and on whom you are dependent for your job"—the power condition. In the no-power condition, they met a colleague with no authority.

These researchers found that adults did not expect persons in power to be prejudiced. In a second and third study, they explored how targets of prejudice reacted when a person in power expressed prejudice. All three studies controlled for the personal sense of power experienced by adults so that it was clear that differences found at the end of each study were a result of the power condition and not interpersonal feelings of power. The researchers explain that in each study the power structures were the same because power structures can affect emotional reactions.

The second study found that adults had a more negative emotional reaction to prejudice from a powerful person than from one without power over them. In a follow-up study some of the participants reacted to prejudice that came from an adult from the same group as the target adult. In the other condition the prejudiced adult was from the target adult's out-group. The researchers found that adults reacted more negatively to a powerful prejudiced person from their in-group, presumably because they may expect to have interactions with this person in the future. A final study focused on sexism as the source of prejudice. The important finding from this study was that when adults expected to have a future interaction with a powerful prejudiced person, they had a more negative emotional reaction than when they did not expect to have any more interaction with the prejudiced person.

These results can help us understand why members of less powerful groups, such as ethnic minorities or women, in an organizational hierarchy may be more negatively affected by a prejudiced teacher, supervisor, or other leader. These results may also help us to understand how power conditions can affect adults when the possibility of prejudice is present. If a powerful person is perceived to be prejudiced against you because of your social group, this prejudice will have a greater negative impact than if it comes from a less powerful source. So we can conclude that power differentials matter more when prejudice is involved. If the prejudice of a powerful supervisor or teacher has such a negative impact on a subordinate adult or youth, we might speculate that this would also affect motivation and productivity, which may further perpetuate a cycle of stereotyping and lack of power in the social hierarchy. The researchers suggest that this indicates that special care should be taken not to place persons with high levels of prejudice in positions of power, particularly in school and work settings. The effects are even more insidious when persons are implicitly prejudiced rather than explicitly or overtly so. The prejudiced person is not only unaware of the prejudice but will vehemently deny it. This makes it all the harder to eradicate these power/prejudice dynamics.

Maybe the Status Quo Has Too Much Power

Positive changes begin with identifying the status quo and understand what keeps it in place. The **status quo** is based on power (see Chapter 6). An established social order or system of power hierarchies is maintained by an overwhelming set of psychological biases (Kay, Banfield, & Lauren, 2010). **System justification theory (SJT)** suggests there is a strong psychological motivation in favor of order that causes people to defend and maintain power hierarchies and social order. SJT describes how those in charge perpetuate myths about the legitimacy of the social order and the importance of maintaining it, as well as how those who are disadvantaged by those myths continue to cling to them. Many years of research support this theory:

> People are motivated not only to hold favorable attitudes toward themselves and toward members of their own groups . . . but also to hold favorable attitudes toward the existing social system and the status quo. What is especially significant is that system justification motives are sometimes capable of overriding ego and group justification motives associated with the protection of individual and collective interests and esteem. The consequence of this psychological bias is that persons in power *and those without power* are both psychologically resistant to change. (Jost & Banaji, 1994, p. 912, italics added)

In recent U.S. politics, an example of this theory may be seen in the fact that poor as well as middle-class people often support cutting taxes for the wealthy, even when this means a reduction in vital social services for the very needy such as healthcare and food stamps. This is a curious phenomenon. The book *What's the Matter With Kansas* details how the state of Kansas, once a bastion of social liberalism, became one of conservatism (Frank, 2004). Poor and middle-class people in Kansas seem to justify the values of conservatives who want things to stay the same rather than change to serve their interests. While Kansas is not representative of the entire United States, and we cannot ignore the Occupy Wall Street protest that began in New York City in 2011–2012 and spread across the nation, it is clear that sometimes social groups vote against their best interests in order to maintain the status quo. There may be situations in which you might have wished to maintain the status quo, rather than change, even when it would benefit you. Are there other explanations for this?

People are compelled to believe that the world is fair according to SJT and thus believe that the status quo is the way things should be maintained (Jost & Banaji, 2004; Kay et al., 2010). Research that uses manipulation of threats to known systems has been employed to examine how persons react to these possible changes in the social order. Some had extremely negative reactions to the election of the first Black president. The presidency of Barack Obama threatened the status quo. There have been some extreme reactions to this historical first. Many persons questioned the national birth of this president for his first 3 years of office. Perhaps white-skin privilege was threatened, which may explain some of the negative reactions to President Obama. In studies of our tendency to support the current social order it is generally found that:

> [I]n much the same way that depriving someone of water will increase the motivation to find something to drink, or that feeling lonely for an extended period of time will activate the motivation to find social contact—threatening the system justification motive increases activations; that is, it increases [a] desire to see [a] system as just and legitimate. (Kay et al., 2010, p. 315)

If the status quo were deemed to be unfair, persons committed to democracy and equity would want to see these impediments to equality reduced. Fairness is not necessarily that everyone is equal but implies that outcomes should be equitable. Difficulties arise in determining what is fair. One of our challenges is how to define what is fair? This would require clearly defining equality and how it differs from equity.

Stereotyping: Can It Help and Not Harm?

Power affects bias in several ways (Fiske, 2001; Glick & Fiske, 2001; Guinote & Phillips, 2010). There is a strong bidirectional and reinforcing interaction between power and stereotyping that is influenced by which group is paying attention to the other (Fiske, 1993). Persons with less power pay more attention to those with more power because the more powerful control their social outcomes (Barreto et al., 2010). This careful attention allows the less powerful to develop nuanced, complex, individualized, and non-stereotypical impressions of the more powerful. The powerful, on the other hand, pay less attention to those who are less powerful and are more likely to use stereotyping because it is not necessary for them to understand and individuate the less powerful since they don't control their outcomes (Nelson, 2009). Guinote and Phillips (2010) provide real-world validity to this theory in a study of managers and subordinates in the hotel industry.

White, native, English-speaking managers and subordinates working in a restaurant and a hotel in southeast England were presented with descriptions of either an "English" or "Afro-Caribbean" person in the role of a teacher or a DJ. The participants were given general information about the job for which each target was applying and six behavioral sentences that were consistent with previous research showing that Anglo-Saxon persons perceived English people as hard-working, well-mannered, and efficient and that they perceived Afro-Caribbean persons as laid-back, religious, and musically talented. The researchers found that subordinates paid more attention to stereotype-inconsistent information than did managers. They concluded that attention to the stereotype-inconsistent information indicated that the participant perceived the target as a person. Subordinates also paid more attention to the social information provided than did managers. This study suggests that it may be useful to guide persons with power to more carefully process information about people who have less power, thus reducing the impact of power on bias.

Summary

The study of power requires examining inequality. Sociologists and psychologists have documented inequalities among diversity groups in income, college admissions, high-school completion, employment rates and patterns, health outcomes, and health services. On average, these inequalities favor Whites and men. Power dynamics is a term used to represent how power is acquired and maintained and the complex relationships among diversity status, power, and privilege. Social power is the ability to control assets and the access that others have to those assets. Social power often leads to social privilege: access to resources, opportunities, and possibilities that are not easily available to others. This has been referred to as unearned assets of which one is usually not aware. Power concentrated in only one or two groups or where two diversity groups intersect, such as White and male, to the disadvantage of others, raises questions of fairness. A social role reflects one's position in society. Social roles that correspond to diversity group membership have created a social hierarchy where Blacks, Hispanics, women, gays and lesbians, and some other social groups have less power and social status. In some situations, having white or lighter skin means that you are likely to be in an advantageous or powerful position—given a privilege you have not earned, just because your skin-color group is more powerful.

The social influence theory identifies three types of power used to exercise control: (a) legitimate authority that comes from the leader's position; (b) coercive power, based on threats or actual punishment; and (c) reward power, which is the positive opposite of coercive power, but also includes (d) expert and (e) referent influence. The ability to attain and exercise power depends on these basic dimensions of power.

Social influence can also come from other sources: social dominance orientation, social class, and skin color. People with less power than others have a more negative reaction to a situation where a person with power expresses a negative attitude toward them than a person who has an equally powerful social role as the person expressing prejudice. Power affects bias. Persons with less power pay more attention to those with more power because the more powerful control their social outcomes. This allows the less powerful to develop nuanced, individualized, and non-stereotypical impressions of the more powerful. The powerful, on the other hand, pay less attention to those who are less powerful and are more likely to use stereotyping because it is not necessary for them to understand and individuate the less powerful since they don't control their outcomes. This suggests that it may be useful to guide persons with power to more carefully process information about people who have less power, thus reducing the impact of power on bias. Our purpose in this chapter is to present you with some perspectives to help you think critically about power and diversity so you have greater awareness of how they intersect and challenge our sense of fairness.

Questions for Thinking and Knowing

1. Think about your views on whether some diversity groups have more power than others.
2. Do you think there is Black male privilege? In what situations might Black males occupy a position of power, and under what circumstances?
3. Bargh and colleagues (1995) propose that possessing power leads to a strong *approach* motivation, eagerness and energy directed at one's goals. But they find that lacking power is not associated with *avoidance* motivation. How would you describe your approach or avoidance tendencies when you feel you have some degree of power or when you feel you don't?
4. Make a list of the situations in which you feel power as a person and those in which you feel power because of the social group to which you belong. Explain the source of your powerful position. In what situations do you feel you have little or no power?
5. Think about whether and why you agree or disagree with this statement: Social hierarchies are necessary for society to function. Whatever your opinion, what alternatives to hierarchies would be feasible?

Key Terms

Arab Spring
Equity
Expert influence
Fairness
Intersectionality
Objective SES
Power dynamics
Privilege
Referent influence
Relative deprivation
Social class
Social dominance
Social dominance orientation

Social group power
Social influence
Social power
Social role
Social role hierarchies
Social status
Socioeconomic status (SES)
Status quo
Subjective SES
System justification theory (SJT)
Theory of social influence
White-skin privilege

References

Ancis, J. R., & Szymanski, D. M. (2001). Awareness of White privilege among White counseling trainees. *The Counseling Psychologist, 29,* 548–569.

Anderson, S. K., & Middleton, V. A. (2011). *Explorations in diversity: Examining privilege and oppression in a multicultural society* (2nd ed.). Belmont, CA: Brooks/Cole.

Bargh, J. A., Raymond, P., Pryor, J., & Strack, F. (1995). The attractiveness of the underling: An automatic power–sex association and its consequences for sexual harassment and aggression. *Journal of Personality and Social Psychology, 68,* 768–781.

Barreto, M., Ellemers, N., & Fiske, S. T. (2010). What did you say, and who do you think you are? How power differences affect emotional reactions to prejudice. *Journal of Social Issues, 66,* 477–492.

Bynen, R., Moore, P. W., Salloukh, B. F., & Zah, M. (2013). *Beyond the Arab Spring: Authoritarianism and Democratization in the Arab World.* Boulder, CO: Lynne Reinner Publisher.

Christensen, A., & Heavy, C. L. (1990). Gender and social role structure in the demand/withdrawal pattern of marital conflict. *Journal of Personality and Social Psychology, 59,* 73–81.

Cole, E. R. (2009). Intersectionality and research in psychology. *American Psychologist, 64,* 170–180.

Cole, E. R., Avery, L. R., Dodson, C., & Goodman, K. D. (2012). Against nature: How arguments about the naturalness of marriage privilege heterosexuality. *Journal of Social Issues, 68,* 46–62.

Department of Housing and Urban Development. (2005). *Discrimination in metropolitan housing markets: National results from Phase 1, Phase 2, and Phase 3 of the Housing Discrimination Study (HDS).* Retrieved from http://www.huduser.org/portal/publications/hsgfin/hds.html

Eagly, A. (1987). *Sex differences in social behavior: A social-role interpretation.* Hillsdale, NJ: Erlbaum.

Eagly, A., Wood, W., & Diekman, A. B. (2000). Social role theory of sex differences and similarities: A current appraisal. In T. Eckes & H. M. Trautner (Eds.), *The developmental social psychology of gender* (pp. 123–174). Mahwah, NJ: Lawrence Erlbaum & Associates.

Eckes, T., & Trautner, H. M. (2000). Developmental social psychology of gender: An integrative framework. In T. Eckes & H. M. Trautner (Eds.), *The developmental social psychology of gender* (pp. 3–32). Mahwah, NJ: Lawrence Erlbaum & Associates.

Ehteshami, A., & Wright, S. (2007). Political change in the Arab oil monarchies: From liberalization to enfranchisement. *International Affairs, 83,* 913–932.

Eldridge, K. A., Sevier, M., Jones, J., Atkins, D. C., & Christensen, A. (2007). Demand-withdrawal communication in severely distressed, moderately distressed, and non-distressed couples: Rigidity and polarity during relationship and personal problem discussions. *Journal of Family Psychology, 21,* 218–226.

Epley, N., Caruso, E. M., & Bazerman, M. H. (2006). When perspective taking increases taking: Reactive egoism in social interaction. *Journal of Personality and Social Psychology, 91,* 872–889.

Fiske, S. T. (1993). Controlling other people. *American Psychologist, 48,* 621–628.

Fiske, S. T. (2001). Effects of power on bias: Power explains and maintains individual, group, and social disparities. In A. Y. Lee-Chai & J. A. Bargh (Eds.), *The use and abuse of power: Multiple perspectives on the causes of corruption* (pp. 181–193). New York: Psychology Press.

Frank, T. (2004). *What's the matter with Kansas? How conservatives won the heart of America.* New York: Henry Holt and Company.

French, J. R. P., & Raven, B. (1959). The bases of social power. In D. Cartwright & A. Zander (Eds.), *Group dynamics* (pp. 150–167). New York: Harper & Row.

Glick, P., & Fiske, S. T. (2001). An ambivalent alliance: Hostile and benevolent sexism as complementary justifications for gender inequality. *American Psychologist, 56*, 109–118.

Golden, D. (2007). *The price of admissions: How America's ruling class buys its way into elite colleges—and who gets left outside the gates.* New York: Crowne Publishers/Random House.

Goodman, E., Adler, N. E., Kawachi, I. F., Grazir, A. L., Huang, B., & Colditz, G. A. (2001). Adolescents' perceptions of development and evaluation of a new indicator. *Pediatrics, 108*, 1–8.

Guinote, A., & Phillips, A. (2010). Power can increase stereotyping: Evidence from managers and subordinates in the hotel industry. *Social Psychology, 41*, 3–9.

Guinote, A., & Vescio, T. K. (2010). *The social psychology of power.* New York: Guilford Press.

Hammack, P. L. (2008). Narrative and the cultural psychology of identity. *Journal of Personality and Social Psychology Review, 12*, 222–247.

Henry, P. J., & Pratto, F. (2010). Power and racism. In A. Guinote & T. K. Vescio (Eds.), *The social psychology of power* (pp. 341–362). New York: Guilford Press.

Hodge, R. W., Siegel, P. M., & Rossi, P. H. (1964). Occupational prestige in the United States, 1925–63. *American Journal of Sociology, 70*, 286–302.

Hodge, R. W., & Treiman, D. J. (1968). Class identification in the United States. *American Journal of Sociology, 73*, 535–547.

Houser, R. A., & Ham, D. A. (2004). *Gaining power and control through diversity and group affiliation.* Westport, CT: Praeger.

Hunter, M. (2002). If you're light you're alright: Light skin color as social capital for women of color. *Gender and Society, 16*, 175–193.

Jackman, M. R., & Jackman, R. W. (1983). *Class awareness in the United States.* Berkeley: University of California Press.

Jost, J. T., & Banaji, M. R. (1994). The role of stereotyping in system-justification and the production of false consciousness. *British Journal of Social Psychology, 33*, 1–27.

Jost, J. T., & Banaji, M. R. (2004). A decade of system justification theory: Accumulated evidence of conscious and unconscious bolstering of the status quo. *Political Psychology, 25*, 881–919.

Kay, A., Banfield, J. C., & Lauren, K. (2010). The system justification motive and the maintenance of social power. In A. Guinote & T. K. Vescio (Eds.), *The social psychology of power* (pp. 313–340). New York: Guilford Press.

Kerbo, H. R. (2007). Social stratification. In C. D. Bryant & D. Peck (Eds.), *21st century sociology: A reference handbook* (pp. 228–236). Thousand Oaks, CA: Sage.

Khalidi, R. (2011, March 21). The Arab spring. *The Nation.* Retrieved on October 1, 2011 from http://www.thenation.com/article/158991/arab-spring

Kimmel, M. S. (2011). *The gendered society.* New York: Oxford University Press.

Kochhar, R., Fry, R., & Taylor, P. (2011). *Wealth gaps rise to record highs between Whites, Blacks, and Hispanics. Twenty-to-one.* Pew Social and Demographic Trends. Washington, DC: Pew Research Center. Retrieved on December 11, 2012 from http://www.pewsocialtrends.org/2011/07/26/wealth-gaps-rise-to-record-highs-between-whites-blacks-hispanics/

Kraus, M. W., Piff, P. K., & Keltner, D. (2009). Social class, sense of control, and social explanation. *Journal of Personality and Social Psychology, 97*, 992–1004.

Kuhn, D., Nash, S. C., & Brucken, L. (1978). Social role competence in three-year olds and four-year-olds. *Child Development, 49*, 445–451.

Lott, B. (2002). Cognitive and behavioral distancing from the poor. *American Psychologist, 57*, 100–110.

Magee, J. C., & Galinsky, A. D. (2008). Social hierarchy: The self-reinforcing nature of power and status. *Academy of Management Annals, 2*, 351–398.

McIntosh, P. (2009). White privilege and male privilege. In M. S. Kimmel & A. B. Ferber (Eds.), *Privilege: A reader* (2nd ed., pp. 3–25). Boulder, CO: Westview Press.

McLeod, S. A. (2008). *Social roles*. Retrieved on November 7, 2011 from http://www.simplypsychology.org/social-roles.html

Miles, E. W., Hatfield, J. D., & Huseman, R. C. (1989). The equity sensitivity construct: Potential implications for worker performance. *Journal of Management, 15,* 581–588.

Morin, R. (2012). *Rising share of Americans see conflict between rich and poor*. Pew Social and Demographic Trends. Washington, DC: Pew Research Center. Retrieved from http://www.pewsocialtrends.org/2012/01/11/rising-share-of-americans-see-conflict-between-rich-and-poor/

National Bureau of Labor Statistics. (2011). *May 2011 National occupational employment and wage estimates United States*. Retrieved from http://www.bls.gov/oes/current/oes_nat.htm#00-0000

Nelson, T. (Ed.). (2009). *Handbook of prejudice, stereotyping, and discrimination*. New York: Taylor Francis.

Oakes, J. M., & Rossi, P. H. (2003). The measurement of SES in health research: Current practice and steps toward a new approach. *Social Science and Medicine, 56,* 769–784.

Parsons, T. (1939). The professions and social structure. *Social Forces, 17,* 457–467.

Pew Hispanic Center. (2012). *Statistical portrait of the foreign-born population in the United States, 2010*. Table 28: Detailed Occupation, by Region of Birth: 2010. Retrieved on December 22, 2012 from http://www.pewhispanic.org/files/2012/02/PHC-2010-FB-Profile-Final_APR-3.pdf

Pratto, F., Sidanius, J., Stallworth, L. M., & Malle, B. F. (1994). Social dominance orientation: A personality variable predicting social and political attitudes. *Journal of Personality and Social Psychology, 67,* 741–763.

Ramos, J. (2010). *A country for all: An immigrant manifesto*. New York: Vintage Books.

Raven, B. H. (2008). The basis of power and the power/interaction model of interpersonal influence. *Analyses of Social Issues and Public Policy, 8,* 1–22.

Riley, G. (2011). *How young children remain autonomous in expressing their gender identity: Parent perceptions of experiences had by their gender nonconforming child in the early education environment*. MA Thesis presented to Mills College, Oakland, CA, June 2012.

Sandel, M. J. (2011, August 21). If I were President . . . *The New York Times*, p. SR12. Available at http://www.nytimes.com/2011/08/21/opinion/sunday/what-id-do-if-i-were-president.html?pagewanted=all&_r=0

Saulny, S., & Steinberg, J. (2011, June 13). Race remixed: On college forms, a question of race, or races, can perplex. *The New York Times*. Retrieved from http://topics.nytimes.com/top/news/us/series/race_remixed/index.html

Schaefer, R. T. (2008). *Racial and ethnic groups* (11th ed.). Upper Saddle River, NJ: Prentice Hall.

Sebanc, A. M., Pierce S. L., Cheatham, C. L., & Gunnar, M. R. (2003). Gendered social worlds in preschool: Dominance, peer acceptance and assertive social skills in boys' and girls' peer groups. *Social Development, 12,* 91–106.

Sidanius, J., Liu, J. H., Shaw, J. S., & Pratto, F. (1994). Social dominance orientation, hierarchy attenuators and hierarchy enhancers: Social dominance theory and the criminal justice system. *Journal of Applied Social Psychology, 24,* 338–366.

Sidanius, J., & Pratto, F. (1999). *Social dominance: An intergroup theory of social hierarchy and oppression*. Cambridge: Cambridge University Press.

Sidanius, J., & Veniegas, R. C. (2000). Gender and race discrimination: The interactive nature of disadvantage. In S. Oskamp (Ed.), *Reducing prejudice and discrimination: The Claremont Symposium on Applied Social Psychology* (pp. 47–69). Mahwah, NJ: Lawrence Erlbaum Associates.

Soares, J. (2007). *The power of privilege: Yale and America's elite colleges*. Palo Alto, CA: Stanford University Press.

Stahelski, A. J., Frost, D. E., & Patch, M. E. (1989). Use of socially dependent bases of power: French and Raven's theory applied to workgroup leadership. *Journal of Applied Social Psychology, 19,* 283–297.

Stets, J. E., & Burke, P. J. (2000). Identity theory and social identity theory. *Social Psychology Quarterly, 64,* 224–237.

Stevens, M. L. (2009). *Creating a class: College admissions and the education of elites*. Cambridge, MA: Harvard University Press.

Tajfel, H. (1979). Individuals and groups in social psychology. *British Journal of Social and Clinical Psychology, 18,* 183–190.

U.S. Census Bureau. (2011). *Current Population Survey, Annual Social and Economic (ASEC) Supplement*. Table PINC-05: Work Experience in 2010—People 15 Years Old and Over by Total Money Earnings in 2010, Age, Race, Hispanic Origin, and Sex. Retrieved from http://www.census.gov/hhes/www/cpstables/032011/perinc/new05_000.htm

Warner, W. L., Meeker, M., & Eels, K. (1949). *Social class in America*. Chicago: Science Research Associates.

Wiley, S., Philogene, G., & Revenson, T. A. (2011). *Social categories in everyday experience*. Washington, DC: American Psychological Association.

Wise, T. (2005). Membership has its privileges: Thoughts on acknowledging and challenging whiteness. In P. S. Rothenberg (Ed.), *White privilege: Essential readings on the other side of racism* (2nd ed., pp. 119–122). New York: Worth Publishers.

Wise, T. (2008). *White like me: Reflections on race from a privileged son* (revised and updated). Brooklyn: Soft Skull Press.

Chapter 12

The Challenge of Diversity for Institutions

Introduction   327
Portraits of Institutional Bias   329
How Institutional Bias Operates   332
Most Bias is Standard-of-Practice Bias   335
Preventing Institutional Bias is a Challenge   348
Summary   350

When you're walking down the hall and you see that there's nothing but white males that occupy these offices, and rarely do you see any women or minorities, you know that there's a problem somewhere along the line.

Veronica Shinault, former Texaco employee

Introduction

This chapter expands on the Chapter 11 discussion of differences in social power among diversity groups as we examine diversity and bias in institutions. An **institution** is an established entity in which the business, education, healthcare, or social goals of a society are sustained. Banks, schools, corporations, the health industry, higher education, and the like are institutions. Marriage is also a social institution. We present evidence that establishes the existence of disparities between diversity groups on many quality-of-life factors. Disparities do not always denote unfairness. However, we propose that institutional bias may be one cause of these disparities. If it is, institutional bias may be related to inequitable social outcomes based on diversity status.

The Psychology of Diversity: Beyond Prejudice and Racism, First Edition. James M. Jones,
John F. Dovidio, and Deborah L. Vietze.
© 2014 Blackwell Publishing Ltd. Published 2014 by Blackwell Publishing Ltd.

Institutional bias is a social outcome advantage, documented at the institutional level, that favors some groups over others. Discussions of institutional bias use the major demographic groups recognized in the U.S. Census as the unit of analysis, such as male, female, Black, White, Hispanic, Asian, and age categories. Bias at the institutional level may result in disparities in social outcomes among these major diversity groups. It may also be a natural consequence of concentrating power among members of a few socially advantaged groups.

In thinking about disparities in social outcomes these questions arise: Do disparities among diversity groups exist? If so, should we be concerned with why these disparities exist and achieving a more equitable distribution of social outcomes? Are they the result of systematic bias across a society? Institutional bias is more related to disparities in outcomes among diversity status groups than to accounting for these differences. As explained by Jones (1997), bias exists at three levels in society. It can be individual, institutional, and cultural. In this chapter we focus on institutional bias. Sociologists have referred to this as structural bias.

The possibility of institutional bias is examined using **social indicators**. A social indicator is a quality-of-life gauge for a society. It represents how well people in a society are doing in education, work, health, home ownership, and the like. At an international level they are used to compare quality of life among countries. For example, literacy rates are 28% in Afghanistan, 59% in Burundi, and 99% in Canada. An index of gender inequality—differences between men and women in reproductive health, empowerment, and the labor market participation—is 0.07 in Norway (almost equal parity between men and women), 0.48 in Colombia (favoring men), and 0.71 in Afghanistan (heavily favoring men) (United Nations Development Program Report, 2011).

Institutional bias is established, in part, by noting disparities among diversity groups using descriptive statistics of social indicators. The relative standing of diversity groups for each social indicator reflects differences among diversity groups in achieving social goals equitably. These data show the degree to which disparities exist among diversity groups. When these disparities occur, and are closely aligned with diversity status, the possibility that intuitional bias is creating these disparities must be considered. Chapter 11 discussed the close inverse relationship between power and diversity status. This inverse relationship between institutional bias and social indicator disparities may also exist.

Two situational examples will help clarify the notion of institutional bias. Suppose that 57% of the workforce are women and 65% are classified as ethnic minority (Blacks, Hispanics, Asians). All the top-level workforce executives are White men. If this happens consistently for decades, across many institutions, industries, professions and governments, this disparity suggests the possibility of persistent institutional bias. Disparities need not be intentional to be considered bias. The determination of bias is based on the pattern of outcomes and the accompanying evidence of what produces them, whether or not they are intentionally produced.

Consider the National Basketball Association in a second example. Blacks are the majority of players; the highest paid players are Black. This is not an example of institutional bias because Blacks don't dominate all sports fields, have not dominated basketball historically, nor do they dominate any other major institution in our society.

Evidence of disparities must be pervasive, cross-cutting, and to have consistently favored a very limited number of diversity groups to be considered institutional bias. Of course it is also generally true that Blacks are the *best* players. We might speculate why this is the case. We speculate about the reasons for the disparity because distinguishing between bias and merit, when disparities in outcomes exist, is not a simple matter.

This chapter presents social indicator evidence showing disparities in some social indicators for major diversity groups. This institutional bias may be an outcome of inequities in the distribution of social power among diversity groups. These relationships are indicated by demographic profiles of different institutions. In examining these profiles, you can think about the reasons for the bias we discuss and equity and fairness concerns that may be raised. Not all disparities represent bias. When they are pervasive, affect the majority of major diversity groups, and are historically unchanged, they may represent institutional bias.

Affirmative action has been offered as a way to address institutional bias. The logic here is that proactive remedies are needed to reduce institutional disparities. Groups lagging in key social indicators would be given an opportunity to be considered for admission or a job, for example, if their qualifications merited such consideration. We gave some examples of this in earlier chapters and the complexities of this remedy are presented in our last chapter.

Portraits of Institutional Bias

Two examples of institutional bias introduce the ideas we will discuss later. The first example is a story about a corporation that, when confronted with accusations of bias, did something to address the problem. The second concerns a deliberate attempt to use an all-girls classroom to rectify an educational bias that favored boys in math classrooms.

Texaco: Recognizing Diversity Bias and Doing Something About It

In November 1996, Texaco, a global oil and gas company, settled a racial discrimination suit filed by African American employees for a then record sum of over $176 million. Black employees had charged the company with institutional racism, having documented widespread pay inequities and a work environment of fear, humiliation, and insults for minority employees. Company officials settled the lawsuit after the news media disclosed some secretly recorded conversations among top executives. These conversations revealed the attitudes that led to Black employees' feelings of fear and humiliation. Here's one conversation used as evidence of some company executives' attitudes about Black employees:

> *Ulrich* (inaudible): I've heard this diversity thing. You know how black jellybeans agree.
>
> *Lundwall*: That's funny. All the black jellybeans seem to be glued to the bottom of the bag.

Ulrich: You can't just have we and them. You can't just have black jellybeans and other jellybeans. It doesn't work.

Retrieved from http://www.pbs.org/newshour/bb/business/november96/texaco_11-12.html

Racism and bias complaints continued to plague the company after the settlement. Texaco leaders faced the problem and took action to make the corporate culture more diverse. CEO Peter Bajer acted forcefully to reverse the company's negative image and create a corporate climate intolerant of racism and other biases. He stated, "We believe a commitment to real diversity makes good business sense" (Johansson, 2000). Bajer demonstrated his concern about diversity by actively encouraging it. Diversity training workshops were created for all employees, from laborers to board members. Texaco established a Corporate Diversity Council, for open conversations about diversity issues. Texaco used telephone and email hotlines and had a dispute-resolution strategy to address bias problems as they arose.

Three years after the discrimination suit, a lot had changed. Texaco focused on three goals: (a) establishing diversity goals in its workforce; (b) creating racism and sexism prevention programs; and (c) seeking diversity in suppliers and vendors. The settlement required some of these changes but Texaco met and exceeded these goals by establishing policies and procedures to eliminate racism, sexism, and other biases. It also began a diversity scholarship and internship program in engineering, information systems, and international business. It began using recruiting firms that had a good track record of finding minority candidates (Johansson, 2000).

This story shows that institutional bias can be reduced, if not eliminated, even if bias is pervasively systematic. When bias is "in the air," as this chapter's introductory quote states, it can be addressed. Preventing workplace bias depends on forceful actions by company leaders. Texaco succeeded in addressing bias not just because it established programs to promote diversity—many companies do this—but because they created a value for diversity and made everyone accountable for achieving it. In 1998, about 60% of new Texaco employees were minorities and 40% of promotions went to minorities and women. In the first 6 months of 1999, the percentage of promotions to women and minorities went up 15 and 20%, respectively (Johansson, 2000). This was impressive during a rocky economic period when the number of employees at Texaco decreased by 30%.

An All-Girls Math Class: Educational Bias on Purpose

In the Texaco case, individual employees, from top management on down, allowed personal prejudice to influence corporate decisions. The result was an expensive lawsuit to establish equity. In contrast, our next example shows that some bias may be distinctly positive. Teachers and guidance counselors at Capistrano Valley High School in California set up an all-girls college-prep math class (Figure 12.1). Their intent was to improve the math performance of girls doing average or failing work. Teachers wanted to help girls prepare for college using the same college-prep curriculum used for boys. They thought girls would do better in only-girl classes because girls, adhering to a prescribed social role, might not want to be seen as aggressively

Figure 12.1.   Girls Enjoy Excelling in Math as Well as Boys When Given Opportunities to Do So. © lightpoet/Shutterstock.com.

competing with boys in an area where boys have traditionally excelled. They also reasoned that this tendency in girls might be magnified because boys might be a romantic distraction for heterosexual adolescent girls.

After a few weeks the students in the all-girls class started behaving differently than they had in the class with boys. They answered questions excitedly and enthusiastically, had moved ahead in the textbook, and were asking questions about sections that had not been assigned. The girls earned higher final grades than they had in previous math classes. They reported that it was easier to learn in the girls-only math class (O'Dell, 2001). They felt more confident being with girls than with boys, some of whom were more aggressive in answering questions. When asked if they missed having boys in the class, the answer was a resounding "No." Educators suspect that when girls are taught in gender-segregated classrooms they create a sense of camaraderie that boosts their confidence and improves performance. Some girls who took the class would not even have enrolled in a mixed-gender math class. While this story does not apply to all boys and girls in math classes, it does illustrate that sometimes segregating boys and girls in classes may have benefits.

There has been controversy about whether gender or culturally segregated classes or schools are beneficial to disadvantaged groups. There are several questions that need answers before we determine if segregating people based on any salient diversity trait is a good idea. There would need to be documented justification for the benefits of such segregation before its application.

For example, those who favor single-sex education think that gender-mixed classes or schools can be distracting and perhaps reinforce gender stereotypes when boys and girls fall into expected roles. A common stereotype is that boys are good at math— because some boys are good at it, boys are encouraged to be good at math. Another is that girls should not be too aggressive, in answering questions for example. Do these typical views make it a good idea to have segregated math classes?

Research has documented that, on average, males and females have different learning styles (National Association for Single-sex Learning, 2012). Another study has shown that girls perform better in a warm learning environment while boys do better in cooler temperatures (http://www.greatschools.org/find-a-school/defining-your-ideal/single-sex-education-the-pros-and-cons.gs?content=1139, retrieved May 1, 2010). These reasons provide some evidence that a gender-segregated math class may have benefits for girls. We don't know if gender-segregated classrooms have learning benefits for boys. But, they too seem to like it better. Others argue that a single-sex learning environment may have a downside, because it prevents both genders from learning how to socialize with each other. The example of gender-segregated math education focuses on the positive benefits but may be ignoring the downside of gender-segregated education for girls.

How Institutional Bias Operates

Institutional racism and sexism are two of the earliest identified forms of institutional bias. Trinidadian-born U.S. civil rights activist Stokely Carmichael referred to it in an October 1966 address on the University of California Berkeley campus:

> Seems to me that the institutions that function in this country are clearly racist, and that they're built upon racism. And the question, then, is how can black people inside of this country move? And then how can white people who say they're not a part of those institutions begin to move? How can we begin to build institutions that will allow people to relate with each other as human beings?

Institutional racism is defined as:

> established laws, customs, and practices, which systematically reflect and produce racial inequalities in American society. If racist consequences accrue to institutional laws, customs, or practices, the institution is racist whether or not the individuals maintaining those practices have racist intentions. Institutional racism can be either overt or covert (corresponding to de jure [meaning of law] and de facto [meaning of fact], respectively) and either intentional or unintentional. (Jones, 1972, p. 131)

Institutional sexism is similar except that the systematic discrimination is biased against women. Our cultural history of strongly held negative attitudes toward women in the workplace and in higher education and similarly negative attitudes toward Blacks in all social institutions are the origin of some institutional bias. Historically, most institutional bias could be classified as individually mediated, because the bias was intentional and based on well-recognized and acknowledged personal prejudice toward women and Blacks. Similar bias has occurred throughout our history toward persons with non-heterosexual orientations.

Structural discrimination is related to institutional bias but focuses more on the conditions that create inequities. Sociologists refer to structural or unintentional bias as practices that result in outcomes that are substantially worse for some groups than for others. This structural bias is passed on from generation to generation, in informal policies and practices, and negative outcomes accumulate.

The distinction between institutional and structural bias may be difficult to detect. Intention is hard to gauge in persons or institutions. There are some cases of bias at this level that are obviously intentional—bias against gay marriage is often openly critical and intentionally based on religious views. Other types of bias may be more structural. White men continue to be overwhelmingly holders of executive and management positions and other race and ethnicity groups, including women, are more likely to be in clerical or assisting roles. These differences may not be intentional but the patterns, once established, continue. This review of institutional bias focuses on the impact of institutional policies and practices and less on the reasons for them.

The Origins of Institutional Bias: A Case Example

Chapter 4 introduced economist Gunnar Myrdal's pioneering 1940s study that revealed how the institution of slavery and racism affected the lives of former slaves and their descendants (Myrdal, 1944). Myrdal's work demonstrates that individual racism and legally mandated institutional racism resulted in economic and social disparities between the lives of White and Black people. Myrdal's work exposed the impact of combined individual and institutional bias when it showed the extent of dire poverty for Black, compared with White, citizens. His work is credited with influencing the 1954 U.S. Supreme Court decision to end school segregation (Cohen, 2004). After winning the Nobel Prize in Economics, Myrdal influenced President Truman and other leaders and organizations, including the National Association for the Advancement of Colored People (NAACP) to "wage war" on these injustices by framing them as a moral problem (Cohen, 2004).

Types of Institutional Bias

Two types of institutional bias create poor social outcomes (Jones, 1997): (a) **individual-mediated bias** and (b) **standard-of-practice bias**. Individual-mediated bias occurs when a person who is prejudiced against groups has key decision-making authority in an institution. A person's views will tend to promote bias, disfavoring some groups and resulting in poor outcomes for these groups. Institutional bias is a natural extension of individual prejudice. Individual bias filtered through an institution becomes more pernicious and harmful. Individual bias is magnified because institutions may be perceived as legitimate.

Standard-of-practice institutional bias is often difficult to detect. It occurs when an institution systematically advantages one group, such as men, and disadvantages another group, women. For example, across all income categories in most jobs, women earn just 74.5% of what men earn (Bureau of Labor Statistics, 2011; note: these statistics are updated frequently. Citations were correct at the time of printing.). Legislation, signed into law by President Obama in 2009 made it possible for women to have more time to file suit for pay discrimination. This did not have any immediate effect on the gender income gap and is unlikely to do so. Economic, criminal justice, and other social data are used to show that standard-of-practice bias exists. We don't need to apply a moral, ethical, or value judgment to an institution to see bias. Rather, we determine that bias exists by looking at the outcomes of institutional practices and policies.

Education and the workplace (Box 12.1) are two institutions of great importance because they affect everyone (Fassinger, 2008). Women, sexual minorities, disabled persons, and many ethnic groups' social outcomes are challenged by institutional bias (Fassinger, 2008).

Box 12.1.   At a Slaughter House, Some Things Never Die: Tar Heel, North Carolina

It must have been one o'clock. That's when the white man usually comes out of his glass office and stands on the scaffolding above the factory floor. He stood with his palms on the rails, his elbows out. He looked like a tower guard up there or a border patrol agent. He stood with his head cocked.

One o'clock means it is getting near the end of the workday. Quota has to be met and the workload doubles. The conveyor belt always overflows with meat around one o'clock. So the workers double their pace, hacking pork from shoulder bones with a driven single-mindedness. They stare blankly, like mules in wooden blinders, as the butchered slabs pass by. It's called the picnic line: eighteen workers lined up on both sides of a belt, carving meat from bone.

On this day the boss saw something he didn't like. He climbed down and approached the picnic line from behind. He leaned into the ear of a broad-shouldered black man. He had been riding him all day, and the day before. The boss bawled him out good this time, but no one heard what was said. The roar of the machinery was too ferocious for that. Still, everyone knew what was expected. They worked harder. The white man stood and watched for the next two hours as the blacks worked in their groups and the Mexicans in theirs. He stood there with his head cocked.

Who Gets the Dirty Jobs

The first thing you learn in the hog plant is the value of a sharp knife. The second thing you learn is that you don't want to work with a sharp knife. Finally you learn that not everyone has to work with a sharp knife. Whites, Blacks, American Indians, and Mexicans, they all have their separate stations.

The few whites on the payroll tend to be mechanics or supervisors. As for the Indians, a handful are supervisors, others tend to get clean menial jobs like warehouse work. With few exceptions that leaves the Blacks and the Mexicans with the dirty jobs at the factory, one of the only places within a fifty-mile radius in this muddy corner of North Carolina where a person might make more than $8 an hour. (Excerpts from Charles Leduff, in Correspondents of the New York Times (Eds.),

How race is lived in America: Pulling together, pulling apart. New York: Times Books/ Henry Holt Company, pp. 97–98).

This excerpt, from an article on work at a Smithfield pork processing plant, is part of a collection of articles published in 1990 by *New York Times* reporters who developed a series for the *Times* titled *How Race is Lived in America.* A book containing a collection of these articles by that same name was published in 2001. The reporters wanted to answer the question: How are race relations today? They chose to explore the answer to this question by identifying and researching situations and settings where people of different races were in contact. They wanted to find out first hand how the different race and ethnicity groups were treated in the United States and how they experienced relating to those of other races. This excerpt from one of the articles provides a clear example of institutional bias based on race and, in the case of the Mexican workers, on ethnicity or country of origin. There may be many reasons for the kind of stratified bias we see in this example. White men control the majority of better-paid and less labor-intensive jobs while Black and Mexican workers had to do the worst and lowest-paying jobs. When a trend like this is observed we label it institutional bias. The title of the article, shown as the title of this box, illustrates that these patterns have existed for some time and seem entrenched and not likely to change.

Most Bias is Standard-of-Practice Bias

Absolute methods for determining the existence of institutional bias don't exist. But **disparate impact** has been measured using the **four-fifths rule**. The U.S. Equal Employment Opportunity Commission (EEOC) developed this rule in 1978. It is a guideline to provide employers with a uniform set of principles for hiring without discrimination based on age, disability, color, sex, religion, national origin, or race. The EEOC Uniform Guidelines state that a selection rate for any group less than four fifths, or 80%, of the rate for the group with the highest rate will generally be regarded as evidence of disparate impact by the agency charged with protecting employment civil rights. The guidelines are applied where statistical and practical differences exist and are meant to be guidelines, not laws (retrieved on September 18, 2012 from http://www.uniformguidelines.com/uniformguidelines.html).

We will examine examples of standard-of-practice biases in this section. We rely on social indicators from key institutions, including housing, the banking system, the workforce, and the criminal justice system. This section will provide some data to support the view that institutional bias exists. These are the kinds of analyses and data that are used to identify possible institutional bias and may be the basis for individuals to seek remedies for past or current discrimination. Historically, bias in employment and education has been the target of affirmative action. Let's take a look at affirmative action first.

Can Affirmative Action Address Institutional Bias?

President John F. Kennedy created the EEOC in 1961 by Executive Order. He instructed the Commission to use affirmative action to prevent discrimination by all federal contractors. Title VII of the Civil Rights Act of 1964 prohibits employment discrimination on the basis of race, color, religion, sex, or national origin (see Chapter 3). The EEOC now oversees all cases of employment discrimination in hiring, compensation, testing, training, and firing. Race, color, sex, creed and age, disability, and pregnant women are groups protected by legislation from discrimination. In 1973 girls' educational programs, including athletics, was added. The U.S. Office of Education's Civil Rights Office oversees educational institutions. President Lyndon Johnson explained in a 1965 Howard University graduation speech that affirmative action is not just granting rights but making them a factual outcome:

> You do not wipe away the scars of centuries by saying: "now, you are free to go where you want, do as you desire, and choose the leaders you please . . ." This is the next and the more profound stage of the battle for civil rights. We seek not just freedom but opportunity . . . not just legal equity but human ability, not just equality as a right and a theory but equality as a fact and equality as a result.
> (http://www.lbjlib.utexas.edu/johnson/archives.hom/speeches.hom/650604.asp)

Since President Kennedy's executive order, 160 federal affirmative action programs have been established and states and local government programs also exist. Nothing about the Civil Right Act has created more controversy than affirmative action. Affirmative action is intended to protect the rights of, and extend opportunitites to, persons historically underrepresented in employment and education because of discrimination.

Affirmative action programs can be either mandatory or voluntary. Voluntary programs may be reviewed by the EEOC; mandatory programs may be imposed after cases of discrimination are settled, as they were in the Texaco case. Affirmative action programs are special efforts to ensure that the underrepresented groups protected by the civil rights laws are given the same opportunity to be recruited, hired, or admitted to positions as are groups not underrepresented in institutions.

Affirmative action is a remedy for past injustices. Most recently it has been applied to persons with disabilities and persons who are sexual minorities. Affirmative action efforts reflect a moral and social responsibility to correct wrongs imposed on some groups by past discrimination. Arguments have been proposed for and against affirmative action. Misunderstandings about affirmative action have been debated and discussed extensively (see, for example, Plous, 2003; Sowell, 2004). Some argue that affirmative action is not necessary because racism and sexism no longer predominate and equal opportunity already exists (D'Souza, 1996). Affirmative action programs have often been misinterpreted as biased against majority groups, because it creates an unfair advantage for the underrepresented groups. Those with this view argue that the policy unfairly excludes qualified applicants, typically Whites, while accepting less qualified applicants, typcially Blacks and Hispanics. This has been labeled **reverse discrimination**. This argument has been used to challenge the legality of affirmative action programs in colleges and universities, as in the well-known 1978 Supreme Court decision in the Bakke case (see Chapter 3). In 2003, the Supreme Court affirmed the compelling interest and legality of race-based affirmative action in *Grutter v. Bollinger* (see Chapter 1). More recently, the court has reconsidered this ruling in *Fisher v. Texas*, but has not ruled as of this writing.

There have also been a number of state and local legal challenges to affirmative action policies in higher education and employment following the Bakke challenge (Ball, 2000). Treating people differently to correct previous wrongs based on skin color, gender, or ethnicity does seem patently unfair. The problem is how to correct wrongs committed by persons long dead, who used discrimination to favor Whites and men, without disadvantaging those who did not participate in past discrimination. In court cases and other venues, Whites and some Asian students have argued that they are being discriminated against when a student with lower test scores is admitted or employed based on skin color or ethnicity. This practice, at face value, seems to be discriminatory. It would be if test scores were the only criteria used for admission and hiring, and race was applied as an extra bonus score. But even in a race-neutral situation, test scores are not the single deciding factor in admissions; the test score plus ethnicity factor is not the formula used either. Admission formulas are never based only on test scores. If they were the rates of Asians admitted would moderately increase, those of Blacks and Hispanics would sharply decrease, and Whites would remain fairly steady, or slightly decrease (Espenshade & Chung, 2005).

It might be fairer to use income, rather than ethnicity, in an admission formula including many other categories such as class rank, grades, community and school activities, and letters of recommendation. For example, the University of Texas adopted the 10% rule, which provides automatic admission to any student from a public high school in the state who graduates in the top 10% of the class. This policy attempts to create a more racially and ethnically diverse first-year class without explicitly considering race among admission criteria. Evidence shows that it has limited success. Diversity based on income may increase the number of poor White students and high-income Black and Hispanic students.

Affirmative action is not intended to give unfair advantage to some at the expense of others, or to create quotas. It is meant to give everyone a fair chance. If it does this, it is upholding our ideal of equity: No one gets an unfair advantage. Those favoring it see its merit as increasing access to talent and different points of view, thus strengthening an institution's capacity for success. Discrimination has created disadvantaged groups. These groups are legally recognized as needing protection to ensure their rights. The question is how to correct these biases to create equal opportunity without disadvantaging those who already are advantaged.

Home Ownership and Mortgage Lending

Property ownership is considered a measure of success in U.S. society. If all groups have equal access to successful outcomes, then all social groups should have both relatively equal rates of property ownership and access to mortgage loans that are proportional to their representation in the population. For many, home ownership is a primary source of wealth. Blacks seem to be losing gains in home ownership at a

Table 12.1.	Homeownership Rates (%) by Race and Ethnicity of Householder 2009–2011				
Year	Total	Non-Hispanic White	Black	All other races	Hispanic of any race
2011	66.4	74.1	44.8	56.7	46.8
2010	67.1	74.5	45.6	57.2	48.5
2009	67.2	74.5	45	58.4	48.4

Note. Source: U.S. Census Report, Table 16: Homeownership rates by race and ethnicity of householder: 1994 to present. Retrieved from http://www.census.gov/housing/hvs/data/histtabs.html

greater rate than other groups (Austin, 2008). Data from the U.S. Census reveals disparities in home ownership rates for Whites and racial and ethnic minorities. Table 12.1 shows that in 2011, nearly three quarters of Whites (74.1%) owned homes, compared with less than half of Blacks (44.8%) and Hispanics (46.8%). Black home ownership is not only significantly lower than White home ownership, but is also more affected by economic ups and downs. For example, 47.2% of Blacks owned homes in 2000. This increased to 49.1% in 2004, a healthy increase but still well below White rates of ownership. However, at the beginning of an economic recession in 2007, Blacks' home ownership declined to its 2000 level (Mishel, Bernstein & Shierholz, 2008). One reason for the decline is that Blacks were more likely to be targeted for and given subprime mortgages to finance homes and these mortgages have had a very high rate of foreclosure, resulting in home loss (Austin, 2008).

Subprime mortgages, which usually have very disadvantageous terms of repayment, are used by some lenders to finance borrowing for high-risk persons with low credit ratings. Because of the risk these borrowers pose, they are charged a higher interest rate on the loans because they generally would not qualify for a more affordable loan. This puts the subprime borrower at a disadvantage compared with borrowers with conventional loans. The outcome of this kind of systematic economic disadvantage in home loans is that persons with subprime loans are more likely to spiral into debt and fall behind in mortgage and other credit payments. This is a serious problem when home equity is the major investment of a family and the major path to acquiring wealth.

Data collected by an organization concerned with fair lending practices shows that the percentage of all borrowers with high-cost loans varies greatly by U.S. Census survey race categories. Persons in different census race and age categories do not equally receive disadvantageous subprime loans nor do the rates of subprime loans match population statistics. There are significant differences between Black and White homeowners in the percentage of subprime mortgages for each group. The rate of these loans for Black homeowners is close to 55%; for White homeowners, the rate of these loans is only 17% (United for a Fair Economy, 2009). This report also charts the proportion of all borrowers with high-cost home-purchase loans by race and income. Additional disparities are noted when considering the rate of these loans by income category and race. White buyers have a lower rate of these bad loans in all income categories, but the rate declines as you go from lower to higher income groups, as you would expect. However, this is not the case for Black or Latino borrowers, for whom the rates are virtually the same across income categories. These disparities suggest practices that systematically direct Black and Latino buyers to high-cost risky loans, so-called "predatory" loan practices. That these practices produce this disparity is quite clear. Additional evidence is necessary to determine if these practices are an actual policy of lending institutions. Even if not intentional the impact is clear.

Race, Ethnicity, Gender, and Age Disparities in Unemployment

There are widespread differences between men and women and between persons of different ethnicities in workplace pay and rates of promotion (Bureau of Labor Statistics, 2010). There are even differences between subcategories of gender and race such as differences between Black women and White women. This section will provide some of the statistics that demonstrate these disparities.

According to the U.S. Census, women comprise 50.7% of the U.S. population. Should we therefore conclude that women might make up a similar proportion of the workforce? Let's look at the numbers. Women constituted 45% of the workforce in 2008, but during the economic recession of 2009–2010 the rate rose to nearly 50% (Bureau of Labor Statistics, 2010). The proportion of women in the workforce may be rising. Predictions suggest it may be 70% in a few years. So, there does not seem to be any institutional bias against today's working women, but bias may be developing against men. However, this is not the whole story when it comes to examining differences in employment among women from different races. Table 12.2 presents some comparisons in unemployment rates for a variety of diversity-status groups. Looking at unemployment rates can help us understand how various groups are faring economically. There may be many reasons for the differences in unemployment rates that existed for these groups, based on the last U.S. Census. And it would be important to identify and explore these factors to fully understand the institutional

Table 12.2. Unemployment Rates (%) Among Age, Gender, Race, Ethnicity Diversity Groups for First Quarter of 2012

Race	*All*		*Age 18–19*		*Age 24–54*		
	Men	*Women*	*Men*	*Women*	*Men*	*Women*	*Total*
White	8.4	7.3	24.0	31.4	17.4	7.4	7.8
Asian	6.5	6.4	—	—	5.9	5.6	6.4
Hispanic	11.1	11.4	28.4	21.5	9.3	21.5	11.2
Black	15.5	12.6	39.2	31.4	13.5	10.7	14.0
Total	10.5	8.3	24.7		15.9		9.5

Note. Source: U.S. Census reports, Household data, not seasonally adjusted, quarterly averages. Retrieved May 2012 from http://www.bls.gov/cps/tables.htm#empstat

bias that these numbers may represent. Institutional bias is based on outcome disparities which, along with other factors, are often considered as reasons for consistent and persistent gaps in unemployment rates among diversity groups of adults and adolescents. Why do disparities exist in a society that values fairness and equity? We must admit it is easier to identify where disparities occur than explain why they occur. The following paragraphs demonstrate disparities in a variety of outcomes for diverse social groups.

Table 12.2 shows that Asians, both men and women of any age, have the lowest unemployment rates of any group. Does this suggest a bias in favor of hiring Asian workers? Blacks have the highest rates of unemployment across both gender and age groups. There is also a significant difference between the unemployment rates of persons aged 18–19 and those aged 24–54. Some of these differences may be explained by the fact that many 18 and 19 year olds are full-time students, but many more may want to work than these numbers reflect. Thus, there may be an institutional bias against young persons in the workforce.

Equally striking is the long-established difference between Black and White men in unemployment rates. The unemployment rate for Black men is almost twice that for White men, 15.5% and 8.3% respectively. A careful examination of Table 12.2 may bring to mind other disparities that indicate bias in favor of or against one of these categories of age, gender, race, or ethnicity. If these disparities continue after controlling for skill level, educational level, and other factors that might be related to unemployment, perhaps some portion of the disparities can be explained by institutional bias. It may also be true that institutional bias has created disparities in the antecedent conditions necessary for employment and that this mechanism perpetuates instructional bias.

The Criminal Justice System and Ethnicity Disparities

U.S. citizens pledging allegiance to the United States must state a belief in justice for all. Administration of justice therefore should be fair and impartial. However, disparities in criminal punishments show that more lenient penalties have been given to Whites when compared with other ethnic groups since early in our nation's history, and they continue today (Gabbidon & Greene, 2012). One example where fairness does not seem to exist is shown by the data on the differences by ethnicity in marijuana arrest rates in New York City between the late 1990s and 2007. Significant disparities were found in the New York City marijuana arrest rates for persons between 18 and 25 years of age for Blacks, Whites, and Hispanics.

Marijuana possession arrest rates rose sharply from 1995 to 2007. Police officers in New York City targeted marijuana users for a number of reasons during this time. In 2008, the New York Civil Liberties Union reported a 10-fold increase in marijuana arrest rates between 1997 and 2007 and major disparities between arrests rates by gender and ethnicity. Arrest rates were disproportionately high for some groups compared with the relative marijuana use by the group. Blacks accounted for about 52% of marijuana arrests, though that group represented only 26% of the city's population over that time. Latinos accounted for 31% of the arrests but 27% of the population (Levine & Small, 2008). Whites represented only 15% of those arrested, despite comprising 35% of the population. In addition, 91% of those arrested were young men. These figures are based on a report by the Marijuana Arrest Research Project and additional information on these rates is available from the project's website (http://marijuana-arrests.com/about.html).

Levine and Sigel (2013) share arrest records for marijuana use in New York City from 2002 through 2009 showing higher use among Whites than among Blacks. However, despite higher usage rates, the arrest rates for possession of marijuana are lower for Whites. These data suggest that New York City police may target young Black and Hispanic men. If so, is this an institutional bias against them? Perhaps the Black and Hispanic men were being watched more closely (disparate treatment) and this resulted in more arrests. Or that Black and Hispanic young men had higher arrests (adverse impact) because they were more heavily involved in drug sales than other groups. One would need more information from the situation to determine if the difference in arrest rates was because of disparate treatment or adverse impact. What additional information would be needed to make this decision?

Ethnic Disparities in Capital Punishment

Wide disparities exist between the percentage of Blacks executed for committing a capital offense and members of other groups. The U.S. Department of Justice reported that the number of convicted murderers executed as of 2008 was 1,099, of which 1,088 were men. Of this group, 56% were White, 36% were Black, and 9% were Hispanic, Asian/Pacific Islander, or Native American. Although the number of executions is highest for Whites, this is not the whole story. Those who killed Whites, whether they were Black or White, were three times more likely to be sentenced to death than those who killed a Black person and over four times more likely to face the death penalty than those who killed any non-White person including Blacks. Thus it is the race or skin color of the *victim*, not the perpetrator that influenced the likelihood of being charged with capital murder and with receiving the death penalty (Pierce & Radelet, 2005).

Healthcare, Marriage, and Environmental Safety

There is compelling evidence that disparities among diversity groups exist in access to healthcare systems and health outcomes. These disparities may result from institutional bias. For example, death rates for all cancers combined for both men and women are highest among Blacks. The age-adjusted death rate for cancer was 25.4% higher for Blacks (243.1 per 100,000) than for Whites (193.9 per 100,000) in 2001. Black women diagnosed with breast cancer are less likely than White women to survive 5 years after diagnosis. Black men have higher death rates from prostate cancer than any other group classified by ethnicity (retrieved from http://crchd.cancer.gov/cnp/pi-albrecht-pilot.html).

In this instance of a health disparity among ethnic groups it is also necessary to consider that this disparity may have several root causes, such as medical delivery, poor diet, unwillingness to get medical care, inadequate insurance, or inability to afford insurance. There is hope that the 2012 Patient Protection and Affordable Health Care Act will prevent some of the disparities due to lack of healthcare insurance. There are many factors that must be explored to determine if a disparity is caused by institutional bias; it may or may not be.

Over the past decade the debate over the right to marry came to the forefront of the political arena and in the social consciousness of U.S. residents. Same-sex couples and their supporters advocated for the civil right to marry. Persons who felt that the right to marry should be only for a man and a woman advocated just as strongly for the opposite position. This denial of rights to a socially accepted convention for one group is another example of institutional bias. Some people see this bias as morally acceptable. What do you think?

Many toxic waste sites are located in predominantly Black and Hispanic low-income communities (Harding & Greer, 1993; Hynes & Lopez, 2007; Mohai & Saha, 2006; Rosenbaum, 2008). Serious health risks for adults, and even more risks for children, are associated with living near toxic waste sites (Faber & Krieg, 2002). Children under 5 years of age are more susceptible to toxicity. The environmental safety of a neighborhood has been correlated with income and race. This is partly because land in these communities is inexpensive and not highly desirable. It is easier to run highway projects through a poor neighborhood than remove more affluent residents. This further raises toxicity exposure.

Environmental researchers in Massachusetts found that communities of color and working-class communities were surrounded by a great many more hazardous sites and toxic waste facilities than wealthier communities and those with a smaller minority population. In a community with a minority population rate of less than 5%, the mean number of toxic sites was less than three per square mile. In communities where the rate of minorities among the population was as high as 24%, the rate of toxic sites per square mile jumped to 27 (Faber & Krieg, 2002). Communities with a large number of poor ethnic minorities face a cumulative exposure rate that is nearly nine times greater than for communities with much smaller ethnic minority populations (Faber & Krieg, 2002).

Toxins come from soil or paint contamination, polluting industrial factories, power plants, and incinerators. People who are exposed to them have significantly higher incidences of life-threatening disorders such as untreated asthma and cancer. Asthma constricts the lungs making it difficult to breathe. It is chronic and can be fatal if not treated promptly and correctly. All children, in any socioeconomic range, can have asthma; however, the highest rates of asthma and asthma-related deaths occur in poor Black and Hispanic neighborhoods.

In Washington state, families with incomes below $20,000 per year were more than twice as likely to have a child with asthma than other families (Massey, 2004). This seriously debilitating illness has been shown to occur significantly more frequently in children attending low-income schools in New York City (Claudio, Stingone, & Godbold, 2006). The U.S. Environmental Protection Agency (2012) has shown that 10- to 14-year-old Black children are six times more likely to die from asthma than are White children of the same age and this disparity has persisted over many years.

What Makes Institutional Bias so Challenging?

There are competing interests, needs, values, and aspirations among groups and persons in a diverse society. Institutional bias is a byproduct of this competition as people of different backgrounds vie for limited resources in situations where discrimination may have existed or still exists. This competition is natural and expected. If it results in bias that limits diverse representation in our institutions the question of fairness enters the equation. Bias that limits diversity can come from individual actions, institutional or societal structures, or from institutional standards of practice. Valuing and managing diversity is one way to address instances of limited diversity in an institution, especially if it is unintentional. The Texaco Company is a good example of first being forced to address biased practices and then managing diversity well after that.

Institutional bias is a challenge to U.S. principles of equality and fairness. If some social groups are systematically excluded from the privileges, rights, and advantages enjoyed by other groups, our ideals are not realized. It is difficult to detect systematic exclusion. However, as the quote mentioned at the beginning of the chapter implies, sometimes it seems to be everywhere and you know a problem exists.

Institutional bias is like individual prejudice but its effects are more far-reaching and widespread (Jones, 1997). Institutional bias can be thought of as individual prejudice magnified to affect an entire social group rather than just an individual. These biases may result from disparate treatment but even if groups are treated equally, disparate outcomes that seem unfair can occur. White men are overwhelmingly holders of executive and management positions and other groups are more likely to be in subordinate roles. As mentioned in Chapter 11, managers tend to see candidates and subordinates who are like them as more competent and valued.

Some institutional bias reflects organizational practices. These practices are initiated and maintained by people in leadership positions. They may appear to be fair but have created differences in opportunities for notable diversity groups that result in disparities in social indicators. When evidence from social indicators, like those discussed earlier in the chapter, become too disparate to ignore, persons or groups may call attention to the bias and label it as unfair.

Fassinger (2008) identifies four groups that are consistently underrepresented, marginalized, or disadvantaged in contemporary U.S. institutions, especially in the workplace: (a) women, (b) people of color, (c) sexual minorities, and (d) people with disabilities. The model shown in Figure 12.2 identifies the major reasons that undermine valuing and achieving appropriate diversity in the workplace. Some barriers to diversity are external and some internal. External barriers include discriminatory practices, a hostile work environment, poor educational opportunities, and inadequate training. Some workers internalize these external barriers, and accept them as appropriate or at least insurmountable, making them difficult to overcome. As we saw in Chapter 7, internalization of prejudice is an ineffective way of handling discrimination. Barriers to diversity may also be either active or passive. For example, an external barrier to diversity that is active could be biased performance evaluations or unequal pay raises not accounted for by meritorious performance. An internalized passive barrier might be the worker's feelings that something is lacking in herself that would make her successful in achieving a pay raise.

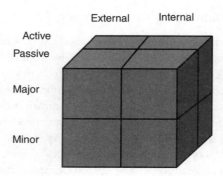

Figure 12.2.   The Theoretical Barriers to Diversity. From "Workplace Diversity and Public Policy: Challenges and Opportunities for Psychology," by R. E. Fassinger, 2008, *American Psychologist, 63,* pp. 252–268.

Effects of Institutional Bias Are Far-reaching

The effects of institutional bias are far-reaching and particularly insidious for two reasons:

1. Individual bias is magnified and its effect more adverse when it is embedded in institutional practices and policies. A person may dislike another individual because of his or her sexual orientation but an institutional policy has a more wide-reaching effect than that of an individual. For example, if the director of human resources for a large hospital corporation has a negative prejudice against gay men, she may refuse to hire anyone she thinks is gay. This informal practice may hurt a few individuals in this woman's hospital, but if this were the policy of most hospitals it would systematically disadvantage an entire group. For this reason, the consequences of biased institutional practices reproduce themselves year after year if left in place.
2. Institutional bias is sometimes very subtle. Perhaps no obvious or overt hostility or prejudice toward any group exists in an institution. A seniority system is an example of how bias may occur unintentionally. Promotion based on seniority is a reasonable and rational policy—the people with the most experience should be in charge. However, seniority contributes to institutional bias when in the past persons of African descent, women, or gays were systematically denied jobs or promotions.

One of the most challenging aspects of institutional bias is determining whether outcomes and opportunities are fairly provided regardless of one's social group status. There is ongoing debate about how to show that the institution's policies have resulted in poorer than expected outcomes for some and better than expected outcomes for others. Another compelling issue involves what we should expect the social outcomes to be for any given group. If everyone has equal access to opportunity, should the outcome be equal results for everyone regardless of race, gender, ethnicity, or sexual orientation? We know this is not possible given naturally occurring differences among individuals. It is more likely that, if all things were equal for all groups, the results for individuals from these groups would not be equal, because we all differ in characteristics like motivation, ability, character, experiences, emotional readiness, and personality traits. Therefore, our successes will naturally vary because they are based on both individual characteristics and whatever access to opportunity a person obtains. For this reason, some have argued that any policy that seeks to create equity in outcomes is trying to overcome the influence of "natural" and "relevant" differences (D'Souza, 1996). But outcomes and opportunities are filtered through social group statuses that are often neither natural nor relevant.

A search for occurrences of institutional bias does not assume that all outcomes for individuals or social groups should be equal. Instead, it seeks to determine if an institution is providing equal access to opportunities for success, and not imposing unnecessary barriers or roadblocks. Each of us should be able to reach our potential, even if our potentials are different. While individual discrimination is illegal, disparities between groups in successful outcomes are not. Showing that disparities exist is not sufficient grounds for determining that discrimination is operating, but these disparities may show how groups are being treated differently.

When we look for evidence of bias, we are more concerned with outcomes than intentions. If rewards for women or persons of color are statistically less frequent than for another social group, institutional practices may or may not account for these differences. To examine bias we need to review policies and procedures at different levels of analysis. One of our challenges in dealing with diversity is to determine how to create a level playing field for all. An institutional bias analysis recognizes that remedies will need to go beyond changing the individual attitudes of explicitly prejudiced people. This could result in dramatic and rapid changes in discriminatory practices.

Emotions May Run High

An individual who perceives that he or she has been treated unfairly generally feels a swift and unpleasant emotional reaction. Feelings of frustration, resentment and anger, and even hopelessness occur. Strong emotional reactions occur because unfairness is at odds with a core principle in our U.S. value system—fairness through respect for individual rights. To correct for past discrimination and unfair treatment, reparations to direct descendants of African-descent slaves have been suggested. Yet persons living in the present day who were not involved with slavery feel this is unfair to them, and resentment builds because they feel strongly that if they had nothing to do with past discrimination and unfair treatment they should not suffer harm or disadvantage. Black persons who have lived with past discrimination and its effects feel resentment too: Why should I not be compensated for the harm my ancestors suffered, and that I suffer because of their disadvantage? When affirmative action, intended as a remedy for past institutional bias, is viewed as unfairly giving priority to someone who is perceived as less qualified than others, the strong and unpleasant emotions associated with unfair treatment are easily understood. However, misunderstandings about affirmative action may be one cause of these strong negative emotional reactions to it and to the concepts of institutional bias and affirmative action (Luppia & Menning, 2007; Mason & Huddy, 2008; Smith, Seger, & Mackie, 2007).

A story about two army sergeants reported in *The New York Times* "How Race is Lived In America" series illustrates the emotional reactions that can occur when a person perceives that institutional bias is affecting them negatively (Correspondents of the New York Times, 2001). President Harry Truman desegregated the U.S. Army in 1948, long before many other American institutions were desegregated (see Chapter 3). Though the army was supposed to be integrated it continued for many years to practice segregation and failed to promote Black persons at the same rate as White persons. Today, however, the army is considered to be a bastion of fairness. This story is about a White drill sergeant who, despite this idealized image of the current army, harbored strong negative feelings because he felt he was not being treated fairly.

At the end of a basic-training cycle, army drill sergeants compete for an award based on their drilling skill. Each sergeant knows that winning the drilling award could lead to promotion and make the difference between scraping by and a better life for a family. Winning the award is important. One of the White sergeants who competed one year and lost became very angry. Senior ranking Black sergeants had given the award to a Hispanic sergeant. Discussing his loss with a friend, the White sergeant stated that he thought he had lost because he was White. He complained that in five of the last six years, the Black sergeants had given the award to a Black or Latino sergeant. The White sergeant felt that a small clique of Black sergeants unfairly disadvantaged him by giving the award to a Hispanic sergeant when his performance had been superior. Determining whether we receive outcomes consistent with our performance is a foundation for determining we are treated fairly. When that determination is negative, resentment is a frequent consequence, no matter what our diversity status may be.

Most desegregated institutions in the United States, and most are, still fail to be truly integrated. Institutions like the armed forces, schools, and most professions can be classified as desegregated since they don't practice open discrimination. Yet many of our institutions are not integrated in the sense that all diversity groups have maximum contact and opportunity. In a **racialized** society where bias has existed for years, it may be difficult to determine who is being treated fairly. A racialized society is one where racial beliefs are actively used to categorize and judge people (Jones, 1997). Although our society may seem to be less racialized today, race categories continue to be used although more subtly. In this condition of uncertainty, a person may feel strong emotions if they are unsure of the fairness of a decision, especially if that decision is being made by a group to which they do not belong. In this situation, the White sergeant felt that he was being disadvantaged by a group of Black sergeants who were giving the advantage to minority sergeants. We learned of similar emotional responses of the young campers in the Robbers Cave experiments from Chapter 6. The issue here is who was best at drilling. Because of past biases in a system that has overwhelmingly favored White soldiers, is it fair to reward the Black sergeant if the two were equally competent at drilling? Past biases make it difficult to determine what is fair.

Maybe Poverty Leads to Institutional Bias

Poverty exists to different degrees in all diversity status groups, and complicates our analysis of institutional bias. Does poverty explain why some institutions appear to be stratified in a way that suggests bias? Let's consider some facts about poverty.

Poverty is not evenly distributed across ethnicity categories. For example, in 2000, only 8% of non-Hispanic Whites lived in poverty, compared with almost 25% of Blacks and 10% of Asians. Poverty rates were almost five times higher (24% vs. 5%) for women raising families alone than for married couples (Dalager & Proctor, 2000). According to the 2010 U.S. Census, 100 million people are either "poor" or "near poor," meaning that almost one third of the population is barely getting by (U.S. Census, 2010); 22% of children living in the United States live in poverty, and the rate is 27% for Blacks and for Hispanics compared with almost 10% for Whites.

As Chapter 3 demonstrates, the history of racism and prejudice has virtually ensured that some ethnic and race minorities are found in the lower economic strata (O'Connor, 2002). So, before we consider the effects of institutional bias, we must be aware that the social forces of poverty have already taken their toll. This makes it difficult to determine whether institutional bias is operating solely or whether other constraints and limitations of poverty are also at work. It is probable that both factors are in play.

In considering the relationship between ethnicity and poverty, we must remember that there is great socioeconomic diversity in all ethnic groups and likewise among both men and women. For example, there are certainly some Blacks who live substantially better than some Whites. However, there is a substantially higher proportion of poor persons among Blacks than Whites in the United States. Blacks have lower employment rates, higher rates of incarceration, lower educational attainment, fewer powerful and high-paying jobs, and poorer overall health (Zack, 2009). In addition, when economic times are bad, or when a disaster strikes, the differences in social inequality become even more apparent (Zack, 2009).

It might seem in some instances that poverty, rather than skin color or gender, is responsible for poor outcomes. William Julius Wilson, a sociologist and professor at Harvard University, suggested this somewhat provocative argument a few decades ago. Wilson argued that skin color discrimination alone could not explain the dire plight of inner city Blacks, because their situation is largely due to macroeconomic forces and inadequate welfare and poverty policies (Wilson, 1987). Wilson's premise was controversial because he went beyond individual discrimination based on skin color to identify economic forces and poverty policies that accounted for adverse impacts (Wilson, 2008, 2009). For Wilson disparate outcomes were due as much, or more, to poverty among African Americans as to racial discrimination. This argument is viewed by some as faulty because it fails to take into account which groups are more likely to be in poverty and why. However, it clearly focuses on a wide array of factors that include institutional bias, historical trends, and cultural tendencies.

Social scientists have been trying to understand poverty, explain its causes, and offer solutions for over a century (Cornfield, 2009; Haskins & Sawhill, 2009; Iceland, 2006).

Women in particular have been negatively affected by poverty, as a result of divorce, because they have traditionally held low-wage positions (teacher, nurse, and childcare worker), or because they are paid less than their male peers (Adair & Dahlberg, 2009; Agee & Walker, 1991). The latter two causes may well be related to institutional bias.

The question Jones (1997) posed years ago remains pertinent today: How much of what we see as inequalities based on diversity characteristics such as skin color, ethnicity, gender, or sexual orientation is a result of the cumulative effects of inequalities at the institutional level, and how much might be due to current low socioeconomic standing for certain groups? Which came first, the racism, sexism, and homophobia, or the poverty? In thinking about the situations that we describe as examples of institutional racism, keep in mind that low socioeconomic standing may be a better explanation than diversity for some of the disparities.

Numerous studies have shown that poverty is strongly negatively correlated with child development. Children in poverty have poorer cognitive and socioemotional developmental outcomes than middle- and high-income children (Duncan & Brooks-Gunn, 2003). Although we know that poverty creates differences in social indicators, it is often difficult to tell how much bias comes from lack of opportunity because of poverty and how much is due to systematic institutional bias.

Preventing Institutional Bias is a Challenge

Solutions for addressing institutional bias are difficult to find. In Chapter 2, we cited a metaphor used by President Lyndon Johnson that compares institutional bias to two runners beginning a race on unequal footing. If runners start in unfair positions, the footrace cannot be concluded fairly. Something must be done to "even the score" or "level the playing field" if a fair race is the goal. When a race is around a track, the starting positions are staggered so that the total distance run by each runner is the same. Jockeys have slightly different weights and so they must carry weights to even out the burden for the horses. Compensating for structural inequalities to make competition fair is standard practice in sports. However, when confronting institutional bias, we have difficulty determining how to get different groups with varying degrees of advantage and disadvantage on an equal footing. How can we approach this problem? The first issue that needs to be addressed in seeking a solution to the problem of institutional bias is determining if the problem exists and if people believe it exists. The second problem then becomes finding a solution to the problem that is perceived as fair in that it benefits all, or at least does not disadvantage anyone unduly.

Valuing Diversity

More and more people recognize that diversity is an important and permanent characteristic of our society. As shown in Chapter 3, diversity has always been a well-recognized feature of the United States. Our society is evolving past a simple recognition of multiculturalism toward the valuing of diversity. Institutions, and often students and employees, argue that diversity is necessary to prepare for living in a multicultural business and social world. And the business community believes that diversity contributes to their bottom line—it is a business necessity. As illustrated in the Texaco example, affirmative diversity means that (a) diversity is recognized and not ignored, (b) diversity is a positive social goal, (c) diversity is valued as a strategy that increases social cohesion and lessens social upheaval, so that (d) organizations and society are strengthened. In most institutions, the term "diversity" refers to persons from a variety of ethnic, socioeconomic, and gender backgrounds. Whites and men often feel excluded from a diversity framework, but if the goal of diversity is to be inclusive of everyone, no identifiable group can be excluded from its purview. Whites and men are diversity groups too.

Some institutions consider diversity as legally necessary to avoid charges of discrimination. Most learn to appreciate diversity as something valuable, perhaps after a discrimination suit, as in the Texaco story. Diversity then becomes not just a legal requirement but also a company asset. Often managers consider that diversity should be sought, cultivated, and managed. This requires making distinctions among affirmative action policies, valuing diversity, and managing diversity. Affirmative action policies are one method of reducing bias, while valuing diversity suggests that an organization or individual understands the importance of diversity for an entire society and for institutional success. An organization manages diversity when it recognizes and seeks diversity to make an institution more successful and able to meet global and national challenges. The purpose of considering diversity is to make sure that all persons who are competent, trained, and interested get to be involved.

As we have seen, people often disagree about the existence of, or remedy for, institutional bias. Those who may be advantaged don't always see the need to address a problem of unfairness because they think things are fair. Things become unfair, they sometimes reason, when unwarranted preferences are given to those disadvantaged others that reduce what they can expect to follow from their hard work and good performance. It seems unfair and difficult to ask a person in an advantaged position to give up some of his or her advantage. Why should those who have already achieved have to give up something? It might be a better idea to think of ways that those who have not had advantaged backgrounds might be given a chance to be advantaged. Broadening the set of criteria for opportunity and merit may be one way to level the playing field. Our resources are not infinite, so simply making more opportunities available to more people may be one way to expand the pie. But in these times resources are shrinking not expanding. How then do we create opportunities that lift all boats? Equitable education and diversity training in higher education may be promising solutions.

Diversity Training in Higher Education

Diversity training in colleges and universities can promote democracy by preparing students to work well with persons from a wide variety of backgrounds (Gurin, Nagda, & Lopez, 2004; Hurtado, 2006). It is effective when well integrated with cultural norms that stress the value of diversity in recruitment, selection, training, evaluation, and dismissal. Fairness has to be applied at all levels. Universities and colleges have established programs to increase student understanding and appreciation of social diversity (Laird, Engberg, & Hurtado, 2005). These programs create situations in which students from different backgrounds can interact and discuss differences in their perspectives and experiences.

Because neighborhoods and schools in the United States are often highly segregated, many students come to relatively diverse higher education settings without ever having experienced diversity first hand. When students learn from diversity programs on campus they are more likely to choose diverse work and living situations (Laird et al., 2005). This may be a way to decrease segregation of social groups. A study of the effects of a diversity program found that at the end of the semester, students who participated in a diversity course had much more positive attitudes toward diversity and more willingness to engage with college students they perceived as different from themselves than those who had not participated (Laird et al., 2005). The researchers concluded that the diversity course was an effective way to influence student attitudes and thus the quality of their interactions with diverse peers compared to enrollment in a management course.

Summary

Institutional bias can take many forms and comes from different sources. It may be intentional or unintentional, subtle or difficult to detect, and it may have negative or positive outcomes. It may stem from individual bias, or it may have an institutional origin. Whatever form it takes, institutional bias leads to disparities based on social categories such as skin color, cultural background, gender, and age. Detecting bias in institutions is a complex task, and is not so much a science as an art.

It is often difficult to prove institutional bias. But we do have an agreed-upon standard, offered by the federal government, that is used to document bias. It is called the four-fifths rule. This rule is the common way that the EEOC calculates whether one group has an advantage in hiring or promotions compared with other groups. If the selection rate for any group is less than 80% of the group with the highest selection rate, the selection process is guilty of producing disparate impact. The four-fifths rule has practical significance. It is easily understood when comparing hiring rates for diversity groups.

Institutional bias has its foundations in institutional racism and magnifies the effects of individual prejudice and bias for two reasons: (a) it spreads instances of individual bias more effectively across decades and groups of individuals; and (b) biases occur as a result of practices that may intentionally and unintentionally promote group inequalities. An individual who is biased against a group of persons can systematically undermine that group because of how he or she can leverage those biases within an institution for maximum effect. But institutional bias can also occur unintentionally with the same effects—differences in access to opportunity and rewards for some groups.

In the economic arena, disparities between Blacks and Whites and between men and women are often the result of bias. In many companies men clearly have an advantage over women when it comes to high status and economic reward. In the area of criminal justice, ethnic minorities experience more severe punishment, profiling, and other unpleasant realities. Institutional bias can also be seen in marriage laws, access to healthcare, and environmental issues such as the areas selected for toxic waste sites. Possible remedies for institutional biases include affirmative action policies, which are both complicated and controversial; diversity training in education; and diversity management in other workplace settings. A major problem is finding a way to address past grievances without harming individuals today who had nothing to do with these past offenses. In the final analysis we have to consider the broad cultural context in which institutional bias occurs. If we consider ourselves to be a nation where justice and equality are our highest ideals, then disparities based on categories that have nothing to do with merit or competence seem patently unfair. How we address institutional bias will depend on individual attitudes and beliefs.

Questions for Thinking and Knowing

1. How are economic trends affecting diverse groups in the United States?
2. What would be a good economic indicator of fairness in the U.S. economy? How should this economic information be disseminated to the public at large?
3. What factors account for the decline in college enrollment for males compared with females?
4. Is racial profiling an effective tool for law enforcement?
5. *The New York Times* series on "race" relations in the United States described in this chapter was conducted over 10 years ago. What has changed since this series was produced? What has remained the same or gotten worse?

Key Terms

Affirmative action
Disparate impact
Diversity training
Four-fifths rule
Individual-mediated bias
Institution
Institutional bias

Institutional racism
Institutional sexism
Racialized
Reverse discrimination
Social indicators
Standard-of-practice bias
Structural discrimination

References

Adair, V. C., & Dahlberg, S. L. (2003). *Reclaiming class: Women, poverty, and the promise of higher education in America*. Philadelphia: Temple University Press.

Agee, M. L., & Walker, R. W. (1991). Feminisation of poverty in America. *Equal Opportunities International, 10*, 24–31.

Austin, A. (2008). *Reversal of fortune: Economic gains of 1990 overturned for African Americans from 2000 to 2007*. Economic Policy Institute Briefing Paper. Retrieved on May 15, 2010 from http://epi.3cdn.net/f205db387e418862d6_c5m6bhw0j.pdf

Ball, H. (2000). *The Bakke case: Race, education and affirmative action*. Lawrence, KS: University of Kansas Press.

Bureau of Labor Statistics. (2010). Labor Force Statistics from the Current

Population Survey. Employment status of the civilian noninstitutional population by age, sex and race. Retrieved from http://www.bls.gov/cps/

Bureau of Labor Statistics. (2011). Women's earnings as a percentage of men's full time wage and salary workers in the United States, 2011 (Chart 1). Retrieved on May 13, 2013 from http://www.bls.gov/ro9/wawomen.htm

Claudio, L., Stingone, J. A., & Godbold, J. (2006). Presence of childhood asthma in urban communities: The impact of ethnicity and income. *Annals of Epidemiology, 16,* 332–340.

Cohen, S. (2004). *The lasting legacy of* An American dilemma. Carnegie Results, Carnegie Corporation of New York. Retrieved on August 13, 2009 from http://carnegie.org/fileadmin/Media/Publications/fall_04americandilemma.pdf

Cornfield, D. B. (2009). Ending poverty in America: How to restore the American Dream. *Social Forces, 87,* 2203–2205.

Correspondents of the New York Times. (2001). *How race is lived in America: Pulling together, pulling apart.* New York: Times Books/Henry Holt Company.

Dalager, J., & Proctor, B. D. (2000). *Poverty in the United States 1999.* U.S. Census Bureau, Current Population Reports P60-210. Washington, DC: U.S. Government Printing Office.

D'Souza, D. (1996). *The end of racism: Principles for a multiracial society.* New York: Free Press.

Duncan, G. J., & Brooks-Gunn, J. (2000). Family poverty, welfare reform, and child development. *Child Development, 71,* 188–196.

Espenshade, T. J., & Chung, C. Y. (2005). The opportunity cost of admission preferences at elite universities. *Social Science Quarterly, 86,* 293–305.

Faber, D. R., & Krieg, E. J. (2002). Unequal exposure to ecological hazards: Environmental injustices in the Commonwealth of Massachusetts. *Environmental Health Perspectives, 110,* 277–288.

Fassinger, R. E. (2008). Workplace diversity and public policy: Challenges and opportunities for psychology. *American Psychologist, 63,* 252–268.

Gabbidon, S. L., & Greene, H. T. (2012). *Race and crime* (3rd ed.). Los Angeles: Sage.

Gurin, P., Nagda, R., & Lopez, G. (2004). The benefits of diversity in education for democratic citizenships. *Journal of Social Issues, 60,* 17–34.

Harding, A. K., & Greer, M. L. (1993). The health impact of hazardous waste sites on minority communities: Implications for public health and environmental health professionals. *Journal of Environmental Health, 55,* 6–9.

Haskins, R., & Sawhill, I. V. (2009). *Creating an Opportunity Society: Economic mobility, children and families, education, federal budget, marriage and family formation.* Washington, DC: Brookings Institution Press.

Hurtado, S. (2006). Diversity and learning for a pluralistic democracy. In W. R. Allen, M. Bonous-Hammarth, & R. Teranishi (Eds.), *Higher education in a global society: Achieving diversity, equity, and excellence* (pp. 249–293). Oxford: Elsevier.

Hynes, H. P., & Lopez, R. (2007). Cumulative risk and a call for action in environmental justice communities. *Journal of Health Disparities Research and Practice, 1,* 29–57.

Iceland, J. (2006). *Poverty in America: A handbook* (2nd ed.). Berkeley: University of California Press.

Johansson, P. (2000). Texaco three years after the fall. Retrieved on January 4, 2010 from http://www.socialfunds.com/news/print.cgi?sfArticleId=131

Jones, J. (1972). *Prejudice and racism.* New York: McGraw-Hill.

Jones, J. (1997). *Prejudice and racism* (2nd ed.). New York: McGraw-Hill.

Laird, F. N., Engberg, M. E., & Hurtado, S. (2005). College students' experiences with diversity and its effects on academic self-confidence, collective agency, and disposition toward critical thinking. *Research in Higher Education, 46,* 365–387.

Levine, H. G., & Sigel, L. (2013). Online library about marijuana possession, arrests, race, and police policy in New York City and beyond. Retrieved from http://marijuana-arrests.com/nyc-pot-arrest-docs.html

Levine, H. G., & Small, D. P. (2008). *Marijuana arrest crusade: Racial bias and police policy in New York City, 1997–2007.* New York: New York Civil Liberties Union. Available from http://www.nyclu.org/files/MARIJUANA-ARREST-CRUSADE_Final.pdf

Luppia, A., & Menning, J. O. (2007). Politics and the equilibrium of fear: Can strategies and emotions interact? In R. Neuman, G. E. Marcus, A. N. Crigler, & M. MacKuen (Eds.), *The affect effect: Dynamics of emotion in political thinking and behavior* (pp. 337–356). Chicago: University of Chicago Press.

Mason, L. H., & Huddy, L. (2008) *Heated campaign politics: An intergroup conflict model of partisan emotions.* Paper presented at the APSA 2008 Annual Meeting, Hynes Convention Center, Boston, Massachusetts. Available at http://www.allacademic.com/meta/p278239_index.html

Massey, D. S. (2004). Segregation and stratification: A biosocial perspective. *Du Bois Review, 1,* 1–19.

Mishel, L., Bernstein, J., & Shierholz, H. (2008). *The state of working America: Economic Policy Institute Report.* Ithaca: Cornell University Press.

Mohai, P., & Saha, R. (2006). Reassessing racial and socioeconomic disparities in environmental justice research. *Demography, 43,* 383–399.

Myrdal, G. (1944). *An American dilemma: The Negro problem and modern democracy.* Piscataway, NJ: Transaction Publishers. Reprinted 1996.

National Association for Single-sex Learning. (2012). *What are some differences in how girls and boys learn?* Retrieved on October 8, 2012 from http://www.singlesexschools.org/research-learning.htm

O'Connor, A. O. (2002). *Poverty knowledge: Social science, social policy, and the poor in twentieth century U.S. history.* Princeton: Princeton University Press.

O'Dell, L. (2001, January 1). A math class of their own. *Los Angeles Times.* Retrieved on October 12, 2012 from http://articles.latimes.com/2001/jan/10/local/me-10623

Pierce, G. P., & Radelet, M. L. (2005). The impact of legally inappropriate factors on death sentencing for California homicides. *Santa Clara Law Review, 46,* 1–47.

Plous, S. (2003). Ten myths about affirmative action. In S. Plous (Ed.), *Understanding prejudice and discrimination* (pp. 206–212). New York: McGraw-Hill.

Rosenbaum, E. (2008). Racial/ethnic differences in asthma prevalence: The role of housing and neighborhood environments. *Journal of Health and Social Behavior, 49,* 131–145.

Smith, E. R., Seger, C., & Mackie, D. (2007). Can emotions be truly group level? Evidence regarding four conceptual criteria. *Journal of Personality and Social Psychology, 93,* 431–446.

Sowell, T. (2004). *Affirmative action around the world.* New Haven: Yale University Press.

United for a Fair Economy. (2009). Sub-prime as a Black catastrophe. Retrieved from http://faireconomy.org/news/subprime_as_a_black_catastrophe

United Nations Human Development Program. (2011). *United Nations Human Development Report, 2011. Sustainability and equity: A better future for all.* Retrieved from http://hdr.undp.org/en/reports/global/hdr2011/

U.S. Census. (2012). *Homeownership rates by race and ethnicity of householder 2009 to 2011.* Retrieved from http://www.census.gov/housing/hvs/

U.S. Environmental Protection Agency. (2012). *Presidential Task Force on Environmental Health and Safety Risks to Children: Coordinated Federal Action Plan to Reduce*

Racial and Ethnic Asthma Disparities. Washington, DC: Environmental Protection Agency. Retrieved on October 12, 2012 from http://www.epa.gov/childrenstaskforce/federal_asthma_disparities_action_plan.pdf

Wilson, W. J. (1987). *The truly disadvantaged: Poverty, the underclass, and social policy.* Chicago: University of Chicago Press. Reprinted 2012.

Wilson, W. J. (2008). The political and economic forces shaping concentrated poverty. *Political Science Quarterly, 123,* 555–571.

Wilson, W. J. (2009). *More than just race: Being black and poor in the inner city.* New York: W. W. Norton and Company.

Zack, N. (2009). Race, class and money in disaster. *Southern Journal of Philosophy, 47,* 84–103.

Chapter 13

The Psychology of Diversity
Principles and Prospects

Introduction   356
Diversity Is Diverse   357
Diversity When It Is All Good   359
Diversity Is Normal   361
Doing Diversity Is Hard   362
Principles of Diversity: What Have We Learned in This Book?   365
Conclusion   371

> *At this University if you are not a minority you are very much discriminated against and do not have as much opportunity. It is as if you are being punished for being a majority!*
>
> White college student

> *Diversity at this university is disgustingly terrible. Something drastic needs to be done to promote a more actively diverse campus, because you can feel the tension around campus if you are of a race that is not mainly the majority race on campus.*
>
> Latino college student

> *Diversity can be good and bad at the same time. Diversity helps to broaden how people think about the world yet many people end up being cheated when diversity becomes a key issue.*
>
> White college student
> Blue Hen Poll (2012)

The Psychology of Diversity: Beyond Prejudice and Racism, First Edition. James M. Jones,
John F. Dovidio, and Deborah L. Vietze.
© 2014 Blackwell Publishing Ltd. Published 2014 by Blackwell Publishing Ltd.

Introduction

This book is about the psychology of diversity. Diversity is a both a compelling interest and a compelling challenge of the twenty-first century. Psychologist Daryl Smith calls it an *imperative!*—"Diversity is a powerful agent of change . . . an imperative that must be embraced if colleges and universities are to be successful in a pluralistic and inter-connected world" (Smith, 2009, p. 3). The indisputably growing diversity across the United States and around the globe creates a new world, socially, politically, and eco-nomically. Understanding the psychology of diversity can help us, individually and collectively, make informed and responsible decisions that will shape this new world.

This book has focused on the psychology of diversity in multiple ways by (a) highlighting basic psychological processes that are triggered when we encounter people who are different from us in significant and salient ways; (b) examining how people cope and adapt to being treated differently by others because of their social status; (c) exploring the dynamics of mental representation and social interac-tion across individuals, institutions, and cultures; (d) analyzing how differential bases of power, privilege, and status affect these interactions; and (e) identifying the effects of diverse contexts on the thoughts, actions, and feelings of all people in them.

As we have seen throughout this book, diversity is an expanding characteristic of our society and poses challenges to us every day. Some suggest that diversity itself is natural and is not the challenge; rather, it is the issue of how we choose to deal with diversity that is the challenge. To some extent that is true. As we saw in Chapter 3, the United States has always been diverse along ethnic, religious, racial, nationality, regional, and class lines. How we have dealt with it, though, has changed and evolved over time.

We present evidence that diversity or difference per se can trigger basic psychologi-cal responses that often make us defensive, dismissive, and distance ourselves from others. The structure and function of our brains and hormones can play a critical role in how we perceive and respond to others who are different from us. On the other hand, people in the United States hold true to the ideal that we are all created equal and we each have the right to freedom and the pursuit of happiness. Most of us embrace core U.S. values, such as equality and opportunity for all, but our differences intrude on these values, and we make judgments about each other based on some-times superficial differences. Dissimilarities often lead to discrimination and inequality, and social injustice ensues.

Hostility and negativity associated with prejudice and racism lead to the social exclusion of diverse groups and pose significant challenges to how we handle diversity. But reducing this bias, though very significant, is not enough. To create relationships, settings and contexts, institutions and organizations, and society, it is necessary to both reduce or eliminate discrimination and bias *and* discover and implement ways to achieve the benefits that diversity offers.

In this book, we focus our attention on these challenging issues of diversity. For example, personally and as a society should we emphasize the distinctiveness of social groups or the commonalities that people share within and across groups? Both per-spectives are important to diversity, and choosing one over the other seems clearly to be unwise. Therefore, in this book we aim for a more expansive perspective that emphasizes a both/and rather than an either/or approach.

Diversity is like a Rorschach inkblot test. In this test, people look at a series of large ambiguous inkblots and describe what they see and the meaning that comes to mind. Different people see different things in each inkblot, depending on their experiences, emotional state, needs, and wishes. Similarly, different people view diversity differently. Some Whites may see it as something that excludes them. People who belong to an underrepresented group but are not Black or Latino may also feel that diversity does not include them. In addition, there are many different bases for diversity in a given context (see also Chapter 10), among which are race, ethnicity, gender, immigrant status, nationality, sexual orientation, age, physical disability status, geographical region, socioeconomic status, religion, values, beliefs, cognitive style, identity, and preference.

As one university student put it in response to a survey of attitudes about diversity on their campus: "Diversity is used in so many ways I usually do not know how to interpret the word when I hear it being thrown around on campus" (Blue Hen Poll, 2012). Because diversity applies to so many types of difference, it is hard to understand what it means. In this book, we have focused on the psychology of diversity principles to help us understand the dynamics of diversity. We emphasized both what is common among different types of diversity (e.g., the ways people react to difference) and how different forms of diversity are distinct. We illustrate diversity dynamics at the micro-levels of the brain up to the macro-levels of social structure. We describe processes within and between diverse groups. We may not have a simple and succinct answer to the student, but we hope we have brought better understanding of the ways in which diversity influences and is influenced by basic psychological processes.

In this chapter, we review some of the compelling issues posed by diversity. We then discuss some of the challenges *of* diversity, including the diversity within diverse groups and intersection of multiple group identities within individuals. We examine the growing complexity these forms of diversity and intersectionality produce. We next consider some of the benefits of diversity for people, educational institutions, and organizations. This chapter also considers some of the obstacles or challenges *to* diversity posed by biases and basic psychological and institutional processes and practices. In the final section, we review what we hope you have learned from this book.

Diversity Is Diverse

In a wide-reaching Supreme Court decision about affirmative action, Justice Sandra Day O'Connor acknowledged that diversity is a compelling interest in higher education, the military, businesses, and society in general (see Chapter 1). But what is diversity? Throughout this book we have seen that it is an elusive concept.

Although race and ethnicity have largely been the focus of diversity in our society, gender has also been an important focus of diversity efforts in the area of equal pay and equal access to certain professions (Moss-Racusin, Dovidio, Brescoll, Graham, & Handelsman, 2012). Disability status, age, sexual orientation, religion, socioeconomic status, culture, and immigration status, when added to the mix, make the picture more complicated. When we further consider the intersections of these multiple groups within a person, labeled intersectionality (Purdie-Vaughns & Eibach, 2008), it becomes even more daunting to create diversity contexts that benefit everyone, without unduly harming anyone. This section explores some factors that need to be considered in our exploration of diversity.

Diversity is not merely a new term for race and ethnicity. Diversity captures the idea that we are different from each other in myriad ways. In addition, in some situations some differences matter more. For example, on the athletics field, gender may matter more than race. However, diversity also includes the idea that we are similar in many ways. These facts contribute to the complexity that diversity challenges us to address. For example, race recedes in significance when people share similar characteristics, for example, students attending the same school (Hehman, Stanley, Gaertner, & Simons, 2011). People are both different in some aspects and the same in others. Hence a **both/ and paradigm** is necessary to analyze and understand diversity.

It is also important to note that diversity resides within individuals (intersectionality) and groups. Most frequently, we think of diversity as differences between groups of people: members of one racial group are different from members of another racial group. But each of us belongs to multiple groups and see ourselves as a complex intersection of identities. For example, you can be a woman, an athlete, and a Republican and have multiple defining characteristics: campus leader, member of a Greek organization, Hispanic. And so one could say, we are individually diverse just like settings, institutions, and societies are diverse.

We all have many characteristics that make up who we are, and each of them can influence our behavior. For example, we saw in Chapter 8 that Asian American women did better on math problems when their cultural identity was salient, but worse when their gender identity was salient (Shih, Pittinsky, & Ambady, 1999). An Asian American woman is both Asian and a woman! The implications of one aspect of diversity may be quite different from those of another and each can influence behavior depending on the setting or context.

Diversity also characterizes groups. Groups are not monolithic, despite the general tendency to stereotype them. Racial identity is a good example. For some Blacks, racial identity is a central aspect of who they are; for others, an emphasis on commonalities with other individuals is paramount; while for others, Blackness is a driving force behind all they think and do (Sellers, Rowley, Chavous, Shelton, & Smith, 1997; see Chapter 8). Some older Americans embody negative aging stereotypes, and others do not. When they do, their health status deteriorates more quickly. Among people aged 49 and under, those who held negative age stereotypes were found to be significantly more likely to experience heart problems as they grew older than those who had positive age stereotypes when they were younger (Levy, Zonderman, Slade, & Ferrucci, 2009).

So here is a challenge: Is it possible to be welcoming and supportive and draw benefits from each of these dimensions of diversity? If we treat each person as an individual, the differences these categories represent may lead to adverse consequences for people who belong to more than one of these groups. In the diversity debate, every group does or should count, and so should every person. This dilemma is captured nicely by optimal distinctiveness theory (Brewer, 1991; see Chapter 6).

Optimal distinctiveness theory proposes that people prefer membership in small groups to satisfy their competing motives for differentiation and assimilation. Hornsey and Hogg (1999) tested this idea by assessing the strength and inclusiveness of one's superordinate identity as a student at the University of Queensland in Australia. Students were divided into two groups, math/science or humanities majors. Results showed that the more inclusive their superordinate identity as a University of Queensland student, the more positive bias students showed toward their own major. In other words, the more being a student at the university defined a person, the more he or she needed to differentiate and claim a subgroup identity.

The good news from optimal distinctiveness theory is the benefit of balance. Diversity cannot be successful in an all-or-none, zero-sum, either/or framework. Such a framework promotes competition between and among people and groups; and the more diversity there is, the more competition there is. There are times when we all belong to the same team and draw positive benefits from that. There are times when we need to be different or distinctive and draw positive benefits from that. All of us have these same general needs. Creating a balance over contexts and across time provides much greater flexibility for pursuing a diversity agenda in which everyone can get the support and opportunities they seek. If diversity is a compelling interest because it benefits everyone, then we may have to recognize that those benefits may be different for different people at different times. A both/and framework may offer the best approach to reaping the positive benefits of diversity.

Diversity When It Is All Good

All the challenges to diversity do not come from bias and discrimination. Diversity is not simply about good versus evil, or right versus wrong. Challenges to diversity also occur when two good ideas, beliefs, principles, or practices conflict with one another. Achieving one may undermine pursuit of the other. The greater the diversity of background, motivations, expectations, and needs in a given context, the greater the probability that two valid and desirable objectives may clash.

Consider again the First and Fourteenth Amendments to the Constitution. As we saw in Chapter 3, the First Amendment grants freedom of speech, while the Fourteenth Amendment grants equal protection to all citizens under the law. Hate speech poisons learning or work environments and its targets seek protection by the Fourteenth Amendment. The utterers of hate speech avow their free speech rights as granted by the First Amendment.

As we noted in previous chapters, our culture, institutions, and history influence the values that shape our responses to diversity. In the United States, we value both the First and Fourteenth Amendments, which creates a challenge to diversity. Other countries see things differently. The Canadian Human Rights Act, for instance, prohibits by law "hate propaganda," including hateful messages about minority groups posted on the internet. The South African Constitution requires tolerance of every religion.

Many challenges to diversity involve tension between values that are perceived to be in conflict. Consider, for example, another student's point of view:

> I am all for diversity but lowering the standards of the University in order to accept more diverse individuals and change the face of the University is an injustice to the students who have to work with these ill equipped individuals in the classroom. (Blue Hen Poll, 2012)

This student's perspective pits diversity against merit. By this logic, a White student with a SAT score of, say, 1200 deserves to be admitted to a university more than a Black student with a score of 1135. Admitting the Black student over the White student may enhance diversity but it undermines meritocracy, this logic suggests. However, the perception of conflict between diversity and merit is partially false because it supposes that measures of potential capability are fair and unbiased (Walton, Spencer, & Erman, 2013). If they are not fair and unbiased, how can there be a general standard of merit? When this systematic bias occurs, it leads to institutional bias (see Chapter 11).

Walton and colleagues reviewed a large body of research and found that measures of intellectual ability systematically underestimate the academic potential of people from groups that are negatively stereotyped in academic settings. Black and Latino students who reported experiencing more stereotype threat (see Chapter 8) had lower GPAs, and this was particularly true when they had few ethnic minority professors. In addition, when they analyzed the findings of over 39 laboratory studies in five countries, these researchers found that the performance of students experiencing stereotype threat underestimated their ability (indicated by their performance when stereotype threat was removed) by 20% of a standard deviation. The standard deviation of the SAT is 100, so removing stereotype threat could increase our hypothetical Black student's score by 20 points. Furthermore, the standard error of difference (SED) of the SAT is 60 points. This means that if the SAT scores of two people are within 60 points of each other, they do not differ in either math or verbal ability. If we add 20 points for the stereotype threat effect and 60 for the difference error, the two scores are 1200 and 1205. So if subtle forms of bias exist in the context of measuring ability, we cannot conclude that a White student's 1200 SAT is superior to a Black student's 1135 score.

What's the point here? Diversity should not be thought of as operating at the expense of fairness, of individual liberties and rights, or of overall institutional quality. There is a wide range of relevant qualities that constitute merit, and there are many biases in standards of merit. For some groups, such as racial or ethnic minority groups, people see a trade-off between group membership and standards, while for other groups they don't think in the same terms.

For instance, in many private colleges, sons and daughters of alumni are admitted with lower SAT scores, on average, than other students. In many universities, athletes have, on average, lower SAT scores than non-athletes. These preferences are all diversity issues. Do they sacrifice quality? Do they seek quality in other areas? The mission of a university is also broad. It is not simply to have the highest average SAT scores of the incoming class, but also to produce graduates who are psychologically healthy, socially comfortable, civic minded, skilled, and productive members of society. SAT scores alone do not predict this.

Approaches that benefit one person or group may sometimes disadvantage another. In many cases, though, it is the perception of being disadvantaged rather than the actual impact of policies that challenges diversity. A major factor in people's opposition to programs promoting diversity is their perception of how the policy might disadvantage them personally and their group generally (Lowery, Unzueta, Knowles, & Goff, 2006).

Diversity not only poses challenges to society; because social change is often needed to accommodate—and to benefit from—diversity, individuals and societies present many challenges to achieving diversity goals. In the next section we illustrate the benefits, and then after that we consider the challenges to diversity.

Diversity Is Normal

In the movie *Wall Street*, Gordon Gekko asserted that greed is good. We assert that diversity is normal and that, in general, it is good. How we deal with it, though, may not be. The good: Diversity brings different perspectives, experiences and abilties that may enrich a setting or context and pursuit of a goal. The bad: Diversity is also the basis of war, genocide, aggression, and oppression. Differences do matter. This is not an assertion of political belief or ideology or even a value judgment about society. It is a summation of what science tells us about life on the planet.

Human diversity is essential to successful evolution and overall advancement of the species. The value of diversity comes from an ability to adapt to changing circumstances, the flexibility that comes from variety, and the role of complexity in protecting against the genetic devastation that occurs when an organism is dependent on only one mode of behavior. Financial advisors warn people about investing in a single company or industry; they recommend a "diverse portfolio." Farmers have learned not to depend on a single crop ("mono-cropping")—not only will the same crop deplete nourishment from the soil faster, but also it makes farmers vulnerable to devastation caused by blights or insects. The boll weevil, a type of beetle, infested cotton crops in the United States in the 1920s, financially devastating farmers who relied solely on cotton for their income. Whether in business, art, health, propagation of the species, or basic human understanding, diversity is valuable.

There is ample social science evidence that a wide range of benefits accrue from racial, ethnic, and social class diversity on college campuses. Bowen and Bok (1998) tracked almost 80,000 undergraduate students who matriculated into 28 selective colleges in 1951, 1976, and 1989. They analyzed the experiences and consequences of higher education on students from different racial/ethnic groups over these three generations. Using data on salaries, workforce participation, family structure, civic engagements, and leisure activities, they found that students accepted into elite campuses through race-sensitive admission policies did extremely well after graduation in terms of economic, educational, and civic contributions to society.

In addition, this series of studies demonstrated the remarkably high levels of community service and civic engagements of students of color while attending college and in subsequent years. Black graduates of selective colleges, even more than Whites, are highly engaged in civic activities. This evidence bodes well for the contributions of diversity to a strong and engaged multiracial democracy.

The Intergroup Relations Program for first-year college students (Gurin, Nagda, & Lopez, 2004) was a more focused study of the benefits of diversity (see Chapters 1 and 10). A key element of this program is the Intergroup Dialogues Course. This course, recognizing that diversity is more than skin deep, is based on five principles for bringing diversity and democracy into alignment: (a) presence of diverse others, (b) discontinuity from pre-college experiences, (c) equality among peers, (d) discussion under rules of civil discourse and normalization, and (e) negotiation of conflict. Participants came from diverse backgrounds, and the curriculum consisted of readings, lectures and papers, and intergroup dialogues.

The intergroup dialogues brought together students from two different identity groups that had a history of disagreements over group-relevant policy issues. Several measures were taken 3 years later, during the students' senior year. Results showed that Intergroup Relations Program participants, compared with students in a control group, were more likely to believe that differences were not divisive, conflict was not bad, and learning about other groups was desirable and worthwhile. The students in the program were also more likely to be interested in politics and to participate in campus civic and political activities. They also felt they were more likely to be active in the community and to promote racial/ethnic understanding once they graduated.

Another larger study, the Michigan Student Survey (MSS), examined similar participation and attitude data from a larger cohort of University of Michigan students who entered in 1990. The MSS data showed that White students who lived in predominantly White segregated communities prior to college report more contact with students of color while in college, and this contact was largely positive in terms of cooperative and personal relationships, interracial understanding, and perspective taking (Gurin et al., 2004).

An empirical analysis of learning outcomes demonstrates that students across racial and ethnic groups report positive relationships between student learning and classroom diversity. Indeed, White students with the most experience with diversity during college reflected the largest growth in complex thinking processes, motivation, postgraduate degree aspirations, and commitment to intellectual and academic skills.

Similarly, students who experienced the most diversity in the classroom and in casual interactions with peers reported the most civic engagement and cross-racial interactions after graduation. These students were also most likely to accept the idea that group differences are compatible with the interests of the broader community. Gurin et al. (2004) conclude that diversity of the student body is critical to fulfilling higher education's mission to enhance learning and encourage democratic outcomes and values.

Doing Diversity Is Hard

Attempts to increase diversity in a setting and realize its beneficial consequences will make any situation more complex. Following are some of the challenging issues that efforts to create and support diverse settings must take into account.

Diversity Demands Change

Diversity demands change. Unwanted change threatens both the structure of society and individual security. Laws and policies are designed to create stability and social order, but diversity changes the complexion of a society, introduces new ways of doing things, and suggests alternative values. Societies experience cultural inertia (Zárate, Shaw, Marquez, & Biagas, 2012). At the institutional level, a society may invoke new laws and policies to protect the status quo (Chapter 3). At the individual level, people tend to believe that "what is" is best, and they resist changes to the ways things are (Chapter 6). Thus, the history of the United States reflects a series of new laws designed to limit the threat of diversity, such as anti-immigration laws and policies limiting the opportunities of members of racial and ethnic minority groups. But laws have also been passed that increase diversity in institutions and societies, including affirmative action and immigration laws (see Chapters 3 and 12).

Diversity Sometimes Stands Opposed to Fairness

What is fair to one person may not be to another; what seems fair at one point in history may become unfair later. Affirmative action is an important way to create opportunity and minimize discrimination for some but may be perceived as a reverse form of bias for others. What is fair? Any perception that a program or outcome is unfair challenges one's acceptance of it. And when individuals feel they are treated unfairly because they've not been rewarded, particularly when another person who has performed the same or more poorly has been, they resent it. Racialized resentment has been shown to be a major factor affecting opposition to policies presumed to benefit minority groups and women, for example, affirmative action, Black and White political candidates, and in other circumstances where individuals feel that race is being used to justify rewards, celebration, or positive feelings that are presumably undeserved (Wilson & Davis, 2011).

Further, as shown in the Walton et al. (2013) research, fairness judgments may be applied at several points, including historical circumstances, situational factors, and outcomes. What is fair is not simple to determine, and diversity considerations make it even more complicated.

Bias Has Deep-seated Psychological Roots and Consequences

We are all susceptible to biases against diversity. Mental shortcuts help us deal with day-to-day living, but they also increase the likelihood of biased judgments against people who are outside our in-group (Chapter 5). Our brains are organized to detect and categorize differences, which increases the chances of distancing ourselves from others. Preferences for one's own race and gender begin early in life and increase with age (Chapter 10). In adulthood preference for, and sensitivity to, one's own group further divides us into in-groups and out-groups (Chapter 6).

A range of personality variables relating to ethnocentrism—support for hierarchical group relations, respect for authority and tradition, low tolerance for ambiguity, cognitive rigidity, and need for closure—predict greater prejudice (Chapter 4).

Furthermore, people who are racists also tend to be sexist, anti-Semitic, homophobic, Islamophobic, anti-immigrant, and biased against homeless people.

Bias is often unconscious and subtle When people are unaware of their own bias, they are unable to avoid it, and they often reject the idea that they are biased at all (Chapter 7). Therefore it is easy for people to think they are unbiased, which may make bias difficult to detect and address.

People's reactions are subtle and complicated No two people react the same, and there are many different ways people react to being victimized by discrimination. Reactions to being stigmatized, marginalized, or discriminated against include sensitivity to racial rejection, internalization of the stigmatized status, and justification of the system that marginalizes you (Chapter 8). Even when people do not endorse the way society stigmatizes their group, simply being aware of social stereotypes arouses stereotype threat, which leads people to act in negative stereotype-confirming ways, even when it is not in their best interest. Thus, the performance and well-being of racial and ethnic minorities can be adversely affected even in the absence of immediate discrimination. These subtle processes make efforts to create favorably diverse environments and settings, ones that create full participation and meet established goals and objectives, that much harder to achieve.

Diversity Complicates Interpersonal and Intergroup Interactions

People are typically wary of those who are different. Wariness leads to low expectations and even to anxiety. We project our negative expectations onto those who are different, and our insecurity leads the other person to behave in ways that confirm the appropriateness of the wariness (Chapter 9). Concepts like pluralistic ignorance describe this gap in mutual understanding and subsequent behavioral conflict.

Some differences carry inherent conflict Cultural differences are often reflected in different values, perceptions, goals, and experiences (Chapter 10). Therefore, different cultures may at times be in direct conflict. Disparities in education, wealth, and health all create differences that may oppose one another. Policies that benefit one group may unintentionally conflict with the ends of another.

Power and control are unevenly distributed across social groups The several consequences of uneven power differentials are that fairness and justice are calculated differently, stereotyping is more prevalent among the powerful, and self-interest can widen the gaps (Chapter 11). These differences in power and control complicate how people respond to diversity.

Different groups often interpret and understand diversity in different ways Diversity is often associated with uncertainty about society and one's place in it. While some people may see promise in the change, others feel threatened and seek to justify the current social structure. **Cultural inertia**—the desire to avoid cultural change if it alters the status quo and forces you to change or, conversely, to ride the wave of change if it carries you to a better position in society—can influence whether one desires or resists change. Multiculturalism requires little change by minorities but more by majorities. Assimilation requires little change by majorities and more by minorities (Zárate & Shaw, 2010; see also Chapter 12). Members of racial and ethnic minority groups tend to see promise while members of majority groups tend to see problems (Chapter 11). When people disagree about what diversity is, what it means, or whether it is good or bad, that is certainly a challenge to how we react to diversity.

Further, sometimes personality factors may not lead to opposition but to a reframing of what diversity is. People high in social dominance (anti-egalitarian) broaden the meaning of diversity to non-racial groups when racial diversity is low, but people low in dominance (egalitarian) do it when racial diversity is high. The less clearly delineated the meaning of diversity, the more people construe its meaning to fit their social motivations (Unzueta, Knowles, & Ho, 2012).

In summary, the barriers to achieving diversity are big ones. They reside in human nature, are tied to the important roles of groups in our evolution and in contemporary life, and to motivations to preserve the structure of society and the nature of culture as they are. But the value that diversity offers makes it important that we confront these barriers individually and as a society.

Principles of Diversity: What Have We Learned in This Book?

The challenges to diversity are many and potent. These challenges are also complex, often involving competing positive values. It is obvious that there is no simple or easy answer to address the complexities of diversity, but psychological research and theory provide some guidance. In this section, we identify some "lessons learned" about human psychology based on empirical evidence presented in this book that can help us achieve the benefits that diversity offers.

Bias Against Diversity Is Not Inevitable

Our brains are structured in ways that make us alert to difference and threatened by uncertainty (Chapter 7). We evolved successfully because of our capacity to understand the world around us. Often that leads us to oversimplify the world, dividing others into in-group and out-group members and stereotyping members of other groups (Chapter 5). But all these processes are highly flexible; we are intellectually agile and emotionally labile. Noticing difference may be an innate capacity, but responding negatively to it is not.

As early as 6 months of age, infants can discriminate individual faces from their own and other races, but process all faces equally well. But by 9 months of age, the ability to process other-race faces as effectively as own-race faces is typically lost—infants lose the ability to distinguish members of other races from one another. Research suggests that this is an important step toward developing in-group bias. This step can be attenuated, if not eliminated, by exposing infants to diversity. Regularly showing White infants pictures of Chinese faces enables 9-month-old infants to maintain their ability to process Asian faces as efficiently as White faces and as accurately distinguish different Chinese faces from one another (Anzures et al., 2012; Heron-Delaney et al., 2011).

Diversity Presents Opportunities to Learn

Because of our fundamental drive to understand our world better, we learn from novel situations and from people who are different from us in salient and important ways (Chapter 5). Throughout our life, we balance security with our desire for novelty. Infants vacillate between the security of their parents and the adventure of exploring their surroundings. Don't you easily get bored with the same old routine? People crave new experiences and ideas, as well as comfort and security. Diversity offers these new opportunities. Across all societies, cultures value both security and openness to change (Schwartz, 1992), and individuals balance the need for certainty with an appetite for novelty. Diversity thus does not have to be feared; people can be motivated by fundamental drives to seek diversity.

Interaction Improves Attitudes Toward Other Groups

People who have frequent and positive interactions with members of other groups develop more favorable attitudes toward diversity (Pettigrew, 1998; Pettigrew & Tropp, 2011). These effects apply cross-culturally for a range of different groups and occur even when this contact is not entirely voluntary, and even for groups with whom we have not had direct contact. One reason why contact improves attitudes is that it helps us see others in more personalized ways, which in turn helps us appreciate them as individuals and undermines stereotypes. Cooperative contact is particularly effective for improving intergroup relations, in part because it changes the typical "we–they" way we see our groups to a more inclusive "we" (Chapter 5). Having superordinate goals—goals that neither group can achieve alone but can accomplish only if they work together—can reduce even intense conflict between groups (Chapter 6).

Diverse Contexts Promote Flexibility, Adaptability, and Creativity

Sometimes social and cultural diversity is experienced in a way that challenges stereotypical expectations (Chapter 5). When contexts are diverse, we interact with people who are different from us in varying ways as we have noted (Chapter 10). Good things can happen when those diverse experiences challenge expectations or stereotypes we may have of people from different groups. But stereotypes are not reality. Others may behave in ways that challenge our stereotypes of them. When this happens, we may abandon the stereotype as wrong, or look for other information that supports it, or simple reexamine it. The process of making these determinations may both suppress stereotyping and enhance creative thinking (Crisp & Turner, 2011). For instance, White students show greater integrative complexity when they work in groups that include either a racial or an opinion minority (Antonio et al., 2004) or, more generally, when they have more racially diverse friends and classmates. In addition, people who have more culturally diverse experiences become more creative and socially adaptable

(Leung, Maddux, Galinsky, & Chiu, 2008). Thus, diversity has many personal benefits for majority-group members.

Personal Motivation Can Limit or Prevent Bias

Many theories of prejudice emphasize personality and other individual-difference factors that lead to prejudice and discrimination (Chapter 4). However, other personality dimensions are related to motivations to not be biased. For example, people differ in their tendency to be internally or externally motivated to respond without prejudice (Plant & Devine, 2009). People who are internally motivated try to inhibit their intergroup biases because such prejudice violates their personal standards and values; people who are externally motivated avoid being biased because they are concerned about what other people think of them. Both internal and external motivations reduce bias, but internal motivation does so more generally and effectively. In addition, although implicit biases, which are automatically activated and often unconscious (Chapter 7), often produce subtle bias and discrimination, when people who desire to be non-prejudiced learn that their behavior does not conform to their standards, they attempt to adjust their behavior and try harder to live up to their standards in the future.

Belief That Biases Can Be Changed Increases People's Interest in Diversity

Many majority-group members avoid interacting with members of other groups because they are concerned about appearing biased (Chapter 7). However, they are more interested in and comfortable with diversity when they believe that they can do something about their biases. Majority-group members who believe prejudice is malleable rather than relatively fixed are more interested in interracial activities relating to race or diversity or activities to reduce their prejudice (Carr, Dweck, & Pauker, 2012). They are also more comfortable in interracial interactions (Chapter 9). In an experimental study, students who were taught a more malleable belief became more interested in interracial interactions, while students who were taught a fixed belief became more anxious and unfriendly in interracial interactions. The important point here is that your beliefs may affect your diversity-related attitudes and behaviors, but it is possible to develop a set of beliefs that are associated with pro-diversity behaviors.

People Can Learn To Be Unprejudiced

A person who is motivated to be unprejudiced can take positive action (Chapter 10) when he or she becomes aware of prejudiced behavior (Chapter 9). With some training, such individuals can learn what situations activate prejudices and how to replace their biases with positive responses. When students received feedback on their degree of racial bias, saw a video about the prevalence of implicit bias in society, and were trained in five bias-reducing techniques, they became more aware and concerned about their own prejudice behavior, were more motivated to recognize and change it, and scored lower on implicit prejudice as much as 2 years later (Devine, Forscher, Austin, & Cox, 2012).

Approach and Avoidance Motivations Are Keys to Diversity Dynamics

Diversity (i.e., difference) often fosters avoidance (Chapter 9), and thus diversity cannot be achieved in a climate dominated by avoidance motives. As we saw in Chapter 10, though, people can adopt different perspectives on diversity. **Prevention focus** and **promotion focus** are two terms that have been shown to explain how people differ in their motivations to interact with others (Shah, Brazy, & Higgins, 2004). Prevention focus involves being motivated by feelings of duty, obligation, or responsibility, and people try to avoid such situations. Promotion focus involves desires to support others or to achieve some desired goals, and we tend to seek or approach these types of situations. Prevention motives have been shown to be related to bias against an out-group (Shah et al., 2004). Promotion motives, by contrast, reduce even spontaneously activated biases and stereotypes (Richeson & Nussbaum, 2004). In addition, when people adopt a frame of mind in which difference is respected, such as a multicultural perspective, both majority and minority groups are more engaged in their intergroup interactions and are more attentive to each other than when they try to ignore differences, such as when they adopt a colorblind perspective (Vorauer & Sasaki, 2009).

Individual Ideology and Values Determine Diversity Attitudes, Support, and Actions

As we have noted, responses to diversity are complex, and opposition to diversity is not simply a case of dislike of other groups. Often values come into conflict (Chapter 10). Many people oppose programs, such as affirmative action, that are designed to promote diversity because they believe that these programs are unfair, rewarding group membership rather than individual merit (Chapter 12). For example, people with strongly held meritocratic values tend to also be strongly opposed to affirmative action (Son Hing, Bobocel, & Zanna, 2002). However, when presented with information that current discrimination interfered with minorities' opportunities to get what they deserved (a violation of meritocracy), the same people became less opposed to affirmative action and more supportive of programs that would assist members of minority groups. In addition, when Whites believe that they did not fairly merit their social advantages over other groups, they also become more willing to support affirmative action and programs to assist minority groups (Lowery, Chow, Knowles, & Unzueta, 2012). Fairness is the fabric of human relationships (Chapter 5); it is essential to coordination and social life. People will generally do what is fair. How diversity is framed thus determines whether people will support or oppose diversity programs.

People Are Resilient in the Face of Discrimination

Discrimination damages people materially as well as psychologically (Chapter 8). In general, when we perceive discrimination directed at us because of our group membership, our psychological health suffers. However, targets of discrimination are often resilient to the damage. Despite long-term racial discrimination in America, Blacks do not have lower self-esteem than Whites (Twenge & Crocker, 2002). Being rejected by others is harmful, but group identification often offsets the harmful effects of rejection. This does not, however, make discrimination at the individual level less painful or harmful. Nevertheless, attributional ambiguity, racial centrality, and a multicultural perspective have all been shown to buffer against these negative effects (Crocker & Major, 1989; Sellers et al., 1997; Vandiver, Cross, Worrell, & Fhagen-Smith, 2002). Also, identifying with one's racial or ethnic group provides social support that buffers us against bias. For example, internalizing homophobia among lesbian, gay, and bisexual men and women undermines psychological health, but the damage is alleviated when they receive social support and effectively regulate their emotional responses (Hatzenbuehler, Nolen-Hoeksema, & Dovidio, 2009).

Respect Promotes Diversity Among Members of Racial and Ethnic Minority Groups

As we discussed in Chapter 9, members of traditionally disadvantaged groups are not interested in being tolerated or in being simply liked: they prefer to be respected (Bergsieker, Shelton, & Richeson, 2010; Shnabel, Nadler, Ullrich, Dovidio, & Carmi, 2009). One consequence is that colorblind approaches to workplace diversity have adverse effects on racial and ethnic minorities. For example, when a company's publicity showed low minority representation and a colorblind diversity philosophy, African American professionals reported low motivation to consider working for the company and little institutional trust (Purdie-Vaughns, Steele, Davies, Ditlmann, & Crosby, 2008). Low representation and an emphasis on competition over relationships had the same negative effects for women. Within an organization, when White employees hold colorblind diversity beliefs, racial minority coworkers perceive greater discrimination and become less psychologically engaged in the organization (Plaut, Thomas, & Goren, 2009).

Support for Diversity Is Greatest When it Includes Your Group

Who does diversity refer to? For many Whites the answer is "not me." A series of studies demonstrated that many Whites associate multiculturalism with exclusion (Plaut, Garnett, Buffardi, & Sanchez-Burks, 2011). White, Black, Asian, Hispanic, and other non-White ethnics completed an IAT (described in Chapter 7) that measured the strength of implicit automatic associations between the terms "multiculturalism" or "colorblindness" and "exclusion" or "inclusion." Whites had a strong tendency to pair multiculturalism with exclusion and colorblindness with inclusion. Ethnic/racial minorities showed no such tendency.

In a follow-up study, White participants read a news story about multiculturalism that explicitly mentioned in the final paragraph that multiculturalism was inclusive of all groups including Whites. This paragraph was omitted in the control group. Participants then took the same IAT as the previous study. When Whites were included in the concept of multiculturalism, the association between exclusion and multiculturalism disappeared and they were more likely to support diversity in their organization (Plaut et al., 2011).

These studies are important because they help us understand the negative attitudes about diversity expressed by the college student at the beginning of this chapter. When Whites feel excluded from the meaning of diversity, they tend to withhold support for it, and may at times actively oppose it. The researchers conclude that "interest in diversity or in supporting diversity efforts, does not rely simply on one's membership in a 'minority' or 'White' group but rather may rise and fall with the incorporation of multiculturalism in the self-concept" (p. 346). We could say "We are all multiculturalists now!" (Glazer, 1997).

Programs to Promote Intergroup Relations Can Succeed

Interventions to combat prejudice, improve intergroup relations, and promote diversity must overcome habits of mind (Chapters 7 and 11) and social forces that teach, motivate, and reinforce bias (Chapters 10 and 11). Nevertheless, social policies and specific programs can be effective. School desegregation was one of the earliest diversity-focused programs. Over the years, many approaches have been tried and their success has been mixed or not adequately evaluated (Stephan & Stephan, 2001; Stephan & Vogt, 2004). These include multicultural education, diversity training, intergroup dialogues, intercultural training, cooperative learning, conflict resolution training, and morals education (Chapter 11).

Cooperative learning is the most successful and empirically supported method for improving intergroup relations. These programs typically provide opportunities for elementary and secondary school students to experience face-to-face, cooperative interaction. Jigsaw classrooms, in which each student has information necessary to solve a group problem, bring children together in order to produce maximum performance. Such classroom strategies lead to stronger interpersonal friendships across racial and gender boundaries, as well as better problem-solving performance (Chapter 6). These programs have been shown to improve intergroup relations by increasing empathy, fostering cross-race friendships, and encouraging children to help their classmates (Chapter 10). However, we should note that recent research has failed to find these positive benefits for intergroup relations (Bratt, 2008).

Trust Is Crucial for Dealing with Difference and Change

Trust is basic to the success of any relationship. This is true even of relationships that cross group boundaries (Chapter 6), and experience with diversity can enhance intergroup trust (Hou & Wu, 2009). Transparency and trust, for example, are important to building and maintaining the perception that a university is committed to its stated diversity goals (Pepper, Tredennick, & Reyes, 2010). When students perceive that their university is committed to diversity, they experience less racial tension, hostility, and discrimination on campus. Trust is also a critical factor for positive intergroup relations between immigrant and native-born students in secondary schools in Denmark (Dinesen, 2011).

Organizational Values, Goals, and Practices Determine the Success of Diversity Efforts

Organizational cultures can change more rapidly than national cultures, and thus organizations have the potential to adapt to and benefit from diversity more effectively. However, realizing the benefits of diversity in organizations does not just happen: it results from organizational leadership, values, and goals (Chapter 12). Diversity has positive effects in businesses because it promotes creativity and often leads to better functioning work groups (Jehn, Northcraft, & Neale, 1999). A company's diversity reputation is also linked to investor confidence, and diversity of leadership is linked to bottom line performance of Fortune 500 companies (Roberson & Park, 2007). However, managing diversity is not a simple matter, and not all methods are equally effective. Reducing managerial bias through diversity training and diversity evaluations was least effective at diversifying management by gender and race/ethnicity (Kalev, Dobbin, & Kelly, 2006). Mentoring and networking were somewhat more effective in reducing isolation of employees from marginalized groups. The greatest gains in managerial diversity came when responsibility for diversity was assigned to a person and an office. Simply valuing diversity is not enough; making an organizational commitment is necessary (see Chapter 12).

Conclusion

A large body of research informs the analysis of prejudice and discrimination, but the psychology of diversity demands that we understand human psychology and social organization and behavior more broadly. Diversity is not just about race and ethnicity, and it is not limited to biases that undermine fairness, opportunity, and well-being. It is a challenge to the core principles of democracy, liberty, and justice. It is also fundamental to how we perceive, understand, and respond to our social worlds. We have attempted to demonstrate these complexities by illuminating the challenges that diversity presents, the mechanisms by which we perceive and respond to human differences, and the opportunities and benefits afforded by successfully enhancing and managing diversity.

There are many perspectives on diversity and they are often based on opinion, beliefs, and values. Our aim in this book has been to bring scientific evidence to bear on understanding diversity and the debates that arise around it. We believe that by laying a scientific foundation for the diversity discussion, we go beyond opinion to help readers understand the complexities and the many sides of the issues.

As the quotes at the beginning of this final chapter suggest, diversity means different things to different people. It is easy to draw battle lines and to characterize individuals as either part of the problem or part of the solution. But we are strongly against such either/or thinking, preferring instead a both/and approach. If diversity among us is an inevitable consequence of the dynamics of contemporary global and electronic evolution, differences among us and their consequences, intended or not, must be addressed not avoided. Reverting to the past for justification of the present condition does not work. There is something great about the American experiment in democracy that drives through many natural aversions to understand, and benefit, from differences among us. Our belief in freedom, fairness, and liberty is strong. Our ability to achieve it, though, is tested at every point in our nation's history. But we struggle, fight, and make progress.

This book has explored the implications of a psychology of diversity for understanding the complexities of living in an increasingly global society, and functioning daily in increasingly diverse institutions. Basic human tendencies challenge us to make growing diversity an asset to society. The psychology of diversity helps us to understand the barriers as well as the advantages and opportunities that diversity presents. This book has taken us "beyond prejudice and racism" to recognize the challenges of diversity psychologically, morally, and practically for us all personally, for our society, and our future.

Questions for Thinking and Knowing

1. Which of the diversity principles presented in this chapter best inform or reflect your understanding of diversity? Which do you see operating in your own experience?
2. Which strategies for coping with diversity—in the context of fairness—do you see as most promising?
3. In what ways are you diverse? What aspects of your personal diversity do you acknowledge, and how do they affect what you think and do?
4. Consider the three quotes that began this chapter. Which of these comes closest to your own view of diversity? Think about the view that you least agree with. What is the merit of that perspective?
5. Describe one way the material in this book can help you address diversity in your personal life.
6. Is the SAT a valid predictor of college performance? If not, how can it be used to make selection decisions? Also if not, how can we calculate merit?

Key Terms

Both/and paradigm
Cooperative learning
Cultural inertia

Prevention focus
Promotion focus

References

Antonio, A. L., Chang, M. J., Hakuta, K., Kenny, D. A., Levin, S., & Milem, J. F. (2004). Effects of racial diversity on complex thinking in college students. *Psychological Science, 15,* 507–510.

Anzures, G., Wheeler, A., Quinn, P. C., Pascalis, O., Slater, A. M., Heron-Delaney, M., . . . Lee, K. (2012). Brief daily exposures to Asian females reverses perceptual narrowing for Asian faces in Caucasian infants.

Journal of Experimental Child Psychology, 112, 484–495.

Bergsieker, H. B., Shelton, J. N., & Richeson, J. A. (2010). To be liked versus respected: Divergent goals in interracial interaction. *Journal of Personality and Social Psychology,* 99, 248–264.

Blue Hen Poll. (2012). 2012 University of Delaware Blue Hen Poll. Undergraduate Student Survey, May 2012. Available from http://www.udel.edu/bluehenpoll

Bowen, W. G., & Bok, D. C. (1998). *The shape of the river: Long-term consequences of considering race in college and university admissions.* Princeton, NJ: Princeton University Press.

Bratt, C. (2008). The jigsaw classroom under test: No effect on intergroup relations evident. *Journal of Community and Applied Social Psychology,* 18, 403–419.

Brewer, M. B. (1991). The social self: On being the same and different at the same time. *Personality and Social Psychology Bulletin,* 17, 475–482.

Carr, P. B., Dweck, C. S., & Pauker, K. (2012). Prejudiced behavior without prejudice? Beliefs about the malleability of prejudice affect interracial interactions. *Journal of Personality and Social Psychology,* 103, 452–471.

Crisp, R. J., & Turner, R. N. (2011). Cognitive adaptation to the experience of social and cultural diversity. *Psychological Bulletin,* 137, 242–266.

Crocker, J., & Major, B. (1989). Social stigma and self-esteem: The self-protective properties of stigma. *Psychological Review,* 96, 608–630.

Devine, P. G., Forscher, P. S., Austin, A. J., & Cox, W. T. L. (2012). Long-term reduction in implicit racial prejudice: A prejudice habit-breaking intervention. *Journal of Experimental Social Psychology,* 48, 1267–1278.

Dinesen, P. T. (2011). Me and Jasmina down by the schoolyard: An analysis of the impact of ethnic diversity in school on the trust of schoolchildren. *Social Science Research,* 40, 572–585.

Glazer, N. (1997). *We are all multiculturalists now.* Cambridge, MA: Harvard University Press.

Gurin, P., Nagda, B., & Lopez, C. (2004). The benefits of diversity in education for democratic citizenship. *Journal of Social Issues,* 60, 17–34.

Hatzenbuehler, M. L., Nolen-Hoeksema, S., & Dovidio, J. F. (2009). How does stigma "get under the skin"? The mediating role of emotion regulation. *Psychological Science,* 20, 1282–1289.

Hehman, E., Stanley, E. M., Gaertner, S. L., & Simons, R. F. (2011). Multiple group membership influences face-recognition: Recall and neurological evidence. *Journal of Experimental Social Psychology,* 47, 1262–1268.

Heron-Delaney, M., Anzures, G., Herbert, J. S., Quinn, P. C., Slater, A. M., Tanaka, J. W., . . . Pascalis, O. (2011). Perceptual training prevents the emergence of the other race effect during infancy. *PLoS ONE,* 6, e19858. doi:10.1371/journal.pone.0019858.

Hornsey, M. J., & Hogg, M. A. (1999). Subgroup differentiation as a response to an overly inclusive group: A test of optimal distinctiveness theory. *European Journal of Social Psychology,* 29, 543–550.

Hou, F., & Wu, Z. (2009). Racial diversity, minority concentration, and trust in Canadian urban neighborhoods. *Social Science Research,* 38, 693–716.

Jehn, K. A., Northcraft, G. B., & Neale, M. A. (1999). Why differences make a difference: A field study of diversity, conflict and performance in workgroups *Administrative Science Quarterly,* 44, 741–763.

Kalev, A., Dobbin, F., & Kelly, E. (2006). Best practices or best guesses? Assessing the efficacy of corporate affirmative action and diversity policies. *American Sociological Review,* 71, 589–617.

Leung, A. K., Maddux, W. W., Galinsky, A. D., & Chiu, C.-Y. (2008). Multicultural experience enhances creativity: The when and how. *American Psychologist,* 63, 169–181.

Levy, B. R., Zonderman, A. B., Slade, M. D., & Ferrucci, L. (2009). Age stereotypes held earlier in life predict cardiovascular events in later life. *Psychological Science, 20,* 296–298.

Lowery, B. S., Chow, R. S., Knowles, E. D., & Unzueta, M. M. (2012). Paying for positive group esteem: How inequity frames affect Whites' responses to redistributive policies. *Journal of Personality and Social Psychology, 102,* 323–336.

Lowery, B. S., Unzueta, M. M., Knowles, E. D., & Goff, P. A. (2006). Concern for the in-group and opposition to affirmative action. *Journal of Personality and Social Psychology, 90,* 961–974.

Moss-Racusin, C. A., Dovidio, J. F., Brescoll, V. L., Graham, M. J., & Handelsman, J. (2012). Science faculty's subtle gender biases favor male students. *Proceedings of the National Academy of Sciences of the United States of America, 109,* 16474–16479.

Pepper, M. B., Tredennick, L., & Reyes, R. F. (2010). Transparency and trust as antecedents to perceptions of commitment to stated diversity goals. *Journal of Diversity in Higher Education, 3,* 153–162.

Pettigrew, T. F. (1998). Intergroup contact theory. *Annual Review of Psychology, 49,* 65–85.

Pettigrew, T. F., & Tropp, L. R. (2011). *When groups meet: The dynamics of intergroup contact.* New York: Psychology Press.

Plant, E. A., & Devine, P. G. (2009). The active control of prejudice: Unpacking the intentions guiding control efforts. *Journal of Personality and Social Psychology, 96,* 640–652.

Plaut, V. C., Garnett, F. G., Buffardi, L. E., & Sanchez-Burks, J. (2011). "What about me?" Perceptions of exclusion and Whites' reactions to multiculturalism. *Journal of Personality and Social Psychology, 101,* 337–353.

Plaut, V. C., Thomas, K. M., & Goren, M. J. (2009). Is multiculturalism or color blindness better for minorities? *Psychological Science, 20,* 444–446.

Purdie-Vaughns, V., & Eibach, R. P. (2008). Intersectional invisibility: The distinctive advantages and disadvantages of multiple subordinate-group identities. *Sex Roles, 59,* 377–391.

Purdie-Vaughns, V., Steele, C. M., Davies, P. G., Ditlmann, R., & Crosby, J. R. (2008). Social identity contingencies: How diversity cues signal threat or safety for African Americans in mainstream institutions. *Journal of Personality and Social Psychology, 94,* 615–630.

Richeson, J. A., & Nussbaum, R. J. (2004). The impact of multiculturalism versus color-blindness on racial bias. *Journal of Experimental Social Psychology, 40,* 417–423.

Roberson, Q. M., & Park, H. J. (2007). Examining the link between diversity and firm performance: The effects of diversity reputation and leader racial diversity. *Group and Organization Management, 32,* 548–568.

Schwartz, S. H. (1992). Universals in the content and structure of values: Theoretical advances and empirical tests in 20 countries. In M. P. Zanna (Ed.), *Advances in experimental social psychology* (Vol. 25, pp. 1–65). San Diego, CA: Academic Press.

Sellers, R. M., Rowley, S. A., Chavous, T. M., Shelton, J. N., & Smith, M. A. (1997). Multidimensional inventory of Black identity: A preliminary investigation of reliability and construct validity. *Journal of Personality and Social Psychology, 73,* 805–815.

Shah, J. Y., Brazy, P. C., & Higgins, E. T. (2004). Promoting us or preventing them: Regulatory focus and manifestations of intergroup bias. *Personality and Social Psychology Bulletin, 30,* 433–446.

Shih, M., Pittinsky, T. L., & Ambady, N. (1999). Stereotype susceptibility: Identity salience and shifts in quantitative performance. *Psychological Science, 10,* 80–83.

Shnabel, N., Nadler, A., Ullrich, J., Dovidio, J. F., & Carmi, D. (2009). Promoting reconciliation through the satisfaction of the emotional needs of victimized and perpetrating group members: The Needs-based Model of Reconciliation. *Personality and Social Psychology Bulletin, 35,* 1021–1030.

Smith, D. G. (2009). *Diversity's promise for higher education: Making it work.* Baltimore: Johns Hopkins University Press.

Son Hing, L. S., Bobocel, D. R., & Zanna, M. P. (2002). Meritocracy and opposition to affirmative action: Making concessions in the face of discrimination. *Journal of Personality and Social Psychology, 83,* 493–509.

Stephan, W. G., & Stephan, C. W. (2001). *Improving intergroup relations.* Thousand Oaks, CA: Sage Publications.

Stephan, W. G., & Vogt, W. P. (Eds.). (2004). *Education programs for improving intergroup relations: Theory, research and practice.* New York: Teachers College Press.

Twenge, J. M., & Crocker, J. (2002). Race and self-esteem: Meta-analyses comparing Whites, Blacks, Hispanics, Asians, and American Indians and comment on Gray, Little, and Hafdahl (2000). *Psychological Bulletin, 128,* 371–408.

Unzueta, M. M., Knowles, E. D., & Ho, G. C. (2012). Diversity is what you want it to be: How social-dominance motives affect con-struals of diversity. *Psychological Science, 23,* 303–309.

Vandiver, B. J., Cross, W. J., Worrell, F. C., & Fhagen-Smith, P. E. (2002). Validating the Cross Racial Identity Scale. *Journal of Counseling Psychology, 49,* 71–85.

Vorauer, J. D., & Sasaki, S. J. (2009). Helpful only in the abstract? Ironic effects of empathy in intergroup interaction. *Psychological Science, 20,* 191–197.

Walton, G. M., Spencer, S. J., & Erman, S. (2013). Affirmative meritocracy. *Social Issues and Policy Review, 7,* 1–35.

Wilson, D. C., & Davis, D. W. (2011). Reexamining racial resentment: Conceptualization and content. *Annals of the American Academy of Political and Social Science, 634,* 117–133.

Zárate, M. A., & Shaw, M. P. (2010). The role of cultural inertia in reactions to immigration on the U.S./Mexico border. *Journal of Social Issues, 66,* 45–57.

Zárate, M. A., Shaw, M., Marquez, J. A., & Biagas, D. (2012). Cultural inertia: The effects of cultural change on intergroup relations and the self-concept. *Journal of Experimental Social Psychology, 48,* 634–645.

Glossary

absolute values   Values that are right for everyone.

acculturation   Similar to socialization (*see below*) but focuses on acquiring knowledge and accepting a different culture.

acculturative stress   The tension caused by the potential conflict between learning one's own culture while adapting to a new one.

affirmative action   Programs and policies used to address institutional bias. These are offered as proactive remedies to reduce institutional disparities. Groups lagging in key social indicators are given an opportunity to be considered for admission or a job if their qualifications merit such consideration. Such actions are designed to minimize discrimination but some people perceive them as a reverse form of bias.

American   Often used to mean U.S. citizens, but actually refers to all persons living in North, Central, and South America.

Americans with Disabilities Act (1990)   A civil rights law that protects persons with disabilities from discrimination in hiring and wages, and requires that reasonable accommodations be made available in the workplace.

amygdala   Within the forebrain, the amygdala is particularly important to how we react to others. The amygdala is sensitive to novel people and objects, and it acts rapidly to signal a threat. When a threat occurs, the amygdala initiates a series of processes that prepare a person for "fight or flight."

Arab Spring   In early spring 2011, citizens in several Arab nations rose up against years of illegitimate and coercive power exercised by dictators through the use of torture, imprisonment, and murder.

attributional ambiguity   The uncertainty about whether negative treatment is the result of bias in other persons or shortcomings in oneself. It has a strong effect on the responses of members of minority groups.

The Psychology of Diversity: Beyond Prejudice and Racism, First Edition. James M. Jones, John F. Dovidio, and Deborah L. Vietze.
© 2014 Blackwell Publishing Ltd. Published 2014 by Blackwell Publishing Ltd.

attribution bias   People explain the causes of behavior (attributions) with internal reasons (the person's personality or disposition) and/or external reasons (some situational influence). People systematically make attributions in ways that make themselves, their group, and members of their group appear in a positive light.

attribution processes   Because people do not have the capacity to process all the information around them, they tend to use abstract basic principles to explain isolated facts. By thinking in terms of what causes a behavior, people do not have to remember separate facts or incidents to feel that they understand a person.

attribution theory   Explains how we come to understand the causes of people's behavior, others' as well as our own. Early research on attribution theory demonstrated that the types of attributions people make are greatly influenced by three dimensions: consensus, consistency, and distinctiveness.

authoritarian personality   The configuration of traits (e.g., respect for authority, intolerance of ambiguity) that produces a personality prone to prejudice, involving a projection of unacceptable impulses (such as anger) onto powerless out-group members.

aversive racism   How people resolve conflicting non-prejudiced explicit attitudes and implicit prejudice; applies to everyday forms of discrimination cross-culturally (at least in Canada, England, and the Netherlands, as well as the United States).

backlash   A negative compensatory response to members of socially devalued groups who display a positive attribute. For example, women who demonstrate high competence tend to be perceived as less warm, which can then be used as a justification for a negative reaction to them.

beneficial diversity   Not only acceptance of differences among people, but a belief that those differences add value to the contexts in which they occur—that organizations, society, and our country are better off when they are diverse.

benevolent sexism   Favorable attitudes toward women are conditioned by their acceptance of men's chivalrous, protective paternalism while staying within prescribed gender roles, and this can have subtle and adverse effects.

biological hierarchy   Biologically defined groups are judged to be superior (men) or inferior (Blacks) and their social status is believed to be genetically determined (superiority and inferiority begins at birth).

Black identity   Associated with changes in how one views oneself, with the goal of acquiring a balanced perspective on positive feelings about being Black, recognizing the potential bias directed against you because you are Black, employing those positive feelings about yourself and your group, and developing effective ways to cope with negative treatment. All demonstrated in a large body of social psychological research.

blatant prejudice   A traditional and overt form of bias that involves the direct expression of negative attitudes leading to discrimination.

both/and paradigm   People are *both* different in some aspects *and* the same in others. This approach emphasizes inclusiveness more than divisiveness which is characterized by an either/or paradigm.

Brown v. Board of Education of Topeka (1954)   State laws that established separate public schools for Black and White students denied Black children equal educational opportunities. The unanimous ruling stated that "separate educational facilities are inherently unequal," thus declaring that de jure, or legal, racial segregation violated the Fourteenth Amendment. This ruling overturned the "separate but equal" doctrine enunciated in the 1896 *Plessy v. Ferguson* decision.

category divide hypothesis When there is conflict between two people from groups that are believed to be different in essential ways, resolving such conflicts is made much more difficult.

cerebral cortex The outermost layer of the brain, made up of two similar-looking halves called hemispheres. The cerebral cortex is associated with three major functions: (a) analyzing and integrating information from various senses; (b) higher-order thinking and abstract problem solving; and (c) performing voluntary actions. When you look at a brain, you mainly see the cerebral cortex because it covers the forebrain, midbrain, and hindbrain.

challenge response When we mobilize our energy and become more involved or immersed in a task; a form of positive engagement—when we try to rise to the occasion.

Chinese Exclusion Act Passed by Congress in 1882, the Act excluded Chinese laborers from entering the United States. The restriction was limited to 10 years but in 1892 the Geary Act extended and strengthened the Chinese Exclusion Act for another 10 years. Ten years later it was extended indefinitely, but finally repealed in 1943.

chronic egalitarian goals Habitual ways of thinking that, when activated, inhibit even implicit biases that are normally automatically activated.

Civil Rights Act (1964) Ended legal discrimination on the basis of race, color, gender, religion, national origin.

cognitive consistency A basic motivation to have one's thoughts and beliefs fit together in a coherent way. When there is a contradiction between beliefs or when new information challenges old knowledge, people experience discomfort and strive to integrate and make sense of the discrepancy.

cognitive dissonance theory Proposes that holding inconsistent thoughts or beliefs arouses psychological tension and discomfort, which people strive to reduce, often by changing their attitudes to be more consistent with their actions.

cognitive diversity Reflects differences in patterns of thinking, analysis, perception, and point of view, including perspectives, heuristics, interpretations, and predictions.

cognitive miser The tendency of people to use mental shortcuts (e.g., generalizations) that reduce the effort needed to process complex information in an efficient but not necessarily fully accurate way. People are motivated to use mental shortcuts when their cognitive capacities are limited or taxed.

collective identity Acknowledging that you belong to a socially defined group and that being a member of that group is important to how you define, describe, and feel about yourself.

collectivism A theory whose proponents focus more on mutual obligations, relationships, and expectations between themselves and groups to which they belong and who tend to subordinate their interests to those of the group.

colorblind An ideology emphasizing that group differences should be ignored and people should be treated as individuals.

colorblind perspective   Proposes that although people do vary in skin color, it is irrelevant and should not be a basis for making important decisions such as hiring for a job or admitting to a school. A colorblind philosophy is not limited to race, but applies to the use of any group characteristic in decision-making.

Comfort v. Lynn School Committee   Beginning in 1988, the Lynn public school system used a voluntary plan to improve racial diversity in its schools and eliminate minority isolation. Under the Lynn Plan, all students had the unconditional right to attend their neighborhood school. However, students could transfer out of their district school and into another if their transfer would have the effect of decreasing racial isolation or increasing racial balance. Conversely, students could not transfer if doing so would detract from either of these goals. As a result of the plan, the student bodies of Lynn schools had become more racially diverse. Parents whose children were denied transfers on race-conscious grounds challenged the transfer provisions of the Lynn Plan, claiming that those provisions violate rights secured to them under the Equal Protection Clause of the Fourteenth Amendment to the U.S. Constitution. In 2003, the U.S. District Court upheld the school district's transfer plan. However, a three-judge panel of the U.S. Court of Appeals reversed this ruling in 2004. The Lynn School Committee petitioned for a rehearing, and in June 2005 a full panel of judges for the U.S. Court of Appeals upheld the Lynn plan.

common in-group identity model   The idea that it is possible to change the ways we think about others by changing the way we think about their group membership. Emphasizing a common group membership can change the way we typically think of others from an "us" versus "them" to a more inclusive superordinate "we" connection.

compelling interest   As enunciated by Justice O'Connor, the legal basis for determining when and how taking race into account may be used to further diversity objectives in higher education. In general terms, it establishes that diversity has an important role to play in higher education.

confirmatory bias   The tendency to seek out information that is consistent with what we expect, dismissing information that is inconsistent. Even if you are hesitant to allow initial attributions to color your feelings and beliefs about another person, the expectations derived from these attributions guide how you weigh subsequent information. The results are ultimately the same, however, biased assessments of the other person that confirm the initial impression.

Confucian dynamism   Variable orientations toward the present (M-time: business time, work time, official) or the future (P-time: playtime, dream time, or social time).

contact hypothesis (theory)   Formalized by Gordon Allport in 1954, this theory originally specified four conditions necessary for intergroup interaction to reduce bias:

- equal status within the contact situation;
- intergroup cooperation;
- shared goals;
- support of authorities, laws, or customs.

More recently, two additional key conditions have been added:

- exchange of information that allows us to make personal connections during these interactions;
- having at least one friend who is a member of the other group.

cooperative learning   Students work in groups to complete tasks collectively in order to reach academic goals. Less competitive in nature than individual learning, students learning cooperatively capitalize on one another's resources and skills. It has been shown to be one of the most successful and empirically supported methods for improving intergroup relations.

coping   Refers to a person's conscious and intentional efforts to regulate behavior (emotion, thought, physiology) or the environment in response to stressful events or circumstances.

correlations   A numerical index, ranging from −1.0 to +1.0, showing the strength and direction of relationship between two variables. A stronger relationship is indicated by a value that deviates more from 0; the sign indicates with the relationship between the two variables is in the same direction (+) or the opposite direction (−).

counter-stereotypic imaging   One of five bias-reducing techniques that involves imagining in detail counter-stereotypic other people who do not fit the typical stereotypes of their group.

Cross Racial Identity Scale (CRIS)   A scale that measures the structure and development of racial identity in African Americans.

cultural bias   The belief that one's cultural heritage is superior to that of other groups is normalized as part of a society's institutions and practices. In some cultures there is a defined social order that promotes the superiority of one skin color, ethnicity, religion, gender, or sexual orientation over others.

cultural diversity   Refers to the variety and extent of cultural differences that exist in a given setting, institution or society, and the nature of the interactions that occur between and among them.

cultural inertia   The desire to avoid cultural change if it alters the status quo and forces you to change; or, conversely, to ride the wave of change if it carries you to a better position in society.

cultural transmission (enculturation)   The process of learning one's own culture, called cultural transmission or enculturation, involves acquiring the knowledge, skills, attitudes, and values that enable a person to become a functioning member of a society.

cultural universalities   Principles, activities, and other elements that all cultures share.

culture   The avenue through which we grow and learn. It is a primary influence on how we think, what we value, what we feel, and how we behave. Culture is a set of tools, real and symbolic, that allows us to share rituals, practices, and customs. This is true whether you conform to prevailing cultural mores, ignore them, or rebel against them.

culture war   A clash between two competing ideas about what is moral, right and good for a society.

decategorization   Refers to when people identify themselves and others primarily as distinct individuals rather than group members.

demographic diversity   Occurs when differences among people are based on social categories or social roles without regard to their psychological salience for the person. These differences usually consist of the same categories as identity diversity (*see below*).

dependent variable   The element that was hypothesized by a researcher to change or vary depending on the independent variable that was manipulated.

descriptive statistics   Summary characteristics and general shape of the data the researcher has collected, such as the mean (average) and standard deviation.

desegregation   Requiring schools to represent appropriate racial and ethnic diversity.

discrimination   Occurs when individuals are treated differently, and usually more negatively, because of their membership in negatively valued groups. Discrimination may result from the actions of individuals or the differential application of laws, social policies, or institutional practices.

disparate impact   Hiring outcomes that fail to meet the 80% selection ratio criterion. *See also* four-fifths rule.

displacement   The process by which an emotion (particularly anger) that is inhibited is redirected in the form of behavior toward another target that was not responsible for arousing that emotion.

disruptive apprehension   The anxiety that accompanies the awareness you are in a stereotype-threating situation.

distributive justice   Concerns whether outcomes in the end are perceived as fair.

diversity   Refers to those characteristics that make us different from one another, including race, ethnicity, gender, demographic differences, country of origin, our culture, sexual orientation, age, values, political affiliation, socioeconomic status, and able-bodiedness. Psychological tendencies, abilities, or preferences also mark diversity.

diversity interactions   One of Milem's three interrelated ways to view diversity: exchanges between and among people who are different.

diversity-related initiatives   One of Milem's three interrelated ways to view diversity: cultural awareness workshops, ethnic studies courses, etc.

diversity science   Examines the ways in which people create, interpret, and maintain group differences and the psychological and societal consequences of these distinctions.

diversity training   The many types of professional development programs that help managers and employees in organizations to avoid bias against persons based on gender, ethnicity, skin color, religion, sexual orientation, and disability. These programs can be voluntary or mandated by the federal Equal Employment Opportunity Commission.

diversity within diversity   Each diversity group contains significant variability, for example, Latino/Latina persons differ in (a) heritage (Mexican, Puerto Rican, Cuban, etc.); (b) generations in the United States; (c) physical appearance; (d) identification with their heritage; and (e) cultural practices.

Dogmatism Scale Measures extremist orientations and rigidity of belief in either a politically conservative or liberal direction.

Don't ask, don't tell The official U.S. policy on gay men and women serving in the military. The policy prohibited military personnel from discriminating against or harassing closeted gay or bisexual service members or applicants, but it barred openly gay, lesbian, or bisexual persons from military service. On July 22, 2011, President Barack Obama, Secretary of Defense Leon Panetta, and Chairman of the Joint Chiefs of Staff Admiral Mike Mullen certified that repeal of DADT would not harm military readiness, and on September 20, 2011 the policy officially ended.

dynamic systems theory States that human behavior is jointly linked to factors occurring within the person (endogenous) and to those occurring in the person's environment (exogenous).

electroencephalography (EEG) Assesses electrical activity in the brain using electrodes pasted temporarily onto the head. Because typically many electrodes are needed, participants often wear special caps with electrodes built in. When neurons in the brain are active, they emit small electrical impulses (microvolts) that EEG detects and analyzes. EEG is especially good at detecting rapid changes in brain activity.

Emancipation Proclamation Made by Abraham Lincoln on September 22, 1862, the proclamation stated that "all persons held as slaves within any State or designated part of a State . . . shall be then, thenceforward, and forever free."

empathy Understanding the perspective of the other person so that we respond emotionally to their situation.

enculturation Refers to the process where parents may want their children to function effectively in their own culture but also teach or expose them to a new culture to prepare them for functioning in a different cultural context. *See also* acculturation.

enemyship The belief that another person holds personal hatred and malice toward you and desires your downfall or attempts to sabotage your progress.

entity theorists People who believe that race is an essential, fixed category of human difference.

epigenetic Refers to the concept that genes are responsible for personal traits, but that cultural, social, and environmental contexts shape how these traits evolve and how we behave.

equity Refers to whether groups are treated in a way that does not unfairly impose economic, social, or other barriers that would prevent them from reaching their full potential.

ethnic identity Refers to the ideas people have of themselves as members of an ethnic group.

ethnicity Refers to a social group that is defined on the basis of cultural criteria.

ethnophaulisms Words that constitute slurs against ethnic groups, and exclusion from U.S. society, for example "mick" (Irish), "dago" (Italian).

evolutionary psychology Focuses on how evolutionary adaptations can influence current behavior, and shows how our past influences our everyday interactions, often in universal ways.

Executive Order 9066   Issued by President Franklin Roosevelt in 1942, this authorized the forcible relocation and internment of approximately 110,000 Japanese nationals and Japanese Americans. Of those interned, 62% were U.S. citizens. The exclusionary order was upheld by the U.S. Supreme Court in 1944. In 1988 Congress passed and President Ronald Reagan signed legislation that apologized for the internment, stating that government actions were based on "race prejudice, war hysteria, and a failure of political leadership." A total of $1.6 billion in reparations were later disbursed by the U.S. government to surviving internees and their heirs.

Executive Order 9981   Signed by President Harry S. Truman on July 26, 1948, this order mandated "equality of treatment and opportunity for all persons in the armed services without regard to race, color, religion, or national origin."

Executive Order 11246   Signed by President Johnson on September 24, 1965, this order required that all federal contractors take affirmative action to ensure that job applicants are judged and employees are treated fairly without regard to their race, color, religion, sex, or national origin. Affirmative action policy established a standard of equal treatment for groups that had been historically disadvantaged and discriminated against, as well as sanctions for violations of non-discrimination practices.

expert influence   Source of power based on people's beliefs that another person has some know-how and understanding that is not yet available to them, which gives the other person social power in the situation.

explicit bias   Preference for or against a social group that a person is aware of and consciously controls. It can be expressed as an attitude, an evaluation, or a behavior.

extended contact hypothesis   Presents the idea that an in-group member's mere knowledge of another in-group member's close positive relationship with a person in an out-group can reduce intergroup bias. For example, White students who know another White person who has a Black, Asian, or Latino friend has more positive attitudes toward that racial or ethnic group than do Whites who do not know such a person.

extrinsic religiosity   Using one's religion to connect to a community, gain social status, or increase personal security.

fairness   A cultural and moral concept indicating that access to opportunities and resources are available to anyone without regard to social group status.

fast-learning system   Memory system that is more conscious, effortful, and intentional. This is the system you use when you encounter new challenges that you want to master. This system allows you to learn quickly from limited exposure, drawing from a range of cognitive resources.

four-fifths rule   A guideline to provide employers with a uniform set of principles for hiring without discrimination based on age, disability, color, sex, religion, national origin, or race. The EEOC Uniform Guidelines state that a selection rate for any group less than four-fifths, or 80%, of the rate for the group with the highest rate will generally be regarded as evidence of disparate impact by the agency charged with protecting employment civil rights.

frustration–aggression hypothesis   Proposes that frustration causes aggression and all aggression can be traced back to some form of frustration.

F-scale   Derived from research on the authoritarian personality, this scale measures anti-Semitism and ethnocentrism without mentioning specifically the groups to which antagonisms were expressed; it is broadly predictive of prejudice.

full participation   An affirmative value that directs institutions to enable people of all identities, backgrounds, or institutional positions to thrive, engage meaningfully in institutional life, and contribute to the well-being of others.

functional magnetic resonance imaging (fMRI)   Measures blood flow within the brain to indicate brain activity. Researchers use fMRI to learn what areas of the brain are active when people are exposed to different stimuli, such as a photograph of a person with light or dark skin, or when they engage in or think about certain activities.

fundamental attribution error   The attributional bias that involves overestimating the role of another's stable character as the cause of his or her behavior.

fundamental preferences   The outcomes we value or prefer.

fusiform face area (FFA)   A distinct brain area located not too far from the amygdala. Whereas the amygdala is part of the brain's general early-warning system, the fusiform face area is specialized to process information about others' faces.

Gentlemen's Agreement 1907   The United States struck an agreement with Japan that promised not to restrict Japanese immigration as long as Japan voluntarily restricted emigration to the United States to upper-middle-class Japanese.

***Grutter v. Bollinger* (2003)**   University of Michigan Law School rejected Barbara Grutter, a White Michigan resident. The Center for Individual Rights filed suit on her behalf, alleging that the university had discriminated against her on the basis of race. She said she was rejected because the Law School used race as a factor, and that the university had no compelling interest to justify the consideration of race in the admissions process. The Supreme Court upheld Michigan Law School.

Haymarket Affair   On May 4, 1886, a rally of laborers in support of an 8-hour work day was held in Haymarket Square in Chicago. Led by anarchists who were mostly German and eastern European immigrants, a bomb was thrown at the police and a riot ensued. Known as the Haymarket Affair, it fueled nativist anti-immigration sentiment.

Health disparities   Racial and ethnic minority-group members typically suffer poorer health and have much higher mortality rates than majority-group members for similar conditions in the United States and across 125 other countries.

***Hernandez v. Texas* (1954)**   This landmark Supreme Court case decided that Mexican Americans, as ethnic minorities, had a right to equal protection under the Fourteenth Amendment. There was no legal requirement that a person was entitled to be tried by a jury of peers, only that no racial, ethnic, or gender groups could be excluded from serving on juries. It held that Mexican Americans had been systematically excluded from serving on juries in Texas.

hostile sexism   Openly negative attitudes and endorsement of negative stereotypes of women.

human capital   The collective skills, knowledge, or other intangible assets of individuals that convey value for the individuals, their institutions, or their communities.

human diversity   Refers to the study of the human species, one of the most widely distributed and varied animal species.

hypothesis An expectation, or prediction, derived directly from a theory. It is an inference based on a set of earlier observations about what will happen under certain conditions.

identity affirmation A way to modify negative stereotype threat effects by embracing group stereotypes and seeking out evaluative diagnostic tasks.

identity diversity Represents differences among people based on sex, gender orientation, religion, race, ethnicity, age, sexual orientation, immigrant status, and so on that are reflected in their affinity for, and identification with, those social categories.

identity safety Systematically identify the identity contingencies that undermine well-being and actively alter their adverse effects, resulting in feelings of social belonging in settings where negative identity contingencies exist.

Illegal Immigration Reform and Immigrant Responsibility Act (1996) Beefed up border patrols, and enhanced enforcement and penalties, inspection, apprehension, and detention. It further forbid employment and sanctioned U.S. businesses for violations. In spite of the law, however, illegal immigration persisted.

illusory correlation The tendency to associate qualities that we see as rare with groups that are small in number; conversely, we link the qualities we view as common with groups that are large.

imagined contact The act of mentally simulating an interaction with a member of another group. Simulating a positive intergroup interaction can help reduce prejudice toward members of the group.

immigration The act of settling in a new country with the desire to remain there permanently.

Immigration Act of 1917 Restricted immigration from Asia by creating an Asiatic Barred Zone.

Immigration Act of 1924 The Act established a formula for immigration that (a) capped total immigration to the United States at 150,000 per year; (b) assigned quotas to specific nations; (c) restricted immigrant visas from quota nations; (d) made it easier to immigrate from non-quota nations by requiring simple proof of residence in the country of origin for at least 2 years prior to emigration to the United States; and (e) limited immigration from Asiatic nations to professionals, clergy, and students.

Immigration and Nationality Act 1965 Abolished the national-origin quotas that had been in place since the 1924 Immigration Act. An annual limitation of 300,000 visas was established for immigrants, including 170,000 from eastern hemisphere countries, with a limit of 20,000 per country. By equalizing immigration policies, the Act resulted in new immigration from non-European nations, which changed the ethnic make-up of the United States.

Implicit Association Test (IAT) In the IAT, people have to make decisions about different groups (such as Anglos and Latinos or Whites and Blacks) in conjunction with positive and negative words. Faster response times reflect stronger implicit associations of different groups with positive or negative words. This test is the most commonly used technique for assessing implicit biases.

implicit bias   Preference for or against a social group that a person may be unaware of and thus cannot consciously control. They may be expressed in one's attitudes, evaluations, or behaviors.

increasing opportunities for contact   One of five bias-reducing techniques that involves seeking opportunities to encounter and engage in positive interactions with counter-stereotypic group members.

independent variable   The element that changes or varies in the way that a researcher has decided to manipulate it.

indirect contact   Involves learning about others' intergroup contact, observing others engaging in intergroup interaction, or imagining oneself interacting with a member of another group.

individual bias   Expressed as a negative attitude about an entire group, resulting in behavior that directly discriminates against a person belonging to that group. Personal expressions and actions of superiority and/or inferiority often represent centuries-old attitudes that have been perpetuated through parenting practices and both institutional and cultural bias.

individualism   A theory whose proponents focus more on rights above duties, a concern for oneself and immediate family, and emphasizes personal autonomy and self-fulfillment, and basing one's identity on personal accomplishments.

individual-mediated bias   Occurs when a person who is prejudiced against particular groups has key decision-making authority in an institution.

individuation   One of five bias-reducing techniques that involves obtaining specific information about group members to prevent drawing stereotypic inferences about them.

inferential statistics   Used to test the researcher's hypothesis, such as the t test, χ^2 (chi-square), and F statistics.

institution   An established entity in which the business, education, healthcare, or social goals of a society are sustained. Banks, schools, corporations, the health industry, higher education, and the like are institutions.

institutional bias   Institutional practices that favor some groups over others. The causes of institutional bias are not always obvious, and may occur without intention and thus is expressed as implicit bias.

institutional racism   Institutional practices that reflect and produce racial inequalities in American society, whether intentional or unintentional, overt or covert.

institutional sexism   Institutional practices that reflect and produce gender inequalities in American society, whether intentional or unintentional, overt or covert, often accompanied by positive attitudes toward women. *See* benevolent sexism.

instrumental preferences   The means by which we pursue preferred outcomes.

integrative complexity   The degree of integration and differentiation of multiple perspectives and dimensions in a person's thinking pattern.

intergroup anxiety   Discomfort associated with anticipating or actually interacting with a member of another group.

Intergroup Dialogues Course   This course, recognizing that diversity is more than skin deep, is based on five principles for bringing diversity and democracy into alignment: (a) presence of diverse others, (b) discontinuity from pre-college experiences, (c) equality among peers, (d) discussion under rules of civil discourse and normalization, and (e) negotiation of conflict. Participants came from diverse backgrounds, and the curriculum consisted of readings, lectures and papers, and intergroup dialogues.

intergroup (versus interpersonal) interaction When you interact with other members of your own group, it is interpersonal. But when you interact with members of another group, these interpersonal interactions become intergroup encounters.

internalized homophobia When negative stereotypes about gays and lesbians become the basis for self-hatred resulting in less self-disclosure to heterosexual friends and acquaintances, less feeling of connection to the gay and lesbian community, and more depressive symptoms and demoralization.

intersectionality A psychological concept referring to the complex interactions that exist for each person, among the various social roles they occupy in a society. All persons jointly occupy different social roles such as woman, teacher, parent, lesbian, White, and so on.

intrinsic religiosity A deep commitment to the principles of religion for the meaning it provides in one's life.

jigsaw classroom The jigsaw classroom gets its name from a jigsaw puzzle, a puzzle for which all the pieces are needed to complete a picture. The strategy is to replace competition in classrooms with cooperation. Instead of students separating themselves from others to work independently or seeking to distinguish themselves from others with superior performance, the jigsaw classroom mandates interdependence and cooperation. Students are placed into learning groups, with each person having responsibility for a proportion of the information needed to complete a task.

Jim Crow Laws State and local laws in the United States enacted between 1876 and 1965 that mandated legal racial segregation in all public facilities in former Confederate southern States.

just-world hypothesis People need to see the world as a just place in which they get what they deserve and deserve what they get. Believing that the world is just makes it seem more predictable and controllable.

lens model Gordon Allport's framework outlining the causes of prejudice, ranging from those very broad and distant to those more narrow and immediate. Moving from the broadest to the most specific, the sources of prejudice are categorized as historical, sociocultural, situational, personality based, phenomenological, and based on the qualities of the target of prejudice.

meritocracy A core belief about how benefits should be earned and bestowed. In theory, merit is objectively determined on an individual basis, such that the better one's performance, the better should be one's rewards.

meta-perceptions Your beliefs about what other people think about you.

minimal groups Reducing what it means to be in a group as much as possible. This technique was used to test how a psychological sense of social identity affects the way people think and act even when there is no consequential relationship between different groups or among members of the same group.

monochronic time (M-time) Characterized by doing one thing at a time in a sequential pattern: following schedules, completing one task before starting another, persisting in goal-directed activities, and disregarding distractions.

Montgomery bus boycott Plans to boycott the Montgomery bus service were put into operation on December 5, 1955, demanding that Black riders be treated with courtesy, Black drivers be hired, and seating in the middle of the bus be handled on a first-come basis. The Montgomery bus boycott expanded to sit-ins, marches, and other forms of passive non-violent resistance.

moral license Frees us from controlling our biases because we have engaged in a prior activity that convinces us that we are not prejudiced and thus no longer have to work at being unbiased.

multiculturalism Social ideology based on the belief that harmony and social justice among different groups can best be achieved if we appreciate our diversity and recognize and accept both positive and negative qualities of different cultural groups.

multicultural perspective Reflects the belief that preserving different cultures or cultural identities within institutions and societies is desirable and beneficial.

Multidimensional Inventory of Black Identity (MIBI) A scale developed to assess dimensions of Black identity.

Multidimensional Model of Racial Identity (MMRI) A theory that most people have a hierarchy of social identities. The place of racial identity in this hierarchy depends on its centrality and salience, the regard you and others have for your group, and the racial ideologies with which you judge yourself and others in your group.

Multigroup Ethnic Identity Measure (MEIM) The most widely used measure of generalized ethnic identity.

multiracial identity A recognized identity classification resulting from the immigration explosion and the desire to claim one's heritage in full measure, as well as greater openness to intimate unions across racial and ethnic lines.

mutual intergroup differentiation Involves maintaining distinct group identities, which limit threats to valued social identity, but within the context of cooperative interdependence between groups.

narrowly tailored In the Supreme Court's majority view, remedies to racial segregation cannot be based on race unless they are in response to individual instances of unlawful discrimination.

nativism A feeling that the large-scale influx of "foreigners" was a threat to the emerging life and culture of the United States.

need for cognitive closure (NFCC) A strong preference and need for having firm answers to questions and understanding of situations compared to confusion and uncertainty.

needs-based model of reconciliation Needs that become important to us when our social identities are activated. In intergroup interactions, members of majority groups or groups that have harmed other groups historically seek to be accepted; members of minority or victimized groups seek to be empowered.

neuroses Psychological problems that impair a person's activities but do not prevent him or her from functioning in society.

Nigresence   The process of becoming Black. Nigresence evolves from an encounter in which a deracialized identity becomes racialized through some sort of negative encounter based on one's race. The deracialized identity is shaken up, challenged, and gives way to a racialized identity—the old identity is demolished and a new frame of reference is adopted.

non-verbal behavior   Our physical actions other than what we say, such as eye contact and gestures.

norms   Informal rules, standards, and expectations within a group powerfully determine how we interact with others, including members of other groups.

objectification   Occurs when a person is treated as a mere body that exists for the sexual use and pleasure of others. Feeling objectified adversely affects people's intellectual and social behaviors.

objective SES   The actual household or individual income reported for an individual or family.

"one drop" rule   Meant that a person with any African blood was socially identified as Black.

optimal distinctiveness theory   Argues that people have simultaneous and competing drives for both distinctiveness and inclusiveness. When inclusiveness exceeds an individual's optimal level—too much "we-ness"—they seek to increase their distinctiveness—more "me-ness." This balancing act implies that when contexts are too homogeneous, too inclusive, diversity should become a more important goal.

out-group homogeneity   The tendency of people to see members of the out-group as very similar to each other, in contrast to perceiving in-group members as more heterogeneous.

own-race bias   The phenomenon that people are better able to distinguish and remember faces of people from their own race than from other races.

perceived discrimination   Involves a person's perception that he or she has been unfairly treated in a given situation. When people perceive they have been discriminated against, whether based on their race / ethnicity or lower socioeconomic status, their physical and psychological health may suffer.

perceptual narrowing   The hypothesis that human perceptual systems are shaped by experience to be optimally sensitive to stimuli most commonly encountered in their cultural environment.

personal identity   Represents what we believe makes us unique compared to all other people. Your experiences, characteristics, talents, and values are distinctive; there is no one else just like you.

personality   Refers to the characteristic way that a particular individual interacts with the social and physical world.

personalization   Exchanging information about each other in a way that conveys each person's unique qualities. When intergroup interactions are personalized, people typically recognize that their stereotypes of the other group are incorrect, which undermines their bias against the group as whole.

perspective taking   One of five bias-reducing techniques that involves adopting the perspective of a person who is a member of a stereotyped group.

phenotypicality   Refers to features of the face that are perceived to be most typical for a member of that racial or ethnic group.

Plessy v. Ferguson (1896) On June 7, 1892, Homer Plessy boarded a car of the East Louisiana Railroad that was designated for use by White patrons only. Although Mr Plessy was only one-eighth Black, under Louisiana state law he was classified as an African American and required to sit in the "colored" car. When he refused, he was arrested and jailed. Plessy argued that his constitutional rights under the Thirteenth and Fourteenth Amendments had been violated. He lost. When Plessy appealed to the Supreme Court, his appeal was rejected, establishing the "separate but equal" doctrine for racial inequality.

pluralistic ignorance A phenomenon that occurs in intergroup racial situations where people mistakenly believe that their interest in interacting with a member of another racial group is not reciprocated, leading both parties to avoid initiating intergroup contact.

polychronic time (P-time) Characterized by doing many things at once, casual disregard for punctuality, and focus on social transactions and affective states.

post-racial Era in America when it was believed that race was no longer a barrier to progress, opportunity or accomplishment and that race no longer mattered and racism was a thing of the past. A substantial body of research demonstrates this to be an inaccurate understanding of the influence of race.

power distance Reflects the relative degree of power between a dominant and subordinate person in a social system (an office, a classroom, a sports team, an airplane cockpit). A boss and an employee are not equals—the boss naturally has more power.

power distance index (PDI) Indicated by the degree to which a subordinate (a) is afraid to disagree with a superior, (b) perceives that the superior makes decisions in an autocratic or paternalistic way, and (c) prefers that the superior makes decisions in an authoritative or paternalistic way.

power dynamics A term that represents how power is acquired and maintained and the complex relationships among diversity status, power, and privilege.

predicament An unpleasant, troublesome, or trying situation from which it is difficult to extricate oneself.

preference diversity Reflects differences in taste and values, including fundamental preferences (the outcomes we value or prefer) and instrumental preferences (the means by which we pursue preferred outcomes).

prejudice Negatively biased attitudes toward, and general unfavorable evaluations of, a group that are then ascribed to individual members of the group. Stereotypes and prejudice often lead to preferential treatment for some groups and discrimination against others.

prevention focus Involves avoiding situations in which interacting with others is motivated by feelings of duty, obligation, or responsibility.

privilege The rights and opportunities that are associated with status in a social hierarchy. The more rights and opportunities a person possesses, the more privileged they are. Privilege is often an indicator of social and economic inequality among social groups.

procedural justice Emphasizes the importance of seeing that decisions about rewards are made fairly whether the outcome is favorable or not.

promotion focus   Involves seeking or approaching situations in which one is motivated to interact with others because of desires to support them or to achieve some desired goals.

protective disidentification   The tendency to define or redefine the self-concept so that performance outcomes are not a basis of self-evaluation or personal identity in a given domain. For instance, rejecting academic performance as a basis for self-evaluation.

Protestant work ethic   Values hard work as the basis of individual accomplishment.

psychodynamic theory   A theory developed by Sigmund Freud that explains prejudice, stereotyping, and discrimination as intra-individual processes, as ways to satisfy individual needs grounded in basic life (Eros) and death (Thanatos) instincts.

psychology of diversity   Examines the basic psychological processes that are triggered when we encounter people who are different from us in significant and salient ways, or experience being treated differently by others because of our social status. It further explores the dynamics of mental representation and social interaction across institutions and differential bases of power, privilege, and status. Finally, it identifies the effects of diverse contexts on the thoughts, actions, and feelings of people in them.

psychopathology   A condition that reflects abnormal psychological functioning.

race   A form of social grouping in which observable physical characteristics that distinguish a group of people are linked to a range of other non-visible, but also assumed to be genetically determined, characteristics such as intelligence. The concept of race, and associated beliefs about a hierarchy of races, supported the exploitation of some groups, determined immigration quotas, and justified the subordination of slaves.

racial identity   The degree to which a person identifies with, values, and represents his or her racial group in his or her personal view of self.

racial integration   The idea that people of all races should comingle across all aspects of society on an equal basis. Racial integration is a core principle of fairness and basic civil and human rights.

racialized   When racial beliefs are actively used to categorize and judge people.

racial paralysis   Describes a situation where a person is unable to act when confronted with a situation in which either of two different responses—approach or avoidance—may be interpreted as racial bias.

racial socialization   Refers to verbal and behavioral practices of families that inform a child about how race affects personal and group identity, intergroup and interpersonal relations, and position in the social hierarchy.

racism   The coordinated interaction of individual-level biases such as stereotypes, prejudice, and discrimination with societal- and cultural-level biases. This process creates disadvantaged and advantaged groups based on presumably distinct biological traits.

random assignment   The placement of participants into conditions of an experiment in a way that, on average, would make the groups comparable at the beginning of the study. Thus, any observed difference in performance by the groups cannot be explained by any prior differences among people who were in the two groups.

realistic group conflict theory Seeing other groups as competitors for material resources (e.g., money) arouses bias, leads people to discriminate, and often produces open conflict.

realistic threat The concern that another group will harm our health, take our group's resources (e.g., jobs) or territory.

recategorization Designed to alter group boundaries but by redefining rather than by eliminating group categorization. Recategorization typically involves changing the way people see others from members of different groups to members of the same inclusive group.

referent influence Source of power based on a person's interest in identifying with another person. The person's admiration of the other person and desire to be like the other person gives the other person social power.

Regents of the University of California v. Bakke Allan Bakke, a White man, applied to the University of California at Davis Medical School in both 1973 and 1974 and was denied admission. In both years, Black and Latino/Latina applicants whose grade-point averages and standardized test scores were lower than Bakke's were admitted under a special admissions program that set aside 16 of the 100 available admissions slots for minority applicants. Bakke filed a racial discrimination lawsuit and it was upheld by the California Supreme Court. The university appealed to the U.S. Supreme Court.

rejection sensitivity Refers to the extent to which a person is anxious about being rejected based on his or her group membership. Because people high in rejection sensitivity generally expect to be rejected because of their group membership, they tend to perceive rejection in the ambiguous behaviors of others.

relational demography The idea that both demographic differences and similarities between coworkers and supervisors affect task performance and behavior in organizational settings, but in somewhat different ways.

relative deprivation Reflects the discontent people feel when they compare their positions to others and realize that they have less of what they believe they are entitled to than those around them.

relative values Values that are right for only yourself.

research design A plan for how data will be collected. Research designs use different standards of control that are somewhat similar to quality control standards for any industry.

reverse discrimination The belief that affirmative action programs are biased against majority groups, because they create an unfair advantage for underrepresented groups. Those with this view argue that the policy unfairly excludes qualified applicants, typically Whites, while accepting less qualified applicants, typically Blacks and Hispanics.

right-wing authoritarianism A contemporary measure that refines the theory behind authoritarianism and improves the psychometric properties of the scale. Right-wing authoritarianism involves an inclination to submit to people of greater authority or status, hostility toward deviants and members of other groups, and a strong commitment to the traditional norms and values of one's group.

rugged individualism   A pioneering spirit of personal adventure, self-improvement, and accomplishment that is considered the driving force behind the settling and expansion of the United States.

scapegoating   The phenomenon in which people who are frustrated by one source but are unable to retaliate directly (e.g., because the person or source is unavailable or too powerful) displace aggression in a more socially acceptable way onto a more convenient and socially available person or group.

schadenfreude   The pleasure that we experience when an out-group suffers.

scientific method   A particular problem-solving approach that is common to all sciences that follows a particular logic and a series of prescribed stages beginning with a formal or informal observation about specific events or a pattern of outcomes that is sufficiently important. In psychology, it is the method by which we determine the causes of behavior.

secondary transfer effects   Involve the generalization of the benefits of contact to other types of out-groups. The positive feelings generated by contact with members of one out-group extend to other out-groups that are seen as similar, even though members of these groups were not involved in the intergroup encounter.

self-categorization theory   A theory that distinguishes personal identity from social identity. Different situations make a particular social identity salient, and we respond in ways that represent what a typical group member should think, feel, and do.

self-fulfilling prophecy   This process, by which expectations become reality, happens when the effects of the need for consistency reach much farther than affecting just our own behavior, also shaping others' reactions, leading them to behave in ways consistent with what we expected in the first place.

shooter bias   Numerous studies in psychology present participants with simulated situations in which they have to make a split-second decision about whether to shoot a man who may or may not have a weapon in his hand. Both Black and White college students as well as police officers are more likely to mistakenly shoot an unarmed Black man than an unarmed White man, and they do so faster. They are also less likely to shoot an armed White man than an armed Black man.

slow-learning system   Memory system that records information slowly and is sensitive to repeated patterns, events, and activities. It produces long-term stable knowledge that we can access automatically and unconsciously through sensory cues.

social bias   Personal attitudes, laws, institutional policies, and informal practices that perpetuate race, ethnic, and gender biases. They can sometimes happen without specific people intentionally driving these processes.

social categorization   Occurs when individuals view and arrange themselves and others into social categories based on many different labels like, most commonly, race, religion, socioeconomic status, political affiliation and attitudes, sexual orientation, gender, and the like.

social class   An indicator of social standing comprising two features: (a) material resources or assets and (b) social status in the social hierarchy. Social status is how a person is perceived compared to the social prestige and resources of others.

social cognition   The way we think about others and come to understand our social world.

social construction   When differences between groups do exist, but they are mainly rooted in social and cultural adaptations to different environments and circumstances, for example, the concept of race.

social dominance   A group's status in the social hierarchy is determined by the group's access to and exercise of power.

social dominance orientation (SDO)   Individual differences in the degree to which people endorse and value hierarchical relations between groups and the associated unequal privileges and resources.

social dominance theory   A theory of intergroup relations that focuses on the maintenance and stability of group-based social hierarchies through institutional discrimination, individual discrimination, and widely shared cultural ideologies (i.e., legitimizing myths) that provide the moral and intellectual justification for these intergroup behaviors.

social group power   Acquired, expressed, and maintained by the proportion of high-status social roles occupied by members of that group. These power differences constantly affect the interactions among social groups and between and among people.

social identity   An identity that you share with others—special others, those in a group that you belong to and care about. These are largely independent ways of thinking.

social identity theory   A highly influential theory that introduced the distinction between collective (social) and personal identity. It originally proposed that people derive self-esteem from their membership in socially valued groups and thus try to distinguish their group from other groups in favorable ways. This theory explains when and why individuals identify with and behave as members of specific social groups.

social indicators   Measures of social outcomes for members of a society such as employment rates and healthcare statistics. Social indicator measures are used to determine whether, and the extent to which, bias has occurred.

social influence   A concept that assumes that people influence the social behavior of other persons through a variety of person-to-person and group interactions.

socialization   What parents do with their children to prepare them to function effectively as adults in our society. Socializing children is not only done by parents but also by other family members (like grandparents, uncles/aunts and older siblings) as well as by other adults (like coaches, teachers, religious leaders) and often peers as well.

social power   The ability to control assets and the access that others have to those assets.

social role   Represents a set of expectations for the position an individual occupies in a group or society. It substantially determines how a person will behave and interact with others. A social role also conveys access to social status, social dominance, and to privilege.

social role hierarchies   Stratification systems that reflect status and privileges given to persons who occupy particular social roles in a society. These hierarchies convey more privileges and status to some based on their actual or perceived contributions to the well-being of society or according to the status given to particular social roles.

social role theory   Proposes that people infer the qualities of groups based on the different roles that members of a group occupy—women are nurturing because they are mothers.

social status   The prestige associated with your position in society. It is a combination of education, job status, and income.

socioeconomic status (SES)   Determined by a subject's financial resources, access to educational opportunities, and participation in social institutions.

soto   When affective bonds with others are weak.

standard-of-practice bias   When regular, sanctioned institutional practices produce outcomes and opportunities that favor some groups more than others. These practices represent the standard operations that define institutional policies and programs that govern hiring, production, promotion, and employee relations.

status quo   The current state of affairs in a society, institution, or organization and existing customs, practices, and social role hierarchies (see definition above). The existing rules, customs, and cultural practices recognized by persons in a society or organization. Often persons resist changing the status quo even if the existing rules, customs, or cultural practices do not give them an advantage.

stereotype boost   When the stereotype about one's group is positive, performance gets better when one's group affiliation is made salient.

stereotype content model   Describes how the content of group stereotypes is determined by how a group is perceived on two dimensions, warmth and competence.

stereotype disconfirmation   Experiences with a member of a group who displays qualities that are inconsistent with beliefs about what that group is like. A first-hand experience with a person who disconfirms a group stereotype can weaken a person's stereotypes of the group.

stereotype replacement   One of five bias-reducing techniques that involves replacing stereotypical responses with non-stereotypical responses.

stereotypes   Beliefs about qualities associated with particular groups and their members. Stereotypes are also based on the social roles that a person usually occupies—leader, officer, cleaner. Group stereotypes distinguish a group from others. They represent social perceptions about consistent qualities presumed to be shared by all members of a group.

stereotype threat   Proposes that situations containing cues making a negative stereotype about your social group salient and your awareness of the possibility that your performance will confirm it creates anxiety and undermines your performance.

stigma   A "stain" or a symbol indicating that a person is worthy of rejection or special, usually negative, treatment.

stress   When the resources needed to manage a particular situation are perceived to be more than you possess, you feel anxiety and negative arousal.

structural discrimination   Related to institutional bias but focuses more on the conditions that create inequities. Sociologists refer to structural or unintentional bias as practices that result in outcomes that are substantially worse for some groups than for others. This structural bias is passed on from generation to generation, in informal policies and practices, and the negative outcomes accumulate.

structural diversity   One of Milem's three interrelated ways to view diversity: numerical and proportional representation.

subjective culture   Refers to the influence of cultural standards and practices on what is considered right and wrong, good and bad, acceptable and unacceptable; and which human categories are important, how they are perceived and valued, and the course of interactions within culturally diverse contexts.

subjective SES   A concept related to objective SES that refers to the perception that an individual has of their social status in a society. This perception may be related to objective SES.

subtle prejudice   A modern form of bias that may be unrecognized or unacknowledged that leads people to discriminate in indirect and rationalizable ways.

superordinate goals   Outcomes that are mutually desired by different groups that can be accomplished only if the groups work together.

suppression   Directed at one's inner thoughts and which involves conscious attempts to inhibit the activation of negative attitudes, feelings, or beliefs when we sense that we are beginning to experience them.

symbolic racism   The expression of prejudice in the form of opposition to policies that support minority groups is closely tied to political behavior (e.g., opposition to bilingual education).

symbolic threat   Involves perceptions that another group challenges our core values and way of life.

system justification theory (SJT)   Suggests there is a strong psychological motivation that causes people to defend and maintain power hierarchies and social order. SJT describes how those in charge perpetuate myths about the legitimacy of the social order and the importance of maintaining it as well as how those who are disadvantaged by those myths continue to cling to them.

system-justifying ideologies   Cultural belief that rationalizes inequalities between groups that contributes to the status quo and makes the advantaged status of some groups over others appear fair and reduces the likelihood that these advantages will be questioned as illegitimate.

tempoagnostic   Where time holds personal and cultural meaning but has no inherent value—a person cannot save time, invest time, or even waste time.

temponomic   Where time is an unseen arbiter of values, accomplishments, order, and sometimes character. Time directly affects behavior—efficiency, punctuality, discipline, productivity, and achievement are often measured against a template of time.

terror management theory   Anything that makes us aware of our mortality, increases existential threat, and leads us to reaffirm things we believe in so we can continue to "live on" after our material deaths.

The Equal Rights Amendment (ERA)   Declared that "Equality of rights under the law shall not be denied or abridged by the United States or by any State on account of sex." The law was passed by Congress in 1972 and over a roughly 10-year period was ratified by 35 of the necessary 38 states required to become law. Finally in 1982, the effort to obtain ratification from three more states was abandoned.

The Five Civilized Tribes   Cherokee, Muscogee (Creek), Seminole, Chickasaw, and Choctaw nations were all forced to relocate from the southeastern United States to Indian Territory, in what is now eastern Oklahoma, because of the Indian Removal Act.

theory   An abstract explanation about a natural social phenomenon. It must be coherent and internally consistent. It must also be testable.

theory of social influence   This theory identifies three types of power that people use to exercise control (*see* social influence) over others: (a) legitimate authority that comes from the leader's position; (b) coercive power, based on threats or actual punishment; and (c) reward power, which is the positive opposite of coercive power. The theory also includes (d) expert influence and (e) referent influence. The ability to attain and exercise power depends on these basic dimensions of power.

The Trail of Tears   The forced march west of the Five Civilized Tribes which led to great suffering from exposure, disease, and starvation and large-scale deaths en route to their destinations.

threat response   Seeking to escape a situation or to protect ourselves against harm.

Title IX of the Education Amendments of 1972   Stipulated that no person shall, on the basis of sex, be excluded from participation in, be denied the benefits of, or be subjected to discrimination under any education program or activity receiving Federal financial assistance. Title IX is most notably invoked to support participation of women in athletics. But it also prohibited any educational institution receiving Federal financial assistance from denying admission to any course of study on the ground of blindness or severely impaired vision.

TRIOS   Acronym for Time, Rhythm, Improvisation, Orality, and Spirituality. A theory which represents the cultural capital that Africans brought with them to the New World. TRIOS is associated with characteristics that are useful for coping and adapting to threatening and uncertain contexts. TRIOS characteristics include flexible and creative responses to unexpected threats and challenges, using verbal and non-verbal communication to share information and knowledge, establishing group boundaries and creating group cohesion, adopting ways to be in synch with situations and contexts one is in, acute focus on the demands and opportunities of the immediate context, and drawing upon a spiritual belief in a power beyond oneself to make sense of one's predicament and alternative positive possibilities.

uchi   When affective bonds with others are strong.

ultimate attribution error   The tendency to attribute negative behaviors of outgroups to dispositional qualities (bad behavior is because he is a bad person) and positive behaviors to external forces (the teacher felt sorry for him so gave him a good grade).

universal context of racism (UCR)   This approach proposes that racism is a chronically accessible explanation for negative outcomes and motivates targets to be vigilant and wary. Belonging to a racial group that is socially salient and historically stigmatized renders the possibility of race-based bias highly accessible. The accessibility of race bias has the potential to influence interpretations of an individual's experiences and expectations, the goals they set and the likelihood they attain them.

values   Desirable trans-situational goals, varying in importance, that serve as guiding principles in people's lives.

voice   The opportunity to participate in and have influence on decisions that affect you.

Voting Rights Act of 1965   Outlawed literacy tests and provided for the appointment of Federal examiners with the power to register qualified citizens to vote. It also applied a nationwide prohibition of the denial or abridgment of the right to vote because of race or color.

White identity   How Whites view themselves, including the degree of invisibility of whiteness, the acceptance of White privilege, and belief in a colorblind ideology.

white-skin privilege   Special opportunities or rights given to a person merely because they have "white" or "light" skin. These privileges are often unearned and unrecognized by persons who gain opportunities based on them. These privileges advantage some groups more than others simply based on phenotypic differences.

worldview   A person's concept of what the world is and should be like, and the role one has or should have in it.

Index

Page numbers in *italics* denote figures, those in **bold** denote tables.

absolute values   280, 377
accents   130–1
acceptance   68, 168, 192, 212, 228, 246
acculturation   212–13, **212**, 377
acculturative stress   211, 377
adaptability   14–15, 366–7
adaptation   21, 32, 63, 94, 118, 175, 212, 213
Adorno, Theodor   94, 95, 96, 98, 111
advertising   43, *159*
affirmative action   74–7, 329, 336–7, 377
   opposition to   108–9
age discrimination   339–40
Allport, Gordon   90, 106, 380–1, 388
   The Nature of Prejudice   252
Allport's Lens Model   90–3, *91*
American, definition of   34, 56, 377
American Indians *see* Native Americans

Americans with Disabilities Act (1990)   73, 377
amygdala   174, 178, 179, 183, 377
Anderson, Sharon   300, 303, 304
animals
   behavior   118–19
   social categorization   129–30
anti-bias education   28–9
anti-Semitism   31–2, 65, 89, 94, 95, 105, 154
Arab Spring   311, 377
Aronson, Elliot   125, 165, 166
Asian Americans   13, 78, 217–18, 227, 229, 230, **283**, 308, 358
Asiatic Barred Zone   69
attribution bias   121, 378
attribution processes   120–4, 378
attribution theory   120–1, 378
attributional ambiguity   209, 218–19, 223–4, 377
authoritarian personality 94–6, 378
aversive racism   193–4, *194*, 249, 378
avoidance   242

backlash   157, 378
Bajer, Peter   330
Bakke, Allan   75, 337
behavioral consistency   127
behavioral science   11–13
beneficial diversity   68, 378
benevolence values   272
benevolent sexism   62–3, 378
Bennett, William   285
bias   7, 365–6
   cultural   43–4, 391
   explicit   40, 188–92, *191*, 384
   implicit   40, 188–92, *191*, 195–8, 384, 387
   individual   37, 42–3, 387
   individual-mediated   333, 387
   institutional *see* institutional bias
   intergroup   187–95
   perceptions of   288–9, *289*
   personal   33, 41, 43, 44
   prevention of   291–3
   racial   133, 182, 191, 193, 197, 198, 245, 250, 288, 292, 367

The Psychology of Diversity: Beyond Prejudice and Racism, First Edition. James M. Jones, John F. Dovidio, and Deborah L. Vietze.
© 2014 Blackwell Publishing Ltd. Published 2014 by Blackwell Publishing Ltd.

bias (*cont'd*)
  recognition of   133–41
  reduction of   316–20
  roots of   363–4
  social *see* social bias
  standard-of-practice   335–48, 387, 396
Bickman, Leonard   109
biological hierarchy   378
biology   32
Black identity   8, 225, 378
blatant prejudice   109–11, 378
both/and paradigm   358, 378
Boudlal, Imane   281, *282*
Bradwell, Myra   62–3, 110
Bradwell v. State of Illinois (1872)   63
brain
  bias in   173, 175, 179
  evolution   175
  organization   175–8
  structure and function   176–8, *177*
Brewer, Jan   79
Brooks, David   154
Brown, Linda   70–1, *70*
Brown, Oliver L.   70–1
Brown v. Board of Education of Topeka (1954)   69, 70–1, 76, 239, 266, 378–9
Buchanan, Patrick   287–8
Bush, George H.W.   31

Capistrano Valley High School   330–2
capital punishment   341
Carmichael, Stokely   332
Carswell, G. Harrold   17
category divide hypothesis   210, 251, 379
cerebral cortex   178, 379
challenge response   180, 379
change   363
chi-square test   49
Chinese Exclusion Act (1882)   61, 379
chronic egalitarian goals   198, 379

circles of inclusion   291
citizenship   15, 57–8, 59–61, 71
civil rights   68–80
  and diversity   68–72
Civil Rights Act (1866)   61
Civil Rights Act (1964)   72, 74, 75, 336, 379
Civil Rights Movement   11, 69, 72–3, 306
Clinton, Bill   106
closeness   275
cognitive consistency   120, 124–8, 379
cognitive control   178–9, 197
cognitive dissonance theory   125, 379
cognitive diversity   9, 379
cognitive miser   120, 379
Coleman, Mary Sue   76
collective identity   224–31, 379
collective threat   227
collectivism   **276**, 278–80, 379
color line   11, 56
colorblind perspective   18, 285–6, 380
colorblindness   369, 379
Comfort v. Lynn School Committee   81, 380
Commission on Civil Rights   70
common in-group identity model   136–7, 380
compelling interest   3–24, 380
competition   152–3, 161–4
confirmatory bias   126–7, 380
conflict   162–4
conformity   99–100
Confucian dynamism   280, 380
contact hypothesis theory   252, 380–1
contemporary prejudice   192–5
Cooke, Jack Kent   269
cooperative learning   370, 391
coping   206, 220–4, 391
correlations   48, 391
counter-stereotypic imaging   293, 391
counterculture   74
creativity   14–15, 366–7

criminal justice system   340–1
Cross Racial Identity Scale (CRIS)   226–7, 391
cultural bias   43–4, 120, 391
cultural competence training   28–9
cultural conditioning   63–4
cultural difference   207–11
cultural diversity   266, 283–93, **283**, *284*, **285**, 391
cultural inertia   364, 391
cultural transmission *see* enculturation
cultural universalities   45, 381
culture   12, 44, 265–98, **276**, 381
  definition of   268–72
  subjective   269, 397
culture peace   289–91, 294
culture war   287–9, 381

dance of life   279
data analysis   49
Dawes General Allotment Act   61
decategorization   134–6, *136*, 382
decision-making   275
demographic diversity   9, 79–80, 382
dependent variable   48, 382
descriptive statistics   49, 382
desegregation   239, 266, 382
Devine, Patricia   188
Diallo, Amadou   174–5, 180
difference   17–18, 81–2
  brain response to   179–83
  prejudice against   94–6
  stress caused by   213–30
discrimination   32, 37–40, 311, 368–9, 382
  perceived   213–14, 220–4, 390
  reverse   288, 336, 393
  structural   332–3, 396–7
disparate impact   335, 382
displacement   94, 382
disruptive apprehension   214, 382
distributive justice   37, 382

diversity 3–24, 357–9, 382
  barriers to 344
  benefits 14–17, 359–61
  challenges 17–19
  definition 4, 6–9
  normality of 361–2
  responding to 154–5
  valuing 348–9
diversity interactions 9, 382
diversity science 12–13, 28
diversity training 28–9, 349–50, 382
diversity within diversity 13–14, 33, 82–3, 382
diversity-related initiatives 9, 382
Dogmatism Scale 96, 383
Dollard, John 93
don't ask, don't tell 16, 73–4, 383
Doob, Leonard 93
dual identity 281–2, *282*
DuBois, W.E.B. 11, 56, 225
Dukakis, George 31
dynamic systems theory 30, 383
dynamics of diversity 57–68

Eagleman, David 173
Eckford, Elizabeth 266, *267*
economic differences 62
education
  anti-bias 28–9
  cooperative learning 370, 391
  diversity training 28–9, 349–50, 382
  single-sex learning 330–2, *331*
Education Amendments (1972) 73
EEG 177, 383
Eichmann, Adolph 105
electroencephalography *see* EEG
Elk, John 61
Elk v. Wilkins (1884) 61
Elliot, Jane 117–18
Emancipation Proclamation 60–1, 383
emotional reactions 345–6
empathy 254, 383
empowerment 246, 247, 328
enculturation 211, 270, 381, 383

endogenous factors 30
enemyship 278–9, 383
entity theorists 184–5, 383
environmental safety 341–2
epigenetics 30, 383
Equal Employment Opportunity Commission 75
equal opportunities 16
Equal Rights Amendment (ERA) 73, 397
equality 10–11
  barriers to 5
equity 6, 14, 37–8, 39, 301, 319, 383
ethnic diversity 61–2
ethnic identity 8, 228–31, 383
ethnicity 31, *78*, 357–8, 383
ethnocentrism 95, 229, 283, 363
ethnophaulisms 64, 383
evolutionary psychology 118–19, 383
exclusion 17, 290–1
Executive Order 9066 69, 384
Executive Order 9981 70, 384
Executive Order 11246 74–5, 384
exogenous factors 30
expert influence 311, 384
explicit bias 40, 188–92, *191*, 384
extended contact hypothesis 255, 384
extremism 153–4
extrinsic religiosity 106, 384

F statistic 49
F-scale 95, 96, 385
fairness 30, 37–40, 122, 301, 316–20, 384
  diversity and 363
fast-learning system 187, 384
Faubus, Orville 266
favoritism 291–3
fight or flight 178
Fisher v. Texas 337
Fitzgerald, F. Scott 210
Five Civilized Tribes 58, 398
flexibility 14–15, 366–7
fMRI 176–7, *176*, 385

forebrain 177–8
four-fifths rule 335, 384
Freud, Sigmund 93
Friedan, Betty 72–3
frustration–aggression hypothesis 93–4, 384
full participation 5–6, 385
functional magnetic resonance imaging *see* fMRI
fundamental attribution error 121–2, 385
fundamental preferences 3–24, 385
fusiform face area (FFA) 183–7, *185*, 390

Gaertner, Samuel 28, 74, 109, 132, 134, 136–9, 163, 166, 167, 186, 193, *194*, 206, 244, 249, 358
Garcia, James 205–6
gays *see* GLBT persons
Geary Act (1892) 61
gender roles 32, 310
gender similarity 5
gender stereotyping 62–3
genetic variation 32
Gentlemen's Agreement (1907) 69, 385
Gladwell, Malcolm 265, 267
Glazer, Nathan 62, 286, 370
GLBT persons 16, *33*, 89–90, 209, 210–11
  bias against 189
  same-sex marriage 342
  see also homophobia
Golding, William 118
Gratz v. Bollinger (2003) 76
Green Circle program 291
groups 28, 358
  membership 128–33
  minimal 131, 388
  out-group homogeneity 132, 390
  relations between 164–8
Grutter, Barbara 75–6
Grutter v. Bollinger (2003) 75–6, 81, 240, 337, 385

Hall, E.T.   279
Haslam, S. Alexander   103–4
hate groups   103–4
Haymarket Affair   65, 385
health disparities   250–1, 341–2,
    385
Hennessey, David   64
Hernandez v. Texas (1954)   71, 385
heterosexism   44–5
hindbrain   177
hippocampus   179
Hispanics   13, 15, 33, 49, 78, 189,
    227, 229, **283**, 290, 302, 303,
    306–8, 312, 314, 316, 320, 328,
    336, 337, 338, **339**, 341, 342,
    346, 358, 369
historical perspectives   55–86
Holocaust   94, 105
    see also anti-Semitism
home ownership   337–9, **338**
homophobia   44–5, 89–90
    internalized   211, 388
Hopwood v. Texas (1996)   83
Horton, Willie   31
hostile sexism   110, 385
Hruska, Roman   17
human capital   14–17, 385
human diversity   30–1, 385
human genome   12
Huntington, Samuel P.   163
hypothesis   46, 386

identity affirmation   227, 386
identity diversity   9, 386
identity fusion   *150*
identity safety   285, 287, 386
Illegal Immigration Reform and
    Immigrant Responsibility Act
    (1996)   79, 386
illusory correlation   125–6, 386
imagined contact   256, 386
immigration   57–9, *59*, *60*, *68*, *73*,
    78–80, *78*, *79*, 386
    and ethnic diversity   61–2
    quotas   **67**
    see also citizenship
Immigration Act (1917)   69, 386
Immigration Act (1924)   66, 386

Immigration and Nationality Act
    (1952)   66
Immigration and Nationality Act
    (1965)   72, 79, 386
immigration policy   65–8
Implicit Association Test (IAT)
    40–1, 189, 386
implicit attitudes   194–5
implicit bias   40, 188–92, *191*,
    248–51, 387
    acknowledging   196–7
    controlling   197–8
    in healthcare   250–1
importation   57–8
increasing opportunities for
    contact   293, 387
independent variable   47–8, 387
Indian Citizenship Act (1924)   61
Indian Removal Act (1830)   58
indirect contact   255, 387
individual bias   37, 42–3, 387
individual rights   80–1
individual-mediated bias   333, 387
individualism   276–80, **276**, 387
individuation   293, 387
inferential statistics   49, 387
ingratiation   247, *247*
Innocence Project   184
institutions   327, 387
institutional bias   8, 38, 43,
    327–54, 387
    case histories   329–32
    challenges of   343–4, *344*
    definition   328
    effects of   344–5
    origins of   333
    prevention of   348–50
    types of   333–5
institutional racism   332, 387
institutional sexism   332, 387
instrumental preferences   9, 387
integration *see* racial integration
integrative complexity   290, 387
interethnic relations   275
intergroup anxiety   242–3, 387
intergroup bias   187–95
Intergroup Dialogues Course   15,
    387–8

intergroup (versus interpersonal)
    interaction   29, 239–62, 366,
    370–1, 388
    positive aspects   252–7
    psychological challenges
    241–51, *245*, *247*, *248*
internalized homophobia   211,
    388
intersectionality   160, 308–10,
    309, 388
intrinsic religiosity   106, 388

Jackson, Andrew   58
Jackson, Jesse   179
Jay, John   56
Jefferson, Thomas   3, *58*
Jews   15, 31, *35*, 65, 137–8, 163,
    240, 280
    anti-Semitism   31–2, 65, 89, 94,
    95, 105, 154
jigsaw classroom   165–6, 388
Jim Crow Laws   71, 388
Johnson, Lyndon B.   38–9, 74,
    336, 348
just-world hypothesis   122–3,
    388
justice   122
    distributive   37, 382
    procedural   37, 391

Kelley, Robin   12
Kelman, Herbert   140
Kennedy, John F.   336
Khakpour, Porochista   281–2
Killens, John Oliver   147, 150
King, Martin Luther   81, 117, 266,
    285
King, Rodney   289

labor force, trends in   29
language diversity   80
    accents   130–1
Latinos   29, 33, 38, 46, 75, 78, 82,
    134, 155, 160, 166, 167, 168,
    189, 192, 206, 209, 214, 217,
    218, 223, 224, 227–30, 240,
    246, 250, 254, 255, 281, **283**,
    316, 339, 346, 360

learning opportunities 366
learning orientation 286
Lens Model (Allport) 90–3, *91*, 388
lesbians *see* GLBT persons
Lincoln, Abraham 42, 60, 383
Lucy, Autherine 266
Lynn, Massachusetts case 76–7

Machiavelli, Niccolò 278
majority 72–3
marriage 341–2
Martin, Trayvon 175
McCarran, Pat 66
McDougall, William 62
McIntosh, Peggy 300, 312, 313
Melville, Herman 239, 241
memory 179
    faces 184
Mencken, H.L. 36
meritocracy 18, 360, 388
meta-perceptions 242, 388
Mexican Americans 33, 71, 229, 313, 334–5
    see also Hispanics; Latinos
Middleton, Valerie 303, 304
Mills, Judson 125
minimal groups 131, 388
minorities 33, 78–80, *78*, *79*, 82–3
misidentification 184
mixed race 13, 14, 78, 300
model minority 13
monochronic time (M-time) 279, 389
Montgomery bus boycott 389
moral license 197, 389
mortgage lending 337–9
motivation 367
Mullen, Mike 74, 383
multicultural perspective 18, 285, 286–7, 389
multiculturalism 289, 369–70, 389
Multidimensional Inventory of Black Identity (MIBI) 225, 226, 389
Multidimensional Model of Racial Identity (MMRI) 225–6, 389

Multigroup Ethnic Identity Measure (MEIM) 228–9, **229**, 389
multiple identities 151–2, 308–10
multiracial identity 230–1, 389
Muslims 135, 153–4, 281–2, *282*
mutual intergroup differentiation 166–7, 389
Myrdal, Gunnar 333

narrative 206
narrowly tailored 81, 389
Native Americans 56, 58, 61, 78
    cultural conditioning 63–4
    Five Civilized Tribes 58, 398
    Trail of Tears 58, 398
nativism 63, 64, 66, 68, 69, 389
Naturalization Act (1790) 58, 65
Nazi Germany 31, 95, 105
need for cognitive closure (NFCC) 98, 286, 389
needs-based model of reconciliation 246, 389
negative responses to diversity 64–5
negative social bias 33
neuroses 93, 389
New Democrat Network 74
Nigrescence 226, 390
non-verbal behavior 242, 249, 390
norms 99–100, 390

Obama, Barack 55, 74, 122, 137, 158, 163, 288, 319
objectification 159–60, *159*, 390
objective socioeconomic status 316, 390
O'Connor, Sandra Day 3, 5, 75–6, 240, 290, 357
"one drop" rule 230, 390
optimal distinctiveness theory 150–1, 359, 390
organizational culture 371
out-group homogeneity 132, 390
own-race bias 183, 390

Panetta, Leon 74
Parks, Rosa 71–2
Patient Protection and Affordable Health Care Act (2012) 342
perceived discrimination 213–14, 390
    coping with 220–4
perceived similarity 5
perceptual narrowing 271, 390
personal bias 33, 41, 43, 44
personal identity 149–51, *150*, 390
personality 89–116, 390
    authoritarian 94–6, 378
    and prejudice 92–3
personalization 134, 390
perspective taking 293, 390
phenotypicality 185–6, 390
physical characteristics 30–1
Plaut, Victoria 28
Plessy, Homer 68–9
Plessy v. Ferguson (1896) 69, 71, 239, 391
pluralistic ignorance 219, 242, 391
political protest *311*
politics, and prejudice 107–9
polychronic time (P-time) 279–80, 391
population growth 58–9
positive identity 152–4
post-racial 288, 391
poverty 347–8
Powderly, Terence 65
power 310, 311, 312–13
    awareness of 304–5
power distance 268, 274, 391
power distance index (PDI) 274–5, 391
power dynamics 305–7, 391
    reducing bias in 316–20
power values 272
Pratt, Richard 63–4
predicament 208, 391
preference diversity 9, 391
preferential treatment 17, 32, 33, 75, 108
    see also prejudice

prejudice   5, 23, 32, 35–7, *35*, 36, *36*, 64, 80–1, 90, 356, 391
  acceptability of   **190**
  against difference   94–6
  Allport's Lens Model   90–3, *91*
  blatant   109–11, 378
  combating   291–3
  contemporary   192–5
  normality of   99–111
  overcoming   367–8
  and politics   107–9
  psychodynamic theory   92, 93–4, 99, 392
  and religion   106–7
  subtle   109–11, 397
prevention focus   368, 391
Price, Henry   63
privilege   300, 306, 313, 391
  awareness of   304–5
procedural justice   37, 275, 391
promotion focus   368, 392
protective disidentification   215, 392
Protestant work ethic   276, 392
psychodynamic theory   92, 93–4, 99, 392
psychological disengagement   223
psychological time   279–80
psychology of diversity   7, 27–53, 392
  definition   30–3
psychopathology   90, 392

quotas   67

race   12, 31, *78*, 357–8, 392
race preferences   270–2, *271*
race similarity   5
racial bias   133, 182, 191, 193, 197, 198, 245, 250, 288, 292, 367
racial hierarchy   31
racial identity   8, 225–8, 392
  and collective threat   227
racial integration   68, 213, 392
racial paralysis   219, 392
racial socialization   212, 392
racialized society   346, 392

racism   5, 12, 23, 41–2, 64, 329–30, 356, 392
  aversive   193–4, *194*, 378
  contemporary   194–5
  institutional   332, 387
  symbolic   192, 397
  universal context (UCR)   221–2, 398
Raheim, Salome   299
random assignment   47, 392–3
realistic group conflict theory   162, 393
realistic threat   163, 393
recategorization   134, 136–8, *139*, 164, 393
referent influence   311, 393
Regents of the University of California v. Bakke   75, 393
Reicher, Stephen   103–4
rejection identification   220–1
rejection sensitivity   221, 393
Rejection Sensitivity Questionnaire   221
relational demography   4, 393
relative deprivation   301, 393
relative values   280, 393
religion   4, 9, 23, 28, 29, 30, 44, 49, 56, 57, 61, 62, 70, 74–5, 81, 99, 111, 135, 153–4, 280–3
  extrinsic religiosity   106, 384
  and prejudice   106–7
  see also Jews; Muslims
research designs   45–9, 393
resilience   368–9
respect   369
reverse discrimination   288, 336, 393
Ricci v. DeStefano (2009)   39–40
Richards, Michael   42–3
right-wing authoritarianism   96–7, **97**, 393
  and social dominance   104–5
Roosevelt, Franklin   69
Rosenberg, Simon   74
rugged individualism   276, 394

scapegoating   94, 394
schadenfreude   153, 394

scientific method   45–6, 47, 394
Scott, Dred   59–60
Scott, Natasha   300
Sears, Robert   93
secondary transfer effects   253, 394
self-categorization theory   148, 394
self-esteem   215, *216*, *270*
self-fulfilling prophecy   127–8, 394
self-promotion   247
self-protection   222
sexism   110
  benevolent   62–3, 378
  hostile   110, 385
  institutional   332, 387
Shephard, Matthew   89–90, 304
Shinault, Veronica   327
shooter bias   181–2, *181*, 394
Shurz, Carl   63
single-sex learning   330–2, *331*
skin color   32, 33, 312–13
"skyboxification"   302, *303*
slavery   37–8, 58
slow-learning system   187, 394
Smith, Daryl   356
social belonging   290–1
social bias   34–41, 394
  layers of   42–5
  negative   33
  research designs   45–9
  structure of   41–5
social categorization   28, 128–33, *130*, 394
social class   315–16, 394
social cognition   119–28, 394
social construction   31, 395
social creativity   152
social distinctions   28
social dominance   100–4, 307, 395
social dominance orientation (SDO)   101–4, **101**, *102*, 314, 395
  and authoritarianism   104–5
social dominance theory   92, 100–4, 314–15, 395

social group labels 33–4
social group power 103–4, 307, 395
social identity 149–51, *150*, 395
social identity theory 148, 395
social indicators 43, 328, 395
social influence 311, 395
social mobility 152
social networks 175
social power 300
social privilege 300, 320
social role 155–61, 299–325, 395
social role hierarchies 307, 395
social role theory 63, 156–7, *157*, 396
social status 307, **308**, 396
socialization 211, 395
  racial 212, 392
socioeconomic status (SES) 284, 314, 396
solidarity 123, 149, 153
soto 277, 396
Sotomayor, Sonia 265, 307
Spinoza, Baruch 188
standard-of-practice bias 335–48, 387, 396
status quo 318, 396
Steele, Shelby 108–9
stereotypes 31, 32, 34–5, 185, 319–20, 396
stereotype boost 217, *218*, 396
stereotype content model 34, 396
stereotype disconfirmation 253, 396
stereotype replacement 293, 396
stereotype threat 209, 214–20, *216–18*, 396
stigma 207–11, 396
  stress caused by 213–30

stress 396
  acculturative 211, 377
  stigma and difference 213–30
structural discrimination 332–3, 396–7
structural diversity 9, 397
subjective culture 269, 397
subjective socioeconomic status 315, 397
subtle prejudice 109–11, 397
superiority 152–3
superordinate goals 165, 397
suppression 196, 397
symbolic racism 192, 397
symbolic threat 163, 397
system justification theory (SJT) 155–61, 318, 397
system-justifying ideologies 110, 160, 397

t test 49
Tajfel, Henri 129
Taney, Roger B. 60
tempoagnostic view 279, 397
temponomic 279, 397
terror management theory 123–4, 397
Texaco 328–30
The Human Stain 208
theory 46–7, 398
theory of social influence 311, 398
Thind, Bhagat Singh 65
threat response 123–4, *124*, 162–4, 180, 398
time 279–80
  monochronic 279, 389
  polychronic 279–80, 391
Title IX of the Education Amendments (1972) 398

Trail of Tears 58, 398
TRIOS 222, 398
Truman, Harry S. 68, 70
trust 370
Tuskegee Airmen 15–16

uchi 277, 398
ultimate attribution error 122, 398
unconscious goals 197–8
unemployment 339–40, **339**
United States v. Bhagat Singh Thind (1923) 66
universal context of racism (UCR) 221–2, 398
universalism values 272, **273**

values 272–4, **273**, 368, 399
  absolute 280, 377
  cross-cultural 273
  relative 280, 393
Vazquez, Evaristo 205–6
visibility 206
voice 275, 399
Voting Rights Act (1965) 72, 399

White identity 8, 227–8, 399
white-skin privilege 313, 399
Whitman, Charles 174, 178
Whitney, Eli 58
women
  benevolent sexism 62–3, 378
  prejudice against 36–7
Women's Movement 69
women's rights 72–3
Woodward, Isaac 69–70
worldview 278, 399
  verification 224

Zimmerman, George 175